# JESUS OF NAZARETH

# Jesus of Nazareth: Lord and Christ

*Essays on the Historical Jesus and New Testament Christology*

*edited by*

Joel B. Green *and* Max Turner

William B. Eerdmans Publishing Company
Grand Rapids, Michigan

The Paternoster Press
Carlisle, UK

Published jointly 1994 by
Wm. B. Eerdmans Publishing Co.
255 Jefferson Ave. S.E., Grand Rapids, Michigan 49503
and by The Paternoster Press
P.O. Box 300, Carlisle, Cumbria, CA3 0QS, UK



Printed in the United States of America

**Library of Congress Cataloging-in-Publication Data**

Jesus of Nazareth: Lord and Christ: essays on the historical Jesus
and New Testament christology / edited by Joel B. Green and Max Turner.
p. cm.
Includes bibliographical references (p. xxx-xxx) and indexes.
ISBN 0-8028-3750-6
1. Jesus Christ — Historicity. 2. Bible. N.T. — Criticism, interpretation, etc.
I. Green, Joel B., 1956– . II. Turner, Max, 1947– .
BT303.2.J456 1994
232.9′08 — dc20 93-39543
CIP

**British Library Cataloguing in Publication Data**

Jesus of Nazareth: Lord and Christ —
Essays on the Historical Jesus and New Testament Christology
I. Green, Joel B. II. Turner, Max
232.908

ISBN 0-85364-560-4

# Contents

# Preface

"The problem of the historical Jesus is one of the most important themes in New Testament scholarship."[1] This judgment of I. Howard Marshall is no less true today than it was when he wrote *I Believe in the Historical Jesus* almost two decades ago. If anything, the validity of his verdict — both for the New Testament academy and for the larger churched and unchurched population — has been further substantiated. In the intervening period, some scholars have taken an increasingly gloomy attitude toward the possibility of knowing much about Jesus from the canonical Gospels, while others have begun moving the whole discussion into fresh areas of creative inquiry, and with new energy. Moreover, in this last decade of the second millennium, new "biographies" of Jesus are appearing at an astonishing rate, and that from major and so-called secular publishing houses. Even if these books include sometimes outlandish claims about the person of Jesus, they nonetheless bear witness to a renaissance of general interest in Jesus of Nazareth.

Fueling this interest more often than not is a corresponding preoccupation with the degree to which our understanding of Jesus influences the shape of faithful life in the church and in the world today. The biographies just alluded to, for example, such as those by A. N. Wilson, S. T. Mitchell, and Bishop Spong,[2] are clear in their agenda to rescue Jesus from the church and so present a Jesus more tolerant, less divine, and more like their authors. That the church is always in danger of reshaping Jesus in its own image is undeniable, with the

1. I. H. Marshall, *I Believe in the Historical Jesus* (London: Hodder and Stoughton; Grand Rapids, Michigan: Wm. B. Eerdmans; Exeter: Paternoster, 1977) 9.

2. A. N. Wilson, *Jesus* (New York: W. W. Norton, 1992); S. Mitchell, *The Gospel according to Jesus: A New Translation and Guide to His Essential Teachings for Believers and Unbelievers* (New York: HarperCollins, 1991); J. S. Spong, *Born of a Woman: A Bishop Rethinks the Birth of Jesus* (San Francisco: HarperCollins, 1992). For a review of these and similar works, see J. B. Green, "Jesus in the Popular Press: Recent Biographies in Review," *RADIX Magazine* 21 (1993) 24-29; also N. T. Wright, *Who Was Jesus?* (London: S.P.C.K; Grand Rapids, Michigan: Wm. B. Eerdmans, 1992).

consequence that good, historical scholarship, scholarship that allows its own presuppositions and motives to be challenged by this Jesus, is always needed.

The question addressed by other studies, however, is nuanced in a quite different direction. Here the issue revolves around the degree to which the apostolic church, as represented in the pages of the New Testament, was *already* reshaping Jesus to support its own agenda. The peril of modernizing Jesus is not merely a temptation for our own age; it was there for the very first who proclaimed and worshiped Christ too. In his survey of *The Origins of New Testament Christology,* Marshall clearly articulates the central problem here: "It has always been a vital question in Christology to discover how far the impact made by the earthly Jesus and his own understanding of his person can sustain the weight of the Christological construction put upon them by the early church."[3]

Not least because of his unremitting commitment to the faith and life of the Christian church and his gracious consideration for students of the faith, Howard Marshall has devoted considerable attention to issues of this sort. Even while he was becoming known as one of the leading authorities on Luke-Acts, many of us were being introduced to him through his publications on Jesus and christology — the aforementioned volumes as well as *The Work of Christ, Last Supper and Lord's Supper,* and such essays as those eventually collected in *Jesus the Saviour.*[4]

Long before evangelical biblical scholarship as a whole had begun to reach the level of maturity that could lend itself to the production of a tome like *Dictionary of Jesus and the Gospels,* for which Professor Marshall played a key role as Consulting Editor,[5] many theological students and pastors looked to him for help in coming to terms with the sometimes arduous tensions between critical scholarship and faith. When asked repeatedly, Why Scotland for postgraduate work?, one of us (JBG) has had a ready answer, To study with a major New Testament scholar who remained committed to and involved in the local church: Howard Marshall. Here is a scholar whose writing, lecturing, *and preaching* have sought always fully to serve the Christian church, joining "together the two so long divided, knowledge and vital piety." It is illustrative of Professor Marshall's own sense of vocation and commitment that, when play-

3. I. H. Marshall, *The Origins of New Testament Christology,* 2d ed. (Downers Grove, Illinois: InterVarsity, 1990) 13.

4. I. H. Marshall, *The Work of Christ,* CEP (Exeter: Paternoster; Grand Rapids, Michigan: Zondervan, 1969); *idem, Last Supper and Lord's Supper* (Exeter: Paternoster; Grand Rapids, Michigan: Wm. B. Eerdmans, 1980); *idem, Jesus the Saviour: Studies in New Testament Theology* (London: S.P.C.K.; Downers Grove, Illinois: InterVarsity, 1990).

5. J. B. Green and S. McKnight, eds.; I. H. Marshall, consulting ed., *Dictionary of Jesus and the Gospels* (Downers Grove, Illinois: InterVarsity; Leicester: Inter-Varsity, 1992). Marshall himself contributed important christological articles on "Son of Man" (775-81) and "Lamb of God" (432-34).

fully asked whether he experienced the writing of his massive commentary on the Third Gospel[6] as an act of worship, without a moment's hesitation he answered, "Yes."

It is equally characteristic of him that despite his heavy load of lecturing, research, writing, editing,[7] and speaking commitments, Professor Marshall has not only found time to chair the Tyndale Fellowship New Testament Study Group, but has also been actively involved both with the student Christian Union, in its witness to the University, and in the leadership of Crusaders, a young people's Christian movement. Not many of us can claim their theological teaching to address such diverse audiences.

The theme for this symposium, "Jesus of Nazareth: Lord and Christ," echoes the language of Peter's sermon at Pentecost. There, in Acts 2:22, 36, we find a proclamation that combines inseparably the historical Jesus and christology. We offer these essays in tribute to one who has always sought to do the same — Howard Marshall, mentor, colleague, churchman, brother, friend.

JOEL B. GREEN
MAX TURNER

6. I. H. Marshall, *The Gospel of Luke: A Commentary on the Greek Text,* NIGTC (Exeter: Paternoster; Grand Rapids, Michigan: Wm. B. Eerdmans, 1978).

7. In addition to editing the important symposium on *New Testament Interpretation: Essays on Principles and Methods* (Exeter: Paternoster; Grand Rapids, Michigan: Wm. B. Eerdmans, 1976), Professor Marshall replaced Professor F. F. Bruce as editor of *Evangelical Quarterly* from 1981 onward.

# Contributors

CLINTON E. ARNOLD, Associate Professor of New Testament, Talbot School of Theology, La Mirada, California, U.S.A.

C. K. BARRETT, Emeritus Professor of Divinity, University of Durham, England

RICHARD J. BAUCKHAM, Professor of New Testament Studies, St. Mary's College, University of St. Andrews, St. Andrews, Scotland

HANS F. BAYER, Dozent in New Testament Exegesis, German Theological Seminary, Gießen, Germany

GEORGE R. BEASLEY-MURRAY, Senior Professor of New Testament Interpretation, Southern Baptist Theological Seminary, Louisville, Kentucky, U.S.A.

CRAIG L. BLOMBERG, Associate Professor of New Testament, Denver Seminary, Denver, Colorado, U.S.A.

DARRELL L. BOCK, Professor of New Testament Studies, Dallas Theological Seminary, Dallas, Texas, U.S.A.

PEDER BORGEN, Research Professor of New Testament, Department of Religious Studies, University of Trondheim, Norway

GARY M. BURGE, Associate Professor of New Testament, Wheaton College, Wheaton, Illinois, U.S.A.

D. A. CARSON, Research Professor of New Testament, Trinity Evangelical Divinity School, Deerfield, Illinois, U.S.A.

JOHN W. DRANE, Director of the Centre for the Study of Christianity and Contemporary Society, University of Stirling, Scotland

JAMES D. G. DUNN, Lightfoot Professor of Divinity, University of Durham, England

RUTH B. EDWARDS, Senior Lecturer in New Testament, University of Aberdeen, Scotland

PAUL ELLINGWORTH, Translation Consultant, United Bible Societies; Honorary Lecturer in New Testament, University of Aberdeen, Scotland

E. EARLE ELLIS, Research Professor of Theology, Southwestern Baptist Theological Seminary, Fort Worth, Texas, U.S.A.

GORDON D. FEE, Professor of New Testament Studies, Regent College, Vancouver, B.C., Canada

RICHARD T. FRANCE, Principal, Wycliffe Hall, Oxford, England.

JOEL B. GREEN, Associate Professor of New Testament, American Baptist Seminary of the West and Graduate Theological Union, Berkeley, California, U.S.A.

ROBERT H. GUNDRY, Professor of New Testament and Greek, Westmont College, Santa Barbara, California, U.S.A.

†DONALD GUTHRIE, Former Vice-Principal, then President, London Bible College, Northwood, Middlesex, England

RICHARD N. LONGENECKER, Ramsay Armitage Professor of New Testament, Wycliffe College, University of Toronto; and Graduate Professor, Centre for the Study of Religion, University of Toronto, Ontario, Canada

LEON MORRIS, Former Principal, Ridley College, Melbourne, Australia

GRANT R. OSBORNE, Professor of New Testament, Trinity Evangelical Divinity School, Deerfield, Illinois, U.S.A.

REINER RIESNER, Dozent für Neues Testament, Evangelisch-Theologische Facultät des Universität, Tübingen, Germany

ECKHARD J. SCHNABEL, Dozent für Neues Testament, Bibelschule Wiedenest, Bergneustadt; and Freie Theologische Akademie, Gießen, Germany

GRAHAM N. STANTON, Professor of New Testament Studies, King's College, University of London, London, England

ANTHONY C. THISELTON, Professor of Christian Theology and Head of the Department of Theology, University of Nottingham, England

STEPHEN H. TRAVIS, Vice-Principal and Lecturer in New Testament, St. John's College, Nottingham, England

MAX TURNER, Director of Research and Lecturer in New Testament, London Bible College, Northwood, Middlesex, England

DAVID WENHAM, Tutor in New Testament, Wycliffe Hall, Oxford, England

# Abbreviations

## I. Ancient Literature

### *A. Apocrypha*

| | |
|---|---|
| Bar | Baruch |
| Bel | Bel the Dragon |
| 1-2 Esdr | 1-2 Esdras |
| 1-2-3-4 Macc | 1-2-3-4 Maccabees |
| Sir | Sirach |
| Tob | Tobit |
| Wis | Wisdom |

### *B. Pseudepigrapha and Early Christian Writings*

| | |
|---|---|
| *Apoc. Bar.* | *Apocalypse of Baruch* |
| *Apoc. Elijah* | *Apocalypse of Elijah* |
| *Apoc. Mos.* | *Apocalypse of Moses* |
| *Barn.* | *Barnabas* |
| *Did.* | *Didache* |
| *1 Clem.* | *1 Clement* |
| *Ep. Apost.* | *Epistle to the Apostles* |
| *Ep. Arist.* | *Epistle of Aristeas* |
| Eusebius | |
| *Hist. Eccl.* | *Historia Ecclesiastica* |
| Gregory the Great | |
| *Hom.* | *Homilies* |
| *Herm. Man.* | *Hermas, Mandate(s)* |
| *Herm. Sim.* | *Hermas, Similitude(s)* |

| | |
|---|---|
| Ign. *Eph.* | Ignatius, *Letter to the Ephesians* |
| *Phld.* | Ignatius, *Letter to the Philadelphians* |
| *Rom.* | Ignatius, *Letter to the Romans* |
| *Smyrn.* | Ignatius, *Letter to the Smyrnaeans* |
| Irenaeus | |
| *Adv. Haer.* | *Adversus haereses* |
| Jerome | |
| *Contra Pelag.* | *Dialogue against the Pelagians* |
| *Jos. As.* | *Joseph and Asenath* |
| *Jub.* | *Jubilees* |
| Lactantius | |
| *Inst. Div.* | *Divine Institutes* |
| *L.A.E.* | *Life of Adam and Eve* |
| *Pss. Sol.* | *Psalms of Solomon* |
| *Sib. Or.* | *Sibylline Oracles* |
| *T. Abr.* | *Testament of Abraham* |
| *T. Ash.* | *Testament of Asher* |
| *T. Benj.* | *Testament of Benjamin* |
| *T. Dan.* | *Testament of Daniel* |
| *T. Iss.* | *Testament of Issachar* |
| *T. Job* | *Testament of Job* |
| *T. Jud.* | *Testament of Judah* |
| *T. Levi* | *Testament of Levi* |
| *T. Mos.* | *Testament of Moses* |
| *T. Naph.* | *Testament of Naphtali* |
| *T. Sim.* | *Testament of Simeon* |
| *T. Zeb.* | *Testament of Zebulun* |

### *C. Dead Sea Scrolls and Related Texts*

| | |
|---|---|
| CD | *Hôdāyôṭ* or Cairo (Genizah text of the) *Damascus (Document / Rule)* |
| 1QH | *Hôdāyôṭ* or Thanksgiving Hymns from Qumran Cave 1 |
| 1QIsa[a] | First copy of Isaiah from Qumran Cave |
| 1QM | *Milḥāmāh* or War Scroll from Qumran Cave 1 |
| 1QS | *Serek hayyaḥad* or Rule of the Community or Manual of Discipline from Qumran Cave 1 |
| 1QSa | Appendix A, *Messianic Rule,* to 1QS |
| 1QSb | Appendix B, *Rule of Benediction,* to 1QS |
| 4QFlor | *Florilegium (Eschatological Midrashim)* from Qumran Cave 4 |
| 4QPrNab | *Prayer of Nabonidus* from Qumran Cave 4 |

| | |
|---|---|
| 4QpIsa | *Pesher on Isaiah* from Qumran Cave 4 |

### *D. Targumim*

| | |
|---|---|
| *Tg. Neb.* | *Targum of the Prophets* |
| *Tg. Onq.* | *Targum Onqelos* |
| *Tg. Ps.-J.* | *Targum Pseudo-Jonathan* |

### *E. Rabbinic Literature and Tractates*

| | |
|---|---|
| *ʾAbot* | *ʾAbot* |
| *ʾAbot R. Nat.* | *ʾAbot de Rabbi Nathan* |
| *b.* | Babylonian Talmud |
| *Ber.* | *Berakot* |
| *Bik.* | *Bikkurim* |
| *Ḥag* | *Ḥagiga* |
| *Ker.* | *Keritot* |
| *Ketub.* | *Ketubot* |
| *m.* | Mishna |
| *Mek.* | *Mekilta* |
| *Mid.* | *Middot* |
| *Midr.* | *Midraš* |
| *Pes. Rab.* | *Pesiqta Rabbati* |
| *Qidd.* | *Qiddušin* |
| *Rab.* | *Rabbah* |
| *Sanh.* | *Sanhedrin* |
| *Šabb.* | *Šabbat* |
| *Soṭa* | *Soṭa* |
| *Taʿan.* | *Taʿanit* |
| *Yebam.* | *Yebamot* |
| *Yal.* | *Yalqut* |

### *F. Other Ancient Authors and Writings*

| | |
|---|---|
| Hippocrates | |
| *Morb. Sacr.* | *De Morbo Sacro* |
| *Nat. Hom.* | *De Natura Hominis* |
| Horace | |
| *Epod.* | *Epodes* |

| | |
|---|---|
| Josephus | |
| *Ag. Apion* | *Against Apion* |
| *Ant.* | *Antiquities of the Jews* |
| *J.W.* | *Jewish Wars* |
| Juvenal | |
| *Sat.* | *Satirae* |
| Philo | |
| *Decal.* | *De Decalogo* |
| *Fug.* | *De Fuga et Inventione* |
| *Gig.* | *De Gigantibus* |
| *Migr. Abr.* | *De Migratione Abrahami* |
| *Op. Mundi* | *De Opificione Mundi* |
| *Plant.* | *De Plantatione* |
| *Praem. et Poen.* | *De Praemiis et Poenis* |
| *Quaest. in Gen.* | *Quaestiones et Solutiones in Genesin* |
| *Quaest. in Exod.* | *Quaestiones et Solutiones in Exodum* |
| *Rer. Div. Her.* | *Quis Rerum Divinarum Heres Sit* |
| *Somn.* | *De Somniis* |
| *Spec. Leg.* | *De Specialibus Legibus* |
| *Virt.* | *De Virtutibus* |
| *Vit. Cont.* | *De Vita Contemplativa* |
| *Vit. Mos.* | *De Vita Mosis* |
| Philostratus | |
| *Vit. Apoll.* | *Vita Apollonii* |
| Plato | |
| *Leg.* | *Leges* |
| *Tim.* | *Timaeus* |
| Polybius | |
| *Hist.* | *Histories* |
| Tacitus | |
| *Hist.* | *Historiae* |
| Virgil | |
| *Eclog.* | *Ecologe* |

## II. Modern Literature

| | |
|---|---|
| AAUHR | Acta Universitatis Upsaliensisi Historia Religionum |
| AB | Anchor Bible |
| *ABD* | *Anchor Bible Dictionary* |
| *ABR* | *Australian Biblical Review* |
| ACNT | Augsburg Commentary on the New Testament |

| | |
|---|---|
| AGSU | Arbeiten zur Geschichte des Spätjudentums und Urchristentums |
| AnBib | Analecta biblica |
| *ANRW* | *Aufstieg und Niedergang der römischen Welt.* Edited by Hildegard Temporini. Berlin: Walter de Gruyter |
| *ASTI* | *Annual of the Swedish Theological Institute* |
| ATANT | Abhandlungen zur Theologie des Alten und Neuen Testaments |
| BAGD | Arndt, William F.; and Gingrich, F. Wilbur. *A Greek-English Lexicon of the New Testament and Other Early Christian Literature.* A Translation and Adaptation of the Fourth Revised and Augmented Edition of Walter Bauer's *Griechisch-Deutsches Wörterbuch zu den Schriften des Neuen Testaments und der übrigen urchristlichen Literatur.* 2d ed. Revised and augmented by F. Wilbur Gingrich and Frederick W. Danker from Walter Bauer's 5th ed., 1958. |
| *BARev* | *Biblical Archaeology Review* |
| BBB | Bonner Biblische Beiträge |
| *BBR* | *Bulletin of Biblical Research* |
| BDF | Blass, F.; and Debrunner, A. *A Greek Grammar of the New Testament and Other Early Christian Literature.* Translated and revised by Robert W. Funk |
| BENT | Beiträge zur Einleitung in das Neuen Testament |
| BETL | Bibliotheca ephemeridum theologicarum lovaniensium |
| BEvT | Beiträge zur evangelischen Theologie |
| BH | Biblische Handbibliothek |
| *BHH* | *Biblisch-Historisches Handwörterbuch* |
| *Bib* | *Biblica* |
| *BibSac* | *Bibliotheca Sacra* |
| *BJRL* | *Bulletin of the John Rylands University Library of Manchester* |
| BJS | Brown Judaic Studies |
| BNTC | Black's New Testament Commentary |
| *BTB* | *Biblical Theology Bulletin* |
| BWANT | Beiträge zur Wissenschaft vom Alten und Neuen Testament |
| *BZ* | *Biblische Zeitschrift* |
| BZNW | Beihefte zur *ZNW* |
| CBC | Cambridge Bible Commentary |
| *CBQ* | *Catholic Biblical Quarterly* |
| CEP | Contemporary Evangelical Perspectives |

| | |
|---|---|
| *ChrCent* | *Christian Century* |
| *CJT* | *Canadian Journal of Theology* |
| CMG | Corpus Medicorum Graecorum |
| *ConNT* | Coniectanea neotestamentica |
| CRINT | Compendia rerum iudaicarum ad novum testamentum |
| *CSR* | *Christian Scholars Review* |
| *CThM* | *Calwer Theologischen Monographien* |
| CTL | Cambridge Textbooks in Linguistics |
| *DivTh* | *Divus Thomas* |
| EB | Echter Bibel |
| EBC | Expositor's Bible Commentary |
| EBib | Etudes biblicos |
| *EDNT* | *Exegetical Dictionary of the New Testament* |
| EH | Europäische Hochschulschriften |
| EHS | Einleitung in die Heilige Schrift |
| EKKNT | Evangelisch-Katholischer Kommentar zum Neuen Testament |
| *EstBíb* | *Estudios bíblicos* |
| *EstEcl* | *Estudios Eclesiásticos* |
| ET | English Translation |
| *ETL* | *Ephemerides theologicae lovanienses* |
| ETS | Erfurter theologische Studien |
| *EvQ* | *Evangelical Quarterly* |
| *EvT* | *Evangelische Theologie* |
| *ExpTim* | *Expository Times* |
| FB | Forschung zur Bibel |
| FF | Foundations and Facets |
| FRLANT | Forschungen zur Religion und Literatur des Alten und Neuen Testaments |
| GNB | Good News Bible |
| GNS | Good News Studies |
| *GTJ* | *Grace Theological Journal* |
| *HBT* | *Horizons in Biblical Theology* |
| HeyM | Heythrop Monographs |
| HNT | Handbuch zum Neuen Testament |
| HNTC | Harper's New Testament Commentary |
| HTKNT | Herders theologischer Kommentar zum Neuen Testament |
| *HTR* | *Harvard Theological Review* |
| HTS | Harvard Theological Studies |
| *HUCA* | *Hebrew Union College Annual* |
| *IBS* | *Irish Biblical Studies* |
| ICC | International Critical Commentary |

| | |
|---|---|
| *IDB* | *Interpreter's Dictionary of the Bible* |
| *Int* | *Interpretation* |
| IRT | Issues in Religion and Theology |
| *ISBE* | *International Standard Bible Encyclopedia*, revised |
| *JBL* | *Journal of Biblical Literature* |
| *JBR* | Journal of Bible and Religion |
| *JETS* | *Journal of the Evangelical Theological Society* |
| *JJS* | *Journal of Jewish Studies* |
| *JSNT* | *Journal for the Study of the New Testament* |
| JSNTSS | Journal for the Study of the New Testament Supplement Series |
| JSOTSS | Journal for the Study of the Old Testament Supplement Series |
| JSPSS | Journal for the Study of the Pseudepigrapha Supplement Series |
| *JTS* | *Journal of Theological Studies* |
| KEK / KKNT | Kritisch-exegetischer Kommentar über das Neue Testament |
| *LB* | *Linguistica Biblica* |
| LCL | Loeb Classical Library |
| LD | Lectio divina |
| LoF | Library of Fathers |
| LSJ | Liddell-Scott-Jones, *Greek-English Lexicon* |
| *LTK* | *Lexicon für Theologie und Kirche* |
| MeyerK | H. A. W. Meyer, *Kritisch-exegetischer Kommentar über das Neue Testament* |
| MNTC | Moffatt New Testament Commentary |
| $NA^{26}$ | Nestle-Aland, *Novum Testamentum Graece*, 26th ed. |
| NCBC | New Century Bible Commentary |
| NEB | New English Bible |
| NEcB | Neue Echter Bibel |
| *Neot* | *Neotestamentica* |
| NIBC | New International Biblical Commentary |
| NICNT | New International Commentary on the New Testament |
| *NIDNTT* | *New International Dictionary of New Testament Theology* |
| NIGTC | New International Greek Testament Commentary |
| NIV | New International Version |
| *NovT* | *Novum Testamentum* |
| NovTSup | Novum Testamentum, Supplements |
| *NRT* | *La nouvelle revue théologique* |
| *NTA* | *Neutestamentliche Abhandlungen* |
| NTC | New Testament Commentary |
| NTD | Das Neue Testament Deutsch |

| | |
|---|---|
| *NTS* | *New Testament Studies* |
| OBO | Orbis biblicus et orientalis |
| OBT | Overtures to Biblical Theology |
| *OCD* | *Oxford Classical Dictionary* |
| ÖTK | Ökumenischer Taschenbuch-Kommentar |
| PGC | Pelican Gospel Commentaries |
| *PGM* | *Papyri graecae magicae.* Edited by K. Preisendanz |
| *PRS* | *Perspectives in Religious Studies* |
| PTMS | Pittsburgh Theological Monograph Series |
| QD | Questiones disputatae |
| *RAC* | *Reallexikon für Antike und Christentum* |
| *RB* | *Revue biblique* |
| RBS | Risk Book Series |
| *RefTR* | *Reformed Theological Review* |
| *ResQ* | Restoration Quarterly |
| *RevExp* | *Review and Expositor* |
| *RevQ* | *Revue de Qumran* |
| *RevScRel* | *Revue des sciences religieuses* |
| *RevThom* | *Revue thomiste* |
| *RHPR* | *Revue d'histoire et de philosophie religieuses* |
| *RivBib* | *Rivista Biblica* |
| RNT | Regensburger Neues Testament |
| RSV | Revised Standard Version |
| SB | Sources bibliques |
| SBEC | Studies in the Bible and Early Christianity |
| *SBET* | *Scottish Bulletin of Evangelical Theology* |
| SBLDS | Society of Biblical Literature Dissertation Series |
| SBLMS | Society of Biblical Literature Monograph Series |
| SBLSCS | Society of Biblical Literature Septuagint and Cognate Studies |
| SBLSP | Society of Biblical Literature Seminar Papers |
| SBM | Stuttgarter biblische Monographien |
| SBT | Studies in Biblical Theology |
| SC | Sources chrétiennes |
| *ScEccl* | *Sciences Ecclesiastiques* |
| *ScriptBull* | *Scripture Bulletin* |
| SHM | Studies in the History of Missions |
| SJ | Studia Judaica |
| *SJT* | *Scottish Journal of Theology* |
| SNT | Studien zum Neuen Testament |
| SNTSMS | Society of New Testament Studies Monograph Series |
| SNTU | Studien zum Neuen Testament und seiner Umwelt |
| SNTW | Studies of the New Testament and Its World |

| | |
|---|---|
| *ST* | *Studia theologica* |
| STDJ | Studies on the Texts of the Desert of Judah |
| Str-B | H. Strack and P. Billerbeck. *Kommentar zum Neuen Testament* |
| SUNT | Studien zur Umwelt des Neuen Testaments |
| SVC:TSECLL | Supplements to Vigiliae Christianae: Texts and Studies of Early Christian Life and Language |
| SVTP | Studia in Veteris Testamenti Pseudepigrapha |
| *SWJT* | *Southwestern Journal of Theology* |
| *TBei* | *Theologische Beiträge* |
| *TDNT* | *Theological Dictionary of the New Testament* |
| *TDOT* | *Theological Dictionary of the Old Testament* |
| THKNT | Theologischer Handkommentar zum Neuen Testament |
| *TLZ* | *Theologische Literaturzeitung* |
| TNTC | Tyndale New Testament Commentary |
| TPINTC | Trinity Press International New Testament Commentary |
| *TQ* | *Theologische Quartalschrift* |
| *TRE* | *Theologische Realenzyklopädie* |
| *TrinJ* | *Trinity Journal* |
| *TRu* | *Theologische Rundschau* |
| *TS* | *Theological Studies* |
| TU | Texte und Untersuchungen |
| *TynB* | *Tyndale Bulletin* |
| *TZ* | *Theologische Zeitschrift* |
| UCP | University of Canterbury Publications |
| UCP:NES | University of California Press: Near Eastern Studies |
| *USQR* | *Union Seminary Quarterly Review* |
| *VD* | *Verbum Domini* |
| *VE* | *Vox Evangelica* |
| VTSup | Vetus Testamentum, Supplements |
| WBC | Word Biblical Commentary |
| WMANT | Wissenschaftliche Monographien zum Alten und Neuen Testament |
| WUNT | Wissenschaftliche Untersuchungen zum Neuen Testament |
| *ZNW* | *Zeitschrift für die Neutestamentliche Wissenschaft* |

# I. Jesus, the Synoptic Gospels, and Acts

# Jesus and the Wild Animals (Mark 1:13): A Christological Image for an Ecological Age

Richard Bauckham

## 1

Modern NT scholarship is historically situated. It inevitably approaches the texts with concerns that derive from its cultural context, both Christian and secular. Such concerns can be heuristically useful, but they can also limit and distort our perceptions of the texts. In the present context of ecological crisis, in which it has become urgently necessary that Christian thinking recover a sense of human beings' place within God's creation, as fellow creatures with other creatures in the community of creation, new concerns are slowly bringing neglected aspects of the texts to light. At the same time it is becoming painfully obvious that much modern interpretation of the NT has been consciously and unconsciously influenced by the prevalent ideology of the modern West which for two centuries or so has understood human history as emancipation from nature. This modern ideology imagined human beings as the omnipotent subjects of their own history, and history as a process of liberation from nature, so that, freed from a limited place within the given constraints of the natural world, human beings may freely transform nature into a human world of their own devising. This rejection of human embeddedness in nature and of the mutual interrelations between human history and the rest of nature, in favor of an assumed independence of and supremacy over nature, is, of course, the ideological root of the present ecological crisis. Biblical theology has not escaped its influence, which appears in the strong tendency to set history against nature and salvation against creation. The assertion of salvation history and / or eschatology as the key concepts of biblical theology has at least tacitly endorsed the modern understanding of history as emancipation from nature. References to nature in the NT, especially the Gospels, have been persistently understood from the perspective of modern urban people, themselves wholly alienated from nature, for whom literary references to nature can only be symbols or picturesque illustrations of a human world unrelated to nature. But once the prevalent modern ideology is questioned, as it must be today, we are freed to read the NT differently. We can recognize that, in continuity with the OT tradition, it assumes that humans live in mutuality with the rest of God's creation, that salvation history and eschatology do not lift humans out of nature but heal precisely their distinctive relationship with the rest of nature.

However, to recognize that a concern with the human relationship to the rest of creation is a genuine aspect of the texts must not mean that we read into the texts our own particular ecological concerns, which arise from our own specific situation at a highly critical juncture in the history of creation on this planet. Before the texts can be relevant to our situation we must place them in the very different context of concern with the human relationship to nature to which they originally spoke. This task takes us into a whole area of historical scholarship — the study of ancient perceptions of the human relationship to nature and of the way such perceptions corresponded to ecological realities — which has been almost as neglected as the specifically biblical aspect of it. The present chapter is a preliminary contribution to the task: an ecological reading of one very brief but significant NT text. The attempt will be made both to understand the text in its original context, especially against the background of early Jewish perceptions of the relation between humans and wild animals, and then to indicate its new relevance today, when recontextualized in our situation of ecological destruction.

Our text is a mere four words of Mark's Gospel: Jesus "was with the wild animals" (ἦν μετὰ τῶν θηρίων). But the brevity of the statement should not mislead us into thinking it incidental. In Mark's concise account of Jesus in the wilderness (1:13) no words are wasted. In these four words, Mark takes up the question of the human relationship to wild animals and gives it a key place in the christological program which the prologue to his Gospel is designed to set out. Dealing with the human relationship with wild animals evidently belongs to Jesus' identity and mission as the messianic Son of God. Our text provides us with a christological image, unique to Mark's Gospel, sadly neglected in the Christian tradition, but, once its background is understood, of considerable symbolic resonance and ripe for contemporary retrieval. It is one of the biblical resources for developing a christology whose concern for the relationship of humanity to God will not exclude but include humanity's relationship to the rest of God's creatures.

## 2

On the significance of Mark's statement that Jesus was with the wild animals, broadly three lines of interpretation have been proposed:[1]

1. E. Fascher, "Jesus und die Tiere," *TLZ* 90 (1965) 561-70, provides an overview of interpretations (in German literature only) up to 1961.

(1) The wild animals are simply part of the setting in the wilderness, mentioned in order to stress the solitude: Jesus' lack of human companionship.[2] However, it is very doubtful that the animals would appear in this role in so concise an account, where otherwise every feature is charged with theological significance.

(2) The animals are to be associated with the demonic and seen as allies of Satan in his attack on Jesus. The scene is understood as a kind of holy war, with Satan and the wild animals ranged on one side, and Jesus and the angels on the other.[3] However, several important points can be made against this interpretation. First, the text is quite explicit about the role of the angels.[4] They do not belong to the armies of heaven, protecting Jesus or fighting with him against evil. They are ministering angels, present to provide for Jesus' needs (διηκόνουν αὐτῷ), almost certainly to provide him with food.

Second, the animals are not portrayed as antagonistic to Jesus, as Satan is. If Mark intended to line them up with Satan against Jesus and the angels, he has expressed himself very badly. Εἶναι μετὰ τινος can refer to mere physical proximity (Matt 5:25; John 9:40; 12:17; 20:24, 26), but it frequently has a strongly positive sense of close association in friendship or agreement or assistance (Matt 12:30; 26:69, 71; 28:20; Luke 22:59; John 3:2; 8:29; 15:27; 16:32; 17:24; Acts 7:9; 10:38; 18:10; Rom 15:33; Ign. *Phld.* 3:2; cf. the positive but less strong sense in John 3:26; 13:33; 14:9; 16:4; 17:12). In Mark's usage elsewhere the idea of close, friendly association predominates (3:14; 5:18; 14:67; cf. 4:36). Thus in Mark 1:13 the phrase ἦν μετὰ τῶν θηρίων, in the absence of any other indication of the kind of relationship envisaged, may convey a more or less strongly positive sense of association,[5] but it certainly does not express hostile confrontation.[6]

Third, there is no good evidence that in Jewish thinking the wild animals were regarded as demonic or as allies of Satan. The evidence usually cited for this does not in fact demonstrate it. There are indeed passages in which dangerous animals are used as metaphors of Satan or demons (Luke 10:19; 1 Pet 5:8;

2. E.g., W. Foerster, "θηρίον," *TDNT* 3:134; other references in U. Holzmeister, "'Jesus lebte mit den wilden Tieren': Mk 1,13," in *Vom Wort des Lebens: Festschrift für Max Meinertz,* ed. N. Adler (Münster: Aschendorff, 1951) 85-86; E. Grässer, "KAI HN META ΤΩΝ ΘΗΡΙΩΝ (Mk 1,13b): Ansätze einer theologischen Tierschutzethik," in *Studien zum Text und zur Ethik des Neuen Testaments: Festschrift zum 80. Geburtstag von Heinrich Greeven,* ed. W. Schrage (Berlin / New York: de Gruyter, 1986) 184 n. 24.

3. E. Best, *Mark: The Gospel as Story* (Edinburgh: T. & T. Clark, 1983) 57; other references in Grässer, "KAI HN META ΤΩΝ ΘΗΡΙΩΝ," 149 n. 27.

4. Grässer, "KAI HN META ΤΩΝ ΘΗΡΙΩΝ," 149.

5. So Holzmeister, "'Jesus lebte mit den wilden Tieren,'" 86 (quoting Wohlenberg); A. Vargas-Machuca, "La tentación de Jesús según Mc. 1,12-13: ¿Hecho real o relato de tipo haggádico?" *Estudios Eclesiásticos* 48 (1973) 172; Grässer, "KAI HN META ΤΩΝ ΘΗΡΙΩΝ," 149. But by not recognizing that the expression can express mere physical proximity, they put the point too strongly.

6. Εἶναι μετὰ τινος can express the physical proximity of someone known from other information to be hostile (Matt 5:25; John 9:40), but it cannot itself convey hostility. Therefore, if it is the hostile confrontation between Jesus and the animals that matters to Mark, he has oddly failed to express it, while using a phrase which instead could readily suggest peaceable and friendly association.

*Jos. As.* 12:9-10; cf. Ps 91:13), just as they appear, in the Psalms, for example, as metaphors for human enemies (e.g., Pss 10:9; 17:12; 22:12-13, 16, 21; 58:4-6; 118:12; 140:3). This is a natural metaphorical usage which tells us nothing about the significance of actual animals in a narrative such as Mark 1:13. It no more means that such actual animals are demonic than the fact that, for example, the lion is used as a symbol of the Messiah (Rev 5:5) means that actual lions are allies of the Messiah. There are also passages in which desolate places are portrayed as inhabited both by wild animals of the desert and by demons (Isa 13:21-22; 34:13-15; Rev 18:2). This shows that places uninhabitable by humans were associated both with wild animals and with evil spirits, and so helps to explain why Jesus encounters both Satan and the wild animals in the desert. The desert is a realm of threat to humans, and its inhabitants, whether animal or demonic, seem alien and threatening to humans. But again this does not make the animals themselves demonic or allies of Satan.

Finally, wild animals frequently appear in the OT and later Jewish literature as inimical to humans and threatening human life and livelihood. Of special interest here are a series of closely related passages in the *Testaments of the Twelve Patriarchs* (*T. Naph.* 8:4, 6; *T. Iss.* 7:7; *T. Benj.* 3:4-5; 5:2), which will be quoted and discussed more fully in section 3 below. In these passages wild animals are mentioned in parallel with Satan or demons as threats to humanity. But this does not make them demonic. It merely shows that wild animals were perceived as menacing human beings, as the demons do also in different ways. The animals and the demons appear as different kinds of nonhuman enemies of humanity. This evidence is relevant to Mark 1:13 — which, as we shall see, does need to be read against the background of the common Jewish view of wild animals as threats to humanity — but it does not prove that Mark portrays Jesus in conflict with the wild animals, as he is with Satan.

(3) According to the third line of interpretation, Jesus is portrayed at peace with the wild animals as the paradisal state of humans and animals was supposed to be in Jewish thought. By means of this motif Mark represents Jesus as the eschatological Adam who, having resisted Satan, instead of succumbing to temptation as Adam did, then restores paradise: he is at peace with the animals and the angels serve him.[7] This is the interpretation which has been argued most fully and persuasively in recent discussion,[8] and probably now commands

7. For older literature taking this view, see Vargas-Machuca, "La tentación de Jesús," 170 n. 33, 173-74 n. 45.

8. See esp. J. Jeremias, "Ἀδάμ," *TDNT* 1:141; W. A. Schultze, "Der Heilige und die wilden Tiere: Zur Exegege von Mc 1 13b," *ZNW* 46 (1955) 280-83; A. Feuillet, "L'épisode de la Tentation d'après l'Evangile selon Saint Marc (I,12-13)," *EstBíb* 19 (1960) 49-73; Vargas-Machuca, "La tentación de Jesús"; Grässer, "KAI HN META TΩN ΘHPIΩN." H.-G. Leder, "Sünderfallerzählung und Versuchungsgeschichte: Zur Interpretation von Mc 1 12f.," *ZNW* 54 (1963) 188-216, rejects the idea of an Adam typology, but accepts a reference to the OT expectation of peace with the wild animals in the messianic age.

the support of a majority of exegetes.[9] I shall broadly agree with it, but I shall shift the emphasis which most of its advocates have given. They generally fail to give the motif of Jesus' being with the wild animals any independent significance of its own, but tend to see it either as making a christological point — that Jesus is the new Adam — purely for its own sake or as just a way of expressing Jesus' victory over evil and inauguration of the kingdom. That Mark or his tradition should have been genuinely interested in affirming that the kingdom of God inaugurated by Jesus includes peace with wild animals seems not to occur to them.[10] It needs to be asked whether they are projecting their own lack of interest in the human relationship with nonhuman creatures back onto Mark.

## 3

The four words of Mark 1:13 in which we are interested form part of Mark's prologue (1:1-15), which introduces Jesus as the messianic Son of God embarking on his mission to inaugurate the kingdom of God. Following his anointing with the Spirit at the baptism, the Spirit drives Jesus into the wilderness (v 12) for a task which evidently must be fulfilled before he can embark on his preaching of the kingdom (v 14). Of Jesus' period in the wilderness Mark recounts:

> He was in the wilderness for forty days, being tempted by Satan.
> And he was with the wild animals (ἦν μετὰ τῶν θηρίων).
> And the angels ministered to him (1:13).

The wilderness, of course, had gathered rich symbolic associations in Jewish tradition,[11] but we should not be distracted by the symbolism it carries in the fuller Matthean and Lukan accounts of the temptation. Nor should we describe Mark 1:13 as Mark's temptation narrative, as is still commonly done.[12] The testing by Satan is for Mark only the first of three encounters, all important. So the wilderness as the place of Israel's testing, after the Exodus, which is

9. Among recent commentaries on Mark, see R. Pesch, *Das Markusevangelium,* vol. 1, HTKNT 2 / 1 (Freiburg / Basel / Vienna: Herder, 1976) 95-96; J. Gnilka, *Das Evangelium nach Markus,* vol. 1, EKKNT 2 / 1 (Zürich: Benziger / Neukirchen-Vluyn: Neukirchener, 1978) 57-58; W. Schmithals, *Das Evangelium nach Markus,* 2d ed., vol. 1, ÖTK 2.1 (Gütersloh: Mohn / Würzburg: Echter, 1986) 92-93; R. A. Guelich, *Mark 1–8:26,* WBC 34A (Dallas, Texas: Word, 1989) 38-39.

10. Grässer, "ΚΑΙ ΗΝ ΜΕΤΑ ΤΩΝ ΘΗΡΙΩΝ," is an exception.

11. See U. Mauser, *Christ in the Wilderness: The Wilderness Theme in the Second Gospel and Its Basis in the Biblical Tradition,* SBT (London: SCM, 1963) chs. 2–4; G. H. Williams, *Wilderness and Paradise in Christian Thought* (New York: Harper, 1962) 12-20.

12. E.g., J. D. Kingsbury, *The Christology of Mark's Gospel* (Philadelphia: Fortress, 1983) 68-69; Guelich, *Mark 1–8:26,* 36.

certainly significant in the Matthean and Lukan temptation narratives, is probably not determinative of the significance of the wilderness here, while the period of forty days is more likely to echo the period in which Elijah was fed by an angel in the wilderness (1 Kgs 19:4-8) than the forty years of Israel's wanderings in the wilderness.[13]

In Mark 1:13 the wilderness carries its most fundamental biblical and natural significance: it is the nonhuman sphere. In contrast to the cultivated land, where humans live with their domesticated animals, the wilderness was the world outside human control, uninhabitable by humans, feared as it threatened to encroach on the precarious fertility of the cultivated land and as the haunt of beings hostile to humans. It was the natural home not only of the wild animals but also of the demonic.[14] Hence Jesus goes into the wilderness precisely to encounter the beings of the nonhuman world. He must establish his messianic relationship to these before he can preach and practice the kingdom of God in the human world. Significantly, none of the three kinds of nonhuman being he encounters in the wilderness — Satan, the wild animals, the angels — subsequently appears in Mark's narrative of Jesus' activity in the human world.

The order of the nonhuman beings in Mark 1:13 — Satan, the wild animals, the angels — is not accidental. Satan is the natural enemy of the righteous person and can only be resisted: Jesus in the wilderness wins the fundamental victory over satanic temptation which he can then carry through against the activity of Satan's minions in the human world later in the Gospel (cf. especially 3:27).[15] The angels, on the other hand, are the natural friends of the righteous person: they minister to Jesus as they did to Elijah in the wilderness (1 Kgs 19:5-8) and to Adam and Eve in paradise (*b. Sanh.* 59b).[16] Between Satan and the angels the wild animals are more ambiguous: they are enemies of whom Jesus makes friends. This is the point I shall shortly establish.

We must first ask: What animals are Mark's θηρία? The word usually refers to wild animals in distinction from animals owned by humans, and usually to four-footed animals in distinction from birds, reptiles, and fish (so Gen 6:20; 7:20; Ps 148:10; Hos 2:18; 4:3, LXX; *1 Enoch* 7:5; *Apoc. Mos.* 29:13; Jas 3:7; *Barn.* 6:18), though snakes can be called θηρία (Gen 3:2, LXX; Acts 28:4–5; *Herm. Sim.* 9:26:1, 7; cf. Josephus *Ant.* 17.117). However, the word can also have the

13. The forty days Moses spent on Mt. Sinai (Exod 24:18) and the forty days Adam spent fasting and standing in the river (*L.A.E.* 6:1-3) are scarcely relevant. Feuillet, "L'épisode de la Tentation," attempts to link all the motifs in Mark 1:13 with Israel's wanderings in the wilderness, while also accepting the themes of the new Adam and the restoration of paradise.

14. J. Pedersen, *Israel: Its Life and Culture* (London: Oxford University / Copenhagen: Pio / Povl Branner, 1926) 454-60; Williams, *Wilderness and Paradise*, 12-13.

15. For this interpretation of 3:27, see E. Best, *The Temptation and the Passion: The Markan Soteriology*, SNTSMS 2 (Cambridge: Cambridge University, 1965) 15.

16. The reference to *L.A.E.* 4, given by Jeremias, "Ἀδάμ," 141 n. 6, and repeated mechanically by many others, is not relevant. *L.A.E.* 4:2 says that Adam and Eve in paradise ate the food of angels, not that angels fed them.

more limited sense of beasts of prey or animals dangerous to humans. Though sometimes given by the context or an adjective (cf. Gen 37:20, 32; Lev 26:22; Job 5:22-23; Hos 13:8, LXX; Tit 1:12; Josephus *Ant.* 17.120), this sense of dangerous beast of prey seems sometimes required by the word θηρίον without further indication of it (e.g., Josephus *Ant.* 2.35; Acts 11:6; Ign. *Eph.* 7:1; *Rom.* 4:1-2; 5:2; *Smyrn.* 4:2; Philostratus *Vit. Apoll.* 4.38).

This linguistic phenomenon corresponds to an ancient tendency, at least in the Jewish tradition, to consider wild animals primarily as threats to humanity, either directly threats to human life (Gen 37:20, 33; Lev 26:6, 22; 2 Kgs 2:24; 17:25-26; Prov 28:15; Jer 5:6; Lam 3:10-11; Ezek 5:17; 14:15; 34:25, 28; 13:7-8; Amos 5:19; *Pss. Sol.* 13:3; *T. Abr.* A 19:14-15; Rev 6:8) or, by attacks on flocks and herds and crops, threats to human livelihood (Lev 26:22; 1 Sam 17:34-37; Hos 2:12; Amos 3:12; John 10:12). The sense of wild animals as threatening belongs to the prevalent conceptualization of the world as conflict between the human world (human beings, their animals, and their cultivated land) and wild nature. Not many wild animals (as distinct from birds and fish) were hunted for food in Jewish Palestine, and so interest in wild animals tended to be limited to those which were threats to humanity. Seeing these animals purely from the perspective of sporadic human contact with them can produce a distorted and exaggerated view of their enmity to humans, as can be seen in a remarkable passage of Philo of Alexandria (*Praem.* 85–90), who portrays wild animals (θηρία), meaning the dangerous beasts of prey, as engaged in a continuous war against humans, constantly awaiting the opportunity to attack their human victims. That Philo, living in Egypt, thinks this is true of the Indian elephant is only mildly surprising, but that he considers the Egyptian hippopotamus to be a man-eater[17] shows the level of paranoia involved. Alien and excluded from the human world, wild animals had human fears projected onto them. It is also worth noting that the staging of conflicts between people and wild animals in the Roman amphitheatres, in which of course the animals were provoked into antagonism, would have heightened first-century people's sense of the enmity of wild animals. Of course, ancient peoples who perceived wild animals primarily as a threat did not notice that they themselves were also a threat to wild animals by steadily reducing their habitats as they extended the area of cultivated or deforested land.

We need not limit the θηρία of Mark 1:13 to the somewhat dangerous animals that might be encountered in the wilderness of Judea:[18] leopards, bears, wolves, poisonous snakes (cobras, desert vipers, and others), and scorpions. The

17. Cf. *Historia Monachorum in Aegypto* 4.3, where the hippopotamus is a threat — but to farmers' crops, not to human life. See also F. S. Bodenheimer, *Animal and Man in Bible Lands,* Collection de Travaux de l'Academie Internationale d'Histoire des Sciences 10 (Leiden: E. J. Brill, 1960) 51-52.

18. Mark does not, of course, specify the area geographically, beyond implying that it was accessible from the Jordan.

word does not prohibit well-informed readers from thinking also of other animals: hyenas, jackals, caracals (the desert lynx), desert foxes, Fennec foxes, wild boars, wild asses (the onager and the Syrian wild ass), antelopes (the desert oryx and the addax), gazelles, wild goats (the Nubian ibex), porcupines, hares, Syrian hyraxes, spiny mice, gerbils, sand rats, and jirds.[19] But both the word usage and the habits of thought which went with it would be likely to bring especially the dangerous animals to mind. Mark portrays Jesus in peaceable companionship with animals which were habitually perceived as inimical and threatening to humans. For clues to the meaning of this portrayal, we must turn now to the way in which the Jewish religious tradition understood the enmity between humans and wild animals and the ways in which it envisaged a healing of this enmity.

## 4

The Jewish tradition, against which Mark 1:13 should be read, saw the enmity of wild animals as a distortion of the created relationship of humans and wild animals and the result of human sin. In creation God established human dominion over the animals (Gen 1:26, 28; Ps 8:6-8; Sir 17:2-4; Wis 9:2-3; *Jub.* 1:14; *2 Enoch* 58:3; Philo *Op. Mundi* 83–88, 148; *2 Apoc. Bar.* 14:18; 4 Ezra 6:54),[20] which should have been peaceful and harmonious, but was subsequently disrupted by violence (cf. *Apoc. Mos.* 10–11). The Noahic covenant took account of this violence. As a result of the Noahic covenant, human dominion now involves permission to kill animals for food (Gen 9:3; Josephus *Ant.* 1.102), whereas according to Genesis (followed by many later Jewish writers) both humanity and the wild animals alike were originally vegetarian (Gen 1:29-30). The Noahic covenant also introduces the fear of humans by animals (Gen 9:2), presumably in order to protect humanity, now that violence has disrupted the originally peaceable relationship of humans and animals. But many later Jewish writers, not distinguishing the original institution of human dominion from its reformulation in the Noahic covenant, took the animals' fear of humans to be intrinsic to the human dominion as such (Sir 17:4; *Apoc. Mos.* 10:3; *Gen. Rab.* 34:12; cf. *T. Naph.* 8:4; *T. Benj.* 5:2). The animals are conceived as properly

19. For this (not exhaustive) list of animals to be found in such areas of Palestine, I am indebted to H. B. Tristram, *The Natural History of the Bible,* 10th ed. (London: SPCK, 1911); F. S. Bodenheimer, *Animal Life in Palestine* (Jerusalem: L. Mayer, 1935); G. Cansdale, *Animals of Bible Lands* (Exeter: Paternoster, 1970). Some OT passages are informative as to the animals generally associated with the desert: Deut 8:15; Job 24:5; 39:6-8; Isa 13:21-22; 32:14; 34:11-15; Jer 2:24; 5:6; 10:22; Zeph 2:14-15; Mal 1:8.

20. Several of these passages (Sirach, Wisdom, Philo, *2 Baruch,* 4 Ezra) are discussed by J. R. Levison, *Portraits of Adam in Early Judaism: From Sirach to 2 Baruch,* JSPSS 1 (Sheffield: JSOT, 1988) 36-37, 55-56, 66-73, 119-20, 131-32.

servants of their human rulers. Their fear of humans is the proper attitude of awe and respect owed by obedient subjects to their king (cf. Philo *Praem.* 89; *Op. Mundi* 148).

However, the situation in which wild animals were commonly perceived as menacing and humans went in fear of them was not even in accordance with the terms of the Noahic covenant, which promised that animals should go in fear of humans. This situation was sometimes understood as a reversal of the human dominion over the animals, resulting from human sin. Instead of humans ruling the animals, the animals rule humans (cf. *T. Naph.* 8:6). When, according to the *Apocalypse of Moses,* Seth is attacked by a wild animal and Eve demands to know why the animal is no longer afraid to attack the image of God, to which it was subjected in Eden (10:1-3), the animal points out that the situation is Eve's fault, "since the rule of the beasts (ἡ ἀρχὴ τῶν θηρίων) has happened because of you" (11:1).[21]

In the face of this situation, Jewish literature envisaged two ways in which the true relationship of humans and animals might be restored: one individual, one eschatological. In the first place, it could be thought that the truly righteous person should enjoy the relationship to animals which God originally intended for humanity. The earliest expression of this idea is found in Job 5:22-23, where Eliphas argues that the righteous person will be protected from all natural threats to human life, including that from wild animals:

> At destruction and famine you shall laugh,
> and shall not fear the wild animals of the earth.
> For you shall be in league with the stones of the field,
> and the wild animals shall be at peace with you.[22]

This passage notably does not refer to the idea of human dominion over the animals, and certainly not to the way this dominion was often interpreted in later Jewish literature, as requiring the fear, submission, and service of wild animals to humanity. Instead, it portrays a covenant of peace, a pact, between the righteous person and all God's creatures, even the stones of the field.[23]

In the rest of the passage of the *Apocalypse of Moses,* to which we have already referred, "the rule of the beasts" proves not to be an entirely accurate statement of the situation after the fall. Seth commands the animal to have regard for the image of God in him, and the animal accordingly flees from him (12:1-2). Evidently, Seth is a righteous person, who can therefore still exercise,

21. D. A. Bertrand, *La Vie Grecque d'Adam et d'Eve,* Recherches Intertestamentaires 1 (Paris: Maisonneuve, 1987) 118, takes this to mean that Eve's own rebellion set a precedent for the animals.

22. Biblical quotations in this section are from the NRSV.

23. The reference to stones is usually thought to be problematic, but it may well mean what the extant text says, implying that the stones will not frustrate agriculture; cf. R. Murray, *The Cosmic Covenant,* HeyM 7 (London: Sheed & Ward, 1992) 198 n. 14.

to some degree at least, the human dominion over the animals. Here it is accepted that, as a result of the fall, the animals are hostile to humanity (11:2), but the righteous person is at least protected from them.

Later the rabbis taught that the righteous person will rule the animals, but the unrighteous will be ruled by the animals (*Gen. Rab.* 8:12: *b. Sanh.* 38b: *b. Šabb.* 151b).[24] The same contrast appears in a series of passages in the *Testaments of the Twelve Patriarchs,*[25] in which the patriarchs warn their descendants that if they are wicked they will be subject to the wild animals, but if they are righteous they will exercise dominion over the animals — that is, they will subdue the animals and the animals will fear them:

> If you achieve the good, my children, men and angels will bless
> you,
> and God will be glorified through you among the Gentiles.
> The devil will flee from you:
> wild animals (τὰ θηρία) will be afraid of you,
> and the Lord will love you,[26]
> and the angels will stand by you. . . .
> The one who does not do good, men and angels will curse,
> and God will be dishonoured among the Gentiles because of him.
> The devil will inhabit him as his own instrument.
> Every wild animal will dominate (πᾶν θηρίον κατακυριεύσει)
> him,
> and the Lord will hate him. (*T. Naph.* 8:4, 6)

> You do these as well, my children,
> and every spirit of Beliar will flee from you,
> and no act of human evil will have power over (κυριεύσεται) you.
> Every wild creature you shall subdue (πάντα ἄγριον θῆρα
> καταδουλώσεσθε),
> as long as you have the God of heaven with you,
> and walk with all mankind in sincerity of heart. (*T. Iss.* 7:7)

24. Cf. J. Cohen, *"Be Fertile and Increase, Fill the Earth and Master It": The Ancient and Medieval Career of a Biblical Text* (Ithaca / London: Cornell University, 1989) 87, 100-101, 103, where additional references are given.

25. The general scholarly opinion that the *Testaments of the Twelve* is an originally Jewish work, which has received some Christian editing, is challenged by the argument of H. W. Hollander and M. de Jonge, *The Testaments of the Twelve Patriarchs: A Commentary,* SVTP 8 (Leiden: E. J. Brill, 1985) 82-85, that the *Testaments* as we have them are a Christian work, whose Jewish sources cannot be reconstructed. But it is in any case probable that the passages quoted here preserve Jewish traditions.

26. This line is omitted in some manuscripts, but the parallel with the last line of v 6 shows that it is most probably original; cf. Hollander and de Jonge, *The Testaments of the Twelve Patriarchs,* 318.

> For the person who fears God and loves his neighbor cannot be plagued by the spirit of Beliar since he is sheltered by the fear of God. Neither man's schemes nor those of animals (θηρίων) can prevail over (κυριευθῆναι) him, for he is aided in living by this: by the love which he has toward his neighbor. (*T. Benj.* 3:4-5)
>
> If you continue to do good, even the unclean spirits will flee from you and wild animals (τὰ θηρία) will fear you. (*T. Benj.* 5:2)[27]

The idea of reversal of dominion is evident in these passages, where the use of κατακυριεύω and καταδουλόω echoes Gen 1:26, 28. (The LXX uses ἄρχω for the dominion [רדה] over the animals [Gen 1:26, 28; cf. also *Barn.* 6:18] and κατακυριεύω for the subduing [כבשׁ] of the earth [Gen 1:28: 9:1, 7; cf. also *Barn.* 6:17], but at least in Gen 9:1, 7, where the LXX differs from the MT in referring to the subduing of the earth,[28] it is clear that in context this includes the dominion over the animals. Κατακυριεύω is used for dominion over the animals in Sir 17:4, LXX, and for dominion over all creatures in *Herm. Man.* 12:4:2.)[29]

Of particular interest in these passages from the *Testaments of the Twelve* is the way the devil and angels are correlated with the wild animals, just as they are in Mark 1:13. However, it is unlikely that there is a direct literary relationship between the *Testaments of the Twelve* and Mark 1:13,[30] since in the *Testaments of the Twelve* the relationships of the wicked and the righteous to other beings are not limited to their relationships to the devil, the wild animals, and angels, but also include their relationships to God and to other humans. This also shows that in these passages the wild animals are not represented specifically as the agents or allies of the devil, but simply as one category of living being, who behave differently toward the righteous and the wicked, as do also God, the angels, the devil, and other humans. In *T. Naph.* 8:4, 6, the complete set of five relationships appear; in *T. Iss.* 7:7 and *T. Benj.* 3:4-5, the reference is to evil spirit(s), humans, and wild animals; in *T. Benj.* 5:2, only evil spirits and wild animals appear. The general point is that the righteous and the wicked enjoy

27. Translations from H. C. Kee, "Testaments of the Twelve Patriarchs," in *The Old Testament Pseudepigrapha,* ed. J. H. Charlesworth, vol. 1 (London: Darton, Longman and Todd, 1983) 813-14, 804, 825-26. For the idea that Beliar (Satan) will flee from the righteous person, see also *T. Dan* 5:1; *T. Sim.* 3:5; Jas 4:7; *Herm. Man.* 12:4:7.

28. On this difference, see Cohen, *Be Fertile and Increase,* 26-27.

29. In this passage the human dominion over all creatures seems to provide the basis not only for mastering (κατακυριεύω) the commandments given by the Shepherd, but also for dominating (κατακυριεύω) the devil (12:4:7; 12:6:2, 4; cf. 5:1:1; 7:2; 9:10; 12:2:5). Since this is connected with the notion that the devil will flee from the righteous person (12:4:7), there may be some connection, via common tradition, between Hermas and the *Testaments of the Twelve.*

30. Murray, *The Cosmic Covenant,* 128 (following H. A. Kelly), suggests that *T. Naph.* 8 is dependent on Mark 1:13.

different kinds of relationship (beneficial for the righteous, detrimental to the wicked) to other living beings, who are comprehensively specified in *T. Naph.* 8:4, 6, and selectively instanced in the other passages. In Mark 1:13, however, it is not Jesus' relationships with all other living beings which are depicted, but his relationships with precisely the three kinds of living being he could encounter in the wilderness, rather than in the human world. In a general sense the passages in the *Testaments of the Twelve* enable us to see that Mark 1:13 depicts relationships with other beings which characterize a righteous person, but in its selection of three such relationships it must have a more specific purpose in view.

For a clue to this more specific purpose, we must turn to the second way in which Jewish literature envisaged that the originally intended relationship of humans and wild animals might be restored. This is the eschatological expectation that the righting of all wrongs in the messianic age of the future would bring peace between wild animals and humans. For example, Hosea's promise of the renewal of God's covenant with his people,[31] when their punishment is over, includes a covenant God makes with the animals for his people's sake:

> I will make for you a covenant on that day with the wild animals, the birds of the air, and the creeping things of the ground; and I will abolish the bow, the sword, and war from the land; and I will make you lie down in safety. (Hos 2:18).

Here protection from wild animals is linked with protection from war, as it is in Lev 26:6; Ezek 34:25-29 (cf. 14:15-18). Since birds and creeping things are mentioned, the thought is not primarily or exclusively of the threat to human life from dangerous wild animals, but of the threat to human livelihood from all animals which consume or destroy the produce or the domestic animals of humans (cf. Hos 2:12; Lev 26:22). The covenant with the animals is therefore not unconnected with the promise of plenty which is characteristic of such prophecies of an ideal time to come (Hos 2:22; Lev 26:4-5; Ezek 34:26-27, 29; Zech 8:12).

The classic scriptural expression of the hope of peace between humans and wild animals is, of course, Isa 11:6–9:

> The wolf shall live with the lamb,
> the leopard shall lie down with the kid,
> the calf and the lion and the fatling together,
> and a little child shall lead them.
> The cow and the bear shall graze,
> their young shall lie down together;

31. Murray, *The Cosmic Covenant*, 27-32, discusses the whole passage (Hos 2:2-23), arguing that it turns on the "cosmic covenant" of 2:18.

and the lion shall eat straw like the ox.
The nursing child shall play over the hole of the asp,
  and the weaned child shall put his hand on the adder's den.
They will not hurt or destroy on all my holy mountain;
for the earth shall be full of the knowledge of the LORD,
  as the waters cover the sea.

It is important to notice that this passage belongs in the context of the account of the messianic king and his righteous rule (11:1–5).[32] It has often been misunderstood by modern readers as depicting simply peace between animals, as well as between animals and humans. In fact, it depicts peace between the human world, with its domesticated animals (lamb, kid, calf, bullock, cow), and the wild animals (wolf, leopard, lion, bear, poisonous snakes), which were normally perceived as threats both to human livelihood (dependent on the domestic animals) and to human life. Human children, rather than adults, appear for the same reason that the domestic animals are represented mainly by their young: children (cf. Lev 26:22; 2 Kgs 2:23-24) and young animals (cf. 1 Sam 17:34-35) were especially vulnerable to wild predators. That the expectation is controlled by the prevalent perception of enmity between the human world and the dangerous wild animals is shown by the fact that there is no mention of peace between the predatory wild animals and the *wild* animals (such as gazelles or antelope) which they usually hunt and kill, but only of peace between the predatory wild animals and the domestic animals which they sometimes attack.[33] Of course, the former is also *implied*, both in the fact that the bear and the lion become vegetarian (11:7) and the snakes harmless (11:8), and in the cessation of all harm and destruction (11:9), which must mean also that humans are to be vegetarian. The picture is of a restoration of paradise ("my holy mountain" is Eden, as in Ezek 28:13-14) and the original vegetari-

32. Murray, *The Cosmic Covenant*, 103-5.

33. So the Isaianic vision is closer than Murray, *The Cosmic Covenant*, 108, allows to the account of the mythical ideal land of Dilmun in the Sumerian poem "Enki and Ninhursaga":

In Dilmun . . .
no lion kills,
no wolf carries off a lamb.
Unknown is a dog harassing kids,
unknown is a hog devouring grain.
(If) a widow spreads malt on the roof
no bird of the skies comes foraging,
no pigeon gorges itself (?)

(quoted in Murray, *The Cosmic Covenant*, 108). Cf. also Virgil *Eclog.* 4.21-25; 5.60-61; Horace *Epod.* 16.33. H. Jeanmaire, *Le Messianisme de Vergil* (Paris: J. Vrin, 1930) 194-95, points out the parallel between the Sumerian poem and Virgil's fourth Eclogue, in order to suggest that the idea of peace between the animals in a terrestrial paradise had wide currency, with ancient origins.

For the wild animals of Isa 11:6-7 as threats to farm animals, see Cansdale, *Animals of Bible Lands*, 108, 112, 118, 119; Bodenheimer, *Animal and Man in Bible Lands*, 42.

anism of all living creatures (Gen 1:29-30), but it is presented from the perspective of ancient people's sense of threat from dangerous wild animals.[34] That threat is to be removed, the enmity between humans and wild animals healed. The emphasis is on peaceable relationships (as in Job 5:22-23) rather than the human dominion over the animals, but there is at least a hint of the latter (strong enough to be taken up, as we shall see, in later Jewish literature) in v 6. It seems that the wild animals are to become domestic animals, herded by a child along with the animals which humans now keep for their own purposes. But, since they are evidently not to be killed for food, we should not take the point too literally. When the writer wishes to envisage peace between humans and wild animals, he thinks naturally of the peaceable relationship already existing between humans and their domestic animals (leaving aside the slaughter of animals for food) and extends it to include the wild animals too.

In a later passage in the book of Isaiah, depicting the new heavens and the new earth (65:17), 11:6-9 is taken up in an abbreviated form:

> The wolf and the lamb shall feed together,
> the lion shall eat straw like the ox;
> but the serpent — its food shall be dust!
> They shall not hurt or destroy
> on all my holy mountain,
> says the LORD. (Isa 65:25)

Here an explicit allusion to Genesis (3:14) has been introduced, presumably implying that although the original harmony of humans and animals will be restored, the serpent which was responsible for first disrupting that harmony will continue to serve its punishment.

Isaiah 11:6-9 continued to inspire postbiblical Jewish expectations of the messianic age. In the third *Sibylline Oracle* it is very faithfully paraphrased:

> Wolves and lambs will eat grass together in the mountains.
> Leopards will feed together with kids.
> Roving bears will spend the night together with calves.
> The flesh-eating lion will eat husks at the manger
> like an ox, and mere infant children will lead them
> with ropes. For he [God] will make the beasts on earth harmless.
> Serpents and asps will sleep with babies

34. Therefore I do not accept the neat distinction suggested by Murray, *The Cosmic Covenant*, 34: "The Bible contains, in fact, two models for thinking about humans and animals: one paradisal, the other this-worldly and realistic. The first way uses the picture of peace *with and between* wild animals as a metaphor for cosmic and social peace; the second way sees peace *from* them as a practical aspect of desired *šalom*." He does not recognize that the second model includes peace between wild animals and domestic animals, and so gives more emphasis than is justified to the first model in his interpretation of Isa 11:6-9 (*The Cosmic Covenant*, 105-9).

> and will not harm them, or the hand of God will be upon them. (*Sib. Or.* 3:788-95)[35]

Philo takes up the hope in very much his own way.[36] Having spoken, in the passage to which we have already referred, of the continuous war in which all wild animals are engaged against humans, he expresses the hope that it will come to an end:

> This war no mortal can quell; that is done only by the Uncreated, when He judges that there are some worthy of salvation, men of peaceful disposition who cherish brotherly affection and good fellowship. . . . Would that this good gift might shine upon our life and that we might be able to see that day when savage creatures become tame and gentle. But a very necessary preliminary to this is that the wild beasts within the soul shall be tamed. . . . For is it not foolish to suppose that we shall escape the mischief which the brutes outside us can do if we are always working up those within us to dire savagery? Therefore we need not give up hope that when the wild beasts within us are fully tamed the animals too will become tame and gentle. When that time comes I believe that bears and lions and panthers and the Indian animals, elephants and tigers, and all others whose vigour and power are invincible, will change their life of solitariness and isolation for one of companionship, and gradually in imitation of the gregarious creatures show themselves tame when brought face to face with mankind. They will no longer as heretofore be roused to ferocity by the sight, but will be awe-struck into respectful fear of him as their natural lord and master, while others will grow gentle in emulation of the docility and affection for the master shown for instance by

35. Translation from J. J. Collins, "Sibylline Oracles," in *Old Testament Pseudepigrapha,* 1:379. Lactantius *Inst. Div.* 7.24.12, quoting this passage, was the first to suggest that it was Virgil's source for his picture of paradise in *Eclog.* 4.21-25 ("the herds shall not fear the great lions. . . . The serpent, too, shall perish. . . ."). J. B. Mayor, "Source of the Fourth Eclogue," in J. B. Mayor, W. W. Fowler, and R. S. Conway, *Virgil's Messianic Eclogue: Its Meaning, Occasion, and Sources* (London: J. Murray, 1907) 87-140, examined the parallels between the fourth Eclogue and both Isaiah and the third Sibylline Oracle, concluding that Virgil knew either Isaiah or a source which reproduced Isaiah more fully than the third Sibylline Oracle. Since Mayor wrote, the possibility that Virgil knew either Isaiah or the third Sibylline has often been discounted (see J. Carcopino, *Virgile et le Mystère de la IV^e Églogue* [Paris: L'Artisan du Livre, 1930] 69-70; H. J. Rose, *The Eclogues of Vergil* [Berkeley / Los Angeles: University of California, 1942] 194), but the only parallel to the idea of peace between animals in Greek or Roman literature seems to be Horace *Epod.* 16.33, while Carcopino's suppositon of Pythagorean influence on both Virgil and Horace is vague. In view of Virgil's own reference to the Cumean Sibyl (*Eclog.* 4.4), it remains possible that he knew a Jewish Sibylline text and accepted it (as it was intended to be accepted by pagans) as a genuine Sibylline oracle.

36. That Philo has Isaiah 11 in mind is suggested by the fact that he not only refers to the wolf and the lamb (*Praem.* 87), which was a virtually proverbial image (Matt 10:16; Luke 10:3; Acts 20:29), but also to all the other wild animals which appear in Isaiah 11: bears, lions, leopards, poisonous snakes, while adding some more exotic examples (*Praem.* 89–90).

> the little Maltese dogs, who express their fondness with the tails which they so cheerily wag. Then too the tribes of scorpions and serpents and the other reptiles will have no use for their venom. The Egyptian river too carries man-eating creatures called crocodiles and hippopotamuses in close proximity to the inhabitants of the country, so too the seas have multitudinous species of very formidable animals. Among all these the man of worth will move sacrosanct and inviolate because God has respected virtue and given it the privilege that none should imagine mischief against it. (*Praem.* 87–90)[37]

Several points are of special interest in this passage. In the first place, it seems that Philo brings together the idea that the truly righteous person will enjoy peace with wild animals and the eschatological expectation of a time when the wild animals will cease to be a threat to humans. At first he seems to be speaking in terms of the former idea, but it then becomes clear that he does envisage a time when there will be a sufficiently widespread change of heart in human beings to bring about a general peace with the animals. Second, like Isaiah 11, he expects the wild animals to become like domestic animals. Third, it is clear that what he envisages is a restoration of the human dominion over the animals given at creation.

The restoration of human dominion is also the theme of the adaptation of Isa 11:6-9 in *2 Apoc. Bar.* 73:6. In the context of an account of how all the evils of life in the present age will be abolished in the messianic age to come, this verse predicts:

> And the wild beasts will come from the wood and serve men,
> and the asps and the dragons will come out of their holes to subject
> themselves to a child.[38]

Since the following verse predicts that women will no longer suffer pain in childbirth (cf. Gen 3:16), it is clear that a restoration of paradisal conditions is envisaged. These conditions include the restoration of human dominion over the animals, which involves not only that the wild animals become tame like domestic animals, but also that they serve humanity like domestic animals. The author has found this notion in Isa 11:6, and deduced that, if the animals subject themselves to the child in that verse, then the reference to the child again in v 8 must have the same sense.

Finally, Papias quotes, as words of Jesus transmitted by John the elder, a prophecy of the paradisal age of the future which is closely dependent on Jewish apocalyptic tradition. Following an account of the extraordinary fruitfulness of the earth (cf. *2 Apoc. Bar.* 29:5; *1 Enoch* 10:19),[39] the prophecy continues:

37. Translation from F. H. Colson, *Philo*, vol. 8, LCL (London: Heinemann / Cambridge, Massachusetts: Harvard University, 1939) 365, 367.

38. Translation from A. F. J. Klijn, "2 (Syriac Apocalypse of) Baruch," in *Old Testament Pseudepigrapha*, 1:645.

39. For other parallels, see J.-D. Dubois, "Remarques sur le Fragment de Papias cité par Irénée," *RHPR* 71 (1991) 6-8.

> all the animals feeding on these fruits produced by the soil will in turn become peaceful and harmonious toward one another, and fully subject to man (*subiecta hominibus cum omni subiectione*). (*ap.* Irenaeus *Adv. Haer.* 5.33.3)[40]

Here Isa 11:6–9 is interpreted in a way similar to *2 Apoc. Bar.* 73:6, as implying the subjection of animals to humanity, but the link with the paradisal fruitfulness of the earth is novel. Presumably the idea is not only that all the wild animals will be vegetarian, but also that there will no longer be any competition between animals or between animals and humans for limited resources. Vegetarian abundance will guarantee both peace between animals and the restoration of human dominion in its original form, so that the animals willingly obey their human rulers.

## 5

If we ignored the context of Mark 1:13, we might classify Jesus, in terms of the Jewish traditions we have examined, simply as the individual righteous person who is at peace with the wild animals. But Jesus in Mark's prologue is no mere individual. He is the messianic Son of God. When he resists Satan in the wilderness, he does so, not as merely an individual righteous person, but as the messianic Son of God on behalf of and for the sake of others. Similarly it is the messianic peace with wild animals that Jesus establishes. He establishes it only representatively, in his own person, and so the objection that a restoration of paradise should not be located in the wilderness is beside the point. More to the point is that all the wild animals of Isaiah 11, with the exception of the lion (unless the forests of the Jordan valley may be included in Mark's wilderness), would be most easily encountered in the wilderness. Jesus does not restore the paradisal state as such, but he sets the messianic precedent for it.

Whether, in that case, Mark 1:13 should be said to embody a new Adam christology is more doubtful. Proponents of the view that Mark 1:13 refers to the paradisal state of peace with the wild animals, eschatologically restored, have usually linked this idea with that of Jesus as the new or eschatological Adam, who resists the devil, whereas Adam and Eve succumbed, and who restores the peaceful relationship with other creatures which Adam and Eve disrupted. Such an implication cannot be ruled out, but there seems to be no other trace of a new Adam christology in Mark. So it may be more relevant to recall that Isa 11:6-9, the classic vision of the messianic peace with wild animals, is connected with Isa 11:1-5, the classic prophecy of the Davidic Messiah. The peace with wild animals belongs to this Messiah's righteous reign. Mark's account of Jesus' baptism (1:9-11), in which he is anointed with the Spirit (Isa 11:2) and

40. Translation from J. B. Lightfoot, J. R. Harmer, and M. W. Holmes, *The Apostolic Fathers* (Leicester: Inter-Varsity, 1989) 322.

addressed as God's Son (Ps 2:7), identifies him as this Davidic Messiah,[41] who therefore inaugurates the messianic age not only by overcoming Satan, but also by establishing the messianic peace with wild animals. Against the background of the Jewish eschatological expectation, the latter has a real significance in its own right. It is not simply a symbol of Jesus' victory over Satan or of his inauguration of the age of eschatological salvation.[42] Peace with wild animals is actually one aspect of eschatological salvation. There is no reason to doubt that first-century people, who were well aware that they shared the world with wild animals, would be interested in this aspect of salvation for its own sake.

Mark's simple phrase μετὰ τῶν θηρίων, indicating a peaceable and friendly companionship with the animals, contrasts with the way the restoration of the proper human relationship to wild animals is often portrayed in the Jewish literature. The animals are not said to fear him, submit to him, or serve him. The concept of human dominion over the animals as domination for human benefit is entirely absent. The animals are treated neither as subjects nor as domestic servants. In its image of peaceable companionship Mark 1:13 is closest, among the passages we have discussed, to Job 5:22-23 and Isa 11:6-9. Jesus does not terrorize or dominate the wild animals, he does not domesticate them, nor does he even make pets of them. He is simply "with them." But the real beauty of that phrase in Mark 1:13 will only appear fully when we recontextualize the image in our own context and our very different perception of the human relationship to wild animals.

The context to which Mark 1:13 originally spoke was one in which wild animals threatened humanity and their wilderness threatened to encroach on the human world. The messianic peace with wild animals promised, by healing the alienation and enmity between humans and animals, to liberate humans from that threat. But our context is one in which it is now clearly we who threaten the survival of wild animals, encroach on their habitat, and threaten to turn their wilderness into a wasteland they cannot inhabit. To make the point one need only notice how many of the animals Jesus could have encountered in the Judean wilderness have become extinct in Palestine this century: the bear, the onager, the desert oryx, the addax, the ostrich, and no doubt others. Others, such as the leopard and the gazelle, would not have survived without modern conservation measures. Mark's image of Jesus' peaceable companionship with the animals in the wilderness survives this reversal of situation and its pregnant simplicity gains a new power. For us Jesus' companionable presence with the wild animals affirms their independent value for themselves and for God. He does not adopt them into the human world, but lets them be themselves in peace, leaving them their wilderness, affirming them as creatures who share the world with us in the community of God's creation.

41. Kingsbury, *The Christology of Mark's Gospel*, 60-68.
42. *Contra*, e.g., Vargas-Machuca, "La tentación de Jesús."

Most of the Christian tradition in the modern period, understanding the God-given human dominion over the animals as permission to treat them with regard to nothing other than their usefulness to humans, has encouraged and colluded with modern Western society's spoliation of the earth, which is currently exterminating whole species daily. In this situation we urgently need to retrieve another perspective, which the Christian tradition has occasionally glimpsed, most famously and clearly in the life of Francis of Assisi.[43] This is the possibility of living fraternally (I use the word because of Francis's sense of all creatures as sisters and brothers) with wild creatures, and experiencing thereby the grace of otherness which God gives us in the diversity of the animal creation and which is missed when animals are reduced merely to usefulness or threat. Mark's image of Jesus with the wild animals can be retrieved as the christological warrant for and symbol of this possibility, given in creation, given back in messianic redemption. It is a symbol. It does not in itself constitute an ethic of animal rights. But since it is precisely the modern demythologizing of nature which has turned it into a mere object of human use and exploitation, our need is very much for religious symbols of the human relationship to nature, as many people in the green movement realize. Mark 1:13 offers us perhaps a christological alternative to the Green Man.

43. For the perception of the relation between humans and animals in the medieval tradition of stories of saints and animals, as well as by Francis, see R. Bauckham, "Attitudes to the Non-Human Creation in the History of Christian Thought," in *Stewarding Creation* (Bristol: Regius, forthcoming).

# The Kingdom of God and Christology in the Gospels

George R. Beasley-Murray

That the Gospels were written in the light of the resurrection faith of the primitive Christian communities has become a self-evident truism to the vast majority of NT scholars. One of the first things that I learned about the Gospels was that they were written backward. That is, they started from the astonishing news that the crucified Jesus was alive from the dead. This set the events surrounding his death in a wholly new light, for since the resurrection of Jesus was clearly an act of God the whole process of his arrest, trial, and crucifixion was seen in accordance with the divine purpose, and was therefore so proclaimed. Inevitably the events in the public ministry of Jesus were similarly interpreted, and the whole story of Jesus, beginning with the baptism of John, became part of the gospel preached, and at length the gospel written. That was all very reasonable, and obvious when once pointed out. What was not made clear to me, however, was the inference drawn that the Easter experiences of the early disciples (not merely of the Twelve) led to the replacement of their early incomprehension by enthusiastic interpretations of the way and the words of Jesus, as prophets gave utterances in the name of the risen Lord and teachers freshly interpreted and elaborated his sayings and doings. This process is thought to have gone on not only among Jewish believers in Palestine but also in the Diaspora and in Gentile churches in the wider world, till at length the original picture of Jesus and his movement became smothered under an overlay of enthusiastic proclamation of the risen Christ.

Surprisingly little questioning has been done among critical scholars concerning this assumed process of development of the Jesus tradition. On the contrary, F. Young spoke for many of her contemporaries when she affirmed, "We do not have the evidence available now to speculate realistically about Jesus' so-called Messianic consciousness. . . . The implicit claims were not merely made explicit, but developed by the faith of the church."[1] There is little doubt that a considerable proportion of NT scholars today share that conviction. Rudolf Bultmann certainly did, but from a point of view peculiar to his philosophical outlook: "What can be said about the historical Jesus," he wrote, "belongs to the realm of the Χριστὸς κατὰ σάρκα. That Christ, however, does not concern us. What went on within Jesus' own heart I do not know, and I do not want to know."[2] His own pupils and colleagues, as we are all aware, reacted to that attitude. Ernst Käsemann made it known that he and some of his friends were "obliged to set limits to the proposition that the event of Easter was the foundation of the Christian kerygma and (were) compelled to enquire as to what the significance of the historical Jesus for faith may be." It had become clear to them that "only the proclamation of Jesus can enable us to encounter the historical Jesus and to comprehend his history"; hence, "everything will depend on defining in a new and better way the relationship of the message of Jesus to the proclamation about the Crucified and Risen One."[3] To achieve that end a caveat is entered: ". . . every departure from historical criticism, distinguishing as it does between authentic material and what dates from after Easter, prevents a proper interpretation."[4] So the distinction between pre- and post-Easter traditions of sayings of Jesus is the primary issue of historical criticism in the quest for recovering the authentic proclamation of Jesus. In practice, of course, that depends on one's choice of criteria of authenticity. Experience has shown that that is a highly subjective decision, leading to some extraordinary variations in reconstructions of the historical Jesus.

John Crossan, for example, in his recent reconstruction of the ministry of the historical Jesus, certainly took great pains to scrutinize carefully the text of the Gospels, and equally great pains to eliminate any possible influence of the resurrection of Jesus on the Evangelists' portrayal of his life and teaching. This, together with his own criteria of authenticity and comparison with non-canonical sources, led him to slim down considerably the selection of sayings of Jesus which he could safely use. The result of this process is a depiction of Jesus as a radical Galilean peasant, whose understanding of the kingdom of God was more akin to that of the Greek Cynics than to that of OT prophets and apocalyptic proclaimers, including John the Baptist.[5] It is instructive to compare

1. "A Cloud of Witnesses," in *The Myth of God Incarnate,* ed. J. Hick (London: SCM, 1977) 18.

2. "Zur Frage der Christologie," in *Glauben und Verstehen,* 1:101; cited by W. Marxsen, *The Beginnings of Christology: A Study of Its Problems,* Facet Books, Biblical Series 22, ed. J. Reumann (Philadelphia: Fortress, 1969) 9.

3. "New Testament Problems of Today," in *New Testament Questions of Today* (Philadelphia: Fortress, 1967) 12.

4. Käsemann, "On the Subject of Primitive Christian Apocalyptic," in *New Testament Questions,* 113.

5. *The Historical Jesus: The Life of a Mediterranean Jewish Peasant* (San Francisco: Harper, 1991). Note especially the statement in his conclusion: "The Historical Jesus was, then, a *peasant*

his approach to the Gospel traditions with that of J. P. Meier, also a Catholic scholar concerned to reveal the historical Jesus; he has required a large volume to clarify the presuppositions needed for such a project, which will be undertaken in a second volume. His first criterion of authenticity is that of "embarrassment" (seen, for example, in the baptism of Jesus by John, and Jesus' ignorance of the time of the end, Mark 13:32). In discussing this matter Meier waxes eloquent:

> An intriguing corollary arises from these cases of "embarrassment." All too often the oral tradition of the early Church is depicted as a game of "anything goes," with charismatic prophets uttering anything or everything as the words of the Lord Jesus and storytellers creating accounts of miracles and exorcisms according to Jewish and pagan models. The evangelists would simply have crowned this wildly creative process by molding the oral tradition according to their own redactional theology. One would get the impression that throughout the first Christian generation there were no eyewitnesses to act as a check on fertile imaginations, nor original-disciples-now-become-leaders who might exercise some control over the developing tradition, and no striking deeds and sayings of Jesus that stuck willy-nilly in people's memories. The fact that embarrassing material is found as late as the redaction of the Gospels reminds us that beside a creative thrust there was also a conservative force in the Gospel tradition.[6]

That "conservative force" alongside the "creative thrust" needs to be reckoned with more than is commonly done in our treatment of the Gospel traditions. How often one has heard a saying of Jesus in the Gospels dismissed without adequate reason, or simply because it "suits" the post-resurrection situation of the early Christians! It seems to be assumed that the disciples' experiences of the presence of the risen Lord were bound to transform their recollection of the teaching of Jesus in the direction of changing its content. On the contrary, is it not altogether more likely that those experiences threw a flood of light on that teaching, so that what before was mystifying now became crystal clear? And would that not apply above all to utterances of Jesus concerning the nature of his mission from God? Jürgen Moltmann appears wholeheartedly to agree with that sentiment. With all his emphasis on the importance of the resurrection of Jesus in the christological reflection of the early church he recognizes that we have no grounds for assuming that it led to a significant modification of its presentation of Jesus. He affirmed:

---

*Jewish Cynic* [author's italics]. His peasant village was close enough to a Greco-Roman city like Sepphoris that the sight and knowledge of Cynicism are neither inexplicable nor unlikely. But his work was among the farms and villages of Lower Galilee" (421-22).

6. *A Marginal Jew: Rethinking the Historical Jesus,* vol. 1: *The Roots of the Problem and the Person* (Garden City, New York: Doubleday, 1991) 169-70.

> Historically speaking, it is inadmissible to assume that on the basis of its experience with the risen and present Christ the Christian community projected anything into the history of Jesus which was inconsistent with the remembrance of him as he was during his lifetime. Historically it is more plausible to assume that the experience of the present Christ and the remembrance of the Christ of the past corresponded, and complemented one another; for the fundamental assertions 'Jesus is the Christ' and 'Christ is Jesus' identify remembrance and experience, experience and remembrance.[7]

That statement was made in connection with the investigation of the Gospels to examine what they reflect of Jesus prior to the resurrection. Moltmann started with a consideration of the "messianic secret." I would ask the simpler but related question as to what there was in the ministry of Jesus which led to the interpretation of Easter in terms of his exaltation as Lord and Messiah at God's right hand and his death as redemptive. Appearances of a beloved teacher after his death would by no means necessarily have that significance, and certainly it would not follow from the reconstructions of Jesus' ministry offered by some scholars of late. On the basis of the Gospels themselves the answer to the question raised above is transparently clear: it is the unique nature of the proclamation of the kingdom of God by Jesus, attested in every strand of the Gospel tradition. Note the use of the term "unique" in that assertion. Many prophets and apocalyptists in Israel preached the coming of the saving sovereignty of God; the hope was shared by Israel's Diaspora; adherents of religions other than Israel's (notably Zoroastrianism) looked for a Deliverer and Deliverance; and of late we have been reminded by B. Mack and J. Crossan that Greek philosophers had their own understanding of the kingdom of God.[8] This is fine, it attests the reality of the work of the Spirit of God in all times and places, and we have no wish to diminish its significance. But the uniqueness of Jesus is seen in his relation to God's saving sovereignty as its Mediator, alike in his ministry, in his death and resurrection, and in its consummation, and moreover in the remarkable fact that each element of that mediatorial work finds place in his teaching recorded in the Gospels. I am perfectly aware that that statement will appear to many as incompatible with modern scholarship, but reflection on the issues for a full half a century has convinced me of its rightness. The remainder of this article must be devoted to salient features in the Gospels concerning the relation of Jesus and the kingdom of God.

We begin with the summary of the proclamation of Jesus in Mark 1:15. Mack regards it as composed by Mark for his own purpose, namely to show Jesus as an apocalyptic preacher, but since Jesus was no such person this element

7. *The Way of Jesus Christ: Christology in Messianic Dimensions* (San Francisco: Harper, 1990) 137.

8. B. Mack, "The Kingdom Sayings in Mark," *Forum* 3 (1, 1987) 3-7, 11-14; Crossan, *Historical Jesus*, 76-80, 290-91.

in Mark's representation of Jesus must be dismissed.[9] In so judging the logion Mack is out of harmony with NT scholarship. There is ground for attributing the summary not to Mark, but to early Christian catechesis.[10] Whether it originated there or with Mark, its positive relation to the records of the preaching of Jesus in all the Gospel sources suffices to show that it is an accurate summary.[11] Its meaning, after a century of debate, is tolerably clear: "God's sovereignty as the sovereignty which comes is now coming to pass."[12] "The new aeon in its present-future identity of operation has already broken in."[13] "The unsurpassable future of God has begun."[14] Those are various ways of taking into account the full implications of the twofold statement:

> "The time [for the fulfilment of the promise of the kingdom] has become completed,
> The kingdom of God has become near."

In other words, the saving sovereignty of God awaited in the future has begun.

Of itself the statement could be interpreted simply as an announcement that the hour of God's redeeming intervention in the world has struck, with no implication as to the role of Jesus in it other than as a prophet to whom the fact has been revealed. There is, however, a whole range of sayings of Jesus that compel us to interpret the summary as declaring the inauguration of the kingdom of God through the presence, the deeds, and the word of Jesus as the instrument of the kingdom. For example, when the disciples of Jesus are criticized for not participating in a fast day he replies, "The friends of the bridegroom cannot fast while the bridegroom is with them, can they? As long as they have the bridegroom with them they cannot fast." Here the emphasis lies not on the inappropriateness of fasting during a wedding celebration,[15] but to do it in the presence of the bridegroom. The point of the parable, in the words of L. Goppelt, is: "Fasting . . . is suitable for one who awaits God's rule, not for the one who brings it."[16] The parable of the Strong Man bound by the Stronger (Mark 3:27 par.) is suitably set by Mark in the context of the charge that Jesus performs his exorcisms through having a liaison with the devil. The thrust of the saying

9. "Kingdom Sayings," 3-7.

10. So E. Lohmeyer, *Das Evangelium des Markus,* KKNT (Göttingen: Vandenhoeck & Ruprecht, 1963) 29-30; W. Trilling, *Christusverkündigung in den synoptischen Evangelien* (München: Kösel, 1969) 53.

11. For substantiation of this, see G. R. Beasley-Murray, *Jesus and the Kingdom of God* (Grand Rapids, Michigan: Wm. B. Eerdmans, 1986) 355 n. 7.

12. J. Becker, *Das Heil Gottes,* SUNT 3 (Göttingen: Vandenhoeck & Ruprecht, 1964) 206.

13. Trilling, *Christusverkündigung,* 48.

14. G. Gloege, *Das Reich Gottes und Kirche im Neuen Testament* (Gütersloh: C. Bertelsmann, 1929) 111.

15. As Jeremias interprets it, "νύμφη, νυμφίος," *TDNT* 4:1103; *idem, Parables of Jesus,* rev. ed. (London: SCM, 1963) 117.

16. "Πίνω," *TDNT* 6:140.

is that Jesus, far from being the devil's associate, has overcome him, and therefore exercises his power to release his captives. Ernst Percy perfectly expressed its implication for Jewish hearers: "Where Satan is driven back, the rule of God begins."[17] That deduction is explicitly drawn in the Q saying Matt 12:28 / Luke 11:20: "If it is by the Spirit [Luke: "finger"] of God that I am casting out the demons, then the kingdom of God has come right to you." The same significance is attached to the healings of Jesus in the Q saying Matt 11:5-6 / Luke 7:22-23, utilizing Isa 35:5-6; 61:1 (plus allusions to Isa 26:19; 29:17-19; 42:6-7). The logion in Matt 11:12 / Luke 16:16 goes beyond the healings of Jesus, and refers to his ministry generally in its relation to the kingdom of God. The original form of the saying may have utilized various shades of meaning of the Aramaic term פרץ, and if so it would be rendered literally:

> "The kingdom of heaven is powerfully breaking into the world,
> and powerful people are powerfully attacking it,"[18]

again strikingly asserting the coming of the kingdom in the mission of Jesus. Sayings with a similar import may be seen in the L tradition (Luke 4:16-21; 17:20-21) and M (Matt 13:44-46).

All the utterances of Jesus here cited refer to the inbreaking of the kingdom of God through his action and his imperious word. Most NT scholars today are ready to acknowledge that they give expression to the consciousness of Jesus as being the Bearer, or better the Mediator,[19] of the kingdom of God in the present. What, however, of the kingdom of God in the future? Many of the most characteristic sayings of Jesus concern the future coming of the kingdom of God (e.g., the Beatitudes, the Lord's Prayer, and parables such as those of Matthew 25 — the Ten Maidens, Talents, Sheep and Goats). What role in relation to the future of the kingdom does Jesus in his teaching envisage for himself? I am persuaded that the familiar formula "now and not yet" does not do justice to our Lord's message both with respect to the presence and the future of the kingdom of God. Rather, we are called on to acknowledge that the kingdom which is to complete God's purpose in creation is that which has been inaugurated through Jesus, even as the kingdom which has been introduced by him is none other than the kingdom which is to issue in the new creation. Both these aspects are present in the parables of Growth (the Sower, Seed Growing Secretly, Mustard Seed, Wheat and Tares), and both are implied in the watchword of Jesus, "Seek first the kingdom . . . and the rest will be

17. *Die Botschaft Jesu* (Lund: Gleerup, 1953) 179.

18. See Beasley-Murray, *Jesus and the Kingdom of God*, 92-94.

19. The term "Mediator" is used of Jesus in this context by Käsemann, notably as follows: ". . . he [Jesus] enters on his proclamatory function as, so to speak, the incarnation of the divine promise; he can no longer be subsumed, as can the Baptist, under the category of forerunner but, if a category of some sort must be used, only under that of mediator who brings in the eschatological age by the act of announcing it" ("Apocalyptic," 122).

yours as well" (Matt 6:33 / Luke 12:31).[20] In that case we are bound to affirm that Jesus is the Mediator of the saving sovereignty of God in every phase of its manifestation, now and in the future.

But if we are to speak of "the future" from the standpoint of Jesus in his ministry, it was not only ambiguous but ominous. Jesus will have been perfectly aware of the increasing danger of his situation — from Pharisees and lawyers on account of his attitude to the oral law, from the leading priests through his popularity among the people, and from Herod after the death of John the Baptist.[21] More important than the pressure of outward circumstances, however, will have been his understanding of his mission in relation to the kingdom of God, not least in the light of the OT scriptures. He will have pondered frequently the psalms which speak of the Righteous Man who suffers at the hands of the wicked (Pss 22, 34, 69, etc.), the frequent fate of prophets who proclaim the kingdom of God and Day of the Lord, the task and destiny of the Servant of the Lord set forth in the Servant Songs of Deutero-Isaiah, and the sufferings of the martyrs in the catastrophic era of Antiochus Epiphanes, remembered annually in the Feast of Dedication and illuminated in the book of Daniel. The kingdom of God is fundamentally God putting forth his almighty power to save. If we can let that slip from our minds at times it is doubtful that Jesus ever could have done so. Old Testament prophets and early Judaism alike were looking for a second exodus; that undoubtedly was interpreted by many in Jesus' time primarily in terms of deliverance from an oppressive power greater than Pharaoh, but for Jesus it will have meant a redemption from far more powerful foes than Rome, including the evil of the human heart, which led Jesus to call for Israel's repentance, and a corresponding transformation of being.[22] Accordingly it is not surprising that we read words of Jesus that conjoin the kingdom of God with expectation of his impending suffering and death.

One such saying is the enigmatic Luke 12:49-50:

> I came to bring fire to the earth,
> and how I wish that it were already set alight!
> But I have a baptism with which to be baptized,
> and how I am hemmed in until it be completed!

The combination of fire and flood in relation to divine judgment was long prefigured for the Jew by the flood in Noah's day and the destruction of Sodom

20. The maxim appears to entail the twofold meaning, "Seek above all else to enter the kingdom," and "Seek above else to serve the kingdom," with emphasis on the latter. See the excellent exposition in R. A. Guelich, *The Sermon on the Mount: A Foundation for Understanding* (Waco, Texas: Word, 1982) 341-49.

21. See, e.g., J. Jeremias, *New Testament Theology* (London: SCM, 1971) 278-80; H. Schürmann, *Jesu ureigener Tod: Exegetische Besinnungen und Ausblick* (Freiburg: Herder, 1975).

22. Note the implications of the second exodus in Isa 51:9-11; Jer 31:31-34; Hos 2:14-23; and cf. Ezek 36:24-32.

and Gomorrah, and it occurs in Isa 30:27-28; Ezek 39:22; 2 Pet 2:5-6; *Sib. Or.* 3:689-90. The extraordinary feature of this double saying, however, is its conjuncture of Jesus inflicting judgment on the world and enduring judgment for the world. The representative of the kingdom thus is sent to bring judgment and suffer judgment.

What is presented obscurely in Luke 12:49-50 is exhibited with clarity in the sayings of Jesus in the Last Supper narratives:

> This is my body. . . .
> This is my blood of the covenant. . . .

Here is a double parable of self-giving on behalf of others ("on your behalf," Luke and Paul; "on behalf of all," Mark). The mention of covenant blood reminds of the covenant with Israel at Sinai (Exod 24:8) and of the new covenant to be made in the last days (Jer 31:31-34). As Behm stated, the new covenant is "a correlative of the βασιλεία τοῦ θεοῦ"; its purpose is to put into effect the eschatological saving will of God.[23] For this reason the statement in Luke 22:29-30a deserves more attention than is sometimes given it:

> I covenant with you,[24]
> as my Father covenanted with me a kingdom,
> that you may eat and drink at my table in my kingdom. . . .

The difference between reading "a kingdom" as the direct object of "covenant," instead of "eat and drink at my table in my kingdom," is not great; the latter clause could define the sense of the former. The important thing is the explicit linking of the covenant with the gift of the saving sovereignty as the fruit of Christ's death. Hence the pertinence of Mark 14:25: Jesus will not drink the produce of the vine "till I drink it in a new way in the kingdom of God." Luke has in addition to this a similar saying relative to the meal before it starts (22:16), thereby indicating that Jesus set the whole meal in anticipation of the kingdom of God. By this means the Lukan tradition frames the Last Supper in affirmations of the death of Jesus in prospect of the kingdom of God.[25]

In view of these passages[26] the predictions of the passion should be taken with due seriousness, especially Mark 8:31 and 9:31 (10:32-34 does appear to

23. "Διαθήκη," *TDNT* 2:134.

24. Διατίθεμαι is a correlative of διαθήκη and should be so translated. See the discussion in R. Otto, *The Kingdom of God and the Son of Man* (London: Lutterworth, 1943) 292; and A. Schlatter, *Das Evangelium des Lukas aus seinen Quellen erklärt* (Stuttgart: Calwer, 1960) 424.

25. Luke 22:15-18 may be a brief summary of the Last Supper in its aspect of fulfillment of Passover; see L. Goppelt, "ποτήριον," *TDNT* 6:153-54; J. Jeremias, *The Eucharistic Words of Jesus* (London: SCM, 1956) 99-100; H. Schürmann, *Der Passamahlbericht Lk 22:(7-14) 15-18* (Münster: Aschendorff, 1953) 48-50.

26. The passages are extensively discussed in E. Schillebeeckx, *Jesus: An Experiment in Christology* (New York: Crossroad, 1979) 303-6.

have been expanded in the light of the events of the trial and death of Jesus). The former appears to mirror the sufferings of the Righteous Man at the hands of the unrighteous, the latter more especially those of the Servant of the Lord, who is the Righteous Man *par excellence,* but suffering not merely through the unrighteous but for them. In Mark 9:31 ("The Son of Man is to be handed over to human hands"), the verb is probably to be understood as a divine passive; Mark uses it frequently in the passion narrative of human actions (Judas, the high priests, Pilate, the soldiers), but behind them all stands the Father, working his salvific purpose through the Mediator of the saving sovereignty (in Rom 8:32 this tradition is linked with Abraham's offering of Isaac, and could conceivably have been in mind from the beginning, in view of the importance of that event in the thought of the Jews).

All three predictions conclude with an affirmation of the resurrection of the Son of Man "after three days," a feature which has strengthened the conviction of many who view the predictions as *vaticinia ex eventu.* On the other hand, vindication through exaltation is a fundamental element of the varied patterns in Israel of the expectation for God's servants who suffer for his name. "Many are the afflictions of the righteous, but the LORD delivers him out of them all," sang the psalmist (Ps 34:20); after the rise of apocalyptic that becomes vindication in the judgment and resurrection for the kingdom of God (cf. Wis 2:10–5:23). The Servant of the Lord in Isa 52:13–53:12 is to be "lifted up and exalted and very high" in virtue of his fearful sufferings (52:12-13; cf. 53:10-12). Reflection on the martyrs for God's cause led to similar expectations for them (cf. Dan 12:2; *T. Job* 33:2-3; *Apoc. Elijah* 37:3-4). Since in Judaism the rejected prophets of God were commonly thought to have been killed by their contemporaries, they too were expected to share in the vindication of the martyrs (note also that the Servant in the Servant Songs functions as prophet — e.g., Isa 49:1-6; 50:4-9; cf. 61:1-3). All this applies in a special way to Jesus, not only because expectation of resurrection after death was a vivid element alike in the hope of his people and of himself, but still more because it is bound up with his call to be mediator of God's saving sovereignty. The most notable feature of the salvation of the kingdom is resurrection to life in God's new world. If Jesus contemplated mediating the life of the kingdom of God in the future he could do no other than believe that after his self-offering unto death God would raise him to his presence as firstfruits of the dead.[27]

It may be objected that one should not cite the sayings that represent Jesus as the Son of Man as though their authenticity can be taken for granted. True, but it was desirable to conjoin the passion predictions with the logia concerning his anticipation of death for the kingdom of God. These predictions, moreover, illustrate one aspect of the Son of Man sayings generally — namely, they all

27. On the fascinating question of the third day ("after three days," consistently in Mark) see Beasley-Murray, *Jesus and the Kingdom of God,* 246-47.

relate to the service of the kingdom of God by the one so named. Virtually all those that relate to the ministry of Jesus (Mark 2:10, 28; Matt 11:19 par.; 8:20 par.; Luke 19:10) reflect opposition to Jesus, and should be bracketed with those that treat his rejection and impending suffering and death for the saving sovereignty; and self-evidently the Son of Man parousia sayings have to do with the consummation of the kingdom of God. In view of the incontrovertible element in the authentic sayings of Jesus of his role to be the instrument of the kingdom, the insistence that the application of the expression "Son of Man" to Jesus "is anchored in the primitive tradition firmly to the prophetic tradition"[28] is highly questionable.

We are all aware of the problems surrounding the use of the expression "Son of Man" in the Gospels, and it may well be that at this stage we have to be satisfied with solutions that are no more than probable and plausible. If it be so that in Galilean Aramaic "son of man" could be used (by whatever route proposed) as a surrogate for "I," like our English term "one" (a usage I very commonly employ in lecturing),[29] that by no means excludes the possibility of reference to the "one like a son of man" in Dan 7:13-14, to whom the kingdom of God is given as the representative of "the people of the saints of the Most High" and also as representative of the Most High himself. In the Son of Man sayings that relate to the parousia it is undeniable that Dan 7:13-14 is being concretized and applied to Jesus; in view of that event forming the conclusion of the coming of the kingdom which is in process of coming in the ministry, death, and resurrection of Jesus, it is completely comprehensible that Jesus should have used that same image of Daniel 7 in relation to his total service of the kingdom.

The question of the relation of the personal use of the term in the Gospels and its parallel use in the *Similitudes of Enoch* is perhaps eased by the increasing trend to date the latter around the second quarter of the first century of our era. That would make it roughly contemporary with or soon after the ministry of Jesus, and suggests not so much the dependence of one on the other as contemporaneous interest in and use of Daniel's visions. The author of the *Similitudes* speaks of "that Son of man" (of Daniel's vision), the Gospels use uniformly "the Son of Man"; both are titular, but whereas in the former the Son of Man is revealed exclusively in the judgment at the end of the age, Jesus appropriates the symbol to bind in one the varied aspects of his task of mediating the kingdom of God. Such a use, of course, is completely outside the range of vision of the author of the *Similitudes*.

28. Käsemann, "Apocalyptic," 115.

29. See G. Vermes, "The Use of בר נשא / בר נש in Jewish Aramaic," in M. Black, *An Aramaic Approach to the Gospels and Acts*, 3d ed. (Oxford: Clarendon University, 1967) 310-28; and his own work, *Jesus the Jew* (New York: Macmillan, 1973) 163-88; Jeremias, *New Testament Theology*, 261 n. 1. I do not think J. Fitzmyer's objections to Vermes's position are strong enough wholly to negate it (*A Wandering Aramaean: Collected Aramaic Essays*, SBLMS 25 [Chico, California: Scholars, 1979] 143-60).

The unity of the work of Jesus as Son of Man is illustrated in a single saying, Mark 14:62. Standing on trial for the ministry he has exercised, Jesus is demanded to declare whether he is the Messiah. He confesses that he is, and knowing full well the consequences of what he says he goes on to expound the nature of his messiahship: he will be revealed in theophanic glory as the Son of Man, exalted by God as the Lord at his right hand, thereby fulfilling Daniel's vision of the coming of the kingdom of God. For that he is condemned to death.

The christological implications of these varied elements in our Lord's teaching are immense. To some they are simply unbelievable,[30] to others offensive.[31] Nevertheless there is an increasing acknowledgment that they have a deep root in the soul of Jesus from which they ineluctably grew, namely his Abba consciousness, with the all but inevitable corollary of his understanding of himself as standing in relation to the Father as son.

The precedents for this in the religious traditions of the Jews are familiar enough: the nation Israel as the son of God (Exod 4:22-23); the king as the representative son of God (Ps 2:7; and especially 2 Sam 7:14); the development from that of the concept of the Messiah as Son of God;[32] the application of the term to especially worthy Israelites, such as the "righteous" among the Jews (Sir 4:10; Wis 2:18; *Jub.* 1:24-25) and charismatic miracle workers and mystics.[33] While these are illuminating precedents it would be unreasonable to view Jesus' Abba address to God as determined by them. On the contrary, it is surely an expression of his experience of God, rooted in and developed during the unrecorded years prior to his ministry.

Joachim Jeremias performed a notable service to NT scholarship in clarifying and emphasizing the uniqueness and significance of this phenomenon. "It expresses," said he, "the heart of Jesus' relationship to God. . . . Abba as a form of address to God *expresses the ultimate mystery of the mission of Jesus.*"[34] The idea expressed in the italicized sentence has caught the imagination of

30. "I, for one, simply cannot imagine a sane human being, of any historical period or culture, entertaining the thoughts about himself which the Gospels, as they stand, often attribute to him" (J. Knox, *The Death of Christ* [London: Collins, 1967] 58).

31. It led D. Strauss to make his famous charge as to the "fanaticism" of Jesus relative to the parousia teaching of Jesus: "Such a thing as he has here prophesied of himself cannot happen to a man. If he prophesied the like of himself and expected it, then to us he is a fanatic *(Schwärmer);* if he uttered it of himself without any real conviction, then he was a braggart and a deceiver" *(Das Leben Jesu für das deutsche Volk bearbeitet* [Leipzig: F. A. Brockhaus, 1864] 236).

32. This appears to be reflected in 4QFlor 1:6-7, 1QSa 2:11ff., and the references to the Son of God in the Daniel apocryphon in Cave 4. H. Braun asserted that this understanding of the Messiah was not unique to Qumran but is "simply Jewish" (*Qumran und das Neues Testament* [Tübingen: J. C. B. Mohr (Paul Siebeck), 1966] 76).

33. See D. Flusser, *Jesus* (New York: Herder and Herder, 1969) 93-94; Vermes, *Jesus the Jew,* 206-10; M. Hengel, *The Son of God: The Origin of Christology and the History of Jewish-Hellenistic Religion* (Philadelphia: Fortress, 1976) 42-43.

34. *New Testament Theology,* 67-68.

scholars of late. It has given rise to the conviction that here is the clue to the messianic consciousness of Jesus and the mission to which that gave rise. Edward Schillebeeckx is among those so convinced:

> Jesus' message and praxis of salvation for all Israel without exception, indeed including all that was abandoned and lost — that in particular — are difficult to place in a historico-religious context. For that reason we are bound to enquire whether Jesus' message and praxis do not become intelligible only when we presuppose his special, original religious apprehension of God.

Schillebeeckx finds the answer to that "enquiry" in the Abba experience of Jesus, defined as "that experience as the soul, source and ground of Jesus' message, praxis and ministry as a whole." Hence he affirms:

> The Abba experience would appear to be the source of the peculiar nature of Jesus' message and conduct, which without this religious experience, or apart from it, lost the distinctive meaning and content actually conferred on them by Jesus.[35]

This, I am persuaded, is a valid insight. It raises a strong query against the suggestion that the concept of Jesus as the Son has its origin in that of the eschatological Son of Man. Consider, for example, the comment of E. Lohmeyer on Mark 13:32:

> It is scarcely accidental that it (the title 'the Son') emerges in an apocalyptic connection, as all designations of the dignity of Jesus are of this origin; and it is yet less critical to suspect it, for what conceivable reason exists that the primitive Christian faith should exclude its Lord from this knowledge? Hence one may say that the designation 'Father and Son' belongs not only to the oldest tradition, but also to the preaching of Jesus, for it is also the pure consequence of taking over the title Son of Man.[36]

In view of the fundamental nature of Jesus' Abba experience this must be judged to be a mistake, but it does remind us of the close relation between the concepts Son of Man and the Son (of God). C. F. D. Moule is among those who have emphasized this feature. He pointed out the resemblance between Dan 7:9-14 and Psalm 2: the imagery of old age in the depiction of God stands for Fatherhood, the one like a son of man represents the royal Son; accordingly Son

35. *Jesus,* 266-67. See further W. Pannenberg, *Jesus — God and Man* (London: SCM, 1968) 324-37; I. H. Marshall, *The Origins of New Testament Christology* (Leicester: Inter-Varsity, 1990) 117; S. Kim, *"The 'Son of Man'" as the Son of God,* WUNT 30 (Tübingen: J. C. B. Mohr [Paul Siebeck], 1983) 74-75; Moltmann, *Way of Jesus Christ,* 53, 90-91; M. J. Borg, *Jesus: A New Vision* (San Francisco: Harper, 1987) 49-50.

36. *Markus,* 283. For comparable views see E. Sjöberg, *Der verborgene Menschensohn in den Evangelien* (Lund: Gleerup, 1955) 187ff.; E. Schweizer, "υἱός κτλ.," *TDNT* 8:372.

of Man turns out to approximate Son of God. Moule adds: "It is organic to the ministry of Jesus that the Son of God shows himself as the frail and vulnerable Son of Man. The two are identical in reality, long before ingenious exegetical connections are spun round them."[37] Whether "frail and vulnerable" is suitable language to attach to the one like a son of man in Daniel 7 may be queried, but the point made is clear, as is the priority of the concept Son of God to Son of Man. It is not irrelevant to mention that in the Fourth Gospel the Son (of God) and Son of Man are frequently used interchangeably; in John 5:25-27 their functions are identical, yet the expression "the Son" is the basic element in the christology of that Gospel. That accords with the Abba experience of Jesus and its corollary of Jesus as son of the Father, hence the Son in a unique sense.

In Judaism, to be a son entails not only privilege but obedience to one's father. This holds good of the relationship of Israel to God as son. To be set in relation to God and to be set to service for God are propagated together in Israel's history, as Exod 19:4–6 illustrates. For Jesus, therefore, the consciousness of God-relatedness will have been accompanied by a sense of vocation and of representation. This finds expression in the controverted Matt 11:27, where the notion of choice of the Son by the Father is bound up with the Son's vocation to reveal him with accompanying authority and power. Status, commission, and authority belong together in this declaration of the Son's relation to the Father, and it remains firmly set within the biblical tradition. By contrast the severe limitation of the authority of the Son in Mark 13:32 is surprising, and yet it is completely harmonious with the message and ministry of Jesus. The frequently voiced objections to the logion have rarely taken into account the eschatological significations of "the Son" and "the Son of God," or the relation of both to the Son of Man, and the fundamental element of obedience and subordination in the notion of "son" in Israel, as with Jesus generally in the Gospels.

This all leads us to say that a conviction of Jesus that he stood in relation to God as Son, understood in the context of the service of the kingdom of God which was at the center of his life, would readily coalesce with a sense of vocation to carry out the function of the Son of God as interpreted within the tradition of his people. As Son of Man he is charged with authority to act for God in the service of his saving sovereignty (Mark 2:10), yet also to represent the people to whom the rule is promised (Mark 2:28). His service includes the function of suffering, that the rule of God may be salvation for the world (Mark 8:31, etc.), but he is also to act as the agent of its consummation in judgment and salvation (Luke 12:8-9, etc.). These varied christological titles accordingly denote the present and future status and function of him who bears them. Jesus is the

37. *The Origin of Christology* (Cambridge: Cambridge University, 1977) 24-27. This interpretation is expounded in detail by Kim in *Son of Man,* the thesis of which is: "With the Son of Man . . . Jesus intended to reveal himself to be the divine figure who was the inclusive representative (or head) of the eschatological people of God, i.e. the Son of God who was the head of the sons of God" (36).

Son, and as the obedient Son he will share the Father's glory when it pleases the Father to reveal the kingdom. He is the Son of God, and with the kingdom will appear as Judge and Redeemer. He is the Son of Man, and at the end will complete the tasks of the Son of Man for God and the redeemed.

All this is said of the man Jesus, and virtually all of it has proceeded from a consideration of the Synoptic Gospels and teaching of Jesus presented therein. This limitation has been deliberate, partly to keep to territory commonly agreed as most trustworthy, and still more because, unlike Bultmann in his statement earlier quoted, we (as the majority of Christians) are deeply interested to know and understand what Jesus said about his relation to God and his place in God's purpose for the world. Nevertheless we acknowledged at the beginning of our study that every word and deed of Jesus recorded in the Gospels is written in the light of the Easter event. We are bound to ask therefore what the significance of the resurrection of Jesus is that makes the Gospels unthinkable without it. On the least estimate it is God's great endorsement of all that Jesus said, and did, and was, and is. The last two words "and is" are themselves a corollary of the resurrection, and Christian faith has ever confessed, "Christ, being raised from the dead, will never again die" (Rom 6:9). Moreover, the two greatest teachers of the church have made clear to us the indissoluble unity of the death and resurrection of Jesus: the Fourth Evangelist in John 12:31-32, whereby we know that in the crucifixion and resurrection of Jesus the judgment of the world took place, and humankind all over the world are henceforth experiencing the power of his life; and Paul, who in 2 Cor 5:17–19 declares that in the crucified and risen Jesus the world was reconciled and is continuing to receive the reconciliation, the new creation came into being and believers continue to experience it. In that twofold event of crucifixion-resurrection the consummation of God's purpose for the world was assured and mirrored, for the resurrection of Jesus is the one clear clue we have concerning the nature and significance of the parousia of the Son of Man.

Accordingly the question of Jesus himself comes to us, who spend much time studying his words, with deeper significance than it could ever have had for those to whom it was first addressed: "What do you think about the Christ?" Hear the answer of one man who reflected long and hard on the question: "Jesus' life, cross and resurrection in the power of the Spirit reveal the depth of the Father-Son relationship, and raise the problem of the Trinitarian God."[38] If the life, death, and resurrection of Jesus raise the problem of the Trinity, that can only be on the ground that the salvific functions of Jesus as the Son, Son of God and Son of Man, point to and are rooted in an ontological relation of Jesus and God. His function as Mediator of the kingdom of God attained new dimensions in his death and resurrection, particularly when viewed as the introduction of the new creation. And his resurrection looks to the consummation of creation in the parousia, when every creature and all creation will be

38. Schillebeeckx, *Jesus*, 641.

subjected to God. These are functions impossible to envisage any human being accomplishing, unless that human being is one with the being of God. The doctrine of the Trinity was forced on us not by the dogmaticians but by the history of Jesus; but strangely the revelation of God in Jesus has enlarged the horizons of our understanding of God in an unexpected manner. The reverse, of course, is also true, that the doctrine of the Trinity explains in an unexpected manner the mystery of Jesus, but as Schillerbeeckx observed, the way is from Jesus to the Trinity, not from the Trinity to Jesus:

> Only in the light of Jesus' life, death and resurrection can we know that the Trinity is the divine mode of God's perfect unity of being. Only on the basis of Jesus of Nazareth, his Abba experience — source and soul of his message, ministry and death — and his resurrection, is it possible to say anything meaningful about Father, Son and Spirit.[39]

In that case the concern of the entire ministry of Jesus, continuing in and from Easter and pressing on to the parousia,[40] is the concern of the trinitarian God — namely, the coming of the kingdom of God. This is why Jesus was "sent." His mission was the mission of God, and it continues in the mission of the church. The kingdom of God is still "at hand"![41] That means that we must think of the Trinity in dynamic terms working toward the goal of creation. The literary labors of J. Moltmann are directed to the endeavor to persuade the church of that truth, which he sees as the burden of the biblical revelation. He wrote:

> The scarlet thread that runs through the biblical testimonies might be called the history of the kingdom of God. But what this history of the kingdom of God is about is really the trinitarian history of the kingdom. It does not merely run its course on earth — which is to say outside God himself — as dogmatic tradition ever since Augustine has maintained. On the contrary, it takes place in its earthly mode within the Trinity itself, as the history of the kingdom of the Father, the Son and the Spirit.[42]

The christology of the kingdom of God thus leads to the understanding of Jesus as the Son with the Father and the Spirit within the Trinity, a dynamic unity pursuing the goal of gathering humanity into its own fellowship. We are invited not only to contemplate it and enjoy it, but to share in the accomplishment of the trinitarian goal. Therein lies the high privilege of our calling.

39. Schillebeeckx, *Jesus,* 658.

40. In God's time there is no delay of the parousia.

41. "It is for us to see the kingdom of God as always coming, always pressing in on the present, always big with possibility and always inviting immediate action" (W. Rauschenbusch, *A Theology for the Social Gospel* [New York: Macmillan, 1917; reprint ed., Nashville: Abingdon, 1978] 14).

42. *The Trinity and the Kingdom of God* (London: SCM, 1981) 95.

# Jesus and the Beginnings of the Mission to the Gentiles

Eckhard J. Schnabel

In his Inaugural Lecture, I. H. Marshall asserted that "Jesus saw his task as the renewal of the people of Israel who had fallen away from the true relationship to God. Although he restricted his activity almost exclusively to the Jews, he showed a particular concern for the poor and the outcasts of society, which suggests that in principle he was open to the inclusion of Samaritans and Gentiles under God's Kingdom."[1] Among the implications regarding the common basis in the teaching of Jesus, Paul, and John he pointed out that "for all the three teachers the salvation events are regarded as the fulfilment of Old Testament prophecy and that the area of fulfilment is the people of Israel now open in its membership, at least in principle, to all who accept Jesus as Lord."[2]

Indeed, Jesus has been called "the primal missionary": his conduct was the starting point of the early Christian mission.[3] Since the early Christian movement saw the mission to the Gentiles as a logical feature of its mission,[4]

1. I. H. Marshall, "Jesus, Paul and John," *Aberdeen University Review* 51 (1985) 18-36 (= *Jesus the Saviour: Studies in New Testament Theology* [London: SPCK; Downers Grove, Illinois: InterVarsity, 1990] 35-56 [42]). The Inaugural Lecture to the Chair of New Testament Exegesis in the University of Aberdeen was delivered on November 9, 1983.

2. Marshall, "Jesus, Paul and John," 52-53.

3. M. Hengel, "The Origins of the Christian Mission," in *Between Jesus and Paul: Studies in the Earliest History of Christianity* (London: SCM, 1983) 48-64, 166-79 (62), referring to E. Grässer, "Jesus in Nazareth," *NTS* 16 (1969-70) 22. The point may be raised whether the one intended reader of a *Festschrift* appreciates detailed footnotes in a document put together as a sign of personal appreciation. However, as Howard Marshall himself is not disinclined to relevant if not detailed documentation of the scholarly tradition history, as any reader of his *The Gospel of Luke* would know, I considered it to be acceptable to include it.

4. Cf. E. P. Sanders, *Jesus and Judaism* (Philadelphia: Fortress, 1987) 220.

the issue of Jesus' position regarding the Gentiles is of fundamental importance.[5] This question has been answered in basically two ways.[6]

First, Jesus did not sanction a mission to the Gentiles. There are at least three versions of this position. (1) Jesus forbade his disciples on principle to engage in a mission among Gentiles; the Gentiles are thought to be brought into the kingdom of God by God's own action in the last days as fulfillment of the prophetic vision of the nations' pilgrimage to Zion.[7] (2) Jesus deliberately limited his ministry to Israel, not wanting his disciples to witness to non-Jews; the conception of an active Gentile mission derives from the Hellenistic Jewish Christians in Jerusalem or from Paul.[8] (3) A more cautious version of this view is the opinion that Jesus did not express any conviction about the Gentiles and the kingdom of God since his vision concentrated on the restoration of Israel.[9]

Second, the Gentile mission originated with Jesus in some way or other. (1) One view holds that Jesus limited his ministry to Israel while envisaging a future inclusion of the Gentiles in the kingdom of God, with the resurrection and the Great Commission being the starting point of the universal mission of the disciples.[10] (2) Another view affirms that Jesus' vision was concentrated on Israel, that the positive encounters with Gentiles were unplanned exceptions, that there is no clear evidence for the assumption that he advocated a future inclusion of the Gentiles, but that Jesus' ministry and some of his sayings opened up perspectives which logically led to the early Christian Gentile mission.[11]

5. *Pace* Hengel, "Origins," who claims that this question is "a secondary problem."

6. For reviews of the history of research see particularly F. Hahn, *Das Verständnis der Mission im Neuen Testament*, WMANT 13 (Neukirchen-Vluyn: Neukirchener, 1963) 19-22; D. T. Bosch, " 'Jesus and the Gentiles' — A Review after Thirty Years," in *The Church Crossing Frontiers: Essays on the Nature of Mission*, ed. P. Beyerhaus and C. F. Hallencreuz (Uppsala: Gleerup, 1969) 3-19; H. Frankemölle, "Zur Theologie der Mission im Matthäusevangelium," in *Mission im Neuen Testament*, ed. K. Kertelge, QD 93 (Freiburg: Herder, 1982) 93-129 (100-102); W. G. Kümmel, "Das Urchristentum. II. Arbeiten zu Spezialproblemen. e. Mission und Stellung zum Staat," *TRu* 52 (1987) 268-85 (268-78).

7. Cf. J. Jeremias, *Jesu Verheißung für die Völker*, 2d ed. (Göttingen: Vandenhoeck & Ruprecht, 1959) 32-33, 47ff., 60ff.; also B. Sundkler, "Jésus et les païens," in *Contributions à l'étude de la pensée missionaire dans le Nouveau Testament*, ed. B. Sundkler and A. Fridrichsen, Acta Seminarii Neotestamentici Upsaliensis 6 (Uppsala: Neutestamentliche Seminar zu Uppsala, 1937) 1-38; H. Stoevesandt, *Jesus und die Heidenmission* (Diss. theol., Göttingen, 1943) 141ff.

8. Cf. H. Kasting, *Die Anfänge der urchristlichen Mission: Eine historische Untersuchung*, BEvT 55 (München: Kaiser, 1969) *passim;* Frankemölle, "Mission im Matthäusevangelium," 117-18.

9. This view is held, with variations, by A. von Harnack, *Mission und Ausbreitung des Christentums in den ersten drei Jahrhunderten*, 4th ed. (1924) 1:39ff.; Hengel, "Origins," 54ff., 62; Sanders, *Jesus*, 221.

10. Cf. M. Meinertz, *Jesus und die Heidenmission*, NTA 1:1-2, 2d ed. (Münster: Aschendorff, 1925) 84ff. *et passim;* similarly D. Bosch, *Die Heidenmission in der Zukunftsschau Jesu. Eine Untersuchung zur Eschatologie der synoptischen Evangelien*, ATANT 36 (Zürich: Zwingli, 1959), 76ff., 193ff. *et passim;* more recently, *idem*, *Transforming Mission* (Maryknoll, New York: Orbis, 1991) 29-31, 39ff., 64-65.

11. Cf. Hahn, *Mission*, 19-32; Bosch, *Heidenmission*, 16-17; R. Pesch, "Voraussetzungen und

(3) A third view asserts that Jesus himself was consciously involved in outreach to Gentiles and may therefore be regarded as the first missionary to the Gentiles.[12]

I propose to proceed in the following manner. We will first review three basic facts which are most relevant for our discussion: the relationship between Jews and Gentiles, the vigor of the early Christian mission to the Gentiles, and the evidence in the Gospels for a link between Jesus and the concern for Gentile mission. Second, we will investigate Jesus' encounters with Gentiles and relevant statements about Gentiles in order to determine whether the Gospel narratives give a reliable portrait of the missionary concerns of Jesus.

## 1. Basic Facts

***1.1. Jews and Gentiles.*** The attitude of the pagan world toward the Jews was mixed. There were on the one hand those who were impressed with the integrative potential of Israel's monotheistic faith and with the ethical rigor of the corresponding praxis.[13] As a result there were Gentiles who decided to become Jews, despite the social alienation from their old context demanded by the Jewish cultic regulations. Besides these "proselytes" there were "God-fearers," people who remained sympathizers and who took over several of the (less strict) Jewish laws. On a more official level, in the Diaspora Jews were generally appreciated as loyal citizens. Many Hellenistic cities welcomed them as traders. Around 200 B.C.E. Antiochus III Megas settled 2,000 Jewish families from Mesopotamia in Lydia and Phrygia to consolidate his strategic interests in these regions (Josephus *Ant.* 12.148-53). Around 139 B.C.E. further Jews migrated to Asia Minor (cf. 1 Macc 15:16-23).[14]

On the other hand, there was a hostile attitude vis-à-vis the Jews which

---

Anfänge der urchristlichen Mission," in *Mission im Neuen Testament,* 11-70 (36-38, 54ff.); cf. Hengel, "Origins," 63.

12. Cf. F. Spitta, *Jesus und die Heidenmission* (Giessen: Alfred Töpelmann, 1909) 72ff., 109ff.; A. Schlatter, *Der Evangelist Matthäus,* 6th ed. (Stuttgart: Calwer, 1963) 277-78, 339, 701-2; similarly D. A. Carson, "Matthew," in *The Expositor's Bible Commentary,* ed. F. E. Gaebelein (Grand Rapids, Michigan: Zondervan, 1984), 202, 248, 596-97; evidently also I. H. Marshall, *Luke: Historian and Theologian* (Exeter: Paternoster, 1970) 140-41; *idem, The Gospel of Luke,* NIGTC (Exeter: Paternoster, 1978) 768, 903-4; R. T. France, *Matthew: Evangelist and Teacher* (Exeter: Paternoster, 1989) 232-35.

13. F. Millar wrote recently that "no full and satisfactory study of proselytism in the Graeco-Roman period has yet been written" (E. Schürer, "Gentiles and Judaism: 'God-Fearers' and Proselytes," in *The History of the Jewish People in the Age of Jesus Christ (175 B.C.–A.D. 135),* ed. G. Vermes, F. Millar, and M. Goodman (Edinburgh: T. & T. Clark, 1986) 3:1:150-76, 150.

14. Cf. G. M. Cohen, *The Seleucid Colonies. Studies in Founding, Administration and Organization* (Wiesbaden: Steiner, 1978) 4ff., 87ff.; P. Trebilco, *Jewish Communities in Asia Minor,* SNTSMS 69 (Cambridge: Cambridge University, 1991) 5ff.

should not be underestimated.[15] This attitude was the effect of official manipulations of public sentiments in times of crises, or the result of the provocation which the nonconformistic and yet attractive Jewish religion constituted for non-Jews (particularly the refusal to intermarry and the impossibility of cult and table fellowship). There was an anti-Jewish propaganda which sometimes resulted in outright persecution. Polemical and mocking remarks about Jews are to be found in writings of Cicero, Seneca, Quintilian, Juvenal, and Tacitus.[16]

It is disputed whether there was an active Jewish missionary effort among Gentiles. Some scholars interpret the available literary and archeological evidence as indicating that there must have been an "advertising" activity by Jews among Gentiles.[17] Others deny that there was an active Jewish mission to Gentiles.[18] It seems to be true, at any rate, that in most cases the impetus for conversion had to come from the Gentile. "It was extremely unusual for any Jew in the first century A.D. to view the encouragement of gentiles to convert to Judaism as a praiseworthy act."[19] The number of proselytes was probably not very high.[20] The barriers for Gentiles wanting to become Jews were considerable. The main hindrances were the requirement of separation (corresponding to the prevention of assimilation for the Jews) and the close relation between nation and religion.[21]

15. See generally J. N. Sevenster, *The Roots of Pagan Anti-Semitism in the Ancient World,* NovTSup 41 (Leiden: E. J. Brill, 1975); M. Stern, "The Jews in Greek and Latin Literature," in *The Jewish People in the First Century,* CRINT 1, ed. S. Safrai and M. Stern (Assen: Van Gorcum, 1974 / 76) 2:1101-59; Schürer, *History,* 150-58; N. R. M. de Lange and C. Thoma, "Antisemitismus I. Begriff / Vorchristlicher Antisemitismus," *TRE* 3:113-19; J. G. Gager, *The Origins of Anti-Semitism: Attitudes toward Judaism in Pagan and Christian Antiquity* (New York: Oxford University, 1983).

16. Cf. Cicero *pro Flacco* 28.67; Juvenal *Sat.* 6.160; 14.96-106; Tacitus *Hist.* 5.8 (M. Stern, ed., *Greek and Latin Authors on Jews and Judaism* [Jerusalem: Israel Academy of Science and Humanities, 1974-84] 1: nos. 68, 298, 301; 2: no. 506). The Alexandrian anti-Jewish polemic can be illustrated by the apologetic text *Contra Apionem* of Josephus.

17. Cf. H. Solin, "Juden und Syren im westlichen Teil der römischen Welt: Eine ethnisch-demographische Studie mit besonderer Berücksichtigung der sprachlichen Zustände," *ANRW* 2.29.2:587-789, 1222-49; 616 n. 45; also Schürer, *History,* 153-59.

18. Cf. recently M. Goodman, "Proselytising in Rabbinic Judaism," *JJS* 40 (1989) 175-85; S. McKnight, *A Light among the Gentiles: Jewish Missionary Activity in the Second Temple Period* (Minneapolis: Fortress, 1991).

19. Goodman, "Proselytising," 175, who concludes from the (scarce) evidence in the Talmud that no Amoraic text reports a tanna of the second century C.E. making a positive statement on proselytizing; the first such positive statements come from the third and the early fourth century. Goodman (184-85) advances the hypothesis that Jewish interest in a "mission to convert," based on a conviction that this was a natural corollary of religious belief, increased during the third century C.E. as a result of the effectiveness of the energetic Christian mission.

20. Cf. Solin, "Juden und Syren," 610ff., who states that among the inscriptions from Rome only six refer definitely to proselytes (623 n. 55). Differently Schürer, *History* 160-61, who regards the success of the assumed Jewish mission as "considerable."

21. Cf. M. Hengel, *Judentum und Hellenismus,* WUNT 10, 2d ed. (Tübingen: J. C. B. Mohr [Paul Siebeck], 1973) 560ff.; Solin, "Juden und Syren," 616. Cf. Tacitus *Hist.* 5.5.2: "Those who cross over into their manner of life adopt the same practice, and, before anything else, are instructed

When the Jews read the Scriptures with a view to establishing the attitude toward the Gentiles in their own time and in the future of the promised Messiah, they read of a pilgrimage of the nations to Zion (Isa 2:2-3; 60:3-4; Zech 8:20-23; Mic 4:1-2) and of Gentiles worshiping God in all parts of the earth (Isa 45:6; 59:19; Mal 1:11; cf. Isa 45:22; 49:6, 23; 56:6-8; Zech 2:11; Mic 7:17), but they would also read of a future destruction of the Gentiles (Isa 54:3; Mic 5:10-15; Zeph 2:10-11).[22] Early Jewish literature reflects this ambiguity: hope is expressed that many Gentiles will share Israel's salvation (Tob 14:6-7; *1 Enoch* 90:30-33; *Sib. Or.* 3:616, 716-18, 752-53) and there are predictions of their destruction on account of their idolatry and sexual immorality (Sir 36:7-9; *1 Enoch* 91:9; Bar 4:25, 31-32, 35; 1QM 12:10; *T. Mos.* 10:7; *Jub.* 23:30; *Pss. Sol.* 17:25-27; *Sib. Or.* 3:517-18, 669-72, 761). Sanders seems to be correct when he states that "the evidence does not permit a precise account of the views of Jesus' contemporaries about Gentile conversion at the end-time . . . most Jews who thought about the matter one way or the other would have expected many Gentiles to turn to the Lord when his glory was revealed."[23]

***1.2. The Early Christian Gentile Mission.*** When we turn to the evidence for the early Christian Gentile mission in the letters of Paul and the book of Acts, it appears that no Jewish Christian group disapproved of a mission to the Gentiles as such.[24] The disagreements which underlie the discussion of Paul in his letters to the Galatians and to the Romans concerned only the terms and conditions of the Gentile mission. The movement started by Jesus saw the Gentile mission as an entirely natural venture.

When the Christians of the Jerusalem church were forced to flee to other regions they seem to have regarded it as the natural thing to spread the gospel beyond the confines of Judea, not needing specific guidance from the Spirit.[25] This matter-of-factness included going to Samaria and preaching about the Messiah (Acts 8:4-5). The boundary between Jews and Samaritans was crossed by Philip and then by Peter and John with apparently no compunction about the legitimacy of such a move (8:5-25). When Philip's preaching met with dramatic success, the Jerusalem apostles evidently wanted to examine this new advance with care, but the report of the visit of Peter and John (8:14ff.) does not hint at any reticence regarding the possibility of faith of Samaritans. On

---

to despise the gods, disown their native land, and regard their parents, children, and brothers as of little account."

22. The latter point is emphasized by Sanders, *Jesus,* 213ff., who argues against Jeremias, *Jesu Verheißung, passim,* and J. Riches, *Jesus and the Transformation of Judaism* (London: Darton, Longman & Todd, 1980).

23. Sanders, *Jesus,* 218.

24. Cf. Kasting, *Anfänge,* 110-14.

25. I. H. Marshall, *The Acts of the Apostles: An Introduction and Commentary,* TNTC (Leicester: Inter-Varsity, 1980) 156.

the contrary, the apostles are described as "preaching the gospel to many villages of the Samaritans" (8:25).

The conversion of the Ethiopian court official (8:26-39) does not pose any problems for Philip, who had the confidence of the Jerusalem leaders (cf. 6:5). We do not know whether the Ethiopian was a Gentile God-fearer or, as a proselyte, "a Jew of a peculiar sort" whose status in the Jewish community was evidently ambiguous.[26] That Luke reports no problems regarding the conversion of the Ethiopian may of course be due to the fact that he returned immediately to his own, distant country without having contact with the Palestinian church.[27] We should notice, however, that Luke ends the story with a note of joy (8:39).

The longest single story in Acts (10:1–11:18) recounts the conversion of Cornelius, the Roman centurion, and his family. The fundamental problem, which is overcome by God giving supernatural guidance to Peter, is not the Gentile mission *per se*, that is, not the recognition that the gospel is for the Gentiles as well as for the Jews,[28] but the apartheid of Jewish Christians and believers among the Gentiles, particularly in the area of forthright fellowship at the table and communal living.[29]

When Luke points out that the Christian refugees from Jerusalem who reached Phoenicia, Cyprus, and Antioch "spoke the word to none except Jews" (11:19), he may emphasize the fact that evangelizing the Gentiles had already been initiated by Peter and approved by the Jerusalem apostles.[30] When some of them started to preach Jesus Christ as Lord before a Gentile audience, many believed. Marshall observes that whereas it had taken divine intervention to persuade Peter to take the step to preaching to the Gentiles, "here it seems to have happened almost casually without any issues of principle arising at the outset or later."[31]

Finally, when the church was prompted by God's Spirit to release Barnabas and Paul for the mission to the Gentiles (13:2), the possibility of such a mission seems to have posed no problem. The fasting and praying (13:3) no doubt took place as spiritual support for their future work,[32] rather than being a time of

26. For the status of the proselyte in Judaism, cf. S. J. D. Cohen, "Crossing the Boundary and Becoming a Jew," *HTR* 82 (1989) 13-33 (28-30).

27. Marshall, *Acts,* 160.

28. *Pace* Marshall, *Acts,* 181; and R. Pesch, *Die Apostelgeschichte,* EKKNT 5:1-2 (Zürich: Benziger; Neukirchen-Vluyn: Neukirchener, 1986) 330: "Der Judenmissionar Petrus . . . wird gegen seinen Widerstand zum Heidenmissionar."

29. Note the repeated reference to eating / food (γεύομαι, 10:10; φαγεῖν, 10:13, 14; 11:7; συνεσθίω, 11:3; also 11:8) as well as to the house of Cornelius (οἶκος, 10:2, 22, 30; 11:12, 13, 14) and the house of Simon in which Peter stayed (οἰκία, 10:6, 17, 32; 11:11). The emphasis on the house of Cornelius is further seen in the verbs εἰσέρχομαι (10:27, 28; 11:3) and ἐπιμένω (10:48), used in the same context.

30. Cf. Pesch, *Apostelgeschichte,* 1:351.

31. Marshall, *Acts,* 201.

32. Cf. Marshall, *Acts,* 216; cf. E. Haenchen, *Die Apostelgeschichte,* 13th ed. (Göttingen: Vandenhoeck & Ruprecht, 1961) 380.

"distinguishing between spirits" (cf. 1 Cor 12:10), assessing whether a mission to the Gentiles was a viable option.

There was a group in the Jerusalem church who opposed admitting Gentile converts into the community of believers without circumcision (and possibly also adherence to food laws) being demanded of them (Gal 2:12; Acts 15:1). We have no idea, however, how large and how influential this group of "right wing Jewish Christians in Jerusalem" were, but nothing suggests that they were dominant in the church.[33]

***1.3. The Gospels and the Mission to the Gentiles.*** It is a fair assumption that the early Christians had developed a theology of missions which included the mission to the Gentiles. The theology and the praxis of the apostle Paul, whose missionary ministry began just three or four years after the death and the resurrection of Jesus,[34] is the most obvious case in point. Without doubt such a theology of mission would not have been uniform, as the dispute between Paul and "those of the circumcision" shows.

Less conspicuous is the fact that all four Gospels show a discernible interest in missionary outreach to the Gentiles, although the degree to which this interest is a central or a more peripheral motif varies. I will not attempt to present the full evidence at this point. A rather sketchy review of Matthew's Gospel and some hints regarding the Gospel of Luke must suffice.

In his opening sentence Matthew links Jesus with David and Abraham (Matt 1:1). This can be interpreted in terms of the conviction that the hope of a "new creation" is fulfilled in Jesus Christ, who is the messianic king of Israel and heir to the Davidic promises and who is the one through whose ministry God's promise to the patriarchs that all the nations of the earth will be blessed is being realized.[35] That Jesus' designation as "son of Abraham" marks him not only as a true Jew but as the instrument of divine blessing for the nations (taking

33. Marshall, *Acts,* 202.

34. Assuming that his sojourn in Arabia (Gal 1:17) was not a spiritual retreat for purposes of meditation and that the time in Syria-Cilicia (Gal 1:21) was not devoted to the pursuit of personal interests but missionary outreach (cf. Gal 1:23 and the probable background of 2 Cor 11:32-33 and Acts 9:24-25); cf. Marshall, *Acts,* 174; F. F. Bruce, *The Epistle to the Galatians,* NIGTC (Grand Rapids, Michigan: Wm. B. Eerdmans, 1982) 96, 104-5; recently M. Hengel, "Der vorchristliche Paulus," in *Paulus und das antike Judentum,* ed. M. Hengel and U. Heckel, WUNT 58 (Tübingen: J. C. B. Mohr [Paul Siebeck], 1991) 177-291 (220).

35. Cf. W. D. Davies and Dale C. Allison Jr., *The Gospel according to Saint Matthew,* ICC (Edinburgh: T. & T. Clark, 1988 / 91) 1:159-60, who interpret βίβλος γενέσεως in terms of "book of origin." Carson *(Matthew,* 61) disagrees with the "increasingly popular view," advocated by Zahn, Davies, Hill, Maier, and others who see the phrase as a heading for the entire Gospel. Even though it is true that no occurrence of the expression βίβλος γενέσεως for a book-length document has been discovered, and that it should therefore be taken as a heading to 1:2-17 or to 1:2-25, it is not impossible to assume, on the basis of Matthew's use of γένεσις, that the Evangelist wants Jesus Christ understood as a new beginning in the sense of a new creation (cf. R. T. France, *Matthew,* TNTC [Leicester: Inter-Varsity, 1985] 73).

up Gen 12:3; 18:18; 22:18) is indicated (1) by the fact that Abraham is regularly seen in critical distance to Israel (Matt 3:9; 8:11; 22:32) and (2) by the end of the Gospel (28:19-20), where the commission to evangelize the nations clearly implies the universality of the salvation taught and brought by Jesus.[36]

The first reported speech by human beings is the inquiry of Gentile magi who have come from the East to worship the King of the Jews (2:2) — before Jesus' task to Israel has even begun and in tragic contradistinction to the leaders in Jerusalem. "Thus the commission to be the Son of Abraham (1:1) is here already going into effect."[37] And the first "action" of Jesus, the infant Messiah, takes him to Egypt (2:13-15), another element in the introduction which points outside Israel.[38] The first episode of Jesus' ministry in Galilee and his first reported words in the main body of the narrative (4:18-22) are his commissioning of Simon Peter and Andrew, James and John to follow him and to become "fishers of people" (4:19). Since the last reported words of Jesus, which conclude the entire narrative (28:18-20), contain the commission to make disciples of all nations, the ἄνθρωποι in 4:19 may well imply a universal dimension.[39]

When Matthew outlines "the programme of Jesus' active ministry" in 4:23-25,[40] he implies that the Galilean ministry (v 23) had an impact on non-Jews as well: the news of Jesus reaches Syria and the Decapolis. Coming after a reference to "all Galilee" and determined by ὅλη, Syria is most likely not a reference to the Roman province nor to the Jewish population living in *Palaistine Syrie* but to the territory extending from Damascus to Antioch and eastward and implies non-Jews hearing from Jesus.[41] Whether the reference to the Decapolis (v 25) is intended to imply Gentiles among the "great crowds" who followed Jesus is unclear: it may refer, together with the other regions listed in v 25 (Galilee, Jerusalem, Judea, Perea ["from beyond the Jordan"]) and with the exception of Samaria, which is not mentioned, with salvation-historical import to the ancient "holy land";[42] if the reference is determined by the contemporary

36. J. Gnilka, *Das Matthäusevangelium*, 2 vols., HTKNT 1, 2d ed. (Freiburg: Herder, 1988) 1:7.

37. Cf. H. J. B. Combrink, "The Structure of the Gospel of Matthew as Narrative," *TynB* 34 (1983) 61-90 (77); also Davies and Allison, *Matthew*, 1:253.

38. Cf. France, *Matthew: Evangelist and Teacher*, 233. Davies and Allison, 1:281 n. 53, find it questionable that the references to Egypt further the Gentile theme, referring to U. Luz, *Das Evangelium nach Matthäus*, EKKNT 1 (Zürich: Benziger; Neukirchen-Vluyn: Neukirchener, 1985-90) 1:129, who allows, however, that such a hint is "durchaus möglich."

39. Similarly Davies and Allison, *Matthew*, 1:398: "Perhaps Matthew thought of the Gentiles as included in the ἀνθρώπων.''

40. Davies and Allison, *Matthew*, 412; quoting B. Gerhardsson, *The Mighty Acts of Jesus according to Matthew* (Lund: Gleerup, 1979) 23.

41. Thus recently Gnilka, *Matthäusevangelium*, 1:108; Davies and Allison, *Matthew*, 1:417. Luz, *Matthäus*, 1:181 with n. 16, sees a reference to the entire Roman province but interprets in terms of Gentile recipients of the news of Jesus' ministry as well. Συρία is a *hapax legomenon* in Matthew.

42. Cf. G. Lohfink, "Wem gilt die Bergpredigt? Eine redaktionskritische Untersuchung von Mt 4.23–5.2 und 7:28f," *TQ* 163 (1983) 264-84 (275-76); France, *Gospel*, 105; Gnilka, *Matthäusevangelium*, 1:108-9; with caution Luz, *Matthäus*, 1:180-81.

historical situation, however, the Gentile majority of the Decapolis cannot *a priori* be excluded.

In the Sermon, followers of Jesus are described as "the salt of the earth" and "the light of the world" (5:13-14). Both γῆ and κόσμος cannot be made to refer to the land of Israel[43] but have a universal reference. These verses imply therefore a universal mission of the disciples,[44] at least for the Evangelist. The significance of this universal dimension is highlighted by the fact that 5:13-16 may be regarded as a "summary statement of the task of the people of God in the world."[45] The narrative section 8:1–9:34, which reports on Jesus' healing ministry, recounts in central position encounters of Jesus with Gentiles: the healing of the centurion's servant (8:5-13) and the healing of the Gerasene demoniacs (8:28-34).

Moving to the later sections of the Gospel, we notice that the last element of Matthew's general description of the "signs" indicating that Jesus is coming back (24:4-14) is the feature that "this gospel of the kingdom will be preached throughout the whole world, as a testimony to all nations" (24:14). The end of the world cannot come until the gospel has penetrated ἐν ὅλῃ τῇ οἰκουμένῃ and has reached outside the Jewish world to πάντα τὰ ἔθνη.[46] The first pericope of the passion narrative (26:6–27:66), Jesus' anointing at Bethany (26:6-13), ends with the pronouncement that "this gospel will be preached in the whole world" (26:13). The phrase ἐν ὅλῳ τῷ κόσμῳ is even more all-inclusive than the corresponding phrase in 24:14.[47] The resurrection narrative (28:1-20) ends with Jesus declaring his universal authority and giving the disciples the commission to "make disciples of all nations." The Great Commission is the last and therefore perhaps the most relevant definition of the λαός whom Jesus will save according to the announcement of the angel (1:21) — the identification of "his people" as people of all nations is the resolution of a theme that has been implied (2:1-12), predicted (8:11-12), and clarified (15:21-28) earlier in the Gospel.[48]

One can make a similar case for the other Gospels. All four Gospels

43. *Pace* W. J. Dumbrell, "The Logic of the Role of the Law in Matthew 5:1-20," *NovT* 23 (1981) 1-21.

44. Cf. Davies and Allison, *Matthew,* 1:472, 479; Gnilka, *Matthäusevangelium,* 1:135-36, who, however, regard the statements as redactional, "presupposing" the Gentile mission. Schlatter, *Matthäus,* 146, states: "Der Beruf der Jünger hat keine Grenzen; sie sind zur Menschheit gesandt. Das letzte Wort des Evangeliums: *eis panta ta ethne* 28.19 ist auch das erste, das den Jüngern ihren Beruf zeigt." Similarly G. Strecker, *Die Bergpredigt* (Göttingen: Vandenhoeck & Ruprecht, 1984) 52: "An der Durchführung des Missionsauftrages entscheidet sich das Jüngersein."

45. Thus the heading for this pericope in Davies and Allison, *Matthew,* 1:470. Gnilka, *Matthäusevangelium,* 1:133, categorizes the statements as "Definitionssätze."

46. Cf. J. W. Thompson, "The Gentile Mission as an Eschatological Necessity," *ResQ* 14 (1971) 18-27.

47. Thus France, *Gospel,* 363.

48. Cf. M. A. Powell, "The Plot and Subplots of Matthew's Gospel," *NTS* 38 (1992) 187-204 (196 n. 27).

express a discernible interest in mission to the Gentiles.[49] Now it is a fair assumption that in their selection of the available teaching of Jesus the Evangelists wanted to be relevant to the needs of his church. It is spurious, however, to argue that since they were interested in the relevance of the teaching of Jesus rather than in its origin they felt free to create sayings or settings which suited their purposes. As regards this question of authenticity, the case of Luke's Gospel seems to be particularly relevant. Luke is the only Evangelist who wrote a sequel to his portrait of Jesus, narrating the mission of the early Christians after the ascension and the giving of the Spirit. A key point of this second volume is the desire to show how the gospel of salvation in Jesus Christ was meant for the Gentiles as well as for the Jews[50] and how the problem of continuity between the message of "the things that have been fulfilled among us" (Luke 1:1, NIV), which retain their moorings in OT prophecy, and the fact of the early Christians' turn to the Gentiles can be explained.[51] If Luke had these concerns, and if he designed a two-volume project right from the start,[52] the manner in which Luke refers to Gentiles warrants the conclusion that his references to Jesus' encounters with and sayings about Gentiles are not apologetically motivated redactional clarifications and justifications. Luke's "special material" on Gentiles either consists of OT quotations or remains implicit. Note (1) how the references to Gentiles in 2:32 and 3:4-6 are allusions to OT prophecy not developed in the respective contexts; (2) how the allusion to the Gentile mission in the commissioning of the Seventy-two remains implicit; (3) how the saying about those from all four corners of the earth (paralleled in Matt 8:11) is not developed either; and (4) how the command to evangelize in 24:47 (roughly paralleled in Matt 28:19) refers to "all nations" as the target group and the starting point (Jerusalem) of the mission without being expanded along the lines of Acts 1:8.

It is further evident that the references to Gentiles are on a more modest scale than those in Matthew and in Mark. (1) Note how Luke omits Mark's reference to Jesus' foretelling the preaching to the Gentiles (Mark 13:10) as well

49. See generally the sketch of Hahn, *Mission,* 95-115. For Mark see specifically Z. Kato, *Die Völkermission im Markusevangelium,* EH 23:252 (Frankfurt / Bern: Lang, 1986); K. Stock, "Theologie der Mission bei Markus," in *Mission im Neuen Testament,* 130-44; for Luke see S. G. Wilson, *The Gentiles and the Gentile Mission in Luke-Acts,* SNTSMS 23 (Cambridge: Cambridge University, 1973) 29-58; for John see R. Schnackenburg, *Das Johannesevangelium: Ergänzende Auslegungen und Exkurse,* HTKNT 4:4 (Freiburg: Herder, 1984) 58-72; M. R. Ruiz, *Der Missionsgedanke des Johannesevangeliums,* FB 55 (Würzburg: Echter, 1987); T. Okure, *The Johannine Approach to Mission,* WUNT 2:31 (Tübingen: J. C. B. Mohr [Paul Siebeck], 1988).

50. Marshall, *Luke,* 20.

51. Pesch, *Apostelgeschichte,* 1:33-34, pointing out that Luke sees the solution of this problem of continuity in the soteriological will of God, which is universal and which can be traced in history as well as in the hardening and impenitence of part of Israel.

52. Cf. M. Hengel, *Zur urchristlichen Geschichtsschreibung* (Stuttgart: Calwer, 1979) 38, who speaks of the "historical and theological unity" of Luke-Acts; cf. Pesch, *Apostelgeschichte,* 1:29.

as the healing of the Syrophoenician woman (Mark 7:24-30) together with the preceding section on ritual purity (Mark 7:1-23), a sequence of pericopes which in Mark and Matthew imply — in hindsight quite powerfully — a christological justification of the mission to the Gentiles. (2) Luke omits the geographical reference to Caesarea Philippi as the locale where Peter confesses Jesus as the Messiah and where a new people of God is established (Luke 9:18). (3) Luke omits the phrase "for all the nations" from the quotation of Isa 56:7 used by Jesus to explain his demonstration in the temple (19:46).

Thus we see a very strong link between Jesus and a concern for mission among Gentiles in the Gospels. Although the Evangelists, particularly Matthew, portray Jesus as limiting his ministry to Israel, they all point out that the vision of Jesus was larger — and not only his vision for the future, but the reality of his ministry as well. And this nexus between Jesus and mission among Gentiles cannot simply be ascribed to the aetiological interests of the Gospel writers.

## 2. Jesus and the Gentiles

Before we return to our investigation of Jesus' encounters with Gentiles it will be helpful if we pause to define the concept of "mission," something often neglected by NT scholars. They sometimes seem to be content with a vague notion of "mission" or they work with a one-sided concept of "mission" as implying by necessity a move to a different geographical locality.

***2.1. Defining "Mission."*** As for a working definition, we may understand "mission" as referring to a movement which stands out from the surrounding environment with regard to convictions and practice (implying the general validity of the truth held and practiced) and which aims at and works toward winning others for its cause as a result of its self-understanding.[53] In other words, the term "mission" applies where a person or a group of persons conveys to other persons a new interpretation of reality (including God, the plight of humanity, salvation), imparts a new way of life as a substitute for his or her old way of life, and achieves integration into the community. The concept "convey" may imply geographical movement ("take from one place to another") or communication of ideas ("express in words"). Thus, this "conveying to others" may happen by actice expansive proclamation (centrifugal movement of mission) or by "winning presence" (centripedal movement of mission). The result of mission is conversion, characterized by the adoption of new convictions, the adoption of new practices, and the integration into the new community.

53. Cf. Frankemölle, "Theologie der Mission," 99.

As regards the procedures of conversion to Judaism the following observations apply. First, there was no official conversion ceremony in pre-rabbinic Judaism. Conversion was a private affair. There existed no authorized courts performing a ceremony and no central registry for converts. There was evidently no set of specific requirements that had to be met by the Gentile for a conversion to be considered valid. The criteria the rabbis used to distinguish between a Gentile and a convert are unknown. "Circumcision was the only essential requirement."[54] Second, still along the same lines, some Jewish communities allowed God-fearers to join, at least in the sense of a loose affiliation which allowed participation in the synagogue services.[55] However, the evidence for this comes from Greek cities like Aphrodisias, Miletus, and Panticapaeum, and it is not clear whether the same practice was found in Palestinian cities. Third, in the eyes of the Jews even the proselyte apparently did not "become" a Jew, since he or she did not achieve real equality with the native Jews but became "a Jew of a peculiar sort," and this peculiarity was evidently hereditary.[56] Fourth, terminological categories are vague.[57] Gentiles who expressed sympathy for the Jews and their faith may be designated as "sympathizers": they admired some aspect of Judaism, acknowledged the power of the God of the Jews, may have benefited the Jews, or may have been conspicuously friendly. They may also have practiced a few or many of the Jewish rituals and venerated the God of the Jews while denying or ignoring the pagan gods; such sympathizers may be more specifically called "adherents" (usually called "God-fearers").[58] We may speak of a "convert" (proselyte) if a sympathizer went beyond this and joined the Jewish community, worshiping the God of Israel and following the stipulations of the law not as perhaps a convenient supplement to his or her current

54. Cf. S. J. D. Cohen, "The Rabbinic Conversion Ceremony," *JJS* 41 (1990) 177-203 (193). Analyzing *b. Yebam.* 47a-b and tractate *Gerim* 1:1, Cohen concludes that the rabbinic conversion ceremony of the primary text *b. Yebam.* 47a-b, apparently deriving from the mid-second century C.E., is not primarily an initiation ritual but an attempt "to regulate and formalize what until then had been an entirely personal and chaotic process" (203; referring for confirmation to M. Goodman, "Proselytising in Rabbinic Judaism," *JJS* 40 [1989] 175-85 [184]). Recently G. Gilbert, "The Making of a Jew: 'God-Fearer' or Convert in the Story of Izates," *USQR* 44 (1991) 299-313, discussing the conversion story of Izates as narrated in Josephus *Ant.* 20.34-48, argues that circumcision was not regarded as necessary for establishing Jewish identity.

55. Cf. Cohen, "Boundary," 32.

56. Cf. Cohen, "Boundary," 29-30. An example is the regulation in *m. Bik.* 1:4-5 which stipulates, among other things, that Gentiles converted to Judaism may not recite liturgical references to "our fathers"; cf. S. J. D. Cohen, "Can Converts to Judaism Say 'God of Our Fathers'?," *Judaism* 40 (1991) 419-29.

57. For the following cf. Cohen, "Boundary," 15-31.

58. For the current discussion on the existence of "God-fearers," see T. M. Finn, "The God Fearers Reconsidered," *CBQ* 47 (1985) 75-84; R. S. MacLennan and A. T. Kraabel, "The God-Fearers — A Literary and Theological Invention," *BARev* 12 (1986) 46-53, 64; L. H. Feldman, "The Omnipresence of the God-Fearers," *BARev* 12 (1986) 58-69; Trebilco, *Jewish Commentary,* 145-66.

way of life but as a substitute for the old way of life. Joining the Jewish community as such is not sufficient for "religious conversion" (as distinguished from "nominal conversion"), since the status of the Gentile slaves who "became" Jews (through the administration of circumcision and later manumission) and the social integration as result of intermarriage were not the result of a new devotion to the God of Israel.

The various levels of affiliation of Gentiles to the Jewish faith and the Gentile conversion to Judaism make us cautious not to interpret "hangers-on" as converts nor to posit a rigid initiation ceremony.[59] The central process of conversion involves a change of basic convictions about God and salvation, a change of everyday behavior on the basis of God's revealed will, and the integration into the community of those who share the same beliefs and practice the same ways.

Returning to our discussion of Jesus' relationship with Gentiles in practice and in proclamation, we will proceed with three questions in mind: (1) Is a change of fundamental convictions involved or envisaged, including a substitution of beliefs? (2) Is a substitutional adoption of a new (Jewish? or "kingdom-related"?)[60] way of life involved or envisaged? (3) Is loyalty to Jesus and / or integration into the community of his followers involved or envisaged?

***2.2. Jesus' Encounters with Gentiles.*** (1) Summary statements. The summaries of Jesus' ministry indicating its effect on the Gentile population of the Decapolis (Matt 4:24-25) and the region about Tyre and Sidon (Mark 7:7-8) do not imply an active endeavor to reach Gentiles. The picture is more like that of the success of the Jewish faith in pagan surroundings, with the perhaps decisive difference, though, that this success did not come in trickles but in a rush of people. "A great multitude" and "great crowds" came to hear Jesus and "followed" him (Matt 4:25). The verb ἠκολούθησαν does not necessarily connote discipleship but refers here to a more loose attachment to Jesus as he moved about in Galilee. Neither a change of convictions nor the adoption of a new way of life is implied, as in the case of the disciples who left their boat, their nets, and their father when they "followed" Jesus (Matt 4:18-22 par. Mark 1:16-20). But the effect of Jesus' ministry on Gentiles living in Galilee and adjacent areas should not be denied.

(2) The first encounter with a pagan which the Gospels report in more detail is the meeting with the centurion of Capernaum (Matt 8:5-13 par. Luke 7:1-10).[61] Being a soldier, he presumably was a God-fearer rather than a full-

59. Despite the baptism practiced by John, since this was not an initiation ceremony proper but a prophetic call to repentance and to anticipation of the awaited Messiah.

60. The relation between the two needs to be further discussed. Such a discussion, involving a consideration of Jesus' view of the law, of the criteria for being an "insider" in the kingdom of God, and of his eschatology, would take us too far into other areas.

61. For the historical reliability see recently, with positive results, U. Wegner, *Der Hauptmann*

fledged proselyte, but he still could have enjoyed a loosely affiliated membership in the local synagogue community.[62] Was he converted? (a) Jesus "marveled" (ἐθαύμασεν only here in Matthew) at his "faith" (πίστις), whose greatness is the soldier's understanding of the secret of Jesus' authority.[63] Is this faith "conversion"? The centurion, who already venerates the God of Israel, trusts Jesus. Even though the basis of this trust is not spelled out, it may be inferred from his comment about Jesus' authority (Matt 8:9). It is more than trust in Jesus as a powerful miracle worker; he trusts Jesus to do what only God can do. It is trust as a result of acceptance of Jesus' message about the kingly rule of God who alone can do the impossible as manifest in his own ministry. So we may assume a change of convictions regarding the locus of God's power. (b) The centurion had already adopted at least some Jewish practices. Did he qualify for Jesus as an "insider" regarding the kingdom of God? Possibly, as Jesus comments by referring to those coming "from east and west" to be joined to the fathers of Israel at the consummation of the messianic kingdom (8:11; cf. Luke 13:28-29) — that is, to Gentiles.[64] (c) The centurion "loves" the Jewish nation and (helped financially to) build the synagogue (Luke 7:5). A corresponding "love" for Jesus and devotion to his and his disciples' needs are not reported. This confirms the historical reliability of the narrative: Matthew did not present the centurion as the first Gentile follower of Jesus who supported the Lord and the disciples. However, it does not allow us to draw conclusions about his conversion.[65] Since the sources relate only the healing of the servant but remain silent regarding the subsequent involvement of the centurion, we must suspend judgment. However, the saying about the "many from east and west" (Matt 8:11-12) clearly implies integration into the community of those

---

*von Kafarnaum (Mt 7.28a; 8.5-10, 13 par Lk 7.1-10): Ein Beitrag zur Q-Forschung,* WUNT 2:14 (Tübingen: J. C. B. Mohr [Paul Siebeck], 1985) 403-28.

62. The way the "elders of the Jews" speak of him may be understood to imply distance ("he loves our nation," Luke 7:5 — i.e., he still belongs to another ἔθνος), indicating perhaps (1) that he had not "become" a Jew through circumcision or (2) that he did not belong to the synagogue community. This piece of evidence is not conclusive, however, as our observations on Gentile conversion to Judaism show. Still, it is difficult to imagine how a centurion who had become a proselyte, substituting his old way of life with the practice of Jewish laws, could have retained his post.

63. Cf. Carson, *Matthew,* 202.

64. Davies and Allison, *Matthew,* 2:27-29, interpret the "many" who come from east and west in terms of "unprivileged Jews . . . because they have not lived in the land or heard Jesus" (28). Dale C. Allison Jr., "Who will Come from East and West? Observations on Matt 8:11-12 — Luke 13:28-29," *IBS* 11 (1989) 158-70, argues that the original saying was passed down without a specific context and spoke of the eschatological ingathering of dispersed Jews, while the new context suggested identification with Gentiles. As regards the different context of Matt 8:11-12 and Luke 13:28-29, Carson, *Matthew,* 202, points to the alternative that Jesus as itinerant preacher said similar things more than once. If the saying belonged originally to the context of Matt 8:5ff., the presence of the Gentile Cornelius determines the referent of the "many" from east and west.

65. *Pace* Schlatter, *Matthäus,* 275, who speaks of the centurion's "Anschluß an Jesus."

who have experienced God's salvation (Abraham, Isaac, Jacob) — that is, into God's people.

Thus, whether or not Jesus regarded the centurion of Capernaum as a converted Gentile, it seems obvious that he speaks of the basic reality of Gentiles belonging to the kingdom of God. Even though the saying reflects the OT prophecies of Gentiles coming to Jerusalem, thus implying the "centripedal" effect of "mission,"[66] we may still speak of the implication of "mission" (defined in the sense above, which does not include the categories centripedal / centrifugal) to the Gentiles nevertheless.[67] And we note that as Jesus does not take up a specific OT reference to the eschatological pilgrimage, the statement about believing Gentiles who find their way into the kingdom does not presuppose any assumption about who plays the active part — remembering that the centurion came to "faith" as a result of Jesus' activity and the news thereof.

(3) The second encounter of Jesus with an individual pagan is with the Gerasene demoniac (Mark 5:1-20 par. Luke 8:26-39 par. Matt 8:28-34). Regarding the question whether the pagan was converted, it may be significant that Matthew has two persons whereas Mark and Luke have only one: Matthew possibly had independent knowledge of a second demoniac, while the other two Gospels focus either on the fiercest of the two or (my suggestion) on the one with the more lasting results after the deliverance from the spirits.[68] We notice (a) a change of convictions, as the man is delivered from the violent manipulation of the evil spirits (Mark 5:15) and as he realizes that to stay with Jesus is more important than to return to his home.[69] (b) The life of the healed man would naturally have differed dramatically from his old way of life. Since this change came as a result of a miraculous healing, it is uncertain whether we can also assume a spiritual change resulting from a knowledge of Jesus' message of the kingdom of God. On the other hand, he was not just an "emotional

66. Emphasized by Gnilka, *Matthäusevangelium,* 2:303.

67. Unless we interpret in terms of "Matthew's eschatological expectations," assuming that the land has been transcendentalized and that the realization of these promises takes place not in this world but in the world to come (thus Davies and Allison, *Matthew,* 2:29). The argument that the Gentiles cannot be in view since in that case Jews would be regarded as condemned, which is not Matthew's position, is not conclusive; in view is not the condemnation of all Jews but the reconstitution of the Israel of God consisting of "the international fellowship of those who believe in the Messiah" (D. Wenham, *The Parables of Jesus* [London: Hodder & Stoughton, 1989] 131).

68. The argument about Mark and Luke singling out the fiercest was already put forward by the Church Fathers. Access to independent tradition on the part of Matthew is assumed by W. Grundmann, *Das Evangelium nach Matthäus,* THKNT 1, 6th ed. (Berlin: Evangelische, 1986) 262-63; Carson, *Matthew,* 217. France, *Gospel,* 163, explains with the witness theme and sees all personal details concerning the men "almost entirely omitted." Davies and Allison, *Matthew,* 2:80, prefer to "remain unenlightened."

69. The "worship" (Mark 5:6) is presumably a gesture of submission on the part of the spirits; cf. J. M. Nützel, "προσκυνέω," *EDNT* 3:419-23 (420). One should not read too much into this term regarding the attitude of the man himself.

conquest."[70] He obeys Jesus, who told him to go home and tell the people what had happened. Indeed, he goes beyond this and proclaims in the entire town (καθ' ὅλην τὴν πόλιν, Luke 8:39) and in the Decapolis (Mark 5:20) what had happened through Jesus. (c) The healed Gentile is dismissed by Jesus, but with a task to perform, implying that he is accepted.[71] For the readers of Mark and Luke, "the story is a paradigm of what conversion involves: the responsibility to evangelise"[72] — that is, to evangelize people in one's home and hometown, even Gentiles. The message the man proclaimed was limited, but at its center was the news of Jesus.

Thus, although Jesus himself does not involve himself in preaching in the Gentile areas of the Decapolis, he sends a Gentile who has grasped something of his dignity with the task of telling others what God (Luke 8:39) has done through Jesus. If the incident is historical,[73] it shows that Jesus' ministry was not restricted entirely to the Jews but implied an openness for mission to the Gentiles.[74]

(4) The third encounter between Jesus and a specific Gentile is told in the story of the Syrophoenician woman (Mark 7:24-30 par. Matt 15:21-28). (a) The discussion of the woman's convictions concerning Jesus is hampered by the fact that again we are not given much information about the content of her faith. Jesus calls her faith "great" (μεγάλη, Matt 15:28). The "greatness" of her faith, as can be deduced from her reply (15:27 par.), should be seen in the fact that she acknowledges Israel's covenantal prerogatives and blessings, not arguing against the apparent unfairness of some being children and others being "dogs under the table," while she trusts God to extend his mercies even to Gentiles, as he now feeds the "children" through Jesus, even though they have no inherited right to receive them.[75] We do not know how the

70. The term is taken from F. Solmsen, *Isis among the Greeks and Romans* (Cambridge, Massachusetts: Harvard University, 1979) 83, who uses it to designate an acceptance of the cult of Isis which falls short of "conversion" (quoted by Cohen, "Boundary," 31 n. 64).

71. Thus Marshall, *Luke,* 341. Cf. J. A. Fitzmyer, *The Gospel according to Luke,* AB 28-28A (Garden City, New York: Doubleday, 1981 / 85) 735: "The cured demoniac, who desired to stay with him, thus becomes a pagan disciple."

72. Marshall, *Luke,* 341. Cf. Fitzmyer, *Luke,* 740: "He sends him on a missionary errand"; when he adds: "that is not yet of Christian discipleship, since the time for Gentile disciples has not yet come in the Lucan story," he contradicts his earlier statement (see preceding footnote). Like many others, Fitzmyer seems to have become the victim of a *petitio principii:* there can be no pagan disciples during Jesus' ministry before his death, and any evidence to the contrary must therefore be explained differently. However, if this Gerasene demoniac indeed became a disciple, and if he was a Gentile (a fact which Fitzmyer emphasizes), then he was (perhaps the first?) pagan disciple.

73. Cf. Marshall, *Luke,* 335-36, for arguments in favor of historical reliability.

74. Cf. Kato, *Völkermission im Markusevangelium,* 59, who remarks that Mark presents the tradition of the earthly Jesus giving a commission of proclamation to a Gentile who is to preach the mercy of the God of Israel for the Gentiles.

75. Cf. Schlatter, *Matthäus,* 491; Carson, *Matthew,* 355-56, emphasizing the historical perspective of the narrative (353-54); for the latter see also Davies and Allison, *Matthew,* 2:544-45,

woman came to have such "great faith." (b) However, there is no hint of an adoption of a new way of life, and (c) no reference to a desire to join the followers of Jesus.

Thus we may not speak of the "conversion" of a Gentile occasioned by Jesus' presence. What we do have, however, is the recognition on the part of Jesus that God's grace is now freely available to non-Jews as well, while retaining the salvation-historical privilege of Israel. Relevant in this respect is Mark's notice (Mark 7:24b) that even though Jesus did not want his presence in the Gentile territory near Tyre to be known, "he could not be hid": his significance as bringer of salvation cannot be limited to Israel but forces its way beyond the Jewish borders.[76]

5. If the 4,000 of Mark 8:1-10 par. Matt 15:32-39 who spent three days with Jesus were indeed Gentiles, we would need to infer from the frequent association of large crowds with Jesus' healing and teaching (Mark 1:31-32, 45; 2:2; 3:7-8, 20; 4:1-2; 6:32-44) that besides healing the sick Jesus also preached to those present — that is, to Gentiles. This may have been deliberate. Whether one accepts G. Dalman's reconstruction of Jesus' itinerary in 7:31, which takes Jesus from Tyre north to Sidon across to Caesarea Philippi down to the Sea of Galilee at Hippos, or that of F. G. Lang, which takes Jesus from Tyre via Sidon across Lebanon to the territory of Damascus which bordered on the eastern territory of Sidon and then southeast through the Decapolis, perhaps via the cities of Dium, Abila, Gadara, and eventually through Hippos to the Sea, the conclusion is the same: "Jesus took a longer than necessary journey to reach the Sea of Galilee in the area of the Decapolis."[77] When we understand this episode against the background of the earlier feeding of the 5,000 in Galilee (Mark 6:30-44 par.), and if we assume the possibility that the miracle, though real, is a symbol for the anticipation of the messianic banquet, we may infer that Jesus demonstrates here his openness to give Gentiles a share in fellowship with God. In the first feeding which involved Jews, Jesus did not want to leave the crowds "like sheep without a shepherd" (Mark 6:34) — that is, he is the

---

who conclude: "One wonders whether a story whose import is so ambiguous could have been created for the express purpose of granting instruction on the Gentile problem."

76. Cf. Kato, *Völkermission im Markusevangelium,* 88.

77. R. A. Guelich, *Mark 1–8:26,* WBC 34A (Dallas: Word, 1989) 393; referring to G. Dalman, *Sacred Sites and Ways: Studies in the Topography of the Gospels* (New York: Macmillan, 1935), 200-201; and F. G. Lang, "'Über Sidon mitten ins Gebiet der Dekapolis': Geographie und Theologie in Markus 7.31," *Zeitschrift des Deutschen Palästina-Vereins* 94 (1978) 145-60. The difficulty of the itinerary and certain linguistic peculiarities make it impossible to regard Mark 7:31 as the free invention of the Evangelist; thus R. Pesch, *Das Markusevangelium,* HTKNT 2:1, 4th ed., 2:2, 2d ed. (Freiburg: Herder, 1984) 1:393, regarding the itinerary as a combination of traditional materials; and J. Gnilka, *Das Evangelium nach Markus,* 2 vols., EKKNT 2 (Zürich: Benziger; Neukirchen-Vluyn: Neukirchener, 1978 / 79) 1:296, who opts for a free creation of v. 31. The historical reliability is defended by G. Maier, *Matthäus-Evangelium* (Neuhausen: Hänssler, 1979 / 80) 1:550- 51, taken up by Carson, *Matthew,* 357-58.

true shepherd of Israel. In the second feeding Jesus takes action on account of his compassion for the crowd who are hungry and who might faint on the way.

Thus, again, the salvation-historical thrust of his mission to Israel is not jeopardized, while a mission to Gentiles becomes possible as a result of their weakness and helplessness. If Jesus ministers to Gentiles in the same way as he ministers to Jews, even in the context of God's miraculous provision of necessities of life, there can be no barriers preventing a mission to the Gentiles. The Gentile crowd who gathered around Jesus is not portrayed as a converted community of Jesus. But the possibility of treating the Gentiles like the Jews when it comes to showing God's mercy has been established in a fundamental way.

(6) Jesus' demonstration in the temple (Mark 11:15-17 par. Matt 21:12-17 par. Luke 19:45-46) is relevant for the subject under discussion. Two factors tie the episode to the Gentile theme: (a) the locus of the demonstration in the Court of the Gentiles where the commercial proceedings were allowed, and (b) Jesus' quotation from Isa 56:7 referring to God's house as "a house of prayer for all the nations" (Mark 11:17), linked with the allusion to Jeremiah's woe oracle against the temple (Jer 7:11-15 [7:11]) implying God's judgment on the center of the (old) covenant people. Without going into details and without considering the messianic implications,[78] we establish the fact that the symbolic action of Jesus in the Court of the Gentiles, together with his explanation by the double quotation, can be regarded as constituting "a decisive hour of salvation history" — as judgment on the temple and as Gentile participation in the worship of the one God are announced.[79] This is confirmed by the violent reaction of the chief priests, the scribes, and the leaders of the people (Mark 11:18; Luke 19:47).

If Jesus indeed understood his action with the accompanying explanation as an announcement of the destruction of the temple (cf. Matt 21:18-22 and 24:2, 15-21 par.), speaking in the same vein of legitimate Gentile worship of the God of Israel, he implies the establishment of a new people of God consisting of Jews and Gentiles.

***2.3. Jesus' Sayings about Gentiles.*** (1) Luke 4:25-27. In his preaching in Nazareth Jesus reacts to the hostility of the listeners by saying that no prophet is accepted in his hometown. He elaborates by pointing to the OT prophets Elijah and Elisha, whose ministry, in times of unbelief, brought no blessing to Israel but rather to a Sidonian widow and a Syrian general. In the context of the unbelief in Nazareth this reference constitutes a warning that a comparable

78. Cf. recently J. Maier, "Beobachtungen zum Konfliktpotential in neutestamentlichen Aussagen über den Tempel," in *Jesus und das jüdische Gesetz*, ed. I. Broer (Stuttgart: Kohlhammer 1992) 173-213.

79. Cf. Kato, *Völkermission im Markusevangelium*, 109ff., defending the historicity of the reference to the Gentiles; cf. also Pesch, *Markusevangelium*, 2:199.

situation has developed, with the consequence that there may be other potential beneficiaries — outside Nazareth, even outside Israel. Howard Marshall thinks that the universalistic tone of vv 25-27 "is strange at this early point in the ministry of Jesus," and, although surely authentic, may well stem from another (later?) context.[80] Whatever the tradition history of the saying, unless we must assume that Jesus' universalistic vision developed slowly as a result of his rejection in Israel, nothing speaks against an implicit reference to a "mission" to the Gentiles made early in his ministry. Two facts may be seen as confirmation: the potential non-Jewish beneficiaries are mentioned without special emphasis,[81] and the implication is stated with reference to OT prophecy. Of course, in this passage Jesus does not speak of conversions of Gentiles occasioned by missionary outreach, not even by implication, and can therefore hardly be taken as a specific justification for a universalistic mission to the Gentiles. He moves from his hometown not to Gentile territories but to "Capernaum, a city of Galilee" (4:31).

(2) Matthew 5:13-14. Followers of Jesus are the "salt of the earth" and the "light of the world." As the effect of both salt and light is "centrifugal," so the existence of disciples is portrayed as a mission with universal significance, whatever the specific symbolic associations may be. And as the effect of salt and light is visible, so the universal mission of Jesus' followers leads to tangible results.

(3) Matthew 10:18. The reference to future hardships of the disciples as missionaries who witness in areas where local Jewish councils have jurisdiction as well as in areas with pagan rulers speaks of opportunities for witness before such pagan governors and kings and before other Gentiles. Since the disciples are passive, being taken into custody, it is difficult to speak of an active mission. All Jesus says is that even in such trying circumstances the Spirit would help them to spread the gospel message.

(4) Matthew 13:38. In his interpretation of the parable of the tares,[82] Jesus identifies the world as the locus of the kingdom of God. The brief statement "the field is the world" assumes a mission beyond Israel, but this is not a main point of the parable.

(5) Matthew 22:1-14; cf. Luke 14:15-24. In the parables of the wedding banquet and of the tenants the people who are eventually invited to the feast come from "the thoroughfares" and "streets" (Matt 22:9-10) and from "the

80. Marshall, *Gospel*, 180.

81. Cf. J. Nolland, *Luke 1–9:20*, WBC 35a (Dallas: Word, 1989) 201, who, however, sees "in the flow of the immediate narrative" no reference to the universalism of the Gentile mission (203); thus also R. L. Brawley, *Luke-Acts and the Jews: Conflict, Apology, and Conciliation*, SBLMS 33 (Atlanta: Scholars, 1987) 6-27.

82. Cf. G. R. Beasley-Murray, *Jesus and the Kingdom of God* (Grand Rapids, Michigan: Wm. B. Eerdmans, 1986) 135, for a defence of authenticity; also C. L. Blomberg, *Interpreting the Parables* (Leicester: Inter-Varsity, 1990) 198-99.

highways and hedges" (Luke 14:23), respectively. A call goes out to a wider circle of people to be invited to the messianic banquet of the kingdom of God. The replacement guests have been taken as referring not only to Jewish outsiders such as tax collectors, prostitutes, and sinners but, by implication, to the largest group of outsiders of all — namely, to Gentiles.[83] If this is correct, a mission to Gentiles is at best implied. The servants of the king do not figure prominently in the parable and should not simply be identified with the disciples as missionaries.[84]

(6) Mark 13:10; cf. Matt 24:14. Jesus points out that in the midst of the birth pains of the messianic kingdom which moves toward its consummation, the "gospel of the kingdom" is preached throughout the world "as a testimony to all nations." The ascription to redaction[85] or early Christian tradition[86] of Mark 13:10 is dependent on the assumption of Jesus' expectation of an imminent end and linked with an attitude which deems it impossible to reckon with genuine prophecy. If we do not doubt the latter, and if we proceed from the assumption, which can be defended from the evidence in the Gospels, that Jesus assumed an interval between his death and resurrection and the parousia, the statement may be understood as a prophetic commission by Jesus of mission to the Gentiles.[87] Even though the Gentile mission is made explicit, the circumstances and even the effect are left open: the phrase "as a testimony" implies that the gospel will bring either salvation or

83. Cf. Wenham, *Parables,* 135. See also Fitzmyer, *Luke,* 1053, who regards this motif as a Lukan allegorization of the original parable, however.

84. Further references to Gentiles in Jesus' parables have been seen in the birds of heaven who nest in the mustard plant (Matt 13:31-32; cf. Davies and Allison, *Matthew,* 2:420), in the "others" to whom the vineyard is given (Matt 21:33-46 [v 43 par.]; cf. Wenham, *Parables,* 130-31), and in the sheep which the shepherd brings from outside the fold into one flock (John 10:1-18 [v 16]; cf. Wenham, *Parables,* 104). Since these references are more implicit than explicit (cf. the caution of Blomberg, *Parables,* 248, 285) and since Jesus does not identify the Gentiles in the respective contexts, we would not advance the discussion by considering these passages further.

85. Cf. W. Marxsen, *Der Evangelist Markus: Studien zur Redaktionsgeschichte des Evangeliums,* 2d ed. (Göttingen: Vandenhoeck & Ruprecht, 1959) 119-20; more recently Kasting, *Anfänge,* 108; G. Strecker, "Das Evangelium Jesu Christi," in *Jesus Christus in Historie und Theologie* (Tübingen: J. C. B. Mohr [Paul Siebeck], 1975) 503-48 (523, 535-40).

86. Cf. Hahn, *Missions,* 31, 57-63; with caution, *idem,* "Die Rede von der Parusie des Menschensohnes Markus 13," in *Jesus und der Menschensohn,* ed. R. Pesch and R. Schnackenburg (Freiburg: Herder, n.d.) 240-66; followed by Pesch, *Markusevangelium,* 2:266ff., 285; E. Brandenburger, *Markus 13 und die Apokalyptik,* FRLANT 13 (Göttingen: Vandenhoeck & Ruprecht, 1984) 30-32, 41, 149-53 (but perhaps redaction). A different view is that of G. D. Kilpatrick, "The Gentile Mission in Mark and Mark 13:9-11," in *Studies in the Gospels,* ed. D. E. Nineham (Oxford: Blackwell, 1955) 145-58, who interprets in terms of a preaching of the gospel to Jews outside Palestine.

87. Authenticity is defended by G. R. Beasley-Murray, *Jesus and the Future: An Examination of the Criticism of the Eschatological Discouse, Mark 13* (London: Macmillan, 1954) 194ff.; cf. Bosch, *Heidenmission,* 149-90; Wilson, *Gentiles,* 19-27 (who follows Jeremias's apocalyptic interpretation, however). Cf. the detailed source- and tradition-analytical study of D. Wenham, *The Rediscovery of Jesus' Eschatological Discourse* (Sheffield: JSOT, 1984), with its implications for authenticity: "the onus of proof must be on those who deny the teaching to Jesus, not on those who affirm it" (373).

curse, depending on how people receive it. Again, the profile of Gentile mission remains vague.

(7) Mark 14:9 par. Matt 26:13. Jesus' announcement that the anointing in Bethany will be mentioned when "the gospel is preached in the whole world" assumes a Gentile mission and again does not elaborate its character.

(8) Matthew 28:18-20 (cf. Luke 24:47). The most comprehensive statement about a mission to the Gentiles is given by the risen Christ.[88] The statement describes the authority of the missionaries, which is Christ's own authority (v 17b), the charge to go to πάντα τὰ ἔθνη, to make disciples, to baptize, and to teach (vv 18a-20a), as well as the promise of Jesus' enabling presence. As regards Jesus' sayings involving Gentiles, this passage alone includes all elements of "mission": Jesus envisages a change of fundamental convictions ("make disciples . . . teaching them"), the adoption of a new way of life ("to observe all"), loyalty to Jesus ("all that I have commanded"), and integration into the community of his followers ("baptizing them . . . teaching them").

## 3. Conclusions

The mission to the Gentiles assumes more specific characteristics in the context of Jesus' encounters with Gentiles than in his teaching. This fact speaks against the assumption that the Evangelists created the references to a Gentile mission out of their own contexts. At the same time it anchors the reality of the later early Christian Gentile mission firmly in the ministry of Jesus.

As regards the question of authenticity, we may further point to the fact that the Gentile mission pericopes in the Gospels hardly answer the pressing questions which were discussed as a result of the later Gentile mission, such as the question whether converted Gentiles should be circumcised and which parts of the law apply for Gentile converts.[89]

As further confirmation of the possibility of Jesus anticipating a universal mission among Gentiles by his disciples we notice that important elements of Jesus' teaching had no reference to the law.[90] In other words, most of the teaching of Jesus could be lifted without too much difficulty from the Jewish context with a view to applying it to Gentiles who became followers of Jesus (e.g., Mark 2:17; 8:35).

Jesus' welcoming posture regarding Gentiles fits with his concern for those

88. For details cf. J. Lange, *Das Erscheinen des Auferstandenen im Evangelium nach Matthäus,* FB 11 (Würzburg: Echter, 1973); B. J. Hubbard, *The Matthean Redaction of a Primitive Apostolic Commissioning: An Exegesis of Matthew 28:16-20,* SBLDS 19 (Missoula: Scholars, 1974). As regards authenticity, Carson, *Matthew,* 592, observes that "the temptation to ascribe authenticity to 'tradition' but not to 'redaction' must be resisted."

89. Extending the argument for Matt 8:5-13 of Wegner, *Hauptmann,* 403ff.; cf. Davies and Allison, *Matthew,* 2:18.

90. Cf. E. Best, "The Revelation to Evangelize the Gentiles," *JTS* 35 (1984) 1-30.

looked down upon by many of his contemporaries — "sinners and tax collectors," women, lepers, and Samaritans. Since Jesus' concern for the outsiders of Jewish society which often ended in fellowship around the table is generally regarded as authentic, both the criterion of coherence and that of dissimilarity can be cited in favor of the reliability of the tradition which speaks of Jesus' concern for the Gentiles.

We conclude, therefore, that the Gospels portray Jesus as ministering to Israel with salvation-historical priority as the people of God. At the same time his ministry was not confined to Jews but extended beyond the boundaries defined by the Sinai covenant. His encounters with Gentiles indicated, sometimes quite clearly, that the gospel of the kingdom of God establishes a new covenant community which encompasses Jews and Gentiles alike. In anticipation of things to come Jesus spoke of a future universal mission of his disciples, the profile of which he delineated after his death and his resurrection.

# Good News to Whom? Jesus and the "Poor" in the Gospel of Luke

Joel B. Green

## 1. Introduction

One of the curious features of the Third Gospel is that, having been anointed to proclaim good news to the poor (4:18), Jesus is found repeatedly frequenting the homes of the wealthy (e.g., 5:29; 7:36; 14:1; 19:5). Inasmuch as "evangelizing the poor" stands at the head of Jesus' missionary program in the Third Gospel,[1] we might anticipate that Jesus' behavior would take a different turn, that we would find him repeatedly with "the poor." This is not the case.[2] Indeed, one searches Luke's Gospel in vain for any narration of Jesus' preaching good news *to the poor,* explicitly named, so that L. Schottroff and W. Stegemann can wonder if Luke should not be called "pastor of the wealthy."[3] Assuming that "poor" is primarily an economic term for Luke, this dissonance between the announced purpose and actual ministry of Jesus is striking. Robert Tannehill has attempted to relativize this disjunction by drawing attention to the ample instruction about possessions in the Gospel — teaching, he maintains, that is motivated by a concern for the poor.[4] He also points to Jesus' apparent com-

1. That Luke 4:16-30 sets forth the missionary agenda for Jesus in the Third Gospel is now universally agreed. See the survey of recent discussion on this pericope in C. J. Schreck, "The Nazareth Pericope: Luke 4:16-30 in Recent Study," in *L'Évangile de Luc — The Gospel of Luke,* revised and enlarged edition of *L'Évangile de Luc: Problémes littéraires et théologiques,* ed. F. Neirynck, BETL 32 (Leuven: Leuven University, 1989) 399-471.

2. Attempts to posit the equation, Luke's "people / crowds" = peasants = "the poor," only beg the question with which this essay is concerned — namely, the degree to which a social group (in this case, "peasant") can be defined in purely economic terms; on this question vis-à-vis peasants, see T. Shanin, ed., *Peasants and Peasant Societies: Selected Readings,* 2d ed. (London: Basil Blackwell, 1987).

3. L. Schottroff and W. Stegemann, *Jesus and the Hope of the Poor* (Maryknoll, New York: Orbis, 1986) 67-68.

4. R. C. Tannehill, *The Narrative Unity of Luke-Acts: A Literary Interpretation,* vol. 1: *The Gospel according to Luke,* FF (Philadelphia: Fortress, 1986) 127-32.

mitment to producing disciples who are concerned for the poor. As important as these observations may be, they suggest rather indirect ways for Jesus to fulfill his own statement of primary mission.

In this essay, we will explore another reading of the mission of Jesus to the poor in Luke. First, we will set a context for our discussion by taking note of the current interest in wealth and poverty in the Third Gospel, and raising central questions about its assumptions. From this vantage point we will examine selected materials from the Gospel itself — the Lukan vocabulary of poverty and those Lukan texts delineating explicitly the mission of Jesus. On this basis, we will argue that economic readings of Jesus' mission to the poor are much too narrow, that Luke himself portrays Jesus' mission to the "poor" against a larger backdrop. In "evangelizing the poor," we will argue, Jesus in the Third Gospel is concerned fundamentally with those defined as "them," as outsiders — a social state that may or may not have economic roots.

## 2. Jesus, Luke, and the "Poor" in Recent Study

In characteristic fashion, H. J. Cadbury anticipated by some sixty years the contemporary fascination with Lukan economics. He observed that Luke has a special interest in issues of poverty and wealth motivated not so much by his sympathy for the poor as by his appreciation of the responsibilities of "the privileged classes."[5] Subsequent Gospels research, in which the atomizing tendencies of much tradition-historical study occupied a position of preeminence, diverted attention away from the prospect of developing a "Lukan theology" of any kind, including a Lukan understanding of wealth and poverty. In addition, until the 1970s, whenever the message of the Third Gospel was reviewed, otherworldly and end-time-related pre-understandings largely kept Luke's social concerns from materializing as consequential for any understanding of the heart of his Gospel.[6] More recently, the scholarly terrain has undergone a remarkable metamorphosis, so that anyone wanting to comment on the Third Evangelist's "option for the poor" must first stand in a very long queue indeed.[7] In his

5. H. J. Cadbury, *The Making of Luke-Acts* (London: Macmillan, 1927) 260-63.

6. Cf. D. M. Scholer, "The Magnificat (Luke 1:46-55): Reflections on Its Hermeneutical History," in *Conflict and Context: Hermeneutics in the Americas,* ed. M. Lau Branson and C. R. Padilla (Grand Rapids, Michigan: Wm. B. Eerdmans, 1986) 210-19.

7. D. L. Mealand (*Poverty and Expectation in the Gospels* [London: S.P.C.K., 1980] 103-4) lists most of the relevant literature from 1891 to 1976. For recent surveys, see F. Bovon, *Luke the Theologian: Thirty-three Years of Research (1950-1983),* PTMS 12 (Allison Park, Pennsylvania: Pickwick, 1987) 390-400; J. R. Donahue, S.J., "Two Decades of Research on the Rich and Poor in Luke-Acts," in *Justice and the Holy: Essays in Honor of Walter Harrelson,* ed. D. A. Knight and P. J. Paris (Atlanta: Scholars, 1989) 129-44. Recent studies include M. V. Abraham, "Good News to the Poor in Luke's Gospel," *Bible Bhashyam* 14 (1-2, 1988) 65-77; P. H. Davids, "Poverty and Wealth," in *Dictionary of Jesus and the Gospels,* ed. J. B. Green and S. McKnight (Downers Grove, Illinois:

survey of NT ethics, A. Verhey aptly summarizes a now widely held view: "From the very beginning, Luke's story of Jesus emphasizes his solidarity with the poor."[8]

That the Third Gospel tells the story of Jesus as "good news to the poor" is self-evident. Thus, for example, the terminology of poverty in the NT congregates especially in Luke-Acts: πενιχρός — Luke 21:2 (otherwise absent in the NT); ἐνδεής — Acts 4:34 (otherwise absent from the NT); and πτωχός — Luke 4:18; 6:20; 7:22; 14:13, 21; 16:20, 22; 18:22; 19:18; 21:3 (Matthew — 5x, Mark — 5x, John — 4x, Paul — 4x, James — 4x, Revelation — 2x).[9]

Of greater consequence, Jesus was anointed by the Holy Spirit in order "to preach good news to the poor" (εὐαγγελίσασθαι πτωχοῖς — 4:18), and this divine portfolio is underscored again in 7:22 (πτωχοὶ εὐαγγελίζονται) by way of demonstrating Jesus' identity as the Anticipated One. Moreover, in addition to material shared with Mark related to wealth and possessions (e.g., Mark 10:21, 25 // Luke 18:22, 25; 12:13-17 // 20:20-26; 12:41 // 21:1-4) and with Matthew (e.g., Matt 5:40, 42 // Luke 6:29-30; 6:25-33 // 12:22-32; 8:20 // 9:58), Luke

---

InterVarsity, 1992) 701-10; T. D'Sa, "The Salvation of the Rich in the Gospel of Luke," *Vidyajyoti* 52 (4, 1988) 170-80; J. Dupont, O.S.B., "The Poor and Poverty in the Gospels and Acts," in *Gospel Poverty: Essays in Biblical Theology* (Chicago: Franciscan Herald, 1977) 25-52; P. F. Esler, *Community and Gospel in Luke-Acts,* SNTSMS 57 (Cambridge: Cambridge University, 1987) 164-200; R. Gnuse, *You Shall Not Steal: Community and Property in the Biblical Tradition* (Maryknoll, New York: Orbis, 1985) 102-7; J. L. González, *Faith and Wealth: A History of Early Christian Ideas on the Origin, Significance, and Use of Money* (San Francisco: Harper & Row, 1990) 78-86; B. Gordon, *The Economic Problem in Biblical and Patristic Thought,* SVC:TSECLL 9 (Leiden: E. J. Brill, 1989) 61-76; M. Hengel, *Property and Riches in the Early Church* (Philadelphia: Fortress, 1974) 23-34; L. J. Hoppe, O.F.M., *Being Poor: A Biblical Study,* GNS 20 (Wilmington, Delaware: Michael Glazier, 1987) 153-60; T. Hoyt Jr., "The Poor in Luke-Acts" (Ph.D. diss., Duke University, 1975); L. T. Johnson, *The Literary Function of Possessions in Luke-Acts,* SBLDS 39 (Missoula, Montana: Scholars, 1977); *idem, Sharing Possessions: Mandate and Symbol of Faith* (Philadelphia: Fortress, 1981) esp. 11-25; R. J. Karris, O.F.M., "Poor and Rich: The Lukan Sitz im Leben," in *Perspectives on Luke-Acts,* ed. C. H. Talbert (Edinburgh: T. & T. Clark, 1978) 112-25; I. H. Marshall, *Luke: Historian and Theologian* (Grand Rapids, Michigan: Zondervan, 1971) 122-23, 141-44, 206-8; J. Navone, S.J., *Themes of St. Luke* (Rome: Gregorian University, n.d.) 103-17; R. F. O'Toole, *The Unity of Luke's Theology: An Analysis of Luke-Acts,* GNS 9 (Wilmington, Delaware: Michael Glazier, 1984) 129-35; W. E. Pilgrim, *Good News to the Poor: Wealth and Poverty in Luke-Acts* (Minneapolis, Minnesota: Augsburg, 1981); J. S. Pobee, *Who Are the Poor? The Beatitudes as a Call to Community,* RBS 32 (Geneva: WCC, 1987); T. E. Schmidt, *Hostility to Wealth in the Synoptic Gospels,* JSNTSS 15 (Sheffield: JSOT, 1987) 135-62; Schottroff and Stegemann, *Jesus,* esp. 67-120; D. P. Seccombe, *Possessions and the Poor in Luke-Acts,* SNTU B6 (Linz: Fuchs, 1983); Tannehill, *Narrative Unity,* 127-32.

8. A. Verhey, *The Great Reversal: Ethics and the New Testament* (Grand Rapids, Michigan: Wm. B. Eerdmans, 1984) 93; cf. W. Schrage, *The Ethics of the New Testament* (Philadelphia: Fortress, 1988) 159-61.

9. J. P. Louw and E. A. Nida, eds., *Greek-English Lexicon of the New Testament Based on Semantic Domains,* 2 vols. (New York: United Bible Societies, 1988) 1:527, 564; 2:311. They also mention γυμνιτεύω (NT — 1x), πένης (NT — 1x), πτωχεία (NT — 3x), and πτωχεύω (NT — 1x), but these are absent from the Lukan corpus. Cf. E. Bammel, "πτωχός," *TDNT* 6:902, 905-7.

records a number of unique passages relevant to our subject: for example, Mary's Song (1:46-55); the first blessing with its corresponding woe (6:20, 24); further instruction on giving and receiving (6:27-36); the story of the rich fool (12:13-21); the parable of the shrewd manager (16:1-13); the story of the rich man and Lazarus (16:19-26); the question of guests at dinner (14:13, 21); and the encounter between Jesus and Zacchaeus (19:1-10).[10] Irrespective of source-critical considerations, the pervasiveness of this theme in the narrative as a whole, coupled with its emphatic placement in Jesus' inaugural address, bespeaks its centrality to the Lukan portrayal of Jesus' ministry and the way of discipleship.

Given this state of affairs, the critical question is this: For Luke, who are the "poor"? To whom did Jesus come announcing good news? Students of Luke have not altogether ignored this question heretofore; some have even raised it explicitly.[11] Though one always enters with caution the minefield of generalizations, in this case it is not difficult to summarize briefly the prevailing answer to our query. Recent studies of the poor in Luke have largely kept at center stage the economically destitute.[12] Some interpreters have been quick to argue that "economic destitution" is not the whole story here, that the poor were forced by their circumstances to a position of dependence on Yahweh. As Pobee notes, "The poor know their need and, therefore, can rely only on God."[13] This added nuance, however, does not detract from the semantic bottom line: The vocabulary of poverty in Luke is generally understood as referring to relative economic position. Thus, for Schottroff and Stegemann, "It is clear in all strata of the Jesus tradition that when the synoptic Gospels speak of the 'poor' [= *ptōchoi*] they are in fact thinking of extreme want and often even of destitution."[14] Karris

10. For convenient summaries of ways in which Luke's special concern for the rich and poor comes to the fore in Lukan redaction (*contra* Mealand, *Poverty and Expectation,* 16-20), see Esler, *Community and Gospel,* 165-69; Donahue, "Two Decades," 131-35.

11. See esp. Pilgrim, *Good News,* 17; Hoyt, "Poor," iii.

12. The outstanding counter-example among recent studies is Seccombe, *Possessions and the Poor.* He argues that "poor" refers to "Israel," standing in need of salvation. Seccombe's argument is grounded in his observation that Luke has drawn on psalmic and especially Isaianic demarcations of the "poor" as "the nation Israel suffering and in great need" (39). This is a helpful perspective, though it is worth asking what has happened to the hermeneutical history on which Seccombe's point is based once it is located within the Lukan narrative as primary intra-text (cf. R. Albertz, "Die 'Antrittspredigt' Jesu im Lukasevangelium auf ihrem alttestamentlichen Hintergrund," *ZNW* 74 [1983] 182-206 [184-86]). Thus, e.g., his early equation of "poor as Israel" does not grapple with the reality that already in the Lukan birth narrative Israel is presented as divided. More importantly, as Seccombe recognizes, his understanding of "poor" is developed primarily from the Magnificat and the Nazareth sermon and cannot be employed in other contexts in the Gospel (apart from, perhaps, 7:22). Elsewhere, "poor" for Seccombe refers to the economically needy.

13. Pobee, *Who Are the Poor,* 18. This emphasis arises largely from studies of the vocabulary of poverty in the OT — cf., e.g., G. J. Botterweck, "אביון," *TDOT* 1:27-41 (35-41); H.-J. Fabry, "דל," *TDOT* 3:208-30 (226-29); H.-H. Esser and C. Brown, "πτωχός," *NIDNTT* 2:821-29 (821-24); Bammel, "πτωχός," 888-94.

14. Schottroff and Stegemann, *Jesus,* 16.

defines the poor in Luke as "the indigent, those who lack the necessities, those who need alms."[15] Although he is sensitive to wider concerns in Luke, Pilgrim has it that "the poor belonged essentially to two groups: those who sought to earn their own livelihood, and those who lived off subsidy."[16] And Hoppe writes, "Luke's use of the word 'poor' focuses on the economically poor. . . ."[17]

By what route have students of Luke arrived at definitions of this sort? In many cases, this linking of the words "poor" and "poverty" with the concept of "economic marginality" is largely assumed. For others, it has become almost axiomatic that Jesus' announcement of good news to the poor must be understood against its background in the OT and against the backdrop of socio-economic developments — taxation, landed wealth, the plight of the peasantry, and so forth — in first-century Palestine. Regardless of the rationale, the consequence is to portray the Lukan Jesus as intimately and emphatically concerned with persons who lack the essential means of livelihood, who live in a continuous state of destitution and need.

This near consensus is not surprising given mid- and late-twentieth-century conceptualizations of class and class situation. For M. Weber, the general contours of whose analysis are representative, "class situation" is a measure of one's capacity to procure goods, gain a position in life, and find inner satisfactions — a capacity which derives from one's relative control over goods and skills and their income-producing uses within a given economic order.[18] Hence, " 'property' and 'lack of property' are . . . the basic categories of all class situations."[19] Accordingly, the rich control the market through their monopolization of capital, wealth accumulation, and the purchasing of goods. The poor are slaves, paupers, debtors, and "the declassed." In between are the "middle classes," people who make their living through acquired skills or from their limited property.

We are not suggesting that Lukan scholars have gone to Weber for critical assistance as much as that Weberian-type categories have often been operative at an unacknowledged level. The question is, Would Luke and his auditors have understood this way of putting matters? That is, given the reality that all language is embedded in culture,[20] to what degree are our perceptions on this matter determined by social systems alien to the Third Evangelist?

15. Karris, "Poor and Rich," 112-13.

16. Pilgrim, *Good News,* 43.

17. Hoppe, *Being Poor,* 160.

18. M. Weber, *Economy and Society: An Outline of Interpretive Sociology,* 2 vols., ed. G. Roth and C. Wittich (Berkeley: University of California, 1968) 1:302; cf. 1:302-7, 2:926-32; *idem, The Theory of Social and Economic Organization,* ed. T. Parsons (New York: Free, 1947) 424-29.

19. Weber, *Economy and Society,* 2:927.

20. Cf. M. Stubbs, *Discourse Analysis: The Sociolinguistic Analysis of Natural Language* (Chicago: University of Chicago, 1983) 8; G. Brown and G. Yule, *Discourse Analysis,* CTL (Cambridge: Cambridge University, 1983) 27-31; P. Cotterell and M. Turner, *Linguistics and Biblical Interpretation* (Downers Grove, Illinois: InterVarsity, 1989) 68-72. This point is made in a way germane to

How might one address this question? One obvious approach would be to engage in a full examination of the relevant vocabulary in OT and Septuagintal contexts. The diachronic data thus assembled would not be decisive for our purposes, but would provide important information related to how Luke and his auditors might have heard these terms.

Luke's preferred term for "poor" is πτωχός, which in the LXX usually translates עני, דל, אביון, and רוש. Other terms belong to this semantic field, however — 22 others in the Hebrew Bible, according to F. I. Andersen and A. D. Forbes.[21] Happily, although no one seems to have conducted an exhaustive analysis of this semantic domain, enough has been done so that we are able to put forward two widely recognized observations that have direct bearing on our question.[22] (1) Words of this domain characteristically embrace both socio-economic and religious connotations. Persons thus described might be utterly destitute or they might have small property holdings, but the fundamental portrait is one of persons who have given up their independence, who are susceptible to exploitation by those with power, and who must look beyond themselves for help — help that comes, ultimately, from God. (2) Hence Yahweh is understood as the deliverer and protector of the poor, the one who grants mercy to the poor, judges those who pervert justice, and vindicates the poor in the face of their enemies. *That is, the emphasis falls on the relationship between God and the poor, with the former extending grace to the latter, who find themselves increasingly at the periphery of society.*

This relational aspect of the notion of "poor" is an important one, for it prepares us for another key ingredient of the presupposition pool[23] Luke and his audience will have shared. The most material disclosure about wealth and poverty in Greco-Roman antiquity would have been the relative subordination of things economic to other issues of social relationship. Thus, the level of one's wealth was of little consequence except insofar as that wealth might be translated into status.[24] This reality immediately calls into question attempts to categorize Jesus and members of the early Jesus-movement as "lower class" or "middle class,"[25] assuming that by "class" we have to do with "relation to the means of

---

our project in B. J. Malina, "Interpreting the Bible with Anthropology: The Case of the Poor and Rich," *Listening* 21 (1986) 148-59 (148-52).

21. F. I. Andersen and A. D. Forbes, *The Vocabulary of the Old Testament* (Rome: Pontifical Biblical Institute, 1989) esp. 18.

22. In addition to the studies listed above, n. 12, see H.-J. Fabry, "חסר," *TDOT* 5:80-90.

23. "Presupposition pools" provide the backdrop of a discourse and are constituted from general knowledge and the situational context of the discourse, along with the information related in the already completed portion of the discourse itself. See Brown and Yule, *Discourse Analysis*, 79-83.

24. Cf. R. Duncan-Jones, *The Economy of the Roman Empire: Quantitative Studies*, 2d ed. (Cambridge: Cambridge University, 1982); E. A. Judge, *Rank and Status in the World of the Caesars and St. Paul*, UCP 29 (Canterbury: University of Canterbury, 1982).

25. *Pace* Hengel, e.g., *Property and Riches*, 23-30; W. Stegemann, *The Gospel and the Poor* (Philadelphia: Fortress, 1984) 22-31.

production" or even "persons who share such-and-such a standard of living." The abundance or lack of money, on its own, simply did not have this immediate a determinative function. Nor can one think primarily in terms of those who own the means of production and those who do not; as M. I. Finley has observed, ". . . the slave and the free wage labourer would then be of the same class . . . as would the richest senator and the non-working owner of a small pottery. This does not seem a very sensible way to analyse ancient society."[26] The inappropriateness of any narrow focus on relative wealth as a measure of social relations in antiquity can be further highlighted with reference to Zacchaeus — a wealthy man who was nevertheless an outsider due to his role as a chief toll collector (Luke 19:2, 7).[27]

Thus, while wealth was required if one were to reach the upper echelons of Roman nobility, it was not enough. For our purposes, then, "class" as an economically determined nomenclature should be replaced with reference to "status honor." Here we refer to the determination of social boundaries by means of positive and negative social estimations of honor. Status situation is reflected in the style of life expected of those who belong, the restrictions applied to the inner group of social discourse vis-à-vis the style of appropriate interaction with those within and outside the status circle.[28] Status honor is a measure of social standing that embraces wealth, but also other factors, including access to education, family heritage, ethnicity, vocation, religious purity, and gender. In the Greco-Roman world, then, poverty is too narrowly defined when understood solely in economic terms.

Reflection on the assumptions behind current studies of the "poor" in Luke raises two points of tension. The first arises from an examination of the presupposition pool Luke would have shared with his Greco-Roman audience, specifically as this question relates to the discourse meaning of "poor." The second, to be taken up now, concerns the actual portrait of Jesus and the "poor" in the Third Gospel: To whom do we actually find the Lukan Jesus proclaiming good news?

## 3. The Gospel of Luke: Who are the Poor?

In this essay it will not be possible for us to survey in an exhaustive way all of the Lukan material germane to our subject. Instead, we will focus on two lines of evidence — the first related to Luke's use of the vocabulary of poverty, the

26. M. I. Finley, *The Ancient Economy* (Berkeley: University of California, 1973) 49.

27. On which, see further below. On the evolving status of *publicani* and, to a lesser degree, toll collectors, in Roman antiquity, see E. Badian, *Publicans and Sinners: Private Enterprise in the Service of the Roman Republic* (Ithaca, New York: Cornell University, 1972).

28. Weber, *Economy and Society*, 2:926-39. See also C. W. Mills, *The Power Elite* (London: Oxford University, 1956); Finley, *Ancient Economy*, 50-51; W. A. Meeks, *The First Urban Christians: The Social World of the Apostle Paul* (New Haven: Yale University, 1983) 53-55.

second to key passages in the Third Gospel where the purpose of Jesus' mission is formulated.

*3.1. Luke and the Language of Poverty.* In his two-volume work, Luke uses four words from the semantic field of "poor" in the NT. In Acts 4:34, he employs the term ἐνδεής, "needy," in the phrase οὐδὲ γὰρ ἐνδεής τις ἦν ἐν αὐτοῖς, borrowed from Deut 15:4 (LXX). The material, economic connotations of this term are clear in the context of this Lukan summary though it also points qualitatively and transparently to the experience of *koinonia* among these early believers. Ἐνδεής appears only here in Luke-Acts.

Also appearing a single time in Luke-Acts is πενιχρός. In the NT this term occurs only in Luke 21:2, in Luke's depiction of the poor widow at the temple treasury. Its usage parallels the description of this "poor widow" in 21:3, this time using the term πτωχός, apparently for linguistic variation. The context suggests the woman's material deficiency (cf. 21:4). At the same time, closer co-textual consideration suggests an additional nuance. Luke's narrative draws a transparent nexus between this episode, wherein Jesus compares the widow's offering with that of the rich (21:1-4), and the immediately preceding portrait of the teachers of the law as those who devour widows' homes (20:45-47). This connection is evident from the introduction to the second story (ἀναβλέψας δὲ εἶδεν), from the repetition of the term χήρα (20:47; 21:2, 3), and from the parallelism of theme.

The four phrases used in 20:46 to characterize the teachers of the law are all forms of paralinguistic social deixis.[29] In their own ways, they each illuminate the attempt of the teachers of the law to lay claim to honor.[30] The referent of στολή in the first clause, περιπατεῖν ἐν στολαῖς, is not immediately clear. An outer garment is clearly intended, and K. H. Rengstorf proposes that, by the first century, στολή could refer to the festive garment worn to celebrate the Sabbath,[31] but this is uncertain. In the LXX στολή refers especially to the outer garment by which a person is noted for his or her status (e.g., Gen 41:14, 41-42; Esth 6:8; 1 Chr 15:27; 2 Chr 5:12; 1 Macc 6:15).[32] Elsewhere in the Third Gospel (as throughout Roman Palestine)[33] clothes can signify social meaning and status. For example, in 16:19, the rich man dresses in purple and fine linen — in other words, he is extravagantly wealthy (cf. 7:25). In 8:26-35, the Gerasene demoniac is introduced naked, symbolizing his madness and exclusion from

29. See S. C. Levinson, *Pragmatics,* CTL (Cambridge: Cambridge University, 1983) 54-94.

30. H. Moxnes (*The Economy of the Kingdom: Social Conflict and Economic Relations in Luke's Gospel,* OBT [Philadelphia: Fortress, 1988]) demonstrates the relation between concerns with wealth and positioning for status among Jesus' opponents in the Third Gospel.

31. K. H. Rengstorf, "Die στολαί der Schriftgelehrten. Eine Erläuterung zu Mark. 12,38," in *Abraham unser Vater: Juden und Christen im Gespräch über die Bibel. Festschrift für Otto Michel zum 60. Geburtstag,* AGSU 5, ed. O. Betz, M. Hengel, and P. Schmidt (Leiden: E. J. Brill, 1963) 383-404.

32. Cf. U. Wilckens, "στολή," *TDNT* 7:689.

33. Cf. G. Hamel, *Poverty and Charity in Roman Palestine, First Three Centuries C.E.,* UCP:NES 23 (Berkeley: University of California, 1990) 73-93.

the community (v 27); following the exorcism, he is clothed (v 35) — that is, restored to reputable status and to the community.[34] In the present pericope, then, teachers of the law are portrayed as those who enjoy parading around in clothes signifying their importance.

The other three descriptive phrases —

φιλούντων
ἀσπασμοὺς ἐν ταῖς ἀγοραῖς
καὶ πρωτοκαθεδρίας ἐν ταῖς συναγωγαῖς
καὶ πρωτοκλισίας ἐν τοῖς δείπνοις —

continue Jesus' critique of the public behavior of the teachers of the law. Each phrase parallels the other, with the result that three major public arenas are mentioned — the marketplace as social center, the synagogue, and the banquet room — together with symbols of honor appropriate to each. Interestingly, each is paralleled elsewhere in Luke's Gospel. In 11:43, the Pharisees are condemned for loving the best seat in the synagogue and salutations in the marketplace, and in 14:7-11, Jesus warns his fellow guests against choosing seats of honor, lest a more distinguished guest arrive. The latter pericope repeatedly underscores issues of honor (cf. πρωτοκλισία — vv 7, 8; ἔντιμος — v 8; φίλος — v 10; ἀνώτερος — v 10; τότε ἔσται σοι δόξα ἐνώπιον πάντων τῶν συνανακειμένων σοι — v 10; ὑψόω — v 10) and shame (cf. αἰσχύνη — v 9; ἔσχατος — v 10; ταπεινόω — v 11), suggesting a concern with those who by their actions claim unwarranted honor. In short, the teachers of the law, Luke tells us, enjoy being treated as persons of status, as though they were wealthy benefactors.

If Luke draws a connection between the teachers of the law of the first scene and the wealthy of the second, can we say the same of the widows? Some exegetes find in 21:1-4 an affirmation of the poor widow's exemplary piety. In relation to the preceding, however, where we learn that widows' houses are devoured by the religious leadership, another reading seems preferable. That is, in 21:1-4 Jesus laments the travesty of a religious system which leads to this poor widow's behavior. She is a victim of the system; in effect, in giving all she had, her house has been devoured. The result of this narrative strategy is to juxtapose the rich, as those of honorable status and positions of power, with the poor widow, who enjoys no such honor and has become their victim.

Luke's obvious term of choice is πτωχός, found ten times in the Third Gospel. We have already noted its appearance in 21:3. A further category of usage embraces the appearance of the term in 18:22 and 19:8, where the rich find that an appropriate response to Jesus is to give to the poor (πτωχοί). These poor are those in need of alms.

More interesting and pervasive in Luke is the use of this term in association

34. See Moxnes, *Economy of the Kingdom*, 90-93.

with other descriptive terms, especially in lists. In fact, the remaining seven appearances of the term fall into this category:

| **4:18** | **6:20** | **7:22** |
|---|---|---|
| Poor | Poor | Blind |
| Captive | Hungry | Lame |
| Blind | Mournful | Leper |
| Oppressed | Persecuted | Deaf |
| | | Dead |
| | | Poor |

| **14:13** | **14:21** | **16:20, 22** |
|---|---|---|
| Poor | Poor | Poor |
| Maimed | Maimed | Ulcerated |
| Lame | Blind | Hungry |
| Blind | Lame | |

From a narratological point of view, this sort of accumulation of adjectives slows the progression of the story and so draws special attention to this facile means of amplifying what sort of person is (1) the unexpected recipient of good news (4:16-30; 7:18-23) and blessedness (6:20-26), and (2) the normally excluded who are now welcomed (14:12-14, 15-24; 16:19-31).[35] We may note that in each case "poor" stands at the head of the list, except in 7:22, where it appears in the final, emphatic position. As such it interprets and is amplified by the others. The impression with which one is left is that Luke is concerned above all with a class of people defined by their dishonorable status, their positions outside circles of power and prestige, their being excluded. The conjunction of these words in these Lukan lists points to the challenging dimensions of the new era Jesus proclaims, a reign that embraces those marginalized by religious leaders, those thus defined as outsiders.

This insight is underscored by other terminological phenomena in the Gospel of Luke. Attention to the vocabulary of wealth directs us immediately to 1:51-53, where the proud and mighty are contrasted with the humble, the rich (who are well fed) with the hungry. Similarly, in 12:16-21 and 16:19-31 the rich are those with significant resources at their disposal, and who fail to consider the plight of others in their daily existence. Interestingly, in 14:12 "rich neighbors" are catalogued with one's "inner circle" — friends, brothers, kin — persons with whom one enjoys relationships of equality and mutuality. Like "poor," "rich" is not simply a term economically defined. It is related to issues of power and privilege, and social location as an insider.

35. Cf. B. Dupriez, *A Dictionary of Literary Devices* (New York: Harvester Wheatsheaf, 1991) 9-12, 32-33, 390-91.

Finally, we may recall the earlier work of J. A. Sanders, who saw the connection between Luke's word-families and lists of excluded persons at Qumran.[36] In the Rule of the Congregation, the parameters of the convocation of the whole assembly are set, and they exclude those who are afflicted in the flesh, those with injured feet or hands, the lame, blind, deaf, dumb, and so on (1QSa 2:5-7). In the War Scroll, those excluded from participation in the eschatological battle are named: boys, women, the lame, blind, crippled, and those with a permanent bodily defect or bodily impurity (1QM 7:4-6).

Whether or not the Lukan material arose in an attempt to contradict membership legislation of this sort, the effect is the same, for it is clear that Luke is concerned to overturn any overly narrow notion of election. Thus, terminological juxtapositions in the Third Gospel emphasize the inclusiveness of the community being created by Jesus. In this context, "poor" has become a cipher for those of low status, for those excluded according to normal canons of status honor in the Mediterranean world. Although "poor" is hardly devoid of economic significance, for Luke this wider meaning of diminished status honor is paramount.

To whom is the good news announced in Luke? Who are the poor? This first line of evidence demonstrates that Luke's story does indeed reflect the wider concern in Roman antiquity with "status honor." "Poor" is not to be narrowly understood along economic lines, but also as a measure of belonging, a matter of group definition. In the Third Gospel, "good news to the poor" is preeminently a gracious word of inclusion to the dispossessed, the excluded.

***3.2. Luke and Jesus' Commission.*** This assessment may be supported further by a brief investigation of those passages in the Third Gospel where the purpose of Jesus' mission is formulated. There are three such passages: 4:16-30; 5:27-32; and 19:1-10.

Luke 5:27-32 and 19:1-10 are similar in a number of key ways. Both narrate the encounter of Jesus with a toll collector.[37] Both disclose the generally poor status of toll collectors in the eyes of the Pharisees and teachers of the law (5:30) and the general public (19:7). Both name toll collectors as "sinners" — by means of vituperative apposition in 5:30 (cf. 7:34; 15:1; 18:11) and, in 19:7, by an added descriptive paraphrase. Both illustrate behavior becoming a dis-

36. J. A. Sanders, "The Ethics of Election in Luke's Great Banquet Parable," in *Essays in Old Testament Ethics: J. Phillip Hyatt, In Memoriam,* ed. J. L. Crenshaw and J. T. Willis (New York: Ktav, 1974) 245-71.

37. On this nomenclature, see Badian, *Publicans and Sinners;* J. R. Donahue, S.J., "Tax Collectors and Sinners," *CBQ* 33 (1971) 39-61. Ἀρχιτελώνης is otherwise unattested, and O. Michel ("τελώνης," *TDNT* 8:97-99; cf. F. Godet, *A Commentary on the Gospel of St. Luke,* 2 vols., 5th ed. [Edinburgh: T. & T. Clark, n.d.] 2:216) speculates that Zacchaeus is thus named as the head of a group of tax farmers collecting customs on goods passing from Perea to Judea. Although Zacchaeus presumably had some such role, it may be that Luke has created this title in order to further the parallel between Zacchaeus and the rich ruler (ἄρχων) of 18:18-30.

ciple: Levi leaves everything, follows Jesus, and throws a feast in Jesus' honor;[38] Zacchaeus declares that he is making fourfold restitution to those he has defrauded and gives half of his goods to the poor. And both generalize from this encounter to clarify the contours of Jesus' mission: "I have not come to call the righteous but sinners to repentance" (5:32) and "For the Son of Man came to seek and to save the lost" (19:10).

What is of consequence for our reading of these texts is the unenviable and well-attested low social status of toll collectors throughout antiquity, both among Jews and Gentiles.[39] In the present contexts, their low status is further highlighted by their identification as "sinners." Attempts like that of E. P. Sanders to identify "sinners" as "the wicked"[40] are of little help here, for there hardly seems to have been any unanimity on the characterization of paying taxes or collecting them as unlawful within first-century Judaism (cf. 3:12-13). Marcus Borg refers to "sinners" as those who "did not accept in practice the Pharisaic program of holiness for Israel and could not be trusted with regard to tithing and cleanness,"[41] but even this more fluid definition seems too narrow, focused as it is on a Pharisaic agenda. As J. D. G. Dunn has documented, in the factional context of the era in question a "sinner" would be one whose behavior departs from the norms of an identified group whose boundaries are established with reference to characteristic conduct.[42] That is, "sinner" receives concrete explication especially in terms of group definition; a "sinner" is an outsider.

This concern with group boundaries is manifest in our stories. Thus, Luke reports the shock of the bystanders at Jesus' willingness to eat with Levi and his guests and with Zacchaeus and his household. Refusal to share a meal with another serves an important function in this and other cultural contexts: It signifies social ostracism, the designation of someone as excluded from an identified group.[43] In this case, Jesus' host and fellow guests were regarded as persons of a lower status to be avoided, especially at the table.

Moreover, Luke 5:27-32 is narrated in such a way as to indicate that Jesus'

38. J. A. Fitzmyer, S.J. (*The Gospel according to Luke,* 2 vols., AB 28-28A [Garden City, New York: Doubleday, 1981 / 85] 1:589) draws attention to the *inclusio* marked by vv 27, 32: "Jesus *calls* Levi to follow him, because he has come to *call* not the righteous but sinners to reform." Hence Levi's response to Jesus (vv 28-29) gives concrete expression to the repentance of v 32. On Zacchaeus, see below.

39. See, e.g., Michel, "τελώνης"; Donahue, "Tax Collectors and Sinners"; Schottroff and Stegemann, *Jesus and the Hope of the Poor,* 7-13.

40. E. P. Sanders, *Jesus and Judaism* (London: SCM, 1985) 177; see 177-79.

41. M. J. Borg, *Conflict, Holiness and Politics in the Teachings of Jesus,* SBEC 5 (Lewiston, New York: Edwin Mellen, 1984) 84.

42. J. D. G. Dunn, "Pharisees, Sinners, and Jesus," in *The Social World of Formative Christianity and Judaism: Essays in Tribute to Howard Clark Kee,* ed. J. Neusner et al. (Philadelphia: Fortress, 1988) 264-89 (275-80).

43. See M. Douglas, "Deciphering a Meal," in *Implicit Meanings* (London: Routledge and Kegan Paul, 1975) 249-75; Borg, *Conflict,* 80.

opponents have one view of things, the narrator and Jesus another. Thus, Jesus' associates at the table are regarded as "toll collectors and *sinners*" by the Pharisees and teachers of the law, whereas the narrator had identified them only as "toll collectors and *others*."[44] The word "sinners," then, is introduced by Jesus' opponents (cf. 7:34, 39; 15:2); when Jesus borrows the word he turns it on its head, as if to say, "You may call these people 'sinners,' but people like Levi are precisely those to whom I have come to extend the call to discipleship."

The story of Zacchaeus in 19:1-10 is more complicated for two reasons. First, it follows 18:1-43 and appears at the close of the Lukan Travel Section, on the heels of an extensive treatment of the notions of "sinner" and "toll collector."[45] Hence, many of the concepts with which Luke characterizes Zacchaeus have already come in for interpretive development, and this earlier material occupies a prominent position in the presupposition pool Luke has helped construct to this juncture; our understanding of the present encounter must be shaped by the development of the narrative as a whole to this point, and especially by the immediately preceding chapter. Second, Luke 19:1-10 has also been the focus of lengthy scholarly discussion: Does Zacchaeus defend himself in 19:8 as one who already gives alms; or does he proclaim a new set of behaviors as a result of an experience of repentance?[46]

Irrespective of how one answers this latter query, Zacchaeus is pointedly portrayed as an outsider. This is most evident from v 7: ". . . everyone murmured, saying, 'Jesus has gone in to be the guest of a sinner!'" Labeling him thus, they vocalize his unacceptability, his social distance from them. The same point is made in a different way in v 3: καὶ ἐζήτει ἰδεῖν τὸν Ἰησοῦν τίς ἐστιν καὶ οὐκ ἠδύνατο ἀπὸ τοῦ ὄχλου, ὅτι τῇ ἡλικίᾳ μικρὸς ἦν. English translations generally find an explanation for Zacchaeus's inability to fulfill his quest to see Jesus in his shortness. But shortness of stature is no necessary obstacle to seeing a parade. People of reputation, of status, are granted a view by others, irrespective of their height. The shared opinion about Zacchaeus — he is a sinner — would work against the granting of such privileges in his case. Reading ἀπὸ τοῦ ὄχλου as causative[47] suggests that Zacchaeus is the man for whom the crowd would not make room. The obstacle is the crowd (as in 18:35-43), not Zacchaeus's height.

With this understanding in hand, we may exploit what are already un-

44. J. Nolland suggests that Luke substitutes "others" for Mark's "sinners" because "others" must now include Jesus' disciples (*Luke 1–9:20,* WBC 35A [Dallas, Texas: Word, 1989] 245), but this does not explain the introduction of "sinners" in vv 30, 32.

45. Cf. the recent treatment of this material in D. A. Neale, *None But the Sinners: Religious Categories in the Gospel of Luke,* JSNTSS 58 (Sheffield: JSOT, 1991).

46. See the recent installments to this debate in D. Hamm, S.J., "Luke 19:8 Once Again: Does Zacchaeus Defend or Resolve?" *CBQ* 107 (1988) 431-37; D. A. S. Ravens, "Zacchaeus: The Final Part of a Lucan Triptych?" *JSNT* 41 (1991) 19-32.

47. Cf. Luke 21:26; 22:45b; 24:41; Acts 12:14; 20:11; 22:11; BDF §210.1.

mistakable connections between Luke 19:1-10 and the preceding material,[48] which serve to present Zacchaeus in a positive light. Neither Zacchaeus nor the widow of 18:1-8 is put off by their obstacles. Like the toll collector of 18:9-14, Zacchaeus is socially ostracized but nonetheless receives grace. Like the children of 18:15-17, this man receives Jesus' attention. As in the story of the blind man of 18:35-43, so the crowds stand in the way of Zacchaeus's encounter with Jesus.

Perhaps the most impressive parallels are between the stories of the rich ruler and Zacchaeus. The first man is a ruler (ἄρχων), Zacchaeus is a "ruling" toll collector (ἀρχιτελώνης). According to his self-evaluation, the ruler keeps the commandments, while Zacchaeus is, according to popular opinion, a "sinner." The ruler is counseled to sell all he has and give to the poor; Zacchaeus sells half of his possessions and gives the proceeds to the poor. The ruler is very wealthy; Zacchaeus is wealthy. At the conclusion of the first story, Jesus was asked, "Who then can be saved?" At the conclusion of the second, Jesus asserts, "Today, salvation has come to this house."

Two observations must be made explicit. First, in the preceding eighteen chapters of his Gospel, Luke has consistently portrayed people with money and power, recipients of honor in their own social world, in a negative light, but he has presented toll collectors, despised in their social world, positively. Hence Luke may refer to Zacchaeus as "wealthy," but he does not in any way fit the profile we have come to associate with "the rich" in Luke's Gospel; that is, his is not a position of extensive relationships of reciprocity among the respectable of his community, nor does he find in his wealth a source of security before or apart from God. *The chief characteristic of Zacchaeus is not that he is wealthy but, in contrast to the ruler, that he is (1) a social outcast who is (2) willing to put his money in the service of the needy through his generosity.* Second, whether "salvation" for Zacchaeus assumes his spontaneous repentance on the occasion of Jesus' visit or presupposes a history of "producing fruit in keeping with repentance" (3:8, 12-13), it at least means that the previously excluded Zacchaeus is restored to the community of Israel as a son of Abraham.[49] The presentation of Zacchaeus is mixed: he is a "ruler," but he rules only toll collectors and is poorly regarded by the populace; he is wealthy, but his wealth has not bought him honor and friends, and he places his wealth in the service of justice. In a paradoxical way befitting Luke's portrayal of salvation-as-status transposition, Jesus' encounter with Zacchaeus is a proclamation of good news to the poor.

We may now focus briefly on Luke 4:16-30, which marks the opening of Jesus' public ministry and sets the course of his mission. Two issues require notice.[50] First, we should call attention to the structure of the Isaianic citation

48. Cf. J. O'Hanlon, "The Story of Zacchaeus and the Lukan Ethic," *JSNT* 12 (1981) 2-26 (9-11).

49. Cf. Ravens, "Zacchaeus," 27.

50. See further J. B. Green, "'Proclaiming Repentance and Forgiveness of Sins to All Na-

in 4:18-19. (1) The first three lines each end with "me," repeating the pronoun in the emphatic position. This underscores in the clearest possible way the inexorable relation of the Spirit's anointing and the statement of primary mission, "to proclaim good news to the poor." (2) As a consequence, the three subsequent infinitive phrases appear in parallel and in a position subordinate to Jesus' statement of primary mission. Thus:

Spirit of the Lord is upon *me,*
  For he has anointed *me;*
To preach good news to the poor he has sent *me:*
  To proclaim for the captives **release,**
    and to the blind sight;
  To send forth the oppressed in **release;**
  To proclaim the year of the Lord's favor.

In effect, then, the three subordinate clauses — "to proclaim . . . to send . . . to proclaim" — amplify Jesus' first mission statement.[51] Hence, in this co-text, the category "poor" is interpreted above all as embracing those who need "release." Importantly, "release" is developed throughout Luke-Acts as *forgiveness of sins* — with its social ramifications, since forgiveness provides entry (back) into the community (cf., e.g., 5:31-32; 7:36-50; 15:3-31; 19:1-10; Acts 15:8-9); and as *freedom from the binding power of Satan,* a freedom which also signifies wholeness and acceptance in the community.[52]

Second, what is the relation between Jesus' inaugural citation of Isa 61:1-2 / 58:6 and his mention of Elijah and Elisha? Nolland has provided a helpful summary of the interpretive options taken by recent scholarship.[53] Here we may observe simply that Jesus' words draw a comparison between his ministry and theirs, between the recipients of his ministry and those of theirs. In this context, the role of Elijah and Elisha as agents of healing to outsiders is paramount. Elijah is sent to a woman, a non-Jew, a widow — surely a person of low status. Elisha encounters a non-Jew, too, a Syrian whose disease, leprosy, served as a further marker of his socio-religious distance from the community of God's people (Leviticus 14). With reference to these examples, Jesus underscores that "good news to the poor" embraces the widow, the unclean, the Gentile, those of the lowest status.

Taken together, these three statements of ministry — 4:16-30; 5:27-32;

---

tions': A Biblical Perspective on the Church's Mission," in *The World Is My Parish: The Mission of the Church in Methodist Perspective,* ed. A. G. Padgett, SHM 10 (Lewiston, New York: Edwin Mellen, 1992) 13-43; cf. H. J. B. Combrick, "The Structure and Significance of Luke 4:16-30," *Neot* 7 (1973) 27-47.

51. *Contra,* e.g., NRSV.

52. Cf. J. B. Green, "Jesus and a Daughter of Abraham (Luke 13:10-17): Test Case for a Lukan Perspective on the Miracles of Jesus," *CBQ* 51 (1989) 643-54; *idem,* "Church's Mission."

53. Nolland, *Luke,* 200-201.

and 19:1-10 — point to Jesus' mission as opening the way for the inclusion of people in God's dominion who otherwise have no apparent claim on God. They have been made outsiders in the social systems of the ancient Mediterranean world. They are the poor to whom Jesus proclaims good news.

## 4. Conclusion

The current emphasis in Lukan studies on the material, this-worldly focus of Jesus' message in the Third Gospel represents a helpful advance on the spiritualized and end-time-oriented interpretations of previous decades. We have demonstrated, however, that this emphasis has not gone far enough toward a grounding of Luke's message in its own context. Consequently, we have pointed to the danger of interpretive strategies which operate from too narrow or anachronistic a base — in this case, an unexamined "materialistic exegesis" — while allowing that the material side of Luke's message has often been and cannot be overlooked. A fuller appreciation of the "poor" in the Third Gospel embraces Luke's concern for the economically destitute but also recognizes how economic concerns must be integrated more fully into an understanding of the human condition and social dynamics in the first-century Roman world. And this allows for a fuller appreciation of the Lukan portrait of God's gracious visitation. In Luke, Jesus repeatedly goes to those on the outside; this is his mission.[54]

54. The original stimulus for this investigation was provided by my association with the Berkeley Emergency Food Project. The social-scientific material informing this essay was shaped in conversation with Frances S. Adeney, Ph.D., and Susan S. Phillips, Ph.D. An early draft of this paper was presented to the Section on Synoptic Gospels, Society of Biblical Literature; it has also benefited from interaction with Stephen C. Barton, Ph.D., and Professor I. Howard Marshall's New Testament Seminar, King's College, University of Aberdeen.

# "Your Faith Has Made You Whole": The Evangelical Liberation Theology of Jesus

Craig L. Blomberg

Twenty-five years after the publication of G. Gutiérrez's seminal work, liberation theology remains as controversial as ever.[1] It has made only modest inroads into the Western historical-critical establishment. Evangelicals for the most part continue to view it with great suspicion.[2] Meanwhile, in the Two-Thirds World, various theologies of liberation frequently predominate over all other Christian ideologies. And increasingly, liberationists' praxis and reflection are demonstrating more sophisticated hermeneutical procedures and clearer biblical grounding.[3] Above all, the historical Jesus appears central to their enterprise.[4] To what extent may Jesus of Nazareth be legitimately viewed as a role model to justify liberationists' agendas?

The question, of course, is a large one and has been answered variously. The purpose of this essay is far more modest: to investigate one important formula of healing attributed to the Synoptic Jesus and to demonstrate its appropriateness as a label for representative, authentic healings as well as correlate these findings with some observations on his teachings on wealth and poverty. In so doing, we will suggest that the concept of "an evangelical liberation theology"[5] well

1. G. Gutiérrez, *A Theology of Liberation* (Maryknoll, New York: Orbis, 1968; rev. ed. 1988). In a personal conversation in Lima, Peru, during June of 1990, Gutiérrez stressed that he believes he has been frequently misunderstood and misrepresented in North American circles by both conservatives and liberals.

2. E.g., H. Belli and R. Nash, *Beyond Liberation Theology* (Grand Rapids, Michigan: Baker, 1992).

3. C. Rowland and M. Corner, *Liberating Exegesis: The Challenge of Liberation Theology to Biblical Studies* (London: SCM, 1989); A. F. McGovern, *Liberation Theology and Its Critics* (Maryknoll, New York: Orbis, 1989).

4. See esp. J. L. Segundo, *The Historical Jesus of the Synoptics* (Maryknoll, New York: Orbis, 1985).

5. Cf. R. J. Sider, "An Evangelical Theology of Liberation," *ChrCent* 97 (1980) 314-18.

captures the meaning of a major swath of Jesus' words and works; the two adjectives need not be pitted against each other. What is more, this conjunction helpfully delineates the difference between the historical Jesus and the most popular contemporary historical-critical reconstructions of his life and significance, which tend to be neither evangelical nor liberationist.[6]

## 1. "Your Faith Has Made You Whole"

The formula for consideration appears in four distinct episodes in the life of the Synoptic Jesus: ἡ πίστις σου σέσωκέν σε (Mark 5:34 [par. Matt 9:22; Luke 8:48]; Mark 10:52 [par. Luke 18:42]; Luke 7:50; 17:11-19). In three of these passages, σῴζω obviously has to refer at least to physical healing; in Luke 7:50 it must refer at least to spiritual salvation. Numerous traditio-critical analyses of this pronouncement argue that it goes back to Jesus, but that he originally used it to refer only to physical healing. In tradition and redaction, however, the formula took on its added spiritual significance.[7] It is our contention, conversely, that Jesus originally spoke these words, in each of the four contexts in which they are preserved, to refer to *both* physical and spiritual wholeness, and that later development of the Synoptic tradition, like church history more generally, could not easily hold these two elements together.

The semantic range of σῴζω in the OT includes both physical and spiritual healing, though both are by no means present in every usage of the term.[8] In the four Synoptic passages, however, material in the immediate context in each case suggests a dual reference. In Mark 5:34b, Jesus declares, "Go in peace and be healed of your affliction." The former clause more naturally suggests personal, inward well-being; the latter, continued physical health.[9] In Mark 10:52b, Mark follows Jesus' declaration with the observation that Bartimaeus "received his sight and followed him." The second verb is widely acknowledged to refer to discipleship.[10] Luke 17:19 finds Jesus telling the Samaritan leper that his faith has saved him, when in fact all ten lepers have already been healed. What therefore distinguishes this one? Presumably the answer is that he is "saved" in an additional sense, namely, being made spiritually right with God.[11] In Luke

6. Cf., most recently, J. P. Meier, *A Marginal Jew* (Garden City, New York: Doubleday, 1991); J. D. Crossan, *The Historical Jesus* (San Francisco: HarperCollins, 1991).

7. So, e.g., J. A. Fitzmyer, *The Gospel according to Luke*, 2 vols., AB 28-28a (Garden City, New York: Doubleday, 1981/85) 2:1156.

8. G. Fohrer and W. Foerster, "σῴζω, σωτηρία, σωτήρ, σωτήριος," *TDNT* 7:973-78.

9. E. Schweizer, *The Good News according to Mark* (Richmond: Knox, 1970) 118; W. L. Lane, *The Gospel according to Mark*, NICNT (Grand Rapids, Michigan: Wm. B. Eerdmans, 1974) 194.

10. J. Gnilka, *Das Evangelium nach Markus*, vol. 2, EKKNT 2 (Zürich: Benziger; Neukirchen-Vluyn: Neukirchener, 1979) 111; H. Anderson, *The Gospel of Mark*, NCBC (London: Marshall, Morgan & Scott, 1976) 259.

11. C. H. Talbert, *Reading Luke* (New York: Crossroad, 1986) 165; C. A. Evans, *Luke*, NIBC (Peabody, Massachusetts: Hendrickson, 1990) 250.

7:50 only a spiritual sense is demonstrably present, but one suspects that Luke might imagine the woman to have been previously healed by Jesus, since he redactionally juxtaposes 7:36-50 with another passage about healed women who became Jesus' followers (8:1-3).[12]

In fact, many commentators acknowledge these dual referents at the redactional level of each of these four passages. But they usually dispute that such a combination can be traced back to the earliest stages of the tradition. A careful application of the various criteria of authenticity suggests otherwise. The logion considered by itself can surely make a substantial claim to authenticity. It is attested twice in triple-tradition material and twice in L material. It appears in multiple forms: three times in accounts of healing miracles, one time also as part of a call story or paradigm (Mark 10:46-52), and once as part of framing material for a parable. Saving faith in the epistles and the later NT church is almost wholly dissociated from physical healing, but a spiritual interpretation of Jesus' words is also largely discontinuous with first-century Judaism.[13] An underlying Semitic original is easily reconstructible (אֱמוּנָתֵךְ הוֹשִׁיעָה אוֹתָךְ), in which "faith" would best be interpreted as confidence or trust in Jesus. And this interpretation coheres with the Synoptic Jesus' characteristic use of the term.[14]

When one turns to the use of Jesus' logion in each of its four specific contexts, an application of the criteria again yields positive results. In a *Sitz im Leben Jesu,* the most important kind of healing which the hemorrhaging woman would have sought would probably not have first been either physical or spiritual, as we tend to define those terms, but ritual.[15] The malady had persisted twelve years (Mark 5:35), so it was not likely constant or severe. Nothing in the passage can prove that the woman had begun to believe in Jesus as Messiah or to want to become a disciple. But the continuous ritual stigma and ostracism which her disease perpetuated would make her crave a cure for her affliction. And ritual uncleanliness affected the whole individual — body and soul. So Jesus' pronouncement of wholeness is most naturally viewed as a declaration concerning her entire person.

Mark's redactional activity in 5:21-43 is largely limited to the intercalation of the two miracles of healing and resurrection.[16] Verses 25-34 are primarily a traditional unit, with the logion in question functioning as the climactic pronouncement of the original pericope.[17] As with the concluding logia of full-fledged pronouncement stories, Jesus' decisive word thus lays the greatest claim

12. A suggestion inspired but not directly stated by J. J. Kilgallen, "A Proposal for Interpreting Luke 7, 36-50," *Bib* 72 (1991) 305-30. Cf. the discussion below.

13. N. Perrin, *Rediscovering the Teaching of Jesus* (New York: Harper & Row; London: SCM, 1967) 136.

14. A. J. Dewey, "The Synoptic Use of ΠΙΣΤΙΣ: An Appeal for a Context-Sensitive Translation," *Forum* 5 (1989) 83-86.

15. M. J. Selvidge, *Woman, Cult, and Miracle Recital* (Lewisburg: Bucknell, 1990) 91-93.

16. R. Pesch, *Das Markusevangelium,* 2 vols., HTKNT 2 (Freiburg: Herder, 1977) 1:295.

17. R. A. Guelich, *Mark 1–8:26,* WBC 34A (Dallas: Word, 1989) 291-94.

to authenticity of the various parts of the passage. Mark does not seem to emphasize the woman's faith in Jesus himself, inasmuch as the passage contains hints of superstitious or quasi-magical belief in the power of his clothing (vv 27-28). Matthew understandably and characteristically abbreviates these verses, so as better to highlight the woman's faith (Matt 9:22).[18] Matthew more consistently, though not uniformly, accentuates disciples' faith, whereas Mark tends to stress the lack of trust of those who come to Jesus or purport to follow him.[19] All of these factors combine to suggest that Jesus' words about the woman's faith are not a Markan creation.

"Go in peace" is clearly a Semitic formula and recurs in Luke 7:50. Vernon Robbins has argued that "be freed of your affliction" is the Greek counterpart and hence a Markan addition.[20] But a Semitic substratum is equally plausible. Behind ἴσθι ὑγιής could lie the verb רָפָא; behind μάστιξ, a participial form of חָלָה. Interestingly, forms of both of these words appear in Isaiah 53 (vv 5, 10) in contexts in which spiritual and not merely physical affliction and health come to the fore. If it is regularly granted that Mark sees Jesus' words to the woman as implying holistic healing, it does not seem inappropriate to attribute the source of Mark's conviction to Jesus' originally intended meaning.[21]

In Mark 10:52, the two-pronged nature of Jesus' healing ministry emerges from Mark's comments which follow Jesus' declaration. Because Mark states that Bartimaeus "followed" Jesus "on the road," most commentators take this to be a redactional addition of the theme of discipleship to what was originally just a miracle of physical healing. A few deny that discipleship is involved even at the Markan level.[22] At the same time, Matthew is the Synoptist who most frequently adds ἀκολουθέω to his sources, while here the verb is securely embedded in the triple tradition (cf. Matt 20:34; Luke 18:42). Luke demonstrates how redactional activity can make the meaning of "follow" unambiguous; he has the blind man glorify God, an undeniably spiritual act. Yet even without such explicit clarification, Mark's Bartimaeus can still call Jesus "Son of David" (Mark 10:47, 48), implying some kind of messianic associations.[23] But again the criterion of divergent patterns from redaction comes into play, since Matthew is the Evangelist most to emphasize this title. An even more decisive

18. W. D. Davies and D. C. Allison Jr., *A Critical and Exegetical Commentary on the Gospel according to Saint Matthew*, vol. 2, ICC (Edinburgh: T. & T. Clark, 1991) 130.

19. C. D. Marshall, *Faith as a Theme in Mark's Narrative* (Cambridge: Cambridge University, 1989) 101-10, 123-32, has helpful and detailed discussions of the integrity of the theme of faith in this passage and in 10:46-52, which Mark did not first introduce.

20. V. K. Robbins, "The Woman Who Touched Jesus' Garment: Socio-Rhetorical Analysis of the Synoptic Accounts," *NTS* 33 (1987) 510.

21. B. Blackburn, *Theios Anēr and the Markan Miracle Traditions*, WUNT 2:40 (Tübingen: J. C. B. Mohr [Paul Siebeck], 1991) 261-62, and n. 134.

22. E.g., Lane, *Mark*, 389; more tentatively, C. E. B. Cranfield, *The Gospel according to St. Mark* (Cambridge: Cambridge University, 1977) 346.

23. H. K. Nielsen, *Heilung und Verkündigung* (Leiden: E. J. Brill, 1987) 25.

application of this criterion is the observation that this is the only healing miracle in Mark in which Jesus allows the healed person to accompany him. All these factors combine to suggest that Mark saw Bartimaeus's healing as both physical and spiritual and that he derived this understanding from the tradition.

Form-critical considerations suggest that this tradition is most likely authentic. Verse 52 provides the climax to what Dibelius explicitly labeled a paradigm (i.e., pronouncement story).[24] Despite the healing, the miraculous element recedes into the background so that Jesus' declaration can take center stage. As noted above, the climactic sayings of pronouncement stories are most likely authentic. Pesch comes to a similar conclusion by identifying v 52b as equivalent to the acclamation notice in a miracle narrative.[25] More specifically, M. G. Steinhauser has analyzed this passage as a "call story," with vv 51-52 occupying the position of the sign to verify the call. He goes on to note that no other Synoptic passage adds ἀκολουθέω to a healing miracle but that this verb does naturally appear as the original conclusion to call stories (cf. Mark 1:18; 2:14).[26] Bartimaeus's discipleship is therefore a necessary and integral part of the story from the earliest stages of the tradition. Its multiple attestation and thoroughly Semitic milieu support a verdict of historicity as well.

The dynamics of Luke 17:11-19 are somewhat less straightforward. Ten lepers have already left Jesus for the priest and discovered that en route they were "cleansed" (ἐκαθαρίσθησαν), a term which again probably focuses first of all on ritual wholeness,[27] as the temple authorities would confirm. But after the Samaritan, and he alone, returns to give thanks, Jesus once again utters, ἡ πίστις σου σέσωκέν σε. Does this mean that the physical healing of the others was revoked? Or were the other nine healed by means of something other than faith? The most natural assumption would surely be that all remained physically healed by simple virtue of their appeal to Jesus (v 13) but that the Samaritan's faith enabled him to be "saved" in an additional, and hence spiritual, sense.[28]

A substantial majority of traditio-historical analyses of this passage nevertheless attribute v 19 to Luke's redaction, often along with v 11, as part of his framing of an otherwise traditional pericope.[29] A more careful structural analysis of the text, however, suggests that v 19 parallels v 14 more closely than

24. M. Dibelius, *From Tradition to Gospel* (New York: Scribner, 1965) 43.

25. Pesch, *Markusevangelium,* 2:174.

26. M. G. Steinhauser, "The Form of the Bartimaeus Narrative (Mark 10.46-52)," *NTS* 32 (1986) 589.

27. J. J. Pilch, "Understanding Biblical Healing: Selecting the Appropriate Model," *BTB* 18 (1988) 60-66.

28. See n. 11 above. I. H. Marshall, *The Gospel of Luke,* NIGTC (Exeter: Paternoster; Grand Rapids, Michigan: Wm. B. Eerdmans, 1978) 652, thinks the other nine had simply a less complete faith.

29. E.g., G. Petzke, *Das Sondergut des Evangeliums nach Lukas* (Zürich: Theologischer, 1990) 154.

v 11. After Luke's introductory verse, the text divides into two closely parallel segments: vv 12-14 and vv 15-19, each with three components. First, one or more people approach Jesus and address him, crying out (vv 12-13, 15-16). Second, Jesus responds to the addressees (v 14a, vv 17-18). Third, a statement of healing ensues (v 14b, v 19). Unless one is prepared to jettison v 14b as redactional and / or unhistorical, there is no reason to reject v 19.[30] But without v 14b there would be no account of any kind of healing in the passage; the very core of the pericope would be expunged.

Unlike the two Markan passages already treated, this one of course is not multiply attested. But there is good reason to attribute it to L,[31] and to place a fair measure of confidence in the historicity of the L material. To be sure, Luke's distinctive concerns come to the fore with the appearance of his favorite term σῴζω, but given the parallel occurrences of the formula of v 19 in Mark's text, Luke has clearly not invented its usage here. And given his distinctive emphasis on the social or this-worldly side of salvation,[32] accounting for his inclusion of this episode which portrays a Samaritan in a positive light, he is not likely to have distracted from a physical healing by adding a spiritual element not already present in the tradition. The climactic position of Jesus' words, finally, for the third consecutive time argues for their authenticity.

Luke 7:50 is the only one of the four occurrences of our formula in which it cannot be demonstrated that both physical and spiritual healing were present. Interestingly, however, it is not the spiritual element, usually held to be the later redactional emphasis in the various passages, but the physical side which is absent. It is, of course, usually maintained that vv 36-50 have a complex tradition-history, in which v 50 is one of the latest elements added.[33] A few have argued for keeping v 50 with other traditional elements, while still separating off other later accretions.[34] Once again, however, a structural analysis yields quite different results. To begin with, vv 36-50 must be distinguished from the anointing of Jesus at Bethany in Mark, Matthew, and John. Some assimilation of traditions may have occurred but the two traditions remain largely independent and reflect separate events from quite different periods and settings in Jesus' ministry. Luke is again drawing on L.[35]

The parable of vv 41-43 is closely linked to its framing material. Both the story and the setting contain three main characters, and they are intended to

30. W. Bruners, *Die Reinigung der zehn Aussätzigen und die Heilung des Samariters Lk 17,11-19* (Stuttgart: KBW, 1977), develops a similar structure, paralleling vv 11-12a and 15-16, 12b-13 and 17-18, and 14 and 19. Because Bruners finds Lukan redaction in each section, however, he attributes the whole passage to Luke.

31. W. Wiefel, *Das Evangelium nach Lukas* (Berlin: Evangelische Verlagsanstalt, 1988) 153.

32. Of a voluminous literature, cf. most recently, H. Moxnes, *The Economy of the Kingdom: Social Conflict and Economic Relations in Luke's Gospel,* OBT (Philadelphia: Fortress, 1988).

33. F. Bovon, *Das Evangelium nach Lukas,* vol. 1, EKKNT 3.1 (Zürich: Benziger; Neukirchen-Vluyn: Neukirchener, 1989) 385-89.

34. Most recently, see J. Nolland, *Luke 1–9:20,* WBC 35A (Dallas: Word, 1989) 352.

35. Marshall, *Luke,* 304.

correspond to each other. The woman corresponds to the debtor forgiven more, the Pharisee to the debtor forgiven less, and the creditor to Jesus speaking on behalf of God.[36] The narrative introduction sets up the contrast between the Pharisee and the woman by alternating the focus between them. Verse 36 introduces the Pharisee; v 37, the woman. Verse 38 describes her anointing of Jesus, while v 39 portrays Simon's indignant response. The sequel to the parable continues this contrast. Verses 43b-47 narrate Jesus' reply to Simon, and vv 48-50 convey Jesus' response to the woman. These two sections in turn subdivide into three parallel parts: a pronouncement concerning the person addressed (vv 43b, 48), one or more contrasts (vv 44-46 — between the woman and Simon; v 49 — the contrasting response of the guests), and a closing and climactic conclusion concerning the woman (vv 47, 50). Not one of the standard tradi-tio-historical dissections of the passage respects these thematic parallels and contrasts;[37] the passage was more likely a unity from the outset.

The older Roman Catholic view that the woman is saved as a result of her love is now largely abandoned, including in many Catholic circles.[38] Verse 47 is rightly understood as meaning that Jesus can *say* (λέγω) that the woman is saved "because she loved much." In other words, her love demonstrates her faith.[39] But this presupposes some prior encounter with Jesus for which she is now thanking him. John Kilgallen thinks she had received forgiveness through the ministry of John the Baptist, and that Luke is hinting at this through his redactional relocation of the parenthesis of vv 29-30, and through the juxtaposition of 7:18-35 more generally.[40] But, notwithstanding the reference to "the son of man" in v 34, this does not as easily fit her lavish outpouring of love and perfume upon *Jesus*. Gerd Petzke objects to the authenticity of v 50 on the grounds that it belongs to a miracle story.[41] Indeed, the only other time the Synoptic Jesus declares a specific person's sins forgiven is in the context of an explicit healing — that of the paralytic of Mark 2:1-12 pars. (see vv 5, 7). But one could argue in the opposite direction that the presence of vv 47 and 50 thus suggests that the woman's previous encounter with Jesus was an occasion in which he had healed her of some physical affliction.

Interestingly, the majority of Catholic history makes such an assumption explicit by identifying this woman with Mary Magdalene, from whom Jesus exorcised seven demons (8:2).[42] Modern scholarship of most theological tradi-

36. C. L. Blomberg, *Interpreting the Parables* (Downers Grove, Illinois: InterVarsity, 1990) 184-86.

37. See the helpful survey in Wiefel, *Lukas,* 153-54.

38. J. de Urrutia, "La parábola de los dos deudores Lc 7,39-50," *EstEcl* 38 (1963) 472-73.

39. J. Jeremias, *The Parables of Jesus* (London: SCM, 1972) 127.

40. J. J. Kilgallen, "John the Baptist, the Sinful Woman, and the Pharisee," *JBL* 104 (1985) 675-79.

41. Petzke, *Sondergut,* 99; so too H. Klein, *Barmherzigkeit gegen über den Elenden und Geächteten* (Neukirchen-Vluyn: Neukirchener, 1987) 40.

42. Still vigorously defended, e.g., by A. Feuillet, "Les deux onctions faites sur Jésus, et Marie-Madeleine," *RevThom* 75 (1975) 357-94.

tions largely rejects this equation, inasmuch as the text of Luke never makes it, though early attestation of the tradition can be found in Ephraem of Syria (*Hymn* 1.176-77), Tertullian (*De Pudicitia* 11.2), and Gregory the Great (*Hom.* 25.1.10). Modern redaction criticism does helpfully suggest, though, that Luke's insertion of 8:1-3 at this point reflects the theme of "Jesus and Women" which unites these verses with 7:36-50.[43] Whether or not the unnamed woman at Simon's house was Mary, might this juxtaposition not also reflect awareness of some tradition in which the woman who anointed Jesus did so out of thanksgiving for previous healing? Ben Witherington allows this at least a "slim possibility."[44] John Kilgallen believes that the unnamed woman who anointed Jesus became a symbol not only of repentance and forgiveness but also of the women who followed Jesus because he had healed them.[45] It is a short step, indeed, from this conclusion to the inference that Luke believed the unnamed woman herself to have been previously healed.

At any rate, what is clear is that the passage speaks unambiguously about the forgiveness of sins. One cannot defend a unilateral tendency of the tradition to develop from physical healing only to physical plus spiritual healing. If physical healing is not presupposed in the background to this passage, we have an example of only spiritual healing at the earliest stage of the story. And, as with Luke 17:11-19, given Luke's greater interest in the socio-physical side of salvation, he has not likely created the current emphases of this story. The OT links throughout ch. 7 with the Elijah-Elisha cycles speak less for Lukan midrashic creativity[46] than they do for authenticity by the criterion of Semitic background. Jesus' formula of salvation, finally, stands, as it has previously, as a fitting declarative climax to a pericope, in a position which strongly supports its authenticity.

In sum, ἡ πίστις σου σέσωκέν σε should be accepted as an authentic logion of Jesus in each of the four Gospel contexts in which it appears. It should be interpreted in at least three and perhaps all four of these contexts as implying holistic salvation of body and soul, in both this life and the next. A good English translation of this sense would be "Your faith has made you whole." What is more, this double referent for salvation stems from the historical Jesus and not merely from later tradition and / or redaction.

But what of the rest of the Synoptic tradition? It is time to turn from intense scrutiny of a tiny percentage of the Gospel material to paint with broad strokes various patterns which emerge from a brief survey of much larger swaths of the Synoptic strata. Recent study of the historical Jesus, especially within but

43. E.g., Fitzmyer, *Luke,* 1:696.

44. B. Witherington III, "On the Road with Mary Magdalene, Joanna, Susanna and Other Disciples," *ZNW* 70 (1979) 243.

45. Kilgallen, "Luke 7,36-50," 316-17.

46. As in T. L. Brodie, "Luke 7,36-50 as an Internalization of 2 Kings 4,1-37: A Study in Luke's Rhetorical Imitation," *Bib* 64 (1983) 457-85.

by no means limited to liberationist circles, has helpfully focused on Jesus' healings more generally, along with his teachings concerning wealth and poverty, as crucial and representative samplings of his works and words overall.[47] It is our contention that the same holistic gospel of liberation emerges from this kind of survey of the data which our more "microscopic" focus on Jesus' formula of salvation has revealed.

## 2. Jesus' Healing Miracles

It is not our purpose here to argue for the historicity of every passage or every detail within every passage cited. The point rather is to demonstrate a persistent theme or juxtaposition of themes which is not likely to be derived on any large scale from later church influence. Now, to be sure, one can rule narratives of miraculous deeds out of bounds for historical investigation[48] or redefine them sociologically so that they no longer purport to describe genuinely supernatural events.[49] But the former requires an unnecessarily truncated understanding of the legitimate boundaries of historical and scientific investigation.[50] The latter rests on a category mistake; social-scientific analysis rightly investigates the function of miracle narratives but is not in a position to adjudicate on their historicity.[51]

If one applies the standard criteria of authenticity to the Synoptic healing narratives in general, they in fact fare quite well.[52] They find very few parallels in the Judaism of their day; the few other "charismatic holy men" work primarily through prayer and are not equally well-known for their teaching or claims about the in-breaking eschaton.[53] Against Hellenistic backgrounds, Jesus' healings stand out by virtue of their simplicity and directness, that is, their dissociation from most forms of magic.[54] But beyond the pages of the book of Acts,

47. Of recent works, see esp. C. Myers, *Binding the Strong Man: A Political Reading of Mark's Story of Jesus* (Maryknoll, New York: Orbis, 1988).

48. As, e.g., in Meier, *Jesus,* 220.

49. As, e.g., in Crossan, *Jesus,* 303-32.

50. See esp. C. Brown, *Miracles and the Critical Mind* (Exeter: Paternoster; Grand Rapids, Michigan: Wm. B. Eerdmans, 1984).

51. See esp. G. Theissen, *The Miracle Stories of the Early Christian Tradition* (Edinburgh: T. & T. Clark, 1983) 231-64.

52. For full elaboration, see R. Latourelle, *The Miracles of Jesus and the Theology of Miracles* (New York: Paulist, 1988).

53. A. E. Harvey, *Jesus and the Constraints of History* (London: Duckworth; Philadelphia: Westminster, 1982) 98-119.

54. H. C. Kee, *Medicine, Miracle and Magic in New Testament Times* (Cambridge: Cambridge University, 1986); and G. H. Twelftree, "'Eἰ δὲ ἐγὼ ἐκβάλλω τὰ δαιμόνια . . .'," in *Gospel Perspectives,* vol. 6, ed. D. Wenham and C. Blomberg (Sheffield: JSOT, 1986) 361-400; though both stress that at times the differences have been overdrawn.

such healings quickly disappear from early Christian literature, though persisting with much less prominence in some circles until at least the third or fourth centuries. The healings are attested in every Gospel and every Gospel stratum (Mark [e.g., 1:40-45 pars.], Q [e.g., Matt 8:5-13 par.], M [e.g., Matt 9:27-31], L [e.g., Luke 17:11-19], and even the small body of uniquely Markan material [Mark 8:22-26]).[55] They appear combined with multiple forms (as, e.g., in combination with pronouncement stories or call stories as in the passages described above, to which may be added summary statements [e.g., Mark 3:7-12], dialogues [e.g., Matt 11:1-6], and controversies or conflict stories [e.g., Mark 2:1-12 pars.]) and themselves subdivide into multiple forms (as, e.g., with exorcisms and resurrections). Occasionally, two-stage miracles and / or the use of means such as spittle vary the healing narratives from their standard form (cf., e.g., Mark 7:31-35; 8:22-26).

External evidence strongly corroborates the fact that Jesus worked miraculous healings. Other portions of the NT refer back to Christ's wonder-working powers (e.g., Acts 10:38; 1 Cor 15:4-8; Heb 2:4). Apocryphal Christian texts, while fancifully embellishing the accounts of Jesus' ministry, nevertheless bear indirect testimony to his power to heal by focusing considerable attention on this aspect of his career (see esp. the *Infancy Gospel of Thomas* and the *Acts of Pilate*). Non-Christian Jewish sources also admit that Jesus was a healer. Both Josephus (*Ant.* 18.63-64) and the Talmud (*b. Sanh.* 107b) refer to his extraordinary powers in this regard, although the latter source attributes them to a demonic rather than a divine origin.

The healings illustrate a remarkable diversity of themes. At times Jesus heals in response to people's faith (as in the passage with our formula above). Other times he heals in order to produce faith. The latter is particularly common in John (4:53-54; 20:31), but the phenomenon is not absent from the Synoptics (cf., e.g., Matt 8:15, in which Simon's mother-in-law "serves" Jesus after he heals her fever). Sometimes he restores people's physical health out of sheer compassion (e.g., Matt 14:14; 20:34); in other cases, to break down the barriers caused by Jewish ritual taboos (e.g., Mark 1:41; 7:24-30). On occasion, he even more directly challenges Israel's laws and exposes its faithlessness (e.g., Mark 3:1-6; Luke 13:10-17). In John he uses healings to teach about the various possible relationships between sickness and sin (5:14; 9:3). All this variety should guard against any simplistic formula of faith necessarily leading to healing, while preserving God's sovereignty to intervene miraculously when he sees fit.[56]

But the criterion of divergence from redaction suggests that another key theme which is increasingly played down the more the tradition develops is in

55. The rest of this section relies heavily on C. L. Blomberg, "Healing," in *Dictionary of Jesus and the Gospels,* ed. J. B. Green and S. McKnight (Leicester: InterVarsity; Downers Grove, Illinois: InterVarsity, 1992) 299-307, and the literature there cited.

56. A balance reasonably well-achieved by B. Barron in his sympathetic but thoughtful critique, *The Health and Wealth Gospel* (Downers Grove, Illinois: InterVarsity, 1987).

fact the central and most authentic theme to emerge from a study of the healing miracles in a *Sitz im Leben Jesu.* Consistently Jesus refers to his own miracles of healing as corroboration of his claim that with his person and ministry the messianic age or kingdom of God was being inaugurated in human history.[57] Inasmuch as this is the central theme of his teaching overall, by the criterion of coherence, the healing miracles which reflect this theme should be given serious consideration as historical. Some of the most striking examples of this link between Jesus' works and words come via a comparison of nature miracles and parables, as I have elsewhere stressed.[58] But the same point emerges quite clearly from an analysis of the healing miracles too. A few examples must suffice in this context.

In a passage widely acknowledged to be authentic and regularly cited in defense of realized eschatology (Matt 12:28), Jesus declares that his exorcisms demonstrate that the kingdom of God has come upon his generation. A second text well embedded in the core of bedrock sayings material is Jesus' answer to the question of John's disciples about his identity: his healings should demonstrate that he is the one to come (Matt 11:4-6). Characteristic of both of these texts is an indirect christological claim, which later tradition would surely have phrased more explicitly. The same may be said of the account of the healing of the paralytic (Mark 2:1-12 pars.). Jesus works the miracle to prove that he has the authority to forgive sins, a prerogative reserved for God alone (vv 10-11). Yet neither Jesus nor the narrative spells out the appropriate conclusion from this fact; the listener or reader is left to infer it.[59] By way of contrast, in clearly redactional expansions of tradition, the Fourth Evangelist will use a story of Jesus' giving sight to the blind to illustrate the specific claim that Christ is "the light of the world" (John 9:5) or link Jesus' resurrection of Lazarus with the "I-am saying" about the resurrection and the life (11:25). Mark's and Matthew's redactional summaries preserve a closer link with the traditional emphasis,[60] joining Jesus' healing to his preaching under the headline of his call to repentance, "for the kingdom of God is near" (Mark 1:15; cf. Matt 4:23; 9:35; 21:14).

Other specific healing miracles also point by inference to the arrival of the kingdom or of the messianic age. When Jesus heals a deaf-mute, Mark describes the man as one who could hardly talk (μογιλάλος — Mark 7:32), a word found elsewhere in the Greek Bible only in Isa 35:6 (LXX), in which the

57. O. Betz and W. Grimm, *Wesen und Wirklichkeit der Wunder Jesu* (Frankfurt: P. Lang, 1977); M. Trautmann, *Zeichenhafte Handlungen Jesu* (Würzburg: Echter, 1980); L. Sabourin, *The Divine Miracles Discussed and Defended* (Rome: Catholic Book Agency, 1977).

58. C. L. Blomberg, "The Miracles as Parables," in *Gospel Perspectives,* vol. 6, 327-59.

59. Theissen, *Miracle Stories,* 164-65, gives cogent reasons for not relegating vv 5b-10 to later tradition, as is commonly done.

60. Cf. L. E. Keck, *A Future for the Historical Jesus* (Nashville: Abingdon, 1971) 32, on Mark 1:14-15: "This is almost universally acknowledged to be at the same time a formulation by the church and an accurate summary of what Jesus had to say."

prophet is describing the wonders of the age to come, including the fact that the "mute tongue" will "shout for joy."[61] The resurrection of the widow of Nain's son (Luke 7:11-17) strikingly resembles Elisha's raising the son of the Shunammite woman (2 Kgs 4:8-37), especially since Nain was located on a site within a few miles of OT Shunem.[62] Even the crowds pick up on the resemblance as they marvel at the "great prophet" who has arisen among them (cf. Deut 18:18). The category of eschatological prophet is important to the earliest stages of Jewish Christianity (cf. Acts 3:22; 7:37) but quickly falls into disuse and is thus not likely the product of later tradition.[63] So, too, language of the age to come or of the kingdom quickly gives way to Paul's emphasis on justification or John's on eternal life, and to general Christian emphasis on more explicit christology, in ways which suggest that the links between Jesus' miracles and the arrival of the new age are not the products of later Christian reflection.[64]

The accumulation of evidence makes it highly probable, therefore, that physical healing formed a crucial part of the ministry of the historical Jesus. Concern for the physical needs of God's people in particular, and of the whole world more generally, should therefore form a central focus of Christians in every age. Yet Jesus never worked healings as ends in themselves, but as pointers to the arrival of the kingdom of God and, more indirectly, to his messiahship. So too Christians dare not provide for human physical need without also addressing people's areas of spiritual need. More specifically, ministries of physical healing must point beyond themselves to Jesus, the great physician and the savior of our souls as well as our bodies. But this does not mean, for example, that medical missions are merely a "front" for evangelism. Concern for the whole spectrum of human need addresses each aspect of an individual's life as worthy of respect and integrity in and of itself. One hopes that people may be healed in every aspect of their personhood, and one recognizes how interrelated these aspects are,[65] but if circumstances or their own choices prevent healing in certain areas, we must continue to try to work redemptively

61. Guelich, *Mark,* 394.

62. On the parallels see T. L. Brodie, "Towards Unravelling Luke's Use of the Old Testament: Luke 7.11-17 as an *Imitatio* of 1 Kings 17,17-24," *NTS* 32 (1986) 247-67; but, for authenticity, see M. J. Harris, " 'The Dead Are Restored to Life': Miracles of Revivification in the Gospels," in *Gospel Perspectives,* vol. 6, 295-303.

63. See esp. R. N. Longenecker, *The Christology of Early Jewish Christianity* (London: SCM, 1970) 32-38.

64. See in detail Nielsen, *Heilung,* 124-252. After Mark, few NT or later Christian writers kept Jesus' eschatological perspective on healings in the foreground of their theology.

65. It is possible to bring only spiritual or only physical healing to an individual, but the one often logically leads to the other. Cf. W. A. Dyrness, *Let the Earth Rejoice!* (Westchester: Crossway, 1983) 187-88: "The basic reason, of course, for considering matter and spirit as a whole is that from our discussion of creation we have seen that the spirit cannot be made an object of independent attention because it does not exist in isolation from its material context. It is in and through the created order that the human person must express his or her values."

in the remaining areas. Put another way, our gospel is both evangelical and liberationist.

## 3. Jesus' Teaching on Wealth and Poverty

Christian faith should lead to a holistic gospel in the area of finances, economics, and stewardship, too. Again it is interesting to see how the Synoptic teaching attributed to Jesus consistently holds together concepts which believers since have tended to sunder. The blessed poor are both pious and destitute; the rich condemned are both wealthy and godless. A right use of wealth demonstrates generosity and compassion for the physically needy as well as an avoidance of spiritual idolatry. Poverty is never idealized. It should be alleviated because marginalization and oppression can turn people away from the Lord, but wealth tends to do so even more, as people think they can independently supply all their own needs. Mammon may be humanity's greatest idol and competitor with God for personal allegiance, but in the hands of disciples it can be a positive tool for implementing kingdom priorities and bringing people to Christ. Again we must be selective in surveying the evidence, but even a cursory highlighting of some of Jesus' key teachings demonstrates how little subsequent Christian discipleship has been as holistic and balanced as Jesus' own agenda.[66]

As with his healings, there are general considerations for affirming the authenticity of a bipolar interpretation of Jesus' teachings on wealth and poverty which is both evangelical and liberationist. The criterion of dissimilarity again works particularly well. Notwithstanding the exemplary experiments in the early church with communal sharing (Acts 2:43-47; 4:32-36), Christian leaders soon had to struggle with raising funds to provide for needy fellow believers (cf., most notably, 2 Corinthians 8–9). Throughout the history of the church, small groups and various individuals have taken radical vows of poverty; contemporary liberation theology frequently elevates the alleviation of poverty above the mandate to prepare human souls for eternity. But most Christians, ancient and modern, find a gospel of spiritual salvation alone far more comfortable, so that their lifestyles and finances are scarcely affected.[67] Dissimilarity from Jesus' Jewish background is less noticeable, since his ethics finds solid rooting in the OT prophets, but it is not clear that wide numbers of first-century Palestinian

66. Important monographs include M. Hengel, *Property and Riches in the Early Church* (London: SCM, 1974); D. L. Mealand, *Poverty and Expectation in the Gospels* (London: SPCK, 1980); L. T. Johnson, *Sharing Possessions* (Philadelphia: Fortress, 1981); W. Stegemann, *The Gospel and the Poor* (Philadelphia: Fortress, 1984); L. J. Hoppe, *Being Poor: A Biblical Study* (Wilmington: Glazier, 1987); J. M. Bassler, *God and Mammon: Asking for Money in the New Testament* (Nashville: Abingdon, 1991).

67. See esp. J. L. González, *Faith and Wealth: A History of Early Christian Ideas on the Origin, Significance and Use of Money* (San Francisco: Harper & Row, 1990).

Jews were implementing their own scriptural commands any more successfully than subsequent generations of Christians did.[68] The common observation that Jesus' ethic is more admired than obeyed underlines its radical nature and dissimilarity from typical human ideology and practice.[69]

Jesus' teachings on wealth and poverty occur in all the Synoptic strata (Mark [e.g., 10:17-31 pars.]; Q [e.g., Luke 6:20-49 pars.], M [e.g., Matt 25:31-46], and L [e.g., Luke 16:19-31]). They cut across all the major Gospel forms, including hymns (e.g., Luke 1:53), sermons (e.g., Luke 4:18-19), call stories (e.g., Mark 1:16-20 pars.), beatitudes (e.g., Matt 5:3 par.), summary statements (e.g., Matt 7:22 par.), commissioning narratives (e.g., Mark 6:8-9 par.), proverbs (e.g., Luke 9:58 par.), parables (e.g., Luke 12:13-21), and so on. The teaching fits perfectly the fourth decade of first-century Palestine, which was growing increasingly restless with imperial oppression and heavy taxation, yet exactly fits no contemporary mold of the day.[70] Jesus never endorses either the revolutionary violence of the Zealots or the separatistic quietism of the Essenes.[71] Key terms like "the poor" (οἱ πτωχοί) rely on distinctive OT usage. Some of Jesus' words are so potentially embarrassing or misleading that they surely would have been excised by the tradition had it felt free to do so (most notably in the account of the rich young ruler in Mark 10:17-31 pars. or with shorter sayings such as Matt 5:42). Right use of wealth and right response to poverty forms a major theme of numerous parables (e.g., Matt 25:14-30; Mark 4:1-9 pars.; Luke 12:13-21; 14:28-33; 16:1-13, 19-31). Once again we may invoke the criterion of coherence with the bedrock core of the sayings tradition — teaching on the kingdom of God, and particularly that which appears in parabolic form.

Of many passages worthy of note, several focus the issue at hand in particularly helpful ways, blending a right understanding of material possessions with a proper devotion to God. It is frequently alleged that Jesus' first beatitude refers to the materially poor in Luke 6:20 but to the spiritually poor in Matt 5:3. Almost certainly, however, Jesus intended both concepts, even if

68. Nor is Jesus' teaching on wealth as directly tied to the prophetic period (nor to any one other immediate antecedent); see esp. T. E. Schmidt, *Hostility to Wealth in the Synoptic Gospels,* JSNTSS 15 (Sheffield: JSOT, 1987).

69. T. E. Schmidt, "Burden, Barrier, Blasphemy: Wealth in Matt 6:33, Luke 14:33 and Luke 16:15," *TrinJ* n.s. 9 (1988) 186-87, observes, ironically, that spiritualizing Jesus' words on money is most common among those most vociferous about taking the Bible "literally." The problem, of course, emerges because "when luxuriant levels of living are confronted by strong and recurrent opposition in the teaching of Jesus, something has to give. That something is usually the teaching of Jesus."

70. See esp. D. E. Oakman, *Jesus and the Economic Questions of His Day* (Lewiston, New York: Mellen, 1986); R. A. Horsley, *Jesus and the Spiral of Violence* (San Francisco: Harper & Row, 1987).

71. Cf. the esp. well-balanced study of R. J. Cassidy, *Jesus, Politics and Society* (Maryknoll, New York: Orbis, 1978).

the two Evangelists have emphasized different aspects of his meaning.[72] Behind οἱ πτωχοί lie the OT *ʿanāwîm* (as particularly in passages like Isa 61:1), who refer to the faithful remnant in Israel.[73] They are for the most part genuinely economically impoverished, but they also acknowledge their utter dependence on God.[74] It is exegetically irresponsible to argue that God has a preferential option for the poor irrespective of their spiritual openness to him. It is biblically disobedient to ignore the regular scriptural calls to believers to give generously of their goods to help those less fortunate in the world, particularly within "the household of faith" (cf. Gal 6:10).

A similar two-pronged interpretation must be given to Luke 4:18-19. This even more direct quotation of Isa 61:1-2 focuses largely on victims of material and physical oppression and enslavement, but each of the terms is susceptible of a double interpretation which includes spiritual liberation as well. Inasmuch as Jesus astounds his audience by declaring this text to be fulfilled in him even as he speaks (4:21), Jesus' own holistic ministry of meeting needs of body and soul must be viewed as the hermeneutical key to understanding the meaning of his words in this context.[75] Indeed, throughout Luke-Acts, physical blindness and sight, particularly following healings such as those alluded to via the Isaiah quotation here, function as paradigms of spiritual inability and ability to see.[76] The link between teaching and healing is made even tighter by Luke 7:22 (the almost verbatim Lukan parallel to Matt 11:5), because it gives Jesus' reply to John's disciples concerning the poor having good news preached to them a direct antecedent. Jesus' proclamation just as much as his healings should convince John of who Jesus is.[77]

The parables of the rich fool and of the rich man and Lazarus have often been dissected traditio-critically, so that the authentic portions speak only of condem-

72. R. A. Guelich, *The Sermon on the Mount* (Waco, Texas: Word, 1982) 75. F. D. Bruner, *The Christbook* (Waco: Word, 1987) 135, neatly notes the opposing pitfalls: "If we say that 'blessed are the poor in spirit' means 'blessed are the rich, too, if they act humbly,' we have spiritualized the text. On the other hand, if we say that 'blessed are the poor' means 'poor people are happy people,' we have secularized the text."

73. W. Heard, "Luke's Attitude toward the Rich and Poor," *TrinJ* n.s. 9 (1988) 47-80, who also helpfully surveys the numerous other options.

74. K.-P. Jörns, "Armut, zu der der Geist hilft (Mt 5,3) als *nota ecclesiae*," *TZ* 43 (1987) 59-70 — these are those whom the Spirit helps to be materially poor; G. T. Meadors, "The 'Poor' in the Beatitudes of Matthew and Luke," *GTJ* 6 (1985) 305-14 — these are the pious, but faith-commitment of necessity produces social and / or economic oppression.

75. W. Dietrich, "'den Armen das Evangelium zu verkunden'," *TZ* 41 (1985) 31-43; W. W. Klein, "The Sermon at Nazareth (Luke 4:14-22)," in *Christian Freedom: Essays in Honor of Vernon C. Grounds*, ed. K. W. M. Wozniak and S. J. Grenz (Lanham: University Press of America, 1986) 153-72.

76. D. Hamm, "Sight to the Blind: Vision as Metaphor in Luke," *Bib* 67 (1986) 457-77; *idem*, "Paul's Blindness and Its Healing: Clues to Symbolic Intent (Acts 9, 22 and 26)," *Bib* 71 (1990) 63-72.

77. Luke better preserves the original sequence and juxtaposition of passages in Q at this point; see J. S. Kloppenborg, *The Formation of Q* (Philadelphia: Fortress, 1987) 91-92.

nation of the rich. Luke or the tradition is then said to have spiritualized Jesus' meaning so that only the godless rich are to blame. But such dissection is almost certainly wrongheaded. A flurry of recent parable scholarship has demonstrated from numerous angles that the parables should not be "cut out of their frames."[78] And once this advice is heeded, then Luke 12:21 must be included in any legitimate interpretation of the parable of the rich fool. The man had not only accumulated needless wealth; he had taken no thought for God. So too Luke 16:29 demonstrates that the rich man who neglected Lazarus recognized after death that he had also failed to repent (and hence requests for an otherworldly messenger to help his family members do what he had not done). On the other hand, evangelicals often take consolation too quickly in these observations. Whatever godlessness may be implied in the portraits of the two rich men (and whatever piety may be implied in the choice of the name Lazarus for the poor man) are more implicit than explicit.[79] What dominates these two parables is the description of hoarding and self-indulgence of the rich at the expense of the poor, which, almost by definition, proves these men not to be people of God. Given the frightening parallels among many modern Westerners, including some who facilely call themselves Christian, the powerful impression of the damning danger of literal riches must not be blunted.[80]

The story of the unjust steward (Luke 16:1-9) is in some ways the most perplexing of Jesus' parables. Inability to appreciate the picaresque or rogue characters which Jesus more than once utilizes as heroes of his narratives (cf. esp. Luke 18:1-8; Matt 24:43-44) has led to frequent attempts to interpret vv 8-9 in a less than straightforward sense — most notably as irony, interrogative, or sarcasm.[81] Others read in historical reconstructions which make the steward act ethically after his previous embezzlement has been discovered.[82] The most

78. Most recently, see B. Gerhardsson, "If We Do Not Cut the Parables Out of Their Frames," *NTS* 37 (1991) 321-35.

79. See esp. H. Kvalbein, "Jesus and the Poor: Two Texts and a Tentative Conclusion," *Themelios* 12 (1987) 80-87.

80. See esp. J. Ellul, *Money and Power* (Downers Grove, Illinois: InterVarsity, 1984).

81. For the most recent representative of each of these views, see, respectively, S. E. Porter, "The Parable of the Unjust Steward (Luke 16,1-13): Irony *Is* the Key," in *The Bible in Three Dimensions,* ed. D. J. A. Clines, S. E. Fowl, and S. E. Porter (Sheffield: JSOT, 1990) 127-53; D. M. Parrot, "The Dishonest Steward (Luke 16,1-8a) and Luke's Special Parable Collection," *Bib* 70 (1989) 474-95; I. J. du Plessis, "Philanthropy or Sarcasm? Another Look at the Parable of the Dishonest Manager (Luke 16:1-13)," *Neot* 24 (1990) 1-20. All three do a good job debunking the popular recent view represented by the studies in n. 82 below, but Parrot and du Plessis mostly ignore the traditional understanding re-presented here. Porter complains that the steward's cleverness cannot be separated from his specific, ingratiating action, which forms an unworthy example (131), but he gives no reasons for this assertion, which is not self-evident. W. Loader, "Jesus and the Rogue in Luke 16,1-8A: The Parable of the Unjust Steward," *RB* 96 (1989) 518-32, combines the traditional view with a christological interpretation of the steward. But where christology is implicit in the parables it is invariably with the master figures rather than their servants.

82. J. D. M. Derrett, *Law in the New Testament* (London: Darton, Longman, Todd, 1970)

common interpretation throughout church history remains the best — the master is praising the steward's shrewdness, not his dishonesty.[83] Jesus then calls his followers shrewdly to use worldly wealth for kingdom priorities rather than to become enslaved to it, since one cannot serve both God and Mammon (v 13). Taken this way, all of vv 1-13 may be read as an integrated whole; no traditio-critical dissection is needed.[84]

Wolfgang Stegemann captures the contemporary application quite concisely: "we affluent Christians, too, can make friends for ourselves by means of unrighteous mammon. We can become poorer in a purposeful way by giving away part of our wealth to benefit the poorest people of this world."[85] As we do so, we must do it in the name of Jesus, telling the people we help not that our generosity is contingent on their becoming believers but that we believe we have an even greater gift than physical life which they should accept. Otherwise we as rich, or the poor whom we help to become a little richer, will simply be worshiping Mammon rather than God.

The God and Mammon contrast reappears in Matt 6:24 in a context which is particularly crucial for maintaining this balance between earthly and heavenly riches. On the one hand, Jesus commands us to seek to store up spiritual rather than material treasures (vv 19-21). On the other hand, he promises that those who seek first God's kingdom and its righteousness will have all their material needs supplied as well (v 33). Because this promise has patently not been fulfilled for many individual believers, most commentators take it merely as a reference to the eschaton. But it is hard to imagine how the promise of vindication in the distant future can be a strong motive not to be anxious in the present (v 25). The Lukan parallel, however, almost immediately after the call to seek first God's kingdom (Luke 12:31), inserts the command to sell our possessions and give alms (v 33). And the oldest (Markan) form of the dialogue between Peter and Jesus on recompense for the sacrifices of itinerant ministry has Jesus specifically declaring that those who give up family or property for the Lord will receive in return a hundredfold in both categories, not only in the life to come but also in this age (Mark 10:29-30). Inasmuch as the hundredfold addition of family must refer to the larger community of disciples, the extra houses or fields must also be those which belong to fellow believers.[86] Put simply, the reason Christians should be able to expect to have their physical needs cared

---

48-77; J. A. Fitzmyer, "The Story of the Dishonest Manager (Lk. 16:1-13)," *TS* 25 (1964) 23-42; K. E. Bailey, *Poet and Peasant: A Literary-Cultural Approach to the Parables in Luke* (Grand Rapids, Michigan: Wm. B. Eerdmans, 1976) 110.

83. See now esp. J. S. Kloppenborg, "The Dishonest Master (Luke 16,1-8a)," *Bib* 70 (1989) 474-95.

84. Blomberg, *Parables*, 247 and n. 99.

85. Stegemann, *Gospel*, 63.

86. See esp. D. M. May, "Leaving and Receiving: A Social-Scientific Exegesis of Mark 10:29-31," *PRS* 17 (1990) 141-54.

for, when their spiritual priorities are correct, is that Jesus calls all his followers to share their possessions with other Christians in need.[87] But he is not first of all addressing individual believers but his disciples as a community. If Christian communities do seek first God's kingdom, then by definition they will care for the poor within those fellowships. To be blunt, "situations occur where people's needs are not met because followers of Christ have not been obedient in applying the principles that God has outlined in His Word."[88]

So must all Christians do what the rich young ruler would not — sell all and give to the poor — as a prerequisite for discipleship? Clearly not; one need turn no further than the Lukan version of this encounter (Luke 18:18-30) to find closely juxtaposed narratives in which would-be disciples gave up only (!) half (Zacchaeus — Luke 19:1-10) or none of their goods. In the latter instance, they invested their capital to be used for God's kingdom (the parable of the pounds — 19:11-27).[89] Even in the earlier Markan account, it is clear that Jesus' command is based on what stands in the way of this specific individual's ability to become a disciple (Mark 10:21b).[90] But again one should be wary of breathing a sigh of relief too quickly. Robert Gundry provocatively captures the paradox present here: "That Jesus did not command all his followers to sell all their possessions gives comfort only to the kind of people to whom he would issue that command!"[91]

But a balancing text must once again intrude to round out this discussion, yet another text which can lay a good claim to essential authenticity.[92] "For what does it a profit a person to gain the whole world and forfeit his or her soul?" (Mark 8:36). This question must be addressed to all forms of liberation theology which become so preoccupied with issues of peace and justice in this life that they neglect the life to come, which will make the sufferings or joys of this present age pale into insignificance in comparison (cf. Rom 8:18). Genuine, saving faith will of necessity transform the use of one's material possessions (Jas 2:14-17, probably alluding to the teaching of Jesus), but sacrificial care for the poor and struggle against injustice without personal allegiance to Jesus as

87. Guelich, *Sermon on the Mount*, 373.

88. G. A. Getz, *A Biblical Theology of Material Possessions* (Chicago: Moody, 1990) 92.

89. W. E. Pilgrim, *Good News to the Poor* (Minneapolis: Augsburg, 1981) 129-34, deduces from this triad that the middle element is the normative one, but this does not naturally follow. Each prevents any of the other two from being absolutized.

90. D. O. Via Jr., *The Ethics of Mark's Gospel — in the Middle of Time* (Philadelphia: Fortress, 1985) 137, charts a good middle ground between over-absolutizing and over-relativizing the text.

91. R. H. Gundry, *Matthew: A Commentary on His Literary and Theological Art* (Grand Rapids, Michigan: Wm. B. Eerdmans, 1982). Cf. also H. N. Ridderbos, *Matthew* (Grand Rapids, Michigan: Zondervan, 1987) 358: "The man of course did not think that his riches were more than eternal life, but he must have told himself that he did not really have to give up his wealth to gain it."

92. W. Rebell, "'Sein Leben verlieren' (Mark 8.35 parr.) als Strukturmoment vor- und nachösterlichen Glaubens," *NTS* 35 (1989) 202-18. Rebell notes a parallel tradition history to that which we have discussed for the healings — authentic Jesus material originally focused primarily on the kingdom of God but was later christologized and ultimately applied to faith.

Lord accomplish nothing of eternal value. In wealth as in health, we must seek the faith which makes us whole — in body and soul.

## 4. Conclusion

The historical Jesus truly does break all molds, including those of the most recent and comprehensive analyses. The historical-critical establishment, particularly in the United States, continues to reject (or simply ignore) much liberationist thought and almost all evangelical research. In fact, these twin arenas jointly point the way forward to a more sober assessment of the true significance of Jesus' words and works. Ironically, most evangelicals and liberation theologians remain as far from each other as they are from traditional liberalism.[93] With the heresy of the so-called "health-wealth gospel" on the one hand and the reductionism of the historical-critical establishment on the other, a balanced evangelical liberation theology, which takes into account all of the canonical data on Jesus, is desperately needed.[94] While liberalism unjustifiably rejects the majority of the Gospel tradition as inauthentic,[95] conservativism *de facto* ignores a substantial portion of Jesus' priorities in its practice. Evangelicals can supply a crucial orthodoxy; liberationists, a much needed orthopraxy. Together, to the extent that the sovereign Spirit of God makes possible in this age, they could transform the world in the name of Jesus, bringing to individuals, people, institutions, and cultures the faith which liberates, heals, eradicates poverty, and brings forgiveness of sins.[96] Such faith can make women and men of all times and places whole.[97]

93. Ironically, because liberation theology consistently accepts more of the Synoptic Gospels' data as actually reflecting the historical Jesus than does traditional historical-critical study. Cf. the liberal complaint by C. Gudorf, "Liberation Theology's Use of Scripture: A Response to First World Critics," *Int* 41 (1987) 11, that liberationists' historical Jesus is often "unusually ample"!

94. Hopeful pointers in the right direction include A. Kirk, *A New World Coming* (London: Marshall, Morgan & Scott, 1983); C. R. Padilla, *Mission Between the Times: Essays on the Kingdom* (Grand Rapids, Michigan: Wm. B. Eerdmans, 1985); and O. E. Costas, *Liberating News: A Theology of Contextual Evangelization* (Grand Rapids, Michigan: Wm. B. Eerdmans, 1989).

95. For a defense of the substantial historicity of the canonical data, see C. L. Blomberg, *The Historical Reliability of the Gospels* (Leicester: Inter-Varsity; Downers Grove, Illinois: InterVarsity Press, 1987).

96. On a more popular and practical level, particularly helpful and challenging are R. J. Sider, *Rich Christians in an Age of Hunger*, rev. ed. (Dallas: Word, 1990); F. Tillapaugh, *The Church Unleashed* (Ventura: Regal, 1982); and T. Sine, *Wild Hope* (Dallas: Word, 1991).

97. Because of the writings of Professor I. Howard Marshall, I was led to apply for Ph.D. studies in the University of Aberdeen. Because of Professor Marshall's expert supervision and constant encouragement I was able to complete that degree. Because of the cross-cultural education I received living and worshiping among the Scots and learning among a large international (esp. Third World) community of students, I first became sensitized to many of the issues reflected in this essay. It is with profound gratitude for his being a major part of what my wife and I still consider the best three years of our lives (1979-82) that I am deeply honored to have been invited to contribute to such a celebratory volume for Professor Marshall.

# Jesus the Baptist?

R. T. France

Ragnar Leivestad commits himself to the confident claim, "Aside from the crucifixion, the most secure historical fact about Jesus is that he was one of those who came to John the Baptist to be baptized."[1] There can be no doubt that it was in the context of John's baptizing ministry that Jesus' mission took shape, and there seems no reason to doubt the testimony of the Gospels that the model which naturally occurred to Jesus' contemporaries in trying to categorize his ministry was that of a successor to the Baptist (Mark 6:14; 8:28). Indeed, the Synoptic Jesus seems to go out of his way to reinforce the connection when he links himself with John as those whose message the people did not want to hear (Matt 11:16-19), and defends his own authority by an appeal to that of John (Mark 11:27-33). And even the Gospel of John, for all its systematic subordination of John to Jesus (John 1:7-8, 15, 19-27; 3:28-30; etc.), records the parallel ministry of the two baptizing groups centered on John and Jesus in 3:22-23; 4:1-2.

Yet in the Gospel accounts after that point baptism apparently plays no part as a factor in Jesus' ministry, so that when in Matt 28:19 the risen Jesus sends his disciples out to baptize this comes as a bolt from the blue, and looks like a throwback to the earliest phase of the Gospel story. This study aims, then, to consider the relation between Christian baptism and the baptism of John in the light of the relation between John and Jesus in the Gospel tradition. In particular it aims to explore how far Jesus really was, and thought himself to be, what popular opinion made him — a second Baptist.

1. R. Leivestad, *Jesus in His Own Perspective* (Minneapolis: Augsburg, 1987) 32. For a similar estimate see E. P. Sanders, *Jesus and Judaism* (London: SCM, 1985) 91-93.

## 1. The Significance of John[2]

Christian tradition has for so long consigned John to the role of a curtain raiser that it has been necessary for recent scholarship to re-emphasize his importance, both in the Jewish world of his time and in the Gospel tradition.

Some Christians are surprised, even shocked, to discover that Josephus gives a more substantial notice to John than he does to Jesus. (The contrast is even greater if it is concluded that the Christianized version of the *Testimonium Flavianum* is a pure fabrication rather than an adaptation of a less laudatory or even hostile notice by Josephus himself.)[3] The brief account in *Ant.* 18.116-19 shows John not only as sufficiently prominent to draw Antipas's attention and suspicion and to justify his execution as a potential leader of rebellion, but also as so well known and respected that people naturally attributed Antipas's subsequent military defeat to his unjust elimination of John.

Josephus's portrait marks John as what we might call a religious revivalist. As such he does not fit neatly into any of the standard categories of Jewish politics and piety in the first century, since his solitary, ascetic life contrasts even with the monastic regime of Qumran. A similar figure some thirty years later achieves a brief mention in Josephus's autobiography: Josephus in his youth spent three years in search of spiritual purification under the direction of Bannus, an ascetic holy man living in the wilderness (*Vita* 11). There may well have been other such figures, but John is the one who has left the most obvious mark in history.

The Gospels tell us that people saw John as a prophet. Even if not everyone would have subscribed to the dogma that prophecy ceased with Malachi,[4] this designation places him on a level above that of the ordinary religious teacher. Recent studies of the NT period agree in regarding John as a very important figure in the religious world of his day, one who set a new benchmark by which those who followed (including Jesus) must be assessed.

Thus the first of the three sections which make up B. F. Meyer's study of

2. For all aspects of the ministry and significance of John the Baptist see now R. L. Webb, *John the Baptizer and Prophet: A Socio-Historical Study,* JSNTSS 62 (Sheffield: JSOT, 1991). Webb's important study was not available to me when writing the first draft of this paper, but I have taken the opportunity to make appropriate references in the notes.

3. The debate on the *Testimonium Flavianum* shows no sign of slackening. The careful survey by P. Winter in E. Schürer, *The History of the Jewish People in the Age of Jesus Christ (175 B.C.–A.D. 135),* vol. 1, rev. ed., ed. G. Vermes and F. Millar (Edinburgh: T. & T. Clark, 1973) 428-41, shows opinions fairly evenly divided as to whether Josephus wrote anything at this point about Jesus. For a more recent and fascinating account of the debate see J. N. Birdsall, "The Continuing Enigma of Josephus's Testimony about Jesus," *BJRL* 67 (1984-85) 609-22.

4. D. E. Aune, *Prophecy in Early Christianity and the Ancient Mediterranean World* (Grand Rapids, Michigan: Wm. B. Eerdmans, 1983) 103- 6, demonstrates effectively that this was a dogma restricted to certain Jewish circles, and does not represent the general Jewish perception. See further Aune, *Prophecy,* 129-32, for the prophetic character of John the Baptist.

the "aims of Jesus" is devoted to Jesus and John the Baptist, since "the beginning of Jesus' public career is inextricably bound up with the public career of John the Baptist. Both careers were prophetic appeals to the nation."[5] Similarly, J. A. T. Robinson presents the Johannine account of the story of Jesus in three phases, the beginning, the middle, and the end — and "the beginning" is focused on Jesus' early days as a disciple of John and his continuation of John's mission.[6]

Joachim Jeremias[7] wonders what is the right starting point for an account of the proclamation of Jesus, and points out that to start with Jesus' call to repentance in the light of the coming of the kingdom of heaven (Matt 4:17) will not do, since the same call has already been issued by John the Baptist (Matt 3:2). So is John the proper starting point? After a lengthy discussion, he concludes that important as John's ministry was as the context within which Jesus' proclamation must be located, the real starting point is not in the ministry of John himself, but in "the call which Jesus experienced when he was baptized by John."[8]

Few would doubt the importance of that observation, but I wonder whether it does full justice to the significance of John in the Gospel accounts of Jesus' ministry.[9]

## 2. Jesus as John's Successor

Matthew in particular seems keen to stress the continuity between the ministry of John and that of Jesus. Not only do both begin their public ministry with exactly the same proclamation (Matt 3:2; 4:17), but almost every phrase of Matthew's account of John's preaching is echoed, in content and often in phraseology, in his subsequent presentation of the teaching of Jesus. The most obvious such echoes are as follows:[10]

- Matt 3:2; cf. 4:17
- Matt 3:7; cf. 12:34; 23:33
- Matt 3:8; cf. 7:16-20; 12:33
- Matt 3:9; cf. 8:11-12
- Matt 3:10; cf. 7:19
- Matt 3:12; cf. 13:30

5. B. F. Meyer, *The Aims of Jesus* (London: SCM, 1979) 115-28.

6. J. A. T. Robinson, *The Priority of John* (London: SCM, 1985) esp. 168-89.

7. J. Jeremias, *New Testament Theology* (London: SCM, 1971) 42.

8. Jeremias, *New Testament Theology,* 56.

9. For a full study of the relations between Jesus and John the Baptist, which at several points supports the arguments of this paper, see E. Linnemann, "Jesus und der Taufer," in *Festschrift für Ernst Fuchs,* ed. G. Ebeling et al. (Tübingen: J. C. B. Mohr [Paul Siebeck], 1973) 219-36.

10. For a list of further similarities (not limited to Matthew) see Jeremias, *New Testament Theology,* 48.

This is not to suggest that there are no differences between the two preachers and their messages. Matthew 11:16-19 makes their different style and impact vividly clear. But the differences mark not a contradictory direction, but rather a development in which continuity is more evident than discontinuity, and which is in any case required by John's own contrast between his water baptism and the Spirit baptism to be instituted by the "coming one" (Mark 1:7-8).

Matthew's emphasis on the continuity between John and Jesus is supported by the instinctive assumption of Antipas (Mark 6:14), and of people in general (Mark 8:28), that in Jesus John the Baptist lived again.

It is also reinforced by the fact that references to John the Baptist occur quite frequently in the Synoptic accounts of Jesus' ministry, and in each case the inference is suggested that the two men stand in the same prophetic line. In Luke 11:1-4 Jesus teaches his disciples to pray just as John had done. In Matt 11:1-15 Jesus presents himself as the one John was expecting to succeed him, and endorses John's ministry as "more than a prophet," the one in whom the period of preparation has come to an end and the period of fulfillment has dawned. In Matt 11:16-19 John and Jesus, despite their different styles of ministry, are bracketed together as representing the wisdom of God over against the unreceptiveness of "this generation." In Mark 9:11-13 the fate of John (as "Elijah") is a model for that of Jesus (as "the Son of Man"). In Mark 11:27-33 Jesus' counterquestion about the authority of John is not a pointless trick to escape giving a straight answer, but a clear claim to a continuity of mission: the authority by which John operated is that of Jesus also, and the implication that it is a divine authority is barely veiled. In Matt 21:28-32 the parable which follows that claim is applied to the leaders' failure to respond to the teaching of John: their attitude to John's "way of righteousness" is a ready indicator of their response to Jesus' preaching of the kingdom of God. To reject the one is to prove themselves unfit for the other.[11]

Jesus was, in more than a merely chronological sense, John's successor. We shall discuss later whether it is appropriate to describe him as John's disciple. At any rate, he identified himself closely with John's mission, and understood himself as carrying it on where John had left off.

But John's mission was focused, at least in the popular perception which gave him his traditional epithet, in the rite of baptism. What then was the

11. This section of the paper has focused on the Synoptic tradition as developed in Mark and, particularly, Matthew. The element of continuity is less clear in Luke; indeed, H. Conzelmann, *The Theology of St. Luke* (London: Faber, 1960) 22-27, believes that Luke deliberately separates John from Jesus, so that he is not even Jesus' forerunner, but merely "the greatest prophet." J. A. Fitzmyer, *Luke the Theologian* (London: Chapman, 1989) 102-10, defends the traditional view that Luke understood John as Jesus' precursor, though with a less defined sense of continuity than we find in Matthew.

meaning of that baptism, and what place does it have in our understanding of the mission of Jesus?

## 3. The Meaning of John's Baptism[12]

Recent archeological discovery has underlined the importance of ritual washing in Jewish religious life in the Second Temple period. Visitors to the south side of the temple area in Jerusalem are shown an impressive range of what are thought to have been *mikwa'ot,* cisterns allowing total immersion of a worshiper prior to entering the temple. Synagogues, too, had their own *mikwa'ot* (found, e.g., at Masada and at Chorazin), and the Qumran ruins contain prominent, stepped cisterns thought to have been used for ritual ablutions. The Mishnah tractate *Mikwa'ot* shows how significant this aspect of Jewish piety had become by the late second century, and there is no reason to doubt that it was already so at the turn of the era.

But such ablutions were a regular and repeated feature of pious observance,[13] and were a personal and private matter. John's "washing," however, was according to both Josephus and the Gospels a single, public act, marking the end of an old phase of life and the commitment to a new relationship with God ("repentance"). Was there, then, any parallel in current Jewish practice to such an "initiatory" washing?

One such has been suggested at Qumran. Most ablutions at Qumran seem to have fit the general Jewish pattern of repeated purification. But 1QS 2:25–3:12 envisages a man who has refused God's covenant, and whose behavior has rendered him "unclean," so that no ablution can cleanse him; but after a change of heart he may be restored to the community, and then "his flesh is sprinkled with purifying water and sanctified by cleansing water" as part of his rehabilitation to the community. This looks like a more drastic "conversion" experience than that involved in regular ablutions.[14]

That is, however, only a single text. A more obvious parallel is the baptism of proselytes, a regular component in the process whereby a Gentile entered the community of Israel. The origins of the practice are not clear, though its symbolism is obvious. But there is good reason to believe that it was standard

12. For a full study of religious ablution in first-century Judaism see Webb, *John the Baptizer,* 95-162.

13. Note that even Bannus, who is in other respects apparently a close parallel to John the Baptist, used to wash "day and night frequently." In this his practice is closer to that of Qumran than to that of the Baptist.

14. Webb, *John the Baptizer,* 140-52, discusses this text in detail. He goes on to argue from this and other texts that ablutions at Qumran were used for both initiatory and restorative purposes (summary, 159-62).

practice in pre-Christian Judaism,[15] and was therefore the natural background against which John's single "initiatory" baptism would be understood. If the Qumran text just mentioned suggested that washing symbolized readmission to the pure community of the people of God, the baptism of a proselyte marked the initial admission to that community of one who until that point lived in Gentile "uncleanness." It is not just an act of personal piety, but has a community dimension. It is a mark of belonging to the people of God.

Jeremias[16] mentions in this connection that the Hillelite scribes, in order to provide a scriptural basis for proselyte baptism, taught that Israel, too, had undergone "immersion" when they entered the covenant at Sinai (*b. Ker.* 9a; cf. *b. Yebam.* 46b), though it is not clear whether the reference was to the crossing of the Red Sea (cf. 1 Cor 10:1-2) or to the sprinkling with blood in Exodus 24. This is a further indication of the Jewish significance of baptism as a mark of entering (or in the case of Qumran, reentering) the true people of God.

All this suggests that John's choice of baptism as the visible focus of his ministry was intended to symbolize not only, or even primarily, the determination of the individual to lead a new life, but rather the entry into a new community.[17] Its significance was essentially ecclesial.[18]

But of course the striking difference between John's baptism and the baptism of proselytes was that John was calling *Jews* to be baptized. He was thus, in effect, saying to them, "You are not yet the true people of God; that requires more than the accident of birth into the 'covenant community.' Israel is subject to judgement, and it is only those who respond to God's call to repentance who will prove to be truly his people. Without it, you are no better than Gentiles." Here is the classical "remnant" theology of the OT prophets, who persistently attacked Israel's reliance on their covenant status and the temple cult which was its symbol, when their life and worship were no better

15. See the classic study by H. H. Rowley, "Jewish Proselyte Baptism and the Baptism of John," *HUCA* 15 (1940) 313-34; reprinted in his *From Moses to Qumran* (London: Lutterworth, 1963) 211-35. More briefly, J. Jeremias, *Infant Baptism in the First Four Centuries* (London: SCM, 1960) 24-29. Webb, *John the Baptizer,* 122-30, criticizes Jeremias's arguments, and suggests that the lack of clear documentary evidence for proselyte baptism before 70 C.E. indicates that the practice did not antedate the fall of the temple. Even if his dismissal of Jeremias's data is accepted (and it is at several points not a matter of firm proof), it must still be asked whether silence may in this case properly be used as evidence for the absence of the practice. If not by "baptism," how *were* proselytes "enrolled" at an earlier date? All agree that the practice was established after 70 C.E., and the assumption by that date that it was the norm might better be used as evidence that, even if not specifically mentioned earlier, it was already established.

16. *Infant Baptism,* 31-32; cf. *idem, New Testament Theology,* 44.

17. A similar idea may underlie Josephus's statement (*Ant.* 18.117) that John called on his hearers to use baptism not as a means of gaining forgiveness for sins, but as a bodily "consecration" in the light of the fact that their soul was already purified.

18. Webb, *John the Baptizer,* 209, while doubting that proselyte baptism antedates 70 C.E., nonetheless sees it as analogous in important respects to John's baptism.

than that of pagans.[19] In similar vein, John challenges the Israel of his day, "Don't imagine you can say to yourselves, 'We have Abraham as our father.' For I tell you that God can raise up children for Abraham from these very stones" (Matt 3:9).

The statement that John's baptism was focused on "the forgiveness of sins" naturally leads Western minds to think of it as a matter of *individual* piety and salvation. But as B. F. Meyer rightly points out, "It is historically out of the question that John conceived judgment along the individualistic lines characteristic of later Western thought. Rather, he conceived judgment in collective, or better, 'ecclesial', terms, i.e., in terms of 'God's people, Israel'. "[20] Of course it was as individuals responded to John's message that the restored community could come into being; it was precisely by being willing to mark themselves out by baptism from the bulk of the nation that they became members of the "remnant." But the result was not to be a solipsistic experience of salvation, but the renewal of Israel.

It is one of the great merits of Meyer's study of *The Aims of Jesus* that he has emphasized this ecclesial dimension to the ministry of John — and therefore also to that of his successor, Jesus. "The Baptist's career was an *Entscheidungsruf* (call to decision) which implied not a christology but an ecclesiology, not the closed ecclesiology of a reformist sect but the assembling by baptism of an open remnant: the Israel of the converted, soon to be purified by Spirit and fire.' "[21]

This focus on the eschatological renewal of Israel gives added point to the emphatic characterization of John's ministry as taking place "in the wilderness" (Mark 1:3, 4, 12, 13). It was in the wilderness that Israel had been formed into the people of God (Deuteronomy 1–8 *passim*, esp. 8:2-6), and the prophets thereafter looked back to the wilderness experiences as the "honeymoon period" when the relationship between Israel and its God had been pure and unspoiled (Jer 2:2-3). It was natural, then, that eschatological hopes should also focus on a new exodus and a new wilderness experience, when the physical transformation of the wilderness would symbolize the new life of the eschatological Israel (Hos 2:14-15; Ezek 20:34-38; Isa 40:3; 41:18-19; 43:19-21; 44:3-5; etc.). It was this hope which had led the people of Qumran, in obedience to Isa 40:3, to make their home in the wilderness (1QS 8:13-14; cf. 9:19-21), and Josephus records a series of would-be leaders of Israel who typically collected a following in the wilderness area around the Jordan valley in the hope of launching there

19. In speaking of John's as a "remnant theology" I am not wishing to deny a desire on his part to restore *all* Israel to their true obedience as the people of Yahweh, as is argued effectively, e.g., by Sanders, *Jesus,* ch. 3. But such a mission, if it does not result in a response on the part of the people as a whole, becomes inevitably a call to form a true remnant over against the unfaithful majority.

20. Meyer, *Aims of Jesus,* 117.

21. Meyer, *Aims of Jesus,* 220.

the decisive movement for the restoration of Israel.[22] "The wilderness" is where you would expect the renewal of Israel to begin.[23]

The movement launched by John in the wilderness, and popularly characterized as a baptizing ministry, was then in essence a prophetic call for the eschatological renewal of Israel by gathering a repentant and forgiven "remnant" from within Israel. Baptism was the rite of enrollment in this restored Israel, a mark of belonging to the true people of God.[24]

## 4. The Provisional Character of John's Baptism

Josephus does not explicitly mention an eschatological focus to John's preaching (though Antipas's fear of an insurrection resulting may suggest that John was understood to preach not only holiness of life but also the promise of better things to come). But the Gospel accounts are all strongly forward-looking, not only in that John warned people to prepare for divine judgment to come, but also in that he saw himself as the forerunner of "someone stronger" (ἰσχυρότερος), who would so far exceed him in authority that John was not even qualified to act as his slave (Mark 1:7 par.; John 1:27).

The Synoptic tradition identified John as the forerunner predicted in Mal 3:1 and the returning Elijah who is to precede the Day of the Lord in Mal 3:23-24 (*EVV* 4:5-6). Both these passages in Malachi indicate that it will be "the Lord" himself who will follow the forerunner; neither suggests any intermediate messianic figure.[25] To identify John with this forerunner therefore has interesting christological implications, which we cannot explore here.[26] But whatever may have been in the mind of those who first saw John in this light, by the time

22. Theudas (*Ant.* 20.97-98; cf. Acts 5:36), "the Egyptian" (*J.W.* 2.261-63; *Ant.* 20.169-72; cf. Acts 21:38), Jonathan the Weaver (*J.W.* 7.43-44), and cf. the general summary of such insurgents in *J.W.* 2.258-60; *Ant.* 20.167-68. Cf. also, with a less political agenda, Bannus (*Vita* 11).

23. See further U. Mauser, *Christ in the Wilderness* (London: SCM, 1963). Cf. the comment of W. Marxsen, *Mark the Evangelist* (Nashville: Abingdon, 1969) 37-38, on the theological significance of the geographical location: ". . . ἐν τῇ ἐρήμῳ qualifies the Baptist as the fulfiller of Old Testament predictive prophecy. Put in exaggerated form, the Baptist would still be the one who appears 'in the wilderness' even if he had never been there in all his life."

24. See Webb, *John the Baptizer,* 197-202, for a fuller demonstration of how John's baptism was intended to be understood as "an initiation into the 'True Israel.'"

25. See my *Jesus and the Old Testament* (London: Tyndale, 1971) 91-92 n. 31; for an alternative exegesis of Mal 3:1 see P. A. Verhoef, *The Books of Haggai and Malachi* (Grand Rapids, Michigan: Wm. B. Eerdmans, 1987) 287-90, but his interpretation likewise allows for no third (messianic) figure.

26. See my *Divine Government: God's Kingship in the Gospel of Mark* (London: SPCK, 1990) 100-101. See Webb, *John the Baptizer,* 282-88, for a careful analysis of the identity of "John's expected figure," concluding that he is described in terms most clearly appropriate to Yahweh, but suggesting nonetheless that John was thinking of someone distinct from Yahweh who would fulfill his eschatological role as his agent.

the Gospels were written it is likely that John's anticipatory role was understood with regard to *Jesus* as the "stronger one" rather than, as Malachi would more naturally suggest, with reference to the coming of God himself. In the Gospel of John this theme is even more strongly emphasized, with the constant repetition of the superiority of Jesus ("the true light") to John, his "witness" (John 1:8, 15, 19-23, 26-27, 29-33; 3:26-30; 5:33-36).

The principal basis for this contrast between John and Jesus, in both Synoptic and Johannine traditions, lies in the fact that John baptizes merely with water, but his successor will baptize with the Holy Spirit (and, in the Q tradition, with fire). The contrast is particularly strongly drawn out in John 1:26-33, where three times over John describes his own baptism as "in water," in order to point forward to his unknown successor who nonetheless "was before me," and on whom the Spirit descends in order to mark him out as the one who baptizes with the Holy Spirit.

The contrast of water and Spirit is then picked up again in John 3:5, where the new birth which ensures entry to the kingdom of God requires both water and Spirit in order to be effective. The point is developed in the following verses, where flesh and Spirit are contrasted, with the implication that water alone could suffice for a new beginning only at the level of "flesh." Such a distinction between the "outward" and the "inward," the superficial and the effective, is common prophetic usage. It suggests that John's water baptism, on its own, could have only an anticipatory value. The real transformation to which it points is that of Spirit baptism, and Spirit baptism is the mark of the "greater" ministry of Jesus.

The persistent suggestion of a link between John the Baptist and the Qumran community gains some support at this point, since a similar recognition of "Spirit baptism" as the basis of true godliness may be found in 1QS 4:20-22, again in an eschatological context: in the future "visitation" God will eradicate the spirit of falsehood from people's flesh, and will cleanse them with the spirit of holiness, sprinkling them with the spirit of truth as with purifying water.[27] The imagery suggests that at Qumran, too, there was a deliberate contrast between merely external purification ("baptism with water") and a more efficacious cleansing still to come ("baptism with Spirit").

Whether or not John ever had direct links with the Qumran community,[28]

27. I assume, with the majority of interpreters, that the "spirit" referred to here is the Spirit of God rather than a human "disposition." The latter view was argued by P. Wernberg-Møller, "A Reconsideration of the Two Spirits in the Rule of the Community (1QSerek III, 13–IV, 26)," *RevQ* 3 (1961) 413-41; it has recently been strongly supported by R. P. Menzies, *The Development of Early Christian Pneumatology,* JSNTSS 54 (Sheffield: JSOT, 1991) 78-80. For a survey of views on the interpretation of the "spirit"-language in 1QS 3:13–4:26, see A. E. Sekki, *The Meaning of Ruaḥ at Qumran* (Atlanta: Scholars, 1989) 193-219.

28. Robinson, *Priority of John,* 175-76, takes this Qumran text as evidence for his contention that John the Baptist had originally been a member of the Qumran community before he launched into his solo mission.

it is this sort of view of purification which underlies the water / Spirit contrast and the understanding of water baptism as merely an anticipation of the true eschatological cleansing. The real thing is still to come, and it will come with Jesus.

## 5. Why Was Jesus Baptized?

Matthew 3:14-15 betrays an embarrassment, not shared with the other canonical Gospels, over the fact of Jesus' baptism. At a later stage of Christian doctrinal development that embarrassment took the form of a simple syllogism: John's baptism was for the forgiveness of sins; Jesus was baptized by John; therefore Jesus could not have been sinless (as Christian orthodoxy from the NT on declared him to be). It is that syllogism which underlies the text from the second-century *Gospel of the Hebrews,* quoted by Jerome,[29] in which Jesus, urged to join his family in receiving John's baptism, replies, "What sin have I committed, that I should go and be baptized by him? Unless perhaps this very thing I have just spoken is ignorance" (and therefore presumably sinful!).

Matthew perhaps already felt the force of that syllogism, since he defuses its first member by not describing John's baptism, as Mark and Luke do, as "a baptism of repentance for the forgiveness of sins" (Mark 1:4; Luke 3:3; contrast Matt 3:2). But John's objection, "I need to be baptized by you, and do you come to me?" (Matt 3:14), should probably be read in terms not primarily of moral comparison, but of the contrast set out in the previous section: "I need your Spirit-and-fire baptism, and do you come for my water baptism?" Jesus is the one whose sandals he is not fit to untie, and his own water baptism is merely a provisional measure to prepare for the real baptism which Jesus will offer.

Even so, Jesus' reply, "This is the right way for us to fulfil all righteousness," does not seem to offer much help![30] Many commentators, following Cullmann,[31] have explained it in the light of the voice from heaven, with its echo of Isa 42:1, marking Jesus out as the Servant of Yahweh who, while himself guiltless, identifies himself with sinners to the extent of carrying their sin on himself. Matthew 3:15 does not say that, of course, but it is possible to see in the odd use of the term δικαιοσύνη an echo of the repeated יצדיק צדיק of Isa 53:11, where the Servant's role is spelled out as achieving righteousness on behalf of many.

That may well be what Matthew intended. But the fact that Jesus' reply says nothing directly about sin and repentance, and that none of the other canonical Evangelists evinces any such embarrassment, suggests that perhaps

29. Jerome *Contra Pelag.* 3.2.

30. It is surprising that the *Gospel of the Ebionites* (also second century, and quoted by Epiphanius *Panarion* 30.13.7-8), while emphasizing Jesus' superiority to John, leaves Matt 3:15 unaltered apart from substituting "everything" for "all righteousness."

31. O. Cullmann, *Baptism in the New Testament* (London: SCM, 1950) 15-19.

the problem felt by the *Gospel of the Hebrews* was an artificial one. It arose from the assumption, still common today, that John's baptism was all about individual sin and forgiveness. But once it is recognized that John's mission was essentially ecclesial, the problem disappears. Jesus' baptism was not an attempt to find personal forgiveness, but his "vote" for John's program of the restoration of Israel. "Jesus . . . underwent John's baptism in order to take his place among the eschatological people of God that the Baptist was assembling."[32]

By accepting John's baptism, Jesus became a member of his new "remnant" community. Members of that community are later referred to as "John's disciples" (Mark 2:18; Matt 11:2; 14:12; John 1:37). Was Jesus then also at first a "disciple of John"? This was asserted by C. H. Dodd,[33] on the grounds that the Gospels refer several times to Jesus as "coming behind *(ὀπίσω)*" John (Mark 1:7; Matt 3:11; John 1:15, 27, 30). We have been used to treating "after me" in these verses as a statement of temporal succession, but Dodd rightly points out that elsewhere in the NT to "come behind" is regularly a term for the status of the disciple. There would in that case be a delicious irony in the description of Jesus in John 1:27 as "my *disciple,* whose sandal thong I am not fit to untie"![34]

J. Ramsey Michaels[35] suggests that Jesus' original status as a disciple of John was an embarrassment to the Synoptic Evangelists, who have therefore omitted any reference to the parallel ministry of John and Jesus which John records (John 3:22-24; 4:1-2), and deliberately present Jesus' public activity as beginning after the imprisonment of John. John, however, "broke the conspiracy of silence"! This is unnecessarily colorful language, especially since the use of ὀπίσω from which Dodd derived his argument is found in Mark and Matthew as well as in John. The embarrassment may perhaps be more in the mind of a modern author for whom the term "disciple" has developed a quasi-technical sense, with a resultant connotation of inferiority. In any case, none of the Gospels uses this term directly of Jesus in relation to John. But they all agree that Jesus was one of those who came to the Jordan to hear John's preaching, who accepted the baptism for which he called, and who therefore formed the basis of the restored Israel which was the object of his mission. It was as a member of that group that Jesus first came to notice, and it was as a follower of John that people naturally tried to understand him.

This is not the only time in history that a "disciple" has eclipsed his or her leader's reputation. The Gospels suggest that that is just what John, like any good teacher, would have wished for.

32. Jeremias, *New Testament Theology,* 49.

33. C. H. Dodd, *Historical Tradition in the Fourth Gospel* (Cambridge: Cambridge University, 1963) 272-74.

34. Robinson, *Priority of John,* 182-83, accepts Dodd's argument, and refers to similar views expressed earlier by M. Goguel and E. Stauffer.

35. J. R. Michaels, *Servant and Son: Jesus in Parable and Gospel* (Atlanta: John Knox, 1981) 19-22.

## 6. Jesus the Baptist?

We are now in a position to address the issue of whether Jesus was himself a "Baptist." That he was perceived by people at the time as a successor to John the Baptist, and that he did not object to being so perceived, seems clear from our study so far. But did he not only follow on from John's call to repentance, but also continue his practice of baptism?

Here the evidence of the Fourth Gospel is crucial. If it were not for John's Gospel, the *only* direct reference to the practice of baptism in the Gospel tradition (apart from the baptism of John, of course) would be Matt 28:19, and that speaks of the future activity of the disciples, not of the practice of Jesus himself. Moreover, as a result of its sophisticated trinitarian formula Matt 28:19 is very generally assumed to be, if not a gloss to the text of Matthew,[36] at least an anachronistic reading back of the later church's baptismal practice, at a relatively late stage in the Gospel tradition. As historical evidence for baptism in the Jesus movement in the pre-Easter period it is therefore accorded little weight.

It is in fact generally assumed that the Jesus movement was not a baptizing movement during Jesus' lifetime. To quote a few typical examples: "Why did Jesus cease to baptize after the arrest of John? . . . the high probability that he did in fact put an end to his baptismal ministry at this point. . . ."[37] "The absolute silence of the first three evangelists compels us to suppose that Jesus did not continue John's ministry of baptism."[38] "We do not know why Jesus did not practise baptism, although both John and the later Christians did."[39]

That last comment provokes the question why this assumption should be so easily made. If baptism both preceded and followed the historical ministry of Jesus, is an argument from silence sufficient ground to assume that it was not part of the ministry of Jesus too? In light of the clear continuity between the ministries of John and Jesus which we have observed already, is it not the safer assumption that this central part of John's mission also continued under his successor, unless there is specific evidence to the contrary?

That it did so continue at least at first is the clear testimony of the Fourth Gospel (John 3:22-24; 4:1-2). These notices relate to the period between the

36. The only textual evidence for the absence of the reference to baptism and the trinitarian formula in Matt 28:19 is the fact that on a number of occasions in Eusebius's pre-Nicene writings he offers the abbreviated quotation "go and make disciples of all nations in my name," though in other works he cites the full text as we know it. On this basis H. Kosmala, "The Conclusion of Matthew," *ASTI* 4 (1965) 132-47, argued for the shorter text as the Matthean original, but few have been convinced. See to the contrary B. J. Hubbard, *The Matthean Redaction of a Primitive Apostolic Commissioning: An Exegesis of Matthew 28:16-20* (Missoula: Scholars, 1974) 151-75. There is no manuscript evidence for the shorter text.

37. Meyer, *Aims of Jesus,* 129.

38. Leivestad, *Jesus in His Own Perspective,* 37.

39. C. S. Rodd, "Talking Points from Books," *ExpTim* 99 (1987-88) 292.

baptism of Jesus and the imprisonment of John (3:24), a period on which the Synoptic Gospels are silent. They indicate a parallel development of the two "baptist" movements side by side, and some such context is needed to account for the quite natural transfer of members of the one group into the other which is recorded in John 1:35-42. Moreover, this understanding of the beginning of the Jesus movement can not easily be dismissed as a Johannine fiction, in the light of the comment in Acts 1:21-22 that an acceptable witness to the historical ministry of Jesus must be someone who had been part of the movement "the whole time that the Lord Jesus came and went among us, beginning from John's baptism until the day when he was taken up from us."

Evidence for continuing friendly contact between the two groups is found in John 10:40-42, where Jesus escapes from pressure in Jerusalem to the scene of John's earlier baptizing ministry, and there meets with a friendly reception from those who apparently recognize in him John's designated successor. And again the Synoptic tradition reinforces the Johannine, in that in Matt 14:12 it is to Jesus that John's disciples naturally turn after their master's death. Would so cordial a link have been maintained if Jesus had now abandoned the rite which had been the hallmark of their master's ministry?

Those who are inclined to give historical credence to the Johannine notices of Jesus' early baptizing ministry generally take it for granted, on the basis of the silence of the Gospel tradition, that after the arrest of John the baptizing stopped. This is sometimes assumed to be because it was now politically dangerous to be so obviously linked with a prophet who had fallen foul of the establishment;[40] others offer the more theological reason that in the presence of the "coming one" there was no need for the forerunner's rite to be continued and for baptism with water to be offered where Spirit baptism was now available.[41]

But could baptism be so easily dispensed with? If both John and Jesus (while John was still around) had used this visible means of marking out those who opted to join the new community of the restored people of God, how else were new adherents to the Jesus movement to be enrolled? Moreover, if baptism had not been a feature of the Jesus movement during Jesus' earthly ministry, how are we to account for the fact that from the very beginning of the story in Acts it is universally assumed that baptism is the proper and essential means of Christian initiation? (Note, too, the insistence of Acts 1:1-2 that the story in Acts marks not a new beginning but the continuation of what Jesus had already begun.) Perhaps Jesus' command in Matt 28:19 (if, unusually, it is accepted as a historical saying of Jesus) might account for the immediate and universal acceptance of such an innovation, but I would suggest that it is a more economical explanation to interpret the silence of the Gospels as indicating the continuation of John's rite of initiation, rather than its absence.

40. So, e.g., Jeremias, *New Testament Theology,* 46.

41. Leivestad, *Jesus in His Own Perspective,* 37-38; cf. Meyer, *Aims of Jesus,* 129.

The hypothesis of the cessation of baptism during Jesus' ministry raises the interesting (and ultimately unanswerable) question of how those who led the post-Pentecost church were themselves "enrolled." Some of them had received baptism from John, but presumably not all Jesus' disciples were taken over from John. If Christian baptism was a post-Easter innovation, were those previously baptized by John now rebaptized (like the Ephesian disciples of Acts 19:1-7)? And when, if at all, were the others baptized? Did the three thousand baptized on the day of Pentecost (Acts 2:41) include not only new converts but the whole existing Jesus movement?

There are, of course, two references to baptism in the Synoptic tradition of Jesus' sayings before Easter, Luke 12:49-50 and Mark 10:38-39. Both use baptism as a metaphor for Jesus' future suffering, or, as Meyer puts it, his "eschatological vocation."[42] It represents his being set apart for a special role in relation to the time of eschatological fulfillment, a symbolism John the Baptist would surely have recognized. Neither saying relates directly to the practice of baptism, but the choice of metaphor would be the more cogent if baptism had remained a significant feature of the Jesus movement.

There is, then, good reason to believe that baptism did not fall into disuse after the imprisonment of John, only to be reintroduced suddenly after the resurrection, but that it remained for Jesus, as it had been for John, the normal means of enrolling those who joined this eschatological restoration movement. Not only at the beginning, but throughout his ministry, Jesus was a second "Baptist."

## 7. Water and Spirit

This is not to suggest, however, that nothing changed with the end of John's ministry. John baptized with water, but his successor was to baptize with the Holy Spirit. Does this new dimension then not render water baptism unnecessary? Is it not even a potential source of confusion, tempting those who receive it to rest content with the outward at the expense of the inward (a problem which has remained with us ever since)? It is on such grounds, as we have seen, that some explain Jesus' presumed abandonment of baptism.

Yet this does not seem to have been a difficulty for the post-Pentecost church. The gift of the Spirit was a central aspect of their understanding of salvation,[43] but this did not lead to any devaluing of water baptism. Indeed, the two are regularly mentioned in the same breath (Acts 2:38; 8:12-17; 9:17-18;

42. Meyer, *Aims of Jesus,* 217.

43. Note, however, the argument of Menzies, *Early Christian Pneumatology,* in opposition to J. D. G. Dunn, that Luke saw the gift of the Spirit as an endowment for prophetic ministry rather than as of soteriological significance: "Luke . . . does not present reception of the Spirit as necessary for one to enter into and remain with the community of salvation" (279).

10:44-48; 11:15-17; 19:5-6). The coming of the Spirit at Pentecost, far from making water baptism irrelevant, is the point from which the regular practice of baptism becomes explicit in the church. There seems little force, then, in the argument that baptism would have been out of place in Jesus' ministry *before* the outpouring of the Spirit at Pentecost.

It is in any case perhaps too simple to equate the fulfillment of John's prophecy about "baptizing with Holy Spirit" directly and only with the event of Pentecost. John's words do not relate so much to a particular event as to the whole scope of Jesus' ministry. He will operate on a different level from John; he will offer real, inward renewal in contrast with John's external, symbolic washing. In that sense (as John 20:22 also suggests), baptism with the Holy Spirit was already the experience of Jesus' disciples even before the event in the upper room made the reality dramatically visible, and launched these Spirit-filled disciples out on their mission.

Jesus' words to Nicodemus about water and spirit point the same way.[44] Following the repeated contrast between the two styles of "baptism" in John 1:26-33 the most natural reading of 3:5 is that here Jesus refers to both outward and inward washing, to the necessity not only of water baptism but also of spiritual renewal, as indeed the following verses make clear. What then was Jesus asking of Nicodemus (and presumably of other would-be disciples of whom John presents Nicodemus as typical)? Was he to accept water baptism now, but to wait until after Jesus has been glorified for the real thing? And if he was to accept baptism now, was it to be John's baptism (or Jesus' during the brief remaining period before John's imprisonment)? If so, presumably the demand made of Nicodemus could have no bearing on those who followed Jesus after John's imprisonment, if baptism was then in abeyance. It is surely more satisfactory to conclude that to follow Jesus continued to carry the promise made to Nicodemus, of "birth by water and spirit," that they would be baptized into the Jesus movement, and would there experience the inward renewal which he required. Or was it to remain impossible to "enter the kingdom of God" until after Jesus' earthly ministry?[45]

Jesus' ministry, then, is in continuity with that of John, but now including, as John himself had predicted, the new and central element of baptism with the Holy Spirit. This new dimension no more renders water baptism obsolete

44. That this may be pre-Johannine tradition is suggested by the fact that the language of "seeing" and "entering the kingdom of God" is more typical of the Synoptic tradition than of John, who nowhere else uses "the kingdom of God."

45. See the interesting discussion of John 3:3-5 by Robinson, *Priority of John,* 184-85, drawing on the earlier remarks of Armitage Robinson. It must be recognized, of course, that John *is* often interpreted, largely on the basis of 7:37-39, as denying any experience of the Spirit before Jesus' glorification. This is not the place to enter that debate, but an interesting introduction to it is provided by the "debate" between M. M. B. Turner and G. M. Burge in "*The Anointed Community:* A Review and Response," *EvQ* 62 (1990) 253-68.

during Jesus' ministry than it did in the post-Pentecost church. For Jesus, as for John and for Jesus' followers after his death and resurrection, baptism remains the proper symbol of entry into new life, of belonging to the eschatological people of God.

## 8. The Great Commission

When at the end of Matthew's Gospel Jesus sends his disciples out to "make disciples of all nations," the first element in that disciple-making is baptism, followed by teaching (these being the two participles which function together to specify the nature of "disciple-making"). In the light of our previous discussion this may not have been the complete surprise which most commentators have to assume. Rather than introducing a new rite, oddly reminiscent of John's practice which, *ex hypothesi,* Jesus had earlier deliberately abandoned, the risen Jesus is in fact simply instructing his followers to continue with the practice which has throughout his ministry been the normal and expected visible form of "disciple-making." There are surprises enough in the christology of these verses (Jesus' universal kingship, the inclusion of all nations, the trinitarian basis of discipleship, the substitution of Jesus' commands for those of God as its focus, the assurance of Jesus' permanent presence) without introducing another with the "reinvention" of baptism.

The sequence of the two elements in disciple-making (baptizing . . . teaching) does not correspond to most current church practice, at least where the baptism of adults is concerned. We generally baptize only *after* extensive teaching and examination. Baptism thus becomes a retrospective mark of having become a disciple, rather than an element in disciple-making. Is there then anything to be said for reexamining our practice in the light of the sequence of the two participles in Matt 28:19-20?

This has been argued passionately in a surprisingly little-known book by R. Brow, *Go Make Learners: A New Model for Discipleship in the Church.*[46] In a wide-ranging study of the NT, Brow argues that baptism was not the culmination but the beginning of the process of becoming a disciple. Converts in Acts were baptized immediately, not after extensive preparation and examination. From "the biblical practice of immediate baptism" Brow argues that the Christian church is to be understood on the model of a school, in which people are enrolled, by baptism, *in order to* learn. The baptized community is a community of learners, not of those who have already arrived. Baptism is a mark of commitment to learn, not a sort of "graduation."

46. Wheaton: Harold Shaw, 1981. The cover carries the opinion of J. I. Packer: "Some books can be safely ignored, but not this one." Unfortunately, at least on this side of the Atlantic, I fear that Packer's words have not been heeded.

Brow therefore believes that the order of the participles in Matt 28:19-20 is both deliberate and highly significant. By baptizing we mark people out as "learners," and it is then our responsibility to make sure that they find within the church the opportunity to learn "all that Jesus commanded." There are clearly important implications from this thesis both for the theology of baptism (and in particular the rationale of infant baptism) and for its pastoral outworking, in the debates which rage between the "indiscriminate" and "rigorist" approaches. It was the insistent pressure of these pastoral questions, and his experience of working them out in practice in his ministry in Anglican churches in Canada, which led Brow to write *Go Make Learners*, and I commend his book to the attention of those who wish to pursue them. For our present purposes, however, I believe that his "school-enrollment" model helps us to understand the function of baptism within the Jesus movement, both before and after Jesus' death and resurrection.

But discipleship is not a merely intellectual process, and baptism is not into an educational program but into a relationship. It is "into the name of the Father and of the Son and of the Holy Spirit." We do not here need to pursue the issue of the authenticity of this phrase as a saying of Jesus, on which I have commented elsewhere.[47] The solemn formula serves to identify the personal allegiance which baptism denotes, the Master into whose "school" the disciple is thus initiated.

For John the Baptist the "object" of the baptized's commitment was of course the God of Israel. In Christian baptism this remains true, but the coming of Jesus has led to a fuller understanding of who that God is. Jesus was to "baptize with the Holy Spirit," and the Holy Spirit now appears within the formula denoting the object of baptism. But even more remarkably so does the Son, whom any Christian reader knows can be no other than Jesus himself. Thus Jesus the Baptizer takes his place alongside Father and Holy Spirit as the object of that baptism.

It is here, above all, that the new dimension of Christian baptism is seen. It is in this respect in particular that the baptism of John must prove inadequate. Jesus has continued it with a new level of significance, to the extent that John's baptism alone will no longer suffice. That is why in Acts those who have been baptized only with the baptism of John stand in need of further instruction (Acts 18:24-26), and even of rebaptism (19:1-7).

Here, as elsewhere in Jesus' dealings with the preceding forms of religion, the balance between continuity and discontinuity has to be carefully discerned. I have argued above that there was a greater degree of continuity between John the Baptist and Jesus than is generally admitted, to the extent that Jesus could properly be recognized as a second Baptist. But the second does not merely

47. *History, Criticism and Faith*, ed. C. Brown (London: Inter-Varsity, 1976) 130-31; R. T. France, *Matthew: Evangelist and Teacher* (Exeter: Paternoster, 1989) 316-17. Cf. above, n. 36.

replicate the ministry of the first, but carries it to a higher level, as John himself had said he must: "He must increase, but I must decrease." To stay as a disciple of John the Baptist once the "stronger one" has come is to miss the fulfillment of God's purpose for the restoration of his people. It is in the christological crescendo of the Great Commission that John's ministry is finally fulfilled, and sent into honorable retirement.

# Disciples of Jesus

Leon Morris

The term μαθητής was in common use in the Greek writings for a learner, a student. But in an educational system very different from any of those with which we are familiar in modern times there came to be a special significance in the master-student relationship. Students not only learned facts, but came to take up the essential position of their revered teachers. They accepted not only the teachings but also their teachers. It was not simply a matter of acquiring useful knowledge but of coming to follow a whole way of life.[1] This might refer not only to the following of a living teacher, but to a wholehearted acceptance of the teachings of someone who had long since died. There were disciples of Plato, for example, who lived long after the death of that great teacher. They wholeheartedly accepted what he had taught and gladly identified themselves with him.

Of course, there was wide variation. Teaching some things must have been more or less routine. We do not know all the details of the way people learned to write, for example. But obviously there had to be a good deal of standard instruction in conveying the techniques of using the materials commonly employed in putting words in written form. This must have been the case also in the acquiring of other routine skills. Such instruction would not necessarily involve personal attachment to a teacher. But where more was involved than the acquisition of a technique, the acceptance of the revered teacher's essential position was a characteristic of most studies.

We must also be on our guard against subconsciously assuming that the learning process then was much the same as ours today. The cost of writing materials and the difficulties involved in using the materials then available meant that our habit of making notes would not have been the method then. Certainly a good deal more emphasis was placed on memory than is the case with us, and disciples would commit to memory quite long

1. K. H. Rengstorf says of the corresponding verb, μανθάνω, that it "denotes from the very outset an intellectual process which serves to develop the personality" ("μανθάνω," *TDNT,* 4:393).

passages,[2] even whole books.[3] And there may well have been other important differences.

It would of course have been possible to acquire the technique of writing without accepting the positions held by the teacher. But in the absence of detailed information about scribal schools we do not know how common this was. We do know that the term μαθητής, while it could signify simply a learner, came to have the fuller meaning of one who accepted the teacher. In other words, while it could denote someone in the role of an apprentice to a trade, it could also convey the fuller sense of students committed to the position of the master teachers they followed.

How fully this was accepted in OT Israel is not clear. The disciple-teacher terminology is certainly not found in the writings available to us. But instruction did of course take place: how else can a body of learning be passed on from generation to generation? There was certainly a respect for "wisdom" in ancient Israel, and this implies a system of instructing neophytes. The word *talmidh* (the Hebrew equivalent of μαθητής and a term commonly used in the later rabbinical schools) occurs only once in the OT (1 Chr 25:8), and that for the instruction given to budding temple musicians. But this does not tell us what happened in the training of scribes like, for example, Ezra (Ezra 7:1-6, 11-12). We are left to surmise. It is possible that there was something not fundamentally different from the Greek process. Or the Israelites may have developed a different system. We simply do not know.

## "Disciple" in the New Testament

"Disciple," μαθητής, occurs 73 times in Matthew, 46 times in Mark, 37 times in Luke, 78 times in John, and 28 times in Acts. Interestingly, it is found nowhere else in the NT. The corresponding verb, μαθητεύω, is much rarer, being found three times in Matthew and elsewhere only once in Acts. But the number of occurrences of the noun show that discipleship was a significant concept in

2. M. J. Wilkins quotes Schürer, "Instruction consisted in a continuous exercise of the memory. For since the aim was to imprint on the pupil's mind the whole subject, in all its countless details, and since moreover the oral Torah was not to be written down, one lesson could never suffice. The teacher had to repeat his material with his pupils over and over again" (*The Concept of Disciple in Matthew's Gospel,* NovTSup 59 [Leiden: E. J. Brill, 1988] 119).

3. B. Gerhardsson makes it clear that a very great deal was committed to memory in the rabbinic schools. "A fully-qualified *tanna,*" he says, "must know (repeat) all the most important collections of tradition (in the form in which they existed at that time): Mishnah, Sifra, Sifre and Tosefta, in the same way as a Scripture specialist (קרא) must know (read) the whole of Scripture accurately (certainly also from memory) — the Law, the Prophets and the writings" (*Memory and Manuscript* [Lund: Gleerup, 1961] 96). See further R. Riesner, *Jesus als Lehrer: Eine Untersuchung zum Ursprung der Evangelien-Überlieferung,* WUNT 2:7 (Tübingen: J. C. B. Mohr [Paul Siebeck], 1981).

early Christianity. With this we should take the corresponding verb μανθάνω (Matt 11:29; John 6:45), though it is not nearly as significant as the noun, being used only six times in the Gospels (and nineteen times elsewhere in the NT). We should also notice the verb ἀκολουθέω, "follow." This may be used of a literal following, as when two blind men followed Jesus, calling on him for help (Matt 9:27). But a teacher like Jesus moved about from place to place, and the person who followed him literally as he journeyed might come to be understood as one who accepted him and was committed to his teaching. "Follow" thus can have a meaning like "be a disciple" (Matt 9:9, etc.). Peter could say, "We have left all and followed you" (Mark 10:28).[4]

Jesus was not the only Palestinian figure to have disciples at that time. There were, for example, disciples of John the Baptist (Matt 9:14; Mark 2:18; Luke 11:1; John 1:35) and those of the Pharisees (Matt 22:15-16).[5] It is clear that in a general way in both these cases the disciples were those who adhered to the accepted teaching of a great teacher (John) or of an important sect (the Pharisees).[6] In the Fourth Gospel we read of Pharisees who claimed to be disciples of Moses (John 9:28), which appears to mean that they claimed to be the authentic heirs of the teaching of that great man of old.

The Baptist's disciples acted as his messengers when in prison he wanted to put a question to Jesus (Matt 11:2; Luke 7:18). The implication is that these were people who were identified in some way with the Baptist and whom he could trust. Earlier they had gone to Jesus, whether with or without John's knowledge and authority, to ask why it was that Jesus' disciples did not engage in the religious practice of fasting, whereas they and the Pharisees did so (Matt 9:14 [some MSS add "often" or "much"]; Mark 2:18). This perhaps indicates that the way inculcated by John was somewhat ascetic and that his disciples took seriously the importance of self-discipline. The only other place where Matthew mentions them is after John had been executed by Herod the tetrarch. John's disciples took the body of John and buried it, after which they went and told Jesus (Matt 14:12; cf. Mark 6:29). This may well indicate that they saw the movement John had instituted as being akin to that headed by Jesus.

This is supported by the fact that the Fourth Gospel tells us that the Baptist directed some at any rate of his disciples to follow Jesus and that this was the way Andrew and an unnamed companion became disciples of Jesus (John 1:35-

4. C. Blendinger comments on this usage: "*akoloutheō* is always the call to decisive and intimate discipleship of the earthly Jesus. It always points to the beginning of discipleship. Jn. hints at its spiritual implications for fellowship with the Exalted One (especially 12:26ff.)" ("Disciple," *NIDNTT,* 1:482).

5. It is perhaps curious that we never read of disciples of the scribes, though there must have been scribal schools of some sort.

6. Josephus speaks of Hyrcanus as a disciple of the Pharisees (*Ant.* 13.288), but in view of what we know of the man this can scarcely mean that he wholeheartedly lived by the teachings of the Pharisees. "Disciple" may be used of varying degrees of commitment.

40). The two groups evidently continued in some sort of contact, for John also relates an incident which began with a dispute about purifying and ended with some of his followers complaining about the numbers who had come to follow Jesus, only to be met with the Baptist's joyful acceptance of the fact (John 3:25-30). In this incident it is noteworthy that John's disciples speak of Jesus as he "to whom you have borne witness" (v 26). The usage of "witness" in this Gospel indicates that this is to be taken as a warm endorsement of Jesus. And we should notice the curious incident narrated in Acts wherein Paul came to Ephesus and found "certain disciples" (Acts 19:1).[7] He discovered that they had not even heard of the Holy Spirit; further inquiry revealed that they had been baptized with John's baptism (for which reason some expositors hold that they were not Christians in any sense but followers of the Baptist). But evidently they identified with the Christian movement and readily accepted Christian baptism (Acts 19:1-7). But even before that they are called "disciples."[8]

John's followers engaged in the practice of fasting, in which they contrasted with the disciples of Jesus (Luke 5:33). They evidently also found prayer important, for Luke tells us that the Lord's Prayer was elicited by the fact that some of Jesus' disciples asked him to teach them to pray "even as John taught his disciples" (Luke 11:1).

The disciples were clearly a very important group during the ministry of Jesus, and, as the use of the term in Acts shows, in the life of the early church. The group idea is emphasized by the prevailing use of the plural. Thus Matthew uses the singular only three times, and two of these are concerned with the nature of discipleship in general, with being a disciple of any teacher, rather than specifically with being an individual follower of Jesus (Matt 10:24, 25, 42). Mark invariably has the plural, and Luke too has it except for a few passages referring to the nature of discipleship (6:40; 14:26, 27, 33). John follows this practice throughout Jesus' ministry (he has one singular, in 9:28), but toward the end of his Gospel he has a number of references to individual disciples: the disciple who brought Peter into the courtyard (18:15, 16), Joseph of Arimathea (19:38), "the disciple whom Jesus loved" (19:26, 27; 20:2; 21:7, 20, 23, 24), and the disciple who ran with Peter to the tomb (20:3, 4, 8; v 2 shows that this was the disciple whom Jesus loved).

7. I. H. Marshall denies that they really were disciples: "Paul met some men who *appeared to him* to be disciples. . . . Luke is not saying that the men were disciples but is describing how they appeared to Paul" (*The Acts of the Apostles,* TNTC [Leicester: Inter-Varsity, 1980] 306). F. F. Bruce, however, says, "that these men were Christians is certainly to be inferred from the way in which Luke describes them as 'disciples'; this is a term which he commonly uses for Christians" (*Commentary on the Book of the Acts,* NICNT [Grand Rapids, Michigan: Wm. B. Eerdmans, 1954] 385).

8. "μαθητής for Luke always signifies 'Christian'" (E. Haenchen, *The Acts of the Apostles* [Philadelphia: Westminster, 1971] 553); cf. J. B. Shelton, *Mighty in Word and Deed: The Role of the Holy Spirit in Luke-Acts* (Peabody, Massachusetts: Hendrickson, 1991) 133-36.

## The Call of Jesus

One marked difference between the disciples of Jesus and those of other teachers is that Jesus took the initiative and called people to follow him and be his disciples. The usual practice was for the individual student to choose the teacher with whom he wished to be associated. "Provide thyself with a teacher," said Joshua b. Perahyah (*'Abot* 1:6), and Rabban Gamaliel similarly said, "Provide thyself with a teacher, and remove thyself from doubt" (*'Abot* 1:16). But Jesus called people to leave their occupations and follow him (Matt 4:19; 9:9; Mark 2:14, etc.).[9] That is, the rabbinic model is insufficient to explain Jesus' call to discipleship.[10] There is the implication from the beginning that Jesus is Lord, not simply a teacher as the rabbis were. It is not specifically said of every one of the Twelve that Jesus called him, though it is said that Jesus chose them (Luke 6:13), and John has some statements that show clearly that the choice was that of Jesus. He reports that Jesus asked, "Did I not choose you, the twelve?" (6:70), and in the upper room said plainly, "You did not choose me, but I [the pronoun is emphatic] chose you," and again, "I chose you out of the world" (15:16, 19).[11] Or he may say that the disciples belonged to God and that the Father "gave" them to him (17:6). C. K. Barrett comments, "The disciples belonged to God from the beginning, because from the beginning he had predestinated them as his children."[12]

And when people asked to be permitted to follow him, evidently as disciples, he refused them (Matt 8:19-22; Luke 9:57-62). It was Jesus, not the potential disciple, who determined the relationship. The cured demoniac from Gerasa asked that he might be with Jesus, clearly as a disciple, but was told to go back to his home (Luke 8:38-39). The rich young ruler was challenged to sell all he had and follow Jesus, but the giving up his money proved to be too big a price (Matt 19:21-22) so that Jesus' demand on him led to his rejection as a disciple.

9. There are problems about Jesus' call of the disciples, for example his call of Andrew and Peter from their nets in the Synoptic account and from their adherence to John the Baptist in John. Yet we should bear in mind that in John's Gospel, "Neither does Jesus call, nor John send. The disciples of John recognize the Messiah and spontaneously attach themselves to Him" (L. Morris, *The Gospel according to John,* NICNT [Grand Rapids, Michigan: Wm. B. Eerdmans, 1971] 155). G. R. Beasley-Murray sees this as "a first step towards becoming disciples of Jesus" (*John,* WBC 36 [Waco, Texas: Word, 1987] 26). But our concern here is not with the way the Synoptists relate to the Fourth Gospel, but with the fact that Jesus took the initiative in making disciples.

10. Cf. Martin Hengel, *The Charismatic Leader and His Followers,* SNTW (Edinburgh: T. & T. Clark, 1981) 42-57.

11. "This makes it plain, for those at the Last Supper and for every generation of disciples since, that, however much things may appear, and even feel, to the contrary, it is Christ who has chosen them to be disciples, not they themselves. The initiative in Christian life is with the Lord" (J. Marsh, *The Gospel of St John* [Harmondsworth: Penguin, 1968] 526).

12. C. K. Barrett, *The Gospel according to St. John,* 2d ed. (Philadelphia: Westminster, 1978) 505.

Among those Jesus called and who followed him were people as dissimilar as Simon the Zealot (Luke 6:15), some fishermen (Mark 1:16-20), and Matthew (or Levi) the tax collector (Matt 9:9; Mark 2:14; Luke 5:27-29).[13] Jesus' deliberate choice of a tax collector is significant, for such a person was regarded as an outcast by people like the Pharisees (tax collectors are linked with "the sinners" in Luke 15:1).[14] Jesus wanted disciples, but not in the conventional sense in which his Jewish contemporaries understood the term.

We should see the initiative of Jesus also in the events subsequent to the resurrection. The Gospels make it plain that the disciples were devastated by the crucifixion. They had all fled at the time of Jesus' arrest, and there is no indication of cohesion among them or of any determination to carry on living by the teachings of Jesus in the immediately following time. But when Jesus rose he appeared to them and commissioned them. It is not too much to say that he reconstituted the apostolic band. It was due to him and to no other that they became a cohesive band again, people with a faith and a purpose, and that they went about the task of making disciples. From another standpoint the Gospels bring out the truth that Jesus Christ is Lord.

## The Importance of Jesus' Disciples

The disciples were of critical importance not only for their service of Jesus during his lifetime and not only for the early church but for the whole of Christendom. Jesus committed none of his message to writing (if he wrote anything it has not survived). But he taught his disciples. He entrusted his whole teaching to them. The church throughout the whole world and through all the centuries has depended on the disciples for all their knowledge of who Jesus was and what Jesus did and for the basic message they were to proclaim and by which they were to live.

But nowhere does the NT tell us what a disciple was or what functions a disciple exercised. Clearly a disciple was in some sense a student and constantly received instruction. The large amount of Jesus' teaching recorded in the Gospels is evidence of that. But there was more to being a disciple than being a learner or pupil. Certain truths are told us about disciples and, for example, we find that "a disciple is not greater than the teacher . . . it is sufficient for the disciple that he be as his teacher" (Matt 10:24; cf. Luke 6:40). Jesus goes on to say, "If they called the master of the house Beelzeboul, how much more those of his household?" He is not teaching that the disciples are equal to him, but

13. "Quite apart from temperament and peculiarity of character they form a motley group" (G. Gloege, *The Day of His Coming* [Philadelphia: Fortress, 1963] 246).

14. E. P. Sanders refers to "sinners" as "the wicked," "those who sinned wilfully and heinously and who did not repent" (*Jesus and Judaism* [London: SCM, 1985] 177).

that, as they identify with him, they cannot escape the kind of persecution and criticism their Master faced. The teacher for whose sake disciples must from the beginning be ready to face persecution is one who makes a large claim for himself.

Those called to be disciples of Jesus were called to live lives of service,[15] though in what this service consisted we are not specifically told. But some of them were called to be "fishers of people" (Mark 1:17; Luke 5:10). And, when Jesus sent disciples out on missions, the Twelve (Matt 10:1-42; Mark 6:7-13) and the Seventy (Luke 10:1-20), they were told to cast out demons, heal people, and bring a message of salvation and peace. Such a description of the function of a disciple is not invariable, but there is always the thought of service of some kind. Jesus did not call people to be members of a select academic community.

Jesus made it clear that being one of his disciples meant the utmost in devotion. A disciple of Jesus must bring him such loyalty and love that the closest of earthly ties is but hatred in comparison. Indeed, the disciple must hate even his or her own life also. Jesus demanded a loyalty such that he could say: "Whoever comes to me and does not hate father and mother and wife and children and brothers and sisters, and more, even life itself, cannot be my disciple. Whoever does not carry the cross and come after me cannot be my disciple" (Luke 14:26-27; cf. Matt 10:37-39; 16:24; Mark 8:34). The taking up of the cross is something that must be done daily (Luke 9:23). No one who reads this passage can take discipleship lightly,[16] nor fail to see that it tells us something important about Jesus' understanding of himself.[17]

All this is to demand a loyalty greater than that which anyone who is only a human like other humans can demand. It has important implications for Jesus' understanding of his own person. It makes very clear the fact that discipleship of Jesus is different from discipleship to other teachers and makes far higher demands. As I. H. Marshall points out, discipleship of Jesus

> involved personal allegiance to him, expressed in following him and giving him an exclusive loyalty . . . in every case readiness to put the claims of Jesus

15. E. Käsemann remarks, "After all, Jesus called disciples and did not open a school of perfect theology or of its adepts"; he points to the continuing relevance of this fact, "Grace that is not active is illusion; only discipleship in our everyday life can justify our dogmatics in the face of the world" (*Jesus Means Freedom* [Philadelphia: Fortress, 1972] 60).

16. J. A. Fitzmyer cites J. Schmid, "Only the person who is capable of a radical and painful decision, to set all natural, human relations behind the connection with Jesus (cf. 9:59-62; 8:19-21; 11:27-28) and to give up life itself in martyrdom, can really become a disciple of Jesus" (*The Gospel according to Luke (X–XXIV)*, AB 28A [Garden City, New York: Doubleday, 1985] 1062). Similarly L. Goppelt says, "discipleship meant not only to be together with Jesus, but also to become directed by the course of his life. It produced a total break with the former existence; not only the separation from occupation and family, but also that from one's customary manner of life" (*Theology of the New Testament*, vol. 2 [Grand Rapids, Michigan: Wm. B. Eerdmans, 1982] 101).

17. See further Hengel, *Charismatic Leader.*

first, whatever the cost, was demanded. Such an attitude went beyond the normal pupil-teacher relationship and gave the word 'disciple' a new sense.[18]

Disciples are people who believe in Jesus; Luke in particular speaks of the faith that Jesus expected to find in them (Luke 17:5; 22:32). D. Müller speaks of this as "decisive in understanding *mathētēs* in the gospels,"[19] and despite the paucity of passages which state this explicitly he is surely right. Throughout the Gospels there is everywhere the thought that the disciples have put their trust in Jesus: they really believe in him. Where Jesus is concerned discipleship meant more than learning. It meant faith, wholehearted trust in Jesus as Lord.

## "The Twelve"

All four Gospels make it clear that Jesus had twelve especially close followers whom he chose to be near him, to be the recipients of his teaching, and occasionally to be sent on missions. The earliest literary evidence of a special group of disciples called "the twelve" appears in 1 Cor 15:5 — all the more important since it refers to Jesus' postresurrection appearance to the Twelve as a group in spite of Judas' prior separation from this group.[20] Matthew speaks of "the twelve disciples" (26:20; probably also 20:17)[21] and of "his twelve disciples" (10:1; 11:1; perhaps also Luke 9:1). More usually the Evangelists refer simply to "the twelve" (Matt 26:14; Mark 4:10; Luke 8:1). Matthew once speaks of "the twelve apostles" and lists their names (Matt 10:2-4). That twelve among his followers had a special place is clear from all four Gospels, but mostly the Evangelists refer to "his disciples" or "the disciples."[22]

We often think of "apostles" as being very important in Jesus' ministry, but the word is not common in the Gospels. Luke uses the term 6 times and

18. "Disciple," in *The Illustrated Bible Dictionary*, ed. J. D. Douglas, vol. 1 (Leicester: Inter-Varsity, 1980) 389.

19. "Disciple," *NIDNTT*, 1:489.

20. *Jesus*, 98-106. Sanders regards this testimony as an important voice in favor of the historicity of "the twelve," but argues that "the twelve" is noteworthy for its symbolic significance — that is, its emphasis on the restoration of "all Israel" — and not as a literal designation of twelve special disciples.

21. In both cases there are textual variants, with some MSS omitting "disciples."

22. It is possible to hold that in the use of "disciples" references to the Twelve are few, as P. Parker does. He says, "Of over 230 instances of the term in the gospels about 90 per cent either are not limited to the Twelve at all, or else do not make clear whether these or some larger group is indicated" ("Disciple," *IDB*, 1:845). Technically this is correct, but it is difficult to think that anyone other than the Twelve is in mind in such references as those to disciples being in a boat (Mark 6:45; with Jesus, 8:10), or in a house with him (Mark 7:17; 10:10), or to their coming to him "privately" (Matt 24:3; Luke 10:23). While it is possible to see too many references to the Twelve in the expression "the disciples," it also possible to see too few.

the other three Evangelists once each. It occurs 70 times in the rest of the NT (Acts has it 28 times and Paul 34 times). "Disciple" is a much more significant term for the little group of close followers Jesus called to be with him during his ministry. This is not to overlook the fact that "apostle" had a special importance; the idea in "apostle" is that of "one sent." Jesus not only called people to be with him but sent them out to be his emissaries. The emphatic commission he gave after the resurrection may be a reason for the increase in the use of "apostle" after the Gospels (cf. Matt 28:18-20; Luke 24:49). But Jesus seems rarely to have used the term. He much preferred "disciples."

According to the Gospels, those twelve were especially close to him during his ministry. They received teaching that others did not receive, they were witnesses of happenings that others knew nothing about, and they were commissioned to carry on Jesus' teaching after his death. This little group of key followers of Jesus are of the utmost importance for an understanding of what Jesus was doing. He did not simply broadcast his teaching (though he did make it available to all who would hear). He concentrated on twelve people who would come to know his person and his teaching in a way that others would not, and who, after Jesus died, would continue the movement he founded.

On one occasion he sent them on a mission to the nation of Israel (Matthew 10). He expressly charged them not to go to Gentiles or Samaritans; this was a mission to "the lost sheep of the house of Israel" (Matt 10:5-6). They were to tell the Israelites that "the kingdom of heaven" had "drawn near" (Matt 10:7). The instructions given to them on that occasion reveal a good deal of the message Jesus entrusted to his followers. They had an enduring function, for Jesus spoke of their being on thrones judging the people of Israel at the judgment (Matt 19:28). And, of course, they were with Jesus on the last night of his earthly life, when he gave important teaching and instituted holy communion (Matt 26:20-29).

It is likely that we should see symbolic significance in the number twelve, the number of the twelve tribes of Israel. J. W. Bowman puts it this way:

> Wherever our Lord would appear with his band of "twelve," *the number in itself* would be proclaiming the Gospel message, the more so as the people were familiar with the custom of the prophets and, as we have seen, reckoned Jesus among their number. "Can't you see," it would be saying to Jewry, "this is the Remnant spoken of in the prophets. Open your eyes and see; this is the Messiah and the new Israel!" It may be that this parable in action more than anything else contributed to the rather general impression among both the crowds and his enemies that Jesus *claimed* to be the Messiah, though the Gospel evidence that he ever made such a claim before either group is negligible.[23]

23. *The Intention of Jesus* (Philadelphia: Westminster, 1943) 185-86. G. Gloege points to the twelve patriarchs as "the ancestors of the ancient people of God" and the twelve disciples as "the

Bowman may be somewhat overestimating the effect of the number twelve, but it is difficult to think that among the Jews there would be no significance attaching to this number. There is all the more force in this contention in that Jesus emphasized that his contemporaries did not really understand the OT Scriptures. It would be all the more likely that he would establish a new people who would understand them. And in making a new "people of God" Jesus was making a great claim.

Sometimes Jesus explained a little of what discipleship means. "If you continue in my word," he said to some Jews who believed[24] him, "you are truly my disciples; and you will know the truth, and the truth will set you free" (John 8:31-32). This makes it clear that a continuing faith is an indispensable condition of discipleship. To be a disciple is to have an abiding trust in Jesus. And the consequence of that, and we may feel an explanation of what discipleship involves, is that the believer will know truth. In this Gospel truth is a very important concept, and it is linked with Jesus who could say, "I am . . . the truth" (14:6). Truth liberates, and this liberation is an important part of being a disciple.[25] It is also important for an understanding of the Master. To be a disciple meant to see ultimate truth in him who is the truth.

Elsewhere in John we find the bearing of fruit linked with being a disciple (15:8). It is not certain whether we should understand the text to mean, "My Father's glory is shown by your bearing much fruit; and in this way you become my disciples" (GNB) or "My Father is glorified by this, that you bear much fruit and become my disciples" (NRSV). Either way the bearing of fruit is linked with discipleship. As Jesus understood it, disciples live fruitful lives. They were to be occupied in the service of God, not to be preoccupied with their own status.[26]

## Failures of the Twelve

In view of the high place accorded the disciples in the Gospels, and the charge Jesus gave them after the resurrection, it is important for us to notice that the Gospels

---

ancestors of the new people of God" (*Day,* 245-46). G. Bornkamm also sees twelve as symbolizing the twelve tribes of Israel and reasons "Jesus' disciples were thus conceived as the new people of God of the last days" (*Jesus of Nazareth* [New York: Harper & Row, 1960] 150). See also Sanders, *Jesus,* 95-106.

24. The expression is τοὺς πεπιστευκότας αὐτῷ. John's more usual construction for genuine trust is πιστεύειν εἰς, but he does not always make a hard-and-fast difference between the various constructions. The context shows that these people in one sense believed and in another did not.

25. " 'To know the truth' (8:32) means to come to know God's saving purpose as it is embodied in Christ; and the freedom promised is freedom from sin (8:34), which could not be accomplished under the old covenant but only by the Son" (G. E. Ladd, *A Theology of the New Testament* [Grand Rapids, Michigan: Wm. B. Eerdmans, 1974] 267).

26. Wilkins cites T. W. Manson, "Discipleship was not matriculation in a Rabbinical College, but apprenticeship to the work of the Kingdom" (*Concept of Disciple,* 110).

speak plainly of their limitations. Our Evangelists make very clear that the Twelve were not superhuman. They were ordinary people, people with limited abilities and all too prone to failure. If called upon to give the names of the Twelve most of us would find the task difficult, a fact which arises not so much from our imperfect memories as that several of them seem not to have been very memorable. Nothing is recorded, for example, of any deeds of Bartholomew or Thaddeus or Simon the Canaanite. And when what they did is recorded, it is sometimes far from creditable. For example, they disputed which of them was the greatest (Mark 9:33-34; Luke 9:46), a dispute which flared up from time to time (cf. Matt 20:20-28; Mark 10:35-45), and continued right up to the last night of Jesus' life, in the upper room (Luke 22:24). The disciples could to the very end be looking for the chief places in his kingdom when it should be established.

They sometimes found Jesus' teaching difficult to understand[27] and were afraid to ask him what he meant (Mark 9:32; Luke 9:45). Caught in a storm at sea, they were rebuked as cowardly and "of little faith" (Matt 8:26; Mark 4:40). When they failed to bring help to a man with a demon-possessed boy they were included in Jesus' rebuke of a "faithless and perverse generation" (Matt 17:17; Luke 9:41).

They gave evidence of a spirit of intolerance, out of harmony with Jesus, when they forbade a man to cast out devils in Jesus' name "because he does not follow with us" (Luke 9:49; a mistake reflecting an attitude that has all too often been repeated throughout the history of the church). A similar spirit was displayed when they wanted to call down fire on a village which refused to receive Jesus (Luke 9:54). They lacked understanding when they rebuked the mothers who brought their children for him to lay his hands on them (Matt 19:13-15; Luke 18:15-16), and again when they wanted to reject the Canaanite woman who came to ask Jesus to heal her daughter (Matt 15:22-28). They did not recognize that defilement is not a matter of externals, of what is eaten, but comes from one's inner being (Mark 7:17-23). They did not understand Jesus' warning against "the leaven" of the Pharisees and of Herod (Mark 8:15-21).

They could be completely out of sympathy with Jesus, for example when he spoke of having food to eat of which they knew nothing and they could think only of literal, physical food (John 4:31-33). Similarly Jesus' conversation with Philip and Andrew before the feeding of the five thousand showed that these disciples had no comprehension of Jesus' ability to meet the needs of the people (John 6:5-9). On a later occasion they were indignant when precious oil was poured over his head instead of being turned into money and given to the poor (Matt 26:6-13).

27. G. Vermes says of the Twelve, "heroic though they may have become after Jesus' death, consecrating themselves whole-heartedly to the continuation of his lifework, they are not depicted in the Gospels as particularly quick at understanding the mind and preaching of their master while he was alive, or brave at the time of his ordeal, when they all deserted him" (*Jesus the Jew* [London: Collins, 1973] 30).

Notable among the disciples was the apostle Peter.[28] This man was capable both of rising to great heights and of falling to abysmal depths. We see both in the incident in which he declared that Jesus was "the Christ, the Son of the living God" and almost immediately rebuked his Master for prophesying that he would die (Matt 16:16-23; Mark's account is much the same, though shorter [Mark 8:31-33]). In both accounts Jesus calls Peter "you Satan" and points out that his mind is not on the things of God but on those of mere humans. Again, Peter saw it as unreasonable that Jesus should ask who touched him after a woman had secured healing by touching him in the crowd (Luke 8:45; Mark has only a reference to "his disciples," Mark 5:31). Peter it was who asked whether he should forgive someone who sinned against him as many as seven times only to learn that "seventy times seven" was more like it (Matt 18:21-22). In the upper room Peter showed himself to be out of harmony with Jesus' teaching by his attitude to the feet-washing (John 13:6-10). He declared his readiness to go to prison and even death for Jesus, whereupon the Master prophesied Peter's threefold denial of him (Luke 22:33-34), a denial which in due course took place, and which all four Evangelists faithfully record. Peter "wept bitterly" (Luke 22:62) when he realized what he had done, but that did not alter the fact that he had done it. It is notable that this leader among the followers of Jesus could fail so signally so often. We need not doubt that his devotion to Jesus was wholehearted, nor that he said and did many fine things. But the picture left by the Gospels is that of a man who all too often failed his Lord.

The culmination of the failure of all the disciples came, of course, at the end of Jesus' life. It was Judas, one of his chosen Twelve, who betrayed him to his enemies, a betrayal that John sees as inspired by Satan (John 13:2, 27; cf. Luke 23:2). In Gethsemane Jesus faced the prospect of a painful and shameful death and was in agony as he prayed. But they were so far from being in sympathy with him what while he prayed they slept (Matt 26:36-45; Luke 22:39-46). And at the moment of crisis "the disciples all left him and ran away" (Matt 26:56). Later, when they heard that Jesus had risen from the dead and had appeared to some women, they refused to believe these "idle words" (Luke 24:11; cf. v 25). Granted that we do not well to sit in judgment on the disciples for failing to rise to the demand for faith, reflecting that we would doubtless have done even worse in such a situation, granted also that I have passed over many incidents which reflect credit on the disciples, the fact remains that there is nothing in their attitude that prepares us to see them as great leaders in the church that would emerge.[29]

28. E. J. Goodspeed points out that "none of the others rose to the commanding stature Peter afterward achieved" (*A Life of Jesus* [New York: Harper, 1950] 74).

29. Cf. C. K. Barrett, "the death of Jesus appears to have broken the spirit and the loyalty of the disciples. Up to a late point in the narrative as we have it they profess that not even death

It is important that we notice the limitations of the disciples. Jesus did not select twelve supermen, people of towering intellect and irresistible drive, to be with him throughout his ministry and to whom he would in due course commit the responsibility of heading up the new movement. He chose twelve ordinary, sinful, limited people. This means that the church was set on its way not on account of the dynamic of the first preachers, but because of the divine power that was imparted to them. C. H. Dodd could say, "It is part of the character and genius of the Church that its foundation members were discredited men," a truth we should reflect on more than we usually do. Dodd goes on, "it owed its existence not to their faith, courage, or virtue, but to what Christ had done with them; and this they could never forget."[30] The church exists because of what God has done in Christ, not because of any outstanding abilities in its first members. The fact that, despite the limitations and the failures of the disciples, Jesus established through them a church that would go through the world, tells us something about the nature of the Lord the Evangelists depict.

## Other Disciples

That the Twelve had a special place is clear from all the Gospels. But it is also clear that followers of Jesus outside the Twelve were important and that they were sometimes called "disciples" (e.g., Matt 5:1; 12:49-50). We are not to think of the teaching of Jesus as something exclusive to which only a few elite followers had access, which only the elite would understand, or to which only the elite might respond. He taught the common people gladly. The Evangelists never deal with the relationship between the two groups, nor do they ever say precisely what constituted a person a "disciple" of Jesus.

There were faithful women who followed Jesus and served him, but the Evangelists say nothing about whether they were called "disciples" or what their relationship was to other followers of their Lord. Women were certainly included among Jesus' adherents. The word μαθήτρια is used of Tabitha (Acts 9:36),[31] but it is not found elsewhere in the NT. That women were numbered among Jesus' followers is clear, but whether the word "disciple" was used of them is not.

The terminology is perhaps unimportant over against the significant fact

---

will cause them to deny or desert Jesus; Peter is specially loud in his protestations, but he is joined by the whole group (Mark 14.31). Yet in the end, all the disciples desert Jesus, Peter denies him, and Judas betrays him." Barrett goes on to speak of "so complete a debacle" (*Jesus and the Gospel Tradition* [Philadelphia: Fortress, 1968] 59).

30. *The Interpretation of the Fourth Gospel* (Cambridge: Cambridge University, 1953) 416 n. 1.

31. BAGD 486 gives the meaning of this word as "a (woman) disciple" and notes its use of Mary Magdalene in the *Gospel of Peter*, as well as its use here of Tabitha.

that Jesus taught women apparently as freely as he taught men. This was an innovation in Jewry, for the rabbis not only did not, but would not, teach women.[32] It is recorded that when Ben Azzai suggested that women be taught the law for some purposes R. Eliezer replied: "If any man gives his daughter a knowledge of the Law it is as though he taught her lechery" (*Soṭa* 3:4). The attitude of R. Jose b. Johanan of Jerusalem is significant: "Let thy house be opened wide and let the needy be members of thy household; and talk not much with womankind" (*'Abot* 1:5). The passage goes on to report "the Sages" as teaching: "He that talks much with womankind brings evil upon himself and neglects the study of the Law and at the last will inherit Gehenna." Conduct "that transgresses Jewish custom" may be explained as "If she goes out with her hair unbound, or spins in the street, or speaks with any man" (*Ketub.* 7:6). Jesus' attitude was in marked contrast. He taught women like Mary of Bethany (Luke 10:38-42) and the one he met near a well (John 4).

The Gospels do not give us a picture of Jesus engaging in evangelistic campaigns, and we certainly cannot think that his main aim was to induce large numbers of people to follow him. He was more interested in proclaiming the truth than in winning a huge following. But he did preach to people who did not number themselves among his adherents. For example, the Fourth Gospel tells us that early in Jesus' ministry "he made and baptized more disciples than did John" (John 4:1; he adds that Jesus himself did not perform the baptisms, but his disciples; but from what we read elsewhere it is clear that no external ceremony constituted people as disciples of Jesus). On one occasion when his mother and his brothers wanted to interrupt his teaching of the people, he said, "Who is my mother and who are my brothers?" He stretched out his hand to his disciples and said, "Look, my mother and my brothers. For whoever does the will of my Father who is in heaven, he is my brother and sister and mother" (Matt 12:46-50). This passage clearly means that the essence of discipleship to Jesus is to be indissolubly linked with doing the will of the heavenly Father.

Luke introduces his "Sermon on the Plain" by saying that there had assembled "a great crowd of his disciples, and a great multitude of the people from all Judea and Jerusalem" (Luke 6:17). This shows plainly that there were many outside the intimate circle of the Twelve who were sufficiently impressed by what Jesus taught to number themselves among his disciples. And since they are distinguished from the "great multitude of the people," this means more than that they simply gave Jesus a hearing. To some degree they were committed to his cause. We should probably say the same about "his disciples" who came to Jesus and heard him deliver the Sermon on the Mount (Matt 5:1).

Jesus diffentiated the discipleship he looked for from his followers from that which the rabbis sought. Students in a rabbinical school aimed at becoming

32. For the place of women in antiquity and specifically among the Jews see my *New Testament Theology* (Grand Rapids, Michigan: Zondervan, 1986) 202-6.

rabbis themselves; any one of them might indeed surpass his teacher. But in the new little group this is not possible. "You," Jesus said,[33] "be not called 'Rabbi,' for one is your teacher and you are all brothers" (Matt 23:8). Disciples of Jesus were not people on the way to becoming rabbis; they were people who were perpetually learning and serving.[34] The term underlined the centrality of Jesus. It put emphasis on the lowly status of all his followers. Every use of the term reminded the hearers of him whose disciples they were.[35]

This would have been assisted by the content of Jesus' teaching, which was marked by a new understanding of the meaning of the OT as well as radically new teaching about himself and the saving act he would accomplish by his atoning death. As R. P. Meye puts it, "Jesus gave to the disciples His own interpretation of the OT and His direct teaching, rather than a catena of traditions to which He simply added His own word. His word superseded all else before."[36] We should also bear in mind that it was central to Jesus' teaching that he would bring salvation by dying for sinners. Though he spoke a number of times of his coming death on the cross this was such a difficult concept for them that the disciples found it very hard to grasp. The originality of Jesus' message meant that discipleship for him and his followers was markedly different from discipleship to the rabbis. It brought them into a whole new world of understanding the Scripture and the will of God for their lives. Jesus commanded his followers to "make disciples of all the nations" (Matt 28:19), and as Matthew puts this at the end of his Gospel, among the final instructions Jesus gave them, it is clearly seen as important.[37] Luke also refers to Jesus' commission to them to preach "to all the nations," adding, "You are witnesses of these things" (Luke 24:47-48). This makes it all the more curious that after the Gospels the term "disciple" occurs 28 times in Acts but nowhere else. We might have expected that Paul would sometimes write about "disciples," but he does not.

33. His "you" is emphatic, "you in distinction from others."

34. "Μαθητής became a convenient vehicle to carry Jesus' concept of vital attachment to himself personally. He was his disciples' supreme teacher and leader (Mt. 23:7-10). They were not to be disciples of any other person, and were never to advance to being called rabbi" (Wilkins, *Concept of Disciple,* 125).

35. Rengstorf emphasizes the differences between Jesus' disciples and those of the rabbis. The rabbinic student aimed to be "like the rabbi, and thus independent of or even superior to him. For the disciple of Jesus, however, discipleship is not a first step with the promise of greater things to come. It is the fulfilment of his destiny. . . . Whereas the תַּלְמִיד־חָכָם hopes in some sense to master the Torah, it is the business of the μαθητής of Jesus to be stamped and fashioned by Him" ("μαθητής," *TDNT,* 4:448-49).

36. "Disciple," *ISBE,* 1:947. He adds, "a consequence was that Jesus' disciples not only often failed to understand Him, but were constantly amazed at what He said and taught."

37. L. Goppelt holds that these words "meant that Jesus would not become the Teacher of the nations when they accepted the teachings of the earthly One like those of a rabbi, but when they turned to the resurrected and exalted One in person" (*Theology,* 2:216). They involve an ongoing discipleship.

Apostles are mentioned much more often after the Gospels, though disciples must have outnumbered apostles in the church, even allowing for the multiplication of false apostles. Perhaps "disciples" became firmly attached to the Twelve. Or it may be that the early church found expressions like "believers" or "brothers / sisters" or "saints" more satisfactory as designations of those who came to accept the way of Jesus.

From Acts we learn that the first followers of Jesus wasted no time in obeying the command to make disciples. On the day of Pentecost, just after the ascension, they proclaimed the gospel forcefully and about three thousand people were converted (Acts 2:41). It is not long before we are reading of "the multitude of the disciples" (Acts 6:2, 7). Throughout Acts the most frequent use of the term is for the believers in a given locality (this usage accounts for about half of the occurrences of the term in Acts).

Mysteries about the NT use of the term "disciple" remain. But clearly it referred to a distinctive form of discipleship, a discipleship in which the learners must always remain learners. Jesus' disciples were (and are) people in a lowly position who could never aspire to the heights of their Teacher. Discipleship tells us something of the greatness of Jesus and the lowliness of his followers. And the limitations of those to whom Jesus committed the task of evangelizing the world spells out something important in a world where people persist in seeing greatness anywhere but in lowly service.

# Matthew 11:19b / Luke 7:35: A Test Case for the Bearing of Q Christology on the Synoptic Problem

D. A. Carson

## 1

As is well known, the Q hypothesis depends on the validity of the argument for the priority of Mark. Conversely, where other arguments over the Synoptic problem appear fairly evenly matched, support for the existence of some form of Q is easily taken as support for the priority of Mark. The complex questions surrounding both Q and the Synoptic problem lie beyond the constraints imposed on this essay; I propose to examine only Matt 11:19b / Luke 7:35, a test case as it were. This pair of passages is frequently taken as a clear instance where Luke has the original form of Q, and Matthew has changed it to support his Wisdom christology. If that thesis stands, it becomes difficult to imagine how Matthew (at this point, at least) could be the prior text. What is sometimes not adequately recognized is that the arguments turn on a number of difficult exegetical questions where certainty is problematic. Indeed, one particular interpretation, I shall argue, regularly receives short shrift, and, if it were to stand, reduces the relevance of these passages to discussion of the Synoptic problem.

In what follows I shall briefly sketch the dominant consensus, then criticize it and offer an alternative exegesis, and, finally, trace the bearing of this exegesis on the Synoptic problem.

## 2

Supporters of the Griesbach hypothesis have argued that Matt 11:2-19 / Luke 7:18-35 is one of many pairs of passages exhibiting "the kind of verbal similarity

. . . which suggests the possibility of direct copying"[1] — the assumption being, of course, that Luke has copied from Matthew. But close study has convinced a majority of scholars that copying has gone the other way — or, more precisely, that both Matthew and Luke used Q,[2] but that Luke shows few signs of having edited Q while Matthew shows rather more signs of having done so.[3]

The argument, in brief, runs like this. The verb ἐδικαιώθη picks up ἐδικαίωσαν in v 29, already judged on other grounds to be pre-Lukan.[4] Since the usage in v 35 cannot easily be seen to be a Lukan redaction of Matt 11:19 (for reasons still to be seen), v 35 is likely also to be pre-Lukan (and thus, granted the parallel with Matthew, presumably Q). Comparison of v 29 with v 35 also suggests that "children" (v 35) is more original than Matthew's "works": a personal subject is demanded for the "justifying" if the alleged parallel between the two verses is to stand. In this view, Luke 7:35 offers a contrast with the immediately preceding verses (the initial καί is usually understood to have adversative force), but links up powerfully with vv 29-30; that is, unlike those who despise the style of both the Baptist and of Jesus (vv 33-34), all Wisdom's children (v 35) justify Wisdom, just as "all the people, even the tax collectors," justify God in vv 29-30.

The link between v 29 and v 35 is judged to be so strong that most scholars conclude that in Luke Wisdom's children are "all the people, even the tax collectors," over against the religious authorities who listened to neither the Baptist nor Jesus. Two features, it is argued, make it unlikely that Wisdom's "children" in v 35 refers to John and Jesus. First, πάντων (attested in most manuscripts[5] and possibly redactional) makes it unlikely there are only two "children";[6] second, it is often pointed out that in Wisdom literature, on which this saying is modeled,[7] Wisdom's "sons" are those who listen to and obey her

1. So W. R. Farmer, *The Synoptic Problem* (New York: Macmillan, 1964) 203, 207.

2. In this essay I use "Q" to refer to Q-material, material common to Matthew and Luke, without prejudice as to whether or not such material ever constituted a single document, and, apart from contextually determined occurrences, without prejudice as to whether or not Q ever existed in any written form.

3. So, e.g., C. M. Tuckett, *The Revival of the Griesbach Hypothesis: An Analysis and Appraisal* (Cambridge: Cambridge University, 1983) 148ff.

4. Here, however, I. H. Marshall, *The Gospel of Luke,* NIGTC (Grand Rapids, Michigan: Wm. B. Eerdmans, 1978) 303, is among those who think the verb has been introduced into v 29 under the influence of v 35.

5. It is absent from D L Θ Ψ $f^1$ 28 700 1241 *al;* it ends the phrase in many manuscripts (A Q *Byz*). Support for the NA$^{26}$ reading comes from B W $f^{13}$ 892. The reading πάντων τῶν ἔργων αὐτῆς finds support only in the second corrector of ℵ.

6. So, *inter alios,* D. R. Catchpole, "Tradition History," in *New Testament Interpretation,* ed. I. H. Marshall (Exeter: Paternoster, 1974) 169; M. J. Suggs, *Wisdom, Christology, and Law in Matthew's Gospel* (Cambridge, Massachusetts: Harvard University, 1970) 35; and earlier, M.-J. Lagrange, *Evangile selon Saint Luc,* 8th ed. (Paris: Gabalda, 1948) *in loc.*

7. So, rightly, A. Feuillet, "Jésus et la Sagesse divine d'après les évangiles synoptiques," *RB* 62 (1955) 161-96. The contrary view of R. Cameron, "'What Have You Come Out to See?' Characterizations of John and Jesus in the Gospels," *Semeia* 49 (1990) 35-69, who argues that the Q references to John the Baptist make him out to be not a biblical prophet but a Cynic, is remarkably

call, rather than those who preach it.[8] Fitzmyer is an exception in that he lumps together John the Baptist, Jesus, and all those who listen to either of them, as Wisdom's children.[9]

There are many variations on and refinements to the interpretation just outlined, and a few scholars who take quite a different view. Some of these options I shall briefly discuss below. For the moment it is only necessary to mention that, by contrast with the Lukan parallel, Matt 11:19 is thought to betray secondary features and a more developed Wisdom christology. In particular, Matthew's τῶν ἔργων (instead of Luke's πάντων τῶν τέκνων) is a self-conscious closing of the *inclusio* opened in Matt 11:2: John the Baptist heard in prison of τὰ ἔργα of the Christ. The works that justify Wisdom in 11:19 — in short, the works of Wisdom — are nothing other than the works of Christ. The implication is obvious: Wisdom has become personified, almost hypostatized, and Christ=Wisdom.

Could such an identification of Jesus with Wisdom already have been found in Q? If πάντων in Luke 7:35 is redactional (and certainly πᾶς is a Lukan word), then Wisdom's *children* in the Q source *might* have been John and Jesus; but in any case Matthew goes beyond this by making Wisdom=Jesus. If the "children" of Luke 7:35 referred in Q only to the disciples of John and Jesus (a stronger possibility if πάντων belonged to Q), then Wisdom still cannot be identified with Jesus since the entire context shows that *both* John *and* Jesus are *envoys* of Wisdom, but not Wisdom itself. In other words, the close association of John and Jesus throughout the three preceding pericopae makes it unlikely that in the Q logion itself Jesus is identified with Wisdom.[10] So Dunn concludes: "*Where Q at most presented Jesus as the envoy of Wisdom and most probably as the child of Wisdom, Matthew clearly took the step of identifying Jesus as Wisdom herself.*"[11] Dunn, of course, is interested in the development of christology, but his views on our pair of texts is widely shared, and, if sustained, obviously bears directly on the Synoptic problem.

---

uncontrolled. In this passage it turns on finding μαλακίαν (cf. Matt 11:8 / Luke 7:25) and related terms in Cynic writers. Cameron fails to mention that the same word-group abounds in Philo, Josephus, and the LXX.

8. E.g., Prov 8:32; Sir 4:11. Cf. U. Wilckens, *Weisheit und Torheit* (Tübingen: J. C. B. Mohr [Paul Siebeck], 1959) 198; D. Lührmann, *Die Redaktion der Logionquelle* (Neukirchen-Vluyn: Neukirchener, 1969) 29-30.

9. J. A. Fitzmyer, *The Gospel according to Luke (I-IX)*, AB 28 (Garden City, New York: Doubleday, 1981) 678-79.

10. So, e.g., G. N. Stanton, "On the Christology of Q," in *Christ and Spirit in the New Testament*, ed. B. Lindars and S. S. Smalley (Cambridge: Cambridge University, 1973) 36.

11. J. D. G. Dunn, *Christology in the Making: An Inquiry into the Origins of the Doctrine of the Incarnation* (London: SCM, 1980) 198 (emphasis his). Similarly, cf. R. H. Gundry, *Matthew: A Commentary on His Literary and Theological Art* (Grand Rapids, Michigan: Wm. B. Eerdmans, 1982) 212-13.

3

In what follows, I want to raise a number of points against this reconstruction. I shall begin with some reflections on Matthew, and then turn to Luke and Q.

(1) Whatever is said about John and Jesus being linked together in Luke 7, the same must be said, *mutatis mutandis,* regarding the link between them in Matthew 11.

The general flow of the preceding verses in both Luke and Matthew is the same. Emissaries from the Baptist approach Jesus, expressing the former's doubt and frankly asking whether or not Jesus is ὁ ἐρχόμενος (Luke 7:19; Matt 11:2). Jesus responds by summarizing his ministry, using the categories of Isa 35:5-6; 61:1-2 (omitting any mention of vengeance), and concluding with an aphorism designed to encourage perseverance on the part of the Baptist (and of later readers) (Luke 7:20-23; Matt 11:4-6). Then, just as John had borne witness to Jesus before the crowd (Luke 3:1-18; Matt 3:1-12), so also now Jesus bears witness to John before the crowds — though as we shall see, it is a peculiar witness that has the effect of pointing out his own unique importance. After a series of difficult rhetorical questions nominally addressed to the crowd, Jesus establishes that John the Baptist is more than a prophet by insisting that he is also someone concerning whom prophecy was uttered (Luke 7:24-27; Matt 11:7-10 — citing Mal 3:1 under influence from Exod 23:20 LXX[12]). We cannot here explore each element in the citation. But even if Mal 3:1 had been exactly quoted, the flow of the argument in both Luke and Matthew demands that if John the Baptist is the prophesied Elijah who prepares the way for Yahweh (Luke 1:76; Matt 3:3) or for the Day of Yahweh (Mal 4:5-6), and John the Baptist is Jesus' forerunner, then Jesus himself is the manifestation of Yahweh and brings in the eschatological Day of Yahweh.[13] Far from breaking up the flow of the passage, the quotation ties it together by showing exactly *how* John the Baptist is more than a prophet:[14] he is greater than any prophet in that he alone serves as the immediate forerunner of Yahweh's gracious self-disclosure in Jesus, preparing the way before him. From the perspective of both Luke and Matthew, doubtless the antecedent prophets had contributed to the corpus of revelation that pointed to the coming of Messiah (the "Christ" in Matt 11:2). But it was John alone who pointed him out and prepared his way directly. That leads to the conclusion expressed in the next verse: John the Baptist is the greatest person born of woman (the text presupposes "up to that time" or the like, or the rest of Luke 7:28 / Matt 11:11 makes no sense). John the Baptist is greater than

12. Cf. R. H. Gundry, *The Use of the Old Testament in St. Matthew's Gospel* (Leiden: E. J. Brill, 1975) 11-12.

13. Cf. R. T. France, *Jesus and the Old Testament* (London: Tyndale, 1971) 91-92 n. 31, 155; D. A. Carson, *Matthew,* EBC 8 (Grand Rapids, Michigan: Zondervan, 1984) 263ff.

14. *Contra* D. Hill, *The Gospel of Matthew,* NCBC (Grand Rapids, Michigan: Wm. B. Eerdmans, 1972) *in loc.* and many others.

Moses, greater than David, greater than Solomon, greater than Isaiah, simply because to him fell the inexpressible privilege of introducing the Messiah to the world. Thus Jesus' witness to John becomes a dramatic way of drawing attention to his own unique identity.

In this light, ὁ μικρότερος in the kingdom who is greater than John is not a reference to Jesus as "the younger," that is, "the lesser" in a purely temporal sense,[15] as if the text is simply saying that Jesus, though younger than John, is in fact superior to him (cf. John 1:15). For that would mean that the greatness of ὁ μικρότερος relative to John is not established on the same basis as the greatness of John relative to the antecedent prophets, and so the flow of the passage would be badly disrupted. Indeed, many scholars affirm that the push to take ὁ μικρότερος to mean "the younger" finds primary impetus in nothing more than the fact that the passage is so difficult. Others hold that the kingdom is entirely future:[16] the least in the kingdom *then* will be greater than John is *now*. But neither Luke nor Matthew deploys such categories in this passage, and in any case the basis for comparing the two patterns of relative greatness would again be destroyed. Many argue that Matthew (but not Luke) presupposes that John the Baptist is himself in the kingdom,[17] largely on the basis of the strict identity between John's message and Jesus' message as reported in Matt 3:2; 4:17. But this is to focus too narrowly on isolated verses without sufficiently observing their redactional contexts. When John announces the coming of the kingdom and calls for repentance, he does so in the context of anticipating the one who follows him (Matthew 3); when Jesus announces the coming of the kingdom and calls for repentance, he does so in the context of his *fulfillment* of the prophecy of Isaiah 9 that a great light would shine in Galilee (Matt 4:12-17) — and this takes place *after* John is imprisoned (Matt 4:12).

If we look for a way to understand our passage, such that the relative greatness of the least in the kingdom over John parallels the relative greatness of John over everyone before him, then a way forward presents itself. John is greater than everyone before him because (as we have seen) it was given to him to point out with greater clarity than had ever been done before the precise locus of God's greatest self-disclosure — Jesus himself, and the dawning of the Day of Yahweh. But John does not envisage any delay in the prospect of apocalyptic judgment (Luke 3:16-17; Matt 3:11-12); that is the genesis of his doubt at the beginning of our passage. He has no theology of the cross (toward which all the Gospel writers press); he has no conception of a kingdom in which tares and wheat must grow together, in which the Spirit must come and empower

15. So *inter alios* O. Cullmann, "Ὁ ὀπίσω μου ἐρχόμενος," *ConNT* 11 (1947) 30; M. Brunec, "De Legationi Ioannis Baptistae (Mt 11:2-24)," *VD* 35 (1957) 262-70; BDF §61(2).

16. E.g., A. H. McNeile, *The Gospel according to St. Matthew* (London: Macmillan, 1915) *in loc.*

17. E.g., W. Wink, *John the Baptist in the Gospel Tradition* (Cambridge: Cambridge University, 1968) 33-35.

Messiah's people before the awful climax. In that sense the least in the kingdom, the lowliest disciple living *this* side of the cross and resurrection, points out Jesus better than the Baptist; and that constitutes the greatness of the least in the kingdom.

Thus Jesus has explained (according to both Luke and Matthew) the role of the Baptist in the stream of redemptive history, but in such a way that he himself is the unique and climactic self-disclosure of God.

Then, in the verses immediately before the text that is the focus of this essay, Jesus compares "this generation" with children in the marketplace who call out to others to join them in their play, and find them unresponsive. Jesus then makes an application to the Baptist and himself, an application still to be explored (Luke 7:31-34; Matt 11:16-19a). Our text follows (Luke 7:35; Matt 11:19b).

Of course, I have neglected to comment on the peculiarities in Luke and Matthew. In particular, Luke draws a contrast between the readiness of the people to hear Jesus' words and the rejection of God's purpose by the Pharisees and scribes (Luke 7:29-30); Matthew includes a difficult logion about the advancing kingdom and John's place in it, returning to the link with the promised Elijah who was to come (Matt 11:12-14; cf. Luke 16:16). In addition, Matthew (as we have seen) incorporates τὰ ἔργα in the initial question (11:2). But the point of this recital of the main thrusts of *both* Luke and Matthew is to stress how similar they are. Throughout both passages Jesus is utterly without peer; at the same time, John is highly praised, located within the stream of redemptive history, and assigned his status because of his relationship to Jesus. And "this generation" is condemned for rejecting *both* John *and* Jesus (no matter how the difficult parable of the children in the marketplace is understood).

What this means, I think, is that it is very difficult to conceive how an ordinary first-century reader (how much less an auditor!) could have associated Matt 11:19b with Jesus but *not* with John, with Matt 11:2 but *not* with 11:16-19a. To argue that 11:19b must refer exclusively to *Jesus'* works (the necessary condition for the argument that Wisdom=Jesus) because of the one-word connection (in another case!) with "works" in 11:2, while ignoring the entire flow of the passage, is exegetically unjustified.[18] This is the elevation of an old-fashioned and doctrinaire form of redaction criticism that makes all the meaning hang on changes, and none of it on the large mass of common material, let alone on the flow of the passage. The changes must not be ignored; I shall return to them. But when Matthew's version is simply read as a flowing account, without reference to Luke, it is very difficult to see how the "works" of 11:19b are exclusively those of Jesus.

(2) Many have pointed out that τὰ ἔργα in Matt 11:2 has the effect of pointing backward to the carefully constructed series of works that *Jesus* performs

18. True, the thrust of the passage immediately establishes Jesus' *superiority* over John, but not on the ground that Jesus = Wisdom.

in chs. 8–9, and therefore John the Baptist can be included with Jesus in 11:19 only if we assume that he too is performing kingdom works.[19] Some, rightly, go farther: the expression in its context is broad enough to embrace not only the works of chs. 8–9 but also the teaching of chs. 5–7 and the mission of ch. 10.

All of these "works," however, are cast as the "fulfillment" of antecedent revelation, the coming of the eschatological kingdom. Thus in the Sermon on the Mount the purpose of Jesus' coming and the burden of his teaching fulfill the law and the prophets (5:17-20; 7:12). Obeying Moses' commands becomes a testimony to who Jesus is (8:1-4); exercising faith in Jesus associates the believer, whether Jew or not, with the patriarchs in the long-awaited kingdom (8:5-13); Jesus' healings fulfill Isa 53:4 (Matt 8:14-17). The coming of the Son of God prompts the demons to ask if he has come to torture them before the appointed time (8:29). Unlike John's disciples, who fast, Jesus' disciples enjoy the presence of the bridegroom (9:14-15 — incidentally another bit of evidence that Matthew does not regard John as already in the kingdom). When the Twelve are sent out (ch. 10), it is because Jesus sees that the harvest-time has already come (9:35-38). What they preach is that the kingdom of heaven is near (10:7).

Much more evidence could be adduced, but the point seems clear enough. Matthew is careful to place Jesus' works in the appropriate place in the stream of redemptive history. But it is vital to recognize that he has already done the same for John the Baptist and his ministry. Not only does Matthew (in line with other Evangelists) point out that John came to fulfill the words of Isaiah (Matt 3:3), but alone among the Evangelists Matthew casts John's baptism of Jesus as a work by which *both* John and Jesus "fulfill all righteousness" (3:15). This does not jeopardize Jesus' uniqueness: the voice from heaven refers to Jesus alone when it declares, "This is my Son, whom I love; with him I am well pleased" (3:17).

That there is an *inclusio* created by τὰ ἔργα (11:2) and τῶν ἔργων (11:19b) we need not doubt; that these words were introduced as Matthean redaction is likely. But in the light of Matthew's emphasis on redemptive history, in the light of the intervening pericopae explaining John's place within that stream, in the light of the OT quotation used to declare that John himself fulfills Scripture, it is hard to see why the *inclusio* should be thought to *exclude* John from the works of 11:19b, or should be thought to label the Baptist's works with *exactly* the same kingdom significance as those of Jesus. The thought, rather, is that both John and Jesus have performed the works that God himself has assigned to them in their respective roles in redemptive history, and "this generation" responds negatively to both. John the Baptist is in this respect associated with Jesus, not driven from him.

19. Cf. esp. R. A. Edwards, "Matthew's Use of Q in Chapter Eleven," in *Logia: Les paroles de Jésus — The Sayings of Jesus,* ed. J. Delobel et al., BETL 59 (Leuven: Leuven University, 1982) 266; also Suggs, *Wisdom,* 56-58; H. Schürmann, *Das Lukasevangelium: Erster Teil: Kommentar zu Kap 1, 1-9.50,* HTKNT 3 / 1 (Freiburg: Herder, 1969) 428.

(3) The major Matthean addition, namely, 11:12-13, is an extraordinarily difficult passage.[20] I have argued elsewhere[21] that this is a form of antanclasis. The verb βιάζεται should be taken as a deponent middle (its predominant usage) *in bonum partem,* referring to the advance of the kingdom; βιασταί and ἁρπάζουσιν should be taken according to their overwhelmingly preponderant usage, *in malem partem,* referring to evil people who have been trying to seize the kingdom, pillage it, rape it (conative present), ever since it appeared and started to make its forceful advance. "From the days of John the Baptist until now," on this reading, uses John as a temporal marker of the *terminus a quo* of the kingdom (without stating that John himself was in the kingdom), and "until now" means up to and including the moment Jesus speaks (with the readers doubtless left to project forward into their own time as well, in a secondary way). This interpretation admirably suits the context.

> The argument up to v. 11 has established John the Baptist's greatness, grounded in his ministry of preparing for and pointing out Christ; and it has anticipated the witness of those in the kingdom who are even greater than John because the least of them testifies to Christ yet more clearly. Now, Jesus goes on to say, from the days of the Baptist — i.e., from the beginning of Jesus' ministry — the kingdom has been forcefully advancing. . . . But it has not swept all opposition away, as John expected. . . . Simultaneous with the kingdom's advance have been the attacks of violent men on it. That is the very point John could not grasp. Now Jesus expressly affirms it.[22]

Probably in Matthew's mind these attacks are not just of one kind. They include the attacks by Jewish leaders now intensifying (9:34; 12:22-24), the materialism that craved a political Messiah and the prosperity he would bring but not his righteousness (11:20-24), and the potential for serious persecution (10:16-42).

Whether or not this interpretation is correct, what is surely clear is that these two difficult verses, however interpreted, turn on sequence ("From . . . until now"), on history, on development. In short, they make what might be called some redemptive-historical distinctions — distinctions that simultaneously establish, on the one hand, the respective roles of John the Baptist and of Jesus, and, on the other, the superiority of the latter over the former. In other words, these redemptive-historical distinctions reinforce the approach to 11:2-16 being argued for here.[23]

(4) As we have seen, Dunn argues that Matthew (but not Luke or Q)

20. For a useful survey of the options, cf. B. D. Chilton, *God in Strength: Jesus' Announcement of the Kingdom* (Freistadt: F. Plöchl, 1977) 203ff.

21. Carson, *Matthew,* 265ff.

22. Carson, *Matthew,* 267.

23. Indeed, F. Mussner, "Der nicht erkannte Kairos (Mt 11, 16-19 = Lk 7, 31-35)," *Bib* 40 (1959) 599-612, argues that the "heilsgeschichtliche Auffassung" of both these passages runs right through *both* the text *and* the source, and is ultimately traceable to Jesus.

is the first to make the explicit identification of Jesus with Wisdom. Dunn sees the same pattern elsewhere, and if he is right then his interpretation of this passage might be judged to have more cogency. But in each case his arguments are less than convincing. When he compares Matt 11:25-30 with Luke 10:21-22,[24] he rightly sides with those who do not see in the initial parallel (Matt 11:25-27 = Luke 20:21-22) a background in Wisdom, but rather in the identification of Jesus with Israel in (or of) the last days. The closest parallels are in OT election passages. Matthew 11:28-30, however, without parallel in Luke, is Matthew's addition to the Q passage, and this (Dunn and others[25] argue) has been modeled on Sirach 51, especially vv 23-26, where the teacher of Wisdom invites pupils to put their necks under Wisdom's yoke, and offers his own testimony regarding the rest he himself has found in his labor under this yoke. But the differences between this passage and Matt 11:28-30 are at least as remarkable as the similarities. Ben Sira invites people to take on the yoke of Wisdom, which is nothing other than studying Torah, as the means of gaining acceptance and rest; Jesus offers eschatological rest, not to the student of Torah, but to the weary who come to him and adopt his teaching — and this teaching stands, as the next two pericopae show (12:1-8, 9-13), in some distinction to traditional understandings of Torah, and focuses on Jesus himself, the Lord of the Sabbath(-rest). Thus Jesus replaces the centrality of Torah (cf. 5:17-20). Matthew's own context makes adequate sense, indeed better sense, without here reading in Jesus' identification with or fulfillment of Wisdom. True, Wisdom and Torah are tightly tied together in Sirach 51, and Matthew probably knew this passage. But the Evangelist is much closer to insisting on Jesus' identification with or fulfillment of Torah than of Wisdom.

Dunn's treatment of the remaining two passages (Luke 11:49-51; Matt 23:34-36; Matt 23:37-39 / Luke 13:34-35)[26] does not prove any more convincing. Indeed, on the face of it one might reasonably argue that Luke is more interested in personifying Wisdom than is Matthew (cf. Luke 11:49), but that neither Evangelist specifically identifies Jesus with Wisdom.

(5) Although Wisdom is already personified in the OT (e.g., Job 28; Proverbs 1, 8) and certainly developed in Jewish tradition into a quasi-personal hypostasis expressing the mind of God,[27] and although this background sometimes serves in the NT as a vehicle for christology, yet here Wisdom is best seen in its more common and traditional guise. The purpose of Matthew 11 is not to establish a Wisdom christology, but to set out the place of John the Baptist,

24. *Christology in the Making,* 198-201.

25. E.g., J. Zumstein, *La condition du croyant dans l'Evangile selon Matthieu* (Göttingen: Vandenhoeck & Ruprecht, 1977) 140ff.

26. *Christology in the Making,* 201-4.

27. See G. Fohrer and U. Wilckens, "σοφία κτλ," *TDNT* 7:465-526; F. Christ, *Jesus Sophia,* ATANT 57 (Zürich: Zwingli, 1970) 13-60, 156-63; Dunn, *Christology in the Making,* 168-76.

and therefore *a fortiori* of Jesus, in the stream of redemptive history. The addition of Wisdom christology in v 19b would have added little to the argument.[28]

The proverb should be read in the light of the immediately preceding parable: God's Wisdom is vindicated (ἐδικαιώθη) by her actions, which in the context refer to the respective lifestyles and ministries of both John and Jesus. Wisdom is much concerned with right living under God. Both John and Jesus have been roundly criticized for the way they live and for what they teach. But Wisdom has in fact been vindicated by her works; that is, both John with his asceticism and Jesus with his *Weltoffenheit* act in accord with God's Wisdom, and their respective lifestyles and emphases are acknowledged as hers (they are *her* works) and justify her claims. Wisdom is justified by her effects, and the effects are good in both cases. On this reading, Wisdom is not a personification of Jesus, and the thrust of Matthew's form of the logion is only a whisker away from that of Luke (as we shall see).

(6) Turning now to the parallel in Luke, once again one wonders if some of the interpretations of the proverb have depended rather too narrowly on certain redactional features *at the expense* of the entire text. The first of these features is the lengthy addition of Luke 7:29-30. As we have seen, many scholars draw a tight connection between v 29 and v 35, largely because both verses deploy the verb δικαιόω. On this basis, "All the people, even the tax collectors" (v 29) becomes equivalent to "all her [i.e., Wisdom's] children" (v 35), set over against "this generation" (v 31) who are more narrowly identified with the Pharisees and scribes (v 30). Perhaps the strongest form of this argument has been put by du Plessis,[29] who finds a basic chiastic parallelism in vv 29 and 35:

| | |
|---|---|
| v 29 | *All the people . . . acknowledged* that *God's way was right* |
| v 30 | But the Pharisees . . . rejected God's purpose for themselves |
| vv 31-34 | To what, then, can I compare the children of this generation |
| v 35 | But *wisdom* is *proved right* by *all her children* |

Du Plessis then notes the following formal parallels between v 29 and v 35:

28. The detailed reasons put forward by Suggs, *Wisdom,* in defense of Wisdom christology here are not convincing, but take us beyond the scope of this essay. On many points Suggs is followed by F. W. Burnett, *The Testament of Jesus-Sophia: A Redaction-Critical Study of the Eschatological Discourse in Matthew* (Lanham: University Press of America, 1981).

29. I. J. du Plessis, "Contextual Aid for an Identity Crisis: An Attempt to Interpret Luke 7:35," in *A South African Perspective on the New Testament,* ed. J. H. Petzer and P. J. Hartin (Leiden: E. J. Brill, 1986) 124-25.

v 29: καὶ πᾶς ὁ λαός . . . ἐδικαίωσαν τὸν θεόν
v 35: καὶ ἐδικαιώθη ἡ σοφία . . . πάντων τῶν τέκνων

Indeed, if one eliminates the common elements, du Plessis argues, not only must one argue that Wisdom's children are "all the people" but that "God's counsel" (v 30) = "Wisdom."

Despite the formal plausibility of this approach, several factors weigh against it. The internal members of the chiasm are not parallel in tone, grammar, vocabulary, or thrust. The only point of comparison is the Pharisees (along with, presumably, the scribes) and "the people of this generation." In any case, the sheer length of the third member makes the proposed chiasm suspect, unless there is powerful countervailing evidence. So what we have, then, is not a believable chiasm, but simply the parallels between v 29 and v 35 that have long been noted by scholars. Moreover, in the tight form of the parallelism that du Plessis proposes, there is a sleight of hand operating. Strictly speaking, on formal grounds we should conclude that God = Wisdom. The only reason why du Plessis can change this to the proposition that "God's purpose" or "God's counsel" = Wisdom is that he has drawn τὴν βουλὴν τοῦ θεοῦ from v 30 back into v 29. Of course, if one "justifies" God's purpose, presumably one also justifies God. The fact remains that the *formal* elements of the alleged parallelism are not as tight as first appears.

Granted that the passage moves on to include vv 31-34 before allowing v 35 to stand (with whatever degree of parallelism we might conclude it has with v 29), it seems best to discern a slightly different flow of thought from that which leaps so quickly from v 29 to v 35. It is true that "all the people, even the tax collectors," justified God (v 29), while the Pharisees and scribes, representing the leaders and thus (under an essentially tribal covenant) the people as a whole, "the people of this generation," rejected God's counsel (v 30). This latter rejection is represented in the parable (vv 31-32) and then explained with reference to the rejection of both the Baptist and Jesus (vv 33-34). And (But?) Wisdom is justified by all her children — surely, in this sequence, not least by John and Jesus; perhaps, following v 29, *a fortiori* by John and Jesus.

(7) There are four minor exegetical details in Luke 7:35 that need weighing (namely, καί, πάντων, ἀπό, and the aorist tense), but before turning to them, the parable itself and its interpretation (both similarly expressed in Luke and Matthew) must be considered. The overwhelming majority of interpreters hold that in both Gospels the children who play the flute and sing a dirge, inviting others to join them, represent Jesus and John respectively; the children who refuse to play represent "this generation" (Matthew) or "the people of this generation" (Luke). Most commentators who discuss the matter acknowledge that this alignment is (superficially at least) a trifle messy. The parable is introduced by asking what this generation is like; we are told, "*They* are like children sitting in the marketplace and calling out to each other. . . ." But in the usual

interpretation, *They* do not call out in dance and dirge, but sulkily refuse to cooperate. These difficulties have generated some negative comment. "The comparison is not exactly expressed," writes Creed. "It is John and Jesus — not this generation — who are the counterparts to the children who invite their fellows to joy or to mourning — in each case without success."[30] Klostermann thinks the present text is corrupt;[31] McNeile says of Matthew, "Strictly speaking 'this generation' was similar, not to the children who uttered their complaints but to those who refused to play; for the προσφωνοῦντα can hardly be the Pharisees, demanding this and that manner of life from the Baptist and Jesus: they made no such demand."[32]

The usual way of avoiding this difficulty is by supposing that the ὁμοιώσω / ὅμοιός εἰσιν language reflects an Aramaic idiom meaning, "It is the case with X as with Y" — and "Y" may be the entire story.[33] That is certainly how the introductions to many of the kingdom parables work. "The kingdom of heaven is like a man who sowed good seed in his field" (Matt 13:24); the kingdom of heaven is not like a man at all, but it is the case with the kingdom of heaven as with (the story of) the man who, etc. Even so, this explanation is perhaps less convincing in Matt 11:16-19 / Luke 7:31-34. It is a commonplace that "parable" covers an extraordinarily wide range of forms (including proverbs, maxims, similes, comparisons, stories embodying some truth, riddles, and more).[34] By the same token, the way they are introduced may vary. Our text may be a more-or-less straightforward comparison, and if so it is essential to think clearly about what things (or people) are being compared. Moreover, unlike many of the kingdom parables where the nature of the comparison (an impersonal noun like "kingdom" coupled with a "man") forces the interpreter to see the point of comparison lying between the kingdom and the thrust of the entire narrative, here there is no narrative (there is no plot line), and people are being compared with people.

In short, we are driven to weigh an alternative proposal, recently defended by O. Linton.[35] In this interpretation, the people of this generation are represented by those who played the flute and sang a dirge; John the Baptist and Jesus are those who would not play their games. The children calling to the others are not demanding anything extraordinary or extravagant. They are simply demanding that John and Jesus join them for their feasts and festivals

30. J. M. Creed, *The Gospel according to St. Luke* (London: Macmillan, 1930) 108.

31. E. Klostermann, *Das Matthäus-Evangelium,* 2d ed. (Tübingen: J. C. B. Mohr [Paul Siebeck], 1927) 99.

32. *Matthew,* 157.

33. See J. Jeremias, *The Parables of Jesus,* 2d ed. (London: SCM, 1963) 100-101; M. Zerwick, *Biblical Greek Illustrated by Examples* (Rome: Biblical Institute, 1963) §65. This is the approach taken, e.g., by Gundry, *Matthew,* 212.

34. C. H. Peisker and C. Brown, "Parable, Allegory, Proverb," *NIDNTT* 2:743-60.

35. "The Parable of the Children's Game," *NTS* 22 (1976) 159-79.

— that is, that they fit in. Judith was praiseworthy because "she fasted all the days of her widowhood, save the eves of the sabbaths, and the sabbaths, and the eves of the new moons and the new moons, and the feasts and joyful days of the house of Israel" (Jdt 8:6). In other words, she knew there was "a time to weep and a time to laugh; a time to mourn and a time to dance" (Eccl 3:4). Certainly there is evidence that Jesus and his disciples did not fast the way John and the Pharisees and their disciples did (Mark 2:18-22; Matt 9:14-17; Luke 5:33-39); indeed, just before this evidence we are also told that Jesus was charged with eating with tax collectors and sinners (Mark 2:16; Matt 9:11 [cf. Luke 5:30]). In short, Jesus did not behave as some people thought a pious Jew should. As for John the Baptist, his obvious asceticism (remember his diet!) would not have prepared him for joyous celebrations of feasts.

The feasting / fasting opposition is in any case probably symbolic of larger questions of perceived appropriateness. John came and preached repentance, and the severity of both his lifestyle and his message were judged "over the top." Jesus comes with much more *Weltoffenheit*, insisting fasting is unsuitable at the wedding feast over which he presides. His conduct and his message demonstrate that he cannot be domesticated.

And so the opposition sets in. John is invited to lighten up: "We played the flute for you," but he would not dance. Jesus is invited to the sobriety of popular religion: "We sang a dirge," but he would not mourn.[36] The Jewish authorities demand that both John and Jesus conform to the dictates of custom that has all the force of religious mandate, but they will not oblige.

From the parable the text turns to the explanation of the criticism offered by this generation. This generation is convinced it knows *why* John will not lighten up: "He has a demon" (Matt 11:18; Luke 7:33). They also think they know *why* Jesus will not toe the line: "Here is a glutton and a drunkard, a friend of tax-collectors and sinners" (Matt 11:19; Luke 7:34). John and Jesus belong together and can be dismissed together precisely because neither will conform to religious expectations.

A number of details might support this interpretation.[37] First, the historical order, John the Baptist preceding Jesus, agrees with the order of the explanation (Matt 11:18-19a; Luke 7:33-34), and we should perhaps expect it to occur in the rhyme itself; on the traditional interpretation, it does not agree with the rhyme. Of course, one might argue that the parable was a well-known couplet that could not reasonably have been reversed, or that this is another example of hysteron-proteron. Nevertheless, when the argument of the chapter turns on who is first and who is second in chronological appearance, and when the explanation itself follows this chronological order, then all things being equal

36. Of course, we must not suppose the rhyme invites John and Jesus to reverse their roles. That would be to confuse the parable and its application, to force the parable to run on all fours.

37. In part I follow Linton; here and there I diverge from him, nowhere more forcefully (as we shall see) than in his treatment of Matt 11:19b / Luke 7:35.

that interpretation seems best which follows the same order in the rhyme: John is attacked first, and then Jesus.

Second, when we compare the rhyme, where the entire content is nothing other than what some children *say* (Luke: λέγει; Matthew: λέγουσιν), with the application or explanation that follows, where the burden of the content again lies in what the critics *say* (Luke: λέγετε; Matthew: λέγουσιν), it appears that "the *tertium comparationis* lies in the comments, in what the children *say* about their comrades, and what people *say* about John and Jesus."[38]

Third, if the rhyme is a Greek rendering of an underlying Semitic couplet, the parataxis must not mislead. The thought may well be (and is in any case perfectly allowable even as the Greek stands), "When we played the flute for you, you did not dance; when we sang a dirge, you did not cry."

To be frank, I am not certain if this interpretation is correct. Certainly the objections against it do not appear very substantial. For example, not a few scholars have objected to this view on the ground that it makes John and Jesus correspond to the passive participants in the parable, the active role being reserved for the children who call out in the marketplaces and who represent the people of this generation. But the fact that John and Jesus take the initiative over against the religious establishment throughout the Gospels as a whole does not mean they must take the initiative in every pericope. Again, Fitzmyer objects to this interpretation on the ground that "it may be allegorizing the passage more than is called for."[39] But that presupposes that there is some standard as to how much "allegorizing" is allowed. Over against the rigid school of Jeremias, recent parable research has shown that "allegorizing" of some elements in a narrative parable provides no evidence for later development. Weder distinguishes parabolic (as opposed to allegorical) elements as those tied to the narrative flow and therefore lacking *independent* existence both in the narrative and its interpretation.[40] In other words, where so-called "allegorizing" elements are tied both to the parable and to its interpretation, contributing to the thrust of the former and the power of the latter, they are better thought of as legitimate parabolic elements. By such standards no charge of undue allegorizing can be brought against this passage. In any case such discussion applies primarily to *narrative* parables; the present passage does not qualify. I can think of no reason and know of no research that establishes this sort of comparison as too "allegorizing."[41]

38. Linton, "Children's Game," 173.

39. *Luke,* 679.

40. H. Weder, *Die Gleichnisse Jesu als Metaphern* (Göttingen: Vandenhoeck & Ruprecht, 1978) 69-75.

41. If it be objected that the word παραβολή is not used to refer to this passage, the interpretation offered here is strengthened, for R. A. Edwards, *A Theology of Q* (Philadelphia: Fortress, 1976) esp. 58-78, has drawn attention to the extraordinarily high concentration of "comparison" utterances in Q material.

Even if this interpretation is not finally adopted, it makes the next step in my argument only marginally more difficult, and will not detract from my main points.

(8) On the reading I have advanced here, "this generation" has been venting its criticism of John and Jesus. But that is not the last word. The purpose of Matt 11:19b / Luke 7:35 is to cast the lifestyles of John and of Jesus in a different light. That brings us to the minor exegetical details to which I have already alluded:

(a) καί: The overwhelming majority of scholars detect adversative force in this conjunction, some comparing *atque* and drawing attention to parallels in the Fourth Gospel.[42] At one level that approach is doubtless justified. Still, more needs to be said. It is an axiom of linguistics that no two words or expressions long occupy *exactly* the same semantic space. Differences in emphasis, overtone, associations, intensity, or the like are always to be found. We must therefore ask the paradigmatic question, Why is καί found in both Matthew and Luke, instead of ἀλλά or some other adversative? What does this choice signify, and how can it best be represented in English?

I have looked at every instance in the NT where the major grammars find alleged instances of adversative καί. Many of them are best translated by an English "but." Nevertheless, I think I can detect a common element, a possible reason why a word normally rendered "and" was chosen. The adversative force of what follows is usually ironic, or is a slightly distanced reflection, or is slightly aphoristic; alternatively, the adversative relationships between, say, two connected clauses, is established by the content of the clauses (as in Hebrew antithetic parallelism), such that a "but" would be a trifle heavy-handed whereas an "and" is more subtle and in such a context more suggestive and powerful.

So here. Perhaps in this case an appropriate English orthography to get across the same idea would be a new paragraph beginning with "And." The new paragraph would signal not a new thought, but a dramatic conclusion. The movement of thought (on the assumption that the parable is to be interpreted as outlined above) would be as follows. The people of "this generation" criticize both John and Jesus for their respective lifestyles and ministries, comparing them with unresponsive children. Their harsh judgments are recorded. Pause. New paragraph. "And Wisdom is justified in (all) her children / works." Of course, the καί is logically adversative. Stylistically, however, the choice of καί means that the concluding proverb bears a subtle reevaluation of the same phenomena in John and Jesus that have been criticized by "this generation" — one that moves off in quite a different direction, and implicitly condemns the evaluation of "this generation." (This approach to καί could also be adapted to more traditional interpretations of the parable and its explanation, though perhaps not with quite as much force.)

(b) πάντων: The text-critical question is difficult: the text of NA[26] is not

42. So A. Plummer, *The Gospel according to S. Luke*, 4th ed., ICC (Edinburgh: T. & T. Clark, 1901) 208.

powerfully supported[43] but becomes reasonably persuasive only because it is tangentially supported by the manuscript evidence that attests πάντων at the end of the verse. But how did it get there? If we suppose that it was displaced from its original location, represented by the NA[26] text, by some stylist who thought it fit better at the end, then the support for inclusion is very strong. If instead we suppose that πάντων was a marginal gloss that a later copyist felt must be inserted somewhere, and chose the end of the clause, then the question becomes, How did the marginal gloss arise? If it arose because of someone's theology (attempting a link with v 29? forcing the text to bear a more general application?), then support for inclusion is quite limited. But if the marginal gloss arose because an early copyist neglected to include it at its proper position (immediately after the preposition), and placed it in the margin so it would not be overlooked by the next copyist, then the evidence for inclusion returns to substantial strength. Several other possibilities come to mind.

If we assume that πάντων is original (whatever its location), we must ask what function it serves in the text as we have it before we can reasonably ask if it is redactional. The majority opinion among scholars today is that it rules out the view that Wisdom's children are John and Jesus. Luke 7:35 thus gets tied to v 29, and Wisdom's children are none other than ὁ λαὸς ἀκούσας καὶ οἱ τελῶναι, thus removing v 35 from any direct relevance to the immediately preceding verses (vv 31-34).

But if the interpretation advocated in this essay is correct, we may not be forced to choose. Verse 35 is tied to both its context and to the earlier redactional statement (vv 29-30). If v 35 is tied to the parable and its explanation, it provides, as we have seen, the counterpoint explanation of the lifestyles and ministries of John the Baptist and Jesus. If πάντων were not present, or if the text had read "both her children," then it would have been most natural to link this concluding proverb exclusively to vv 31-34. But with πάντων present the *application* of the proverb to John and Jesus is still just as effective as if it were not present, but the application cannot easily be *limited* to them. Thus the burden of the proverb and its location point unerringly to John and Jesus as Wisdom's children; the inclusion of πάντων and the echoing link with v 29 suggests a further application to their disciples, and, implicitly, to the followers of Jesus among the readers of the book.[44] It is *always* true that Wisdom is justified by her children, even if that truth is preeminently displayed in John and Jesus. As for those who have drawn attention to the fact that in the relevant literature Wisdom's sons are those who listen to and obey her call, not those who preach it (Prov 8:32; Sir 4:11; 15:11) — and therefore conclude that in Luke 7:35 Wisdom's children cannot be John and Jesus[45] — on this interpreta-

43. Cf. n. 4, *supra.*

44. Fitzmyer, *Luke,* 681, reaches similar conclusions on somewhat different grounds.

45. See n. 8, *supra.*

tion John and Jesus are not doing the "calling" or "preaching" in the marketplaces at all. Rather, it is their conduct that is being evaluated. Even on a more traditional interpretation of the parable and its explanation, it is not John and Jesus *qua* preachers who are being discussed, but John and Jesus *qua* Wisdom's envoys.

When we ask (still assuming that πάντων is part of the text) whether or not πάντων was part of Q (on the assumption of the existence of Q), we face the problem that if Q included πάντων we must explain why Matt 11:19b has dropped it, when on the face of it inclusion might have marginally strengthened Matthew's argument (assuming πάντων would in that case have been modifying ἔργων). Someone might argue that Matthew has a tendency to abbreviate his sources (judging by what he does with Mark), and that in changing τέκνων to ἔργων he dropped πάντων from his Q-source on these stylistic grounds. This sequence of judgments becomes unnecessary, of course, if we assume that Q (if it existed) did *not* include πάντων. In that case there is nothing to explain in Matthew; what must be explained is why Luke added it. Demonstrably Luke has a small penchant for πᾶς. Coupled with his concern to make the double link of the proverb (i.e., both with John / Jesus and with v 29, which Luke has also added), this penchant justifies the tentative conclusion that πάντων was not in his source. But this tentative conclusion holds up whether his source was Q or Matthew. In other words, one could as readily infer from these judgments the priority of Matthew and Luke's dependence on Matthew as the existence of Q.

(c) ἀπό: Several have argued that this preposition must be taken in some Aramaic sense (either *min*, or *min q'dâm*): either "in view of," "on account of" (which makes adequate sense of Matthew but not of Luke), or "in front of" and hence "over against" — that is, Wisdom is justified *over against* her children (= this generation), almost *despite* her children.[46] Methodologically, however, it is a dubious procedure that makes an interpretation depend on a semitism (as opposed to a Semitic enhancement):[47] one must assume that the translator / evangelist was incompetent. It is appropriate to appeal to a semitism if one cannot make sense of the passage any other way (which is not the case here); it is appropriate to appeal to a putative Aramaic underlay if what is at stake is no more than a Semitic enhancement (presupposed in the earlier discussion of

46. J. Jeremias, *Parables*, 164 n. 43, takes *min q'dâm* to mean "in view of," citing J. Wellhausen, *Das Evangelium Matthaei* (Berlin: Georg Reimer, 1904) 55. But the latter understands the Aramaic expression to mean "in front of / against." In this he is followed by Linton, "Children's Games," 177-78.

47. In current linguistic theory, a semitism in a Greek text is a word or expression or construction that does not make sense in Greek, but can be explained *only* by appealing to a putative Semitic underlay. A Semitic enhancement is a word or expression or construction that occurs in Greek (however rarely), that makes adequate sense in Greek, but that occurs much more frequently in the text than would have been the case if there had not been any possibility of Semitic underlay.

the ὅμοιος word group). It is not appropriate to take ἀπό in a sense utterly unknown to Greek readers, unless there really is no other reasonable choice.[48] This factor surely eliminates the view that the "children" refer to this generation.[49] Taking the preposition to mean "in view of" or "on account of" makes sense with Matthew's "works" but not with Luke's "children." On the ground that the simplest explanation is best (all other things being equal), it seems wiser to take ἀπό in its well-attested sense of "by," occasionally used in Hellenistic Greek in a sense not easily distinguishable from ὑπό (with the passive) to express agency and sometimes means.[50]

Wisdom is justified, vindicated, by her effects — whether the "works" of John and Jesus (Matthew) or her children and their lifestyles and ministries (primarily John and Jesus, but derivatively all those who hear Jesus' words and acknowledge that God's way as expressed in those words is right — so Luke).

(d) Many scholars have argued that the aorist ἐδικαιώθη is gnomic — that is, that it is timeless, not past-referring.[51] That is doubtless correct, but in itself it cannot establish that Matt 11:19b / Luke 7:35 was originally an independent logion. Even if this proverb had been attached to the parable and its explanation from its inception, it would still be best to take it in a "gnomic" sense, since the ostensible setting of the utterance places John in the past but Jesus in the present. Besides, even when proverbs are *applied* to concrete historical settings they are usually *cast* in a timeless structure. In short, although it is entirely plausible that the proverb led an independent existence, we have no evidence for it except what we have here, where it is firmly attached to what precedes it. The alignment of the order of the pericopae in Matt 11:2-19 and Luke 7:18-35 (redactional insertions aside), including the final proverb, forcefully argues either for direct borrowing or for a common source.

(9) Finally, we must weigh the common judgment that τῶν ἔργων in Matt

48. The study of H. Sahlin, "Traditionskritische Bemerkungen zu zwei Evangelienperikopen," *ST* 33 (1979) 77-84, treating both Matthew 11 and Luke 7, is especially guilty on this score.

49. Cf. the preceding two notes. Perhaps I should add that, whether one is thinking of Matt 11:19b or of Luke 7:35, the interpretation of W. J. Cotter, "Children Sitting in the Agora: Q (Luke) 7:31-35," *Forum* 5 (1989) 63-82 — that "the seemingly opposite roades to *[sic]* wisdom which John and Jesus represent in the unit, are blessed as two viable and sure routes to *[sic]* their one Mother [= Wisdom]" — is contextually unattached and syntactically unjustified. Equally difficult to defend is the view of R. Leivestad, "An Interpretation of Matt 11:19," *JBL* 71 (1952) 179-81, to the effect that the "works" performed are those of the Jews, and the σοφία is not divine wisdom but the wisdom of the Jews: the utterance is ironic, such that "wisdom is justified by her deeds" is roughly equivalent to "the tree is known by its fruit." Leivestad acknowledges there is no parallel use of σοφία in the NT, but compares Job 12:2 ("No doubt but you are the people, and wisdom shall die with you").

50. Cf. Schürmann, *Lukasevangeliums*, 427 n. 145.

51. Some recent grammarians have argued that the aorist tense is not temporally determined in any mood, including the indicative. Whether the action is past-, present-, or future-referring is established on other grounds than the morphology of the verb. Cf. esp. S. E. Porter, *Verbal Aspect in the Greek of the New Testament, with Reference to Tense and Mood* (Bern: Peter Lang, 1989).

11:19b is secondary and was generated by the use of τὰ ἔργα in Matt 11:2, leaving τῶν τέκνων in Luke 7:35 to be the original by default. Since virtually no one holds that Matthew copied from Luke, and if direct borrowing from Matthew to Luke is ruled out by the conclusion that Matthew's form is secondary, we are driven back to Q, and the assumption that Luke has preserved Q at this point.

If we may leave aside the proposal that an Aramaic original was variously pointed "servants" and "works" (if for no other reason than that τέκνα is an odd way to render "servants"), we must ask if a plausible case can be made for Luke adapting Matthew as his source — that is, for Luke changing τῶν ἔργων to τῶν τέκνων. One might argue that τῶν τέκνων was introduced to establish a connection of persons (as opposed to "works") with vv 29-30. But there is no use of τέκνον in vv 29-30, and in any case we have already found substantial reasons for seeing the *primary* link lying between v 35 and vv 31-34, not between v 35 and vv 29-30. It has also been suggested that Luke was influenced by παιδίοις in v 32. The hypothesis is hard to disprove, but the least that must be said against it is that (a) Matthew also had that word before him, or (b) if Luke had been set on making a connection between v 35 and v 32 it is strange that he did not choose the same word.

On balance, then, it is somewhat more likely, so far as this word is concerned, that Matthew is secondary, and to that extent there is an implicit support for Q.

## 4

Quite apart from any contribution to the exegesis of Matt 11:19b / Luke 7:35 that this essay makes, its bearing on the Synoptic problem can now be briefly stated.

Methodologically speaking, the emphasis in this discussion has been on the importance of the large-scale movement of the flow of thought in Matthew 11 and Luke 7 when trying to evaluate the contribution of minute scraps of data — and vice versa.

The meanings of the two passages are remarkably similar; Luke probably sees an extension of the application of the proverb beyond John and Jesus to those who hear Jesus' words and perceive that God's way, expressed in Jesus, is right — but this is a secondary application. Arguments for a fully-fledged Wisdom christology in Matthew — arguments which by implication would make Matthew secondary, and therefore support the Q-hypothesis — are exceedingly weak. Matthew appears more primitive in the omission of πάντων; Luke appears more primitive in his use of τέκνων. But as we have seen, the Q-hypothesis applied to this pair of passages allows for both claims of primitiveness; it is marginally more difficult for a theory of Matthean priority to do so. But the margin is slight.[52]

52. This essay is offered to Professor Howard Marshall with enormous appreciation for the masterly way he combines meticulous attention to detail, large-scale vision, and transparent concern for the well-being of other believers. *In multos annos!*

# Structure and Christology in Mark 1:21-45

Grant R. Osborne

As is the case with the other Gospels, there are almost as many different "outlines" of Mark's structure as there are scholars.[1] Ancient narrative does not lend itself well to modern structural approaches, and the Gospels often tend to be more cyclical than linear in their organization. Nevertheless, there is certainly a structural relationship between the pericopes of Mark, and so the search will continue.

In terms of macrostructure, 1:21-45 is part of the first major section of Mark following the prologue, 1:16–3:6.[2] The primary thrust of this first section is not merely conflict versus popularity but more the authority of Jesus as it confronts the three primary groups with which Jesus interacts — the disciples (1:16-20), the crowds (1:21-45), and the religious leaders (2:1–3:6). Their diverse reactions to that authority — following Jesus totally, flocking after him, and opposing him totally — form the dynamic of this section. Christology intertwines with soteriology as each group is forced to respond to God's presence in Jesus. In this sense, the christological revelations of 1:1-15 are acted out in the human dramas of 1:16–3:6.

The structure of 1:21-45 itself is quite debated, with several different approaches. One popular approach finds a concentric structure employing chiasm. Didelberg and Mourlon Beernaert[3] develop a seven-part chiasm: A (vv 21-27), B (v 28), C (vv 29-31), D (vv 32-34), C′ (vv 35-38), B′ (v 39), A′ (vv

1. One of the most impressive qualities of Professor Marshall was the extent to which he made his students feel as if they were already scholars, and that he was looking forward to seeing their work. As a mentor, he had a gift for encouragement. It is indeed a privilege to participate in this *Festschrift* in his honor. The two elements of this study, structure and christology, have always been visible in I. Howard Marshall's many works, and thus this seems an apt topic for this *Festschrift*.

2. While some such as H. Anderson, *The Gospel of Mark*, NCBC (London: Oliphants, 1976); and J. Gnilka, *Das Evangelium nach Markus*, 2 vols., EKKNT 2 (Neukirchen-Vluyn: Neukirchener, 1978/79), believe that the first section ends at 3:12, I agree with the majority position that it ends at 3:6. Mark 3:7-12 is another of Mark's summary sections and forms a transition between the two parts but relates more to what follows.

3. P. Didelberg and P. Mourlon Beernaert, "Jésus vint en Galilée," *NRT* 98 (1976) 306-23 (esp. 315-17).

40-45). The strong points of this — the centrality of the summary section of vv 32-34 and the parallelism between v 28 and v 39 — are vitiated by the lack of parallels between vv 21-27 and vv 40-45 and between vv 29-31 and vv 35-38. On the other hand, Clark[4] finds a five-part chiasm in 1:21–2:12: A (1:21-28), B (1:29-34), C (1:35-39), B′ (1:40-45), A′ (2:1-12). This proposition depends partly on taking 2:1-12 with 1:21-45 rather than with 2:13–3:6. While others have argued for this,[5] the rhetorical development of 2:1-12 seems to move deliberately from popularity (2:2, 4, which summarizes the theme of 1:21-45) to opposition (2:6-12), which becomes the key element of 2:1–3:6. Moreover, the inner ring (vv 29-34 and 40-45) and center (vv 35-39) of Clark's proposal have even more difficulties than that of Didelberg and Mourlon Beernaert.[6]

Since 2:1–3:6 does seem to employ a chiastic arrangement (A [2:1-12], B [2:13-17], C [2:18-22], B′ [2:23-28], A′ [3:1-6]),[7] such an arrangement for 1:21-45 is certainly possible. I find two possible concentric arrangements. If we proceed from 1:16-20, a six-part chiasm could make sense: A (vv 16-20), B (vv 21-28), C (vv 29-31), C′ (vv 32-34), B′ (vv 35-39), C′ (vv 40-45). The core would consist of two miracle sections (vv 29-31, 32-34), with Capernaum miracles the inner ring (vv 21-28, entering Capernaum; vv 35-39, leaving Capernaum), and discipleship sections the outer ring (vv 16-20, calling the first of the Twelve; vv 40-45 with many seeking Jesus). If we restrict ourselves to 1:21-45, there could be a five-part chiasm, A (vv 21-28), B (vv 29-31), C (vv 32-34), B′ (vv 35- 39), A′ (vv 40-45). The summary section (vv 32-34) would form the core, with the inner ring (vv 29-31, 35-39) centering on Jesus and his disciples and the outer ring (vv 21-28, 40-45) on Jesus' effect on the crowds. However, these too are artificial and do not do justice to the linguistic links (there are few such for any of the suggested chiastic arrangements) or the themes of the sections. Chiasm is always possible if one chooses a single theme from each section and ignores the others. But true chiasm must demonstrate linguistic connections as well as a congruence of major themes.[8] Both are lacking here.

4. D. J. Clark, "Criteria for Identifying Chiasm," *LB* 35 (1975) 63-72 (esp. 67-70).

5. See M. A. Tolbert, *Sowing the Gospel: Mark's World in Literary-Historical Perspective* (Minneapolis: Fortress, 1989) 131-36, who organizes the opening chapters of Mark on the basis of the geographical comment, "and passing along by the Sea of Galilee," which occurs in 1:16; 2:13; 3:7; 4:1. With this clue she sees 2:1-12 more as the final of four healing stories after the call of the first disciples (1:16-20), with 2:13-14 (the call of Levi) opening the second section, followed by four controversy stories. Tolbert's model certainly posits a close rhetorical unity between 1:16–2:12 and 2:13–3:6, and I find it attractive, especially since she has given greater place to the call of Levi as a second discipleship unit. However, as I shall indicate below, 2:1-12 should be taken with 2:13–3:6 rather than with 1:16-45.

6. See the excellent detailed critique of both chiastic proposals in J. Dewey, *Markan Public Debate: Literary Technique, Concentric Structure, and Theology in Mark 2:1–3:6* (Chico, California: Scholars, 1980) 173-79.

7. See Dewey's excellent work in *Markan Public Debate, passim.*

8. See Dewey's excellent discussion of criteria for discovering concentric arrangements in Mark in *Markan Public Debate,* 132-36.

A linear progression is more *a propos* to the unit. The themes build on each other to a climax in v 45, where Jesus becomes so popular that he can no longer minister in the towns due to the huge throngs that congregated to him. Here vv 21-34 are widely seen as a Sabbath day's ministry on Jesus' part, but that has come under dispute. The double time notes of v 32 (ὀψίας δὲ γενομένης, ὅτε ἔδυ ὁ ἥλιος) remove vv 32-34 from the Sabbath (which ended at dusk) and more likely connect vv 32-34 with vv 35-39. The double time notes of v 35 (πρωῒ ἔννυχα λίαν) duplicate the style of v 32 and indicate an event which took place the same night. Therefore it is more likely that Mark organized the section around a day's activities (vv 21-28, 29-31) and a night's activities (vv 32-34, 35-39).

Yet the actual structure is more complex than this. There is a distinct progression from the healing of one (vv 29-31) to the healing of many (vv 32-34) to the preaching to all (vv 35-39; cf. πάντες in v 37). Around this progression vv 21-28 functions as an introduction and vv 40-45 as a conclusion. Moreover, christology is central throughout the developing narrative. Therefore, we must note the linear development and interaction of structure and christology pericope by pericope.

## 1. Authority in Word and Deed (1:21-28)

The entry into Capernaum (v 21a) is presented here as a first stop on a missionary tour; Jesus and his disciples "fish for souls" (1:17) via teaching (1:21-22) in Capernaum. It has been common to think of Matthew as stressing Jesus' teaching and Mark as stressing Jesus' action. However, France[9] shows conclusively how central Jesus' teaching ministry was for his messianic role according to Mark. Jesus is called "teacher" 10 times (versus 6 in Matthew) and is described as "teaching" 15 times (versus 9 in Matthew). Moreover, most of these occur in Markan summaries and show his own interests. Jesus as teacher is essential to Markan christology. Jesus' first ministry in Capernaum sets the tone for the christological development of his Gospel. Jesus is the hidden epiphany of God, revealed already at the baptism as the "beloved Son" (1:11) and now astounding the people with his teaching. Moreover, as the content of the temptation narrative in 1:12, 13 may have been omitted partly because it is programmatic for the cosmic conflict theme of the rest of Mark's Gospel, so the content of Jesus' teaching may have been omitted here partly because it is programmatic of Jesus' ongoing teaching in the rest of this Gospel.

The "amazement" of the people (v 22a) is also a Markan theme. Mark uses five different verbs a total of 24 times to describe the wonder of those who

9. R. T. France, "Mark and the Teaching of Jesus," in *Gospel Perspectives*, vol. 1, ed. R. T. France and D. Wenham (Sheffield: JSOT, 1980) 101-36.

come in contact with Jesus' teaching and deeds. These have christological significance, alluding to that aura of marvel and fear reminiscent of OT theophanies and stressing the revelatory content of Jesus' teaching here. Jesus' teaching "overwhelms" (the meaning of ἐκπλήσσεσθαι) the people, but it must be noted here that wonder is not yet belief. The awe of the crowds is the natural response, but it is as yet enigmatic.[10]

The reason (γάρ) for this wonder (v 22b) forms the heart of this passage. Once more we are introduced to a major Markan term: ἐξουσία occurs 10 times in Mark, and on each occasion it is found in sections where Jesus' God-given "authority" is emphasized.[11] In fact, in 1:27, where it is in *inclusio* with v 22, it is a "new teaching" seen in his deeds as vehicles of divine revelation. Note how many christological themes coalesce at this point. Jesus speaks with ἐξουσία because he is Messiah and Son of God (1:1, 11) who has been endowed with the Holy Spirit (1:10, 12) and thus preaches a "new teaching" (1:27) — the gospel of the time of fulfillment when the kingdom (1:15) will break out in acts of teaching (1:22) and power (1:23-27).

The Markan καὶ εὐθύς (v 23) links the words and the deeds inextricably together. There are many signs of Markan redaction in this passage[12] — for example, the Markan terms and themes already noted and the use of εὐθύς and key words to link sections. Mark has carefully crafted vv 21-22, 23-27 to dramatize how Jesus' teaching and actions worked together to demonstrate his ἐξουσία.

The exorcism of the man possessed by an "unclean spirit" (Mark's favored expression for the demon-possessed, occurring eleven times in his Gospel, to stress the "ritually unclean" effects on the victims) follows the "classical" form, as Guelich points out:[13] encounter (v 23a), defense (vv 23b-24), command to depart (v 25), exorcism (v 26), and the crowd's reaction (v 27). The primary debate here centers on the significance of the interchange between the demon

10. B. D. Chilton, "Exorcism and History: Mark 1:21-28," in *Gospel Perspectives,* vol. 6, ed. D. Wenham and C. Blomberg (Sheffield: JSOT, 1986) 257, says, "Within the Markan style of presentation, Jesus is disclosed as wielding a divine but confusing authority, both to his contemporaries and to Mark's readers."

11. This understanding of ἐξουσία has been challenged by D. Daube, "Ἐξουσία in Mark 1:22 and 27," *JTS* 39 (1938) 45-59 (*The New Testament and Rabbinic Judaism* [= London: Athlone, 1956] 205-33). He argues that Jesus is seen as an ordained scribe with the "license" to make authoritative pronouncements on Torah rather than one of the "unordained" laypersons who only appealed to tradition. However, A. W. Argyle, "The Meaning of Ἐξουσία in Mark 1:22, 27," *ExpTim* in 80 (1969) 343, shows that this was not the normal meaning of ἐξουσία in the first century, and rightly questions whether such a technical demarcation would fit first-century Judaism. Few scholars have followed Daube on this, and the suggestion, while interesting, is doubtful.

12. For detailed discussion see R. Pesch, *Das Markusevangelium,* 2 vols., HTKNT 2 (Freiburg: Herder, 1977) 1:119-20; R. H. Stein, "The 'Redaktionsgeschichtliche' Investigation of a Markan Seam (Mc 1,21f)," *ZNW* 61 (1970) 70-94; Chilton, "Exorcism and History," 253-71; and R. Guelich, *Mark 1-8:26,* WBC 34a (Dallas: Word, 1989) 55.

13. Guelich, *Mark,* 55.

and Jesus. It has been common for scholars to discover in the demon's cry, "I know who you are, the Holy One of God" (1:24), a defensive maneuver by which the demon sought to gain an advantage over Jesus in the cosmic war. In the ancient world, names contained spiritual power, and the demon would be trying to gain mastery over Jesus by uttering his "secret name" or essence.[14]

This has been challenged recently by Koch and Guelich,[15] who say that in ancient texts the utterance of an honorific title in an exorcism setting exhibits not cosmic conflict but acquiescence to a superior authority. In this sense the demon would be recognizing Jesus as "the Holy One of God" and pleading with Jesus not to "destroy" him (v 24). Guelich connects this with his view of the "messianic secret,"[16] in which the commands that the demons "be silent" (1:25, 34; 3:11) are not power encounters but injunctions to secrecy "because they knew him" (1:34; cf. 3:11, "not to make him known").

The position of Koch and Guelich is very viable, both because it makes sense of the Markan language and because it would highlight even further the christological force of the title, "the Holy One of God." However, the language of this passage draws me back to the more common view. While demonic conflict is not uppermost in 1:34 or 3:11, the larger context here makes it probable that a conflict setting is present. Markan theology stresses the cosmic war (as in the "binding of the strong man" in 3:27), and vv 24-25 favor this perspective for 1:23-27. As Fitzmyer notes,[17] ἀπόλεσαι reflects the belief that the demons and their control over human beings would be "destroyed" before the Day of the Lord when God would gain control on behalf of his people (cf. 1QM 1:10-14; 14:10-11) by casting the demons into the abyss (Luke 8:31; Rev 20:10-11). I see defiance rather than acquiescence in the language of v 24. Moreover, Kee has noted[18] that ἐπιτιμᾶν of v 25 stems from the technical Semitic word גער, used in the Qumran texts and elsewhere to designate the command by which God or his emissaries force evil powers into submission. Jesus' command rings with finality. With a single word Jesus gains total control,

14. Among others, see O. Bauernfeind, *Die Worte der Dämonen im Markusevangelium* (Stuttgart: Kohlhammer, 1927) 3-10, 28-31; W. L. Lane, *The Gospel according to Mark,* NICNT (Grand Rapids, Michigan: Wm. B. Eerdmans, 1974) 74.

15. D.-A. Koch, *Die Bedeutung der Wundererzählungen für die Christologie des Markusevangeliums* (Berlin: de Gruyter, 1975) 57-61; Guelich, *Mark,* 57-58.

16. R. A. Guelich, "Mark, Gospel of," in *Dictionary of Jesus and the Gospels,* ed. J. B. Green and S. McKnight (Downers Grove, Illinois: InterVarsity; Leicester: Inter-Varsity, 1992) 521.

17. J. A. Fitzmyer, *The Gospel according to Luke,* vol. 1, AB 29 (Garden City, New York: Doubleday, 1981) 545-46. Chilton, "Exorcism and History," 258, notes the oddness of the demon speaking of being "destroyed," since language of "binding" or "tormenting" is more common in an exorcism, which involves expulsion rather than destruction as a rule. Chilton believes that the close proximity of this to the temptation narrative (1:12, 13) "presupposes that the rule of the demons has been broken, and that a new era dawns."

18. H. C. Kee, "The Terminology of Mark's Exorcism Stories," *NTS* 14 (1968) 232-46 (esp. 235).

and the demons are forced to exit the unfortunate man. The terminology describing the exit of the demons in v 26, ἐξῆλθεν ἐξ αὐτοῦ, is a verbatim repetition of Jesus' command in v 25, emphasizing the extent of their obedience. Truly with Jesus the kingdom has entered the world (1:15) and demonic forces are now on the retreat.

The demon's recognition title, ὁ ἅγιος τοῦ θεοῦ (v 24), was not really a messianic title in Judaism. It is used for commissioning in the OT (Judg 13:7; 16:17), and in the NT is found only here and in John 6:69. Here it is used like the "son of God" title (1:1, 11) to refer to his special relationship to God. It is not without reason that some of the christological high points of Mark are found on the lips of demons — "Holy One of God" (1:24), "Son of God" (3:11), "Son of the Most High God" (5:7). All are connected to Jesus' unique sonship and serve the dual purpose of stating that authority by which Jesus defeats the demons and reminding the reader of the true significance of this one who does such "marvelous" things.[19]

Graham Twelftree has shown in a significant work[20] that Jesus used readily recognizable techniques (primarily in comparison with Jewish exorcistic activity) as an exorcist of his day. Twelftree notes six areas of parallel between Jesus and his contemporaries: an initial dramatic confrontation, in which the demons cry out in distress; the words of the demons as they seek to defend themselves against Jesus by disarming him; Jesus' words of exorcism, binding and casting the demons out; the demonic plea for leniency (in Mark 5:10-12 but not here); and the violent cure. Each is found in contemporary accounts and shows that in the broad sense Jesus was indeed a first-century exorcist.

Yet the differences are also startling. Twelftree notes five areas:[21] the absence of mechanical devices (e.g., burning incense, amulets, herbs, etc.);[22] the refusal to use "proofs" to demonstrate success; the absence of prayer in Jesus' exorcisms; the refusal to invoke other authorities like Solomon or the Spirit of God or angelic forces;[23] and the absence of the binding formula. In conclusion, Jesus' exorcisms were commonly recognized as such, but they departed in sig-

19. This has been challenged by G. Twelftree, "ΕΙ ΔΕ . . . ΕΓΩ ΕΚΒΑΛΛΩ ΤΑ ΔΑΙΜΟΝΙΑ . . . ," in *Gospel Perspectives,* vol. 6, 361-400 (esp. 376-77), who argues that both "the Holy One of God" here and "Son of the Most High God" in 5:7 connote no more than one who has a special relationship with God in the first century. While such is possible in light of first-century usage, it is not likely for Mark. The high christology of Mark 1 and the buildup of terms used by the demons in Mark (Twelftree strangely does not discuss "Son of God" in 3:11) make a titular force more likely for Mark. In short, Twelftree's point is indeed possible for the *Sitz im Leben Jesu* (though it is not as likely for 3:11 or 5:7) but not for Mark's portrayal.

20. Twelftree, "ΕΚΒΑΛΛΩ," 368-87. (See also his *Jesus the Exorcist,* which was unavailable to me.)

21. Twelftree, "ΕΚΒΑΛΛΩ," 383-85.

22. Apollonius and some rabbis also relied only on their word of authority. However, this was still highly unusual.

23. Again, Apollonius and some of the rabbis parallel Jesus here.

nificant ways, primarily in the authority he possessed in and of himself. He needed no aids, no formulas, no outside help. Most significantly, for Jesus (and Mark) the exorcisms functioned as part of the kingdom message (cf. 1:14-15, following vv 12-13); in Jesus the kingdom has arrived and the powers of the demonic realm are being broken (cf. 3:27).

In v 22 the bystanders were astonished. Now in v 27 "all" (ἅπαντες) are astounded. As in v 22 the term for amazement (here ἐθαμβήθησαν) connotes both wonder and dread. No one can escape the incontrovertible reality of Jesus, the "Holy One of God," in all his power and authority. The inclusion of "new teaching" (v 27) with the "teaching" of v 22, as stated above, shows that in Jesus' authoritative deed a "new teaching" was exemplified, that the kingdom age had begun (1:15) and a new power was present in the world. This is the only place in the Gospels in which a miracle is called "teaching" (Luke 4:36 has, "What kind of utterance is this?"). The meaning is similar to John's "sign" theology, stressing the christological significance of Jesus' miracle here. Both in his synagogue teaching and in the synagogue miracle the onlookers discovered διδαχὴ καινή. Jesus' authority in word and deed will dominate the ensuing chapters. The reader identifies with the disciples, crowds, and leaders as each group encounters this authority and thereby is confronted in turn with the reality of God in Jesus.

The theme of Jesus' increasing popularity begins in v 28 and will control the rest of this chapter. The language is very strong. The verb of the "spread" (ἐξῆλθεν) of the report is the same one used for the expulsion of the demon in vv 25-26. This does not constitute (as some have tried to argue) a "second exorcism," but it is likely that Mark has chosen his words carefully to link the "casting out" of the demon with the sensational effect it evoked. The news could not be held back but swept throughout the "whole region of Galilee" (cf. 1:33-34, 39, 45). The publicity bandwagon is starting to roll.

## 2. Healing Peter's Mother-in-Law (1:29-31)

Jesus departs from the synagogue and enters a home, but the authoritative activity continues. The Markan καὶ εὐθύς, the note on the departure from the synagogue, and the naming of the disciples present are all structural markers that connect this story with vv 16-20 (Simon and Andrew, James and John were the four present in vv 16-20) and vv 21-28. The narrative flow of the whole is predominant, and Robbins makes this part of "the initial phase of the teacher / disciple relationship."[24] The addition of the four names (rather than just Simon's) is hardly accidental and is intended to make this an extension of

24. V. K. Robbins, *Jesus the Teacher: A Socio-Rhetorical Interpretation of Mark* (Philadelphia: Fortress, 1984) 108, speaking of 1:14–3:6 as a unit.

1:16-20. The two sides of Mark — christology and discipleship — blend into a deeper unity, for here Jesus' authority directly touches his disciples' lives.[25] Moreover, the three activities of teaching, exorcism, and healing are programmatic for the ministries of both Jesus and his disciples in the rest of the Second Gospel. In 3:14; 6:7, 13 these are the same core activities that Jesus passes on to his disciples.

Each of the miracles in 1:21-45 occurs in response to the initiative of others. In v 30b, the second καὶ εὐθύς of the pericope emphasizes their report to Jesus regarding Simon's fevered mother-in-law. The disciples, in keeping with Jesus' ἐξουσία portrayed in vv 23-28, show their dependence on Jesus. In vv 18, 20 they had left everything to follow him. Now Simon relinquishes his mother-in-law into Jesus' care. The simplicity of Mark's description of the miracle — Jesus comes, takes her hand, raises her up, the fever departs, she ministers[26] to them — is in keeping with Mark's interest in action. The emphasis in this episode is on Jesus' authority and its results upon the disciples.

### 3. Miraculous Ministry in the Evening (1:32-34)

This summary passage is closely connected to both vv 21-31 and vv 35-39 via the double time note ὀψίας δὲ γενομένης, ὅτε ἔδυ ὁ ἥλιος. In the first instance it is the final event of the "day in Capernaum" set of activities (vv 21-34); in the second instance it forms the nighttime activities (vv 32-39) following the Sabbath events of vv 21-31. Mark's hand is evident in "all the sick," "the whole city," "many sick," "many demons," and the silencing of the demons. The majority of scholars[27] affirm the pre-Markan origin of the pericope but see Markan emphases in the details. The expanded focus of Jesus' miraculous ministry is evidenced not only in the many miracles he performs on this occasion but also in the public setting of the story. The scene moves from inside Simon's home to outside his "door," with the impression that "the whole city" is gathered

25. Guelich, *Mark,* 61, believes that Mark found this pericope in a traditional complex with vv 32-34 and 35-39, arranged in a temporal sequence: during the day (vv 29-31), after sunset (vv 32-34), and the following morning (vv 35-39). This may be true, but in the Markan context the temporal link is stronger with vv 21-28, comprising the Sabbath events in Capernaum.

26. There is some debate as to the significance of διηκόνει αὐτοῖς. Some, like E. Schweizer, *The Good News according to Mark* (Richmond: John Knox, 1970) 53, believe that this indicates "the specific manner of discipleship for a woman," while the majority take this more generally of her activity as hostess. Certainly the word is used of the angels "ministering" to Jesus in 1:13 and is used in a discipleship sense in 9:35 and 10:43-45. While this latter technical meaning could be hinted at here, it is difficult to prove without stronger contextual markers. At best, such would be secondary to the primary, non-technical use of διηκόνει.

27. E.g., Pesch, Grundmann, Lane, Anderson, Lohmeyer, Guelich; *contra* Koch, Gnilka, who believe it is entirely the product of Mark's hand.

"around" it (v 33). There are two major parts to the story:[28] the gathering of the needy and indeed of all the citizens (vv 32-33) followed by the healing of both the sick and the demon-possessed (v 34).

Verse 32 dramatically pictures the stream of the sick and demon-possessed to Jesus. Travel was restricted on the Sabbath, so it is natural that people would wait for the beginning of the new day (indicated by ὅτε ἔδυ ὁ ἥλιος) to bring the needy to Jesus. The primary stress is on πᾶς, which expands the themes of 1:21-31 to depict Jesus as the healer of "all" in need. This, combined with ὅλη in hyperbolic fashion, presents Jesus as related to "all." Mark specifies the two groups (the ill and the demon-possessed; cf. Luke 4:40, which has simply "those sick with various diseases") to summarize the events of vv 23-28, 29-31, as well as to anticipate the miracles of v 34.

Verse 33 develops further the theme of Jesus' tremendous popularity with the common people (cf. v 28). The strong verb ἐπισυνηγμένη (συνάγειν is more common) pictures the throngs "gathered together around" the door of Simon's home and provides a vivid word-picture of the extent of Jesus' fame. The popularity motif progresses from his initial fame in v 28 to the "whole city" of v 33 and then to "everyone" in v 37 and "everywhere" in v 44. These dynamic scenes combine to present Mark's emphasis on Jesus' universal popularity.

One point of tension concerns the switch from πᾶς in v 32 to πόλλη in v 34. Several[29] believe they are synonymous due to a semitism (in which πόλλη means "all"). The switch would then be stylistic. Others[30] find meaning in the switch, namely that Jesus ministered to "all" but healed only the "many" who came to him in faith. On the basis of Markan parallelism the former is more likely (cf. 10:45, "a ransom for many"). Such a switch in meaning would be unlikely in a context (1:21-45) that emphasizes so greatly the universal results of Jesus' authority. Moreover, the parallel passages in Matt 8:16 ("many" . . . "all") and Luke 4:40 ("all" . . . "each") favor synonymity.

Once more the demons "know Jesus," and once more Jesus silences them. However, here the cosmic conflict of vv 24-25 is not part of the meaning. Rather, at this point Mark introduces the reader to the "messianic secret." The phrase was first coined by W. Wrede to describe those places where Jesus enjoins silence on the part of demons (1:34; 3:12), those healed (1:43; 5:43; 7:36), and his disciples (8:30; 9:9) as to who he really is. Without going into depth on the many ramifications,[31] this concept is valid on three levels. As to the *Sitz im Leben Jesu,* Jesus

28. Guelich, *Mark,* 64, finds an ABA pattern with the gathering and healing of the sick (A) surrounding the stress on the whole city (B). This has merit, but there seems to be a more linear development with the gathering of the sick and the whole city in vv 32-33 leading to the healing of the "many" in v 34.

29. E.g., Lagrange, Lane, Guelich.

30. E.g., Pesch, Grundmann, Gnilka.

31. For more extensive discussion, see C. M. Tuckett, ed., *The Messianic Secret,* IRT 1 (Philadelphia: Fortress, 1983); and Guelich, "Mark, Gospel of," 521-22.

undoubtedly commands silence because the Jewish people cannot understand him as a suffering Messiah rather than a conquering Messiah and because he does not want people flocking to him only as a wonder worker. As to the *Sitz im Leben Kirche,* this is part of Mark's theme regarding the hidden epiphany of Jesus Messiah, Son of God (1:1). The reality of who Jesus is can never be understood merely on the basis of wondrous deeds; this demands the supernatural revelation of God himself, primarily in the passion and resurrection of Jesus (cf. 9:9; 15:39). At the literary level, the messianic secret serves to highlight the unfathomable popularity of Jesus among the people. The more he commands silence, the more those healed proclaim his glory (cf. 1:45; 7:36-37; cf. 2:12; 5:19-21). At the same time, Jesus' desire to avoid publicity does not prohibit him from performing miracles; compassion for the needy has priority. It seems that the significance of Jesus both entails hiddenness and ensures proclamation.

The abbreviated summary of 1:32-34 has four functions: summarizing the themes of exorcism and healing from vv 21-31; presenting Jesus as the compassionate healer who cares for all who come to him; demonstrating further the incredible growth of his popularity; and contrasting the latter with Jesus' desire to remain incognito.

## 4. Departure, Prayer, and Itinerant Preaching (1:35-39)

As already stated, Mark's use of a second, double time-note in v 35 (cf. v 32) ties this closely together with vv 21-34, again with a mixture of tradition and redaction.[32] In the context of this unit, v 35 constitutes a double departure from Capernaum, first for prayer (v 35) and then for preaching (v 38). The accent is on Jesus' expanded ministry in relation to both God (prayer) and "all of Galilee" (preaching). Jesus' departure "while it was still dark" gives the impression of intense seriousness: he wants to get away from the pressing crowds in order to be alone with his Father.

The departure εἰς ἔρημον τόπον employs a Markan phrase (Matthew and Luke utilize it only when following Mark) found mainly in passages (e.g., 1:45; 6:31-33) where Jesus escapes the crowds by seeking a "wilderness-type place." There is a probable allusion back to 1:12-13 when Jesus is comforted in the "wilderness" during his temptation by Satan. Since there was no "wilderness" in the region near Capernaum, the emphasis is more theological than geographical.[33] In connection with 1:12-13, Mark probably is noting the crowds as a

32. E.g., W. Kirchschlager, "Jesu Gebetsverhalten als Paradigma zu Mk 1,35," *Kairos* 20 (1978) 303-10, argues that v 35 exhibits a catechetical form with decided Semitic flavor. Non-Markan terms also include κατεδίωξεν (v 36), ἀλλαχοῦ (v 38), and κωμοπόλεις (v 38).

33. See U. W. Mauser, *Christ in the Wilderness: The Wilderness Theme in the Second Gospel and Its Basis in the Biblical Tradition* (London: SCM, 1963) 104-8; Lane, *Mark,* 81, for further discussion of these points.

source of temptation to Jesus (cf. v 34). The people sought a prophetic wonder worker and centered on the sensational rather than the spiritual ministry of Jesus. In the "remote place" Jesus sought solace and escape from such temptation. In vv 12, 13 the angels provided that comfort. Here Jesus turns to the Father.

Morning prayers in a time of need are recorded in Pss 5:3; 55:17; 88:13. Accounts of Jesus at prayer are infrequent in Mark, occurring only in 6:46 (in the midst of the discipleship failure of 6:45-52) and 14:32-33 (Gethsemane). Therefore prayer in Mark is connected with crisis, in this case the crisis of popularity (cf. vv 36-37). The resultant desire to be with the Father is natural; Jesus seeks a new strength to face the occasion and continue his true mission to fulfill the Father's will by proclaiming the kingdom message (vv 38-39). The search for Jesus (vv 36-37) reemphasizes his great fame. The central point is the statement that "all" (πᾶς) were seeking Jesus, thus continuing the "all" / "many" from vv 32, 34. The popularity of Jesus has grown from the citizens of Capernaum (v 27) to the regions of Galilee (v 28) to "the whole city" (v 33) to "all" (v 37).

It is implicit in Jesus' response (v 38) that he wants to avoid the crowds that are clamoring for him. In response to the disciples' statement (v 37), he responds, "Let's go elsewhere" (v 38). Jesus not only wants to leave the place of popularity in order to be with the Father (v 38) but also to fulfill the Father's directive to preach the gospel.[34] Yet this refusal to don the mantle of wonder worker is not primary in the text; rather, it is implied in the larger interplay within the narrative. It is clear in v 39 that Jesus never refuses to heal or cast out demons. He centers on preaching but continues to show compassion to the needy. Mark's emphasis is the movement in Jesus' ministry from miracles to preaching, from deeds back to the centrality of word. There is a kind of chiasm, as vv 21-28 teach an authority of word and deed and then the succeeding pericopes move from his deeds (vv 29-34) to his words (vv 35-38). Again an expansion occurs as Jesus' ministry moves from Capernaum (vv 21-34) to the surrounding towns (v 38) to all of Galilee (v 39).

The summary of Jesus' gospel proclamation (1:14-15) is undoubtedly meant to provide the content of κηρύσσειν in vv 38-39. Jesus says that preaching the gospel is "why I have come" (v 38). Some read this as Jesus' divine directive to preach (thus a summary of his mission as a whole),[35] but it more likely (with ἐξέλθειν repeated from v 35) refers to the reason Jesus has left Capernaum to expand his ministry (thus referring primarily to the immediate context).[36] As in v 39, Mark regularly connects preaching and exorcism (e.g., 3:14, 15; 6:12, 13). This functions here as a summary of the "authority in word and deed" in vv 21-28, only now it is expanded to all of Galilee.

34. So Pesch, *Markusevangelium,* 1:138-39; W. Grundmann, *Das Evangelium nach Markus,* THNT 2 (Berlin: Evangelische Verlagsanstalt, 1968) 48-49.

35. So Swete, Grundmann, Lohmeyer, Gnilka.

36. So Pesch, Lane, Guelich.

Several themes come to the forefront in vv 35-39. The priorities of prayer and preaching function as a clarification of the place of the miraculous in Jesus' ministry. The latter was not the focus but rather functioned as a supplement to the priority of the Father and of the gospel in Jesus' ministry. In fact, the reason for Jesus' two "departures" are just these — to be with the Father (v 35) and to proclaim the truths of the kingdom (vv 38-39). Also, here we see Jesus negating the temptation which popularity represented. God and his will are first, not the insistent clamor of the people.

### 5. The Healing of the Leper (1:40-45)

This episode has no time note (cf. vv 29, 32, 35) to link it with the preceding and may be here more for topical reasons. It concludes the ministry and popularity of Jesus among the people (vv 21-39) and provides a transition to the confrontation with the leaders (2:1–3:6). By culminating the motifs of Jesus' authority (healing a leper was equated with raising the dead in 2 Kgs 5:7 and rabbinic circles) and fame (it is now so great that he cannot enter any city at all, v 45), this pericope points backward to the christological themes of vv 21-39. By introducing the question of the law (v 44) this paragraph points forward to the legal controversies of 2:1–3:6.

There are two major sections in this story, each with two parts. The healing episode consists of the leper's believing request (v 40) and the miracle itself (vv 41-42); the aftermath consists of the commands for silence and priestly confirmation (vv 43-44) and the resultant publicity and increase in popularity (v 45). There is an AB:AB pattern consisting of a request (A) and a response (B), in the first pair directed from the leper to Jesus and in the second pair from Jesus to the leper.[37]

The leper comes to Jesus with a degree of faith. Mark gives a vivid description via three parallel participles: beseeching, kneeling, and saying. While some have seen worship, perhaps even conversion, in the kneeling, that goes beyond the evidence. However, in his "If you choose, you can make me clean" (v 40), there is a certain faith in Jesus' healing power; and the leper becomes the archetype of the pattern already noted in 1:21-45, that the initiative is with the needy person.

Jesus' response (v 41) contains the most difficult text-critical problem of

37. The outline would change if one were to agree with Koch, *Wandererzählungen,* 74-75; Guelich, *Mark,* 72; or M. Wojciechowski, "The Touching of the Leper (Mark 1, 40-45) as a Historical and Symbolic Act of Jesus," *BZ* 33 (1989) 114-19 (esp. 114-16) that v 45 was a later Markan redaction. Then there would be three parts (vv 40, 41-42, 43-44) with a Markan conclusion (v 45). However, even if v 45 were a late redactional addition (I prefer to see here a Markan reworking of the traditional ending), it would be integral to the final form of the story, and I prefer the outline above.

the passage. The majority of the texts have σπλαγχνισθείς, and all versions but the NEB (which has "in warm indignation") follow the majority reading. However, the majority of commentators[38] prefer ὀργισθείς (supported by only D a d ff[2] r[1] Ephraem but preferable as the more difficult reading). It is easy to understand why later scribes would replace the theologically difficult "angry" with "pity," but hard to see how the reverse would occur. Moreover, the immediate context, with çmbrimhs9menov in v 43, makes "became angry" more understandable.[39] Therefore, it is more likely that Mark originally spoke of Jesus' "anger" rather than his "pity."

Some have interpreted this as the leper's anger at his terrible situation,[40] others of a spiritual power stirred up in Jesus by the man's plight.[41] Neither fits the context, however, for in the first case it is difficult to understand why later scribes would want to change the text, and in the latter case there is no hint in the context of any such spiritual force. It is far more likely that Jesus' anger is directed at the dilemma of God's people caught up in sickness and sin, and at the power of evil that is behind this perversion of God's creation (as also in Mark 3:5; 7:34; 8:12; 9:19; 10:14). As Lane notes,[42] this explains why several elements common to exorcism narratives are found in this story. In the ancient world, the healing of the sick would be regarded not only as a physical miracle but also as a spiritual victory, a defeat of the evil powers in this world.

It is difficult to know how much christological significance to see in the miracle. Certainly Jesus' "touch" (touching a leper rendered one unclean) results from the "hermeneutic of love"; compassion for the needy outweighs considerations of clean and unclean.[43] Jesus' simple response to the request also has theological connotations. The sovereign declaration, "Θέλω, καθαρίσθητι" (v 41), has christological implications. With his "I do choose," Jesus functions as the son of Yahweh (1:1, 11). This forms a fitting conclusion to this "first act" of Jesus' messianic ministry, for it demonstrates in a powerful way the presence of the kingdom.

In Jesus' injunction to silence, two other remarkably strong verbs come into play. First, Jesus ἐμβριμησάμενος (v 43a), a verb which usually connotes anger (Lam 2:6, LXX; Dan 11:30, LXX; Mark 14:5) or a "deep disturbance" of heart (John 11:33, 38). Here and in Matt 9:30 it has the connotation of a stern command. Again there are several interpretations,[44] but the most likely is a

38. Among others, Pesch, Grundmann, Lane, Anderson, and Guelich.

39. G. Stählin, "ὀργή," *TDNT* 5:427 n. 324, mentions στενάζειν in Mark 7:34 and Jesus' anger in John 11:33, 38 as other parallels.

40. So K. Lake, "'ΕΜΒΡΙΜΗΣΑΜΕΝΟΣ and 'ΟΡΓΙΣΘΕΙΣ, Mark 1, 40-43," *HTR* 16 (1923) 197-98; in Lane, *Mark,* 86.

41. So Pesch, *Markusevangelium,* 1:144; Gnilka, *Markus,* 1:93.

42. Lane, *Mark,* 86. See also Cranfield, Grundmann, Pesch, Guelich.

43. Wojciechowski, "Touching," 118-19, finds a paradox in Jesus' act. Rather than defiling Jesus, the touch cleansed the leper. He believes this extraordinary reversal of the norm to be grounded in Jesus' "special holiness and power in the sacral sphere."

44. (1) Lane and Stählin connect this with Jesus' foreknowledge that the man would disobey

combination of a stern warning to obey both injunctions (to silence and to meeting the legal requirements) with a cosmic warfare overtone (seen in the combination of this with ὀργίσθεις in v 41 and ἐξέβαλεν here in v 43). In this sense there is possibly also double meaning in ἐξέβαλεν (v 43b), the common use by which Jesus "sent him away" and a secondary hint of exorcism.

The prohibition itself is emphatic and absolute, introduced by the double negative μηδενὶ μηδέν. Under no circumstances was the man to divulge what had happened. In healing miracles (e.g., 5:43; 7:36; 8:26) the command to silence plays a different role than in other contexts. With demons (1:34; 3:12) and disciples (8:30; 9:9) the secret is maintained, but those healed disobey the injunction, resulting in even greater publicity. One interesting solution[45] sees Mark as developing pre-Markan tradition, in which the injunctions prohibited the one healed from relating to others the process of healing, following the tendency in magical papyri of keeping such formulas and actions a secret. Mark then understood this "secret" as a desire on Jesus' part to avoid publicity. The thesis regarding the magical formulas is doubtful, for there is no hint that there were any such formulas or actions on the part of Jesus or the early church. However, the theory regarding Jesus' desire to avoid publicity fits the evidence of 1:35, 38. In this sense there is an ironic undertone. The more Jesus sought quiet, the more the very people he sought to help drew greater and greater crowds to him.

This is seen especially in vv. 44b-45. Jesus told the man to follow the legal requirements and show himself to the priests εἰς μαρτύριον αὐτοῖς. The question is whether this should be interpreted as a dative of advantage, "a testimony to them,"[46] or a dative of disadvantage, "a testimony against them."[47] The context favors the former, for the legal steps would testify to the people[48] that the man was now clean. Strathmann, however, argues that whenever μαρτύριον with the dative occurs, it always functions as a legal polemic or prosecution "against" someone.[49] Yet while some contexts are neutral (e.g., Matt 10:18 = Mark 13:9) and others negative (Luke 9:5 = Mark 6:11), Matt 24:14 is primarily positive, describing the good news throughout the world "as a testimony to all nations." Context must decide, and that favors the positive thrust.

---

the command to go to the priest. (2) Cranfield, Pesch, and Jeremias call this a "stern warning" that the man be silent about the miracle. (3) Guelich and Kee see a deliberate hint of an exorcism in which Jesus "sternly rebukes" and then "drives out" (ἐκβάλλειν) the demonic forces behind the situation. (4) Wojciechowski believes that it refers to Jesus' agitation in general rather than anger at the situation.

45. See Pesch, *Markusevangelium,* 1:145-46; and Guelich, *Mark,* 75-76, who build upon U. Luz, "Das Geheimnismotiv und die markinische Christologie," *ZNW* 56 (1965) 9-30.

46. So all versions, Lagrange, Cranfield, Pesch, Gnilka.

47. So Strathmann, Lane, Guelich.

48. The plural αὐτοῖς most likely goes beyond the priests (ἱερεῖ in v 44 is singular) to the community as a whole.

49. H. Strathmann, "μαρτύς," *TDNT* 4:502-3.

The response of the man is all the more interesting in light of this. There is no hint in the context whether the man obeyed Jesus' command. Probably he did. Rather, the text almost gives the impression that he took εἰς μαρτύριον αὐτοῖς (last in v 44) literally and "went out"[50] (first in v 45) "preaching" the news. The terms κηρύσσειν and διαφημίζειν τὸν λόγον refer to the proclamation of the gospel often in Mark (1:14-15, 38-39; 3:14; 5:20; 6:12; 7:36; 13:10; 14:9). Here, of course, the primary meaning is to "proclaim the news" of his healing. However, at the secondary level he becomes in some ways the first missionary of the good news. The success of his mission is obvious: Jesus becomes so popular that he "could no longer go into a town openly but stayed out in the country." While some read this negatively (Jesus' mission was compromised, an ominous portent of the opposition to come in 2:1–3:6), that is not the contextual meaning. Note the *inclusio* of Jesus presence in the ἔρημος τόπος between v 35 and v 45. Jesus began his extended ministry with a journey to the "remote place" in order to be with his Father and ends it with ministry in the "remote places" to the multitudes. This culminates the Markan emphasis on Jesus' growing popularity among the multitudes, developed from v 23 (fame throughout the region) to v 33 (the whole city flocking to him) to vv 37, 39 (ministering throughout Galilee) to v 45 (people coming from everywhere).

The appearance of so many themes from 1:21-39 make vv 40-45 a good choice as the conclusion of this section. First, since Judaism considered the cure of leprosy to be equivalent to raising the dead, this miracle highlights in a special way the theme of Jesus' authority. Indeed, it is the word (v 45) and the deed (vv 40-44) which dominate (cf. vv 21-22, 27). Second, the growing popularity of Jesus culminates in the convergence of people "from everywhere" (v 45) to such an extent that Jesus was kept even from entering the towns. Third, this developing fame was mitigated by misunderstanding, and this led to Jesus' demand that his miraculous ministry be kept secret (v 44). Fourth, the cosmic conflict is hinted at in the language of Jesus' anger (vv 41, 43a) and "casting out" (v 43b) the man. Fifth, Jesus' acquiescence to the Mosaic law is stressed in v 44 and provides a bridge to the conflict over the law in 2:1–3:6. Here he demonstrates that he has no intention of nullifying the law (cf. Matt 5:17-20).

## 6. Conclusion

There is no single structural pattern that alone fits 1:21-45. In one sense, the time notes in vv 29, 32, and 35 control the organization of the pericopes in 1:21-45 and seem to favor a Sabbath day / Sabbath night framework that would

50. See J. Swetnam, "Some Remarks on the Meaning of ὁ δὲ ἐξελθών in Mark 1,45," *Bib* 68 (1987) 245-49, who proves conclusively (*contra* Jeremias, Klostermann, and Elliott) that the phrase refers to the leper rather than to Jesus.

link vv 21-28 with vv 29-31 and vv 32-34 with vv 35-39. In another sense, many scholars favor linking vv 32-34 with vv 21-31 and forming a "day in Capernaum" triad, with vv 35-39 comprising the events of the following morning. Either of these is viable, though the former is preferable due to the time notes, which connect vv 32-34 with vv 35-39. However, the development of themes in this section, centering primarily on christology, favors a more linear approach. The middle three pericopes build on themes introduced by vv 21-28 and in turn develop those themes further. Then vv 40-45 tie the themes together and conclude the whole. Therefore, there is a secondary Sabbath day / Sabbath night sequence and a primary linear sequence, with vv 21-28 the introduction and vv 40-45 the conclusion for a christological montage the inner three pericopes of which develop Jesus' authority in word and deed and his resultant impact on the crowds.

As one might expect, the christological themes of 1:21-45 expand those of 1:1-20, and together the two passages introduce the christological emphases which will predominate throughout the Second Gospel. Since Wrede, there have been many different theories regarding Markan christology. Some view Mark as correcting a false christology, either of a *theios anēr* type (T. J. Weeden) or of an exalted heavenly figure (R. P. Martin). In both cases Mark corrects the false ideas by showing that Jesus is the humble suffering servant as well as the exalted Son of God. Others like Bultmann and some of his followers center primarily on Mark's high christology and see the Jesus of Mark as a gnostic redeemer passing incognito through this world. None of these satisfy, primarily because of their speculative nature. A narrative approach to christology would favor a simpler portrait. The Jesus of Mark is Messiah and Son of God,[51] with 1:1 setting the tone. There are three primary emphases: Jesus fulfills Jewish messianic hopes; he does so via his suffering and death (the major cluster of χρίστος occurs in the passion narrative); and Jesus transcends the messianic office as "Son of God." In this 1:21-45 plays a significant role, for this passage shows that christology for Mark is narrative theology, presented via dramatic confrontations between Jesus and those around him. Two of the groups form the core of 1:21-45 — the crowds and the disciples. The third group, the leaders of the Jews, comes to the fore in 2:1–3:6. These three groups provide the foil for Jesus throughout the rest of the Gospel. The reader knows who Jesus is from 1:1 on, and the tension as the three groups wrestle with his significance characterizes Mark's portrayal. The following themes emerge from 1:21-45 and set the tone for ensuing chapters:

(1) There is a high christology in vv 21-45, developing the earlier theme of Jesus the Son of God (1:1, 11; cf. "the Holy One of God," v 24) who exemplifies "authority" in word and deed (1:21-22, 27, 29-31, 41). This new authority "astounds" (v 22) and "overwhelms" (v 27) the people, who see the hand of

51. See Guelich, "Mark, Gospel of," 518-19; and J. D. Kingsbury, *The Christology of Mark's Gospel* (Philadelphia: Fortress, 1983).

God in Jesus but cannot understand the true meaning of his actions. Only the demon who cries, "I know who you are, the Holy One of God" (v 24), understands, and his outburst is quickly silenced.

(2) This authority is especially evident in Jesus' teaching. Even his deeds are called "a new teaching with authority" (v 27), and Jesus' priorities clearly center on preaching the kingdom message (vv 38-39). It is the true desire and emphasis of his ministry, and the language of v 45 pictures the leper's proclamation as a missionary extension of Jesus' preaching ministry.

(3) Yet Jesus' miracles at the same time exemplify his authority and are a focus of his messianic activity. He is a "healer" of "all" (vv 32, 34), one whose hand is at all times stretched out to the sick (1:29-31, 32, 34, 40-42). However, Jesus never seeks to heal the sick or cast out demons as an end in itself. He responds with divine compassion to the needy, but they must come to him. His desire is to proclaim God's message, and the miraculous is subservient to that rather than controlling his ministry. Jesus' true orientation is to the Father (v 35) and to the Father's message ("that is what I came out to do," v 38), and the miraculous is a supplemental aspect of that overall purpose.

(4) In addition to his healing ministry, Jesus engages in combat against the demonic forces. This cosmic war is seen in two exorcism stories (vv 23-26, 32- 34), though the latter places no emphasis on the cosmic conflict. In addition, the "anger" of Jesus at the leper's plight in vv 41, 43a and the language of "casting out" the leper in v 43b hint at the cosmic conflict. The startling aspect of these stories (indeed, of all exorcism miracles) is that there is never any actual battle. Jesus expels the demons with hardly a conflict, and the battle is over virtually before it can begin.

(5) As a result of his "authority in word and deed," Jesus' fame grows geometrically. The people's amazement (vv 22, 27) leads to his popularity spreading throughout Galilee (v 28). First the whole city of Capernaum gathers (v 33), then "everyone is searching" for him (v 37) and he begins preaching in synagogues throughout Galilee (v 39). Finally, he becomes so famous that he can no longer even enter cities but has to go to "the country" to receive those who flock "from every quarter" (v 45).

(6) Jesus wants no fame, and he continually commands the demons and those healed to be silent regarding the miracle. In one sense the silencing of demons is emblematic of Jesus' total victory in the cosmic war (v 25); in another sense the silencing is to keep them from making his true identity known ("because they knew him," v 34). Jesus refuses to identify with the people's fascination with him as a wonder worker. This is connected to Mark's theme on the hiddenness of Jesus, who cannot be understood apart from the events of the cross and resurrection. It is also connected to Jesus' desire to avoid the sensational, which leads him to go to the "remote places" rather than the densely populated areas. Finally, this is connected in Mark to the unalterable fact that nothing Jesus did could stave off the inevitable fame that attended the revelation of the divine "authority" in him.

# Jesus of Nazareth: A Magician and a False Prophet Who Deceived God's People?

Graham N. Stanton

The relationship of Jesus to first-century Judaism continues to be discussed vigorously.[1] This ongoing debate was sparked off initially by the publication of H. S. Reimarus's *Wolfenbüttel Fragments* between 1774 and 1778.[2] In deliberately provocative comments Reimarus insisted that Jesus did not intend to abolish the Jewish religion and to introduce a new one in its place. The intention of Jesus, Reimarus claimed, was reversed completely after his death by both the actions and the teaching of the apostles. With their abandonment of the law, "Judaism was laid in its grave."[3]

In an equally influential publication two generations later, D. F. Strauss noted that a radical account of the origins of Christianity along these lines had been propounded by "the enemies of Christianity in its ecclesiastical form," and that it had been done "most concisely of all in the *Wolfenbüttel Fragments*," that is, by Reimarus.[4] Although Strauss was sympathetic to many of Reimarus's claims, he knew that any presentation of Jesus as a faithful Jew was built on a one-sided reading of the evidence. Strauss emphasized that there was clear,

1. Earlier, more wide-ranging versions of this paper were given as the Thatcher Lecture at the Uniting Theological College in Sydney on July 18, 1991, and as a lecture or seminar paper at the Universities of Otago (New Zealand), Leiden (the Netherlands), Lancaster, Leeds, Belfast, and Aberdeen. I am grateful for many helpful comments and for the warm hospitality received. Professor Howard Marshall has heard an oral version of this paper, quite unaware (I hope) of the destination of the published version. At least I know that he is keenly interested in the topic and my approach, even if not completely convinced by my arguments. This essay is dedicated to him in deep appreciation of his many major contributions to NT scholarship.

2. Reimarus died in 1768. The *Fragments* were published anonymously by G. E. Lessing. The identity of the author did not become generally known until 1814.

3. Reimarus, *Fragments*, 1.19, ed. C. H. Talbert (Philadelphia: Fortress, 1970) 101. In a note at this point Talbert insists that "this entire argument is an oversimplification by Reimarus."

4. *The Life of Jesus Critically Examined*, §67. I have cited the edition by P. C. Hodgson (London: SCM, 1973) 298; this is G. Eliot's translation of the fourth German edition.

strong evidence within the Gospels to support the opposite viewpoint: Jesus was at odds with the religious leaders of his day.[5]

Reimarus and Strauss both still have plenty of supporters, and many mediating positions are defended. After 150 years of discussion, the relationship of Jesus to Judaism remains a contentious issue, as a cluster of recent book titles confirms: *Jesus the Jew, Jesus and Judaism, Jesus and the Transformation of Judaism,* and *Jesus within Judaism.*[6] Although our knowledge of first-century Judaism has increased enormously in recent decades, the variety of views still on offer is bewildering in its rich profusion.

An impasse has been reached. This is partly because at key points there are crucial gaps in our knowledge. For example, we cannot be certain just what were the conventions of various religious groups on the fine points of Sabbath observance in, say, Capernaum in 30 C.E. In addition, the relevant evidence which has survived is difficult to interpret. Almost all of it has come down to us from a partisan point of view. Whether we are examining the evidence of Josephus, or of the rabbis, or of the NT Evangelists, this fact has to be taken very seriously indeed. However, I do not think that these difficulties should deter critical inquiry. I am convinced that discussion of the relationship of Jesus to contemporary Judaism can be advanced as effectively by opening up unconventional lines of inquiry as it can be by rehearsing familiar arguments. In this essay I shall plot a path which has been neglected in most recent discussion. I shall examine the most widely attested ancient criticism of Jesus of Nazareth: he was a magician and a false prophet who deceived God's people. The barbed criticisms of the opponents of any striking individual are often as revealing as the fulsome praise of close associates, so we do well to take seriously the small number of negative comments about Jesus which have come down to us from antiquity.[7]

I shall start with criticisms of Jesus which are found in Jewish, Christian, and pagan circles in the middle of the second century. I shall then discuss earlier forms of this stock polemic in the writings of Josephus, John, Luke, and Matthew, before turning, finally (and more tentatively), to traditions which go back to the lifetime of Jesus. It is often helpful in studies of earliest Christianity to

5. *Life of Jesus,* 297-300, 599-602.

6. G. Vermes, *Jesus the Jew* (London: Collins, 1973); E. P. Sanders, *Jesus and Judaism* (London: SCM, 1985); J. Riches, *Jesus and the Transformation of Judaism* (London: Darton, Longman & Todd, 1980); J. H. Charlesworth, *Jesus within Judaism* (London: SPCK, 1989). In an intriguing, recent book, *The Historical Jesus: The Life of a Mediterranean Jewish Peasant* (Edinburgh: T. & T. Clark, 1991), J. D. Crossan paints on an even larger canvas and portrays Jesus as a Mediterranean peasant, a Jewish Cynic. Quotations from the Cynic letters and Epictetus are given greater prominence than (for example) the Qumran writings. In effect Crossan downplays the Jewishness of Jesus. See my review in *Theology* 95 (1992) 452-53.

7. It is worth noting that no ancient opponent of early Christianity ever denied that Jesus existed. This is the Achilles' heel of attempts by a few modern scholars such as G. A. Wells to deny that Jesus existed.

work back from later, clearer evidence to more problematic earlier evidence. Of course there is a risk of anachronism, but sometimes risks have to be taken: later traditions may well suggest new questions and new ways of looking at much disputed issues.

Polemical accusations of magic and false prophecy / deception are very closely related to one another. Although in ancient polemic they are sometimes found singly, in many polemical traditions in which only one of the two terms occurs, the other is often implied. There is a third closely related concept which is prominent in polemic: the apparent success of the magician and the false prophet / deceiver is regularly ascribed by opponents to some form of demonic possession. Readers familiar with elementary mathematics will quickly appreciate that I have in mind three overlapping circles in a Venn diagram.

I shall try to show that the accusations that Jesus was a magician and a false prophet who deceived God's people were well known in the middle of the second century in both Christian and Jewish circles; they became part of the stock rabbinic polemic against Jesus. These jibes were probably known to Josephus about 90 C.E.; they were known to and countered by the Evangelists; they were almost certainly used by some of Jesus' adversaries in his own lifetime. If this final point can be established, there are important implications for our appreciation of the relationship of Jesus to the Judaism of his day.

## 1. Justin Martyr, Rabbinic Traditions, Josephus

In the middle of his extended debate with his Jewish adversary Trypho (written about 160 C.E.), Justin claims that the healing miracles of Jesus were the fulfillment of the messianic prophecies of Isa 35:1-7. The miracles of Jesus were intended to elicit recognition of him as Messiah, but many who saw them drew the opposite conclusion: "they said it was a display of magic art, for they even dared to say that he was a magician and a deceiver of the people" (μάγος καὶ λαοπλάνος, *Dialogue* 69:7). From the context in the *Dialogue*, there is no doubt that the term "deceiver" is being used against the background of Deut 13:5 in the special sense of a false prophet who leads God's people astray.[8]

The title of this essay is taken from the double polemical accusation in *Dialogue* 69:7. Justin clearly believes that it was prevalent in the lifetime of Jesus. Was he correct in this judgment? Or do his comments simply reflect Jewish-Christian controversies in the middle decades of the second century? It is not easy to answer these questions — and a great deal is at stake.

To label someone a "magician" and / or a "deceiver" ("false prophet") in antiquity was an attempt to marginalize a person who was perceived to be a

8. The notion of "deception" is widespread in ancient polemic of all kinds, where it is not necessarily linked to false prophecy. False prophecy, however, always involves deception.

threat to the dominant social order. If we can show that these terms, with their roots in Deuteronomy 13 and 18, were used by contemporary opponents of Jesus, an important corollary would follow: the teachings and actions of Jesus must have been considered by some of his contemporaries to be deeply offensive.

The extent to which Justin's *Dialogue* reflects genuine discussion and controversy between Christians and Jews has been keenly debated. The *Dialogue* is highly stylized and far from being a dispassionate verbatim account of a debate between Justin and Trypho. There is at least some truth in Harnack's view that Justin's dialogue with Trypho was in fact the monologue of a victor.[9] However, there is little doubt that the double accusation against Jesus which is recorded in *Dialogue* 69:7, "magician and deceiver of God's people," was being used in Jewish anti-Christian polemic in the middle of the second century, for it is also found in two related rabbinic traditions.[10]

In *b. Sanh.* 43a an anonymous tradition is introduced with the formula, "It is said," an indication that it is a *baraitha,* an old tradition:

> On the eve of Passover Yeshu was hanged. For forty days before the execution took place, a herald went forth and cried, "He is going forth to be stoned because *he has practiced sorcery and enticed and led Israel astray.*" Anyone who can say anything in his favor, let him come forward and plead on his behalf." But since nothing was brought forward in his favor, he was hanged on the eve of Passover. Ulla retorted: "Do you suppose that he was one for whom a defence could be made? Was he not *a deceiver,* concerning whom scripture says (Deut 13:8), Neither shalt thou spare neither shalt thou conceal him? With Yeshu however it was different, for he was connected with the government."

The pronouncement of the herald, "forty days before the execution took place," confirms that this is no casual polemical comment, but a *formal legal accusation* against Jesus.[11] The two verbs, "entice" and "lead astray," have the

9. A. Harnack, *Judentum und Judenchristentum in Justins Dialog mit Tryphon* (Leipzig: J. C. Hinrichs, 1913).

10. For a fuller discussion than is possible here, see D. R. Catchpole, *The Trial of Jesus* (Leiden: E. J. Brill, 1971) 1-71; J. L. Martyn, *History and Theology in the Fourth Gospel,* 2d ed. (Nashville: Abingdon, 1979) 73-81; W. Horbury, "The Benediction of the *Minim* and Early Jewish-Christian Controversy," *JTS* 33 (1982) 19-61; J. Maier, *Jesus von Nazareth in der talmudischen Überlieferung* (Darmstadt: Wissenschaftliche Buchgesellschaft, 1978); G. Twelftree, "Jesus in Jewish Traditions," in *Gospel Perspectives,* vol. 5: *The Jesus Traditions outside the Gospels,* ed. D. Wenham (Sheffield: JSOT, 1985) 289-342.

11. Maier, *Jesus von Nazareth,* has claimed that *b. Sanh.* 43a did not originally refer to Jesus: that identification was made only in post-Talmudic redaction. Horbury, however, has argued strongly that the sentences "on Passover Eve they hanged Jesus" and "Jesus the Nazarene . . . practised sorcery and deceived and led astray Israel" may be older than their immediate context ("Benediction," 57).

same direct object, Israel, and are closely related in meaning, as are the corresponding nouns in the related passage in *m. Sanh.* 7:10-11. Although the comment attributed to Ulla (a late third-century rabbi) may be a later elaboration of this polemical tradition, the reference to Deuteronomy 13 confirms that "entice" and "lead astray" amount to a charge of false prophecy, for in that *locus classicus* these three terms are very closely related.

In *b. Sanh.* 107b the same double accusation is found in the same order:

> One day he (R. Joshua) was reciting the Shema when Jesus came before him. He intended to receive him and made a sign to him. He (Jesus) thinking it was to repel him, went, put up a brick, and worshipped it.[12]
>
> "Repent," said he (R. Joshua) to him. He replied, "I have thus learned from thee: He who sins and causes others to sin is not afforded the means of repentance." And a Master has said, "Jesus the Nazarene *practiced magic and led Israel astray.*"

These two rabbinic traditions are very difficult to interpret in detail, and even more difficult to date with any confidence. Were it not for the close correspondence between these traditions and Justin's *Dialogue* 69:7, it would be tempting to dismiss them as third-century (or even later) Jewish anti-Christian polemic. However, the semitechnical terminology used in Justin Martyr's Greek is almost as close as one could reasonably expect to the Hebrew of the rabbinic traditions.[13] Equally important, the order in which the accusations are cited is the same. In Deuteronomy the discussion of enticement to apostasy and false prophecy in ch. 13 which is referred to in *b. Sanh.* 43a *precedes* detailed reference to various forms of magic and sorcery in ch. 18.[14] The order of the discussion in Deuteronomy is followed in *Mishnah Sanhedrin* 10–11 (where there is no reference to Jesus), but it is reversed in Jewish polemic against Jesus, both in Justin's *Dialogue* and in *b. Sanh.* 107b and 43a. Since direct dependence is very unlikely, the similar wording and the correspondence in order strongly suggest independent use of a stock polemical tradition.

If this double accusation echoed polemical passages in the NT Gospels, the close correspondence in terminology and in order might be coincidental. But this is not the case. Jesus is not called ὁ μάγος in the NT. Although the πλάνος accusation occurs explicitly (as we shall see) in redactional passages in the Gospels, there are no grounds for suspecting literary dependence. So the jibes against Jesus which are found both in Justin's writings and in rabbinic traditions have not been taken directly from the canonical Gospels. They put

12. See esp. E. Bammel, "Jesus and 'Setting up a Brick,'" in *Judaica*, Kleine Schriften 1 (Tübingen: J. C. B. Mohr [Paul Siebeck], 1986) 204-8.

13. See esp. Martyn, *History and Theology*, 79 n. 110.

14. In Deuteronomy rejection of magic in 18:9-14 is followed immediately by the promise of the "prophet like Moses" and discussion of true and false prophecy in 18:15-22. However, the latter passage does not seem to be in view in either of the two rabbinic traditions quoted above.

us in touch with an independent negative assessment of Jesus which appears to have been widespread by the middle of the second century, if not earlier.

There is a further example of this double accusation in the *Acts of Thomas*, a third-century writing which very probably incorporates earlier traditions. In a strongly polemical passage in ch. 96, Charisius rounds on his wife Mygdonia: "I have heard that that *magician and deceiver* (ὁ μάγος ἐκεῖνος καὶ πλάνος) teaches that a man should not live with his own wife. . . ." He said to her again, ". . . be not led astray by deceitful and vain words nor by the works of magic." The phrase "magician and deceiver" recalls Justin's *Dialogue* 69:7 and the rabbinic allegations against Jesus. The same phrase is used in ch. 102, and again (though in separate sentences) in chs. 106–7.[15]

These passages in the *Acts of Thomas* are very different from the examples of this allegation which have been referred to above. Here there is hardly a trace of Christian-Jewish polemic or apologetic, and with the exception of ch. 48 (where Jesus is referred to with the single accusation πλάνος), they are made against the apostle Thomas, not Jesus. But there is no doubt at all that Thomas is an *alter ego* of Jesus.[16] The use of the phrase μάγος καὶ πλάνος can hardly be a coincidence. In the *Acts of Thomas* a "stock" Jewish criticism of Jesus has survived in a very different setting. This confirms that it was a widespread and well-known polemical accusation.

A further example of this double accusation is found in the *Testimonium Flavianum,* the paragraph about Jesus in Josephus *Ant.* 18.3.3. In its present form it cannot have been written by the Jewish historian *c.* 93-94 C.E., for several phrases are undeniably Christian assessments of the significance of Jesus. The key question, debated since the sixteenth century, is whether the whole five-sentence paragraph is a later Christian interpolation, or whether a Christian scribe has added a few phrases (and perhaps altered a few words) in a "neutral" or mildly hostile account of Jesus which was originally written by Josephus himself.

Over the last decade or so several influential voices have supported the latter view.[17] I believe that this is much the more likely solution. For our present

15. The English translation is taken from E. Hennecke, *New Testament Apocrypha,* vol. 2, ed. R. McL. Wilson (London: Lutterworth, 1965). The Greek text is from *Acta Apostolorum Apocrypha,* 2.2, ed. M. Bonnet (Hildesheim: G. Olms, 1903; reprint ed., 1959). The reference in ch. 48 to Jesus as ὁ πλάνος is noted, but without discussion, by Martyn, *History and Theology,* 79 n. 110; and by A. Strobel, *Die Stunde der Wahrheit* (Tübingen: J. C. B. Mohr [Paul Siebeck], 1980) 90, but they do not refer to chs. 96 or 106–7. A. F. J. Klijn, *The Acts of Thomas* (Leiden: E. J. Brill, 1962) 271, includes a note on the "sorcerer" accusation which is made against Thomas in numerous passages, but does not comment on the πλάνος accusation or on the combination of μάγος and πλάνος noted above.

16. See, e.g., chs. 2, 11, and 45.

17. See esp. E. Bammel, "Zum Testimonium Flavianum (Jos Ant 18,63-64)," in *Josephus-Studien,* ed. O. Betz, K. Haacker, and M. Hengel (Göttingen: Vandenhoeck & Ruprecht, 1974) 9-22 (= Bammel, *Judaica,* 177-89). For a recent careful assessment of the literature, see J. P. Meier, "Jesus

purposes the second sentence is the most important. In the Loeb edition of the writings of Josephus, L. H. Feldman translates it as follows: "For he (Jesus) was one who wrought surprising feats and was a teacher of such people as accept the truth gladly. He won over many Jews and many of the Greeks." Translations along these lines are found in several books on Jesus and the Gospels; they offer a neutral or even mildly *positive* assessment of Jesus. I believe that they are unduly influenced by the view that the whole pericope is a later Christian addition. Without any emendation of the text, the key Greek words can more plausibly be translated to give an ambivalent or even a mildly *hostile* assessment of Jesus — that is, one which can be attributed to Josephus with much greater confidence.

Let us start with the final verb, ἐπηγάγετο, translated by Feldman as "he won over," and by Meier as "he gained a following among." R. Eisler emended the verb to ἀπηγάγετο, and translated it as "seduce."[18] If this proposal is adopted, we are close to Justin's λαοπλάνος and the related rabbinic terms discussed above.

But there is no need to emend the verb. Bauer's lexicon gives "bring on" as the meaning of ἐπάγω, and notes that in figurative usage it usually has the sense "bring something bad upon someone."[19] Hence ἐπηγάγετο in the *Testimonium* can be understood as "brought trouble to," or even "seduce, lead astray."[20] In other words, the verb ἐπάγομαι is only a little less close to πλανάω than ἀπάγομαι.

The preceding two phrases in the *Testimonium* are equally important for our present concerns. The translation of the first is not problematic: the phrase refers to Jesus as "one who did surprising (or unexpected) deeds." Depending on one's perspective, this could refer negatively to a magician, or positively to a miracle worker.

Meier translates the next phrase as "a teacher of people who receive the truth with pleasure," but in a note accepts (correctly) that it could imply simple-

---

in Josephus: A Modest Proposal," *CBQ* 52 (1990) 76-103. Meier argues that with the extraction of the three most obviously Christian statements, the *Testimonium* yields the original or "core" text Josephus wrote, with no need to rewrite any words or phrases in the core. I believe that this solution is correct, but I do not accept all of Meier's translations of what is admittedly difficult and ambiguous Greek. Meier does not discuss the relationship of the original text of the paragraph to the other assessments of Jesus with which I am concerned in this essay.

18. R. Eisler, *The Messiah Jesus and John the Baptist* (London: Methuen, 1931) 61-62.

19. BAGD 281. Josephus *Life* 18 is a good example of the verb in this sense. "Win over" is attested in Thuycidides and Polybius (see LSJ) and Chrysostom (see G. W. H. Lampe, *Patristic Greek Lexicon*), but the verb is rarely used with this positive sense.

20. Bammel notes that *significatio seditionis* is possible for ἐπάγομαι ("Testimonium Flavianum," *Judaica*, 179-81). Meier acknowledges that this is "a possible, though not necessary, meaning of the verb," but does not give supporting references or reasons for rejecting this translation ("Jesus in Josephus," 88 n. 33). M. Smith, *Jesus the Magician* (London: Victor Gollancz, 1978) 178, translates "lead astray" and claims that this sense is implied by the Greek text.

minded enthusiasm, even self-delusion.[21] A decision depends on whether Josephus paints his portrait of Jesus from a mildly hostile or from a "neutral" perspective. I believe that the former is much more likely, though a full defense is not possible here.[22]

In short, in the *Testimonium* Jesus is said to have been a miracle worker / magician who impressed rather gullible people, and led many Jews (and many Greeks) astray. Although the terminology in the terse assessment of Jesus in the *Testimonium* differs from that used in the anti-Christian Jewish polemic quoted by Justin, and in the rabbinic traditions discussed above, there is notable agreement.

In all these summary assessments of Jesus, his actions and his words are linked closely; they are referred to in the same order and in broadly similar ways as those of a "magician" and a "false prophet" who led astray God's people. I do not think that these similarities can be mere coincidence. From these passages, which are all independent of one another, we may conclude that there was a stable form of anti-Jesus polemic which dates from the time of Josephus toward the end of the first century. In the final section of this essay we shall consider its earlier roots.

## 2. Magic, False Prophecy, Demonic Possession

So far we have considered examples of the *double* polemical accusation that Jesus was a magician and a false prophet / deceiver. Both accusations are also found singly. Since, as we shall see in a moment, these charges are closely related to one another, use of one or the other polemical term often carries with it the implications of the other.

The single accusation that Jesus was a sorcerer is found in several passages. In his *First Apology* 30 Justin refers to the claim by his opponents that the miracles of Jesus were done by the use of magical arts. Writing at about the same time as Justin, Celsus repeatedly makes the same accusation, usually when he is citing the polemic of a Jew.[23]

The single accusation that Jesus was a false prophet / deceiver is found even more widely. In ch. 108 of his *Dialogue,* Justin claims that Jewish leaders "appointed chosen men and sent them into all the civilized world, proclaiming that 'a certain godless and lawless sect has been raised by one Jesus of Galilee, a deceiver (πλάνος). . . .'" A Christian redaction of *The Testament of Levi,* which

21. "Jesus in Josephus," 84, and n. 19.

22. See esp. Bammel, "Testimonium Flavianum," *Judaica,* 177-89. Bammel's article is perceptive and generally persuasive, though I am not convinced by his proposed conjectural emendation of ἀγαπήσαντες to ἀπατήσαντες.

23. See *Contra Celsum* 1:6, 28, 68, 71; 2:32, 48-49. On Celsus's Jew, see E. Bammel, "Der Jude des Celsus," in *Judaica,* 265-83.

may well date from the same time as that of Justin and Celsus, alleges that those who plotted to kill Jesus categorized him as πλάνος (*T. Levi* 16:3).[24] As we shall see in the final section of this essay, this line of polemic is also found in the Gospels.

The following passages confirm the close relationship in antiquity between μάγος and ψευδοπροφήτης / πλάνος.

(1) In Acts 13:6-12 Luke records that Barnabas and Paul met a certain magician, a Jewish false prophet named Bar-Jesus, also known as Elymas (τινὰ ψευδοπροφήτην μάγον, v 6). Luke carefully contrasts Paul, who has been filled with the Holy Spirit, with Elymas, who is a son of the devil and full of deceit and villainy (vv 9-10). In this passage "magician" and "false prophet" are almost synonymous; not quite synonymous, however, otherwise one or the other term would be redundant.

(2) In Philo *Spec. Leg.* 1.315, προφήτης and γόης are contrasted, probably with Deuteronomy 13 in mind.

> If anyone cloaking himself under the name and guise of a prophet and claiming himself to be possessed by inspiration lead us on to the worship of the gods recognised in the different cities, we ought not to listen to him and be deceived by the name of a prophet. For such a one is no prophet, but an imposter (γόης), since his oracles and pronouncements are falsehoods invented by himself.

In this passage γόης is used in the general sense of "imposter," "charlatan"; "sorcery" is probably but not necessarily in view. However, "false prophecy" and "sorcery" are associated explicitly in *Vit. Mos.* 1.277, where Philo contrasts the technique of the μάγος with the πνεῦμα προφητικόν.[25]

(3) In Josephus *Ant.* 20.169-72; *J.W.* 2.261-63 (cf. Acts 21:38), we read of an unnamed Egyptian who designated himself as a προφήτης and promised a legitimating miracle: at his command, Jerusalem's walls would fall down. Josephus, however, scornfully labels him as a ψευδοπροφήτης and a γόης.[26]

In *Ant.* 20.97 Josephus refers to a certain sorcerer (γόης) called Theudas who persuaded a large number of people to follow him to the river Jordan: "he stated that he was a prophet and that at his command the river would be parted

24. For a fuller discussion of these passages, see G. N. Stanton, "Aspects of Early Christian-Jewish Polemic and Apologetic," *NTS* 31 (1985) 377-82 (= Stanton, *A Gospel for a New People: Studies in Matthew* [Edinburgh: T. & T. Clark, 1992]) 232-55. See also *The Apocryphon of John* 1:1; Origen *Contra Celsum* 2:1; Chrysostom *Sermons against Judaizers* 5.5.8-9.

25. See G. Delling, "μάγος," *TDNT* 4.358. In most of the passages with which I am concerned, there is no significant difference between μάγος and γόης.

26. See also the descriptions of individual rebels in Josephus *Ant.* 20.97-98; 18.1-10 (and 20.102); and summary passages in *Ant.* 20.167-68; *J. W.* 2.259. For discussion, see D. Aune, "Magic in Early Christianity," *ANRW* 2.23.2, 1528.

and would provide him with an easy passage." Josephus clearly believes that Theudas was a false prophet whose promised miracle was a typical ploy of a γόης.

(4) This close relationship between "magic" and "false prophecy" is by no means confined to Hellenistic Jewish and early Christian writers. A second-century-C.E. papyrus notes that in the eyes of his opponent, the prophet of Apollo is a "hungry γόης."[27] In Philostratus *Life* 5.12 we read that Apollonius does not prophesy on the basis of γοητεία, but on that of divine revelation. Lucian of Samosata *Peregrinus* 13 attacks opponents as "false prophets who are really charlatans and sorcerers." And in an intriguing magical papyrus which is difficult to date (*PGM* 5.110), we read, "I am Moses your prophet."[28]

These passages (which are by no means exhaustive) confirm the close relationship between "magic" and "false prophecy." In ancient polemic reference to one or the other term may well imply the other.[29] From the evidence set out above, it is clear that the allegations that Jesus was a magician and that he was a false prophet who deceived God's people are closely related. They are found in tandem (and, strikingly, in the same order), and also singly in a wide range of writings. The strength of the evidence from the middle of the second century is most impressive. The *Testimonium Flavianum* suggests that the polemic has deeper roots in the first century.

Before we explore the origin of what became stock polemic against Jesus and early Christianity, it will be important to show that there is a third closely related line of polemic in writings from our period. The examples which follow show that in ancient polemic opponents allege that both the "magician" and the "false prophet" are able to act as they do as the result of their close relationship to the devil or to demons.

(1) At the beginning of ch. 69 of Justin's *Dialogue* with Trypho, the chapter which I have taken as my starting point in this essay, Justin notes that both the deeds of the magicians in Egypt and the words of the false prophets in the time of Elijah were the work of the devil. This linking of magic, false prophecy, and the work of the devil is significant. It is found in several passages in Justin and in a wide range of ancient polemical writings.

A further important example of the close relationship of these three concepts occurs at the opening of the *Dialogue*. In his account to the Jew Trypho

27. For details, see BAGD 164.

28. I owe this reference to A. B. Kolenkow, who quotes the passage in full ("Relationships between Miracle and Prophecy in the Graeco-Roman World and Early Christianity," *ANRW* 2.23.2, 1488).

29. In *Jesus the Magician*, 79, Smith goes further and states that "false prophet" and "magician" were often used almost as synonyms. However, in his Appendix B, "Jesus vs. the Prophets," he downplays evidence which suggests that Jesus saw himself and was seen by others as a prophet. P. Samain has also stressed the close relationship between "imposter" and "magician" ("'L'accusation de magie contre le Christ dans les Évangiles," *ETL* 15 [1938] 449-90). I have not been able to consult this article; see the summary in Aune, "Magic in Early Christianity," 1540-41.

of his conversion experience, Justin attaches great weight to the witness of the OT prophets. The fulfillment of their prophecies compels agreement with what they have spoken.

> And also on account of the miracles which they did, they were entitled to belief, for they both glorified the Maker of all things as God and Father, and proclaimed the Christ sent from Him, as His Son, a thing which the false prophets who are filled with the seducing and unclean spirit never did nor even do, but dare to work miracles of a sort to amaze men, and give glory to the spirits of error and demons. (*Dialogue* 7:3)[30]

(2) Celsus's Jew challenges Jesus: "Come let us believe that these miracles were really done by you." He then refers to the works of sorcerers who profess to do wonderful miracles and asks, "Since these men do these wonders, ought we to think them sons of God? Or ought we to say that they are the practices of wicked men possessed by an evil daemon?"[31] There is no doubt or even hesitation about miracles. The key question is whether they were the result of demonic possession or of a special relationship to God.

(3) Within the NT, there are two examples of the close relationship between false prophecy, magic, and demonic possession which was widely accepted in antiquity. Luke's careful contrast in Acts 13:6-12 between Paul and Elymas (noted above) is striking. Luke contrasts Paul, who has been filled with the Holy Spirit, with Elymas, who is a son of the devil and full of deceit and villainy (vv 9-10). Whereas the true prophet acts and speaks as a result of being filled with the Spirit, the false prophet and magician are in league with the devil.

In Rev 16:13-14 three foul spirits like frogs issue from the mouth of the false prophet (and the dragon and the beast); all three are demonic spirits who perform signs. In other words, the "signs" of the false prophet are the result of demonic possession. Revelation 19:20 refers to the signs by which the false prophet deceived (πλανάω) those who had received the mark of the beast.

In the first and second centuries C.E., three closely related concepts are found in polemical traditions which attack Jesus and a wide range of other individuals. General accusations of deception are often given sharper focus by reference to false prophecy. In Jewish polemic which echoes Deuteronomy 13, this is nearly always the case: the "deceiver" is a "false prophet" who leads God's people astray.

30. With some minor modifications I have quoted A. L. Williams's translation (*Justin Martyr: The Dialogue with Trypho* [London: SPCK, 1930]). For a further example from Justin, see *I Apol.* 26 and 56; Menander, a Samaritan and a disciple of Simon Magus, "was possessed by the demons. He deceived many at Antioch by magic arts. . ." (ch. 26).

31. *Contra Celsum* 1:68. I have quoted the translation by H. Chadwick (Cambridge: Cambridge University, 1953). See also *Contra Celsum* 2:49, where Celsus's Jew uses a similar line of argument: Jesus referred to miracle workers whom he clearly regarded as wicked persons and sorcerers (Matt 24:23-27; 7:22-23), so why should one conclude that the miracles of Jesus are those of a god, while those who employ similar miracles are sorcerers?

Although γόης is used in the more general sense of "rogue" or "imposter," where the individual concerned has laid claim to legitimating miracles (and this is the norm, rather than the exception), the label γόης implies sorcery, as, of course, does μάγος.[32]

The claim that an opponent was possessed by demons or in some other way closely related to the demonic world was easy to make and difficult to refute. As we have seen, it was often used in conjunction with allegations of sorcery and false prophecy. These three labels which are so prominent in ancient polemic have a specific social setting. They are used to marginalize and undermine the influence of individuals whose claims and behavior are perceived to pose a threat to the stability of the dominant social order. In short, the polemic is a form of social control.[33] With these considerations in mind, we turn now to the Gospels.

## 3. The Gospels and Jesus

Before considering the possibility that already in his own lifetime Jesus was labeled by his opponents as a magician and a false prophet, we must examine evidence which stems from the hands of the Evangelists. This procedure is in line with the method of "working backwards" from later, clearer evidence to earlier, more problematic evidence which I have used in previous sections of this essay. I take this method to be axiomatic for all critical inquiry into the teaching and actions of Jesus.[34]

In the central chapters of John's Gospel we are able to overhear the disputes between the Johannine community and the local synagogue in the Evangelist's own day. In ch. 7 there are three references to division among the people on account of Jesus (7:12, 25-27, 40). In 7:12 some who are antagonistic to Jesus claim that he is leading the people astray. At the climax of the chapter the officers who were sent by the chief priests and Pharisees to arrest Jesus returned empty-handed, only to be asked why they had failed to bring Jesus with them (v 45). The officers answered, "No man ever spoke like this man!" (v 46). Their positive response to Jesus is immediately undermined by the taunt, "Are you led astray, you also?" (v 47).

32. In the writings to which I have referred, with the exception of Matt 2:1-12, μάγος always has a pejorative sense.

33. For a helpful discussion of the social setting of magic, see Aune, "Magic in Early Christianity," 1510-16. Part of L. T. Johnson's article, "The New Testament's Anti-Jewish Slander and the Conventions of Ancient Polemic," *JBL* 108 (1989) 419-41, is relevant at this point. See also B. J. Malina and J. H. Neyrey, *Calling Jesus Names: The Social Value of Labels in Matthew* (Sonoma, California: Polebridge, 1988) esp. 35-42.

34. I have tried to use this method consistently in my book, *The Gospels and Jesus* (Oxford: Oxford University, 1989).

In both verses reference to "leading astray" is a formal allegation with roots in Deuteronomy 13. In John 4:19 and 9:17 acknowledgment of Jesus as a prophet is shown to be an acceptable if partial response to Jesus. So it is no surprise to find reference to Jesus as a *false* prophet in 7:12, 47, and, by implication, in 7:52. There is little doubt that it is related to the polemic Justin refers to in *Dialogue* 69:7 and 108:2, and to the allegations found in the rabbinic traditions quoted above. In both 7:12 and 47 the claim that Jesus leads the people astray is used to ridicule sympathetic responses to Jesus. This may well have been the context in which this jibe was used in the Evangelist's day. The Evangelist refers to this and other allegations against Jesus because he is confident that his Gospel as a whole is an adequate response.

The claim that Jesus is a magician is not referred to explicitly in the Fourth Gospel. Perhaps this is not surprising, given the absence of references to exorcism in this Gospel and the fact that exorcism is unquestionably the best-attested form of magic among the Jews before Bar Kokhba.[35] Although John 8:48, the allegation that Jesus has a demon, has sometimes been said to be related to the charge that he was a magician,[36] this is unlikely. We noted above that allegations of demonic possession were associated with charges both of sorcery and of false prophecy. Since the latter is so clearly in view in John 7, and since in the immediate context it is the (prophetic) words of Jesus which are being attacked by his opponents, false prophecy rather than sorcery probably lies behind John 8:48.

John 10:19-21 is all of a piece.[37] As in John 7:12, 47, following a division among the people a hostile allegation is used to discredit those who make a sympathetic response to Jesus. Jesus is said to have a demon and therefore to be mad. "So why listen to him as the prophet like Moses?" (cf. *to him you shall listen,* Deut 18:15). Others insist that the sayings of Jesus are not those of one who has a demon. And then, unexpectedly for modern readers, they say, "Can a demon open the eyes of the blind?" Although this final comment might be taken as a rebuttal of an accusation that Jesus is a magician, once again (as in 8:48) false prophecy is more likely to be in view. As we noted above, demon possession is often said to confirm false prophecy as well as sorcery. And there are some Jewish traditions in which the prophet like Moses is expected to perform signs.[38] This hope is reflected in John 6:14; 7:31; 9:16-17, and, we may add, 10:21.

35. So P. S. Alexander, "Incantations and Books of Magic," in E. Schürer, *The History of the Jewish People in the Age of Jesus Christ,* 3.1, rev. ed., ed. G. Vermes, F. Millar, and M. Goodman (Edinburgh: T. & T. Clark, 1986) §32.7, 342-79 (342).

36. Martyn, *History and Theology,* 77, notes in passing that this is a possibility. See also R. Bultmann, *The Gospel of John* (Oxford: Blackwell, 1971) 299 n. 4.

37. The importance of these verses has been regularly overlooked in the standard commentaries and in recent major books on the Fourth Gospel.

38. See Martyn, *History and Theology,* 106-12, with references both to primary sources and to other literature.

In view of the role accusations of demonic possession (and similar charges) play in ancient polemic, it is perhaps not surprising that both parties to the ferocious disputes which lie behind the central chapters of the Fourth Gospel use this taunt. In John 8:44 "the Jews" are said to be "of their father the devil," while in 8:48, 52 and 10:20 Jesus is alleged to have a demon. The Evangelist is confident that his readers will know where the truth lies.

In Luke 23 there are three references to Jesus leading the people astray. In v 2 the verb is διαστρέφω, in v 5 ἀνασείω, and in v 14 ἀποστρέφω. These clauses are certainly not taken from Matthew or from John; in all probability, they come from Luke's redaction of Markan traditions rather than from pre-Lukan material. From Luke's perspective, such charges were mischievous if not unexpected; they were all of a piece with the false allegations brought against Stephen and Paul.[39] I think it probable that Luke was aware of what became the standard polemical claim that Jesus was a false prophet who led the people astray.

I am confident that Matthew's Gospel reflects the double allegation that Jesus was a magician and a false prophet who deceived God's people. The threefold accusation that the exorcisms of Jesus have been carried out "by the prince of demons" (9:34; 10:25; 12:24, 27) is a way of alleging that Jesus is a magician. As we noted above, exorcism is the best-attested form of magic among Jews before Bar Kokhba.[40] The first two of Matthew's three references to this accusation, 9:34 and 10:25, come from the Evangelist's own hand. The third, 12:24, 27, is taken from Mark 3:22 and from Q (= Luke 11:19); Matthew has redacted his traditions at this point. So Matthew clearly has a special interest in this allegation: he is anxious to acknowledge it and to refute it.

At the climax of ch. 12 the tables are turned on the scribes and the Pharisees: they are part of a generation which is possessed by seven evil spirits (12:43-45). They are demon possessed, not Jesus. As in the Fourth Gospel, both sides in this bitter dispute between Christians and Jews trade the same taunt.[41] The threefold accusation that the exorcisms of Jesus have been carried out by dint of collusion with Beelzebul, the prince of demons, is carefully balanced by a threefold insistence that Jesus acts ἐν πνεύματι θεοῦ (12:18, 28, 31-32).

The final words attributed to the Jewish leaders in Matthew refer to the second half of the double allegation with which we are concerned. In 27:63-64 Jesus is referred to as "that deceiver" (ἐκεῖνος ὁ πλάνος) and his life is summed up as "deception" (πλάνη). Once again the Pharisees are singled out as the arch-opponents. They have been conspicuously absent from Matthew's story line since the end of ch. 23, but in 27:62-66 they join the chief priests (whose presence is demanded by the preceding narratives) in petitioning Pilate. The

39. See G. N. Stanton, "Jesus in Lucan Perspective," in *Studia Biblica*, vol. 3, ed. E. A. Livingstone (Sheffield: JSOT, 1980) 345-60.

40. In Acts 19:11-20 Luke almost equates exorcism and magic. See also Josephus *Ant.* 8.45-49; Justin *Dialogue* 85:3; Origen *Contra Celsum* 1:68.

41. For a fuller discussion of these passages, see Stanton, *Gospel for a New People*, 173-79.

whole pericope is thoroughly Matthean, so here we have further evidence of the Evangelist's own special interest in a hostile assessment of Jesus.[42]

This time Matthew does not reply directly to the polemic. He takes great pains to convince the reader that the resurrection of Jesus from the tomb in which he was buried was not the "final deception," but he simply lets the Jewish leaders' critical comments stand. Presumably he is convinced that readers of his gospel will readily agree that the claim of the Jewish leaders that Jesus is a "deceiver" is monstrous; perhaps the closing verses of the Gospel (28:18-20) were intended to prove the point.

The allegation that Jesus was a magician and that he was a false prophet was known at the time the Evangelists wrote. Matthew knew the double form of the accusation. John (certainly) and Luke (probably) are aware that Jewish opponents of Christian claims allege that Jesus was a false prophet who led God's people astray.

The passages from the Gospels discussed so far in this section are all redactional. They put us in touch with the viewpoints of the Evangelists and confirm that they were aware of polemical allegations against Jesus and sought to counter them. Matthew, Luke, and John all wrote in the 80s, at a time of mutual incomprehension, keen rivalry, and sour disputes between Christians and Jews. So it is no surprise to find in the Gospels charges and countercharges concerning the actions and teaching of Jesus.

Does this polemic have roots in the lifetime of Jesus? There are sound reasons for concluding that even in his own lifetime Jesus was labeled "magician" by his opponents.

In Mark 3:22 and independently in Q (Matt 12:24 = Luke 11:15),[43] the exorcisms of Jesus are said to be carried out as a result of Jesus' association with Beelzebul, the prince of demons. We noted above that exorcism was the best-attested form of magic among Jews in the first century and that magicians were regularly said to be demon possessed. Hence there is little doubt that both the Markan and the Q traditions are tantamount to a charge that Jesus was a magician. In his healing miracles and exorcisms Jesus undoubtedly used techniques which would have been perceived by contemporaries to be magical.[44] Since few scholars have any reservations about the authenticity of these two traditions, it is highly likely that Jesus was written off by his opponents as a magician, and thus as a social deviant.

Not surprisingly, already within the pre-Markan tradition and in Q (as well as in the completed Gospels), there is a response to this charge. Followers

42. For details of Matthean vocabulary and style in this pericope, see R. H. Gundry, *Matthew: A Commentary on His Literary and Theological Art* (Grand Rapids, Michigan: Wm. B. Eerdmans, 1982) 540-51.

43. In most recent reconstructions of Q, this tradition is accepted as Q material. See the brief discussion in J. Kloppenborg, *Q Parallels: Synopsis, Critical Notes & Concordance* (Sonoma, California: Polebridge, 1988) 90-92.

44. See Aune, "Magic in Early Christianity," 1523-29; Smith, *Jesus the Magician,* 94-139.

of Jesus would not have transmitted such a hostile assessment of Jesus unless a firm refutation of the allegation were juxtaposed.

The Q pericope contrasts sharply two ways of assessing the exorcising activity of Jesus: is Jesus in league with the prince of demons, or are his actions the result of his relationship to God? Jesus himself claims that his exorcisms were carried out "by the finger of God," as signs of the breaking in of God's kingly rule (Matt 12:28 = Luke 11:20). In later polemic the same issue arises, but without specific reference to this passage. In *I Apol.* 30 Justin notes that critics claim that the miracles of Jesus were done by magic arts rather than as a result of Jesus' relationship to God as his Son. Celsus's Jew argues similarly: on account of his miraculous powers, Jesus gave himself the title God, but in fact they were the result of magical powers gained in Egypt (*Contra Celsum* 1:28). Celsus's Jew closes his remarks addressed to Jesus with the claim that the miracles were the actions of one "hated by God and of a wicked sorcerer" (*Contra Celsum* 1:71); in this way the claim of Christians that Jesus stands in a special relationship to God is undermined.

Mark himself has shaped considerably the traditions he links together in 3:20-35. In a redactional comment in v 30 he points out that the saying of Jesus concerning blasphemy against the Holy Spirit (3:28-29) applies to those who claimed that Jesus was possessed by Beelzebul, and that he cast out demons by the prince of demons (3:22). R. A. Guelich has perceptively summed up the key point Mark is making: "To attribute the work of the Spirit through Jesus to demonic forces is the ultimate calumny for which there is no forgiveness."[45] Once again, as in the Q Beelzebul traditions, there are two opposing assessments of the actions of Jesus: are they to be ascribed to demonic possession or to divine agency?

In Mark 3:22 the opponents are identified as "the scribes who came down from Jerusalem." They represent the dominant social order which Jesus is threatening.[46] Although the reference to Jerusalem is a redactional note from Mark himself, the scribes were probably identified as the opponents of Jesus in the pre-Markan tradition. There is no reason to doubt that both the actions and the teaching of Jesus brought him into conflict from time to time with the religious authorities of the day. In that social setting allegations of false prophecy and sorcery thrive. As we noted above, they are used to marginalize and undermine the influence of individuals whose claims and behavior are perceived to pose a threat to the stability of the dominant social order.

It is more difficult to establish that in his own lifetime Jesus was considered by some to be a false prophet who led Israel astray. In the Gospels there is no specific allegation along these lines. However, cumulative evidence makes this a strong probability.

45. R. A. Guelich, *Mark 1–8:26,* WBC 34A (Dallas: Word, 1989), 180.

46. A. F. Segal's comments are instructive (*Rebecca's Children: Judaism and Christianity in the Roman World* [Cambridge: Harvard University, 1986] 144-45): "The logic from the scribes' perspective is that if Jesus were from God, he could not oppose the ideas of the legitimate authorities of Judea. Since he does oppose them, his power must have other sources."

(1) As we have seen above, Matthew and John, and probably Luke, were aware of this polemical charge. There is no reason to suppose that it first arose at the time they wrote. Tension between Jews who accepted Christian claims about Jesus and those who did not, did not surface overnight in the 80s. Given that Jesus was alleged by some to be a magician, and given the close links between the two allegations to which we drew attention above, it is highly likely that Jesus was said by some to be a false prophet.

(2) John the Baptist was said to have a demon (Q: Matt 11:18 = Luke 7:33). Since neither the Synoptic Evangelists nor Josephus (*Ant.* 18.116-19) attribute miracle-working powers to John,[47] the polemical jibe recorded in Q labels him as a demon-possessed false prophet. Since John and Jesus were associated closely, Jesus was almost certainly also marginalized by some with the same accusation.

(3) Although the Evangelists do not emphasize that Jesus was a prophet, in two sayings, Mark 6:4 and Luke 13:33, Jesus refers to himself as a prophet. A number of other sayings and several of his actions confirm that he saw himself as a prophet.[48] Thus it would be surprising if some opponents did not dub him as a false prophet, perhaps even with Deuteronomy 13 in mind.[49]

I have argued that the double allegation found in Justin's *Dialogue* 69:7 and in the rabbinic traditions quoted above has deep roots. In his own lifetime Jesus was said by some to be a demon-possessed magician. It is probable, but not certain, that he was also said to be a demon-possessed false prophet.

Two corollaries follow. It is generally accepted that in the first and second centuries Christians and Jews were at odds about christology and the law. It is less frequently appreciated that both the actions and the teaching of Jesus were also a source of tension and dispute: they were assessed very differently by his later followers and opponents.

The allegations of the contemporary opponents of Jesus confirm that he was seen by many to be a disruptive threat to social and religious order. His claims to act and speak on the basis of a special relationship to God were rightly perceived to be radical. For some they were so radical that they had to be undermined by an alternative explanation of their source.

The relationship of Jesus to Judaism must be considered from many angles, including the perspective I have adopted in this essay. While I have considered only a few strands of the relevant evidence, I hope I have shown that at least on this issue, Strauss is to be preferred to Reimarus.

47. Cf. also John 10:41. Mark 6:14 is an apparent exception, but on any view this is a puzzling verse.

48. I have summarized and discussed the evidence briefly in *Gospels and Jesus*, 177-83. See esp. D. E. Aune, *Prophecy in Early Christianity and the Ancient Mediterranean World* (Grand Rapids, Michigan: Wm. B. Eerdmans, 1983) 153-89.

49. Strobel, *Stunde der Wahrheit*, goes much further and argues that this accusation was in fact central in the Sanhedrin trial.

# The Son of Man Seated at God's Right Hand and the Debate over Jesus' "Blasphemy"[1]

Darrell L. Bock

## 1. Introduction to the Debate over Historicity

All agree that if the Gospel reports about the trial of Jesus before the Jewish leadership were true, then a crucial puzzle piece would exist in the quest of the historical Jesus. In addition, no part of the trial scene is more important literarily than the saying which causes the high priest and those present at the trial to regard Jesus as having convicted himself. The ripping of the garments and the remarks made after this saying show that the leadership is deeply offended by the defendant's remarks.[2] After Jesus' own testimony, the leadership takes the case to Rome and Pontius Pilate. Clearly this saying plays an important role in the *narrative* portrayal of Jesus' death. With this literary function of the account all agree.

Unfortunately, the premise about the *historical* truthfulness of these reports has been challenged on many grounds.[3] My goal is very modest. Since I

1. I. Howard Marshall's work, *The Origins of New Testament Christology* (Downers Grove, Illinois: InterVarsity, 1976), was the catalyst to my own interest in christology while I was a student. So I am pleased to offer this small token of gratitude by examining the nature and conceptual background of Jesus' blasphemy.

2. On the ripping of garments as a sign of offense, see Gen 37:29; 2 Kgs 6:30; Josephus, *J.W.* 2.316.

3. For a full discussion of the wide range of challenges as they apply to Mark's Gospel, see Robert Gundry, *Mark* (Grand Rapids, Michigan: Wm. B. Eerdmans, 1993) 891-922. I thank Dr. Gundry for letting me see a prepublication draft of the manuscript. Of course, the literature on the trial is enormous. In general, views take a wide range of approaches. Two of the better-known works raising significant doubts about the portrayal of the Sanhedrin trial scene in the Synoptics are H. Lietzmann, "Der Proceß Jesu," *SPAW*, phil.-hist. Kl. 14 (1931) 313-22 (= *Kleine Schriften*, vol. 2: *Studien zum Neuen Testament*, ed. K. Aland, TU 68 [Berlin: Academie, 1958] 251-63); and the development of his view by P. Winter, *On the Trial of Jesus*, 2d ed., rev. T. A. Burkill and G. Vermes, SJ 1 (Berlin: de Gruyter, 1974). Winter attempts to neutralize the Sanhedrin's involvement

cannot deal with all the objections to this scene in this essay, I wish to examine the thrust of the saying of Luke 22:69 in its Jewish background. If this piece of information can be shown to cohere with its historical setting then one key piece of the puzzle for this passage will be laid on the table. So I wish to propose a hypothesis about the conceptual background to this saying and the charge of blasphemy which helps to explain the officials' reaction.

I choose to discuss the Lukan trial scene, though in fact on the point to be developed it makes no difference which version of the saying is analyzed. Luke is unique in not explicitly calling Jesus' saying blasphemy (cf. Mark 14:64; Matt 26:65), and no formal charge emerges so one could argue that it is the least developed account. As I shall show, however, this is more a difference of rhetorical presentation than of substance. Still, for some Matthew and Mark give the most problematic form of the account, so Luke emerges as a potentially fruitful starting point for discussion.[4]

E. P. Sanders offers perhaps the most famous recent challenge to the trial scene and this saying about blasphemy in its Synoptic form (especially that of Matthew and Mark).[5] Of the seven reasons for doubting the authenticity of the trial scene narratives he offers, three revolve around the Son of Man saying I wish to consider.

Briefly stated those three objections are: (1) "the Gospels are surprisingly reluctant to have Jesus admit the supposed charge, though doubtless all the evangelists believed that he was the Christ and also the Son of God." Sanders does recognize Mark's positive version of the reply (14:62), but suggests that it is "possible that all the evangelists, not just Luke, wanted to protect Jesus from being guilty of the supposed charge, even though they all believed that he was

---

by arguing that Jesus' teaching corresponds with Pharisaism and that any Jewish action was in response to Roman political pressure. Among those challenging their skepticism about this scene, see A. N. Sherwin-White, *Roman Society and Roman Law in the New Testament* (Oxford: Oxford University, 1963) 24-47; D. R. Catchpole, *The Trial of Jesus,* SPB 18 (Leiden: E. J. Brill, 1971) 153-220; A. E. Harvey, *Jesus and the Constraints of History* (Philadelphia: Westminster, 1982). Another key collection of essays is *The Trial of Jesus,* ed. E. Bammel, SBT (London: SCM, 1970), esp. D. Catchpole, "The Problem of the Historicity of the Sanhedrin Trial," 45-65; see also the survey of issues in B. Corley, "Trial of Jesus," in *Dictionary of Jesus and the Gospels,* ed. J. B. Green and S. McKnight (Downers Grove, Illinois: InterVarsity, 1992) 841-54.

4. For such skepticism, see Lietzmann, "Proceß Jesu." E. Lohse, "συνέδριον," *TDNT* 7:867-71, recognizes a Lukan source, but his discussion focuses on issues as presented in Matthew and Mark. Catchpole, *Trial of Jesus,* 153-60, gives numerous reasons for seeing a special Lukan source here, rather than mere dependence on Mark. If Luke has independent access to information, then a look at his account is significant in considering the issue. In addition, the less official nature of the blasphemy charge suggests the need for looking at Luke's version on its own terms. For four general approaches to the trials of Jesus and the issue of Jewish versus Roman involvement, see J. Blinzler, *The Trial of Jesus* (Westminster, Maryland: Neuman, 1959) 10-20.

5. *Jesus and Judaism* (Philadelphia: Fortress, 1985) 297-98. Of his seven objections we discuss his nos. 2, 3, and 4 in this essay.

the Son of God." This leads to Sanders's conclusion that "it is more likely . . . that the charge of blasphemy was not firmly rooted in the tradition."

(2) "The exchanges between the high priest and Jesus in the Synoptic accounts, especially in Matthew and Mark, do not carry conviction." Sanders goes on to explain that the temple charge, which in his judgment has the most potential to be historically accurate, is argued by the Synoptics not to be key, since this charge is brought by "false" witnesses (Mark 14:55-59; Matt 26:59-61) and is dropped when Jesus makes his remarks. This observation by Sanders of the Synoptic handling of the charge is correct. In fact, it is apparently such a minor point that Luke fails to mention it at all.[6]

(3) "It is hard, though not impossible, to imagine a chain of transmission which would have passed on the exchanges of the supposed trial." The objection seems to be that since the only "sympathizer" present at the trial was Jesus himself, where could such testimony come from? One can even note that Peter was outside the room where the trial was held.

This last objection can be handled immediately. It is not so hard to imagine various chains of transmission. Luke suggests that Joseph of Arimathea, a member of the council, asked for Jesus' body (Luke 23:50-51). So a "silent sympathizer" may have been present. At the least, if he had not attended the council meeting, he would have had access to the post-trial discussion.

But two other chains of possible transmission still exist. First, surely the leadership would have tried to explain why they "crucified" Jesus or allowed the Romans to do so.[7] Jesus had been a very visible figure of Judaism (so visible that years later Josephus is aware of him). The Jewish relationship to the episode would need clarification. They would have attempted to put their public "spin" on events. The charge that emerges would have the potential to offend Jews in a way other charges would not. The leadership would have to explain such a harsh treatment of a well-known teacher, as well as deal with the teacher's

6. Earle Ellis, in his essay for this volume (192-203), argues that Luke drops the temple charge because it forms a doublet with the Stephen scene in Acts, so Luke saves that issue for that scene. But Luke is capable of producing "doublet scenes," such as his handling of the journey motifs of Jesus and Paul; his handling of the miracles of Jesus, Peter, and Paul; and his presentations of the Peter-Cornelius event and of Paul's conversion show. On Lukan doublets, see J. A. Fitzmyer, *The Gospel according to Luke*, AB 28-28A (Garden City, New York: Doubleday, 1981) 81-82, but these have more to do with sayings than full scenes. On parallel scenes in Luke, see C. H. Talbert, *Literary Patterns, Theological Themes and the Genre of Luke-Acts* (Missoula: Scholars, 1974); R. F. O'Toole, *The Unity of Luke's Theology*, GNS (Wilmington: Michael Glazier, 1984) 62-94. I prefer to see Luke's omission as conscious for another reason. Since the other accounts make it clear that this charge was irrelevant to the trial's outcome, Luke left it out. Regardless of who is right on this detail, it does not alter the point that Jesus' Son of Man response plays a key and decisive role in all of the Synoptic accounts.

7. One can note that possible evidence of such a "spin" on the issue of the resurrection exists (Matt 28:11-15), though some see this as a Matthean apologetic motif. What is clear is that a body was never produced to stop the disciples' declaration of a resurrection.

sympathizers. So the Jewish leadership would be interested in explaining why they had recommended death to Rome. In referring the matter to Rome, they did not need an "official religious" violation, but only a charge that would pressure Rome to deal with a political threat, which is what they bring to Pilate (Luke 23:2-5).

Second, the Roman court, which handled Jesus later, might have interest in making it clear that they were merely following the nation's "religious experts." So they also would have an interest in circulating an account of what took place with this controversial figure. Such reports could involve the knowledge of people in official positions or people connected to them, like the wife of Chuza, or talk circulating in the city. The summary character of the report need not suggest an official account. Either of these options, a Jewish source or one associated with contact with Rome, cannot be demonstrated or denied. They simply note possible options in how information about this event may have circulated. What the options show is that possible chains of transmission exist. Sanders's skepticism on this point is too great.

So we are left with one basic question to pursue. Does the exchange between Jesus and the high priest "carry conviction"? To answer this question I pursue two themes: (1) the concept of blasphemy in first-century Palestinian Judaism and (2) the significance of the temple and Shekinah presence in first-century Palestinian Judaism as a clue to how a heavenly session might be viewed. The two themes need examination because these two themes are combined in Jesus' reply in Luke, which reads, "But from now on the Son of Man will be seated at the right hand of the power of God."

## 2. Blasphemy in First-Century Judaism

A look at the concept of blasphemy against God shows that it is related to the general use of the term of blasphemy against people. In everyday use, blasphemy was usually speech that expressed disrespect or abuse (Bel 14:9; the term is translated "slander" in Matt 15:19). But often the term applied to abuse or reproach directed against God. Leviticus 24:10-23 specifies that blasphemy against God involved anyone who "curses the name" of God (esp. vv 11, 16). But broader usage also exists. One can blaspheme Yahweh without necessarily mentioning his name. Second Kings 19:6 says that the king of Assyria blasphemes by mocking the living God (cf. 2 Kgs 19:4). No other specifics are given. Isaiah 37:6 notes that an Assyrian's statement that God would not deliver Israel is blasphemy. In fact, one could blaspheme by denying God's ability (Ps 74:18), persecuting his people (Isa 52:5), rejoicing in their defeat (Ezek 35:12), slaying them (Tob 1:18 [S]), or insulting the temple (1 Macc 7:35-38). Thus denigration of God's character, insulting God's presence, insulting his people, or acting against them can be called blasphemy.

Later Jewish literature shows that acts can be considered blasphemous in this general sense. First Maccabees 2:6 suggests that actions, not just sayings, are in view, though normally what is said constitutes blasphemy (2 Macc 8:4; 10:34-35; 12:14; 15:24). In Josephus, the term "blasphemy" usually refers to reproach spoken against a person (*J.W.* 1.603; 2.493; 6.320; *Ant.* 7.207, 265). Even Moses can be blasphemed (*J.W.* 2.145), as can the Jews (*Ant.* 18.257). Only rarely is blasphemy in Josephus directed against God (*Ant.* 6.183; 10.233; 20.108; a false charge is discussed in 8.358-59).

The Josephus examples are significant. *Antiquities* 6.183 is a commentary on David's boldness in facing Goliath, who is accused of insulting Israel's army and blaspheming God (1 Samuel 17). In the context of *Ant.* 6.170-82 the only things that Goliath says are insults to Israel's inability to field a man to oppose him. Hence, this blasphemy is tied to the disrespect shown to God's people and army. In *Ant.* 10.231-33 Belshazzar (called Βαλτασάρην in *Ant.* 10.231) uses temple vessels for a party (cf. Dan 5:1-2 LXX). They come from the temple Nebuchadnezzar had conquered as spoil. But Nebuchadnezzar had simply stored them in a temple. Belshazzar insults the deity, in that he drinks from these vessels while blaspheming God. Josephus says that the combination of drinking from these vessels and blaspheming God reflects "audacity." In *Ant.* 20.108 a soldier guarding the temple during the festival of Passover exposes his private parts to the crowd. This act is called "blasphemy" by the crowd.

These examples are interesting in that two of them are related in part to temple elements, just like some of the examples in 1 Maccabees. In addition, both speech and act are regarded as blasphemous. This is not the "technical" blasphemy that results in capital punishment, but the examples do give a sense of how and in what kind of settings the term was used in first-century Judaism.

Most of the modern debate on the historicity of Jesus' blasphemy centers around *m. Sanh.* 7:5, where it is required that one utter the divine name for one to be guilty of the capital offense of blasphemy. That passage reads, "He who blasphemes is liable only when he will have fully pronounced the divine name." The basis for this capital sanction is Lev 24:11-13.

The problems with this more formal, legal definition are well known. Jesus does not utter the divine name explicitly, unless one reads Mark 14:62 and the "I am" reply as an allusion to the divine name, rather than an affirmative reply.[8]

8. This is the approach of Gundry, *Mark,* 891-922. He suggests that Jesus did use the tetragrammaton in alluding to Ps 110:1, but, as was the custom, all reports of such remarks used a euphemism in its place. He defines blasphemy as dishonoring someone by "verbal robbery," citing Mark 2:7; 3:28-30; 7:22; and 15:29 as examples. The most well-known advocate of the equation of "I am" and the tetragrammaton is E. Stauffer, *Jesus and His Story* (New York: Knopf, 1959) 24-26, 177-95. Catchpole, *Trial of Jesus,* 133-35, critiques Stauffer's approach. Gundry's argument is possible and, if it is so, it would solve the legal issue. But it is a particularly subtle argument. The variation in the parallels at this specific verbal point also makes one wonder if a case for authenticity should be built on the basis of the *ipsissima verba,* when there is such variation. So I will take a different, more conceptual track in answering the historicity question, while noting that this other possibility also exists.

So given the possibility Jesus did not utter the divine name but simply answered affirmatively (or ambiguously) and given the nature of how blasphemy as a capital offense operated, is there another way to view Jesus' reply as worthy of the death penalty because of blasphemy?[9]

What is important to note about our summary on blasphemy before offering our hypothesis is that it could involve either word or action and that special sensitivity existed where the temple of God was concerned. The question emerges, Might some combination of these features yield for Jewish ears a blasphemy worthy of death?

## 3. The Hypothesis: The Offense of a Direct Heavenly Session and the Analogy of the Temple

What is clearly asserted in Jesus' remarks is the session of the Son of Man at the right hand of God. It is this reply in all the Synoptics that sparks the movement to condemn Jesus. What is it that is so offensive? To set some context for the answer to this question, it would be good to review how the temple was viewed in first-century Israel.

The temple was one of three key institutions in first-century Judaism, alongside the synagogue and the home.[10] Most of the priestly activity supported the temple, especially that of offering sacrifices (Exodus 25–31; Leviticus 1–9, 16, 21–22; *Epistle of Aristeas* 92–95; Josephus *Ag. Apion* 2.195-96). The temple was viewed as holy ground, a place where God resided in a special way (Exod 40:34-38; Num 9:15-23). Numerous purity laws served to underscore the locale's sanctity (Leviticus 12, 13–15; 22:4-7). The temple ministry was underwritten by taxes and tithes, so that the priesthood and temple were supported by the rest of the nation (Exod 30:13-16; Num 18:13, 20-31; Deut 14:22-27; 18:1-2; Neh 13:11-12). The Herodian temple also was an extensive site, extending some 450 meters from north to south and 300 from east to west. In fact, the temple was so holy that this may be the one locale over which Rome allowed Jewish authorities to have total jurisdiction, perhaps even including the right of capital punishment for offenses made on these grounds.[11]

9. Where Mark 14:62 has "I am," Matt 26:64 has, "you have said so." Luke 22:67 has, "If I tell you, you will not believe; and if I ask you you will not answer." So we speak of either an affirmative or an ambiguous answer. As ambiguous as this initial reply may have been perceived, the subsequent remarks remove ambiguity and become the issue.

10. The following description draws heavily on E. P. Sanders, *Judaism: Practice and Belief 63 BCE–66 CE* (London: SCM, 1992) 47-102, esp. 70-72. Citations from Josephus and Philo that follow are from the LCL.

11. For the possibility that the rights of capital punishment may have been granted the Sanhedrin for this limited area, see Sherwin-White, *Roman Society,* 35-43, as he appropriately refutes Lietzmann's premise that the Sanhedrin had this authority in general. Lietzmann's claim,

For our concerns, the most important feature about the temple was its sanctity. Restricted access was tightened as one came closer to the Holy of Holies. Gentiles could enter only the outer court, and similar restrictions applied to impure Israelites (Josephus *Ant.* 12.145-46; *Ag. Apion* 2.102-5). Impure Jews (e.g., lepers, menstruants) were excluded from the entire temple complex (Lev 15:19-23). Women were restricted to the Court of Women (Josephus *J.W.* 5.199; *m. Mid.* 2:5). Laymen could not enter the court of the priests or the sanctuary. This view was held so strongly that the inner area of the rebuilt temple complex was constructed by 1,000 priests trained by masons for the task (Josephus *Ant.* 15.390). So only the priests could do the work of the temple. All of these descriptions served to communicate the concept of God's holiness.

Even more intense was the restricted access to the Holy of Holies, where God was believed especially to reside. Here only once a year, the high priest could enter, and then only after a long process of preparation (Leviticus 16). How holy was this locale? Perhaps no ancient text indicates the view as clearly as Philo's *Spec. Leg.* 1.72. It reads:

> Right in the middle stands the sanctuary itself with a beauty baffling description, to judge from what is exposed to view. For all inside is unseen except by the high priest alone, and indeed he, though charged with the duty of entering once a year, gets no view of anything. For he takes with him a brazier full of lighted coals and incense, and the quantity of vapor which this naturally gives forth covers everything around it, beclouds the eyesight and prevents it from being able to penetrate any distance.

This citation shows the respect with which God's presence was viewed. Though the high priest was allowed in only once a year, the place was so holy that nothing was seen. Even if Philo's description is an exaggeration, it still indicates how strong a view of God's holiness existed. God was so holy that humans did not have direct access. Only a selected representative could enter into God's presence, and only after much purification. Even the heavenly experiences of Isaiah (Isaiah 6) and Ezekiel (Ezekiel 1) are visions. God's throne is beyond direct human access.

The Maccabean experience confirms this attitude. A reading of 1 Macc 1:29-64; 4:36-58; or 2 Macc 10:1-9 reveals the sense of revulsion at Antiochus Epiphanes's desecration of the temple. God's presence was holy.

But one other detail needs noting. The temple was seen as a model of the heavenly temple. This helped to explain why there was only one temple and why it was taken so seriously. Josephus writes, "In no other city let there be

---

if it were correct, would raise historical questions about a referral to Pilate, as well as the trustworthiness of the Sanhedrin trial scene itself.

either altar or temple; for God is one and the Hebrew race is one" (*Ant.* 4.201). Interestingly, the very next topic discussed is blasphemy: "Let him who blasphemes God be stoned, then hung for a day, and buried ignominiously and in obscurity" (*Ant.* 4.202). Could this suggest a close connection between the temple and the potential for blasphemy?

In *Ant.* 3.180-81, Josephus is very clear about how the tabernacle's design relates to heaven. He notes,

> For if one reflects on the construction of the tabernacle and looks at the vestments of the priest and the vessels which we use for sacred ministry, he will discover that our lawgiver was a man of God and that these blasphemous charges brought against us by the rest of men are idle. In fact, every one of those objects is intended to recall and represent the universe, as he will find if he will but consent to examine them without prejudice and with understanding. Thus to take the tabernacle, thirty cubits long, by dividing this into three parts and giving two of them to the priests, as a place approachable and open to all, Moses signifies the earth and the sea, since these too are accessible to all; but the third portion he reserved for God alone, because heaven is also inaccessible to men.

The rest of the section works out the symbolism in even more detail. What is clear is how the Holy of Holies pictures the heavens and God's presence. A similar view of the earthly temple modeling the heavens appears in Philo *Spec. Leg.* 1.66-67.

In *Ag. Apion* 2.192-95, Josephus follows his description of the creation of the heavens and earth with a description of the temple. In 2.193-95 he says,

> We have but one temple for the one God (for like ever loves like), common to all as God is common to all. The priests are continually engaged in His worship, under the leadership of him who for the time is head of the line. With his colleagues he will sacrifice to God, safeguard the laws, adjudicate in cases of dispute, punish those convicted of crime. Any who disobey him will pay the penalty as for impiety towards God Himself.

Josephus underlines respect both for the temple and for the high priest as God's representative. Other early Jewish texts express similar views about the model of the earthly temple (*1 Enoch* 14:16-18, 20; 26:1-2; *2 Apoc. Bar.* 4:2-6; 59:4; 4Q405 20 ii 21-22), as did later rabbinic Judaism (*b. Ta'an.* 5a; *Gen. Rab.* 55:7).[12]

In sum, the temple is a model of the heavenly temple and God's presence. The Holy of Holies was set apart because it represented God's presence. The

12. R. McKelvey, *The New Temple: The Church in the New Testament* (Oxford: Oxford University, 1969) 25-41, discusses this theme in Judaism, but lacks discussion of Josephus and Philo. For the DSS text, G. Vermes, *The Dead Sea Scrolls in English*, 3d ed. (London: Penguin, 1987) 228-29; J. Strugnell, "The Angelic Liturgy at Qumrân," *VTSup.* 7 (1960) 337.

holiness applied to it would extend in their view to God's presence in the heavens.

The truth of this summary can be seen in the famous exchange that occurs in later Jewish material about the view of Rabbi Aqiba (*c.* 50-135 C.E.).[13] In *b. Ḥag.* 14a the following exchange occurs,

> One passage says: "His throne was fiery flames [Dan 7:9b]; and another passage says, "Till thrones were placed, and One that was ancient of days did sit" [Dan 7:9a]. "There is no contradiction: One [throne] for him, and one for [the son of] David." This is the view of Rabbi Aqiba. Said Rabbi Yose the Galilean to him: "Aqiba, how long will you treat the divine presence as profane! Rather, [it must mean] one for justice and one for grace."[14]

This tradition is so well-known that it is repeated with little variation in *b. Sanh.* 38b and in *Midrash Tanḥuma* (*Qedoshim* §1).

Yose's rebuke of Aqiba shows that the idea of anyone sitting in God's presence was offensive to many rabbis. Aqiba was excused for his view (but stood rebuked), because it was not uttered maliciously. But the question that has never been made entirely clear is why this should be so offensive and how it could be considered blasphemy (or profaning God's presence). Those who have studied the issue of blasphemy and raise this passage as an example of blasphemy that does not fit Mishnaic limits explain in general terms that God's presence is somehow violated, but the conceptual and social rationale for this feeling, other than in some broad sense, has been lacking. What the texts I have cited show is that the temple *and those things and the Person whose presence it represents* were viewed with a special sense of holiness. Everything about practice at the temple declared its sanctity and thus the sanctity of heaven and the God who dwells there. It is this background that explains why Jesus' remark would be seen as blasphemous.

It is now easier to see why Jesus' reply that the Son of Man would be seated at the right hand of the Father is blasphemous to Jewish ears. It was *worse* than claiming that he had the right to go into the Holy of Holies in Jerusalem, the most holy location in the nation of Israel. The remark offended both God and the high priest as God's appointed representative of the people (see *Ag. Apion* 2.192-95). It denied that the high priest and the civil body he chaired had the right to examine Jesus. In fact, it argued for a radical reversal of perception. Rather than the leadership having the right to judge Jesus, this Galilean teacher was claiming the right to represent God's way and be their

13. For a more complete treatment of this material, C. A. Evans, "In What Sense 'Blasphemy'? Jesus before Caiaphas in Mark 14:61-64," *SBLSP 1991*, ed. E. H. Lovering Jr. (Atlanta: Scholars, 1991) 223-27.

14. ET, I. Abrahams, "Hagiga," in *The Babylonian Talmud,* ed. I. Epstein (London: Soncino, 1978) 5.83.

judge. Unlike the high priest, Jesus would have no sacrificial preparation. Unlike the high priest, his was not for a limited visit to atone for national sin. And unlike the prophets, he spoke with no "visionary" claim. Jesus could go directly into the presence of God and would rule, *seated* at God's side. He would be vindicated and would possess much more authority than anyone currently prosecuting him. If Antiochus's actions in the temple had been so offensive as to stir priests to war, how much more would the words of this Galilean about a heavenly session be regarded as an affront to God and Israel's representative legislative body?

Our hypothesis is that the actual naming of God was not necessary for a capital violation of blasphemy here, because Jesus' remarks were so blatant a violation of God's presence in the Jewish view that a reaction was necessary. Whatever the potential of the capital offense of the temple charge as raised in Mark, this Son of Man remark was much more direct in claiming that Jesus could approach God in a way no other human was allowed to do.

If this hypothesis is correct, then it means that the only other element in the saying necessary to establish authenticity is that Jesus spoke of himself as the Son of Man, especially in the apocalyptic sense. That problem and the issues of the trial legalities are too complex to develop in the limited space available here, but the premise that Jesus used the apocalyptic Son of Man to refer to himself has been defended elsewhere, though more work may be needed on this question as well.[15] If an apocalyptic Son of Man saying is possible for Jesus, then there would be no reason to reject the remark as impossible for Jesus. What I maintain is that the heavenly session remark would be inherently, extremely offensive to Jewish ears, because it contains associations between two of the most holy locales within Judaism, the Holy of Holies and the dwelling place of God in heaven.

## 4. Conclusion

Jesus' reply in Luke 22:69 (and its parallels) escapes the historical complaints raised against its view that the leadership saw blasphemy in Jesus' remark. The Gospels agree that the saying about the Son of Man seated at the right hand of God was the

15. On the trial's legal elements in the Markan version, see Sherwin-White, *Roman Society,* 24-47; for a defense of the Lukan version, see Catchpole, *Trial of Jesus,* 157-59, 220; on the Son of Man elements, see A. L. Moore, *The Parousia of Jesus* (Leiden: E. J. Brill, 1966) 182-87; I. H. Marshall, "Synoptic Son of Man Sayings," *NTS* 12 (1965) 327-51, esp. 347; more recently, *idem,* "The Son of Man in Contemporary Debate," *EvQ* 10 (1970) 67-87; *idem,* "The Son of Man and the Incarnation," *Ex Auditu* 7 (1991) 29-43. The most recent monograph reviewing and analyzing the various positions on the trial is M. Myllykoski, *Die Letzten Tage Jesu: Markus und Johannes, ihre Traditionen und die historische Frage,* vol. 1 (Helsinki: Suomalainen Tiedeakatemia, 1991). It was unavailable to me in time for this essay.

key utterance that offended the Jews. If one keeps the view of the Holy of Holies as an analogy for heavenly session, one can see why this remark was offensive, especially given the leadership's past tensions with Jesus over issues related to who has authority to reveal God's way. Our essay has not proven the authenticity of this entire saying, since that would require the examination of additional points. However, it has argued that one hurdle, the nature of Jesus' blasphemy, is clarified when one places the remark in the context of divine presence and temple / heavenly holiness. In short, the words, at least at the point of Jesus' blasphemy, "carry conviction" and should be taken seriously as giving a major clue concerning why the leadership would have pressed for the end of Jesus' ministry.

# Deity-Christology in Mark 14:58

E. Earle Ellis

The dispute between Jesus and Jewish theologians and "churchmen" that finally led to his condemnation to death was a controversy over the interpretation of Scripture. It appears not only in those debates formulated in the Gospels as *yelammedenu* midrashim[1] but also in the reaction to Jesus' forgiveness of sins[2] and to his affirmations at his trial, where charges of blasphemy were leveled at him (Mark 2:7; 14:64).

## 1

By forgiving sins in his own name — that is, as the Son of Man[3] — Jesus implicitly claims a prerogative of God[4] and thus evokes an interchange with the

1. E.g., Matt 12:1-8 (Q) = Mark 2:23-28 = Luke 6:1-5 (Sabbath); Matt 15:1-9 = Mark 7:1-13 (ritual defilement); Matt 19:3-8 = Mark 10:2-12 (divorce); Luke 10:25-37 (love commandment); Matt 21:15-16 (Davidic Messiah); Matt 22:23-33 (Q) = Mark 12:18-27 = Luke 20:27-40 (resurrection). Cf. E. E. Ellis, *The Old Testament in Early Christianity,* WUNT 54 (Tübingen: J. C. B. Mohr [Paul Siebeck], 1991) 96-100. By Q I designate (1) a *Vorlage* common to Matthew and Luke where they diverge from Mark and (2) the Gospel that best retains that *Vorlage.*

2. Matt 9:1-8 = Mark 2:1-12 = Luke 5:17-26 (Q). This triple-tradition episode, found also in a Q *Vorlage,* is at the bedrock of the Gospel tradition. Classical form criticism sometimes regarded Mark 2:5b-10 as secondary (cf. R. Bultmann, *The History of the Synoptic Tradition* [Oxford: Blackwell, 1963] 14-15). It is in general not a reliable guide to questions of historicity, however, because of *inter alia* its mistaken perception of a "folk tradition" transmission of the Gospel traditions. See B. Gerhardsson, *The Gospel Tradition* (Lund: Gleerup, 1986); R. Riesner, *Jesus als Lehrer,* WUNT 2:7 (Tübingen: J. C. B. Mohr [Paul Siebeck], 1988) 1-95, 408-502; E. E. Ellis, "Gospels Criticism," in *The Gospel and the Gospels,* ed. P. Stuhlmacher (Grand Rapids, Michigan: Wm. B. Eerdmans, 1991) 37-41.

3. For a discussion of the issues surrounding this much-discussed term, cf. S. Kim, *"The 'Son of Man'" as the Son of God,* WUNT 30 (Tübingen: J. C. B. Mohr [Paul Siebeck], 1983) 89-93, *passim.*

4. So, Kim, *Son of Man;* E. E. Ellis, *The Gospel of Luke,* NCBC (Grand Rapids, Michigan:

scribes[5] — that is, the Scripture scholars. Both Jesus and they presuppose the biblical teaching that only God can forgive sins.[6] On this theological question both have a common basis of appeal in the received canonical Scriptures[7] and, against the approach of the "history of religions" school, any anecdotal parallels in Jewish apocryphal[8] or in pagan literature are of doubtful relevance for the question in Mark.

By his act of forgiveness Jesus gives a clue to his mysterious self-designation "the Son of Man,"[9] a clue that the scribes grasp better than others. By healing the paralytic, again in his own name, he reinforces the verbal act since both he and they also presuppose the biblical understanding that relates death to sin and healing to God's power[10] and, even more, that attributes to God

---

Wm. B. Eerdmans, 1987) 103-4; V. Taylor, *The Gospel according to St. Mark* (London: Macmillan, 1952) 195; H. Alford, *The Greek Testament,* 4 vols. (London: Rivingtons, 1856) 1:80. Otherwise: C. F. Evans, *Saint Luke,* TPINTC (London: SCM, 1990) 301; F. Bovon, *Das Evangelium nach Lukas,* vol. 1, EKKNT 3 (Neukirchen-Vluyn: Neukirchener; Zürich: Benziger, 1989) 248; C. S. Mann, *Mark,* AB 27 (Garden City, New York: Doubleday, 1986) 224. *Pace* Jeremias (*New Testament Theology* [London: SCM, 1971] 262) and C. Colpe ("ὁ υἱὸς τοῦ ἀνθρώπου," *TDNT* 8:430-31) it is not an assertion that as "God in heaven," so also Jesus, as a man, "has authority on earth to forgive sins" (Q). This is similar to the misunderstanding of the crowds in Matt 9:8.

5. The form is similar to the *yelammedenu* midrash: The scribes' implied biblical question (Mark 2:7; cf. Exod 34:7; 2 Sam 12:13; Isa 43:25; 55:7) is countered by Jesus with another biblical question (2:8-9; cf. Deut 32:39; Ps 103:3-4) and answered by the healing (2:10ff.). Cf. E. E. Ellis, "The Making of Narratives in the Synoptic Gospels," in *Jesus and the Oral Gospel Tradition,* ed. H. Wansbrough, JSNTSS 64 (Sheffield: JSOT, 1991) 320. Cf. Luke 7:47ff.; John 5:14.

6. E.g., Exod 34:7.

7. On the biblical canon of first-century Judaism and its role in the debates between Jesus and other Jewish theologians, cf. Ellis, *Old Testament,* 1-50, 97-98, 125-28.

8. I know of no clear instances. If in the *Prayer of Nabonidus* (4QPrNab; 25 B.C.) the seer offers "forgiveness" (Vermes; otherwise: Burrows), it is no more than an assurance that his prayer "to the Most High God" has been answered and, *pace* Vermes, represents no exception to the Scripture scholars' *dictum* that only God can forgive sin. Cf. G. Vermes, *Jesus the Jew* (London: Collins, 1977) 67-68; M. Burrows, *More Light on the Dead Sea Scrolls* (London: Secker & Warburg, 1958) 400. The same is true of the angelic agent in *Joseph and Aseneth* 14–15 (*c.* A.D. 100?). In *T. Abr.* 14:3-8 (*c.* A.D. 100), Abel at God's appointment offers a provisional human forgiveness that will later be ratified or vetoed by God, who may be identified with Christ (13:4-7) by the (Jewish) Christian author or reviser. Cf. M. R. James, *The Testament of Abraham* (Cambridge: Cambridge University, 1892) 29; E. P. Sanders, "Testament of Abraham," in *The Old Testament Pseudepigrapha,* 2 vols., ed. J. H. Charlesworth (Garden City, New York: Doubleday, 1985) 1:875.

9. The term and the saying are to be taken as dominical unless they can be shown to be secondary (Kümmel). The term is probably (quasi-)titular, and it is specific, not generic (cf. Hare). It has an unclear connotation that is publicly unveiled at Mark 14:62 (cf. Schmithals). Cf. W. G. Kümmel, *Dreissig Jahre Jesusforschung (1950-1980), BBB* 60 (Bonn: Hanstein, 1985) 28-29; D. R. A. Hare, *The Son of Man Tradition* (Minneapolis: Fortress, 1990) 246-49; W. Schmithals, *Das Evangelium nach Markus,* 2 vols. (Gütersloh: Mohn, 1979) 1:152-53; 2:662-63. However, Schmithals mistakenly supposes that "the Son of Man" was identified with Jesus only by the post-resurrection church and that in Mark 14:62 it is Mark's creation.

10. E.g., Exod 15:26; Ps 103:3-4. Cf. J. Pedersen, *Israel,* 4 vols. in 2 (Copenhagen: Branner, [4]1959) I-II:153-56; E. E. Ellis, "Life," in *New Bible Dictionary,* 2d ed., ed. J. D. Douglas (Leicester: Inter-Varsity, 1982) 697-701. Cf. D. L. Bock, "The Son of Man in Luke 5:24," *BBR* 1 (1991) 121.

alone the authority to give life or (truly) to take it away.[11] Jesus is hardly implying merely a human messianic claim, for there is apparently no Jewish tradition that the Messiah or any other creaturely being has the right to forgive sins on his own authority. Furthermore, Jesus does not speak as an agent, priestly or prophetic or angelic, assuring the man of God's forgiveness, nor does he offer the provisional pardon of a human court to be later ratified by God.[12] He makes a flat affirmation of what he and the theologians know to be a prerogative of God and proceeds to ratify it by his own word of life to the paralytic.

The Scripture scholars, who here make their first appearance in the Gospel, are not represented as malicious or prejudiced against Jesus. They make a reasoned judgment based on their biblical understanding and, if Jesus is only a man, they are fully justified. They suspect Jesus of blasphemy here for the same implicit reasons as those spoken explicitly in the only other Gospel passage (before the trial) where the charge of blasphemy appears, John 10:33:[13]

> "We stone you . . . for blasphemy
> That is, because you being a man
> Make yourself to be God."

The unspoken charge in the Synoptics reflects the sharp, though hostile, insight of the theologians into the implication of Jesus' word and deed that is contrasted, in Matthew (12:8), with the superficial apprehension of the crowds. It prepares the way for the second and climactic accusation of blasphemy made against Jesus at his trial.[14]

11. Gen 2:7; 1 Sam 25:29; Job 34:14-15; Ps 73:17, 26; 90:3; cf. Matt 10:28 Q; Ellis, "Life," 698.

12. See above, n. 8. Cf. Str-B 1:495: "[There is] no passage known to us in which the Messiah by virtue of his own authority pronounces to men the forgiveness of sins."

13. Cf. John 5:18; 19:7; 2 Macc 9:12, 28; H. W. Beyer, "βλασφημία," *TDNT* 1:621ff. The first-century Gospel of John is a better index of the force of the charge against Jesus than is a speculative selection 2,000 years later from a broad range of connotations of the term.

14. The episodes of the healing (Mark 2:1-12 + Q) and of the trial (esp. Mark 14:61-64 + Q) agree also in their definition of Jesus' person and role in terms of the Son of Man. They reflect in part a Q *Vorlage,* both in common omissions and in common verbal agreements of Matthew and Luke against Mark (cf. I. H. Marshall, *The Gospel of Luke,* NIGTC [Exeter: Paternoster, 1978] 850; somewhat differently, D. R. Catchpole, *The Trial of Jesus* [Leiden: E. J. Brill, 1971] 220). This raises a certain probability, if not of a proto-Gospel, at least of common pre-Synoptic episodes that the Jacobean-Matthean mission based in Jerusalem and the Petrine (*cum* Mark) mission based for a time in Caesarea included in their congregational readings. Cf. E. E. Ellis, "The Date and Provenance of Mark's Gospel," in *The Four Gospels: 1992,* ed. F. Van Segbroeck *et al.,* BETL 100 (Leuven: Leuven University, 1992) 2:801-16; *idem,* "Making of Narratives," 330-31.

## 2

In the Synoptic accounts of the trial the question of the high priest and the response of Jesus have formed the usual christological issues:

> "Are you the Christ, the Son of the Blessed One?"
> And Jesus said,
> "I am. And you will see the Son of Man
> Seated at the right hand of Power [Ps 110:1]
> And coming with the clouds of Heaven" [Dan 7:13].
>
> Mark 14:61c-62

The high priest asks about Jesus' identity with the anticipated royal Messiah, with an allusion to Ps 2:7 and / or to 2 Sam 7:13-14.[15] Jesus answers affirmatively but proceeds to define the titles "Messiah" and "Son of God"[16] in terms of "the Son of Man."[17] He incurs the charge of blasphemy not by affirming that he was the Messiah, which in Judaism was not a blasphemous claim,[18] but by his further definition of his messiahship in terms of a combination of Dan 7:13-14 (the Son of Man) and of Ps 110:1 (David's Lord seated at God's right hand).[19]

If the trial proceedings are fairly summarized by the Synoptic tradition,[20]

15. This may be a summary designed at the formulation of the Gospel episode, but the high priest was hardly unaware that both 2 Samuel 7 and Psalm 2 were used as messianic texts in contemporary Judaism — e.g., 4QFlor 1:1-2, 10-11, 18-19. Cf. G. J. Brooke, *Exegesis at Qumran: 4QFlorilegium in Its Jewish Context* (Sheffield: JSOT, 1985) 138-39, 147, 209, *passim;* O. Betz, *Jesus, der Messias Israels,* WUNT 42 (Tübingen: J. C. B. Mohr [Paul Siebeck], 1987) 154-68, 327-28.

16. "Son of the Blessed One" is a euphemism substituted by Mark to preserve his different use of the term "Son of God" and perhaps to avoid the use of God's name. Cf. G. Dalman, *The Words of Jesus* (Edinburgh: T. & T. Clark, 1902) 200ff.; Str-B 2:51. Cf. "Son of God" (Mark 1:1) with "Yahweh" (Mark 1:2). See below, n. 54.

17. So J. R. Donahue, *Are You the Christ?* SBLDS 10 (Missoula, Montana: Scholars, 1972) 95, 183-84; otherwise: Hare (*Son of Man,* 208), who argues (213-82) that the eschatological usage is the creation of the early church. But that Jesus used this term of himself both for his earthly ministry and for his future parousia see I. H. Marshall, "Son of Man," in *Dictionary of Jesus and the Gospels,* ed. J. B. Green and S. McKnight (Downers Grove, Illinois: InterVarsity, 1992) 775-81; *idem,* "The Synoptic Son of Man Sayings in Recent Discussion," *NTS* 12 (1965-66) 335-51.

18. Rightly, Catchpole, *Trial,* 132; against J. Blinzler, *The Trial of Jesus* (Westminster, Maryland: Newman, 1959) 106-10.

19. Catchpole, *Trial,* 100-101, may be right in identifying a non-Markan source in the parallel Luke 22:67-68, 70, but that does not exclude the probability that Luke has taken into account Jesus' definition of "Messiah," both in Mark and in a Q tradition, to sum up the high priest's question and Jesus' answer in terms of the Son of God (22:70) as deity. Cf. Ellis, *Luke,* 263-64; J. A. Fitzmyer, *A Wandering Aramean* (Missoula, Montana: Scholars, 1979) 106-7. The later rabbis (R. Jose versus R. Akiba) and modern scholars differ as to whether someone sitting beside God in heaven is a blasphemous idea. Cf. *b. Sanh.* 38b; Catchpole, *Trial,* 140-41.

20. For a cogent survey and evaluation cf. B. Corley, "The Trial of Jesus," in *Dictionary of Jesus and the Gospels,* 841-54; further, S. S. Smalley, "Arrest and Trial of Jesus Christ," *ISBE*$^2$ 2:1049-55. H. Lietzmann, "Der Prozess Jesu," in *Kleine Schriften,* 3 vols. [Berlin: Akademie, 1958-

they reflect a biblical dispute over the nature of Jesus' messianic claims. Indeed, for a *theological* verdict against Jesus they had to address questions of scriptural interpretation. They represent the climax for which Mark (or rather the underlying Synoptic tradition) has earlier prepared his readers:

> The "owner of the vineyard" sent his "beloved Son."
> "David calls [Messiah] Lord; in what way then is he David's son?"
> "Then they shall see the Son of Man coming
> In the clouds with great power and glory."[21]

The charge of blasphemy at the trial is fully understandable if the Sanhedrin understood Jesus to interpret Dan 7:9-14 via Ezek 1:26ff. as a theophany applied to himself and thus to assert his divine status and role.[22] The earlier implicit charge (Mark 2) may explain also Jesus' (occasional) command for silence about his person and work.[23] If so, the command was evidently given not because his messiahship was in some respects future (cf. Schweitzer)[24] or nonpolitical (e.g., Dunn),[25] features that are rather innocuous, but because it involved divine prerogatives and a manifestation of deity that Jesus would disclose in his own terms at his trial. The command at the Transfiguration

---

62] 2:251-63) rejected the historicity of the trial before the Sanhedrin. But see A. Strobel, *Die Stunde der Wahrheit,* WUNT 21 (Tübingen: J. C. B. Mohr [Paul Siebeck], 1980) 6-21, *passim;* D. R. Catchpole, "The Historicity of the Sanhedrin Trial," in *The Trial of Jesus,* ed. E. Bammel, SBT 2:13 (London: SCM, 1970) 47-65; G. D. Kilpatrick, *The Trial of Jesus* (London: Oxford University, 1953) 5-21; A. N. Sherwin-White, *Roman Society and Roman Law in the New Testament* (Oxford: Oxford University, 1963) 24-47.

21. Cf. Mark 12:6ff. parr.; 12:35-37 parr.; 13:24-27 parr. In each passage Matthew and Luke have common readings against Mark, showing that they use a (second) non-Markan source.

22. I.e., as the visible manifestation of Yahweh and as the eschatological judge; cf. Joel 3:9-21 (Yahweh). See below, n. 29. It is true that Messiah was also expected to be Yahweh's agent in judgment (e.g., Isa 11:1-5; 1QSb 5:24-25; cf. G. von Rad, *Old Testament Theology,* 2 vols. [New York: Harper, 1962-65] 2:169ff.; H. Ringgren, *The Faith of Qumran* [Philadelphia: Fortress, 1963] 180ff.), but this only raises in a more acute form the question of the nature of Messiah, who is both David's seed and David's Lord (Mark 12:35ff.; cf. Ps 110:1). The question cannot be limited to the dichotomy, "Is Messiah Yahweh or Yahweh's (creaturely) agent" (cf. Harvey), but must also be posed more broadly: "Is the Messiah as revealed in Jesus both Yahweh and Yahweh's agent?" Still highly instructive for the issue is A. R. Johnson's *The One and the Many in the Israelite Conception of God* (Cardiff, 1961). Cf. A. E. Harvey, "Christ as Agent," in *The Glory of Christ in the New Testament,* ed. L. D. Hurst and N. T. Wright (Oxford: Oxford University, 1987) 239-50.

23. E.g., Mark 1:44 + Q; 7:36 (healings); Mark 1:25 par.; 1:32ff. + Q; 3:11-12 parr.; 5:6 par. (exorcisms); Mark 5:43 + Q (raising the dead); Mark 8:30 + Q (confession of messiahship); Mark 9:9 + Q (Transfiguration); cf. Matt 9:30; Mark 8:26. On the nature of the Gospel parallels, cf. Ellis, "Making of Narratives," 313-27.

24. A. Schweitzer, *The Mystery of the Kingdom of God* (New York: Macmillan, 1950) 114-36; *idem, The Quest of the Historical Jesus* (New York: Macmillan, 1968) 330-97.

25. J. D. G. Dunn, "The Messianic Secret in Mark," *TynB* 21 (1970) 111-12; reprinted in *The Messianic Secret,* ed. C. M. Tuckett, IRT 1 (London: S.P.C.K., 1983) 127-28. For the issues and the debate, cf. Tuckett's introduction (1-28).

explicitly addresses this aspect of his messiahship. The same is true of the silencing of the demons in the exorcisms, as Wrede rightly saw:

> [T]he demons . . . have this knowledge [about Jesus]; it is that of supernatural beings. And the object of their knowledge is equally supernatural; it is not the human Jesus as such, but the supernatural Jesus equipped with the *pneuma* — the Son of God.[26]

All of these features, taken together, argue that "the messianic secret" in the Synoptic tradition, including Mark, is not a secret of some human aspect of Messiah's person but a secret of his "Son of God" status, a secret of his deity.[27]

The charge of blasphemy is, then, an important key to understanding both "the messianic secret" and the meaning of the term "the Son of Man," as Jesus unveils at his trial its earlier enigmatic connotations. It suggests that Dan 7:13-14 was affirmed by Jesus and so heard by his accusers to point beyond an "Adamic" messianic figure, alluding to Psalm 8 and Gen 1:26ff.,[28] to a manifestation of Yahweh in God's throne-room in "a likeness as the appearance of a man," alluding to Ezek 1:26 and Gen 1:26-27.[29] On this understanding the charge has a rationale in Jesus' self-identification with the Son of Man in Daniel 7. But it probably rested not only on this affirmation but also, and perhaps more significantly, on Jesus' alleged claim to destroy and rebuild the "temple" "in three days."

## 3

The accusation by the trial witnesses is expressed in Mark 14:58 as follows:

> "We heard him saying
> 'I will destroy this temple

26. Cf. W. Wrede, *The Messianic Secret* (Cambridge: James Clarke, 1971) 25.

27. Cf. C. F. D. Moule, "On Defining the Messianic Secret in Mark," in *Jesus und Paulus*, ed. E. E. Ellis and E. Grässer (Göttingen: Vandenhoeck & Ruprecht, 1975) 3-4, 242-43; Kim, *Son of Man*, 100-101, with *idem, The Origin of Paul's Gospel*, WUNT 2:4 (Tübingen: J. C. B. Mohr [Paul Siebeck], 1981) 226, 250ff. Somewhat differently, U. Luz, "Das Geheimnismotiv und die markinische Christologie," *ZNW* 56 (1965) 9-30 (= "The Secrecy Motif and the Marcan Christology," in *Messianic Secret*, 75-96): "The Markan christology is to be understood as an attempt not to remove the θεῖος-ἀνήρ christology and 'epiphany' thinking of the Hellenistic community but to make it understandable from the perspective of the cross" (30). But did Mark's recipients have a θεῖος-ἀνήρ christology?

28. Cf. E. E. Ellis, *Prophecy and Hermeneutic in Early Christianity*, WUNT 18 (Tübingen: J. C. B. Mohr [Paul Siebeck], 1978) 167.

29. Cf. Kim, *Paul's Gospel*, 239-43; *idem, Son of Man*, 2-3, 88-89; C. Rowland, *The Open Heaven* (London: S.P.C.K., 1982) 94-98, 107-11; M. Black, "The Throne-Theophany Prophetic Commission and the 'Son of Man,'" in *Jews, Greeks and Christians*, ed. R. Hamerton-Kelly (Leiden: E. J. Brill, 1976) 56-73, 57-58.

(Made with hands [χειροποίητος])
And in three days will build another
(Not made with hands [ἀχειροποίητος]).' "

The saying appears in Matthew, Mark, and John and is probably presupposed by Acts. Yet the accounts vary considerably, suggesting that each is (partially) derived from independent antecedent tradition(s).[30] It fits hand-in-glove with other aspects of the trial, as we shall see below, and has good grounds to be placed there historically.[31]

In both Matthew (26:59-60) and Mark (14:57) the accusation is represented as "false testimony" and is met by Jesus with a noncommittal silence. It is understood by the witnesses to refer to the Jerusalem temple-building (ναός); however, Mark and probably Matthew[32] sharply qualify that understanding. The passage raises several questions: What was the original form of the temple-saying? In what sense is the testimony about it said to be "false"? What are the meanings of the terms "temple," "build," and "three days"?

30. Matt 26:61; cf. 27:40; Mark 14:58; cf. 15:29; John 2:19; cf. Acts 6:14; 15:16. On Luke's tendency to omit a topic that he treats elsewhere in his Gospel or in Acts cf. Ellis, "Making of Narratives," 332-33. The Synoptic trial narrative, or parts of it, has a Q *Vorlage* that is observable in occasional agreements between Matthew and Luke against Mark in wording, omissions, and order. Luke also appears to use yet another special source; cf. J. B. Green, *The Death of Jesus: Tradition and Interpretation in the Passion Narrative,* WUNT 2:33 (Tübingen: J. C. B. Mohr [Paul Siebeck], 1988) 61-66; Catchpole, *Trial,* 153-220.

31. This holds whether or not the saying was combined with another trial-narrative tradition by the Synoptic tradition (or by Mark, as is supposed by D. Lührmann, *Das Markusevangelium,* HNT 3 [Tübingen: J. C. B. Mohr (Paul Siebeck), 1987] 249). Otherwise: J. Gnilka, "Der Prozess Jesu nach . . . Markus . . . ," *Der Prozess gegen Jesu,* ed. K. Kertelge (Freiburg: Herder, 1988) 17-18; R. A. Hoffmann in *Neutestamentliche Studien,* ed. A. Deissmann (Leipzig: J. C. Hinrichs, 1914) 130-39. Such questions and their answers largely depend on the form-critical and source-critical assumptions that the investigator brings to the task.

32. The phrase "temple of God" (Matt 26:61) in the NT elsewhere and in the Apostolic Fathers apparently always refers to the spiritual temple, either to the individual believer's body (cf. 2 Cor 6:14-16 with 1 Cor 6:18-19), to the corporate body of Christ = the church (e.g., 1 Cor 3:16; 2 Cor 6:16; Rev 3:12; cf. *1 Clem.* 23:5; *Barn.* 6:11), or to the heavenly temple (e.g., Rev 7:15; 11:1, 19). This is true also of 2 Thess 2:4 (so Findlay, Frame; otherwise: Best) and of Rev 11:1 (so, e.g., Sweet, Caird, Charles; otherwise: Müller), although the question is disputed both in later patristic and in modern commentaries (cf. Rigaux, Ladd). Cf. E. Best, *A Commentary on the First and Second Epistles to the Thessalonians* (New York: Harper and Row, 1972) 286-87; G. G. Findlay, *The Epistles of Paul the Apostle to the Thessalonians* (Cambridge: Cambridge University, 1904) 170-71; J. E. Frame, *A Critical and Exegetical Commentary on the Epistles of St. Paul to the Thessalonians,* ICC (Edinburgh: T. & T. Clark, 1912) 256-57; B. Rigaux, *Les épitres aux Thessaloniciens* (Paris: Lecoffre, 1956) 660-61; G. B. Caird, *A Commentary on the Revelation of St. John the Divine* (London: Black, 1966) 131-32; R. H. Charles, *A Critical and Exegetical Commentary on the Revelation of St. John,* 2 vols., ICC (Edinburgh: T. & T. Clark, 1920) 1:273; G. E. Ladd, *A Commentary on the Revelation of John* (Grand Rapids, Michigan: Wm. B. Eerdmans, 1972) 149-50; U. B. Müller, *Die Offenbarung des Johannes* (Gütersloh: Mohr, 1984) 206; J. P. M. Sweet, *Revelation* (London: SCM, 1979) 183-84. The OT tabernacle is referred to as "the house of God" (Mark 2:26 + Q) and Herod's temple as "my (= God's) house" that "you have made a den of robbers" (Mark 11:17 + Q).

The temple in Jerusalem is never, in the Gospels, the object of any threat by Jesus, although he calls it "your house," referring to the city that has rejected him, and he predicts its destruction by others.[33] And he never expresses any intention of rebuilding the Jerusalem temple. Against a traditional interpretation of this passage, the temple (ναός) here does not allude to Jesus' prediction about the temple-complex (ἱερόν) in Mark 13:2, as E. Linnemann rightly saw, or to any other saying of Jesus about the Jerusalem temple.[34] The reference to the temple in Jerusalem is part of the falsity of the witnesses' testimony that Mark counters with his qualifiers "made with hands" and "not made with hands."[35]

Almost certainly the phrases "made with hands" and "not made with hands" are not original to the saying of Jesus or to the accusation:[36] (1) They are absent from Matt 26:61, which in this respect is "more simple and original,"[37] from the subsequent accusation at Mark 15:29, and from the Johannine tradition of Jesus' saying, whose form Bultmann regarded as "relatively original."[38] (2) In the context of the trial the phrases make little sense in the mouths of the false witnesses and detract from the force of the accusation.[39] They are very likely Mark's editorial to draw out the true meaning of Jesus' saying and to distinguish the true from the false aspects of the accusation.

Stephen is the first in the NT church to connect "handmade things" with the temple. In his speech at Acts 7:48 he includes the temple among the "things made with hands." But by quoting Isa 66:2, "my hand made all these things" (Acts 7:50), he expands the reference to designate the whole present creation. Stephen thus provides the exegetical rationale for the use elsewhere in the Hellenist mission[40] of the idiom "made with hands" / "not made with hands" for the realities of, respectively, the present creation and the resurrection creation, the present age and the eschatological age, the old covenant and the new covenant. With this understanding Paul in 2 Cor 5:1 can contrast "the earthly house" (ἡ ἐπίγειος οἰκία) with "the building from God . . . , the house not

33. Matt 23:37ff. (Q); Mark 13:2 + Q; 13:14 par.

34. Cf. E. Linnemann, *Studien zur Passionsgeschichte*, FRLANT 102 (Göttingen: Vandenhoeck & Ruprecht, 1970) 118-19, who rejected the historicity of Jesus' saying altogether (116-27), a view she later repudiated.

35. Otherwise: E. P. Sanders, *Jesus and Judaism* (Philadelphia: Fortress, 1985) 61-76, and the literature cited.

36. So, Donahue, *Christ*, 106; cf. D. Juel, *Messiah and Temple*, SBLDS 31 (Missoula, Montana: Scholars, 1977) 117-25, 143-57.

37. H. A. W. Meyer, *Gospels of Mark and Luke* (New York: Funk & Wagnalls, 1884) 180, 191.

38. John 2:19; R. Bultmann, *The Gospel of John* (Philadelphia: Westminster, 1971) 126. Cf. P. Borgen, "John and the Synoptics," in *The Interrelations of the Gospels*, ed. D. L. Dungan, BETL 95 (Leuven: Leuven University, 1990) 432-36. Ἐγείρειν (John 2:19), like οἰκοδομεῖν, can mean "to build" a building. Cf. Callimachus *Hymn to Apollo* 64; J. Schlosser, "La parole de Jésus sur la fin du temple," *NTS* 36 (1990) 401.

39. P. Vielhauer, *Oikodome: Aufsätze zum Neuen Testament* (München: C. Kaiser, 1979) 60.

40. I.e., Mark 14:58; 2 Cor 5:1; Eph 2:11; Col 2:11; Heb 9:11, 24. Cf. E. E. Ellis, "Isaiah in the New Testament," *SWJT* 34 (1991-92) 31-35.

made with hands" — that is, the present creation in Adam with the resurrection creation incorporated in the exalted Christ.[41] Or in Ephesians and Colossians he can contrast the old-covenant circumcision "made with hands" with the circumcision "not made with hands," explained as the believer's corporate identification with Christ's death and resurrection.[42] Similarly, Hebrews (9:11, 24) explains the idiom "not made with hands" as "not of this creation" and describes the resurrected Christ's exaltation as the entering into the holy places (ἅγια) — that is, the temple "not made with hands" in heaven. In the light of this background the phrases "made with hands" and "not made with hands" have a fairly well-defined usage within the mission of the Christian Hellenists. They refer respectively to the present creation and to the resurrection creation, the latter sometimes expressed in terms of Christ's resurrection and sometimes as his identification or association with the eschatological temple.

The phrase "I will build *another* temple" (Mark 14:58) may be the witnesses' misquotation of a saying of Jesus.[43] According to some Jewish traditions Messiah was to build a new temple;[44] according to others God was to do so.[45] However, in Jesus' saying it is the same temple that is destroyed and rebuilt, as the parallels show:

> "The one who destroys the temple and rebuilds it in three days" (Mark 15:29).
>
> "I am able to destroy the temple of God and to build it in three days" (Matt 26:61).
>
> "Destroy this temple and in three days I will raise it up" (John 2:19).

The identification of the temple that is destroyed with the one that is rebuilt excludes another traditional interpretation that identifies the destroyed temple with the Jewish religious system and the rebuilt temple with the church,[46]

41. Cf. E. E. Ellis, "II Corinthians V.1-10 in Pauline Eschatology," *NTS* 6 (1959-60) 211-24 (= *idem, Paul and His Recent Interpreters* [Grand Rapids, Michigan: Wm. B. Eerdmans, 1979]) 35-48.

42. Eph 2:11; Col 2:11-12; cf. 1 Pet 2:4-10; R. J. McKelvey, *The New Temple* (Oxford: Oxford University, 1969) 93-139. Ephesians, Colossians, and Mark's Gospel were probably composed in the same city, Caesarea in Palestine. Cf. Ellis, "Mark's Gospel."

43. In this respect John 2:19 is more original (see above, n. 38), and it involves a subtle distinction between "this temple" in Jesus' word (2:19, 21) and "this temple" in the Jews' question (2:20).

44. Zech 6:12; cf. *Tg.* Zech 6:12; *Tg.* Isa 53:5. Cf. D. D. Edwards, "Jesus and the Temple" (Ph.D. diss., Southwestern Baptist Theological Seminary, 1992) 204-7, and the literature cited.

45. *Jub.* 1:17; cf. Exod 15:17. On the first understanding the high priest could bring to Pilate a political charge against Jesus. On the second he might construe the saying either as an appropriation of God's prerogative or as an implicit claim to deity and, along with the "Son of Man" claim, a basis for the theological charge of blasphemy.

46. E.g., A. Vögtle, "Das markinische Verständnis der Tempelworte," in *Die Mitte des Neuen Testaments*, ed. U. Luz (Göttingen: Vandenhoeck & Ruprecht, 1983) 362-78. It has been a continuing view in modern research since it was broached by J. G. Herder, *Von Gottes Sohn* (Riga, 1797)

although this view comes closer to the meaning of Jesus' saying as it is interpreted by Mark.

The clue that is, I believe, decisive for Jesus' meaning is the phrase "in three days." As D. Juel comments, the phrase "looks suspiciously like a reference to the resurrection [of Jesus]." Considering the use of the phrase or of its equivalent earlier in Mark,[47] one may put it more strongly: "In three days" points to the resurrection of Jesus. In the light of the use of ἀχειροποίητος elsewhere in the Hellenist missions to refer to the new creation brought into being by Christ's resurrection, the temple "made without hands" in Mark 14:58 confirms this understanding of the phrase "in three days."

Mark, then, takes the temple that is destroyed and rebuilt in three days to refer to Jesus' individual body. In this respect he agrees with the interpretation given more explicitly in John 2:21 and with the more allusive Matthean reference to Jesus as "the temple of God."[48] He has prepared his readers for this identification by the midrash on the wicked tenants in which Jesus identifies himself with the rejected stone that becomes the cornerstone of the eschatological temple.[49]

Theologically more significant, Mark attributes to Jesus the claim to raise himself from the dead "in three days," a claim to deity that could hardly be more strongly expressed. If the high priest also suspected this claim to be implicit in Jesus' temple saying, it is understandable that he would view this saying no less than the "Son of Man" claim to be sufficient grounds for the charge of blasphemy of which Jesus was found guilty. The deity-christology that was implicit in Jesus' forgiveness of sins in his own name in Mark 2 becomes explicit at his trial both in

---

135. But see the devastating criticisms of H. A. W. Meyer, *The Gospel of John* (New York: Funk & Wagnalls, 1884) 113-14.

47. Mark 8:31; 9:31; 10:34; Juel, *Messiah,* 118, cf. 143ff. Whether in the mouth and mind of Jesus the phrase meant a literal period of time (cf. Matt 12:40) or only an ultimate eschatological vindication (Luke 13:32) is difficult to decide. Cf. J. Jeremias, "Die Drei-Tage-Worte der Evangelien," in *Tradition und Glaube,* ed. G. Jeremias et al. (Göttingen: Vandenhoeck & Ruprecht, 1971) 221-29.

48. Matt 26:61, probably alluding to Zech 6:12. This was noted already by C. E. Luthardt, *St. John's Gospel,* 3 vols. (Edinburgh: T. & T. Clark, 1876-78) 2:11: At Jesus' death the Jerusalem temple "ceases therewith to be the dwelling of God. . . . But Jesus will raise the temple up again: after three days in his resurrection. . . . From that, then, shall the temple of the New Testament church build itself, Zech vi.12." See above, n. 32.

49. Mark 12:10 + Q. This "temple" is equated by Jesus (Mark 14:58 par.) with his individual body and later, after his resurrection, by his apostles with his corporate body, the church (1 Cor 3:16; 2 Cor 6:16; Eph 2:19-22; cf. Acts 15:6; Heb 3:5-6). The rationale for the expanded reference is provided by the Semitic conception of corporate personality, by Qumran's identification of the eschatological temple with the elect remnant of Israel, and, more specifically, by Jesus' "Last Supper" words and act in which he identifies his followers with his body (Matt 26:26 par.). Cf. A. Cole, *The New Temple* (London: Tyndale, 1950) 49-53; B. Gärtner, *The Temple and the Community in Qumran and the New Testament,* SNTSMS 1 (Cambridge: Cambridge University, 1965) 139, *passim;* G. Klinzing, *Die Umdeutung des Kultus in der Qumrangemeinde und im Neuen Testament* (Göttingen: Vandenhoeck & Ruprecht, 1971) 50-93; H. W. Robinson, *Corporate Personality in Ancient Israel* (Philadelphia: Fortress, 1964) and the literature cited.

his identification of himself with the Son of Man in Daniel 7 and, perhaps more offensively, in his veiled claim to raise himself from the dead.[50]

## 4

Mark alludes to Jesus' deity in contexts other than Mark 14:58. In agreement with the pre-Synoptic episode of "Jesus and the Baptist"[51] he opens with a quotation of Isa 40:3 (1:2) and closes with allusions to Ps 2:7 and Isa 42:1 (1:11). Mark 1:2, 11 are probably *testimonia* excerpted from antecedent midrashim in which the christological understanding of these passages has been worked out.[52] Unlike Matthew and Luke, Mark 1:2 merges Isa 40:3 with an implied reference to God's "coming to his temple" (Mal 3:1):

> Behold, I send my messenger before your [i.e., the Son of God's] face
> Who will prepare your way
> A voice crying in the wilderness
> Prepare the way of Yahweh (κυρίου)
> Make smooth his paths.

Mark's allusion to Yahweh's coming to his temple refers, I suggest, not to the Herodian temple but to his incarnate dwelling in Jesus the Son of Man and prepares the discerning reader for the temple typology that will be elaborated later in the Gospel. Mark is fully aware that the Hebrew texts refer to the coming of Yahweh as Israel's redeemer (Isa 40:3) and judge (Mal 3:1),[53] and in that awareness he expounds them to make an identification *cum* distinction of Yahweh with Jesus Christ the Son of God (Mark 1:1).[54]

The Evangelist also uses the miracles of Jesus to present him as the One who by his sovereign word controls nature (4:35-41; 6:45-52), confers life on the dead (5:21-42), creates matter (6:32-44; 8:1-10), and decrees death (11:12ff., 20-25). While unlike the Gospel of John, he does not call them "signs," it is clear that, no less than John, he regards them as pointers

50. As in other matters, John (10:18) expresses the claim more explicitly. Cf. also Ign. *Smyrn.* 2:2.

51. Matt 3:1-17 = Mark 1:2-11 = Luke 3:2b-22; cf. John 1:19-28. Like the trial narrative this episode has (also) a Q *Vorlage,* which is evident from the agreements of Matthew and Luke against Mark. Whether Mark draws from Q or from a separate tradition is an open question. Cf. Ellis, "Making of Narratives," 324.

52. Cf. Ellis, *Old Testament,* 100-101; *idem, Prophecy,* 150-51, 161-62.

53. It may be that the coming of Yahweh was part of the messianic hope in wider circles of first-century Judaism. Cf. *Pss. Sol.* 17:36 (32): Messiah Yahweh (χριστὸς κύριος). Further, cf. *T. Levi* 8:11; *T. Jud.* 22:2; *T. Naph.* 8:3; *T. Ash.* 7:3, unless these are Christian works or interpolations. Cf. B. B. Warfield, "The Divine Messiah in the Old Testament," in *Christology and Criticism* (New York: Oxford University, 1929) 3-49 = *PTR* 14 (1916) 379-416.

54. Note Mark's (or his tradition's) alteration of "my" in Mal 3:1, LXX, to "your": "Behold, I [Yahweh] send my messenger before *your* face."

to Jesus as One who by his own authority manifests powers exclusive to God.[55]

Of course, Mark's presentation of Jesus as God is veiled, like that of Jesus himself, and it represents only one aspect of the many-splendored reality of the unique person of our Lord. It is in accord with the christology of other NT writers[56] and with the imprecise monotheism of the OT in which God is viewed as a unity in plurality.[57] However, it will pose a problem for those who define monotheism in (later) unitarian categories and then read this definition into pre-Christian Judaism.[58]

The complexity of the doctrine of the person of Jesus Christ in the NT is evident from three centuries of patristic exegesis and debate[59] and, to me personally, from my own Arianism during university days. However, in the revival of unitarian sentiment in some contemporary theology, not unlike that in the eighteenth century,[60] it may be useful to recall a few of the biblical texts and the exposition that led the church away from such conclusions and to the affirmation of the trinitarian God: Father, Son, and Holy Spirit.

55. In the feedings Jesus "looked up to heaven," "blessed," and "gave thanks" (6:41; 8:6-7), showing his relationship to his Father. He does not petition. Mark 10:18 is an *ad hominem* response and tells us nothing about Jesus' morals or about the nature of his person. Similarly, the credo that "Yahweh is one" (**אחד**, 12:29 = Deut 6:4) is not necessarily more unitary than that the married couple is "one" (Gen 2:24).

56. E.g., Paul. Cf. M. J. Harris, *Jesus as God: The New Testament Use of Theos in Reference to Jesus* (Grand Rapids, Michigan: Baker, 1992) 143-85 (on Rom 9:5; Tit 2:13); C. E. B. Cranfield, *The Epistle to the Romans,* 2 vols., ICC (Edinburgh: T. & T. Clark, 1979) 464-70 (on Rom 9:5); E. Best, *Thessalonians,* 272 (on 2 Thess 1:12: perhaps "our God and Lord Jesus Christ" if non-Pauline and late); D. Guthrie, *The Pastoral Epistles,* 2d ed. (Leicester: Inter-Varsity, 1990) 212; and G. D. Fee, *1 and 2 Timothy, Titus* (San Francisco: Harper & Row, 1984) 149 (on the cited tradition at Tit 2:13). Perhaps more decisive than these debated texts is the use of *Old Testament Yahweh Texts in Paul's Christology* (by D. B. Capes; WUNT 2:47 [Tübingen: J. C. B. Mohr (Paul Siebeck), 1992]).

57. Cf. Ellis, *Old Testament,* 112-16; Johnson, *One and the Many,* 13-37; G. F. Moore, *Judaism in the First Centuries of the Christian Era,* 3 vols. (Cambridge, Massachusetts: Harvard University, 1930) 1:360-61: "Monotheism also, the cornerstone of Judaism, remains, as in the Bible, the religious doctrine that there is one God and no other. . . . There is no assertion or implication of the unity of God in the metaphysical sense such as Philo means. . . ." The conception of Yahweh as a corporate personality (Johnson) is based on assumptions different from those in the problem of *Two Powers in Heaven* (by A. F. Segal [Leiden: E. J. Brill, 1977]) discussed by the rabbis in the early centuries of the Christian era.

58. A number of recent writers appear to fall into this anachronism. Cf. J. D. G. Dunn, *The Partings of the Ways* (London: SCM, 1991) 244-47, *passim;* L. W. Hurtado, *One God, One Lord* (Philadelphia: Fortress, 1988) 82, *passim;* A. E. Harvey, *Jesus and the Constraints of History* (Philadelphia: Westminster, 1982) 154-73. Cf. P. A. Rainbow, "Jewish Monotheism as the Matrix of New Testament Christology," *NovT* 33 (1991) 78-91 (88).

59. For perceptive discussions of the issues, cf. B. Lonergan, *The Way to Nicea* (London: Darton, Longman and Todd, 1976); G. L. Prestige, *God in Patristic Thought* (London: W. Heinemann, 1952); C. Stead, *Divine Substance* (Oxford: Clarendon, 1977). For a reasoned rejection of the christology of the patristic creeds, cf. G. W. H. Lampe, *God as Spirit* (Oxford: Clarendon, 1977).

60. There is also a unitarianism that argues that God is "Jesus only." Cf. G. A. Boyd, *Oneness Pentecostals and the Trinity* (Grand Rapids, Michigan: Baker, 1992). But see U. Mauser, "Εἷς θεός und Μόνος θεός in Biblischer Theologie," *Jahrbuch für Biblischer Theologie* 1 (1986) 71-87 (84-85).

# The Essential Physicality of Jesus' Resurrection according to the New Testament

Robert H. Gundry

The present essay, which supplements a somewhat more narrowly focussed one by W. L. Craig,[1] deals with the nature of Jesus' resurrection as the NT presents it. Many believers in the resurrection understand it as a more or less spiritual phenomenon. Some of them say that the story of the empty tomb is unhistorical, the corpse of Jesus having suffered the normal fate of corpses, but that he himself enjoyed resurrection in the form of disembodied exaltation to heavenly existence.[2] Others, putting more trust in the story of the empty tomb, say that the tomb was empty because the corpse of Jesus evaporated, so to speak, and that thus the risen Jesus is nonphysical;[3] or that Jesus' corpse metamorphosed into a living but essentially nonphysical body which

1. W. L. Craig, "The Bodily Resurrection of Jesus," in *Gospel Perspectives,* vol. 1: *Studies of History and Theology in the Four Gospels,* ed. R. T. France and D. Wenham (Sheffield: JSOT, 1980) 47-74. My thanks to Craig for a number of suggestions adopted here.

2. Though she does not deny the emptiness of Jesus' tomb, P. Perkins (*Resurrection: New Testament Witness and Contemporary Reflection* [Garden City, New York: Doubleday, 1984] 84) argues: "Nor . . . can one insist that if a tomb containing the body of Jesus were to be found by archaeologists, the Christian proclamation of Jesus as the one who has been raised and exalted by God would be destroyed and with it the Christian claims about Jesus' place in salvation." Cf. the very influential book by H. Grass, *Ostergeschehen und Osterberichte,* 3d ed. (Göttingen: Vandenhoeck & Ruprecht, 1970).

3. Cf. L. D. Weatherhead, *The Resurrection of Christ in the Light of Modern Science and Psychical Research* (London: Hodder, 1959) 43-57; S. H. Hooke, *The Resurrection of Christ* (London: Darton, Longman & Todd, 1967) 128-33; W. Pannenberg, *Jesus — God and Man* (London: SCM, 1968) 88-106 with 74-88; C. F. D. Moule, "Introduction," in *The Significance of the Message of the Resurrection for Faith in Jesus Christ,* ed. C. F. D. Moule, SBT (London: SCM, 1968) 9-10. Moule thinks of Jesus' material remains as being "taken up into and superseded by" a new and different mode of existence, "rather as fuel is used up into energy." This view of the resurrection then allows him to suggest elsewhere that in his *pre*existence Jesus had, or was, a "spiritual body" (*The Origin of Christology* [New York: Cambridge University, 1977] 139-40).

took on physical characteristics only as the occasion of earthly appearances demanded.[4]

Some but not all who hold these views do so to insulate Jesus' resurrection from the rigors, vagaries, and fluctuations of historical inquiry,[5] perhaps also to soften the supernatural element and thereby avoid sacrificing their intellects, though under the latter motive it is puzzling why the sudden evaporation or metamorphosis of a corpse should be thought very much easier to believe in than the raising of one. But motivation of belief is beside the points of truth or falsity and of significance. If Jesus' corpse suffered the normal fate of corpses, a spiritual resurrection of him is minimally open to historical investigation; for only the claim that the risen Jesus made a number of appearances needs explanation. The evaporation or metamorphosis of a corpse so as to leave an empty tomb leaves the door somewhat more open to historical inquiry; for the emptiness of the tomb, or at least the claim that it was empty, needs to be explained along with the claim that the risen Jesus made a number of appearances. But whatever the fate of his corpse, a Jesus risen only or at least essentially in spiritual form tends to give more explanatory room to psychology and sociology than to history.[6]

I will try to show that the NT presents the resurrection of Jesus in a way that leaves it more open to historical inquiry. My attempt does not imply that

4. M. J. Harris, *Raised Immortal: Resurrection and Immortality in the New Testament* (Grand Rapids, Michigan: Wm. B. Eerdmans, 1983) *passim; idem, From Grave to Glory: Resurrection in the New Testament* (Grand Rapids, Michigan: Zondervan, 1990) *passim.*

5. Cf. the biblical theological description of Jesus' resurrection as eschatological and therefore as not subject, or only restrictedly subject, to the canons of historical research (so, e.g., Perkins [*Resurrection,* 29-30], who infers from the eschatological character of Jesus' resurrection that "the 'bodily' reality involved is discontinuous with the material reality we experience" and thus *not* "a miraculous intervention in the natural order, such as the revival of a corpse," and F. Mussner [*Die Auferstehung Jesu,* BH 7 (München: Kösel, 1969) 123-27], who goes on to weaken the connection with historical inquiry; also R. H. Fuller, *The Formation of the Resurrection Narratives* [Philadelphia: Fortress, 1980] ix-x, 22-23). But why should an eschatological event be considered beyond the pale or at the fringe of historical inquiry if the event is purported to have taken place in time and space and to have provided observable evidence of its occurrence? And it takes more than an *obiter dictum* to establish that eschatology implies discontinuity with present materiality. See H. Harris, *The Tübingen School: A Historical and Theological Investigation of the School of F. C. Baur* (Grand Rapids, Michigan: Baker, 1990) 179-80.

6. Correctly, Harris (*From Grave to Glory,* 103-4) allows historical inquiry to the extent that he sees the tomb of Jesus as empty and his appearances as physical, but disallows historical inquiry to the extent that "there were no witnesses of the Resurrection itself, and in his resurrected state Jesus was normally not visible to the human eye." But the denial that Jesus' resurrection was "even an incident that *could* have been observed by mortal gaze" (italics added) arises out of Harris's definition of resurrection as essentially nonphysical and thereby destabilizes the basis on which he himself argues for openness to historical inquiry. In no way is the present essay intended to comment on the ecclesiastical troubles encountered by him because of the definition. Antisupernaturalism does not characterize his view.

brute facts carry their own interpretation, or that we have direct access to the brute facts concerning the historical Jesus, or even that there are such items as brute facts. Those questions remain open in this essay, as do also philosophical questions of material and personal identity and such like. Nor will I discuss the historicity of Jesus' resurrection. That would require a further effort. I want to find out what the NT *means* when it talks about Jesus' resurrection. Only then will we discover the degree to which historical inquiry may apply to it, and only then will we be able to decide the degree to which dematerializing views represent the NT itself or represent efforts at a cultural translation of it.

My position is threefold: (1) the NT presents a unified view of the nature of Jesus' resurrection; (2) according to that view, he rose from the dead in a physical body; and (3) the physicality of that body forms an essential element of his risen being. The first part of my position disagrees with the view that the NT presents conflicting versions of Jesus' resurrection, such as one version that he rose spiritually to appear luminously and another version that he rose bodily to appear physically.[7] The second part of my position disagrees with the view that the NT presents the risen Jesus as nonphysical. The third part of my position disagrees with the view that though the NT portrays him as occasionally appearing in a physical form, it does not portray that form as essential to his risen being.

## 1. A Presentation of Arguments for the Essential Physicality of Jesus' Resurrection according to the New Testament

We find the earliest literary references to Jesus' resurrection in the epistles of Paul. By his own account, Paul had been a Pharisee (Phil 3:5). According to Josephus *J.W.* 2.8.14 §163, the Pharisees held that the incorruptible (i.e., immortal) soul of a good person passes into another body whereas the incorruptible souls of wicked people suffer eternal punishment. Granted, Josephus used phraseology that reflects Hellenistic dualistic language concerning body and soul rather than the language which Pharisees might have used among themselves. But the really significant point is that he should have mentioned the Pharisees' belief in corporeal immortality at all, and this despite two competing

7. J. M. Robinson, "Jesus: From Easter to Valentinus (or to the Apostles' Creed)," *JBL* 101 (1982) 7-17; *idem, Trajectories through Early Christianity* (Philadelphia: Fortress, 1971) 48-49 n. 43; Fuller, *Formation,* 45-49; cf. 32-34. J. D. G. Dunn (*Jesus and the Spirit* [Philadelphia: Westminster, 1975] 115-22) canvasses other views that see disparity. In Dunn's own view, the first Jewish Christians believed in a physical resurrection of Jesus; Paul substituted a nonphysical resurrection; and Luke and perhaps John reacted against Paul with a return to physical resurrection. In general against Robinson, see G. O'Collins, "Luminous Appearances of the Risen Christ," *CBQ* 46 (1984) 247-54; and W. L. Craig, "A Critical Examination of James Robinson's Proposed Trajectories from Easter to Valentinus and to the Apostles' Creed with Respect to the Resurrection Appearances of Christ," *JSNT* (forthcoming).

considerations: (1) that his Greco-Roman readers were liable to find the belief reprehensible or foolish (witness the Athenian reaction to Paul's preaching of the resurrection in Acts 17:32 — this point stands whether or not we regard the account as historical) and (2) that throughout his book Josephus was trying to make the Pharisees look good in the eyes of his Greco-Roman readers. The Pharisees — among whom Josephus counted himself; so he should have known about their belief — must have held to physical resurrection for him to have attributed to them a Hellenistically phrased position that ran counter to his purpose in writing.

At Acts 23:6-8 the Pharisees' belief in resurrection is distinguished from belief in angels and spirits. The distinction implies belief in the physicality of resurrection. This belief shows up in later rabbinic literature, too.[8] The rabbis even debated whether dead bodies will rise wearing the same clothes in which they were buried.[9] Paul's having been "a Pharisee of the Pharisees" therefore creates the presumption that unless strong evidence to the contrary comes forward, we may assume that his vocabulary of resurrection carries the Pharisaical connotation of physicality. And the theory that physical portrayals of Jesus' resurrection arose later, out of antidocetic tendencies in the early church, will be preempted. Whether Paul thought of the reanimation of the whole person, including the body, or of the reunion of the old but reanimated body with the preserved soul, or of the union with the preserved soul of a new body raised out of the old one (and there may be other possibilities)[10] does not matter a great deal so far as the point of physicality as such is concerned.

In 1 Cor 15:3-4; Acts 13:29-30 Paul's juxtaposing not only Jesus' death but also his burial with his resurrection, the last of which means "raising," entails that the resurrection means the raising of Jesus' buried body.[11] Further descrip-

8. Str-B 3:473-74, 481; 4 / 2:815-16.

9. Str-B 2:551; 3:475.

10. P. Volz, *Die Eschatologie der jüdischen Gemeinde* (Tübingen: J. C. B. Mohr [Paul Siebeck], 1934) 249-55.

11. Some have thought that the mention of Jesus' burial does not prepare for the raising of his physical body, but insures the reality of his physical death (see, e.g., Grass, *Ostergeschehen und Osterberichte*, 146-47). It is true, of course, that burial is often associated with death — but not for insurance of death; rather, as a usual consequence thereof (see the list of references provided by Grass himself). If death leads to burial, resurrection leads to a reversal of burial (cf. Ezek 37:13: "when I open your graves and bring you up from them"). And where in pre-Pauline Christianity do we find evidence of a need to insure the death of Jesus? Later, in Mark 15:44, the question is not whether Jesus has *died,* but whether he has died *already.* The later Gospels ignore this question. In 1 John 5:6-7, which does not, the coming of Jesus Christ in blood as well as water probably denies the Cerinthian or pre-Cerinthian separation of a non-dying spiritual Christ from a dying physical Jesus, so that the resurrection of the indivisible Jesus Christ — if it were in view — would include the physical body. In 1 Cor 15:4 the second ὅτι disengages Jesus' resurrection from his burial no more than the first ὅτι disengages his burial from his death, and no more than the ὅτι in v 5 disengages his appearances from his resurrection. In Acts 13:30 an adversative δέ, "but," forges an adversative link between the entombment of Jesus and his being raised.

tion of the resurrected bodies of believers will add glorification, immortalization, and other enhancements (1 Cor 15:42-44); but the raising of Jesus' buried body provides the physical starting point and *sine qua non* of resurrection. Since Paul is citing tradition, this entailment represents a common, pre-Pauline Christian view, that is, a very early traditional view. Since Paul is citing tradition agreeably, it represents his own view as well as that of Christians before him. And since Paul is citing tradition that provides common ground on which both he and his Corinthian readers stand, it represents a view of Jesus' resurrection that even those at Corinth who denied the future resurrection of believers, and supposedly inclined toward docetism, adhered to.

In the further part of 1 Corinthians 15 Paul writes about the future resurrection of believers after the pattern and on the ground of Jesus' resurrection. His use of the Greek word σῶμα in this discussion therefore says something about the nature of Jesus' resurrection. If the future resurrection of believers will be somatic, so also was Jesus' resurrection, as is only natural to deduce from the aforementioned juxtaposition of burial and raising. Now σῶμα means the physical body. Even as a metaphor it means the physical body, but the physical body as an analogy for something else. Here in 1 Corinthians, for example, Paul's famous metaphor of the body for the church goes down to the physical details of different bodily parts — head, eyes, ears, nose, hands, feet, genitals (12:12-27).

The evidence is massive that σῶμα means a physical body, not a person without reference to the physical body (though by synecdoche it may represent the rest of the person as well).[12] But particularly pertinent to our present topic is Paul's interchanging of σῶμα, "body," and σάρξ, "flesh," in his argument for the resurrection (1 Cor 15:35-40). He does not speak of the resurrection of the flesh, probably because in other associations the word "flesh" connotes weakness and sinfulness; but he does use body and flesh without fundamental distinction in his drawing of analogies to the resurrection. And he even uses the phrase "flesh of human beings" (v 39), which comes as close as possible to equating resurrection of the body with resurrection of the flesh without

12. See R. H. Gundry, *Sōma in Biblical Theology,* SNTSMS 29 (Cambridge: Cambridge University, 1976; reprint ed., Grand Rapids, Michigan: Zondervan, 1987]). The criticism of this book by J. D. G. Dunn (in *SJT* 31 [1978] 290-91) that it proceeds on "an intention to push a line" has no argumentative value. Intentions do not determine the validity or invalidity of arguments. The second, "more serious" criticism that the book wrongly poses the issue "as a sharp either-or between *sōma* = 'the whole person' and *sōma* = 'the physical body alone'" stumbles over the scriptural passages cited by Dunn as undermining this either-or. One might have thought that the first one, for example, favors the either-or in that it takes a mention of the mind as well as of the body to encompass the whole person (Rom 12:1-2). Similarly, one might have thought that the future making alive of believers' mortal bodies in Rom 8:11 favors an understanding of Rom 8:10, "The body [is] dead," in terms of physical mortality, that is, proleptic death (cf. 7:25; 2 Cor 4:10-12), over Dunn's vague understanding in terms of death "in one dimension of his [the believer's] relationships" (Rom 8:10-11). This dimension would have to exclude all physicality if Dunn were to maintain his argument, "Paul can hardly mean that the physical body is dead here and now."

falling prey to the negative connotations that the word "flesh" carries elsewhere.[13]

Paul speaks of earthly bodies as well as of heavenly bodies. He speaks of flesh of birds as well as of flesh of earthbound creatures. The order of the overall analogy does not seem to ascend from flesh to body; for though he moves from flesh (v 39) to body (v 40), he started with body (vv 37-38). Nor does the order of the particular analogies seem to ascend from earth to heaven or from low grade to high grade; for though he moves from seeds up to human beings, he then meanders through beasts, birds, fish, heavenly bodies, earthly bodies, sun, moon, and stars. He stresses differences by saying that we do not sow the seed-like body that will be, by listing widely varying kinds of flesh, and by calling attention to varying degrees of glory. But none of these differences have to do with materiality versus immateriality, just as later the heavenly human being is a human being originating "from heaven" (Paul's own phrase), not a human being made out of heaven as though heaven were an ethereal substance (so we should interpret the earthy human being as originating "from earth" [again Paul's own phrase], not as made of earth — vv 47-48). Also pertinent is Paul's use of οἰκοδομήν, "building," and οἰκοτήριον, "house," terms that connote greater solidity than does ἡ . . . οἰκία τοῦ σκήνους, which means a house that is comparatively unsubstantial, like a tent (2 Cor 5:1-2). C. S. Lewis was following a biblical instinct when in *The Great Divorce* he portrayed heaven and its inhabitants as possessing greater physical density, not less physical density, let alone ethereality.

Moving to the Gospels and Acts, let us note the conjunction of Jesus' empty tomb, the statement "He is risen," and the reported bodily manifestations of the risen Jesus. This conjunction indicates that the Gospels present Jesus' resurrection as physical, even essentially so. Matthew 28:9 reports that women grasped the risen Jesus' feet, John 20:17 that he told Mary Magdalene to stop touching his feet, Luke 24:39-40 that he showed the disciples his hands and feet and invited the disciples to handle him and see, John 20:20 that he showed the disciples his hands and side, and John 20:24-29 that he invited Thomas to feel the scars of crucifixion that remained on his risen body.[14] Luke 24:42-43 reports that the risen Jesus ate food in front of the disciples as part of a demonstration that he was not a spirit.[15] Acts 1:4;[16] 10:41 add that the disciples ate and drank

13. Against Harris, *From Grave to Glory,* 388, where "bodily" is set against "fleshly," as though in Col 2:9 Paul means to imply that though the fullness of deity dwelt in the fleshly body of Jesus during his earthly ministry, that fullness no longer does so. because Jesus now has an unfleshly body.

14. J. M. Robinson ("Jesus: From Easter to Valentinus," 12) sees the following beatitude on those who have not seen yet believe as correcting the materialism of the risen Jesus' appearances earlier in John 20. On the contrary, by compensating for the lack of material evidence once the risen Jesus stopped appearing, the beatitude protects the materiality of his appearances.

15. See Grass, *Ostergeschehen und Osterberichte,* 40-41, on the escalation of evidences for physicality in Luke 24:36-43.

16. Reading συναλιζόμενος instead of the very weakly supported συναυλιζόμενος.

with the risen Jesus.[17] And in Acts 2:26b the citation of Ps 16:9b, "Moreover, my flesh will dwell in hope," with reference to Jesus' resurrection puts a fleshly stamp on it.

It has been said that Jesus reportedly presented himself in material fashion, not to prove that he was physical, but to prove that he was real. But a real what? A real person? That would require only an overpowering vision. Old Testament theophanies, which are sometimes put forward as models of the culturally appropriate way that early Christians used for expressing their experience of the risen Jesus[18] — these theophanies may have portrayed God in human guise, but they fell far short of having him invite his human subjects to handle a body that he had put on just for the human needs of the occasion. And in the NT, the association of Jesus' appearances with his death, burial, and resurrection disfavors OT theophanies as the generative force behind the tradition of his appearances; for OT theophanies had no similar associations with death, burial, and resurrection. The only suitable matrix for the tradition of the appearances is the companion tradition of death, burial, and reversal of death and burial by resurrection. Similarly, the only suitable matrix for the tradition of the risen Jesus' invitation to feel his scars is the desire to prove his physical continuity with the Jesus who had died on a cross. We may say the same with regard to his eating of food. Whether Jesus' body is portrayed as requiring food is beside the point that at least part of his essential being is portrayed as a resurrected physical body.

The implication is not so strong in Mark, because we do not have there a text-critically accepted account of an appearance by the risen Jesus. But the conjunction of the women's coming to anoint his corpse, the young man's reference to him as "the crucified one," his announcement that Jesus "has been raised, he is not here. Look! The place where they laid him," and his reminder that the disciples will see Jesus in Galilee because Jesus is preceding them there

17. According to G. O'Collins (*Interpreting the Resurrection: Examining the Major Problems in the Stories of Jesus' Resurrection* [New York / Mahwah, New Jersey: Paulist] 47-48), Luke mitigates an excessive realism in 24:42-43 by saying in Acts 1:4 that the apostles ate with the risen Jesus, and in Acts 10:41 that they both ate and drank in his company. But Acts 1:4 says that he ate with them, not they with him, so that far from mitigating an excessive realism in Jesus' eating with the apostles, Luke has doubled his emphasis on realism; and after two statements that the risen Jesus ate, the further statement in Acts 10:41 naturally means that the apostles joined him in eating and, as to be expected, that drinking accompanied the eating. O'Collins (40-43) also considers it a problem that if the risen Jesus ate food, "We must face the questions: What happened to the food taken by the risen Jesus? Can a risen body digest food and grow?" Taking a biblical rather than systematic theological or philosophical standpoint (as throughout the present essay), we may ask for evidence that Luke and John would not have answered affirmatively these questions of digestion and elimination. It is another matter whether Paul would have so answered (see the comments below on 1 Cor 6:13, however).

18. J. E. Alsup, *The Post-Resurrection Appearance Stories of the Gospel-Tradition,* CThM A 5 (Stuttgart: Calwer, 1975) 239-74.

all point in the same direction of a physical resurrection. Further factors in Matthew also point in this direction: the conjunction of Jesus' resurrection with the resurrection of saints' bodies (σώματα) that came out of tombs after Jesus' resurrection, entered Jerusalem, and appeared to many (Matt 27:51b-53); also the connection between Jesus' resurrection and the rumor that his disciples had stolen his body — plus an actual appearance in Galilee. These can hardly be understood in any way but physical.

## 2. A Refutation of Arguments against the Essential Physicality of Jesus' Resurrection according to the New Testament

But what of arguments that at least in part the NT portrays Jesus' resurrection as nonphysical? This time I begin with the Gospels and Acts and work backward to Paul. It is often argued that the mysterious abilities of the risen Jesus to appear and disappear suddenly, even to pass through closed doors (Luke 24:31, 36, 44; Acts 1:3; 10:40-41; John 20:19, 26), portray him as essentially nonphysical even though able to project himself occasionally in physical form for the purpose of accommodating himself to the disciples' need of physical verification.[19] If so, however, the Evangelists portray a risen Jesus who deliberately misled his disciples not only by projecting himself physically for the sake of visual verification, but also by leaving the impression of essential physicality through eating food, drinking liquid, subjecting himself to physical contact, and inviting such contact with the scars that he had suffered before his resurrection. The statement attributed to him in Luke 24:39, "A spirit does not have flesh and bones as you see that I have," sounds like a description of essential nature, not like a description of passing accommodation.[20]

19. See, e.g., Harris, *Raised Immortal,* 53-57.

20. According to Harris, *From Grave to Glory,* 404-5, the resurrected body of Jesus "was '*customarily* immaterial' in the sense that in *his customary mode of existence* during the forty days [of post-resurrection appearances], he did not have a material body of 'flesh and bones'. . . . But when, on occasion, he chose to appear to various persons in a material form, this was just as really the 'spiritual body' of Jesus as when he was not visible or tangible." So then Jesus' statement in Luke 24:39 must mean that he has flesh and bones *only at the moment* and that when not appearing to people, as he usually is not, he is a spirit who though having a body does not have flesh and bones. Apart from his misleading the disciples if such was the meaning, we need to ask whether under this view he got a fresh set of flesh and bones every time he appeared to people and, if not (cf. 388: "But these resurrection appearances were certainly not successive reincarnations of Christ"), where the single set was stored and how it managed to stay alive, if it did, during the longer periods of his customary immateriality, and what has happened to those flesh and bones now that he has altogether ceased appearing. Surely these questions are more telling than the question concerning the whereabouts of the risen Jesus' physical body when he was not appearing to the disciples — to which question the answer is easy: if not in heaven, incommunicado on earth. The defense that though turning into flesh and bones under earthly conditions but not under other conditions, the present body of Jesus is the same body under all conditions (392-94 [with appeals to B. F. Westcott and W. J. Sparrow-Simpson], 404-5) — this defense entails the difficulty

Admittedly, there is eating of a meal in the theophany at Gen 18:1-8, but nothing like the risen Jesus' eating and drinking for the express purpose of proving his physicality. It is true that some of the eleven disciples doubted, according to Matt 28:17. But the text does not tell what they doubted or why; so it is reading a lot into the text to say they doubted *that* the risen Jesus was physical or *because* there was so much visual ambiguity that they could not be sure of his physicality. The text localizes the event on an appointed mountain in Galilee. The text says that the disciples saw Jesus. The text says that they prostrated themselves before him. Earlier in his Gospel Matthew stressed their little faith (6:30; 8:26; 14:31; 16:8; 17:20). It was an emphasis peculiar to his Gospel (with the sole exception of 6:30 par. Luke 12:28) and of course had nothing to do with visual ambiguity, since Jesus had not yet died and risen. So it does not seem likely that the doubt in ch. 28 had anything to do with the composition of Jesus' risen body. It probably had to do quite simply with doubt that Jesus *could* have risen despite the physical evidence standing before them.[21] Likewise, the variety which we see in the evangelistic accounts of Jesus' appearances is due to different theological concerns and to multiplicity of sources, not to any ambiguity in what the women and the disciples saw.

The Evangelists who describe the mysterious abilities of the risen Jesus — namely, Luke and John — are none other than the Evangelists who most emphasize his physicality.[22] By twice narrating a visible ascension of Jesus "into heaven" (Luke 24:50-51; Acts 1:9-11; cf. the catching up of Elijah to heaven without death and resurrection or any other transformation according to 2 Kgs 2:1-12), Luke implies that this physicality was not unessential and occasional, but essential and permanent — and Luke is the only NT writer to provide a narrative of the ascension, a fact that strengthens the physical implication over against a false deduction of nonphysicality from Jesus' ability to appear and disappear in Luke's Gospel. John does not provide a narrative of Jesus' ascension, but he does refer to the ascension by quoting Jesus as saying to Mary Magdalene,

---

of having flesh and bones which under unearthly conditions *exist* but do not exist *as flesh and bones.* Otherwise, we are back to the earlier questions of freshness, storage, preservation, and continuance. I regard the observation that neither the disciples nor the women who out of their means ministered to them and to Jesus are said to have offered provisions for his ordinary human need of shelter and food once he had risen (391) as a particularly weak argument from silence for the risen Jesus' essential immateriality, especially in view of his asking for food and in view of the rarity with which this sort of service to him is mentioned prior to the resurrection.

21. Against Dunn (*Jesus and the Spirit,* 123-28, 131, 133), who makes Matt 28:17 his parade example of the ambiguity on the basis of which he casts doubt on the physicality of Jesus' resurrection. Harris (*Raised Immortal,* 20-21) suggests that some of the eleven failed to recognize Jesus because they remained at some distance from him (cf. προσελθών in v 18a). But he appeared to all the eleven; so they all seem to have been at the same distance from him.

22. Additionally, my colleague M. McClymond points out in private communication that "sudden translation of a corporeal body is no more mysterious than a sudden transformation of an incorporeal Jesus from an invisible into a visible state."

"for I have not yet ascended to the Father" (John 20:17). The immediately preceding words, on which the just-quoted "for"-clause depends, read, "Stop touching me." It is hard not to understand John as saying that the risen Jesus not only appeared physically to Mary, but also ascended to appear physically before God his Father. Sometimes Jesus' command to stop touching him is taken as an indication of his essential nonphysicality, as though he meant to say that Mary should learn to think of him from then on in different terms. But he gave the reason why Mary should stop touching him. It was not that he did not want to be thought of as physical. It was that he now needed to ascend to the Father. And when he came back that evening to breathe the Holy Spirit on the disciples he showed them his scars, and a week later invited Thomas to feel them. Apparently ascending to the Father changed nothing with regard to his physicality. Thomas did not feel the scars, not because he could not have done so or because Jesus did not want him to, but because the physical reality was so visually unambiguous, after the ascension as before, that he did not need to (see John 7:37-39 for the necessity that Jesus ascend to the Father between appearances so as to give the Spirit in the second appearance).

So also Revelation 5 portrays Jesus as the lamb in the presence of God. As "standing," Jesus the lamb is risen rather than lying on an altar dead. "As slain" he bears the scars of crucifixion on his physical body *in heaven* just as he bore them on earth when he showed them to his disciples and invited Thomas to feel them.[23] These two items of description — as standing and as slain — show that the risen Jesus is physical in heaven as well as on earth (cf. Paul's contemplation in 2 Cor 12:2-4 of the possibility that he may have been caught up into the third heaven "in the body," that is, in his present body of flesh and blood — a possibility that demonstrates the compatibility of physicality and heavenliness).[24] The physicality of Jesus' resurrection appearances on earth does not seem to have been a passing accommodation to the needs of his earthbound

23. We are not meant to think that John saw the physical form of a lamb, but that he saw Jesus in the physical form of a human being and described him in terms of a sacrificed lamb brought back to life with visible scars remaining.

24. Against Harris (*Raised Immortal,* 121), who equates earthliness with physical decay, and heavenliness with immortality. Besides, we should avoid the assumption that resurrected saints will dwell with God and Christ forever in heaven. Establishing an earthly locale for eternal life are the doctrines of the second coming (a descent from heaven to earth — see esp. 1 Thess 4:16-17; R. H. Gundry, "The Hellenization of Dominical Tradition and Christianization of Jewish Tradition in the Eschatology of 1–2 Thessalonians," *NTS* 33 [1987] 161-69 and esp. 175 n. 29, and other literature cited there against the notion that the catching up of saints to meet the Lord in the air entails a taking to heaven) and of the new creation, in which the New Jerusalem, indwelt by God and Christ, comes down out of heaven to earth (see esp. Revelation 21–22; cf. the description of the "eternal not-handmade house in the heavens," i.e., the new body, as "our building *from* heaven" — 2 Cor 5:1-2; against Harris, *Raised Immortal,* 124-25; *idem, From Grave to Glory,* 425). To the physicality of a renewed earth is matched the physicality of resurrected saints and their resurrected Lord (cf. R. H. Gundry, "The New Jerusalem: People as Place, Not Place for People," *NovT* 29 [1987] 254-64).

disciples. Common authorship of the Fourth Gospel and Revelation would make this argument stronger. But the mere origin of the two books in the same Johannine school (the least that can be said in view of the many interrelationships between John and Revelation) makes the argument strong enough. We can hardly think that in Revelation the risen Jesus is portrayed as physical in heaven simply to accommodate John's need to see and recognize him for who he is, for John portrays himself in 6:9 as quite capable of seeing and recognizing the souls of martyrs for who they are prior to their resurrection. And it is not advisable to think that the Fourth Gospel and Revelation offer competing traditions of nonphysical and physical versions of Jesus' resurrection, perhaps offering the nonphysical for the purpose of negating it with the physical; for the textual evidence favoring a nonphysical version lacks the strength to convince us that there ever was such a version.

An essentially nonphysical resurrection does not necessarily follow from sudden appearance, from sudden disappearance, or from luminosity of appearance. If the shining of Moses' face when he came down from Mt. Sinai did not imply essential nonphysicality, neither does it follow that the shining of the face of the risen Jesus in Rev 1:16 implies *his* essential nonphysicality. The risen Jesus looks luminous only after his earthly appearances to the disciples have ceased and therefore falls due to his heavenly exaltation. No inference concerning nonphysicality can legitimately be drawn. If the sudden transportation of Philip from the desert road near Gaza to Azotus, so that he disappeared suddenly from one locality and appeared suddenly in another, does not imply his essential nonphysicality (Acts 8:39-40), neither do the sudden appearances and disappearances of the risen Jesus carry such an implication. In other words, sudden appearance on a scene does not imply nonphysicality away from the scene, much less nonphysicality at the scene.

The text does not say that the risen Jesus passed *through* a closed door. So under the assumption of a physical resurrection we need not imagine that John wanted us to suppose that one physical body, that of Jesus, passed through another physical body, that of a closed door. All John says is that "Jesus came and stood in the midst" (20:19, 26; similarly, Luke 24:36). We do not know whether John wanted his readers to understand that Jesus' risen body passed through a closed door, or that he gained entry by virtue of the disciples' opening it for him when he came, or that the door did not need to be opened because he came by translation from heaven or elsewhere on earth *directly* into their midst. Since John relates the closed door to the disciples' fear of the Jews and mentions neither a passing through the closed door nor an opening of it, the last possibility seems the most likely. It also seems to fit best John's phraseology of "coming" and "standing in the midst," as though Jesus appeared out of the blue rather than passing *through* anything. In any case, we do know that John stresses Jesus' physicality once the risen Jesus stood in the midst of his disciples.

So also does Luke stress the physicality of the risen Jesus, only without reference to a closed door. Thus we can hardly say that in Luke's Book of Acts Paul heard Jesus speaking but saw only a blinding light because Jesus' post-resurrection physicality lasted only until the ascension and was therefore unessential. The function of the blinding light was not to dematerialize the exalted Jesus; it was rather to strike Paul down and bring him to conversion. Besides, Acts 9:3; 22:6-11 do not say that Paul saw only a blinding light; they say that a blinding light flashed around him, and Acts 26:16 should make us wary of thinking that on the Damascus road Paul did not see the risen Jesus: "For to this end I have appeared [ὤφθην] to you."

The beginning of the risen Jesus' appearances are invariably mentioned, but rarely his disappearances (only in Luke 24:31, apart from the ascension). This textual phenomenon suggests, it has been argued, that after his resurrection Jesus' essential state was one of invisible nonphysicality.[25] Not only does this argument leave the exceptions unaccounted for. It also offers us a *non sequitur:* emphasis on the appearances does not necessarily imply an essential state of invisible nonphysicality. Take the more obvious implication: emphasis falls on the appearances to stress evidence of resurrection. Equal emphasis on the disappearances would be counterproductive in this respect. Moreover, given the strong emphasis on indications of physicality, the appearances imply more naturally that the risen Jesus was not usually with his disciples than that he was essentially nonphysical.

To say that the risen Jesus is portrayed as having the ability to "materialize" and thereby "localize" himself assumes his essential nonphysicality rather than argues for it. The physicality of his body when he appears may equally well imply *coming* rather than materialization — more naturally, in fact, because the Gospels actually use verbs of coming, going ahead into Galilee, and ascending into heaven for the actions of the risen Jesus. These common verbs favor shifts in location rather than shifts in modes of being.

Unless all unmarried people are ghosts, the abolition of the institution of marriage in the resurrection does not imply nonphysicality (Mark 12:25; Matt 22:30; Luke 20:35). Nor does the angel-likeness of resurrected people imply it, for there is more than one possible likeness between them and angels. Luke 20:36 makes it out to be immortality. We might also think of non-marrying as such.[26]

Paul's claim that he has "seen" the Lord (1 Cor 9:1) forestalls interpreting

25. Harris, *Raised Immortal,* 53.

26. Against Perkins (*Resurrection,* 21), who thinks that the Sadducees "mock a literalist version of resurrection" and that Jesus' answer "has already accepted a hellenized spiritualizing of resurrection." On the contrary, the Sadducees mock resurrection as such, because resurrection was understood only in literalistic terms; and nonmarriage does not equate with Hellenistic spiritualization. Also against J. R. Donahue, "A Neglected Factor in the Theology of Mark," *JBL* 101 (1982) 574-78, from which Perkins draws; and Harris, *Raised Immortal,* 123-24, though on 210 Harris interprets Jesus as referring to "the angelic property of deathlessness."

his reference to God's revealing his Son "in" him (Gal 1:16) as an inward experience that excludes an objective vision of physical reality.[27] Paul writes that God will destroy the belly and the foods that we eat to fill it (1 Cor 6:13). But Paul also and immediately writes that the body — that is, the present physical body — is for the Lord and the Lord for it, that it is a "member" of Christ and the "temple" of the Holy Spirit, and later that it will be raised (ch. 15). So we dare not conclude that coming destruction for the belly and its foods implies an essential nonphysicality in the resurrection. By dealing only with the present belly and its foods, this destruction in no way reflects on the makeup of the resurrected body.[28]

The argument that Paul nowhere uses the phrase "the resurrection of the body" stumbles over his writing that the body is raised (1 Cor 15:44). The retort that it is a spiritual body, not a physical body, which is raised mistakes the meaning of "spiritual." Earlier, in 1 Cor 2:13, 15; 3:1, Paul used the word to describe a certain class of Christians as different from fleshly ones. He certainly was not contrasting ghostly Christians with physical Christians, and nobody understands him thus. As he himself said, spiritual Christians are those who are informed by the Holy Spirit (see the whole of 1 Cor 2:10-16). Similarly, in Col 1:9 "spiritual" describes understanding as given by the Holy Spirit, and in Gal 6:1; 1 Cor 14:37 persons as filled with the Holy Spirit. Elsewhere in Paul, "spiritual" describes gifts as given by the Holy Spirit (1 Cor 12:1; 14:1; Rom 1:11); a blessing as given by the Holy Spirit (Eph 1:3; cf. vv 13-14); songs as inspired by the Holy Spirit (Eph 5:19; Col 3:16); the manna, the water-supplying rock, and the law as given by the Holy Spirit (1 Cor 10:3, 4; Rom 7:14, respectively); and the gospel ("spiritual things" in contrast with financial and other support, "fleshly things") as given by the Holy Spirit (1 Cor 9:11; Rom 15:27). Only Eph 6:12 forms an exception by putting "the spiritual things of evil" (τὰ πνευματικὰ τῆς πονηρίας) side by side with "rulerships," "authorities," and "the cosmic rulers of this darkness," all of which stand in contrast with "blood and flesh." But the contrast does not thus lie between immateriality and materiality; rather, between the weakness of human beings and the strength of superhuman beings.[29]

27. In Gal 1:16 ἐν ἐμοί means "in my case," not "inside me." Paul is presenting the revelation as an argument that the Galatians can see personified in his experience. Dunn's explanation of ἐν ἐμοί in terms of subjectivity (*Jesus and the Spirit,* 105-6, 115) slights the element of physical objectivity.

28. Against Harris (*Raised Immortal,* 124), who writes, ". . . Paul hints that the resurrection body will not have the anatomy or physiology of the earthly body."

29. Even R. E. Brown (*The Virginal Conception and Bodily Resurrection of Jesus* [New York: Paulist, 1973] 85-92), who speaks of the resurrected body as only "*less* physical" (italics added), succumbs somewhat to a false understanding of "spiritual" and "flesh and blood." Harris (*From Grave to Glory,* 195, 401-2; *idem, Raised Immortal,* 120-21) inclines to a definition of the spiritual body as a body animated by the human spirit which has been transformed by the Holy Spirit. In support of this definition he cites the parallel with σῶμα ψυχικόν, a body animated by the human soul. But this definition is unnecessarily complicated. The parallel carries a contrast favoring the

Since throughout his letters Paul uses the word "spiritual" not for immateriality but in reference to various activities of the Holy Spirit, we should understand that the spiritual body of resurrection is brought into being by the activity of the Holy Spirit rather than by natural generation. Paul himself goes on to say as much: "the last Adam became a life-producing Spirit" (1 Cor 15:45) — this with specific reference to resurrection of the body, not just to eternal life in general.[30] The statement that the last Adam became a life-producing Spirit links up with "the Lord is the Spirit . . . the Spirit of the Lord . . . from [the] Lord [the] Spirit" (2 Cor 3:17-18) to confirm a reference to the divine Spirit in a "spiritual body." "But the one joining himself to the Lord is one spirit" (1 Cor 6:17) shows that in 1 Cor 15:45 the risen Jesus' having become a spirit does not entail an essential nonphysicality, for in 1 Cor 6:17 Paul is speaking of a human being who exists in an essentially physical body.[31] So we must not infer an essential nonphysicality for the risen Jesus from the spirituality of the bodies of raised believers.[32] Nor must we infer the nonphysicality of the risen Jesus from his having become a life-producing Spirit any more than in the same verse we infer the nonphysicality of the first human being Adam from his having become a living soul.

True, "flesh and blood will not inherit the kingdom of God" (1 Cor 15:50). But "flesh and blood" connotes the frailty of the present mortal body, as Paul's next, synonymously parallel clause indicates: "neither does corruption inherit incorruption." He simply means that the present mortal, corruptible body will not inherit God's kingdom; and he goes on to say that this present mortal, corruptible body will put on incorruption and immortality (1 Cor 15:51-55; n.b. the neuter gender's referring to the body in v 53, and cf. Rom 8:23). This statement sounds not at all like an exchange of physicality for nonphysicality, but like an exchange of inferior physicality for superior physicality — a physicality so superior, in fact, that in 2 Cor 5:1-4 Paul will come to speak not merely of an exchange of bodily characteristics, but of putting on a new, more substantial body over the old, less substantial one. (He mixes the metaphors of dwellings and garments.) So once again we must not infer an essential nonphysicality for the risen Jesus from the incorruptibility and immortality of the bodies of raised believers. Quite the opposite!

---

divine Spirit instead of, rather than in addition to, the human spirit. Any reference to the human spirit would make Paul uncharacteristically contrast the human spirit with the human soul. And we have just seen that with only a single exception, and that one having to do with superhuman rather than human spirits, his other uses of πνευματικός have to do solely with the Holy Spirit.

30. Harris (*From Grave to Glory,* 198) sees a "potential difficulty" in saying that "the spiritual body is simply a body of flesh totally under the control of the Spirit," for then "Jesus had a spiritual body before his resurrection." But here "spiritual" means "*made alive* by the Spirit," not "*controlled* by the Spirit." So also in Rom 8:11: "And if the Spirit of the one who raised Jesus from [the] dead dwells in you, the one who raised Christ from [the] dead will make alive also your mortal bodies through his Spirit that indwells you."

31. Against Harris, *From Grave to Glory,* 404.

32. Also against Hooke, *Resurrection,* 55; Perkins, *Resurrection,* 21.

By the same token, the glory of Christ's risen body does not exclude physicality, but adorns it.[33] It is argued to the contrary that the contrast between "the body of his glory" (Phil 3:21) and "the body of his flesh" (Col 1:22) shows the resurrected Jesus to be essentially unfleshly even though he might appear on occasion as having flesh and bones.[34] But this argument overlooks that in Phil 3:21 "glory" contrasts with "humiliation" and therefore does not in the least denote an unfleshly material out of which the resurrected body is made. In Col 1:22, conversely, "flesh" does identify the material out of which the crucified body of Jesus was made. Perhaps this identification militates against an incipiently gnostic denial of the incarnation (cf. 2:9). Almost certainly it distinguishes the crucified body of Jesus from his metaphorical body, the church, mentioned both before and after in the context (1:18, 24; 2:17, 19; 3:15). There is no contextual reason to think that Paul means to distinguish between the crucified and resurrected bodies of Jesus with respect to essential materiality versus essential immateriality.

Paul's description of the resurrected body as ἀχειροποίητον, "not handmade," does not deny physicality,[35] but denies human origin. God brings the resurrected body into being; the present mortal body is procreated humanly. Similarly, the temple not handmade (Mark 14:58) is a work of divine rather than human artisanship (cf. Acts 7:48; 17:24); the circumcision not handmade (Col 2:11) is divinely performed rather than humanly performed; the tabernacle not handmade (Heb 9:11) is divinely constructed rather than humanly constructed (cf. Heb 9:24); the stone cut out of a mountain without hands (Dan 2:34, 45) represents the kingdom of God as opposed to a human kingdom. Since this stone smites an image and breaks in pieces its iron, brass, clay, silver, and gold, the description of the stone as cut without hands cannot point to immateriality. If circumcision not handmade is nonphysical, it is so because of the description "in the divestment of the body of the flesh" (cf. Eph 2:11), not because of the description "not handmade." This latter description does not touch the question of materiality or physicality.[36]

33. Against Hooke, *Resurrection,* 55-56.

34. Harris, *From Grave to Glory,* 387-88.

35. As thought by Harris, *Raised Immortal,* 114; *idem, From Grave to Glory,* 195.

36. Harris (*Raised Immortal,* 234) tries to steer a middle course between materiality and incorporeality, as though the resurrected body is immaterial yet corporeal: "Paul was implicitly rejecting not only a materialistic view of immortality (since it was a *spiritual* body) but also a spiritualistic view of immortality (since it was a spiritual *body*)." But what makes up the resurrected body if it is neither materialistic (made up of flesh and bones) nor spiritualistic (made up of spirit), both of which descriptions Harris rejects? His definition of "spiritual" as "animated or controlled by the spirit" does not answer this question of constitution. In the absence of an answer, one wonders whether the denial of essential materiality, i.e., essential physicality, may not derive from an assumption that an essential materiality or physicality would entail corruptibility. Harris seems to assume so, for he characterizes a physical body as corruptible and a spiritual body as incorruptible without considering the possibility of a difference between the present physical body as corruptible

The argument that the earliest layers of the NT portrayed Jesus as personally exalted but not as bodily resurrected, and that only later layers portrayed him as also bodily resurrected because people could not conceive of disembodied existence — this argument rests on a failure of observation and a mistaken presupposition. It fails to observe that the earliest datable tradition of what happened to Jesus after his death and burial speaks of his resurrection, not of his exaltation; and it is pre-Pauline, which makes it as early as anything we have in the NT (1 Cor 15:3-7). The argument falsely presupposes that first-century Jews — in particular, those who resisted Hellenism — found it difficult or impossible to conceive of disembodied existence. But Paul had grown up "a Hebrew of the Hebrews" (Phil 3:5), yet spoke of being away from the body and out of the body in a conscious state (2 Cor 5:6-10; 12:2-4; Phil 1:20-24). According to Matthew, the most Jewish of the Gospels, Jesus spoke of those who can "kill the body but cannot kill the soul" (10:28). According to *1 Enoch* 9:3, 10 the souls of righteous martyrs make suit to God; and in 22:3 we read that certain "hollow places have been created . . . that the spirits of the souls of the dead should assemble therein." According to 2 Esdr 7:75-101, at death the soul of the wicked wanders in torture and grief. *Apocalypse of Moses* 32:4 tells Eve that her husband Adam "has gone out of his body" and that she should "rise up and behold his spirit borne aloft to his Maker." And so on and on in non-Hellenistic as well as Hellenistic Jewish literature.[37] And we are supposed to believe that the first Jewish Christians could not conceive of a personally exalted Jesus without inventing the story of his resurrection and an empty tomb? It seems then that the NT presents us with a view of Jesus' resurrection that some people would describe, *have* described, as "crass" and "crude."[38] The NT may be swimming against a strong Platonic current in the stream of Western culture; but we may well hesitate to describe as crass and crude a portrayal concrete enough to examine from a historical standpoint. For historiography, too, has now become deeply embedded in Western culture — and increasingly elsewhere as well.

---

and a future physical body as incorruptible (121). We need to think temporally and ethically as well as constitutionally. In the Pauline and generally biblical view, corruptibility stems from evil, not from materiality or physicality.

37. See Gundry, *Sōma,* 87-109.

38. See, e.g., Perkins, *Resurrection,* 74 ("crudely materialistic images of resurrection"); D. E. Nineham, *The Gospel of St. Mark,* PGC (Baltimore: Penguin, 1963) 321 ("crudely materialistic traits").

# Jesus Christ, the Reception of the Spirit, and a Cross-National Community

Peder Borgen

## 1. Introduction

Two passages will provide the main focus in this essay, Gal 3:1-5 and Acts 15:5-9:

> You foolish Galatians! Who has bewitched you, before whose eyes "Jesus Christ [the] crucified" was so vividly portrayed? This only do I want to learn from you: did you "receive the Spirit" by "works of [the] Law" or by "hearing of [the] faith"? Are you so foolish? Having begun "in [the] Spirit" are you now completing "in [the] flesh?" Have you experienced such things in vain? If so, it really was in vain! Does he, therefore, who supplies the Spirit to you and who works power manifestations among you [do so] by "works of [the] Law" or by "hearing of [the] faith"? (Gal 3:1-5)

> But some believers who belonged to the party of the Pharisees rose up and said, "It is necessary to circumcise them, and to charge them to keep the Law of Moses." The apostles and the elders were gathered together to consider the matter. And after there had been much debate, Peter rose and said to them, "Brethren, you know that from the earliest days God made choice among you, that by my mouth the Gentiles should 'hear the word of the gospel and believe.' And God, the knower of hearts, bore witness to them 'giving them the Holy Spirit' just as he did to us; and he made no distinction between us and them, but cleansed their hearts 'by faith.'" (Acts 15:5-9)

When the Christian message was brought to the non-Jews, and early Christianity became a movement which comprised both Jews and Christians, the church which emerged had to face several difficult problems. They needed to make basic decisions as to what course to follow on questions such as circumcision and Jewish proselytism, cultic calendar, intermarriage between Jews and non-Jews, table fellowship, dietary observances, attitudes and practices toward polytheistic society and cults, different ethical standards and ways of life, and so on. In both passages cited above, cases from the experience of hearing the gospel, of believing, and of receiving the Spirit are used as a decisive argument against the need for Gentile Christians to undergo circumcision. This observation invites further analysis of these passages.

In order to understand better the general historical setting of these two stories about the reception of the Spirit some aspects of the letter to the Galatians should perhaps be outlined. According to this letter, the Jerusalem meeting (Gal 2:1-10) had the function of being a guidepost for Paul and for the leaders of the Jerusalem church in the ongoing struggle about the status of the Gentile Christians. This understanding is confirmed by the fact that Paul connects the dispute at the Jerusalem meeting with the conflict in Galatia. Among the various ways in which Paul makes this connection two should be mentioned.[1]

First, the question of whether Gentile Christians should undergo circumcision is common to both. Circumcision was the central issue at the Jerusalem meeting, as is explicitly stated by Paul in Gal 2:3: "Not even Titus who was with me and who was a Greek was compelled to be circumcised." The same problem was at the center of the Galatian conflict, as seen from Gal 5:2 where Paul writes: ". . . if you receive circumcision, Christ will be of no value to you at all." Paul's concern was caused by the circumstance that some people had come to the newly converted Galatians and wanted to compel them to be circumcised (Gal 6:12). The gravity of this issue as Paul perceives it is also expressed in 5:4, 6, 11 and 6:13, 15.

Second, at the Jerusalem meeting Paul reported on his preaching (Gal 2:2). Paul does not distinguish between his own preaching in Galatia and his preaching prior to the meeting in Jerusalem. His report from Jerusalem in Gal 2:1-10 is rather meant to reinforce his preaching in Galatia — that is, to counter the opponents' misunderstanding of it. Two observations in Gal 2:1-10 demonstrate this: (1) in 2:5, Paul states that his action in Jerusalem was taken for the benefit of the Galatians ". . . in order that the truth of the gospel might remain with you"; (2) the present tense of the verb κηρύσσω used in Gal 2:2 presupposes that Paul preached the same gospel before the Jerusalem meeting and since that time up to the writing of the letter: ". . . I laid before them . . . the gospel which I *preach* among the Gentiles. . . ." F. Mussner makes this point clear: "Und schliesslich geht aus dem 'zeitlosen' Präsens κηρύσσω hervor, dass er dieses spezifike Heiden-Evangelium auch jetzt noch unter den Heiden verkündet und auch bei den Galatern verkündet. . . ."[2]

1. Cf. P. Borgen, *Philo, John and Paul,* BJS 131 (Atlanta, Georgia: Scholars, 1987) 262-64.
2. F. Mussner, *Der Galaterbrief,* HTKNT 9 (Freiberg: Herder, 1974) 102.

Given this, it is possible to draw conclusions from Paul's preaching in Galatia concerning the main points of his preaching at an earlier time, even that of his missionary activity before the Jerusalem meeting. For example, in Gal 5:19-21 Paul explicitly states that he repeats points from his previous preaching to the Galatians.[3] These points are in the form of a list of vices: "Now the works of the flesh are manifest, such as fornication . . . , respecting which I warn you, as I have already previously told you, that those who do such things will not inherit the kingdom of God." Thus Paul's gospel both before, during, and after the Jerusalem meeting included catalogues of vices which served to illustrate the pagan way of life from which the Gentile Christians had turned.

With this background in mind, the question arises whether Paul's argument from the experience of the Galatians as related in Gal 3:1-5 represents a new development in his thinking or if this line of argument also goes back to an earlier time, even to the meeting in Jerusalem and possibly before.

The close parallels between Paul's case history taken from Galatia and Peter's account from Caesarea support the view that both together exemplify one type of argument in the ongoing struggle about the status of Gentile Christians. Although the reference to the Cornelius story in Acts 15:6-9 clearly shows Luke's interpretive and literary creativity, it is probable that instances such as this one and the Galatian episode were referred to at the meeting. Luke, then, had historical and theological basis for using such traditional material as the story about Cornelius, and he built it into his overall scheme of the Acts of the Apostles.

## 2. Paul's Argument from a Case: The Reception of the Spirit by the Galatian Converts (Gal 3:1-5)

Galatians 3:1-5 reports what had happened in the (recent) past when Paul stayed as a missionary among the Galatians. The case concerns the experience of the addressees of the letter, namely their reception of the Spirit. Paul writes to them in the second person plural:

v 2: τὸ πνεῦμα ἐλάβετε

v 5: ὁ οὖν ἐπιχορηγῶν ὑμῖν τὸ πνεῦμα καὶ
ἐνεργῶν δυνάμεις ἐν ὑμῖν

3. For the following, see P. Borgen, *Philo,* 246-47; *ibid.,* "Catalogue of Vices, the Apostolic Decree, and the Jerusalem Meeting," in *The Social World of Formative Christianity and Judaism: Essays in Tribute to Howard Clark Kee,* ed. J. Neusner et al. (Philadelphia: Fortress, 1988) 130-33, 137, 139.

In v 2 Paul uses the traditional formulalike phrase τὸ πνεῦμα ἐλάβετε (cf. Rom 8:15; 1 Cor 2:12; 2 Cor 11:4; Acts 2:38; 8:15, 17, 19; 10:47; 19:2). In Gal 3:5 Paul speaks of the continued presence of the Spirit and specifies that God is the source and that he works "power manifestations" (δυνάμεις). This reception of the Spirit by the Galatian converts was brought about by Paul's missionary preaching of "Jesus Christ crucified" (Gal 3:1), and thus resulted from "a hearing of faith" (ἐξ ἀκοῆς πίστεως, 3:2).

Paul is pointedly critical of the Galatians: "You foolish Galatians! Who has bewitched you . . . ?" (Gal 3:1). "Are you so foolish?" (3:3). "Have you experienced such things in vain? If so, it really was in vain!" (3:4). The phrase "Who has bewitched you?" probably alludes to the intruders who had come to the Galatian converts and troubled them (Gal 1:7).[4]

In Gal 3:5 the danger of their possible deviation is stated more specifically: "Having begun with the Spirit, are you now completing with the flesh?" A. Oepke suggests that Paul's opponents have argued that the Galatians needed a supplement, a completion by "flesh" — that is, circumcision.[5] Since the term "flesh" here alludes to circumcision, the question arises how exactly one should understand the related contrast between "by works of the law" (ἐξ ἔργων νόμου, Gal 3:2, 5) and "by the hearing of faith" (ἐξ ἀκοῆς πίστεως, 3:2).

These two phrases are much debated in NT research. There is a strong exegetical tradition in which the contrast is seen as that of God's gift of grace over and against human self-achievement. In his interpretation of Gal 3:2, H. Schlier formulates this understanding in the following way: "Der Christ lebt sein spezifisches Leben, sein Leben im Geiste oder auch sein 'übernaturliches' Leben nicht aus dem Prinzip (νόμος) und der Kraft (ἔργα) der eigenmächtigen Existenz, sondern aus dem Grund (ἀκοή) and Macht (πίστις) göttlicher Tat."[6]

E. P. Sanders understands the phrases differently. He takes his point of departure in what he regards as Paul's dogmatic conviction that if ". . . the death and resurrection of Christ provide salvation and receiving the Spirit is the guarantee of salvation, *all other means are excluded by definition.*" "What the Galatians hope to achieve by the law *can* come *only* another way, by the death of Christ and by believing."[7] J. D. G. Dunn maintains that Sanders has thereby

4. So E. De Witt Burton, *The Epistle to the Galatians,* ICC (Edinburgh: T. & T. Clark, 1977) 143; H. Schlier, *Der Brief an die Galater,* 5th ed., MeyerK (Göttingen: Vandenhoeck & Ruprecht, 1971) 120-21; H. D. Betz, *Galatians* (Philadelphia: Fortress, 1979) 131.

5. A. Oepke and J. Rohde, *Der Brief des Paulus an die Galater,* 3d ed., THKNT 9 (Berlin: Evangelische Verlagsanstalt, 1973) 101.

6. Schlier, *Galater,* 122. This view was pointedly formulated in the Reformation, and is today followed by scholars such as R. Bultmann, *Theology of the New Testament,* vol. 1 (New York: Scribner, 1951) 254; H. Hübner, *Das Gesetz bei Paulus* (Göttingen: Vandenhoeck & Ruprecht, 1978) 102, where he also cites R. Bultmann, *Theologie des Neuen Testaments,* 7th ed. (Tübingen: J. C. B. Mohr [Paul Siebeck], 1977) 102: ". . . schon die Absicht, durch Gesetzerfüllung vor Gott gerecht zu werden, sein καύχημα zu haben, ist Sünde."

7. E. P. Sanders, *Paul and Palestinian Judaism* (London: SCM, 1977) 484.

drawn ". . . the false conclusion that in disparaging the 'works of the law' Paul is disparaging law as such, has broken with Judaism as a whole."[8] In a later study Sanders places heavier emphasis on Stendahl's hypothesis that Paul dealt with the concrete relationship between Jews and Gentiles.[9] Two quotations from his book, *Paul, the Law, and the Jewish People,* indicate Sanders's main thrust:

> The subject of Galatians is not whether or not humans, abstractly conceived, can by good deeds earn enough merit to be declared righteous at the judgment; it is the condition on which Gentiles enter the people of God.[10]
>
> The debate in Galatians is a debate about 'entry' in the sense of what is essential in order to be considered a member *at all.* Paul holds that faith is the sole membership requirement; his opponents would require also circumcision and acceptance of the Mosaic law . . . it is not doing the law in and of itself which, in Paul's view, is wrong. Circumcision is, from one perspective, a matter of indifference (Gal 6:15). It is completely wrong, however, when it is made an essential requirement for membership.

Paul's phrase the "works of the law" does not refer to "how many good deeds an individual must present before God to be declared righteous at the judgment, but . . . whether or not Paul's Gentile converts must accept the Jewish law in order to enter the people of God or to be counted truly members."[11]

In his essay "The New Perspective on Paul," Dunn restricts the definition of the "works of the law" to Jewish identity markers: ". . . by 'works of the law' Paul intended his readers to think of *particular observances of the law like circumcision and the food laws.*"[12] Thus, he thinks that Paul is not arguing against works, nor even against the Mosaic law as such, but against works that express Jewish nationalistic limitations and prerogatives. God's covenant should no longer be conceived in such nationalistic or racial terms.[13] In his later publications, Dunn does not advocate this restrictive sense of the phrase "works of the law," however. It is Paul's characterization of what the law requires, focused in particular test cases, in particular the undertaking of circumcision and the practice of food laws.[14] In Galatians, "Paul objects to covenantal nomism understood as it then was consistently throughout Judaism — that is, covenantal nomism as restricting the covenant to those

8. J. D. G. Dunn, "The New Perspective on Paul," *BJRL* 65 (1982) 120.

9. K. Stendahl, *Paul among Jews and Gentiles, and Other Essays* (Philadelphia: Fortress, 1976).

10. E. P. Sanders, *Paul, the Law, and the Jewish People* (Philadelphia: Fortress, 1983) 18.

11. Sanders, *Paul, the Law,* 20.

12. Dunn, "New Perspective," 107. A similar understanding of the "works of the law" is held by R. Heiligenthal, "Soziologische Implikationen der Paulinischen Rechtfertigungslehre im Galaterbrief am Beispiel der 'Werke des Gesetzes'," *Kairos* 26 (1984) 38-53.

13. Dunn, "New Perspective," 114-15.

14. J. D. G. Dunn, *Jesus, Paul and the Law* (Louisville, Kentucky: Westminster / John Knox, 1990) 206-64; *idem,* "Yet Once More — 'the Works of the Law'," *JSNT* 46 (1992) 99-117.

within the boundaries marked by the law, to Jews and proselytes."[15] He now criticizes Sanders for making "*too sharp a distinction between entry* (into the covenant) *and continuance* or maintenance of status within the covenant. . . . Consequently *the issue of the continuum between faith and its outworking / corollary was obscured.*"[16]

## 3. Entry into the People of God or Remaining in It?

In general the approach of Stendahl, Sanders, and Dunn is supported by the fact that Paul draws on a widespread formula which was often used when Gentiles, for various reasons, were compelled to become Jews. The formula occurs in Galatians and in Josephus's writings, and also in a fragment from a non-Jew, Ptolemy the Historian (end of first century B.C.E.?). The formula is: ἀναγκάζειν τινὰ περιτέμνεσθαι. Thus:

> Gal 6:12: "they compel you to be circumcised"
> οὗτοι ἀναγκάζουσιν ὑμᾶς περιτέμνεσθαι
>
> Josephus *Vita* 113: "When the Jews would have compelled them to be circumcised if they wanted to be with them, I did not allow any compulsion to be put upon them. . . ."
> τούτους περιτέμνεσθαι τῶν Ἰουδαίων ἀναγκαζόντων, εἰ θέλουσιν εἶναι παρ' αὐτοῖς. . . .
>
> Gal 2:3: ". . . not even Titus who was with me and who was a Greek was compelled to be circumcised."
> οὐδὲ . . . ἠναγκάσθη περιτμηθῆναι. . . .
>
> Josephus *Ant.* 13.318: ". . . he . . . compelled the inhabitants . . . to be circumcised, and to live according to the Jewish laws."
> ἀναγκάσας τε τοὺς ἐνοικοῦντας . . . περιτέμνεσθαι καὶ κατὰ τοὺς Ἰουδαίων νόμους ζῆν
>
> Ptolemy:[17] "The Idumaeans . . . having been subjugated by the Jews and having been compelled to undergo circumcision. . . ."
> ἀναγκασθέντες περιτέμνεσθαι

Although these parallels occur in different contexts, all demonstrate that it was common to regard circumcision as such as a basic identity marker for a Jew

15. Dunn, *Jesus,* 249.
16. Dunn, *Jesus,* 246.
17. Quoted from M. Stern, *Greek and Latin Authors on Jews and Judaism,* vol. 1 (Jerusalem: Israel Academy of Sciences and Humanities, 1976) 356 no. 146.

and that, when needed, Gentiles were forcefully circumcised. By this act they were made citizens of the Jewish nation.

These parallels lend support to the views of Stendahl, Dunn, and Sanders that Galatians deals with the concrete relationship between Jews and Gentiles. They also seem to support the view of Sanders that the theme of Galatians is the controversy surrounding the condition on which Gentiles enter the people of God.

There were several aspects other than circumcision involved in becoming a Jewish proselyte, however. For example, Philo of Alexandria generally concentrates on three aspects.[18] First, the religious conversion. Here the central theme is the change from worshiping many gods to worshiping the One True God. See, for example, *De Virt.* 102-4, and in Paul, Gal 4:8, etc. Second, the ethical conversion. The change here is from pagan vices to the Jewish virtues. See, for example, *De Virt.* 181-82, and in Paul, Gal 5:19-23, etc. Third, the social or national conversion. The proselytes have left their family, their country, and their customs and entered the Jewish nation, "a new and godly commonwealth" (*De Spec. Leg.* 1.51).

From the Jewish side there were subtle discussions about exactly when a Gentile convert received the status of being a Jew. Although the Babylonian Talmud was written at a much later time, *Yebamot* 46a exemplifies how such distinctions could be made: "Is he baptized and not circumcised such a person is a proselyte, for this we find regarding our [fore-]mothers, who were baptized and not circumcised."

More important for the understanding of the Galatian situation is a corresponding but entirely different distinction drawn by Philo in *Quaest. in Exod.* 2:2. He differentiates between ethical circumcision and bodily circumcision: "προσήλυτος is not the one who has circumcised his uncircumcision but the one who [has circumcised] his desires and sensual pleasures and the other passions of the soul. For in Egypt the Hebrew nation. . . ." Philo gives an answer here to the question: When does a person receive status as a proselyte in the Jewish community and cease to be a heathen? In this saying ethical circumcision and not bodily circumcision was the basic requirement for entering the Jewish community. Bodily circumcision was one of the commandments which the proselytes had to obey upon having received the status of a Jew.[19]

Against this background of discussion it can be seen that Sanders's understanding of Galatians is not sufficiently precise. The Galatian converts had turned away from polytheism and from pagan immorality (Gal 4:8; 5:13-25).

18. For the following, see Borgen, *Philo*, 61-71, 207-32.

19. P. Borgen, "Observations on the Theme 'Paul and Philo'," in *Die Paulinische Literatur und Theologie*, ed. S. Pedersen (Arhus: Aros, 1980) 88; *idem, Philo*, 220: "Philo's and Hillel's understanding has thus been that bodily circumcision was not the requirement for entering the Jewish community, but was one of the commandments which they had to obey upon receiving status as a Jew." Dunn uses this quotation as support for his interpretation of Galatians (*Jesus*, 246, 260).

They had received the Spirit both with its power manifestations and with its ethical fruits (3:2-5; 5:22-26).[20] Thus the issue in Galatians is: How shall the Galatian Christians *remain* in the people of God? Accordingly, for Paul the Galatians are in danger of falling away from being members of the people of God, of ". . . turning back again to the weak and beggarly elemental spirits . . ." (Gal 4:9). And they are encouraged to stand firm: "For freedom Christ has set us free; stand fast therefore, and do not submit again to a yoke of slavery" (5:1).

The opponents who had come to the Galatian Christians understood the situation differently from Paul. They wanted to persuade the Galatian Christians to adopt bodily circumcision as a necessary complement to their ethical circumcision. For them this was the requirement for retaining membership in the people of God.

So far it has been seen that some Jews would regard ethical circumcision as the point at which a Gentile convert received the status of "Jew." Bodily circumcision and the other commandments were then to follow in order for them to remain within the Jewish people of God.[21]

When A. Oepke (on the basis of Gal 3:3) suggests that Paul's opponents have argued that the Galatians needed a supplement and a completion by "flesh," that is, by being circumcised, an important question needs to be asked: Could the opponents also have integrated the Galatians' reception of the Spirit into *their* argument? Is there evidence that reception and possession of the Spirit could characterize a Gentile who had become a Jewish proselyte? One passage in Philo shows that it was possible to regard the reception and the indwelling of the Spirit as a phenomenon in the life of the Jewish community as the people of God. The passage is *De Virt.* 212-19, where Abraham, as the prototype of the proselytes, receives the Spirit. Philo tells how Abraham turned from astrology and polytheism to the One God, the Creator. "And therefore, he is the first person spoken of as 'believing God,' since he first grasped a firm and unswerving

20. There is kinship between Paul's understanding and the understanding of some Jews who stressed ethical circumcision, but ignored the observance of bodily circumcision itself, as in Philo *Migr. Abr.* 92. They and Paul rejected the observance of bodily circumcision. There was at the same time a basic difference, since Paul alone gave the ethical life a new and eschatological foundation in the death and resurrection of Jesus Christ. See Borgen, "Observations," 86-87, 91-92; *idem, Philo,* 220, 223, 235, 238-39, 257-58.

21. Basically the same objection to Sanders's understanding was formulated from a different angle by R. H. Gundry, "Grace, Works, and Staying Saved in Paul," *Bib* 66 (1985) 8-9: ". . . the question of staying in *is* the issue, at least the primary one, in Galatians. There, contrary to Sanders' statement that 'the subject of Galatians is . . . the condition on which Gentiles enter the people of God', Paul does not deal with a question whether believing Gentiles had *gotten* in; rather, he deals with the question whether believing Gentiles could *stay* in without submitting to circumcision and keeping other parts of the law." Gundry refers only in a general way to the Jewish background and is thus quite vague in his discussion of the possible view of the Judaizers.

T. Laato, *Paulus und das Judentum* (Abo: Abo Akademi, 1991) 217-21, takes my studies as the starting point in his discussion of Galatians, and stresses that the question in the letter is not entry into the people of God, but remaining in it.

conception of the truth that there is one Cause above all, and that it provides for the world and all that there is therein" (216). As a result of this conversion and as a prototype of proselytes Abraham received the Spirit:

> . . . the divine Spirit,
> which, having been breathed upon him from on high, made its lodging in his soul,
> invested his body with singular beauty,
> his words with persuasiveness,
> and his hearers with understanding.
>
> τοῦ θείου πνεύματος,
> ὅπερ ἄνωθεν καταπνευσθὲν εἰσῳκίσατο τῇ ψυχῇ,
> περιτιθέντος τῷ μὲν σώματι κάλλος ἐξαίρετον,
> τοῖς δὲ λόγοις πειθώ,
> τοῖς δ' ἀκούουσι σύνεσιν (217)

Abraham thus ranked among the prophets (218).

Philo concludes:

> He [Abraham] is the standard (κανών) of nobility for all proselytes, who abandoning the ignobility of strange laws and monstrous customs which assign divine honours to stocks and stones and lifeless (ἀψύχοις) things in general, have come to settle in a better land, in a truly vital (ἔμψυχον) and living (ζῶσαν) commonwealth (πολιτείαν), with truth as director and president. (219)

The model for this new life as member of the Jewish people was thus the reception and indwelling of the Spirit as seen from the picture given of the experience of the proto-proselyte, Abraham.[22]

This passage in Philo's writings shows that Paul's opponents could have integrated the reception of the Spirit by the Galatian (as they saw it: Jewish) proselytes into their strategy for keeping them as members of the Jewish people of God by having them undergo bodily circumcision. They may have taught the Galatians that they would confirm their status as Jews by fulfilling the commandment of circumcision. Paul then emphatically counters that the Galatian converts received the Spirit by accepting (through faith) the preaching of Jesus Christ crucified. Accordingly, they would *remain* members of the people

22. It may be added here that in the book *Joseph and Asenath* Asenath was transformed as she became a Jewish proselyte. Asenath ate the honeycomb which was full of the spirit of life and she was renewed as a person (15:14-16). She was transformed to heavenly beauty (18:6-11), and she received the Spirit of life, wisdom, and truth: "And Joseph kissed Asenath and gave her spirit of life, and he kissed her a second time and gave her spirit of wisdom, and he kissed her the third time and gave her spirit of truth" (19:11).

of God without submitting to circumcision, and thereby become members of the Jewish people under the law of Moses.

## 4. The Argument from a Corresponding Case: The Reception of the Spirit by the Gentiles in Cornelius's House (Acts 10:44-47; 11:1-2, 15-18; 15:6-11)

According to Acts 15:1-2 some men from Judea (v 24, from the church in Jerusalem, but without authorization) went to Antioch and insisted that the Gentile Christians had to become Jewish proselytes in order to be saved: "Unless you are circumcised after the custom of Moses, you cannot be saved" (ἐὰν μὴ περιτμηθῆτε τῷ ἔθει τῷ Μωϋσέως, οὐ δύνασθε σωθῆναι). Conzelmann finds this verse reminiscent of Gal 2:12, where it is told that certain men came from James to Antioch and intervened in the issue of table fellowship between Jewish and Gentile Christians.[23] The situation described by Luke is nearer the situation in the Galatian churches, however.[24] Both in Antioch and in Galatia persons came from the outside as "intruders" and insisted that the Gentile Christians had to undergo circumcision. In Antioch Paul was present, while he had to involve himself in the situation in Galatia by means of a letter. In both places Paul actively took part in the dissent and debate, in Antioch together with Barnabas. Luke tells how this conflict in Antioch was brought to the Jerusalem church, while Paul in Galatians ties the Galatian conflict closely to the Jerusalem meeting which had taken place in the past.

At the meeting in Jerusalem the argument was not based on the reception of the Spirit by the Gentile Christians in Antioch (corresponding to Paul's reference to the experience of the Galatian Christians in Gal 3:1-5). Instead Peter referred to the Cornelius episode (Acts 10:1–11:18) and said: ". . . from the earliest days God made choice among you that by my mouth the Gentiles should hear the word of the gospel and believe. And God, the knower of hearts, bore witness to them, giving them the Holy Spirit just as he did to us . . ." (Acts 15:7-8). Dibelius comments on this point: ". . . this . . . allusion to Acts 10:1ff. cannot be understood by Peter's hearers, though it can by readers of the book. For the latter the Cornelius story has a normative significance . . . and this is the work of the writer Luke. . . ."[25] Many scholars hold a view similar to that of Dibelius,[26] but light may be thrown

23. H. Conzelmann, *Acts of the Apostles* (Philadelphia: Fortress, 1987) 115.

24. Concerning the differences between Acts 15:1-29 and Galatians 2:1-10, see E. Haenchen, *The Acts of the Apostles* (Philadelphia: Westminster, 1971) 462-72, and the books and essays referred to by him on 441-42.

25. M. Dibelius, *Studies in the Acts of the Apostles* (New York: Scribner, 1956) 94-95; ET of *Aufsätze zur Apostelgeschichte* (Göttingen: Vandenhoeck & Ruprecht, 1951) 85.

26. Haenchen, *Acts,* 445; G. Schille, *Die Apostelgeschichte des Lukas* (Berlin: Evangelische, 1983) 319-20; Conzelmann, *Acts,* 116-17.

on Peter's argument from Cornelius's case at the Jerusalem meeting by comparing it with the report on the reception of the Spirit by the Galatians given by Paul in Gal 3:1-5.

There are similarities between Acts 15:6-9 and Gal 3:1-5. Both refer to an incident in the past. Both refer to the reception of the Spirit by converts, the description in Acts 15:6-9 also clearly referring back to Acts 10:44-47 and 11:15. Some of the parallel phrases are:

- Acts 15:8: αὐτοῖς δοὺς τὸ πνεῦμα τὸ ἅγιον
- Acts 10:44 and 11:15: ἐπέπεσεν τὸ πνεῦμα τὸ ἅγιον
- Acts 10:45: ἐπὶ τὰ ἔθνη ἡ δωρεὰ τοῦ ἁγίου πνεύματος ἐκκέχυται
- Acts 10:47: τὸ πνεῦμα τὸ ἅγιον ἔλαβον
- Gal 3:2: τὸ πνεῦμα ἐλάβετε
- Gal 3:5: ὁ οὖν ἐπιχορηγῶν ὑμῖν τὸ πνεῦμα

From these parallels we notice that just as Paul in Gal 3:2 uses a standard phrase to describe the reception of the Spirit, τὸ πνεῦμα ἐλάβετε, so also Luke uses a corresponding standard phrase in Acts 15:8, δοὺς τὸ πνεῦμα τὸ ἅγιον (cf. John 3:34; Luke 11:13; Acts 8:17-18 (cf. 10:45); Rom 5:5; 1 Thess 4:8; 1 John 3:24; 4:13). Just as Paul sees God as the source (". . . he who supplies the Spirit to you . . . ," Gal 3:5), so Luke says that God is the one who gives the Spirit (Acts 15:8). And the wording in Acts 10:47 particularly resembles that in Gal 3:2. Rather varied formulations are then found in the parallels in Gal 3:5; Acts 10:44-45; 11:15.

From Gal 3:1-2 we learn that this reception of the Spirit was brought about by Paul's missionary preaching of "Jesus Christ crucified," and specifically by "a hearing of faith" (ἐξ ἀκοῆς πίστεως). Similarly, in Acts 15:7 it was induced by the Gentiles' hearing of the gospel preached by Peter and their believing on that basis, διὰ τοῦ στόματός μου ἀκοῦσαι τὰ ἔθνη τὸν λόγον τοῦ εὐαγγελίου καὶ πιστεῦσαι. The idea of faith recurs in 15:9. The connection between preaching and the reception of the Spirit is also clear in Acts 10:44 and 11:15.

Paul concludes from the premise of their reception of the Spirit that the Galatian converts should not yield to the circumcision campaign of the intruders. As the conflict in Antioch was brought to Jerusalem, the same dissent also emerged there and Peter argues likewise against "some believers who belonged to the party of the Pharisees" in Jerusalem who "said, 'It is necessary to circumcise them, and to charge them to keep the law of Moses' " (Acts 15:5). Peter contests their view by reporting how the centurion Cornelius and other Gentiles received the Spirit (Acts 10:17–11:19). Further points of agreements between Paul and Luke include the fact that both call circumcision a "yoke" (ζυγός, Gal 5:1 and Acts 15:10), and while Paul speaks of "power manifestations" (δυνάμεις) of the Spirit (Gal 3:5), Luke informs us that Cornelius and the others spoke in glossolalia (Acts 10:46).[27]

Although Luke thus draws on tradition when he tells the story about Peter and the centurion Cornelius,[28] Dibelius and others are right insofar as they maintain that Peter's speech at the Jerusalem meeting (Acts 15:7-11) reveals the literary embellishment of Luke himself. Luke's creative activity can be seen from the fact that he draws a line from Peter's speech at the Jerusalem meeting back not merely to the Cornelius episode, but beyond it to the outpouring of the Spirit at Pentecost too. In his perception, the Cornelius episode was a "Pentecost" for the Gentiles; thus Peter's remark in 11:15: "And as I began to speak, the Holy Spirit fell on them, even as on us in the beginning." Moreover, Luke makes Peter's reference to 10:1–11:18 at the Jerusalem meeting in such an allusive way that only the *readers* of Acts would understand the connection. Given, too, that Acts was probably written between 80 and 90 C.E. — that is, decades after the Jerusalem meeting took place — one might doubt the historical reliability of Luke's report of the meeting.[29]

However, when the Jerusalem meeting is understood as part of an ongoing debate, struggle, and conflict in early Christianity, Luke's use and interpretation of the tradition receives a plausible historical basis. Paul's report and his way of arguing in Gal 3:1-5 offer help at this point. He gives evidence for the fact that an incident of the same nature as the Cornelius episode took place in the early church and played an important role in the dispute about the status of the Gentile converts. Consequently, the traditions about the reception of the Spirit by Cornelius and other Gentiles have a historical basis. Moreover, as shown above, Galatians ties together the Jerusalem meeting, Paul's preaching activity before the meeting, and his "present" struggle in Galatia. It is therefore probable that his position on the Galatians' reception of the Spirit is an example of one kind of argument already more widely employed against those who insisted that Gentile believers should become Jewish proselytes. The similarities between Paul's conversion account from Galatia and Peter's account of Caesarea

27. For an interpretation of δυνάμεις as ecstatic phenomena, see W. Schmithals, *Paul and the Gnostics* (Nashville: Abingdon, 1972) 47; and D. J. Lull, *The Spirit in Galatia* (Chico, California: Scholars, 1978) 69-71. Mussner, *Galaterbrief,* 211, interprets the term to mean charismatic gifts; Betz, *Galatians,* 135, translates the word as "miracles," and states that it remains unclear what kind of miracles Paul has in mind.

28. Concerning the debate on the question of traditions behind the Cornelius episode in Acts, see the survey in Haenchen, *Acts,* 355-57 and 360-63; and esp. K. Haacker, "Dibelius und Cornelius. Ein Beispiel formgeschichtlicher Überlieferungskritik," *BZ* 24 (1980) 234-51. The unevenness and variations among the various sections of Acts 10:1–11:18 and 15:6-9 are discussed in commentaries, and dealt with in a more concise form in such studies as the above-mentioned essays by Dibelius and Haacker.

29. Concerning the date of composition of Acts, see, e.g., Conzelmann, *Acts,* xxxiii, and for the date of the Jerusalem meeting, 121.

support the view that Luke's use of the Cornelius story in Acts 15:7-11 exemplifies a type of argument which was used not merely at the Jerusalem meeting but also more widely both before and after. And by the same token it is probable that cases like the Cornelius incident or the Galatian episode were referred to at the Jerusalem meeting, regardless of whether or not the Cornelius episode was itself specifically included. Luke, it would appear, had good historical and theological basis for using one such tradition (as it happened, the story about Cornelius), and for building it into the overall scheme of the Acts of the Apostles, for this way of arguing had played an important role in the debates on matters related to the Gentile converts in early Christianity.

## 5. Jesus Christ, Jews, and Gentiles

Paul links the Galatians' reception of the Spirit specifically to the proclamation of the crucified Jesus Christ (Gal 3:1-5). The phrase "Jesus Christ the crucified" is one point taken from the christological kerygma (Acts 2:36; 4:10; cf. Matt 20:19; Luke 24:7). This abbreviated form of the kerygma is found also in 1 Cor 1:23 and 2:2, and drawn on in Gal 5:11, 24. Thus the reception of the Spirit by the Galatians was brought about by their "hearing [the proclamation] of faith"[30] when the kerygma about Jesus Christ was proclaimed to them.

In Gal 3:2 the "hearing of the faith" is contrasted with the "works of the law." How can the proclamation of Christ crucified and the hearing of faith be an alternative to the works of the law? Paul's answer is twofold. First, "Jesus Christ crucified" is the foundation for a new kind of community, as in Gal 5:6: "For in Christ Jesus neither circumcision nor uncircumcision means anything. . . ." (See further 6:15 and 3:27-28.) On this basis a new "paradigm" emerged, distinct on the one hand from the Jewish people as the people of the law of Moses and on the other hand from the polytheistic cults and pagan way of life. Second, since it was *the preaching of Christ crucified* that led to the reception of the Spirit, it was demonstrated that this experience happened to the Gentile Christian converts even though they were not Jewish proselytes committed to the law of Moses and obliged to undergo circumcision. Thus, according to Paul, they belonged to the people of God without having become citizens of the Jewish nation.

"Jesus Christ crucified" therefore meant transition away from the *Jewish* "paradigm" as well as away from the pagan one. It would go beyond the limits of this essay to examine further how Paul develops these two themes in his letter. Only a few observations can be mentioned. Paul centers his understanding of the transition around this very point from the kerygma, Christ crucified. This movement away from the Jewish "paradigm" is stated by Paul in Gal 3:13-14:

30. For further discussion of the missionary concept of ἐξ ἀκοῆς πίστεως, see Betz, *Galatians,* 133 n. 50; and Lull, *Spirit in Galatia,* 55 nn. 17-20.

> Christ has redeemed us from the curse of the Law by becoming a curse for us — for it is written, "Cursed is everyone who hangs on a tree" — in order that the blessing of Abraham might come upon the Gentiles through Jesus Christ, that we might receive the promise of the Spirit through faith.

The precise meaning of these verses in their context is problematic and much debated.[31] Only two remarks should be made. First, Paul states here how it has been made possible for the Gentiles to receive the Spirit through faith, the very experience the Galatian converts had received (Gal 3:1-5). Second, Paul says that this new "paradigm" based on "Jesus Christ crucified" was not new, since it was actually the "paradigm" of the "testament" and "promise" given to Abraham, ". . . in order that the blessing of Abraham might come upon the Gentiles through Jesus Christ. . . ."[32] As for the movement away from the pagan "paradigm," Gal 5:24 gives a clue: "And those who belong to Christ Jesus have crucified the flesh with its passions and desires." The term "flesh" refers here back to the catalogue in Gal 5:19-21, which lists idolatry and other pagan vices. Thus the kerygmatic element of Christ's crucifixion is seen as the foundation for the turning away from the pagan way of life.

Turning again to the Acts of the Apostles, an important point of similarity between Paul and Luke can be added: just as the reception of the Spirit by the Galatians resulted from their hearing of Paul's proclamation of the kerygma about Jesus Christ, so also the reception of the Spirit by Cornelius and the other Gentiles came when Peter proclaimed the kerygma (Acts 10:34-42). Again, as Paul did in Gal 3:1, 13, Luke also refers to the crucifixion of Jesus: ". . . him they killed, hanging him on a tree . . ." (ὃν καὶ ἀνεῖλαν κρεμάσαντες ἐπὶ ξύλου, Acts 10:39). It is important that Luke here, as in 5:30, alludes to Deut 21:22, the very OT verse quoted by Paul in Gal 3:13. The application of this OT verse to the crucifixion therefore belonged to an early Christian exegetical tradition utilized by both Paul and Luke. Moreover, the combination of the reception of the Spirit and the proclamation of the kerygma about Christ, both in Gal 3:1-5,

31. Cf. Betz, *Galatians,* 148-53; M. Wilcox, " 'Upon the Tree' — Deut. 21:22-23 in the New Testament," *JBL* 96 (1977) 85-99; F. F. Bruce, "The Curse of the Law," in *Paul and Paulinism: Essays in Honour of C. K. Barrett,* ed. M. D. Hooker and S. G. Wilson (London: S.P.C.K., 1982) 27-36; Dunn, *Jesus,* 225-32.

32. The sharp distinction drawn by Sanders between the Jewish "covenantal nomism" and Paul's "participation theology" is criticized by M. Hooker, "Paul and 'Covenantal Nomism'," in *Paul and Paulinism,* 47-56. She points to the fact that Paul in Galatians 3 implies the concept of covenant when he speaks about the testament meaning the promises given to Abraham and his offspring, promises which were fulfilled in Jesus Christ. Thus the idea of covenant also belongs to Paul's "participation theology" and the contrast between Judaism and Paul should not be as sharply drawn as Sanders does.

For the idea of covenant, see I. H. Marshall, "Some Observations on the Covenant in the New Testament," in *Context: Essays in Honour of P. J. Borgen,* ed. P. W. Boeckman and R. E. Kristiansen (Trondheim: Tapir, 1987) 126-28.

13-14 and in Acts 10:34-44, as also in 11:15 and 15:7-8, demonstrates that Luke's employment of the christological kerygma in the Cornelius story in Acts 10 is not as such due to his own literary creativity, but comes from the tradition which he had inherited.[33] This observation does not mean that Luke has not used his skill as a writer, integrating the tradition into his book and interpreting it within his own view of history, as we have seen.

In spite of this important parallel between Paul and Luke, however, there is also a difference in the way in which they develop the argument further and apply it. Luke does not concentrate on the crucifixion as Paul does, but has a broader range of christological and soteriological points which are relevant to the cross-national perspective of the context:[34] Jesus "is Lord of all" (Acts 10:36), ". . . he is the one ordained by God to be judge of the living and the dead" (10:42), and "every one who believes in him receives forgiveness of sins through his name" (10:43). In addition, the picture of Jesus' ministry would be relevant to the situation: ". . . how God anointed him with the Holy Spirit and with power, who went about doing good, and healing all who were oppressed by the devil, for God was with him . . ." (10:38). Luke's most pointed argument, however, is in the remark which follows the reception of the Spirit: The Gentiles received the Spirit just as the Jewish Christians have, even with particular reference to the Pentecost experience of the Spirit (Acts 2; cf. Acts 10:47; 11:15-17; 15:8-9). Paul does not use this argument, although he makes clear by his use of the first person plural that both Jewish and Gentile Christians have the Spirit. In Gal 3:14 he writes: ". . . that *we* might receive the promise of the Spirit," and in Gal 5:15: "If we live by the Spirit, let us also walk by the Spirit."

Although Luke may himself have influenced these specific points, in general they probably render various emphases which already existed in the kerygmatic tradition. For example, Luke's combination of the point about Jesus' resurrection with his future function as a judge has a parallel not only in the Areopagus speech (Acts 17:31) but also in the missionary kerygma given by Paul in 1 Thess 1:10: ". . . whom he [God] raised from the dead, Jesus who delivers us from the wrath to come." Moreover, the fact that Luke mentions the relevant christological and soteriological points listed above without elaborating upon them theologically also supports the understanding that he reports on motifs which he had received.

A final question is: How can it be explained historically that the Jew Jesus, and the churches' christology, came to create a cross-national community-paradigm *different* from the national community-paradigm of the law of Moses?

33. Contra Dibelius, *Studies in Acts,* 165; Haenchen, *Acts,* 351. For further criticism of Dibelius's analysis and for careful examination of the connection between Peter's speech and the context, see Haacker, "Dibelius und Cornelius," 244-46; R. Pesch, *Die Apostelgeschichte,* vol. 1, EKKNT (Neukirchen-Vluyn: Neukirchener, 1986) 33-34; and A. Dauer, *Beobachtungen zur literarischen Arbeitstechnik des Lukas* (Frankfurt am Main: Anton Hain, 1990) 82-83, 86-87.

34. For the following points, see Haacker, "Dibelius und Cornelius," 245.

No elaborate answer can be given here, but some thoughts can be offered for further consideration. First, this development took place within the context of a process in which different views and lines of action were present. Thus, although it is impossible to give a precise definition of the christology of Paul's opponents in Galatia, it is clear that they regarded the Galatian converts as Jewish proselytes and as members of the Jewish nation. They did not see christology as a foundation for a cross-national community-paradigm as Paul did. Second, the historical fact that Jesus was executed by means of crucifixion within the context of the legal system had the potential to provide an alternative paradigm to the existing model.[35] Such a background would not explain, however, why christology led to a paradigm of a *cross-national* nature rather than merely to a Jewish sect. A possible historical explanation for such a development would be that the historical ministry of Jesus, and thus also his death and subsequent resurrection, was understood to initiate the eschatological era which also should comprise the non-Jewish nations.[36] Thus the crucifixion of Jesus and his association with the inauguration of the eschatological era for both Jews and Gentiles could possibly lead to a new community paradigm, one not based on the division between those circumcised according to the law and those uncircumcised. From its starting point with the historical Jesus, the new paradigm was worked out in the struggle between conflicting viewpoints and conflicting community models.

35. Cf. Hooker, "Paul and 'Covenantal Monism'," 55.

36. Cf. the similar perspective in N. A. Dahl, "The Crucified Messiah," in *The Crucified Messiah and Other Essays* (Minneapolis: Augsburg, 1974) 10-36.

# Christ-Centered Eschatology in Acts 3:17-26

Hans F. Bayer

Considering the importance which has been attributed in recent decades to questions of Lukan christology,[1] eschatology,[2] and the relationship between

1. We merely note some of the important works, particularly on Acts: C. K. Barrett, "Submerged Christology in Acts," in *Anfänge der Christologie,* ed. C. Breytenbach *et al.* (Göttingen: Vandenhoeck & Ruprecht, 1991) 237-44; O. Cullmann, *Heil als Geschichte: Heilsgeschichtliche Existenz im Neuen Testament,* 2d ed. (Tübingen: J. C. B. Mohr [Paul Siebeck], 1967); G. Delling, "Die Jesusgeschichte in der Verkündigung nach Acta," *NTS* 19 (1972-73) 373-89; R. J. Dillon, "The Prophecy of Christ and His Witnesses according to the Discourses of Acts," *NTS* 32 (1986) 544-56; P. F. Feiler, *Jesus the Prophet: The Lucan Portrayal of Jesus as the Prophet Like Moses* (Ph.D. diss., Princeton Theological Seminary, 1986); J. A. Fitzmyer, "Jesus in the Early Church through the Eyes of Luke-Acts," *ScriptBull* 17 (1987) 26-35; E. Franklin, *Christ the Lord: A Study in the Purpose and Theology of Luke-Acts* (Philadelphia: Fortress, 1975); F. Hahn, "Das Problem alter christologischer Überlieferungen in der Apostelgeschichte unter besonderer Berücksichtigung von Act 3,19-21," in *Les Actes des Apôtres: Tradition, Rédaction, Théologie,* ed. J. Kremer (Gembloux / Leuven: Université, 1979) 129-54; M. Hengel, "Christology and New Testament Chronology," in *Between Jesus and Paul* (London: SCM, 1983) 30-47 ( = "Christologie und neutestamentliche Chronologie," in *Geschichte und Urchristentum,* ed. H. Baltensweiler and B. Reicke [Zürich/Tübingen, 1972] 43-67); G. Lohfink, "Christologie und Geschichtsbild in Apg 3,19-21," in *Studien zum Neuen Testament* (Stuttgart: Katholisches Bibelwerk, 1989) 223-43; I. H. Marshall, *Luke: Historian and Theologian,* 2d ed. (Grand Rapids: Zondervan, 1989); P.-G. Müller, *Christos Archegos: Der religionsgeschichtliche und theologische Hintergrund einer neutestamentlichen Christusprädikation,* EH 23: Theologie 28 (Bern: Lang, 1973); J. A. T. Robinson, "The Most Primitive Christology of All?", *JTS* 7 (1956) 177-89; G. Schneider, "Gott und Christus als kyrios nach der Apostelgeschichte," in *Lukas, Theologe der Heilsgeschichte: Aufsätze zum lukanischen Doppelwerk,* BBB 59 (Bonn: Peter Hanstein, 1985) 213-26; G. N. Stanton, *Jesus of Nazareth in New Testament Preaching* (Cambridge: Cambridge University Press, 1974).

2. C. K. Barrett, "Faith and Eschatology in Acts 3," in *Glaube und Eschatologie,* ed. E. Grässer and O. Merk (Tübingen: J. C. B. Mohr [Paul Siebeck], 1985) 1-17; J. T. Carroll, *Response to the End of History: Eschatology and Situation in Luke-Acts* (Atlanta: Scholars, 1988); H. Conzelmann, *Die Mitte der Zeit: Studien zur Theologie des Lukas,* 6th ed., ed. G. Ebeling (Tübingen: J. C. B. Mohr [Paul Siebeck], 1977); E. E. Ellis, *Eschatology in Luke* (Philadelphia: Fortress, 1972); B. R. Gaventa, "The Eschatology of Luke-Acts Revisited," *En* 43 (1982) 27-42; K. Giles, "Present-Future Eschatology in the Book of Acts," *RefTR* 40 (1981) 65-71; 41 (1982) 11-18; W. H. Gloer, ed., *Eschatology*

them,[3] it is useful to investigate the significant contribution of Peter's temple speech (Acts 3:12b-26) to this area of study. In this speech the interplay of christology and eschatology is addressed in a telling way and simultaneously serves as a fundamental motivating factor in Peter's call to repentance.

## 1. The Macrotext and Lukan Eschatology as Background

***1.1. Luke-Acts.*** To begin with, the clarification of the interrelationship between christology and eschatology must be attempted against the background of the purpose and eschatological perspective of Luke-Acts. Only this larger context can provide guidelines along which we may interpret successfully this interrelationship in Peter's second speech.

According to Luke 1:1-4 and Acts 1:1-5, 8, the question of eschatology is *not* central to Luke's purpose. Rather, the carefully researched (ἀκριβῶς) and reliable (ἀσφάλεια) reports[4] of the words and saving deeds of Jesus and the outlook on the Spirit-led expansion of the Gospel as *the confirming work of Jesus after his exaltation*[5] lies in the foreground. On the other hand, Jesus' death and resurrection and especially the continuing deeds of Christ in Acts are presented in a framework of seemingly competing future expectations *(near and far expectation)*, which has led in the past decades to a wide range of positions.[6]

---

*and the New Testament* (Peabody, Massachusetts: Hendrickson, 1988) (esp. F. F. Bruce, "Eschatology in Acts" [51-63]; C. K. Barrett, "The Gentile Mission as Eschatological Phenomenon" [65-75]); J. Ernst, *Herr der Geschichte: Perspektiven der lukanischen Eschatologie* (Stuttgart: Katholisches Bibelwerk, 1987); E. Grässer, *Das Problem der Parusieverzögerung in den synoptischen Evangelien und in der Apostelgeschichte,* 3d ed. (Berlin: Walter de Gruyter, 1977); R. H. Hiers, "The Problem of the Delay of the Parousia in Luke-Acts," *NTS* 20 (1974) 145-55; A. J. Mattill, *Luke and the Last Things: A Perspective for the Understanding of Lucan Thought* (Dillsboro, North Carolina: Western North Carolina, 1979); W. Thüsing, "Erhöhungsvorstellung und Parusieerwartung in der ältesten nachösterlichen Christologie," *BZ* 11 (1967) 95-108, 205-22; 12 (1968) 54-80, 223-40; J. W. Thompson, "The Gentile Mission as an Eschatological Necessity," *ResQ* 14 (1971) 18-27; S. G. Wilson, "Lukan Eschatology," *NTS* 15 (1969 / 70) 330-47.

3. W. Kurz, "Acts 3:19-26 as a Test of the Role of Eschatology in Lukan Christology," in *Society of Biblical Literature 1977 Seminar Papers,* ed. P. J. Achtemeier (Missoula: Scholars, 1977) 309-23; G. W. MacRae, "'Whom Heaven Must Receive Until the Time': Reflections on the Christology of Acts," *Int* 27 (1973) 151-65 (= *Studies in the New Testament and Gnosticism,* ed. D. J. Harrington [Wilmington: Glazier, 1987] 47-64).

4. See I. H. Marshall, *The Gospel of Luke,* NIGTC (Grand Rapids: Wm. B. Eerdmans, 1979) 35, 43-44.

5. Regarding the "deeds of Christ" in Acts, see esp. Acts 1:1-2; 2:33; 3:16 (26). Regarding Acts as confirmation of the Gospel, see W. C. van Unnik, "The 'Book of Acts' — the Confirmation of the Gospel," *Neot* 4 (1960) 26-59.

6. Gaventa, "Eschatology," 27ff., presents a well-informed overview of current positions regarding future expectations in Luke. She identifies the following positions (see also Giles, "Present-Future," 65-66): (1) Because of an unexpected and persistent delay of the parousia, Luke develops his salvation-historical concept as a "solution" (Conzelmann); (2) Luke writes in the

In a recently published study, Carroll questions with good reason whether Luke really instrumentalized the problem of a disappointed near expectation[7] by way of parenetically emphasizing the present (Luke 17:20-21; Acts 3:22-23).[8] He states against Conzelmann's position: "Delay therefore, serves for Luke the opposite function to that identified by Conzelmann. Delay does not oppose but undergirds expectation of an imminent End in Luke's own situation."[9] Both the "today" of repentance, faith, and proclamation of salvation and the expectation of a real, sudden, and near parousia are, according to Carroll, fully present in Luke's report. Only in the light of a lively near expectation does Lukan parenesis retain its urgency.[10]

According to Carroll, Luke is in this regard far less innovative than Grässer[11] and Conzelmann (among others) assume. Rather, Luke concurs basically with known early Christian views of the future. Contrary to Grässer and Conzelmann, Carroll again emphasizes those expressions in Luke-Acts which testify to continued near expectation (see, e.g., Luke 21:29-36; Acts 2:16-21)[12] while upholding salvation-historical events (with a potential delay motif) expected before the end.[13] Furthermore, Carroll reaffirms the view that Luke was much more concerned about causes and interrelationships of events than with time frames (see, e.g., Luke 12:35-48 and Acts 1:6-8).[14] The *certainty* of the sudden coming of Christ (Luke 21:34-35) constitutes the foundation of Luke's portrayed future expectation.[15]

---

expectation of the imminent event of the parousia (Mattill); (3.1) The parousia is being expected by Luke rather soon; there is, however, no imminent expectation (Ellis, Marshall); (3.2) Luke reflects both a near and far expectation of the parousia (S. G. Wilson); (3.3) The delay of the parousia is merely a problem of the community Luke addresses; Luke himself attempts to offset this by maintaining a sure near expectation (Franklin).

7. See the carefully argued study by D. E. Aune, "The Significance of the Delay of the Parousia for Early Christianity," in *Current Issues in Biblical and Patristic Interpretation,* ed. G. F. Hawthorne (Grand Rapids, Michigan: Wm. B. Eerdmans, 1975) 87-109. Aune concludes: "We found no evidence to suggest that the so-called problem of the delay of the Parousia was in fact perceived as a problem by early Christians" (109).

8. Carroll, *Response,* 166, denies that Luke did this (against J. A. Fitzmyer, *The Gospel according to Luke,* vol. 1, AB 28 [Garden City, New York: Doubleday, 1981] 234, who is here influenced by Conzelmann) and remarks (166-67): ". . . Luke's paraenetic interest shifts the center of gravity away from the eschaton toward the sēmeron. . . . Nevertheless, Luke has not, as Fitzmyer claims, dulled the edge of eschatology to make of it a paraenetic device. The eschaton is not 'swallowed up' in the sēmeron."

9. Carroll, *Response,* 166. Marshall, *Luke: Historian and Theologian,* 110 n. 1, prefers to speak on good grounds of "interval" instead of "delay."

10. Carroll, *Response,* 167.

11. Grässer, *Problem, passim.*

12. See also Marshall, *Gospel of Luke,* 781.

13. See Carroll, *Response,* 166-67. See also Marshall, *Gospel of Luke,* 783, who rightly considers it to be a false ". . . assumption that Jesus did not expect an interval before the parousia." Cf. also my study, *Jesus' Predictions of Vindication and Resurrection* (Tübingen: J. C. B. Mohr [Paul Siebeck], 1986) 244-49.

14. See Carroll, *Response,* 165.

15. See Luke 17:22-37; 21:24-36; Acts 1:6-11; 3:19-26; see further Acts 10:42; 17:31. Regarding near expectation, see Luke 18:1-8; 21:32.

As a point of departure we must recognize in the macrotext of Luke-Acts this apparently irreconcilable coexistence of salvation-historical sequences (especially the promises to Israel)[16] on the one hand and expectation of the near end on the other (cf., e.g., Luke 21:5-9 with 21:32). If we can explain the compatibility of this coexistence from the viewpoint of Luke,[17] we may have accomplished historically more than what tradition-historical hypotheses have produced by way of separating at the scholar's desk one strand from the other to produce a "Lukan" (salvation-historical) and a "traditional" (near-expectation) line of transmission. The latter line of argumentation short-circuits the *real* question of *explaining* the stated phenomenon by immediately building hypotheses on this unresolved problem. Luke for his part was able to *live* with these seemingly incompatible factors and views. Why? Precisely this must first be explained! In this regard we should take Luke's theological outlook and the possible historical foundation on which it builds more seriously.[18] Before we attempt to give an answer to this question, the macrotext of Acts must briefly be brought to attention.

***1.2. Acts.*** Narrative criticism convincingly claims that a speech such as the temple speech must be studied in its narrative context[19] in order to clarify its function within a wider framework. A few observations must suffice regarding the larger context of Acts 3.

It is instructive to recognize that the theme of future expectations in Acts breaks off more or less after ch. 3. The outpouring of the Holy Spirit[20] and the mission among the Gentiles[21] are viewed in Acts as fulfilled (or in the process of being fulfilled) eschatological prophecy. Merely the expectation of the parousia with its related events remains.[22] As sure as the outpouring of the Holy Spirit and the mission among the Gentiles has occurred (or is in the process of occurring), the parousia is to be expected.

A brief glance at the first two speeches of Peter shows that the relationship

16. Carroll, *Response,* 167.

17. See the important contribution to this topic by Cullmann, *Heil, passim.*

18. To have set a positive example in doing so is one of the widely recognized accomplishments of the *Jubilar,* I. H. Marshall!

19. See esp. R. C. Tannehill, "The Functions of Peter's Mission Speeches in the Narrative of Acts," *NTS* 37 (1991) 400-414 (400-401 and n. 4).

20. See Ezek 36:25ff.; Isa 31:31-34; LXX Joel 2:28-32; cf. Luke 3:16; Acts 1:5ff.; 2:1ff.; and 1QS 55:20-21. See Giles, "Present-Future," 12, who points to the outpouring of the Holy Spirit as prophecy of the end times: Joel 2:28-29; Zech 1:3-6; Mal 4:5-6; *T. Levi* 18:11; *T. Benj.* 9:3.

21. Isa 49:6. Cf. Matt 24:14; Luke 21:24; 24:47; Acts 11:18; see further Mark 13:10; Matt 24:14; 28:19-20; Luke 1:32; 3:6; 4:25-28; Acts 8:4ff.; 10:10-34.

22. Acts 1:11; 2:17; 3:20; and possibly 7:55-56. Cf. Giles, "Present- Future," 67. The expectations of restoration of the kingdom to Israel (1:6), the expectation of the kingdom (cf. Acts 1:3 with 1:6; see further 8:12; 14:22; 19:8; 20:25; 28:23-31), as well as the resurrection of the dead (Luke 14:11-14; 20:35-36; Acts 4:2; 17:32; 24:15; 26:3) and the final judgment (Acts 4:23; 10:42; 13:41; 17:31; 24:25) are fundamentally related to the parousia. See Hiers, "Problem," 145 n. 3.

between near expectation (displayed, e.g., by the Pentecost speech) and salvation-historical future events (e.g., Acts 1:6-7; 3:19-21) is addressed here in a uniquely concentrated fashion.

On the basis of the first three chapters of Acts it becomes clear that the entire description of ensuing events until Paul reaches Rome is seen within this highly end-time oriented framework. While the Pentecost speech focuses on the presently realized aspects of end-time expectations,[23] the temple speech focuses on present *and* future events. Even if Luke does not frequently return to this eschatological perspective in the course of the unfolding narrative after ch. 3,[24] it is clear that this perspective nevertheless determines the setting in which the ensuing events take place.[25] The context (thematic continuity with ch. 2, thematic discontinuity after ch. 3 with regard to eschatology) thus underlines the fundamental eschatological significance of this speech for Acts.

***1.3. The Context and Emphasis of the Temple Speech.*** The closer context displays the fact that the temple speech not only functions as a response to the healing of the lame but also *interprets* the healing as a manifestation of the active work of the risen Lord. Hamm goes even further and claims that the narrative of the healing explains the speech to a certain degree.[26]

Similar to the Pentecost speech, the temple speech looks back and especially forward.[27] As a review, the speech fulfills the purpose of affirming to the listeners the death and resurrection of Jesus as God's act. As a glance into the present and future, the speech serves as a parameter for the connection between Jewish repentance and the "unraveling of yet awaited end-time events."[28]

***1.4. The Immediate Context of Acts 3:17-21.*** As mentioned above, the close interconnection between christology and eschatology in the temple speech aims at a clear call to repentance. Far from its being sterile orthodoxy, we find a living assurance that Christ is the divinely confirmed leader for all times. In this light alone, the call to repentance is already appropriate and necessary. The eschato-

23. Giles, "Present-Future," 18, remarks: ". . . the death and resurrection of Christ has made future realities present possibilities."

24. Nevertheless, Gaventa, "Eschatology," 34 and n. 28, mentions correctly references to future judgment in Acts 10:42; 17:30-31; and 24:25.

25. This observation points among other factors against the position of Conzelmann, Vielhauer (S. P. Vielhauer, "On the 'Paulinism' of Acts," in *Studies in Luke-Acts,* ed. L. E. Keck and J. L. Martyn [Philadelphia: Fortress; London: SPCK, 1968] 33-50), Haenchen (E. Haenchen, *Die Apostelgeschichte,* 7th ed. [Göttingen: Vandenhoeck & Ruprecht, 1977]), Wilckens (U. Wilckens, *Die Missionsreden der Apostelgeschichte,* 3d ed. [Neukirchen-Vluyn: Neukirchener, 1974]), and others, who claim that a lively expectation of the parousia was no significant theme in Luke's work.

26. D. Hamm, "Acts 3:12-26: Peter's Speech and the Healing of the Man Born Lame," *PRS* 11 (1984), 199-217 (205).

27. Carroll, *Response,* 137ff.

28. This is the sense in which we use the term "eschatology."

logical prospect with the call to repentance (Acts 3:17-21) is further embedded in a preceding "Jesus kerygma" and a following confirmation by Scripture (see below).

The results of our observations thus far may be summarized as follows: (1) The temple speech is highly significant for the Lukan subdomain of eschatology despite the fact that the purpose of Luke-Acts focuses on "Christ assurance." Acts 1–3 does set the "eschatological tone" for the entire book of Acts. (2) In Acts 2 and 3 we find the tension between near expectation (Pentecost speech) and salvation-historical far expectation (temple speech) repeatedly observable in Luke-Acts.

We shall now attempt to demonstrate that a highly Christ-centered eschatology, commencing with the present healing of the lame and the "Jesus kerygma," explains the principal compatibility between far and near expectation of the parousia and simultaneously assigns eschatology its Christ-dependent place.

## 2. Characteristic Elements of Christ-centered Eschatology

***2.1. Christ Is Completely Affirmed by the "God of Our Ancestors."*** In the attempt to formulate a clearer definition of Christ-centered eschatology in this particular context, we stress above all the initiating agency of the "God of our Ancestors." Obviously, this is particularly significant for Peter's Jewish hearers. No other than the God of their ancestors actively affirms the past, present, and future deeds of Christ, more yet, affirms his exalted person (see below).

The *initiative* of God serves as a scarlet thread throughout the entire speech: v 13, ὁ θεός . . . ἐδόξασεν τὸν παῖδα αὐτοῦ; v 15, ὁ θεὸς ἤγειρεν; v 18, ὁ . . . θεός . . . ἐπλήρωσεν; v 20, ἀπὸ προσώπου τοῦ κυρίου (because of ἀποστείλῃ τὸν Χριστόν it is undoubtedly a reference to God); v 21, divine δεῖ and ἐλάλησεν ὁ θεός; v 22, ἀναστήσει κύριος ὁ θεός; v 25, διέθετο ὁ θεός; v 26, ἀναστήσας ὁ θεός . . . ἀπέστειλεν αὐτόν.

Against the solid background of this recurrent emphasis on their ancestors' God as the affirmer of Christ, Peter builds his Christ testimony in a rhetorically fitting manner by referring initially to present deeds of Christ (vv 12, 13a, 16), then by reviewing past events (vv 13b-18), before outlining future deeds of Christ (vv 19-21) following repentance.

***2.2. Christ's Functional and Ontological Eminence.*** "Exaltation" in v 13 refers to the present deed of Christ in healing the lame as *one* consequence of the raising of the Righteous One from death. This signals that Christ is by no means only a matter of past concerns. Exaltation and ὁλοκληρία (v 16) mark the *commencement* of a new thrust of deeds of Christ.

A single outstanding event is the key and *conditio sine qua non* to this new thrust: the resurrection. Peter bridges the two known factors of present healing and past death with the hitherto unknown or rejected fact of Jesus' resurrection (v 15) as the "missing link." Without the witness (μάρτυς,[29] v 15b) to the resurrection of Christ the present healing and past rejection[30] and death of Christ remain virtually unrelated factors to the hearers. Suddenly, the known factors of past death and present healing are related to the same *person.*

Already here we encounter a marked Christ-centered connection of events which remains characteristic of yet unfulfilled salvation-historical occurrences mentioned in this speech. Only in acknowledging the witness regarding the person and work of Christ do seemingly unrelated events become plausible. This will also hold true in understanding time sequences as Christ-dependent occurrences.

While there is predominantly *functional* christology in v 13, we encounter in vv 14-15 predominantly *ontological* descriptions of the one in whom all this holds together: He is the Holy and Righteous One (v 14; cf. Luke 23:47; Acts 7:52; 22:14). The attributive terms "the Holy One"[31] and "the Righteous One"[32] could take up a variety of OT concepts.[33] They at least attribute to Jesus a particular purity and availability to God, perhaps as his special Son (cf. Luke 1:35) and messianic Servant (cf. Acts 4:27, 30; Isa 53:11b), all of which stands in stark contrast to his being rejected by humans (v 14). Jesus' exalted position is further disclosed by the term ἀρχηγός (v 15). The question of the true identity of Christ is thus brought to the point by the paradoxical juxtaposition of τὸν δὲ ἀρχηγὸν τῆς ζωῆς and ἀπεκτείνατε. No greater extremes may be imagined: The head[34] of *life* has been put to *death.* The hearers might already be indirectly challenged to ponder (see 3:20-21) whether they too will reject the vindicated Righteous One.

29. This term is particularly important in Luke: of a total of 35 occurrences in the NT, 13 appear in Acts, 2 in his Gospel.

30. The severity of ἀρνέομαι is emphasized by double reference (vv 13 and 14).

31. As a reference to God: Pss 71:22; 78:41; Isa 1:4; 5:24; 6:3; 10:20; 12:6; 17:7; 31:1; 55:5; 60:9; Jer 2:3; Hos 11:9; 12:1; Amos 4:2; Hab 1:12; Dan 4:19; 3 Macc 2:13; to the king of Israel: Ps 89:19; Isa 43:15; to the ransomer: Isa 47:4; 54:5; to Elisha the prophet: 2 Kgs 4:9; to Aaron, the priest: Ps 106:16 (τὸν ἅγιον κυρίου). Cf. Sir 45:6; Mark 1:24 / Luke 4:34 / John 6:69. The connection of "Servant" and "Holy One" is documented in LXX Dan 3:35: "Abraham, your friend, Isaac your servant, Israel your Holy One."

32. As a reference to God: Ps 129:4; cf. Zeph 3:5; LXX Dan 9:14; *1 Enoch* 38:2; 53:6; to the Son of Man: *1 Enoch* 46:3 ("the righteous Son of Man"). The righteousness of the Messiah is mentioned in Isa 32:1 (cf. 2 Sam 23:3). The righteousness of the Servant is mentioned in Isa 53:11b.

33. The connection between the terms "the Holy One" and "the Righteous" is found in Isa 5:16 with reference to God. Cf. also Isa 33:5-6 and Deut 32:4 *(δίκαιος καὶ ὅσιος κύριος)*; Cf. ὁσίως καὶ δικαίως in 1 Thess 2:10.

34. Cf. LXX Isa 55:4: David as ἄρχων over the Gentiles; cf. (MT) / LXX ἡγούμενος in 1 Chr 17:7; cf. 2 Chr 6:5. While ἀρχηγός can mean source or origin, it is probable that "leader" or "head" is implied here. See the material proximity of this usage to Acts 5:31 (the functional context of 5:31 suggests the meaning of "leader / prince" in conjunction with "savior"; *pace* Delling, "Jesusgeschichte," 381) and the fact that the context of Acts 3:15 permits both interpretations.

The bold and for Jewish ears definitely problematic reference to Jesus as the *object* of faith (v 16) further emphasizes that the one through whom seemingly unrelated past and present events are connected stands as the exalted one in close proximity to the "God of our Ancestors." While the "God of our Ancestors" completely affirms Christ, and Christ himself is endowed with highest eminence, the temple speech stops short of *identifying* Christ as God himself.

The relevance of these observations to our question of the interrelationship between christology and eschatology is that these functional and ontological references disclose the broadly established *eminence* of him who has suffered in the past, who has been vindicated, and who acts presently. Because of this eminence, sealed by the fact that the "God of the Ancestors" fully underwrites his identity and function, future salvation-historical events are fundamentally shaped in terms of content and time frame by Christ himself. The certainty of future events is thus also assured.

With v 16 the subject of the present event of healing is taken up again. Simultaneously, Peter *prepares* the appeal (see vv 17-26) to his hearers to repent and trust this affirmed, eminent leader. The faith of the healed,[35] more precisely his faith in Christ, led to the fact that he was included in God's exceptional work. The God-given faith of the formerly lame provides *by example* a first link between the objective message of Peter and the hearers. They too may receive the gift of this faith.

Beginning with the event of the healing of the lame, vv 12-16 thus develop and communicate the functional and ontological eminence of Christ. Christ's capability of intervening in the present is made possible through the fact that he has been raised from the dead. The divinely vindicated, eminent Christ is thus presented to the hearers in a most actualizing manner. The present eminence of Christ dynamically influences the call to repentance coupled with the eschatological glance into the future.

***2.3. Christ Shapes Eschatology.*** It is no accident that the call to repentance rhetorically marks the center of the speech. As Peter's central concern and aim of the speech, repentance[36] is surrounded by "supportive motivations"[37] (in-

35. See the emphatic repetition of the *name* (v 16) and of *faith* (v 16). Grammatically Peter's faith could also be in view. But the faith of the one administering the healing is never emphasized in Luke (cf. Hamm, "Acts 3:12-26," 204).

36. The call to repentance consists of two imperatives: μετανοήσατε (see Acts 2:38; cf. 26:18ff.) and ἐπιστρέψατε. This pair of terms hints at the fact that repentance is not only turning away from the old ways but also *toward* Christ. The consequence is the forgiveness of sins (see 2:38). See Delling, "Jesusgeschichte," 374, who notes that repentance (2:38; 3:19; 5:31; 17:30) and forgiveness of sins (2:38; 5:31; 10:43; 13:38) are being mentioned "in fast jeder Missionspredigt."

37. See Tannehill, "Functions," 405. The reference to "ignorance" (v 17) as one "supportive motivation" is not a general excuse and dismissal of guilt but rather an expression of hope in the context of the possibility and *necessity* of repentance. Thus far their ignorance paradoxically furthered God's unsearchable ways regarding Christ. It is part of God's counsel (Acts 2:23; cf.

cluding the promise of further salvation-historical blessings) which are used as appeals to the hearers.[38]

The eschatological prospect appended to the call to repentance thus shows that a partial motivation for repentance is derived from the fact that the divinely affirmed and eminent Christ will also act in the future. This goes to show that the question of time frames is clearly secondary. Rather, repentance as the igniting factor for future deeds of Christ is the real concern, coupled with the assurance that Christ as the divine executive will act as surely as he has in the past and present.

Both major views on Luke's eschatology often lack this Christ-centered emphasis.

Position (1) would merely maintain a process-oriented "already — not yet" tension in which some emphasize the "already" (Hamm, Mattill), others the "not yet" (Ridderbos)[39] aspect.

Position (2) maintains that the supposed delay of the parousia gave rise to a deep disillusionment and led to the pneumatological and kerygmatic "substitute theology" of Luke.[40] This occurred in such a way that a real expectation of the dynamic of "already — not yet" was replaced by a de-eschatologized concern for the cares of the growing church[41] (Conzelmann, Vielhauer,[42] Käsemann, Haenchen,[43] Lohfink[44]).

As far as it goes, position (1) appears to be closer to the known facts from the viewpoint of the temple speech, for the following reasons: The "now" in 3:18 is the present time of Peter's preaching.[45] The "not yet" in 3:21 sets out the time of the restoration of all that has been prophesied. Luke does not so much as hint at a different realm of reality between the past event of the crucifixion and future events. References to OT prophecy underline this: v 18 emphasizes the proclamation of the prophesied suffering of the Messiah; v 21 refers to the prophesied expectation of future restoration.

On the basis of our above-mentioned observations it is, however, even necessary to correct position (1) by stating that the focus lies not on a set of *time sequences* (within the "already—not yet" spectrum) but on the *deeds* of the eminent

---

Delling, "Jesusgeschichte," 382). But now they must turn. Regarding the motif of ignorance, Hamm ("Acts 3:12-26," 207) refers to Acts 17:30; Luke 9:45; 18:34; 24:16, 31.

38. Tannehill ("Functions," 406) rightly calls this speech a "repentance speech *par excellence*."

39. H. N. Ridderbos, *The Speeches of Peter in the Acts of the Apostles* (London: Tyndale, 1962) 14.

40. Conzelmann, *Mitte*, 127.

41. Theoretically this position also concedes a "not yet" aspect (cf. Conzelmann, *Mitte*, 10), but it is *de facto* irrelevant. What is presupposed as absolute historical fact is an acute disillusionment regarding the imminent parousia in Luke's and his hearers' thought. Conzelmann (*Mitte*, 87-92, 123-24) gives the impression that Luke maintains the expectation of the parousia merely as an orthodox article of faith.

42. Regarding Vielhauer and Käsemann, cf. Ridderbos, *Speeches*, 15 n. 2.

43. Haenchen, *Acts*, 96.

44. Lohfink, "Christologie," 223ff.

45. See the Joel-citation in Peter's first speech: at least the eschatological "now" has begun in the known space-time continuum.

Christ. Questions of time are simply less crucial than turning to Christ as the divinely affirmed, eminent leader and learning of Christ-shaped future events.[46]

It may, however, be argued that "times of refreshment" and to a certain degree even "restoration" may not be so much Christ-centered as they are God-centered events (see, e.g., v 20, προσώπου). However, as we have noted above, the *initiator* of everything mentioned in this speech is the "God of our Ancestors." Jesus is predominantly the one who *receives* glory from God (v 13), who *has been established* and *sent* to his people for the remission of sins (vv 19 and esp. 26), who is *being rejected* (vv 14, 15a), who is *being raised* from the dead (v 15b), who is *witnessed* to (v 15c),[47] who is the *object* of faith (v 16), who has *been prophesied* (v 18; vv 22-24), who *must be received* into heaven (v 21), and who is *being sent* again (v 20).

Christ is thus presented as the one in whom the counsel of God becomes visible. Nevertheless, Peter does not explicitly state who will bring "times of refreshment" (ἀνάψυξις, v 20) and "restoration of all that has been prophesied" (v 21). Before we attempt to clarify in which way Christ is involved in these events, we must investigate the meaning and message of these two opalescent concepts in order to determine their material proximity to Christ's known future work.

## Excursus

*2.3.1.* καιροὶ ἀναψύξεως. We cannot here engage in an in-depth analysis of this complex phrase. A few remarks must suffice.

To determine the exact reference of the *hapax legomenon* ἀνάψυξις, we are more or less completely dependent on the context of Acts 3:20.[48] Καιροὶ ἀναψύξεως follows a final conjunction with ἄν and prospective subjunctive aorist (ὅπως ἂν ἔλθωσιν). The time frame is thus identified by the context as present-future. Noteworthy is the plural form of καιροί. Luke speaks of absolute end-time events exclusively in the singular (καιρός).[49] Interim times are, however, often referred to in the plural.[50]

46. This also holds true for the Pentecost speech where the *event* of the outpouring of the Spirit marks the inauguration of end times.

47. Cf. K. Haacker, "Verwendung und Vermeidung des Apostelbegriffs im lukanischen Werk," *NovT* 30 (1988) 9-38. Haacker convincingly emphasizes the generally limited Lukan use of ἀπόστολος (cf. Acts 1:21-22) as referring to the Twelve.

48. The noun is merely used in LXX Exod 8:11 (רוחה: "easing of burdens") and in Aq Is 28:12 (undesired refreshment before coming judgment, 28:19-21) as well as Sym Is 32:15 (see below). In Greek antiquity and extrabiblical Koine the sense of "deliverance" can be documented. Cf. Philo *Migr. Abr.* 152: "rest." Cf. A. Dihle, "ἀνάψυξις,'' *TDNT* 9:664. There is also postbiblical rabbinic evidence for the use of the concept of eschatological refreshment in Pirqe 'Abot 4:17.

49. Cf. χρόνος in Acts 1:6; Kurz ("Acts 3:19-26," 309-10 and n. 8) observes that time references such as καιρός, χρόνος, and ἡμέρα in the singular (cf., e.g., Luke 19:44; 21:8; Acts 2:20; 3:20) describe individual events in the present or future. See, however, Luke 12:56; 18:30: here καιρός refers to the present *aeon.* In Acts 2:17-20a there is mention of progressive events in the plural form (outpouring of the Spirit, prophecy, signs and wonders, cosmic events). They all culminate in the single and punctual event of the Day (singular) of the Lord.

50. Cf. Luke 21:24; Acts 1:7. Cf. further Acts 14:17; 17:26, 30.

Louw-Nida[51] rightly connect the three terms ἀνάψυξις (Acts 3:20), ἄνεσις (2 Cor 8:13; 2 Thess 1:7 with eschatological horizon), and ἀνάπαυσις (Matt 11:29) under the semantic subdomain "deliverance from burdens."[52]

Since the context (3:17-21) does not possess any clear delimiting references and the plural of the term points in the direction of a sequence of events, a wide range of documentable, contemporary references including present "refreshment" and "relief"[53] (from the burdens of sin) as well as a chain of future refreshing events before the joy of Christ's parousia may be in view.[54]

This linguistic range of possible references may be complemented by various facets of conceptual theological motifs to which the term might refer. Several possibilities have been suggested:

(1) Apocalyptic reference:[55] Lohfink[56] mentions an attested apocalyptic point of reference.[57] There the beginning of messianic times is described as *uti refrigeret omnis terra.* Lohfink identifies this expression with ἵνα ἀνάψύξαι. Lohfink concludes: "*kairoi anapsyxeōs* stammen also mit Sicherheit aus der jüdischen Apokalyptik."[58] However, this possible reference remains rather weakly attested and linguistically inconclusive.

(2) Pneumatic reference: Lane[59] refers to Sym Is 32:15. Here the coming Spirit from on high is understood as "refreshment." The release which follows forgiveness of sins would be the outpouring of the Spirit and the establishment of righteousness and justice (cf. Isa 32:15ff.). This reference is also weakly documented and presupposes that this term was used in this way before Sym. However, the remarkable *thematic* parallelism between repentance and outpouring of the Spirit in Acts 2:38 compared with repentance and times of refreshment in Acts 3:19-20 does support this point of reference to a certain degree.

(3) Sabbath-rest reference: Ferraro[60] presents the view that ἀνάψυξις in Acts 3:20 is to be viewed against the background of Exod 23:12 (Sabbath Rest) and the understanding of the Sabbath rest in Heb 3:7–4:13 (see Deut 12:9; Numbers 14). While there exists no verbal connection there is a material link between Heb 3:7ff. and Acts 3:20 which is also reflected in the proximity between ἀνάψυξις and κατάπαυσις. Ferraro emphasizes the following parallels:[61]

51. *Greek-English Lexicon of the New Testament,* 2 vols., ed. J. P. Louw and E. A. Nida (New York: UBS, 1988) 1:246-47.

52. See the proximity of the terms ἀναπαύω and ἀναψύχω in LXX Exod 23:12 (textual variants).

53. Besides "relief from trouble," Louw-Nida (*Lexicon* 1:246, 305) offer the meaning of "encouragement" after burdensome trouble, probably on the basis of the verb meaning in 2 Tim 1:16.

54. *Contra* Hamm, "Acts 3:12-26," 208 and n. 30.

55. Generally speaking, the term is not a *terminus technicus* for any concrete expectation of the end times.

56. Lohfink, "Christologie," 223-41.

57. See esp. the so-called eagle vision in 4 Ezra 11:46a.

58. Lohfink, "Christologie," 231.

59. W. L. Lane, "Times of Refreshment: A Study in Eschatological Periodization in Judaism and Christianity" (Ph.D. diss., Harvard Divinity School, 1962) 171-72, 179-80, 205.

60. G. Ferraro, "Kairoi anapsyxeōs: Annotazioni su Atti 3,20," *RivBib* 23 (1975) 67-78 (70).

61. Ferraro, "Annotazioni," 72.

| | | | |
|---|---|---|---|
| Heb: | unbelief | faith | (Sabbath) rest |
| Acts: | ignorance | repentance | times of refreshment.[62] |

We conclude that especially the second and perhaps the third motif might play a part in the connotation of the term in this speech. For lack of further evidence, caution is expedient.

Taking all factors into account, we interpret καιροὶ ἀναψύξεως as any divine intervention (conveyed through the Holy Spirit?) which would relieve and refresh from this world's bonds and burdens (bring occasional release from suppression and establish justice and righteousness, Isa 32:15ff.) as a result of repentance and forgiveness of sins.

*2.3.2.* ἄχρι χρόνων ἀποκαταστάσεως πάντων ὧν ἐλάλησεν ὁ θεός. It is noteworthy that similar to καιροὶ ἀναψύξεως this phrase also speaks of further *events* (in the plural). It is thus likely that a *period of time and a cluster of events* is in view. This is supported by Luke's use of ἄχρι.[63] The diachronic spectrum of ἀποκατάστασις includes "restoration,"[64] "return," and "healing." An eschatological context is documentable, but the term is not limited to it. Although there are no occurrences of the noun in the LXX, the term is used by Philo and Josephus in the Jewish salvation-historical sense of "deliverance" and "return."[65] The term is being used in the Greek of antiquity and Koine in the sense of "bringing back to an original state."[66] Greek inscriptions convey the sense of "repair" of a temple or path.[67] Later rabbinic evidence[68] mentions the Messiah Ben Perez,[69] who is supposed to restore six items, which humanity has lost since the fall of Adam.

For a more specific determination of the phrase in our context it is important to note that restoration refers to *as yet unfulfilled prophecy.*[70] It is therefore legitimate and necessary to consider the broad spectrum of prophecies of restoration which primarily but not exclusively were given to Israel.[71] Hamm conveniently lists important OT

62. Ferraro ("Annotazioni," 75) concludes that ἀνάψυξις (3:20) contains in analogy to κατάπαυσις a reference to the parousia.

63. See Acts 20:6, where ἄχρι ἡμέρων πέντε covers the time span necessary to sail from Philippi to Troas, with the emphasis upon the arrival occurring after five days. See Kurz, "Acts 3:19-26," 311 and nn. 12, 13.

64. Heb 13:19 contains a specialized use of "restoring" Christian fellowship.

65. (1) Philo uses the term with reference to the liberation from Egypt (*Rer. Div. Her.* 293) and to the return of property rights in the year of Jubilee connected with a mystical understanding of the restoration of the soul. (2) Josephus refers to the restoration of the temple after the Babylonian exile (*Ant.* 11.63). For more evidence, cf. A. Oepke, "ἀποκατάστασις," *TDNT* 1:389-90.

66. Cf. the various references in Oepke, "ἀποκατάστασις,'' 1:390. In the medical realm as "healing" (cf. Mark 3:5); in the legal realm as returning possessions (and freeing prisoners; Polybius *Hist.* 3.99.6); in the political arena in the sense of "restoring public order" (Polybius *Hist.* 4.23.1); in the realm of astronomy as the "return of the astronomic cycle to the original position."

67. Oepke, "ἀποκατάστασις," 1:389.

68. *Gen. Rab.* 12; Str-B 1:19.

69. The one who breaks out, Mic 2:13.

70. A. Wainwright ("Luke and the Restoration of the Kingdom to Israel," *ExpTim* 89 [1977] 76-79 [77]) does not convince in limiting the OT reference to the expectation which links restoration with Elijah (LXX Mal 4:6; Sir 48:1-18).

71. Acts 3:21: πάντων, ὧν ἐλάλησεν ὁ θεὸς διὰ στόματος τῶν ἁγίων . . . προφητῶν. Expressions which contain the phrase "everything / all" are to be interpreted strictly according to

allusions: Isa 61:1-2;[72] Isa 49:6b;[73] Amos 9:11-15;[74] and Isa 1:26.[75] He concludes that the phrase refers to the restoration of the Jewish people under God[76] and the restoration of the land[77] for its people (see Acts 1:6).[78] Additionally, there are indications that some OT references are not exclusively given to Israel. Parallel to Luke's emphasis on a general resurrection of the dead (Acts 4:2; 17:32; 24:15; 26:3) and a general last judgment (Acts 4:23; 10:42; 13:41; 17:31; 24:25), especially Ezek 37:21-28, Isa 49:6; 66:18ff.; and Dan 7:27 convey the end-time expectation that not only Israel as a people and land will be restored but *that the Gentiles will participate in this salvation-and-judgment act of God.*[79] Based on the rather general reference to restoration in our context, there may even be a hint of the new messianic creation.[80]

While restoration is more clearly connected to the parousia,[81] it is probable that it includes events prior to the parousia. An interpretive rendering of the phrase would thus be: "He must be received into heaven until all will have been restored of which God spoke through his holy prophets (from the beginning of the world)."[82]

The sequence of events leading to the parousia can thus be identified as events commencing with the present healing of the lame and the proclamation of repentance leading up to repentance with remission of sins. This will lead to times of divine relief from suppressing burdens and refreshment (as the work of the Holy Spirit?). Prior to the parousia, restoration of Israel (as well as the Gentiles) to God and to its land will take place.

We now submit that the above identified "times of divine relief and refreshment" as well as the "restoration of all that has been prophesied" constitute integral elements of Christ's future work. We list the following reasons: (1) the close parallelism in v 20 between times of *refreshment* and the sending

---

the respective context. See, e.g., Luke 21:22: ". . . when all that stands written is to be fulfilled": "all" refers to the prophecy regarding Jerusalem; cf. Marshall, *Gospel of Luke,* 770-71.

72. The year of Jubilee of the Lord and the day of vengeance; Isa 58:6 (cf. Luke 4:18).

73. The Servant as the light of the nations; cf. Acts 13:47 and Luke 2:32; Acts 26:23.

74. Rebuilding of the fallen tent of David; turning of events for the people of Israel; cf. Acts 1:6, 15, 16.

75. Ἐφίστημι (restoration of the judges): "Justice shall redeem Zion, and righteousness her repentant people," Isa 1:27. See further Jer 23:5-6; Ezek 37:21-28; Dan 7:14, 27.

76. Hamm, "Acts 3:12-26," 210. Wainwright ("Luke," 76) believes that restoration includes reinstatement of repentant Israel as the people of God according to Rom 11:20. He further emphasizes the close connection between salvation and restoration of Israel (cf. the future salvation of Israel in Luke 2:38; 21:28; 24:21), including that of Jerusalem (Luke 21:24, 28; cf. Isa 63:17-18; 65:9ff.; Dan 8:9-14). Wainwright further states: "The restoration is not merely to be a reinstatement of Israelites. It will include the coming of others to Jerusalem" (78) (cf. Isa 66:18ff.).

77. Cf. Jer 16:15; 24:6; 50:19. Cf. Sir 48:10.

78. Cf. Tannehill, "Functions," 406.

79. See παλιγγενεσία in Matt 19:28; Rev 21:1-2.

80. See Rom 8:20-21 and the rabbinic reference to creation in *Gen. Rab.* 12 (see above).

81. *Contra* Hamm ("Acts 3:12-26," 214), who fails to convince by pressing the entire speech into a corset of realized eschatology.

82. Literally: "until the completion (ἄχρι) of the times of restoration of all that which God spoke through his holy prophets."

of Christ Jesus suggest that refreshment likewise is being *administered* by Jesus; (2) in the same way as the healing of the lame (see v 13) and possibly forgiveness of sins (vv 19, 26) are Christ's "refreshing" deeds (see v 13), further refreshment will follow; (3) divine release and refreshment may be connected to the work of the Holy Spirit and, according to Acts 2:33, it is Christ who sent the Holy Spirit as his agent; (4) just as Christ's death has been prophesied, likewise prophesied *restoration* is bound up with him since restoration of Israel is a uniquely messianic deed and connotes reinstating justice and proper ownership;[83] (5) in line with the consistent emphasis on the "God of our Ancestors" as the initiator and Christ as the one who administers, it is most plausible that here also Christ *executes* this prophecy.

## 3. Conclusions and Consequences

There arises a convergence of the strands of Lukan study touched on by this essay, namely (1) the relationship of eschatology to christology within the context of the purpose of Luke-Acts and (2) our question regarding the compatibility between far and near expectation in Luke-Acts. In Acts 3:17-26 these strands find their focus in Christ as the divinely affirmed and eminent leader. As prominent as eschatology might seem in Acts 1–3 and as problematic as differences between far and near expectation might appear, Christ-centered eschatology in Acts 3:17-26 is the explanatory key to the latter and the determining factor of the former.[84] Furthermore, this particular emphasis concurs with the purpose of Luke-Acts insofar as the central concern of the temple speech is not eschatology but the call to turn to this eminent and alive leader. The christology we encounter here is characterized by the "God of the Ancestors" who *causes and initiates,* and as such affirms Christ as the eminent leader who *conveys and administers* the counsel of God. Christ in turn is the one who sends the Holy Spirit (Acts 2:33) as divine facilitator (Acts 1:8) of the witnessing believers.

Without Christ *nothing* of God's counsel occurs, in the past, now, or in the future. Christ's eminence dynamically permeates present and future events as well as time frames of future expectations. Without (acknowledging) Christ's powerful eminence, chains of events again disintegrate into unrelated occasions, expectations of future events revert into uncertainty, and dynamic time frames freeze into static sequences.

The *eminence* of Christ thus claims primary attention and shapes events and time frames. His (salvific) *deeds* follow next in importance. *Time frames*

83. See, e.g., Luke 4:18-19 (Isa 61:1-2).

84. Hengel ("Christology," 43) speaks of the "christological consistency" with regard to the boldness of the Greek-speaking Jewish-Christian communities to break with the "ritual regulations of the Torah."

take third place. It is for this reason that near expectation can coexist in a dynamic tension with far expectation, because it is enveloped in the eminence of the person of Christ.

We thus submit, at least regarding Acts 3:17-26, that Lukan eschatology may not even so much be characterized by a *system* of salvation-historical *periods (Heilsgeschichte)* as by its Christ-centered foundation. Time frames are clearly derivative of this vital expectation of end-time events surrounding Christ. Contrary to a position such as that of Conzelmann, a form of near expectation is, however, fully intact. The end *could* be near! No further salvation-historical *conditions* are mentioned *before the end* may come. A delaying time-period may be in view only regarding the possible lack of repentance on the part of the hearers (the restoration of all that has been prophesied may occur at any time). There is thus a dynamic tension between repentance and eschatological events.

The effective work of Christ and his eminent presence is, according to our view, the historically plausible and theologically meaningful "missing link" between the ongoing course of salvation history and a maintained active near expectation.[85] Primary structures of thinking thus follow personal and relational — "Christ-centered" — rather than conceptual, temporal lines. And even if the anticipated *temporal* framework may turn out to be different than expected, *the fundamentals of future expectation remain unshaken.* Near expectation continues to *exist* but only in the context of the certainty of *Christ-centered events* which must take place before the end. As long as there is faith in Christ, no significant event may be missed and no disappointment (including a possible delay of the parousia) may be unbearable. He is alive and, together with the "God of our Ancestors," in control (see, e.g., the divine δεῖ in v 21). Whoever turns to him may rest assured regarding the future.

The tradition-historical question of *when* this deeper Christ-centered link between seemingly competing time expectations arose remains to be investigated. Surely the rise of the confession of the eminence of Christ witnessed to in this speech would also be the *Sitz im Leben* of an understanding of the future as documented in this speech. In other words: as soon as Christ was confessed and preached (see, e.g., Phil 2:4-11) as eminently as in Acts 3:17-26, Christ- and event-centered eschatology, as outlined here, must have already existed.

Kurz[86] claims that "Ac 3:19-26 confirms that Luke's christology is heavily influenced by his eschatology." Our investigation has shown that the inverse is true: Luke's (and the early Christian's) eschatology is heavily influenced and shaped by a vital christology. Is not the parousia itself the crowning *Christ-centered* eschatological event *par excellence?*

85. See Hengel ("Christology," 41), who states that the personal relationship to the exalted Lord is expressed in the κύριος and the μαραναθά acclamation especially in the Greek-speaking part of the earliest Palestinian Jewish-Christian church.

86. "Acts 3:19-23," 318.

# *Imitatio Christi* in Acts

C. K. Barrett

It may be well to begin this essay with a note on my choice of subject. In the *Festschrift* for the late E. Dinkler I wrote a contribution under the title "Theologia Crucis — in Acts?"[1] The common answer to this question is No; Acts has no *theologia crucis*. I was able, however, to conclude my essay with the words,

> It would perhaps be wrong to describe him[2] as either a theologus gloriae or a theologus crucis: he is not sufficiently interested in theology (beyond basic Christian convictions) to be called a theologus of any colour. But he knows that to be a Christian is to take up a cross daily, and what this meant in the first century he has described in vivid narrative. This strictly practical theologia crucis is not contradicted by the fact that his pilgrims can "shout as they travel the wilderness through."[3]

Confronted by the necessity of finding a subject that would both fit the present volume and not take me too far from the work on Acts which at present requires all my attention, I thought that the theme of following Christ and taking up a daily cross might well be continued in a study of the related but wider theme of the imitation of Christ, the living of life patterned on the life of Jesus. If Christians are expected to take up a cross daily (Luke 9:23), we know in whose steps they will be following, a fact that all the Synopticists underline by placing this saying immediately after Jesus' prediction of the suffering and death of the Son of Man. This was my intention; but it has not worked out in this way, and in what follows if (as I hope) my readers find some correct observations about Acts, they will certainly find my mistake.

1. In *Theologia Crucis–Signum Crucis: Festschrift für Erich Dinkler zum 70. Geburtstag,* ed. C. Andresen and G. Klein (Tübingen: J. C. B. Mohr [Paul Siebeck], 1979) 73-84.

2. The author of Acts, hereafter denoted by Luke.

3. Barrett, "Theologia Crucis," 84. Howard at least will need no reference for the quotation within the quotation. It is a pleasure to salute him with it.

The difficulty appears immediately. There is, or at least there appears at first sight to be, very little material with which one can work. The language of imitation is wanting in Acts. The fundamental root is that of the verb μιμεῖσθαι, which, with the cognate noun μιμητής (and the compound συμμιμητής), appears not frequently but in important passages in the NT, especially in the Pauline and Deuteropauline literature. Paul exhorts his readers to imitate him, qualifying the exhortation through his imitation of Christ. The most important passages are in 1 Cor 4:16, μιμηταί μου γίνεσθε, taken up and interpreted in 11:1, μιμηταί μου γίνεσθε, καθὼς κἀγὼ Χριστοῦ. The language of imitation occurs also not in exhortation but as a statement of fact in 1 Thess 1:6, μιμηταὶ ἡμῶν ἐγενήθητε καὶ τοῦ κυρίου. This verse has to do with suffering endured by the Thessalonian Christians, and this theme is made clearer still in 1 Thess 2:14, "You became imitators of the churches of God that are in Judea" ὅτι τὰ αὐτὰ ἐπάθετε καὶ ὑμεῖς. Paul himself (or a Deuteropauline writer) writes in 2 Thess 3:7, 9, αὐτοὶ γὰρ οἴδατε πῶς δεῖ μιμεῖσθαι ἡμᾶς . . . ἵνα ἑαυτοὺς τύπον δῶμεν ὑμῖν εἰς τὸ μιμεῖσθαι ἡμᾶς. In Eph 5:1 is the surprising command, γίνεσθε οὖν μιμηταὶ τοῦ θεοῦ, but it immediately appears that what is in mind is, in practical terms, an *imitatio Christi,* for the next verse continues, περιπατεῖτε ἐν ἀγάπῃ, καθὼς καὶ ὁ Χριστὸς ἠγάπησεν ὑμᾶς. In Hebrews also there is the notion of mediated imitation, that is, the imitation not directly of Christ but of those who set a good example by imitating him: 6:12, μιμηταὶ τῶν διὰ πίστεως καὶ μακροθυμίας κληρονομούντων τὰς ἐπαγγελίας; and 13:7, ὧν . . . μιμεῖσθε τὴν πίστιν. Third John 11 contains the moral precept, which as it stands is not specifically Christian, μὴ μιμοῦ τὸ κακὸν ἀλλὰ τὸ ἀγαθόν.

Philippians 3:17 employs the compound noun and like 2 Thess 3:9 introduces another important word: Συμμιμηταί μου γίνεσθε . . . καὶ σκοπεῖτε τοὺς οὕτω περιπατοῦντας καθὼς ἔχετε τύπον ἡμᾶς. The word τύπος occurs in the NT in various senses. Important for us, in addition to Phil 3:17 and 2 Thess 3:9, are 1 Thess 1:7, where the Thessalonians themselves are said to have provided a Christian pattern for others to imitate, and 1 Tim 4:12; Tit 2:7; 1 Pet 5:3, in which ministers are urged to be (as Paul had been) examples to their people. Other important words, such as ἀρχέτυπος, παράδειγμα, and μίμημα, do not occur in the NT; ἀντίτυπος occurs twice[4] but without relevance to the matter under discussion.

Of the words mentioned, only τύπος occurs in Acts, at 7:43, 44; 23:25. At 7:44 it denotes a pattern or example that is to be imitated, but it is no more relevant to our study than the other two. The language of imitation is not to be found in Acts; nor is the fact to be found without the language. Luke never even points back to his former treatise as supplying a model, or represents the Christian character that he describes as recalling the story of Jesus, the story being presented as an example of Christian behavior.[5] This is part of a larger

4. Heb 9:24; 1 Pet 3:21.

5. It may be said that it was unnecessary for Luke to do this; the Gospel was there and

lacuna in Acts; the book as a whole lays little stress on the ethical component of Christian living.

To say this is not to say that Luke has no interest in the moral consequences of becoming, or being, a Christian. Probably he simply took these for granted. When Peter's audience on the day of Pentecost, at the end of his speech, asks him what they must do, they are bidden to repent; as a result of this they will receive the forgiveness of their sins and the gift of the Holy Spirit. But the sins for which they will be forgiven seem to be primarily those involved in the rejection and crucifixion of Jesus,[6] whom they now in believing Peter's words accept as Messiah and Lord, and there is no indication that the fruit of the Spirit is thought of in such terms as those described in Gal 5:22-23. For Luke the main indication of the Spirit's presence is to be found in inspired speech.[7] The life of those who believe is described in 2:42 as based upon the teaching of the apostles, the fellowship, the breaking of the loaf, and the prayers. It is possible to guess, impossible to prove, that the teaching of the apostles was, or included, moral teaching; on the whole it is more probable that it was teaching about the office and rank of Christ.[8] If the fellowship includes readiness to share one's property with the whole community for the benefit of the needy,[9] this is indeed a high moral act; but Luke does not say this. It is true that in the early years described in the opening chapters of Acts there was probably no need for a great deal of moral teaching. The first believers had been brought up within Judaism and were familiar with its high moral principles. But the lack of interest in moral conversion is even more marked in the later chapters. We hear nothing in ch. 18 of any ethical change in those Corinthians who became Christians; yet these were those to whom Paul wrote: ". . . fornicators, idolaters, catamites, sodomites, thieves, rapacious, drunkards, abusive, highwaymen . . . and such were some of you; but you were washed, sanctified, justified. . . " (1 Cor 6:9-11). It is notorious that Paul's Corinthians had not when he wrote to them become models of ethical achievement, but their lives had been transformed. Acts does not say this, or indeed anything that would lead one to expect it. It is hard to doubt that the Gospels also, like Paul, bear witness to the concern that Christians should possess certain moral characteristics. It is enough to point to such passages as the Beatitudes and the insistence on the command of love to the neighbor, which Luke goes out of his way to emphasize and to illustrate in

---

anyone could read it. This comment might suffice if there were points in Acts that specifically recalled features of the Gospel.

6. 2:38, reading εἰς ἄφεσιν τῶν ἁμαρτιῶν ὑμῶν (with ℵ B vg), *your* sins, the sins that *you* have committed, rather than εἰς ἄφεσιν ἁμαρτιῶν (with D E it sy), which constitutes a formula, the familiar baptism-for-the-remission-of-sins.

7. See 2:4, 18 (not D), 33; 4:8, 25, 31; 6:10; 7:55; 10:44-46; 19:6; and other passages.

8. It is this that has been spoken of, this that needs to be added to practicing Jews to make them practicing Christians.

9. See Rom 15:26; 2 Cor 8:4; 9:13; Heb 13:16.

practical terms. It is surprising that Luke in Acts does not point back to the Third Gospel as depicting the quality of life that members of the young churches should manifest. It is a partial answer that he perhaps felt that he could assume that readers of Acts would have read the earlier work, but this does not explain why (after Acts 1:1) he never refers back to the Gospel.[10]

There is one respect in which narrative material in Acts shows marked parallelism with the story of the Gospel: the arrest, trial, and martyrdom of Stephen and the arrest and various trials of Paul recall a number of features of the story of the suffering and death of Jesus. The points of resemblance have often been remarked and need only brief summary here. The attack on Stephen is explicitly linked with that on Jesus: We have heard him saying that this Jesus will destroy this place and change the customs that Moses delivered to us (Acts 6:14). There is a clear backward reference to the sayings of Jesus that predict the coming end of the temple.[11] Stephen next appears before the high priest and is interrogated by him. Unlike Jesus he answers at length; at the end of his speech (which suggests that Luke may have been thinking of Luke 4:16-30 rather than, or as well as, the Passion in the narrower sense) there is a spontaneous reaction (7:54; cf. Luke 4:28). Stephen cries out (7:55), "I see heaven opened and the Son of man standing at the right hand of God" (cf. Luke 22:69: "Henceforth the Son of man shall be seated at the right hand of the power of God"). He is cast out of the city (cf. Luke 4:29), and in death commends his spirit to Jesus (as Jesus commended his to the Father; cf. Luke 23:46) and begs forgiveness for those who are stoning him (cf. Luke 23:34). It is very difficult to believe that Luke could have written this account of Stephen's martyrdom without calling to mind his own story of the death of Jesus.

The story of Paul is drawn out at greater length, though of course it does not reach the expected climax of the apostle's death. The interplay of Jewish and Roman forces and officials recalls the fundamental pattern of the story of Jesus, and runs back a long way in the story of Acts. Already at 17:7 the Jews at Thessalonica accuse Paul and Silas before the civil authorities of proclaiming Jesus as a rival king; compare Luke 23:2, where Jesus is accused before Pilate of saying that he is an anointed king. The Jews in the temple cry out against Paul, "Away with him!" (αἶρε αὐτόν, 21:36), and after his speech they repeat their cry, "Away with such a fellow from the earth! He is not fit to live" (αἶρε ἀπὸ τῆς γῆς . . . , 22:22). Compare Luke 23:18, "Away with him!" (αἶρε τοῦτον; also 23:21). Throughout the story in Acts (at least until Rome is reached) the Jews show themselves irreconcilably hostile to Paul and out for his blood, but the Roman authorities as consistently pronounce him innocent. Thus the tribune

10. See above and n. 5.

11. 6:14. See C. K. Barrett, "Sayings of Jesus in the Acts of the Apostles," in *À Cause de l'Évangile,* LD 123 (Paris: Cerf, 1985) 684-85; *idem,* "Attitudes to the Temple in the Acts of the Apostles," in *Templum Amicitiae,* ed. W. Horbury, JSNTSS 48 (Sheffield: JSOT, 1991) 345-67, esp. 350-51.

protects him, and believes that he has done nothing worthy of death or bonds (23:29); Felix not only protects him but listens to his teaching (24:23-26); the worst that Festus can say about Paul is that he holds the absurd view that a dead man, Jesus, is now alive (25:19); he has done nothing worthy of death (25:25); Agrippa agrees that if Paul had not appealed to Caesar he could have been set free (26:32). With all these passages compare the repeated assertions of Pilate, backed by Herod, that Jesus is innocent (Luke 23:14, 15, 20, 22). Compare also Luke 23:47, where the centurion, too, declares that Jesus is innocent. In particular it may be noted that as Jesus was struck by one of the high priest's attendants (John 18:22), so also was Paul (Acts 23:2).

These parallels are important. They are generalized, and receive a partial interpretation (of which Luke himself may not have been fully conscious) in 14:22: there is no entering the kingdom of God except through many hardships (διὰ πολλῶν θλίψεων). Behind this, even if not in Luke's own mind, lurks the notion of the messianic affliction, the time of distress that the people of God must expect before the good time to come, a notion that shows itself here and there in the NT and may have provided the earliest interpretation of the suffering and death of Jesus.[12] The parallels, together with Acts 14:22, do much to establish the Lukan kind of *theologia crucis* that may be seen in Acts.[13] It is, however, possible to exaggerate their importance, for they owe something to the inevitable conventions of the martyrology — inevitable, for no one will write a martyrology unless he or she is convinced of the true innocence of the martyr and its logical accompaniment, the belief that the martyr's death was brought about by the malice (which may to some extent be excused by ignorance — Acts 3:17) of the martyr's opponents; and martyrologies will always try to bring out these convictions. Of course Jesus, Stephen, and Paul were innocent men, and this was recognized by fair-minded third parties (unfortunately not available in the case of Stephen). The parallels, moreover, are qualified by divergence. A notable example that will serve as a starting point is the pair of incidents, mentioned above, in which Jesus and Paul are assaulted in court. Jesus responds in dignified terms: "If I have spoken wickedly, bear witness of the wickedness; if well, why are you striking me?" (John 18:23). Paul reacts to the high priest's order that he should be struck on the mouth with the indignant words, "God will strike you, you white-washed wall; do you sit judging me according to the Law and contrary to the Law command me to be struck?" But he had not recognized whence the order came, and when this is pointed out to him he climbs down: "I did not know, brethren, that he was high priest; for it is written, 'Thou shalt not speak evil of a ruler of thy people'" (Acts 23:1-5).

12. See C. K. Barrett, *Jesus and the Gospel Tradition* (Philadelphia: Fortress, 1968) 44-45; W. Bousset, *Die Religion des Judentums,* HNT 21, 3d ed., rev. by H. Gressmann (Tübingen: J. C. B. Mohr [Paul Siebeck], 1926); and many later works.

13. Barrett, "Theologia Crucis."

The two similar but contrasting incidents are interesting in themselves, but also point further. With reference to Paul's appearance before Festus and Agrippa II, G. Stählin wrote,

> Die Szene erinnert in ihrem Rahmen lebhaft an die Sendung Jesu zu Herodes Antipas (Lk 23.7ff.), sowohl in ihrer Begründung, der Ratlosigkeit des römischen Statthalters, der die Neugier des jüdischen Königs entgegenkam, als auch in ihrem Ausgang, der gemeinsamen Überzeugung von der Schuldlosigkeit des von den Juden so hart verklagten, nur mit dem Unterschied, dass Jesus die ganze Szene mit seinem Schweigen, Paulus dagegen mit seiner Rede beherrscht.[14]

Not only in this incident but throughout the Passion Narrative Jesus' silence under questioning is a striking feature — less noticeable in fact in Luke than in the other Gospels. Paul, on the other hand, makes long speeches: in the temple, before the mob, twenty verses, followed by a conversation with a centurion and with the tribune; in the Sanhedrin, two provocative verses, together with the exchange between Paul and those who strike him at the high priest's instance; twelve verses before Felix, followed by frequent discourse on righteousness, self-discipline, and judgment; two verses before Festus, leading up to the appeal to Caesar; twenty-two verses before Festus and Agrippa, followed by interruption and reply (four verses spoken by Paul). It is worthwhile also to recall Stephen's long speech (fifty-two verses) before the Sanhedrin. These observations point to the fact that, for Luke, apostles and others, such as Stephen, are called to be not models but witnesses (1:8); and Luke understands witnessing to be a task that is carried out in speech. It is of course possible to think (and Paul in his letters does think) of witnessing as expressed in manner of life as well as in speech;[15] Luke's own *theologia crucis,* in which the life and suffering of the apostles and others is modeled on the Passion of Christ, points to this conclusion too. But the conclusion is not one that Luke himself explicitly draws. For him, the apostles' testimony is spoken testimony.

Again, we may ask, To what do the apostles bear witness? Primarily to the resurrection of Jesus. This is the stated purpose of their mission according to 1:22: one must be found to take the place of Judas as a witness of the resurrection. This theme is repeated in most of the early occurrences of μαρτύρειν and cognate words. At 2:32 Peter declares, "This Jesus did God raise up, οὗ πάντες ἡμεῖς ἐσμεν μάρτυρες," and it makes no difference to the essential meaning whether we take οὗ to be masculine (*of whom,* i.e., of the risen Jesus) or neuter (*of which fact,* that God raised him from the dead). At 2:40 it is said that Peter further διεμαρτύρατο; the content of his testimony is not expressed, but it clearly looks back to the theme of resurrection.[16] Acts 3:15 is similar to 2:32,

14. *Die Apostelgeschichte,* NTD 5 (Göttingen: Vandenhoeck & Ruprecht, 1962) 305.
15. C. K. Barrett, *The Signs of an Apostle* (London: Epworth, 1970) 42-44.
16. Cf. also 8:25.

and contains the same unimportant ambiguity (οὗ). At 4:33 it is said that the apostles gave with great power τὸ μαρτύριον τῆς ἀναστάσεως τοῦ κυρίου Ἰησοῦ. Acts 5:32 is similar but a little wider in scope: in μάρτυρες τῶν ῥημάτων τούτων, *these things* include the fact that God raised up Jesus "whom you killed, hanging him on a tree," and exalted him to his right hand as Prince and Savior, to give to Israel repentance and the forgiveness of sins. All still turns on the resurrection. It is of course sufficiently obvious that resurrection implies previous death, and in many passages witness to the resurrection is accompanied by explicit reference to the crucifixion; Peter's Pentecost sermon (2:23-24) provides an example that will carry others with it.[17] It is perhaps significant that this passage also refers to the ministry of Jesus, who was marked out by God in mighty works, portents, and signs, which God did by him "in your midst, as you yourselves know" (2:22), and it is perhaps not unreasonable to think that reference to these mighty works may be assumed even in places where they are not explicitly attached to the proclamation of Jesus' crucifixion and resurrection.

We should perhaps also take up here the few references in Acts to τὰ περὶ τοῦ Ἰησοῦ, or similar expressions. According to 18:25 Apollos ἐδίδασκεν ἀκριβῶς τὰ περὶ τοῦ Ἰησοῦ. It is clear that Luke means to represent Apollos as a good man but as an inadequate Christian preacher until he is instructed by Priscilla and Aquila. Is it conceivable that the things concerning Jesus that he taught accurately enough were the characteristics of his ministry but that he did not yet know the saving events (cf. 4:12) of crucifixion and resurrection? We may guess that this was so, but the fact is that Luke does not say so, and he may very well have been anything but clear in his own mind about Apollos's qualifications and deficiencies. It is also against this suggestion that Luke will hardly have wished to allege, in the last verse of his book (28:31), any deficiency in Paul's work as he taught τὰ περὶ τοῦ κυρίου Ἰησοῦ Χριστοῦ (cf. also 28:23, πείθων . . . περὶ τοῦ Ἰησοῦ).[18]

"The things concerning Jesus" may be no more than a variation on the more characteristic "Whom you crucified, whom God raised from the dead," but passages such as 2:22 do suggest some additional interest. This appears to focus on the miracles. So 2:22, quoted above; also 10:38, where Peter asserts that Jesus of Nazareth was anointed with the Holy Spirit and power and went about doing good and healing all who were overpowered by the devil,[19] for God was with him. It is important that Peter continues in 10:39, "We are witnesses of all the things he did in the land of the Jews and in Jerusalem." There is little more, even if we include the passages, noted above, which refer to the things concerning Jesus. Acts 20:35 implies a teaching ministry of Jesus, even though

17. Cf. 3:13-15; 4:10; 10:39, 40; 13:26-31.

18. Cf. also the expression (τὰ) περὶ τῆς βασιλείας τοῦ θεοῦ (1:3; 8:12; 19:8).

19. The reference is presumably to illness, caused (as was believed) by possession.

the words ascribed to him are a Greek commonplace, contained in none of the Gospels. There is no more.[20]

There is, however, enough to show that Luke believed that the testimony of the apostles to Jesus included some reference to his ministry; and to show that the reference was primarily to works of power. The significant words are δύναμις, τέρας, and σημεῖον; and if these are not frequently mentioned in the verbal testimony of the apostles this is supported and supplemented by their acted testimony, for the same words are used in accounts of their ministry. Δύναμις is used of Jesus at 2:22; 10:38; of apostles (or Stephen or Paul) at 1:8; 4:33; 6:8; 8:13; 19:11 (on 3:12; 4:7, see below). Τέρας is used of Jesus at 2:22; of apostles (or Stephen, Paul, Barnabas, or Silas) at 2:43; 4:30; 5:12; 6:8; 14:3; 15:12; cf. 2:19. Σημεῖον is used of Jesus at 2:22; of apostles (or Stephen, Paul, Barnabas, or Silas at 2:43; 4:16, 22, 30; 5:12; 6:8; 8:6, 13; 14:3; 15:12; cf. 2:19. It is worth noting that Luke uses none of these words for the works of Simon the Magus, though he had astonished the Samaritans by his magical practices (8:9, 11). The apostles (and others) may thus be said to have borne witness to Jesus the healer and wonder-worker not only by their words but by their actions, which were an imitation of his. This is true, but it was evidently something of an embarrassment to Luke — a fact which may account for the small extent to which the miracle-working of Jesus appears in Acts. It has often been maintained that the apostles are represented in Acts as θεῖοι ἄνδρες, divine men possessing in themselves a supernatural power by which they could perform miracles, such as healing the sick (and perhaps on occasion striking down the wicked).[21] This is in fact very nearly — not quite — the opposite of the truth. Not quite, because the apostles are, according to Acts, the agents through whom a divine δύναμις works, and signs and portents are done by their hands; they escape dangers, overcome adversaries, and speak with more than human authority. But when questioned about the δύναμις manifested in the healing of a lame man (see 3:12; 4:7, above) they insist in the strongest terms that it is no power of their own. They are purely human agents of the power of another (10:26; 14:14-18). There is here a particularly clear instance of the observation that the theme of Acts is witness rather than imitation.

We should ask further what it is that is being witnessed to, and, to a limited extent and in a questionable manner, imitated in the deeds of the apostles. It is essentially the power of Jesus; and this creates a problem, for it has often been remarked that, among the Gospels, Luke is notable for its insistence on the humanity and compassion of Jesus. It is true that this phenomenon may have been exaggerated; it is interesting to note that the verb σπλαγχνίζεσθαι, with Jesus as subject, occurs in Matthew four times, in Mark three times (and once when Jesus

20. It may be that we should add 27:35, as a reference to the words of Jesus at the Supper and in the feeding miracles. See also 1:4-5 (11:16); 6:14, which hardly count. See Barrett, "Sayings of Jesus," 683-87.

21. See, e.g., J. M. Robinson and H. Koester, *Trajectories through Early Christianity* (Philadelphia: Fortress, 1971) 191.

is asked to have compassion, and does), and in Luke once.[22] But undoubtedly Jesus regularly in Luke shows concern for those in need, the sick, the poor, the under-privileged. This concern is not reflected to any great extent in Acts, except insofar as it is correct that the mission to the Gentiles, who do not observe the Torah which by definition they do not have, is an extension of the mission of Jesus to the *'am ha-aretz.*[23] This observation, however, is not without complications, for Luke omits the healing of the Syrophoenician woman's daughter (the only cure in the Synoptic Gospels performed for the benefit of a Gentile[24]) and omits also the cleansing of all foods (Mark 7:19) — a pronouncement of which one might suppose that Peter had never heard, in view of his shocked refusal to kill and eat one of a miscellaneous collection of animals presented to him in a vision (Acts 10:11-16). There is no doubt that the extension of the gospel to the Gentiles is one of the major themes, perhaps the most important theme, in Acts, and Luke, through the mouths of various speakers, presents various arguments designed to justify it. The miracles that accompany preaching and conversion are marks of God's favor (15:12); the OT foretells the gathering in of the "rest of humankind" (15:15-18); the gift of the Spirit, manifest in inspired speech, to Gentiles equally with the original Jewish disciples, is a clear proof of divine acceptance (11:15-17; cf. 15:8-9). But Luke never points back to the teaching or action of Jesus in his incarnate ministry as calling for the extension; only after the resurrection (Luke 24:47; Acts 1:8) does Jesus predict a mission outside the confines of Judaism. There is a partial exception to this in the favorable attitude of the Third Gospel to Samaritans; but no appeal is made to this in Acts 8.

The sick are healed in Acts. In Acts 3 a lame man is healed; this is an act of power, and the source of the power is discussed in chs. 3 and 4; there is no hint that a lame man excites our pity. The action is of course a εὐεργεσία (4:9), but the main point here is controversial; how can the Jewish court condemn a good deed? In ch. 9 Peter cures Aeneas and raises Tabitha from death; in ch. 14 Paul cures a lame man in Lystra; in ch. 16 he expels a Python spirit from a girl; in ch. 20 he restores Eutychus to the church at Troas; and in ch. 28 he himself escapes a viper's bite and cures the father of Publius of dysentery. All of these are and are represented as acts of power; it is no more than the truth to say that none of them is accompanied by words or other signs of compassion. Paul casts out the Python in Philippi because he is provoked by the possessed girl's prophesying (16:18, διαπονηθείς). This is not to say that Peter and the rest were not compassionate people or that Luke did not believe them to be moved by compassion; he simply does not go out of his way to say that they were concerned to reproduce the compassion of Jesus. This is true also of the many

22. This is a useful pointer, but not proof. It is not confirmed by study of ἐλεεῖν, ἔλεος.

23. See C. K. Barrett, *New Testament Essays* (London: S.P.C.K., 1972) 23-26.

24. The Gerasene (Gadarene) demoniac may be another example, but this is not made explicit.

general references to cures: 4:30; 5:12-16 (including the apparently automatic effect of Peter's shadow); 6:8; 8:6; 15:12; 19:11-12 (including the apparently automatic effect of Paul's napkins and sweatbands). Power rather than compassion is manifested in these summaries, and with them we may put events that issued unfortunately for those concerned in them: 5:1-11 (it is not said that Peter willed the death of Ananias and Sapphira, but he shows no regret); 12:23 (it would go too far to say that Luke gloats over the death of Herod Agrippa, but he gives the impression that Herod got no more than he deserved); 13:10-11 (Paul strikes the magus Elymas blind); 19:16 (it is hard to think that Luke did not enjoy recording the fate of the sons of Sceva). It is only the leaders of the community — apostles, and others such as Stephen, Philip, Paul, and Barnabas — who work miracles; no one is asked or expected to follow their example in this respect, and if they are following the example of Jesus it is only in that they bear witness to the power that God himself is able to exert in his world.

It is often pointed out that in the Third Gospel women play a larger part than might be expected in a religious work of the first century; it may be enough to illustrate this statistically with the observation that the word γυνή occurs in Matthew 29 times, in Mark 16 times, and in Luke 41 times. Something of this recognition of the contribution made by women to the story of Jesus recurs in Acts. Between the ascension of Jesus and Pentecost the apostles meet together with their wives,[25] and with Mary, the mother of Jesus (1:14). It is a negative but not unimportant fact that Ananias and Sapphira are said to be jointly involved in their attempt to cheat the church's pooling of its resources (5:1-11). At 5:14 multitudes of both men and women are said to be added to the community, just as both are baptized at 8:12. Meanwhile both sexes have persecution to endure (8:3, and again at 9:2; 22:4). Tabitha has taken an active share in charitable work, so that the widows she has benefited lament her death (9:36-42). Timothy had the advantage of having as his mother a believing Jewess (16:1); in the same chapter Paul and Barnabas begin their mission at Philippi by conversing with a group of women, one of whom, Lydia, was apparently a person of some distinction (16:13, 14). Among the few converts in Athens was a woman called Damaris (17:34). At Corinth Paul fell in with a married couple, Aquila and Priscilla (18:2), of whom Priscilla may have been the leading partner; at least she is elsewhere named first (18:18, 26). Wives and children join the farewell party at 21:5. Philip has four daughters who prophesy, probably taking a leading part in the life of the church (21:9). Non-Christian women appear too, sometimes joining in opposition to the Christian movement (13:50; 17:4). Felix is joined by his wife Drusilla (24:24),[26] and Agrippa by his sister Bernice

25. Or, with (certain) women; it makes no difference to the present argument.

26. The Western text, if we may find it in the margin of the Harclean Syriac, finds in Drusilla the reason why Felix summons Paul: His wife Drusilla, who was a Jewess, wished to see Paul and to hear the word; so, willing to satisfy her, [Felix] sent for Paul. . . .

(25:13). Women play for Luke a significant part in society, and, in particular, in the Christian movement. It is important simply that they are there; in addition there are at least five of them who take part in the ministry of education and inspiration. All this, however, Luke takes for granted; he does not say that in it the church was following the example of Jesus; apart from Tabitha, the work of the women falls in the general area of witness rather than that of example.

It remains to ask how Luke thought the ethical life of those of whom he writes was formed and encouraged. Some contribution has already been made toward an answer to this question. As far as the earliest, and some of the later, converts were concerned it was possible to assume a foundation in Judaism;[27] there was none better. There was nothing the Christian Jew had to unlearn,[28] little that he had to add. This "little" might be summed up in 2:42, quoted above; the teaching of the apostles must be heard, the fellowship cherished, the common meals attended, and prayers said. Entry into the new community was often[29] marked by baptism, which was into, or in, the name (εἰς τὸ ὄνομα, ἐν or ἐπὶ τῷ ὀνόματι) of Jesus.[30] It is at this point, perhaps, that we come nearest to the notion of an *imitatio Christi,* for the most probable interpretation of "in the name of" is "so as to become the property of," and those who become the property of Christ will follow their Master and aim at becoming like him. The believing obedience that is expressed in baptism results also in the cleansing of their hearts (15:9). Exactly what is meant by this expression is not clear. Spoken by Paul it might be a synonym for justification; standing where it does in the Apostolic Council it may allude to circumcision — not circumcision but faith is what cleanses a person, and cleanses the person inwardly. Moral renewal may be included, but this cannot be inferred with certainty. Reference to the Council suggests the Decree (15:29); it is often said that whereas the Old Uncial form[31] of this is ceremonial the Western[32] is ethical. In fact, both forms[33] are both ceremonial and ethical, the Decree being understood with varying emphasis as circumstances required. The church was prepared to lay down rules or guide-

27. Jesus' interlocutors knew very well that they ought to keep the commandments, including the two represented as the most important.

28. The "But I say unto you" sayings in the Sermon on the Mount on the whole expand and deepen and do not contradict the law.

29. I say "often" rather than invariably; there are passages in Acts where baptism is clearly taken for granted, others (e.g., 13, 14, 17, 20-28) where it is not mentioned. See C. K. Barrett, *Church, Ministry, and Sacraments in the New Testament* (Exeter: Paternoster, 1985) 59-60.

30. I doubt whether it is possible to distinguish between these formulas, which seem to be used indifferently in Acts. See, however, M. Quesnel, *Baptisés dans l'Esprit,* LD 120 (Paris: Cerf, 1985).

31. In B ℵ and others. Here and in the next note there is no need to cite the evidence in full.

32. In D Ir$^{lat}$ Tert and others.

33. See C. K. Barrett, "The Apostolic Decree of Acts 15:29," *ABR* 35 (1987) 50-59.

lines for the moral life of its members, but there is no reference to the example of Jesus, and the Golden Rule, quoted in the Western text (15:20, 29), is quoted in a different, negative, form from that in which it is ascribed to Jesus (Matt 7:12; Luke 6:31).

There remains for consideration one very important passage, Paul's address to the Ephesian elders (20:18-35). Paul presents himself as an example, at the same time making a characteristic "farewell" defense[34] of his behavior, and showing his hearers how they in turn should conduct themselves: πάντα ὑπέδειξα ὑμῖν (20:35). As he worked to help the weak rather than make himself a burden to others, as he bore in mind the words of Jesus, so should they. This last verse in the speech probably carries with it the earlier part: as Paul was faithful in preaching and pastoral work, vigilant to protect the flock against attack, so must his hearers be (20:28). In the speech Paul testifies orally to the witness borne by his life; and v 35 is at least a hint that his life and ministry pointed back to those of Jesus.

In general, however, the apostles and their colleagues are witnesses rather than examples, and the Jesus to whom they bear witness is a savior rather than an example, though the precise sense in which he is a savior is never clarified as it is for example by Paul; it is clear that those who are saved must follow their Ἀρχηγός, even if to follow means to suffer.

34. See J. Munck, in *Aux Sources de la Tradition Chrétienne,* Mélanges offerts à Maurice Goguel (Neuchâtel et Paris, 1950) 155-70.

# James's Speech (Acts 15:13-21), Simeon's Hymn (Luke 2:29-32), and Luke's Sources

Rainer Riesner

## 1. Simeon in Acts 15:14

In Acts 15 we have the Lukan presentation of the so-called Apostolic Council.[1] According to Luke's account, some Pharisaic-minded Jewish Christians demanded that the Gentile Christians should let themselves be circumcised, and so take upon themselves to obey the whole Mosaic legislation (15:5). After the "apostles and the elders" discussed this at length in Jerusalem, Peter raises his voice and, referring to his own experience, appeals for acceptance of the Gentiles without the law (15:8-11). After this Barnabas and Paul relate "the miraculous signs and wonders God had done among the Gentiles through them" (15:12). The final decision is then brought about through the intervention of James, the brother of the Lord. His speech begins with the words: "Brothers, listen to me. Simeon has explained to us how God at first (from the very beginning) looked favorably on the Gentiles, to take from among them a people for his name. The words of the prophets are in agreement with this, as

1. Reviewing a book in which the author had presented the rather uncommon thesis that the place of the crucifixion was on the Mount of Olives, Howard Marshall concluded: "I found this a fascinating book to read, full of fresh ideas, and my nonconformist mind hoped that he might be right and prove the scholars wrong." One of the joys of meeting with Howard Marshall is his notable lack of prejudice and openness to new suggestions, which he always hears accurately before judiciously analyzing them. It is for this reason that I dare to dedicate to him the following contribution in celebration of his 60th birthday. In what follows an interpretation of Acts 15:14 will be introduced that may on first hearing sound somewhat novel. See I. Howard Marshall, Review of *Secrets of Golgotha: The Forgotten History of Christ's Crucifixion,* by E. L. Martin (Alhambra, California: SK Publications, 1988), in *EvQ* 62 (1990) 361-64 (364). For the location of the places of crucifixion and resurrection, cf. R. Riesner, "Golgatha," in *Das Grosse Bibellexikon,* vol. 1, 2d ed., ed. H. Burkhardt et al. (Wuppertal: R. Brockhaus; Giessen: Brunnen, 1990) 480-82. I am most grateful to Mag. theol. Tiina Schilling (Gomaringen) for her help in preparing the English version of this essay.

it is written . . ." (15:13-15). James appeals primarily to Amos 9:11-12, though there are echoes of other prophecies both at the beginning (Jer 12:15 or Amos 7:12) and end (Isa 45:21) of his "quotation." This citation serves James as an introduction for his suggestion that only the four minimal ritual requirements should be put upon the Gentile Christians, and this, presumably, to permit table fellowship with Jewish Christians (15:19-21).

There is a linguistic aspect of note in the speech of James. While the leader of the twelve disciples shortly before (15:7) was called by his most common NT name Peter (Πέτρος), it seems that the brother of the Lord addresses him rather by his original Semitic name Simeon (Συμεών, שִׁמְעוֹן, 15:14). According to E. Haenchen, the whole speech is not originally from James but a construction of Luke. But Luke has taken pains, again according to Haenchen, to give a certain fitting coloring: "Mit der Form Συμεών deutet Lukas an, daß Jakobus, der Herrenbruder, aramäisch spricht."[2] This is indeed the opinion of many modern commentaries on Acts,[3] of which that of J. Roloff may be representative: "Lukas hat diese archaisierende Form wohl gewählt, um das Lokalkolorit zu verstärken."[4]

Rudolf Pesch comes to a quite different conclusion: "Jakobus spricht von Petrus als 'Simeon' (vgl. 2Petr 1,1); der Text bietet die griechische Transkription seines hebräischen Namens. Ob Jakobus mit der Rede von Symeon statt von Kephas Reserven gegenüber dem 'Felsenmann' zum Ausdruck bringt, mag erwogen werden; jedenfalls stoßen wir auf vorluk[anische] Tradition, nicht auf archaisierende Redaktion des Lukas."[5] The supposition that the Hebraic name Simeon indicates a pre-Lukan source was popular among older exegetes, not all of them especially conservative ones.[6] John A. T. Robinson, in his customary

2. *Die Apostelgeschichte* (Göttingen: Vandenhoeck & Ruprecht, 1977) 430.

3. H. J. Cadbury, *The Making of Luke-Acts* (London: S.P.C.K., 1927) 227-28; O. Bauernfeind, *Die Apostelgeschichte,* THKNT 5 (Leipzig: Deichert, 1939) 191; H. Conzelmann, *Die Apostelgeschichte,* HNT 7 (Tübingen: J. C. B. Mohr [Paul Siebeck], 1972) 92; G. Schneider, *Die Apostelgeschichte,* vol. 2, HTKNT 5.2 (Freiburg: Herder, 1982) 182; G. Schille, *Die Apostelgeschichte,* THKNT 5 (Berlin / Ost: EVA, 1983) 320-21; G. Lüdemann, *Das frühe Christentum nach den Traditionen der Apostelgeschichte: Ein Kommentar* (Göttingen: Vandenhoeck & Ruprecht, 1987) 174.

4. *Die Apostelgeschichte,* NTD 5 (Göttingen: Vandenhoeck & Ruprecht, 1981) 231-32.

5. *Die Apostelgeschichte,* vol. 2, EKKNT 5.2 (Zürich: Benziger; Neukirchen-Vluyn: Neukirchener, 1986) 79. Some older scholars had already detected a critical undertone in James's use of "Simeon" — cf. H. A. W. Meyer, *Die Apostelgeschichte,* KEK 3 (Göttingen: Vandenhoeck & Ruprecht, 1870) 332. Others, however, have heard quite the opposite: "Probably the use of this typical Jewish name denotes a close relationship between James and Peter. By calling Peter by his Jewish name, James demonstrates that he agrees wholeheartedly with Peter's account of his visit to Cornelius in Caesarea. Perhaps the use of Peter's Jewish name is meant to influence the Judaizers" (S. J. Kistemaker, *Exposition of the Acts of the Apostles,* NTC [Grand Rapids, Michigan: Baker, 1990] 550-51).

6. E. Preuschen, *Die Apostelgeschichte,* HNT 5.1 (Tübingen: J. C. B. Mohr [Paul Siebeck], 1912) 95; T. Zahn, *Die Apostelgeschichte des Lukas,* vol. 2 (Leipzig / Erlangen: Deichert, 1921) 513-14; E. J. Bicknell, *The Acts of the Apostles,* in *A New Commentary on Holy Scripture,* ed. C. Gore et al. (London: SPCK, 1928) 358; H. W. Beyer, *Die Apostelgeschichte,* NTD 5 (Göttingen: Vanden-

unconventional way, tried to lend further support to this understanding. Supposing that Jude, the brother of the Lord, was the secretary for 2 Peter, where the name Simeon is, indeed, used for Peter (2 Pet 1:1), Robinson concluded concerning James's address in Acts 15:14: "It was in the family."[7]

The distinctive name Simeon here has only rarely been taken to refer to someone *other* than Peter.[8] But I came across this (at the time irritating) claim by R. Feneberg in a semipopular exegetical article: "Beim Apostelkonzil verteidigt zuerst Petrus die Zulassung der Heiden ohne Beschneidung mit Berufung auf diese Erfahrung [der Geisttaufe] beim heidnischen Hauptmann (Apg. 15,7-9). Dann ergreift Jakobus das Wort und erinnert an die Weissagung des Simeon [Lk 2,32], in der die besondere Sendung Jesu inhaltlich benannt ist: Jesus soll aus Heiden ein Volk für Gott gewinnen (Apg 15,14)."[9] His brother W. Feneberg recently adopted this interpretation in an original work on the apostle Paul. There he remarks concerning the speech of James in Acts 15: "Dazu kommt eine persönliche Erfahrung des Bruders Jesu: Symeon hat über das Kind Jesus bereits das prophetische Wort gesprochen, daß sich in ihm Jes[aja] 49,6 erfüllt: Er ist der Gottesknecht, 'bereitet vor allen Völkern, ein Licht zu erleuchten die Heiden und zum Preis deines Volkes Israel' (Lk 2,31f)."[10] At first, I was inclined to dismiss this opinion as absurd.[11] But, as I started to research the matter more closely, the first thing I found was that it is indeed a very old interpretation.

---

hoeck & Ruprecht, 1949) 94-95; J. Kürzinger, *Die Apostelgeschichte,* EB (Würzburg: Echter, 1951) 58. But cf. also W. Dietrich, *Das Petrusbild der lukanischen Schriften,* BWANT 94 (Stuttgart: Kohlhammer, 1972) 312-13.

7. *Redating the New Testament* (London: SCM, 1976) 194. There is another curious similarity between Acts 15:14 ("Men and brothers, listen to me") and Jas 2:5 ("Listen, my beloved brothers"). Kistemaker (*Acts,* 550) points out: "The command *listen to me* occurs nowhere else in the entire New Testament."

8. Those scholars who distinguish Cephas and Simon Peter as two distinct people do not comment on our passage. Cf. K. Lake, "Simon — Cephas — Peter," *HTR* 14 (1921) 95-97; G. La Piana, "Cephas and Peter in the Epistle to the Galatians," *HTR* 14 (1921) 187-93; M. Goguel, *La foi à la resurrection de Jésus dans le Christianisme primitif* (Paris: Payot, 1933) 272-75; D. W. Riddle, "The Cephas-Peter Problem, and a Possible Solution," *JBL* 59 (1940) 168-80; C. H. Henze, "Cephas Seu Kephas Non est Simon Petrus!," *DivTh* 61 (1958) 63-67. Recently, B. D. Ehrman, "Cephas and Peter," *JBL* 109 (1990) 463-74, has warmed to the occasional early church opinion (beginning with the *Epistle to the Apostles* 2 and Clement of Alexandria [in Eusebius *Hist. Eccl.* 1.12.2]), which referred the two names to different people. But this opinion is easily explained by their ignorance of Semitic languages and by the desire to relieve Peter of the Antiochene conflict (Gal 2:12ff.). Cf. Pseudo-Dorotheus (ed. T. Schermann 141, but against this view Hieronymus *Comm. Gal.* 1:2). Ehrman's essay is a good illustration of the problems caused by the belief that one can dispense with Acts as a source enriching and controlling the exegesis of Paul's letters. Unfortunately, Ehrman did not discuss or even mention J. A. Fitzmyer's articles (see below, n. 56) on the problem of the names.

9. "Johannes und Jesus — zwei Rivalen," *Entschluss* 39 (1984) 4-7 (6).

10. *Paulus der Weltenbürger: Eine Biographie* (München: Kösel, 1992) 111-12.

11. Typical is J. W. Packer, *The Acts of the Apostles,* CBC (Cambridge: Cambridge University, 1964) 126: "Identification with anyone else of the name . . . seems entirely out of place."

## 2. A Patristic Testimony

In the year 400 or 401 John Chrysostom preached 55 sermons on Acts[12] in Constantinople (*PGM* 60:13-384).[13] This Church Father was not only an impassioned preacher, but, according to the well-known text-critic C. R. Gregory, "ein klarsehender, scharf denkender, sorgfältig schreibender Philolog, der sich in die heilige Schrift vertieft."[14] Accordingly, Chrysostom, who did not interpret Acts in a purely devotional way, but always sought to give exegetical suggestions, made this tantalizing comment in his thirty-third sermon[15] on Acts 15:14 (*In Acta Hom.* 33:1):

> Καὶ τί φησιν; Ἄνδρες ἀδελφοί, ἀκούσατέ μου. Συμεὼν ἐξηγήσατο. τινὲς τοῦτον εἶναί φασι τὸν ὑπὸ τοῦ Λουκᾶ εἰρημένον· ἄλλοι δὲ ἕτερον ὁμώνυμον τούτῳ. εἴτε δὲ οὗτος, εἴτε ἐκεῖνός ἐστιν, οὐκ ἀκριβολογεῖσθαι χρή, ἀλλὰ μόνον ὡς ἀναγκαῖα δέχεσθαι ἃ ἐξηγήσατο

> And what does he say? "Brothers, listen to me. Simeon has explained to us." Some say, this is the one that Luke told about; some that it refers to another person who had the same name. But it is not necessary to say definitely whether it was this or that one, what is necessary is to accept what he has pointed out.

This represents the longer text-form we have in the edition of J.-P. Migne,[16] following the text of B. de Montfaucon.[17] But there is also a shorter version[18] explained in a catena by the words put in brackets, namely a citation from the *Nunc Dimittis* in the Gospel according to Luke (Luke 2:29):[19]

12. For the earlier date see C. Baur, *Der Heilige Johannes Chrysostomus und seine Zeit II* (München: Kösel, 1930) 84; and L. Meyer, *Saint Jean Chrysostome maître de la perfection chrétienne* (Paris: Beauchêsne, 1933) XXXVI; for the later date, K. Baus, "Johannes Chrysostomus," *LTK*, vol. 5 (Freiburg: Herder, 1960) 1018-21 (1019). On the personality and theology of the Church Father, cf. recently J.-M. Leroux, "Johannes Chrysostomus," *TRE*, vol. 17 (Berlin / New York: de Gruyter, 1988) 118-27.

13. Four earlier homilies on Acts preached at Antioch (*PGM* 51:65-112) do not mention our text.

14. *Einleitung in das Neue Testament* (Leipzig: Deichert, 1909) 369.

15. A modern German translation is lacking, but one can find a rather old one in J. A. Cramer, *Des heiligen Kirchenlehrers Johannes Chrysostomus Predigten und kleine Schriften I / II* (Augsburg / Innsbruck: J. Wolff, 1772). The English-speaking world is well served by P. Schaff, ed., *A Select Library of the Nicene and Post-Nicene Fathers of the Christian Church*, vol. 11: *Saint Chrysostom: Homilies on the Acts of the Apostles and the Epistle to the Romans* (Grand Rapids, Michigan: Wm. B. Eerdmans, 1889) 205-12.

16. *S.P.N. Joannis Chrysostomi . . . opera omnia IX, PGM* 60 (Paris: Migne, 1862) 239.

17. *Ioannis Chrysostomi opera omnia*, vol. 9: *Homiliae LV in Acta Apostolorum* (Paris, 1731) 253 D.

18. H. Savile, *Ioanni Chrysostomi Opera Omnia IV* (Eton, 1613) 795.

19. J. A. Cramer, *Catena in Acta SS. Apostolorum . . .* (Oxford, 1838) 248.

Καὶ τί φησιν; Ἄνδρες ἀδελφοί, ἀκούσατέ μου. Συμεὼν ἐξηγήσατο, ὁ ἐν τῷ Λουκᾷ προφητεύσας· (νῦν ἀπολύεις τὸν δοῦλόν σου, Δέσποτα)

And what does he say? "Brothers, listen to me. Simeon has explained" — the one that in the Gospel of Luke prophesied: ("You now dismiss your servant in peace").

Modern interpretation of Acts has hardly noticed this patristic testimony. There is not even a reference to it in those older Catholic commentaries on Acts, which deliberately referred to patristic writings.[20] F. F. Bruce,[21] who often offers unusual information, does not mention this testimony either. Kirsopp Lake and H. J. Cadbury were exceptions.[22] It was through these authors that S. Giet learned of the striking patristic opinion.[23] He supposed, on the basis of the longer text-form, that the Simeon here referred to the Antiochene "teacher and prophet" Simeon Niger (Acts 13:1) or to some other member of the congregation. This hypothesis was used by Giet to support his more comprehensive thesis that Acts 15:13-21 does not continue the description of the Apostolic Council, but that we have here the account of a different incident. According to Giet, certain problems were discussed in this later meeting — problems that arose in the mixed congregation of Antioch and were then settled through the so-called "apostolic decree" (Acts 15:23-29; cf. 15:19-21). Without knowing this citation from Chrysostom, A. Mentz (whom Giet overlooks) earlier made a similar identification with Simeon Niger, but on the basis of other literary- critical considerations.[24] Among the contemporary commentators, J. A. Fitzmyer[25] and G. A. Krodel[26] consider it at least possible that Simeon Niger was the intended referent of the pre-Lukan tradition, while Luke has identified Simeon with Peter instead.

20. J. E. Belser, *Die Apostelgeschichte* (Wien: Mayer, 1905) 192; E. Jacquier, *Les Actes des Apôtres,* EBib (Paris: Lecoffre [J. Gabalda], 1926) 452; A. Steinmann, *Die Apostelgeschichte* (Bonn: Hanstein, 1934) 160; C. S. Dessain, *Acts,* in *A Catholic Commentary on Holy Scripture,* ed. B. Orchard (London: Nelson, 1953) 1036; A. Wikenhauser, *Die Apostelgeschichte,* RNT 5 (Regensburg: Pustet, 1961) 172.

21. *The Acts of the Apostles,* 3d ed. (Grand Rapids, Michigan: Wm. B. Eerdmans, 1990) 339.

22. *The Acts of the Apostles, The Beginnings of Christianity,* vol. 1.4, ed. F. J. Foakes-Jackson and K. Lake (London: Macmillan, 1933) 175. The tradition was even not discussed by the coeditor of the composite work, F. J. Foakes-Jackson, *The Acts of the Apostles,* MNTC (London: Hodder & Stoughton, 1931) 139.

23. "L'assemblée apostolique et le décret de Jérusalem," *RevScRel* 39 (1951-52) 203-22.

24. "Die Zusammenkunft der Apostel in Jerusalem und die Quellen der Apostelgeschichte," *ZNW* 18 (1917-18) 177-95 (180-82). Mentz thought of Acts 11:27–14:28 and 15:1–16:6 as parallel narratives.

25. "A Life of Paul," in *The Jerome Bible Commentary,* ed. R. E. Brown et al., vol. 2 (London: Chapman, 1968) 220; likewise R. J. Dillon and J. A. Fitzmyer, "Acts of the Apostles," in *Jerome Bible Commentary,* 195. In the re-edition of the commentary this opinion is apparently dropped by R. J. Dillon, "The Acts of the Apostles," in *The New Jerome Bible Commentary,* ed. R. E. Brown et al. (Englewood Cliffs: Prentice-Hall, 1990) 752.

26. *Acts,* ACNT (Minneapolis: Augsburg, 1986) 280.

One must, however, strongly question the identification with Simeon Niger. It is certain that the longer text-form of Chrysostom's remark is secondary to the shorter one. The shorter text-form had already been chosen by P. Schaff in his edition of the Nicene and post-Nicene Fathers.[27] Later E. R. Smothers was to give detailed arguments in support of this text-critical evaluation.[28] As far as the language is concerned, either variant could equally be ascribed to Chrysostom. But the suggestion made in the longer text runs entirely counter to the Father's usual policy, for here the investigation of an exegetical problem is left aside for merely pious reasons. However, we need not rely on internal criteria alone for a decision on this text-critical problem. The known manuscripts of Chrysostom's writings belong clearly to two recensions, and one of these recensions (the one with the long form) is indisputably a secondary revision. This judgment is confirmed by the fact that the existing catenas of Acts use only the unrevised text-form of Chrysostom's homilies. Essentially the same text-critical judgment was reached some time ago by H. Browne,[29] and it was further substantiated more recently by E. R. Smothers[30] through his analysis of the biblical text the manuscripts use in each case. The revised text-form has more thoroughly assimilated the citations to the *textus receptus* of Acts. What is then important for our investigation is that it is the *unrevised* text-form of Chrysostom which gives the shorter text. So both the external and the internal criteria speak for the originality of the short form.

It follows then that Chrysostom clearly identified Simeon in Acts 15:14 with the Jewish prophet of the same name in the Lukan birth narrative (Luke 2:25-35). This identification also fits very well the introductory words of his sermon in which Chrysostom says about James: "See how discerning he is — he gives reasons for his argument both from the old and the new prophets (ἀπό τε νέων, ἀπό τε παλαιῶν βεβαιουμένου τῶν προφητῶν τὸν λόγον)" (*In Acta Hom.* 33 *in initio* [*PGM* 60:239]). The only place in Luke where one can find a "new" prophecy about the Gentiles is in Simeon's oracle in the second chapter of the Gospel. E. R. Smothers, however, thinks Chrysostom arrived at such a (wrong) conclusion only on the basis of the distinctive form of the name "Simeon." This requires us to press the question whether the Church Father merely produces here a well-intentioned exegetical novelty, or whether his affirmation rests in older tradition.

Chrysostom's work apart, we have only one patristic commentary on this passage of Acts: that of Irenaeus — though this writing is less of a commentary than a paraphrase of the text of Acts. Smothers has sought cautiously to deduce

27. *Chrysostom: Homilies,* 205-6.

28. "Chrysostom and Symeon (Acts XV,14)," *HTR* 46 (1953) 203-15.

29. *The Homilies of S. John Chrysostom on the Acts of the Apostles II,* LoF 35 (Oxford, 1852).

30. "Le Texte des Homélies de saint Jean Chrysostome sur les Actes des Apôtres," *RSR* 27 (1937) 513-48.

Irenaeus's opinion on our issue from the words of the single existing Latin text, "*Post quem Iacobus dixit: Viri fratres, Simon retulit*" (*Adv. Haer.* 3.12.14 [ed. W. W. Harvey, 2:69]). The form of the name "Simon" instead of "Simeon" might suggest, according to Smothers, that Irenaeus understood the referent to be Peter.[31] But here too textual criticism must have the last word. According to the stemma of Irenaeus's manuscripts worked out for the newest historical-critical edition[32] we should follow those manuscripts that have the form "*Simeon*."[33] Irenaeus's testimony, then, appears no more decisive than that of Acts itself. Nevertheless, one consideration remains which might incline us to the view that Chrysostom was reproducing a tradition that existed before him. Lake and Cadbury had already found it difficult to explain in other terms how the Church Father could possibly state his opinion so apparently naturally and self-confidently.[34] This observation becomes especially telling when we remember that Chrysostom was for the longest period of his ministry a teacher in the church in Antioch: it was this city that carried many traditions about Peter[35] and also was claimed to be the hometown of Luke, the Evangelist.[36]

## 3. Acts 15 and Luke's Special Tradition

Among the newer commentaries, C. S. C. Williams discusses the question of Chrysostom's comment on Simeon. Without deciding in favor of the alternatives Williams simply comments, "It is striking that Luke should put into James' mouth the 'Hebrew' form of this name found elsewhere in the NT only in 2 Pet i.1."[37] If the unusual Semitic form of the name could convincingly be explained away as a stylistic trick of Luke's, then there would be no need to waste time and energy in the hunt for an older tradition behind Chrysostom's words about Simeon. But if the substance of Acts 15 should prove essentially to derive from

31. "Chrysostom and Symeon," 205.

32. Cf. A. Rousseau and L. Doutreleau, *Irénée de Lyon: Contre les hérésies, Livre III,* SC 210.1 (Paris: Cerf, 1974) 19-23.

33. Smothers, "Chrysostom and Symeon," 240.

34. *Acts,* 175.

35. Cf. G. Downey, *A History of Antioch in Syria from Seleucus to the Arab Conquest* (Princeton: Princeton University, 1961) *passim.*

36. A modern and well-informed defense of the traditional authorship of Luke-Acts (cf. Phlm 24; Col 4:14) is given by C. J. Thornton, *Der Zeuge des Zeugen: Lukas als Historiker der Paulusreisen,* WUNT 56 (Tübingen: J. C. B. Mohr [Paul Siebeck], 1991). For Luke's connection with Antioch, cf. A. Strobel, "Lukas der Antiochener (Bemerkungen zu Act 11,28D)," *ZNW* 49 (1958) 131-34; R. T. Glover, "'Luke the Antiochene' and Acts," *NTS* 11 (1964-65) 97-106; J. A. Fitzmyer, *The Gospel according to Luke,* vol. 1, AB 28 (Garden City, New York: Doubleday, 1981) 41-47. Still worth reading is A. von Harnack, *Lukas der Arzt, der Verfasser des dritten Evangeliums und der Apostelgeschichte,* BENT 1 (Leipzig: Hinrichs, 1906) 15-17.

37. *The Acts of the Apostles,* BNTC (London: Black, 1964) 180.

a pre-Lukan tradition, then it may be altogether worthwhile — inspired by the patristic hint — to pursue the question whether there is not a connection between James's speech (Acts 15:13-21) and Simeon's hymn (Luke 2:29-32). Actually, strong indications speak for the fact that there is an earlier layer of tradition behind this chapter of Acts.[38]

While the linguistic indications of Semitic-colored sources and traditions are in general limited to Acts 1–12, Acts 15 is a clear exception.[39] Here I mention only those observations that pertain to the relevant section, the speech of James (Acts 15:13-21):

(1) ἐπισκέπτεσθαι as the expression for the eschatological intervention of God (Acts 15:14) is a common word in Luke's special sources (Luke 1:68, 78; 7:16; cf. 19:44).[40] A beautiful parallel to an equivalent use of the Hebrew בקר can be found in a newly published Qumran text (4Q521): "The Lord will visit the pious ones (הסידים יבקר) and call the righteous ones by name."[41]

(2) The construction of ἐπισκέπτεσθαι with the infinitive (Acts 15:14) could be due to Hebrew influence.[42]

(3) The idiom λαὸς ἐξ ἐθνῶν (Acts 15:14) — the "*egregium paradoxon*" (to use the words of J. A. Bengel)[43] — does not necessarily need to come from the LXX, but may also be developed on the basis of the Hebrew Bible (Deut 26:18-19).[44]

(4) We have the expression "a people for his name" (Acts 15:14): while this appears neither in the MT nor in the LXX, it is a standard expression in the old Palestinian Targums.[45]

38. So recently, if in very different ways, A. Weiser, *Die Apostelgeschichte*, vol. 2, ÖTK 5.2 (Gütersloh: Gütersloher; Würzburg: Echter, 1985) 367-77; Pesch, *Apostelgeschichte*, 71-74; Lüdemann, *Das frühe Christentum*, 172-79.

39. Cf. R. A. Martin, "Syntactical Evidence of Aramaic Sources in Acts I-XV," *NTS* 11 (1964-65) 38-59; M. Wilcox, *The Semitisms of Acts* (Oxford: Oxford University, 1965) *passim;* M. Black, *An Aramaic Approach to the Gospels and Acts*, 3d ed. (Oxford: Oxford University, 1967) *passim.*

40. Cf. J. Jeremias, *Die Sprache des Lukasevangeliums*, KKNT (Göttingen: Vandenhoeck & Ruprecht, 1980) 73.

41. R. H. Eisenman and J. M. Robinson, *A Facsimile Edition of the Dead Sea Scrolls*, vol. 2 (Washington: Biblical Archaeology Society, 1992) plate 1551. A good photograph may also be found in *BARev* 17 (1991) 65. The text may be relevant for the symbolism of the dove in the story of Jesus' baptism (Matt 3:16 // Mark 1:10 // Luke 3:21-22); cf. D. C. Allison Jr., "The Baptism of Jesus and a New Dead Sea Scroll," *BARev* 18 (1992) 58-60.

42. So E. Delebecque, *Les Actes des Apôtres*, Collection d'Études anciennes (Paris: Société d'édition, 1982) 73-74 n. 14. Cf. also BDF § 392.3.

43. *Gnomon Novi Testamenti*, ed. E. Bengel (Tübingen: Fues, 1855) 480.

44. Against J. Dupont, "ΛΑΟΣ 'ΕΞ 'ΕΘΝΩΝ (Ac 15,14)," *NTS* 3 (1956-57) 47-50 (= *Études sur les Actes des Apôtres*, LD 45 [Paris, Cerf, 1967] 361-65)]; cf. P. Winter, "Miszellen zur Apostelgeschichte 2. Acta 15,15 und die lukanische Kompositionstechnik," *ZNW* 17 (1957) 398-406 (399-402).

45. Cf. N. A. Dahl, "'A People for his Name' (Acts XV.14)," *NTS* 4 (1957-58) 319-27 (320).

(5) In spite of some modern objections,[46] it cannot be denied that the form of the citation of Amos 9:11 in Acts 15:16 is closest not to the LXX but to the OT text in the Damascus Scroll (CD 7:16) and in the collection of messianic testimonies at Qumran (4QFlor 1:12).[47]

(6) The citation of Amos 9:12 in Acts 15:17 is more problematical. Although there are many differences between the text of Amos 9:12 in the LXX and in Acts, there is still a correspondence between these texts, when one compares how essentially the text of Acts differs from the MT. It is therefore possible that in concluding the citation Luke has followed the LXX text rather more closely than in the beginning.[48] But it could also be that both the LXX and Acts 15:17 together rest on a Hebrew text of Amos 9:12 slightly different from that of the MT — or at least that the same reinterpreting Jewish exegesis lies in the background.[49] If "the rest of people will search out God" (יִדְרְשׁוּ אֵל שְׁאֵרִית אָדָם) were read instead of the Masoretic "they will possess the remnant of Edom" (אֶת־שְׁאֵרִית אֱדוֹם יִירְשׁוּ), the changes in the consonants would be so small as to provide a plausible explanation.

(7) The initial phrase καθὼς γέγραπται (Acts 15:15) that corresponds with 4QFlor 1:12 (כאשר כתוב) could suggest that the Amos-citation of Acts also originates from such a compilation.[50]

(8) The way in which James relates the Holy Scripture both to the past and

---

Apparently this criticism was accepted by J. Dupont, "Un Peuple d'entre les Nations (Actes 15.14)," *NTS* 31 (1985) 321-35 (330 n. 7).

46. Cf. E. Richard, "The Old Testament in Acts: Wilcox's Semitisms in Retrospect," *CBQ* 42 (1980) 330-41 (339); J. Dupont, "'Je rebâtirai la cabane de David qui est tombée' (Ac 15,16 = Am 9,11)," in *Glaube und Eschatologie: Festschrift für Werner Georg Kümmel,* ed. E. Grässer and O. Merk (Tübingen: J. C. B. Mohr [Paul Siebeck], 1985) 19-32 (esp. 22-27).

47. So already (for CD 7:16) C. Rabin, *The Zadokite Documents* (Oxford: Clarendon, 1954, 1958) 29. Cf. also W. H. Brownlee, *The Meaning of the Qumran Scrolls for the Bible* (New York: Oxford University, 1964) 88-89; Wilcox, *Semitisms of Acts,* 49; J. de Waard, *A Comparative Study of the Old Testament Text in the Dead Sea Scrolls and in the New Testament,* STDJ 4 (Leiden: E. J. Brill, 1966) 24-26; G. J. Brooke, *Exegesis at Qumran: 4QFlorilegium in Its Jewish Context,* JSOTSS 29 (Sheffield: JSOT, 1985) 210-11.

48. Cf. T. Holtz, *Untersuchungen über die alttestamentlichen Zitate bei Lukas,* TU 104 (Berlin / Ost: Akademie, 1968) 21-27.

49. Cf. M. A. Braun, "James' Use of Amos at the Jerusalem Council: Steps toward a Possible Solution of the Textual and Theological Problems," *JETS* 20 (1977) 113-21 (114-17). I. H. Marshall, *Acts,* TNTC (Leicester: Inter-Varsity, 1980) 262-63, also allows this possibility. In the context of the linguistic situation in Palestine (M. Hengel, *The 'Hellenization' of Judaea in the First Century after Christ* [London: SCM; Philadelphia: Trinity, 1989] 7-29), and given that we have to do with an exchange involving Jews from the Diaspora, we cannot discount the possibility that the discussions at the Jerusalem Council were in Greek (W. Neil, *The Acts of the Apostles,* NCBC [London: Oliphants, 1973] 173). It is another question whether a conservative Jewish Christian like James would base a scriptural proof on the LXX version.

50. This seems possible in the eyes of such different authors as Conzelmann, *Apostelgeschichte,* 84; and Neil, *Acts,* 173.

to the matters then currently under discussion, is reminiscent of the rabbinical method of exegesis in the *Midrash Yelammedenu.*[51]

Paul Feine, whose study is still of interest on issues of Lukan source criticism, has argued that the same written document lies behind much of Luke's special material in the Gospel and chs. 1–12 of Acts.[52] Certain aspects of the language and the contents show, according to Feine, that this writing comes from Jewish-Christian circles in Jerusalem before 70. Feine explicitly left Acts 15 outside this tradition.[53] However, there are some reasons as well for considering whether Acts 15 does not belong with the supposed source. Not only the word ἐπισκέπτεσθαι, which is typical of older sources in Luke, but also the Semitic or even Hebraizing character of the language and a certain closeness to the language and thoughts of the Qumran literature are all reminiscent of the characteristics of Luke's special material in the Gospel.[54] Besides that, some of the themes in Acts 15:14 significantly match characteristic themes of this tradition.

## 4. James's Speech and Simeon's Hymn

Nowhere else in his double work does Luke call Peter Συμεών. The textual history of the beginning of the second letter of Peter with the double name Συμεών Πέτρος (1:1) shows that this Hebraic form of the name was indeed not natural for him. Already the oldest manuscript $P^{72}$, as also Codex Vaticanus, has changed it to the more familiar hellenized form Σίμων.[55] If Luke's intent in Acts 15:14 is simply to give local coloring, why does he not use Συμεών in the Gospel too? If he supposed that the speech of James in Jerusalem was spoken in Aramaic, he must have known that people around Jesus also mostly spoke this language. Readers of Acts who come to this book for the first time without knowing the Gospel would not even be aware that Peter also had another name (whether Simon or Simeon). It is only in the

51. Cf. J. W. Bowker, "Speeches in Acts: A Study in Proem and Yelammedenu Form," *NTS* 14 (1967-68) 96-111 (107-9).

52. *Eine vorkanonische Überlieferung des Lukas in Evangelium und Apostelgeschichte* (Gotha: F. A. Perthes, 1891) 156-212.

53. *Überlieferung,* 211-12.

54. Cf. R. Riesner, "Prägung und Herkunft der lukanischen Sonderüberlieferung," *TBei* 24 (1993) 228-48.

55. Even if both variants find nearly the same support in early manuscripts, Συμεών is clearly the *lectio difficilior.* Cf. B. M. Metzger, *A Textual Commentary on the Greek New Testament,* 2d ed. (London / New York: United Bible Societies, 1975) 699. For the change of both name forms in different textual traditions, cf. J. Blinzler, "Simon der Apostel, Simon der Herrenbruder und Bischof Symeon von Jerusalem," in *Passauer Studien: Festschrift für . . . Simon Konrad Landersdorfer* (Passau: Passavia, 1953) 25-55 (51).

Gospel that this becomes apparent, and invariably in the hellenized form Σίμων;[56] and, indeed, a glance at the distribution suggests that it is there a word that marks a *source* (Luke 4:38; 5:3, 4, 5, 8, 10; 6:14; 22:31; 24:34).[57] That a source has been used also seems to provide the best explanation for the appearance of Συμεών in Acts 15:14; but that accepted, we need to remember that we have then no reason to exclude from the outset the possibility that it referred to someone other than Peter.

Conventional exegesis understands the clause Συμεὼν ἐξηγήσατο in Acts 15:14 to make James refer to Peter's report on Cornelius's conversion (Acts 15:7-11; cf. Acts 10:1–11:18). But it is questionable whether the term ἐξηγεῖσθαι here means simply "explain" or "recount, report."[58] In the Greek of NT times the verb is predominantly used in religious contexts and usually has the sense "to interpret" (e.g., Holy Scripture, dreams, oracles).[59] Most significantly, Philo (*Spec. Leg.* 2.159; *Vit. Cont.* 78) and Josephus (*J.W.* 1.649; 2.162; *Ant.* 18.149) also use words of the ἐξηγ- group with this meaning. And all five uses of ἐξηγεῖσθαι in the Lukan double work (Luke 24:35; Acts 10:8; 15:12,14; 21:19) also refer to such religious matters. Actually, the LXX usually employs ἐξηγεῖσθαι to render ספר, but occasionally it may translate ירה ("teach") as, for example, in Lev 14:57 LXX. John 1:18 (μονογενὴς θεὸς ὁ ὢν εἰς τὸν κόλπον τοῦ πατρὸς ἐκεῖνος ἐξηγήσατο) is the only non-Lukan evidence in the NT, and here, in any case, the meaning "to explain, teach" (as a revelation) provides the apparent nuance. In this instance A. Schlatter has taken פרש as the possible

56. For the different forms of the name, cf. J. A. Fitzmyer, "The Name Simon," in *Essays on the Semitic Background of the New Testament* (London: Chapman, 1971) 105-12; *idem,* "Aramaic *Kepha*' and Peter's Name in the New Testament," in *To Advance the Gospel: New Testament Studies* (New York: Crossroad, 1981) 112-24. C. Roth, "Simon — Peter," *HTR* 54 (1961) 91-97, thought that the name "Simeon" was deliberately avoided in NT times. This thesis is accepted by A. E. Harvey, "The Testament of Simeon Peter," in *A Tribute to Geza Vermes: Essays on Jewish and Christian Literature and History,* ed. P. R. Davies and R. T. White, JSOTSS 100 (Sheffield: JSOT, 1990) 339-54 (353 n. 14) without mentioning the criticisms of Fitzmyer. Harvey sees an admittedly rather complicated redactional link between Symeon's hymn and James's speech: "Luke may have been deliberately seeking to rehabilitate the name when he made a certain 'just and devout' Simeon appear on the scene straight after Jesus' circumcision. The patriarch Simeon . . . had deceitfully insisted on all the men of Shechem being circumcised before putting them to the sword to avenge the abduction of his sister Dinah (Gen. 34); Luke's Simeon reversed this deplorable precedent, and made Jesus' circumcision the occasion to proclaim 'a light to lighten the Gentiles' (Lk. 2.32). So the next Simeon, though normally called Simon, was perhaps deliberately placed in the same succession when, in a discussion whether Gentiles who became Christians should also be circumcised, he was given credit by James for relating how 'God first visited the Gentiles to take out of them a people for his name' (Acts 15.14)" (345).

57. Cf. Jeremias, *Sprache,* 130-31.

58. So G. Schneider, "ἐξηγέομαι," *EDNT,* 2:6.

59. Cf. F. Büchsel, "ἐξηγέομαι," *TDNT* 2:908; C. Spicq, "ἐξηγέομαι," in *Notes de lexicographie néo- testamentaire,* vol. 1, OBO 22.1 (Fribourg: Éditions Universitaires; Göttingen: Vandenhoeck & Ruprecht, 1978) 256-58; W. Bauer, K. and B. Aland, *Wörterbuch zum Neuen Testament,* 6th ed. (Berlin: de Gruyter, 1988) 557-58.

Hebrew equivalent[60] — which is a *terminus technicus* for interpretation of Scripture in the rabbinical writings. Herewith we are near to that interpretation which Chrysostom gave to Acts 15:14. He had understood Simeon's ἐξηγεῖσθαι once as προφητεύειν (*In Acta Hom.* 33:1 [*PGM* 60:239]), but then also as interpretation of earlier prophecies[61] "καὶ καλῶς εἶπεν, Συμεὼν ἐξηγήσατο, ὡς κἀκεῖνον ἑτέρων λέγειν γνώμην" (*In Acta Hom.* 33:2 ([*PGM* 60:240]).

If we may follow this patristic opinion,[62] it solves two problems which otherwise keep provoking literary critical considerations.[63] As many have observed, Peter's speech (Acts 15:7-11) and its supposed summary and rejoinder in Acts 15:13-21 do not appear to fit particularly well. While Peter speaks about the abandonment of circumcision, the brother of the Lord deals rather with the question of table fellowship. If we accept Chrysostom's interpretation, James does not turn back to Peter's statement and also leaves aside the report of Paul and Barnabas, in which they explain the theological significance of God's wonders among the Gentiles (Acts 15:12: ἐξηγουμένων ὅσα ἐποίησεν ὁ θεός);[64] rather, the brother of the Lord offers an independent argument and appeals exclusively to the prophetic testimony of both the present and the earlier period as the basis of his judgment.

This leads us to the question whether Acts 15:14 really could mean that James refers to the interpretation of prophetic passages given by Simeon in the birth narrative in his *Nunc Dimittis* (Luke 2:29-32). There, indeed, an eschatological hope for the Gentiles is mentioned for the first time in the Lukan double work, as echoing the prophecies in Isa 42:6 and 49:6: the messianic child is proclaimed as "the light of the Gentiles" (Luke 2:32a). One could translate Acts 15:14 in an analogous way: "Simeon has expounded to us how God from the very beginning (πρῶτον) looked favorably on the Gentiles to take from among them a people for his name." The adverb πρῶτον emphasizes here, above all, the anticipating initiative of God.[65] Strictly speaking, the phrase "at first" does not fit the story of Cornelius particularly well. For the readers of Acts it was, actually, the Ethiopian eunuch (Acts 8:26-40), and not Cornelius, who was the

60. *Der Evangelist Johannes: Ein Kommentar zum vierten Evangelium* (Stuttgart: Calwer, 1930) 36.

61. Cf. Smothers, "Chrysostom and Symeon," 210.

62. Without mentioning Chrysostom or giving any other argument already A. Mentz, "Zusammenkunft," 182, wrote: "Auf jeden Fall soll doch aber der Satz besagen, daß Symeon aus der Schrift die Möglichkeit der Berufung von Heiden bewiesen hat."

63. Cf. S. Giet, "L'assemblé apostolique," 206-10; Fitzmyer, in "Life of Paul," 220.

64. A certain embarrassment is seen in R. N. Longenecker, "The Acts of the Apostles," in *The Expositor's Bible Commentary,* vol. 9, ed. F. E. Gaebebelein (Grand Rapids, Michigan: Zondervan, 1981) 446: "If, as Luke's account implies, James in summing up made no reference to Paul's and Barnabas' report, this was probably more for political reasons than any of principle."

65. Cf. Dillon, in "Acts," 752. According to the corrected text in the Schaff edition (*Chrysostom: Homilies,* 207), apparently even Chrysostom thought in this way: "But what means it 'How God first (πρῶτον) did visit?' [v. 14.] [It means] from the beginning (ἐξ ἀρχῆς)" (*In Acta Hom* 33:2).

first converted Gentile. Jacques Dupont believes that Luke uses ἐπισκέπτεσθαι(Acts 15:14) to construct a *redactional* bridge to the birth narrative (Luke 1:68, 78).[66] But because, as we have seen, this is rather a word that is typical of Lukan sources, another explanation is preferable: Acts 15:14 could belong to the same tradition as the birth narrative. And there are two further connections between Simeon's hymn and James's speech. On the one hand, in both cases the hope for the Gentiles is connected with the Davidic messianic promise;[67] on the other, while in Luke 2 it is the parents of Jesus who hear Simeon's prophecy, in Acts 15 it is another immediate relative, the brother of Jesus, who (it seems) refers to it.

It would still be interesting to have a final look at the use of Amos 9:11 in early Judaism. As the wording of the Targum shows, the messianic interpretation was in use among the older rabbis.[68] It is true that this passage was not among their favorite messianic prophecies. We find the messianic understanding of this text but once in the Babylonian Talmud (*Sanh.* 96b), while two additional citations of it in the Midrashim do not allow us to draw any messianic conclusions (*Gen. Rab.* 88 [56b]; *Midr. Ps. 76* §3 [171b]; cf. Str-B 2:728-29). In light of these facts it is noteworthy that in the collection of messianic passages from Qumran Amos 9:11 follows immediately after the fundamental prophecy of Nathan in 2 Sam 7:11-14 (4QFlor 1:7-11) and is (just as in the Acts passage) interpreted as refering to the (Davidic) Messiah (4QFlor 1:12). It could be that the verb ἀνορθοῦν in the Amos-citation of Acts 15:17 (Amos 9:12) is a deliberate allusion to 2 Sam 7:13.[69] Because the Amos-citation is used in some Jewish sources but not in either the Lukan double work nor elsewhere in the NT, Dupont attributes to Luke "un certain sens des vraisemblances."[70] But we may question whether this judgment is appropriate; is a pre-Lukan source or tradition not a more probable explanation — especially one which reflects the sort of relationship to the Qumran writings argued by F. Mussner.[71] That question becomes even more pressing when, in bringing this study to its close, we finally take a brief look at our problem from the wider perspective of its historical context.

66. In "ΛΑΟΣ," 362.

67. According to B. Koet, "Simeons Worte (Lk 2,29–32,34c-35) und Israels Geschick," in *The Four Gospels 1992. Festschrift für Frans Neirynck,* ed. F. van Segbroeck, BETL 100 (Leuven: Leuven University, 1992) 1549-69, Simeon's hymn and prophecy function in Luke's double work as a "disclosure," pointing to a Lukan main theme, the salvation of the Gentiles *and* Israel together. In Koet's view there are deliberate reminiscences of Simeon's words in Acts 13:46-47 and 28:26-28. Koet's interest is exclusively redaction-critical, without denying the possibility of older sources or traditions (1549 n. 3).

68. Cf. Dupont, "(Ac 15, 16 = Am 9, 11)," 29.

69. Dupont, "(Ac 15, 16 = Am 9, 11)," 27, 31.

70. Dupont, "(Ac 15, 16 = Am 9, 11)," 28.

71. *Apostelgeschichte,* NEcB 5 (Regensburg: Pustet, 1984) 93.

## 5. The Jewish-Religious Background of James and Simeon

It is often supposed that James, the brother of the Lord, had close affinities with the Pharisees' outlook.[72] There are indications, however, that point in a different direction:

(1) The Jewish Christian historian of the second century, Hegesippus, described James as an ascetic who belonged to both the priestly and the prophetic tradition (Eusebius *Hist. Eccl.* 2.23.4-7). Among all the legendary accretions there could still be an element of historical tradition here.[73]

(2) According to R. J. Bauckham, the letter of Jude is most probably a genuine letter written by another brother of Jesus. This letter is especially characterized by traditions about Enoch and an exegesis which resembles that of Qumran.[74] Bauckham suggests that the Lukan genealogy (Luke 3:23-38) is influenced by the same Enochic thinking. According to Bauckham, this genealogy stems ultimately from a tradition that was first handed down by members of the earthly family of Jesus.[75]

(3) The theory that the letter of James originated, at least, in circles around the brother of the Lord, can still be defended; its Palestinian character is clear, not least in the numerous linguistic and thematic parallels it bears especially to the Qumran literature.[76] But another peculiarity of the writing is its closeness to the Hebraizing special tradition in the Gospel of Luke,[77] which, for its part, also reflects close association with (and deliberate dissociation from) Qumranic ideas.[78] It is improbable that all

72. Cf. esp. M. Hengel, "Jakobus der Herrenbruder — der erste 'Papst'?," in *Glaube und Eschatologie,* 71-104.

73. Cf. J. Daniélou, *The Theology of Jewish Christianity* (London: Darton, Longman & Todd; Philadelphia: Westminster, 1964) 370-72.

74. *Jude — 2 Peter,* WBC 50 (Waco, Texas: Word, 1983).

75. *Jude and the Relatives of Jesus in the Early Church* (Edinburgh: T. & T. Clark, 1990) 315-73.

76. Cf. esp. F. Mussner, *Der Jakobusbrief,* HTKNT 13.1 (Freiburg: Herder, 1964). In his last article, S. Pines, "Notes on the Twelve Tribes in Qumran, Early Christianity and Jewish Tradition," in *Messiah and Christos: Studies in the Jewish Origins of Christianity Presented to David Flusser,* ed. I. Gruenwald et al. (Tübingen: J. C. B. Mohr [Paul Siebeck], 1992) 151-54, connected Jas 1:1 (the Jewish Diaspora as the twelve tribes) with the Qumran War Scroll (1QM 1-2). He also pointed out that the prophet Anna who is linked with the tribe of Asher (Luke 2:36) "is apparently the only individual who is supposed to have lived in the period of the Second Temple or after who is said in either Jewish or Christian writings to have belonged to one of the ten tribes" (154 n. 17).

77. Cf. P. Davids, *The Epistle of James,* NIGTC (Exeter: Paternoster, 1982) 47-49. P. J. Hartin, *James and the Q Sayings of Jesus,* JSNTSS 47 (Sheffield: JSOT, 1991), sees a Matthean-like Q-tradition in the background of James. I will deal with this question on another occasion.

78. Cf. Riesner, "Prägung und Herkunft." But see already *idem,* "Essener und Urkirche in Jerusalem," in *Christen und Christliches in Qumran?,* ed. B. Mayer, ETS NF 32 (Regensburg: Pustet, 1992) 139-55.

of the early Hasidic circles, originating in the Persian era, fully carried out the narrow Essene or rigidly separatist Qumranic way of life.[79] Perhaps one can agree with J. B. Adamson and consider James, the brother of the Lord, as a *hasid,* who was nearer to Essene than to Pharisaic traditions but who was not a Qumran-Essene in the strict sense.[80]

Bo Reicke regarded it as possible that Simeon of Luke 2:25 was an Essene prophet.[81] His hymn resembles (as do the other hymns in the birth narrative) the patterns from Qumran.[82] There could also be a specific linguistic contact, if both σωτήριον μου (Luke 2:30) and ישעכה (1QH 5:12; cf. 1QIs[a] 51:5) are to be considered as titles of the Messiah.[83] If one may regard Simeon as a historical character,[84] one should probably think of him too as a *hasid* with a certain closeness to Essene ideas. Indeed, it may be significant that he is called an ἄνθρωπος εὐλαβής (Luke 2:25). Mathias Delcor has suggested that εὐλαβής could have as its background the Hebrew חָסִד, and the name "Essene" ('Εσσαῖοι, 'Εσσηνοί), which comes from the Aramaic equivalent (חסא could then be translated so into Greek.[85] One cannot even exclude that the Jewish sectarian group had used this name of itself—1QH 7:20 (בְּנֵי חֶסֶד), and the strongly increasing attestation of חסידים / הסיד in the Qumranic writings[86] indeed speaks for it. Simeon is called not only a pious man, but also a righteous one (δίκαιος [Luke 2:25]). We have already seen the juxtaposition of the characteristics "righteous and pious" in the newly published Qumran text 4Q521. If Simeon were a *hasid* rather than a strict Qumran-Essene, it would not be strange that he expected only one Messiah. In the broader movement of groups with Essene leanings there were different ideas about the Messiah, and some within the movement appear to have expected only one person, who had either a more priestly or Davidic character.[87]

79. Cf. J. Maier, *Zwischen den Testamenten: Geschichte und Religion in der Zeit des Zweiten Tempels,* NEcB Ergänzungsband 3 (Regensburg: Pustet, 1990) 260-83.

80. *James — The Man and His Message* (Grand Rapids, Michigan: Wm. B. Eerdmans, 1988) 20.

81. "Simeon 6," *BHH,* vol. 3 (Göttingen: Vandenhoeck & Ruprecht, 1966) 1798.

82. Cf. S. C. Farris, *The Hymns of Luke's Infancy Narratives: Their Origin, Meaning and Significance,* JSNTSS 9 (Sheffield: JSOT, 1985) 67-85.

83. Cf. W. H. Brownlee, "Messianic Motives of Qumran and the New Testament II," *NTS* 3 (1956-57) 195-210 (196).

84. The similarities are not specific enough to make the identification proposed by A. Cutler, "Does the Simeon of Luke 2 refer to Simeon the Son of Hillel?" *JBR* 34 (1966) 29-35.

85. "A propos de l'emplacement de la Porte des Esséniens selon Josèphe et de ses implications historiques, éssenienne et chrétienne. Examen d'une théorie," in *Intertestamental Essays in Honour of Józef Tadeusz Milik,* ed. Z. J. Kapera, Qumranica Mogilanensia 6 (Kraków: Enigma, 1992) 25-44 (35).

86. Cf. J. H. Charlesworth, *Graphic Concordance to the Dead Sea Scrolls* (Tübingen: J. C. B. Mohr [Paul Siebeck]; Louisville: Westminster / John Knox, 1991) 257.

87. Cf. A. Hultgard, "The Ideal 'Levite', the Davidic Messiah and the Saviour Priest in the Testaments of the Twelve Patriarchs," in *Ideal Figures in Ancient Judaism,* ed. G. W. E. Nickelsburg

I do not wish to claim that this essay has demonstrated that the Simeon of James's speech (Acts 15:14) is necessarily the prophet with the same name in the Lukan birth narrative (Luke 2:25), but I hope to have shown that that interpretation is worthy of serious discussion. There is, at least, a tradition inside the ancient church that speaks for such an identification, and there are many exegetical suggestions in John Chrysostom that are still worth listening to today. In any case, it seems noteworthy that a certain closeness to the kind of language and concepts that we know from Qumran connects James's speech (Acts 15:13-21) with Simeon's hymn (Luke 2:29-32), with other parts of Luke's special tradition, and with the letters of Jude and James too. Maybe we have here a fruitful approach for some future explorations into the history of the early church.

---

and J. J. Collins, SBLSCS 12 (Chico, California: Scholars, 1980) 93-110; *idem, L'eschatologie des Testaments des Douze Patriarches*, vol. 3 (Stockholm: Almquist & Wiksell, 1981) 92-123; G. J. Brooke, "The Messiah of Aaron in the *Damascus Document*," *RevQ* 15 / 57-58 (1991) 215-30; and also M. O. Wise and J. D. Tabor, "The Messiah at Qumran," *BARev* 18 (1992) 60-65.

# II. Jesus, Paul, and John

# Patterns of Evangelization in Paul and Jesus: A Way Forward in the Jesus-Paul Debate?

John W. Drane

Ever since F. C. Baur first proposed a dichotomy between the Pauline and Petrine sections of the early church, the issue of Paul and Jesus has never been far from the center of NT studies.[1] Sometimes it has been a simple historical question of whether Paul knew and followed Jesus of Nazareth. At other times it has focused on the problem of whether some continuity can be traced between the teachings of Jesus and Paul. Lurking in the background has always been the theological issue of whether knowledge of or belief in the historical Jesus had any importance for Paul's understanding of the gospel, which was apparently concerned with the "Christ of faith."

Interpreted in the broadest possible terms, our subject is therefore at the heart of much contemporary debate about the NT, and when Howard Marshall became professor of New Testament Exegesis in the University of Aberdeen, he recognized this by choosing it as the topic for his inaugural lecture.[2] The theological question of the relevance of the historical Jesus for Christian faith is obviously crucial to any consideration of NT thinking. Writing in a Decade of Evangelism, I am conscious that it is also central for any meaningful talk of evangelization in the modern church — for if Paul's gospel was in significant respects different from that of Jesus, then we need to ask which version of early Christian belief is most authentically "Christian," and therefore can claim to represent the heart of the Christian message for today. In the effort to elucidate

1. F. C. Baur, *Paulus der Apostel* (Tübingen, 1845; ET: *Paul: His Life and Work,* 2 vols.; London: Williams and Norgate, 1875-76). For a convenient history of the ensuing debate, cf. V. P. Furnish, "The Jesus- Paul Debate: From Baur to Bultmann," *BJRL* 47 (1965) 342-81; reprinted and slightly updated in *Paul and Jesus: Collected Essays,* ed. A. J. M. Wedderburn, JSNTSS 37 (Sheffield: JSOT, 1989) 17-50; T. J. Keegan, "Paul and the Historical Jesus," *Angelicum* 52 (1975) 302-39, 450-84.

2. I. H. Marshall, "Jesus, Paul and John," *Aberdeen University Review* 51 (1985) 18-36 (= *idem, Jesus the Saviour* [London: SPCK; Downers Grove, Illinois: InterVarsity, 1990] 35-36).

some of these questions, I propose to begin with a brief consideration of some of the methodological problems presented by the NT documents, before moving on to outline some of the contours in the debate, and then finally making some suggestions about appropriate models for understanding the relationship between Jesus and Paul, illustrated by reference to their style of evangelization.

## 1

At the methodological level, the debate has often been unbelievably undisciplined. Hardly anyone seems willing to recognize the limitations of the primary source materials, though in many instances these sources are clearly incapable of answering the questions we now wish to put to them.

In the case of Paul there is the obvious fact that, with the possible exception of Romans, all his writings have an occasional character. Paul wrote not to impart some carefully worked-out position which he felt impelled to expound, but because particular problems in the various churches demanded an immediate response from him. Of course, it is not too difficult to identify what he may have been saying in any given context, and to fit that into a more general pattern which we then label "Pauline theology." There is certainly no shortage of scholars ready to make the effort, even if the chances of success are hopelessly disproportionate to the amount of energy expended. Scholarship has become so accustomed to the process that we regularly underestimate — even ignore — the difficulties standing in the way of those who wish to produce such a synthesis of Paul's thinking. Almost every link in the chain of argument has a weakness, for there is not a single epistle for which we can discern an absolutely indisputable context. Even Galatians, which to many seems undeniably devoted to combating some kind of Judaizing influence, cannot be proved to have been written in such a context — while other letters, such as 1 and 2 Corinthians, have a far more uncertain background than that. Moreover, even supposing we were able to contextualize all of Paul's letters quite precisely, we would still be faced with the more difficult problem of deciding what relationship, if any, existed between his *ad hoc* response to a particular situation and his basic theological position as he might express it in more reflective moments.

Right from the outset, therefore, we must guard against being too dogmatic in our assertions about Paul's thinking. Whatever Paul's attitude to the traditions about Jesus may have been, we have no clear statement of it; and even in those instances where a consensus of opinion believes he was referring to such traditions, he does so casually and often ambiguously. It is in any case extremely unlikely that he would have used carefully confirmed quotations to support his arguments. His mode of thinking and writing was much more spontaneous than that (even when quoting the OT, for example), not to mention the fact that he everywhere makes it plain that his main confidence lay not in traditions handed on to him, but in his appointment as an apostle by the risen Lord (e.g., Gal 1:1ff., 11ff.), and in his consciousness that the Spirit of God was working through him (e.g., 1 Cor 7:40).

These uncertainties about Paul's letters are matched by even larger ambiguities about the Gospels themselves, and notwithstanding the renewed confidence engendered by writers of the so-called "Third Quest," much recent writing about Paul and Jesus still betrays too many signs of muddled attitudes toward the Gospel traditions. We can now have direct access only to the end-products of the process of Gospel transmission. But there is no doubt that the NT Gospels represent only a limited selection from the entire Jesus tradition that was available to their authors, and which must presumably have been potentially available to Paul in the fifties of the first century. Documents like *The Gospel of Thomas* imply that authentic Jesus tradition may have been circulating in loosely connected pericopes well into the second century, while the prologue of Luke's Gospel confirms the existence of many collections of traditions at a slightly earlier date (Luke 1:1-4) — and according to the (no doubt exaggerated) statements of John 20:30 and 21:25, there were so many traditions in circulation that the world was too small to contain them all! Even within the range of traditions utilized in the final redaction of the canonical Gospels, it is now generally accepted that these traditions gradually became stereotyped and worn down from much more elaborate accounts, which means that in the pre-literary stage of the Gospel traditions, people of Paul's generation must have been familiar with more comprehensive versions even of those materials to which we ourselves have direct access through the written Gospels — not to mention the further likelihood that someone like Paul may have recognized as Jesus tradition things that we can no longer identify as such simply because they do not feature in the Gospels we now have.

In assessing Paul's relationship to the Gospel traditions, therefore, we are able to make reasonably certain judgments only at those points where contact can be demonstrated between Paul and the traditions which happen to have been preserved in the canonical Gospels. But we cannot ignore the fact that Paul's connections with the Jesus tradition must have been much broader than that. We simply do not know for certain what state the Gospel traditions were in at the time of Paul's ministry. Certainly by the time Mark was writing, the tradition appears to have reached some kind of fixed form, though even Luke's prologue is open to the understanding that the traditions were then in a disorderly form, to which he himself sought to give some order (Luke 1:1-4). In any event, Paul's knowledge of the traditions was probably both broader and narrower than our own: broader in that he had access to material now hidden from us, and narrower in that he may not have known all the material which has come down to us in the canonical Gospels.

There is also the fact that the authors of other NT epistles seem to have been neither more nor less familiar with the Jesus tradition than Paul was. Could it be that the way Paul handles references to Jesus in his letters is not primarily explicable in terms of a distinctive Pauline understanding of the gospel? It has proved relatively easy, and convenient, to explain Paul's infrequent references to the Gospel traditions by appealing to his dynamic, almost existentialist understanding of Christianity. But why then do none of the other so-called "early catholic" epistles show any greater regard for the traditions about Jesus?[3] Are we perhaps looking in the wrong direction when we confine the discussion to the old familiar categories of the Jesus-Paul debate?

## 2

We shall return to this in due course. But since the debate has most often been presented in theological terms, we must, however briefly, review the questions involved from this perspective. Did Paul know about the historical Jesus, and did he care whether he knew him or not? Discussion of this question has tended to concentrate on two major concerns: the interpretation of 2 Cor 5:16, and the relation between tradition and revelation in Pauline thinking.

The statement in 2 Cor 5:16 has been variously interpreted, though very few, if any, would now wish to go along with J. Weiss and regard it as evidence that Paul had actually seen and known the person Jesus of Nazareth.[4] Instead, the debate has tended to center on the notion of knowing Christ κατὰ σάρκα. Bultmann equated this with knowing "the historical Jesus," and so the whole verse can be seen as a disclaimer that this Jesus was of any relevance to Paul's understanding of the Christian faith.[5] The arguments for and against this in-

3. E. Schweizer observes that Paul's knowledge is "more than we find in the epistles of John, comparable roughly to the evidence in Acts" ("The Testimony to Jesus in the Early Christian Community," *HBT* 7 [1985] 89). Of course, both Acts and the epistles of John were compiled by people who also wrote their own Gospels, so presumably they could make some assumptions about how much (or little) their readers would know. In view of the connections that can be traced between Paul and certain aspects of Luke's Gospel in particular (see section 4 below), it is tempting to speculate that Paul may have made similar assumptions based on his commendation of Gospel traditions that were ultimately taken up and used by Luke himself. On the more general point, T. Holz makes a similar observation ("This merits more attention in assessing the whole phenomenon of the Jesus tradition outside the Gospels than it normally receives"), though he fails to develop it. Cf his "Paul and the Oral Gospel Tradition," in *Jesus and the Oral Gospel Tradition,* ed. H. Wansbrough, JSNTSS 64 (Sheffield: JSOT, 1991) 383.

4. According to Weiss, "A personality who inspired such enthusiasm and hatred simply must have drawn the attention of such an earnest and important man as Paul. . . . Paul's experience is inconceivable without such direct or indirect contact with Jesus . . ." (*Jesus im Glauben des Urchristentums* (Tübingen: J. C. B. Mohr [Paul Siebeck], 1910) 23ff. Cf. also his *Paul and Jesus* (ET: New York: Harper, 1909); and F. C. Porter, "Does Paul Claim to Have Known the Historical Jesus?" *JBL* 47 (1928) 257-75. F. F. Bruce seems to agree with Weiss that Paul had met Jesus, but claims that 2 Cor 5:16 is not evidence for it (*Paul and Jesus* [Grand Rapids, Michigan: Baker, 1974] 23).

5. *Glauben und Verstehen* (Tübingen: J. C. B. Mohr, 1933) 190ff.; *idem,* "The Significance of the Historical Jesus for the Theology of Paul," in *Faith and Understanding,* vol. 1 (New York:

terpretation have been well expounded elsewhere.[6] They are not essentially textual or exegetical, and the Pauline statement has become little more than a convenient scriptural launching pad from which the various protagonists can soar into the heights of their respective theological and philosophical orbits.

The debate about revelation and tradition in Paul, however, has a more direct bearing on our subject. When Paul elaborated his faith, what did he think he was doing? Did he believe there was a connection between his own message and that of Christians before him, or did he think of himself as standing outside the mainstream of Christian tradition that had its origin in Jerusalem?

In answering these questions, a great deal of emphasis has been placed on Paul's statements in Galatians 1, especially vv 11-12. According to this understanding, not only is there no reason to suppose that Paul knew of any Jesus tradition and therefore depended on it in some way; but in Galatians 1 he actually denies such dependence.[7] Paul's understanding of the Christian tradition was not of a body of facts handed on in rabbinic fashion: that kind of interest would have been part of what Paul rejects as "works of the law."[8] His insistence on the authority of his own ministry purely on the basis of his encounter with the risen Lord shows that it is the fact of the "Christ event" in the death and resurrection of Jesus that for Paul lay at the heart of Christianity. The exegete as historian can say nothing about the Pauline gospel, for that is part of the Easter faith. Such understanding may be able to tell us that Jesus of

---

Harper & Row, 1969) 220-46; *idem,* "The Primitive Christian Kerygma and the Historical Jesus," in *The Historical Jesus and the Kerygmatic Christ,* ed. C. E. Braaten and R. A. Harrisville (Nashville: Abingdon, 1964) 15-42; *idem, Der zweite Brief an die Korinther,* KKNT 6 (Göttingen: Vandenhoeck & Ruprecht, 1976) *ad loc.* (ET: Minneapolis: Augsburg, 1985). Cf. also W. Schmithals, "Paulus und der historische Jesus," *ZNW* 53 (1962) 145-60.

6. See, among others, J. L. Martyn, "Epistemology at the Turn of the Ages: 2 Corinthians 5:16," in *Christian History and Interpretation: Studies Presented to John Knox,* ed. W. R. Farmer, C. F. D. Moule, and R. R. Niebuhr (Cambridge: Cambridge University, 1967) 269-87; C. F. D. Moule, "Jesus in New Testament Kerygma," in *Verborum Veritas: Festschrift für Gustav Stählin,* ed. O. Bocher and K. Haacker (Wuppertal: Theologischer, 1970) 17; G. N. Stanton, *Jesus of Nazareth in New Testament Preaching,* SNTSMS 27 (Cambridge: Cambridge University, 1974) 86ff.; J. W. Fraser, "Paul's Knowledge of Jesus: II Corinthians V.16 Once More," *NTS* 17 (1970-71) 293-313; *idem, Jesus and Paul* (Abingdon: Marchan Manor, 1974) 46ff.; J. F. Collange, *Énigmes de la Deuxième Épître de Paul aux Corinthiens,* SNTSMS 18 (Cambridge: Cambridge University, 1972) 257-63; C. Wolff, "True Apostolic Knowledge of Christ: Exegetical Reflections on 2 Corinthians 5.14ff," in *Paul and Jesus,* 81-98; O. Betz finds Isa 53:3, 4b illuminating in showing that knowing Christ κατὰ σάρκα actually refers to the unbelieving view that the crucified Jesus was rejected by God — a view that Paul himself had once shared ("Fleischliche und 'geistliche' Christuserkenntnis nach 2.Korinther 5,16," *TBei* 14 [1983] 167-79). According to W. Schmithals, the whole debate is a fuss about nothing, since the verse is a non-Pauline gnostic gloss (*Gnosticism in Corinth* [ET: Nashville: Abingdon, 1971] 302-15).

7. Bultmann, "Significance of the Historical Jesus," 221. Cf. his statements in *Theology of the New Testament* (ET: New York, 1951-55) 1:292ff.; and in *Kerygma and Myth,* 2 vols., ed. H. W. Bartsch (London: S.P.C.K., 1953-62) 1:112-13.

8. Bultmann, *Glauben und Verstehen,* 208.

Nazareth died, but cannot confront us with the kerygmatic declaration that Christ died for our sins.

Taken in isolation, this one statement from Galatians can undoubtedly be made to support such assertions. But we need to compare it with other statements elsewhere, notably 1 Cor 15:3ff. There, using exactly the same technical terms to describe the reception and onward transmission of tradition, Paul stridently affirms that at least part of his gospel consisted of verifiable facts about the historical Jesus. If modern Western readers complain that facts about something like the resurrection can scarcely be amenable to the kind of historical verification that could be claimed for the crucifixion, that would be of no concern to Paul, who viewed the two events as one. Bultmann appreciated this, though it has never been satisfactory to claim, as he did, that Paul had an unfortunate lapse from his insight into the essentially kerygmatic nature of the gospel while he was writing that particular section of 1 Corinthians![9]

In reality, one does not even need to bring in texts from other letters to demonstrate that, whatever Paul meant in Gal 1:11-12, he was not claiming that a factual tradition was unimportant for his own gospel. The immediate context in which the disputed statement is found makes it plain that what Paul understands by the gospel has some clearly defined content and form, which presumably could have been handed on by conventional means (see Gal 1:6ff.). In Galatia, Paul's opponents accused him of having a secondhand knowledge of the gospel — unlike the Judaizers who, as followers of the original Jerusalem apostles, could claim more direct access to the message of Jesus. It is in that context that Paul denies his gospel was received secondhand from others. Indeed, if that is not the point of Gal 1:11-12, then it is difficult to see what Paul is driving at.[10]

In the very next section of Galatians, Paul describes his visit to Jerusalem to see Cephas (1:18ff.), the occasion on which, according to some, Paul did in fact receive at least part of the tradition to which he seems to refer in 1 Corinthians 15 and elsewhere. Though Dodd's oft-quoted observation about the subject matter of their conversation was made more or less intuitively,[11] the vocabulary

9. *Theology of the New Testament,* 1:292ff. On the debate about these two passages, see further my *Paul: Libertine or Legalist?* (London: S.P.C.K., 1975) 19ff.; and F. F. Bruce, "'All Things to All Men': Diversity in Unity and Other Pauline Tensions," in *Unity and Diversity in New Testament Theology,* ed. R. A. Guelich (Grand Rapids, Michigan: Wm. B. Eerdmans, 1978) 82ff.

10. It is at least worth asking whether Paul's need to distance himself from seeming to be a secondhand apostle has not discouraged him from making too much explicit mention of the Jesus tradition in his letters. It is certainly the case that the letters with least mention of Jesus were written against this kind of polemical background. See further n. 38 below; also Drane, *Paul: Libertine or Legalist?,* 22-23; and the comment of B. Gerhardsson: "were the gospel an entity which *could not* be transmitted and taught, then Paul would have had no cause to deny that he had received it in such a way" (*Memory and Manuscript* [Lund: C. W. K. Gleerup, 1961] 265).

11. "We may presume that they did not spend all their time talking about the weather" (C. H. Dodd, *The Apostolic Preaching and Its Developments* [London: Hodder & Stoughton, 1972] 20).

which Paul uses to describe this encounter indicates that he went with the express purpose of obtaining information about such matters from Cephas. The verb ἱστορῆσαι is found nowhere else in Paul (nor, for that matter, in the rest of the NT), so we cannot be absolutely certain how he understood it. But other Greek authors generally use it to describe visits to famous cities and places of interest with a view to gaining firsthand information about them. When Paul writes in this way of his visit to Cephas, it is not unreasonable to suppose that he was seeking information which presumably Peter was in a unique position to give him.[12] Certainly, by the time of his next visit to Jerusalem (Gal 2:1ff.), he had no doubt that his own message could be directly compared with the traditions emanating from Jerusalem.

Some have tried to establish an even closer connection between Paul and the alleged use of rabbinic methods in the transmission of the Jesus tradition in the early church.[13] The problem with this understanding of Paul is the almost total absence of any firm evidence for it. There is no compelling reason for claiming that Paul was rabbinically trained in the first place. Still less can we suppose that the Gospel traditions themselves were the teaching of a rabbi, meticulously preserved and handed on to future generations. The Evangelists do not typically present Jesus in the guise of a rabbi teaching his disciples, and even in the Gospel of Matthew, which comes closest to doing so, there is no hint that Jesus' words should be learned and recited by his followers.

## 3

When we turn to other passages in Paul, we can see that he often includes traditional materials, early credal confessions and hymns, as well as catechetical and parenetical statements that were the common property of the church as a whole. The regular utilization of such material suggests that Paul was con-

12. Cf. G. D. Kilpatrick, "Galatians 1:18 ἱστορῆσαι κηφᾶν," in *New Testament Essays: Studies in Memory of Thomas Walter Manson,* ed. A. J. B. Higgins (Manchester: Manchester University, 1959) 144-49. E. Haenchen agrees with him, and suggests Paul was seeking information from Cephas on moral and practical issues ("Petrus-Probleme," *NTS* 7 [1960-61] 187-97 (= *Gott und Mensch* [Tübingen: J. C. B. Mohr (Paul Siebeck), 1965] 55-67). Gerhardsson links this visit with the mention of a retreat to "Arabia" in the preceding verse, suggesting that after his conversion Paul had taken elaborate steps to rid himself of Jewish knowledge that now as a Christian he believed to be mistaken, before going to Jerusalem to receive the Christian traditions from Cephas (*Memory and Manuscript,* 289-90). Reisenfeld takes a similar line, seeing the Jerusalem visit as a sort of "examination" to determine "whether he . . . had really made the tradition of the words and deeds of Jesus his own, in the form, that is, which those words and deeds had assumed by that date" ("The Gospel Tradition and Its Beginnings," in *The Gospels Reconsidered* [Oxford, 1960] 144). But such suggestions are too subtle and farfetched: cf. J. D. G. Dunn, "The Relationship between Paul and Jerusalem according to Galatians 1 and 2," *NTS* 28 (1982) 461-78.

13. Most notably Gerhardsson *(Memory and Manuscript);* and, more cautiously, W. D. Davies, *Paul and Rabbinic Judaism,* 3d ed. (London: S.P.C.K., 1970).

sciously integrating his own work and ministry into the larger context of primitive Christianity. But our main interest here is his use of materials relevant to the person of Jesus.

Notwithstanding the caution of scholars such as Walter, who "can detect no hint that Paul knew of the narrative tradition about Jesus,"[14] many still believe it is possible to distil from Paul's writings an outline of the life of Jesus not dissimilar from that of the Gospels. The apparent lack of plain evidence did not stop Bruce from claiming that "the outline of the gospel story insofar as we can trace it in the writings of Paul agrees with the outline which we find elsewhere in the New Testament, and in the four Gospels in particular."[15] Dodd pointed out that Paul knew Jesus was born as a Jew (Gal 4:4; Rom 9:5), descended from David (Rom 1:3), had brothers (1 Cor 9:5), worked among Jews and not Gentiles (Rom 15:8), and it was they who were responsible for his death, though he died by the Roman mode of crucifixion (1 Thess 2:15; cf. Gal 2:20; 3:13ff.).[16] Others have added further details to this list.[17]

All such references, however, are more or less incidental, and the real center of interest lies in Paul's actual citations of "sayings of the Lord," which are also known to us from the Gospel traditions. It is often observed how infrequently Paul makes reference to such teachings, and yet it is impossible to deny that he had at least a limited knowledge of them, for in two cases (1 Cor 7:10-11 and 1 Cor 9:14) he explicitly quotes sayings otherwise known to us from the Gospels (cf. Mark 10:1-12; Luke 10:7-8; Matt 10:10). In one further case he says he is referring to a "word of the Lord," though we are unable positively to identify this with any known Gospel tradition (1 Thess 4:15ff.),[18] while in Rom 14:14 it is possible to interpret ἐν κυρίῳ Ἰησοῦ along the same lines, and in this case, plausible Gospel parallels are ready to hand (cf. Matt 15:11).[19] There is also his account of the institution of the Eucharist, which,

14. N. Walter, "Paul and the Early Christian Jesus-Tradition," in *Paul and Jesus,* 60.

15. *Paul and Jesus,* 20. Cf. also his *Paul: Apostle of the Free Spirit* (Exeter: Paternoster, 1977) 95ff.

16. C. H. Dodd, *History and the Gospel* (London, 1952) 64ff.

17. E.g., 1 Cor 11:23-25 mentions the betrayal of Jesus, and the Last Supper seems to be placed in this context by 1 Cor 10:16. Paul also knew that crucifixion implied Jesus died as a criminal (Gal 3:1, 13ff.; 1 Cor 1:23), but he was buried honorably (1 Cor 15:4). Though he accepts the responsibility of the Jews, he insists they were urged on by higher powers (1 Cor 2:8ff.). Cf. D. T. Rowlingson, *The Gospel-Perspective on Jesus Christ* (Philadelphia: Westminster, 1968) 148ff. Galatians 4:4 has also often been taken to refer to the virgin birth, though that is unlikely. W. D. Davies claims that 1 Corinthians 13 is "based upon the life of Jesus" ("The Moral Teaching of the Early Church," in *The Use of the Old Testament in the New Testament and Other Essays,* ed. J. M. Efird [Durham, North Carolina: Duke University, 1972] 321); while Stanton traced the life of Jesus of Nazareth even in the Christ hymn of Phil 2:6-11 (*Jesus of Nazareth,* 101ff.).

18. Not all scholars would agree that we need to find this within the Gospel tradition, of course. Bruce, for example, prefers to believe it was the deliverance of a prophet speaking in the name of Christ to the church (*Paul and Jesus,* 32, 70).

19. C. H. Dodd, "The 'Primitive Catechism' and the Sayings of Jesus," in *More New Testament*

while not agreeing in detail with any of the Gospel accounts now known to us, is nevertheless sufficiently close to them for it to be obvious that they have all come from the same source (1 Cor 11:23-25). His use of the term *Abba* in prayer, especially when linked to the role of the Spirit (Gal 4:6; Rom 8:15), also seems to have undeniable connections with teachings attributed to Jesus himself (e.g., Mark 14:32-42; Matt 6:9ff.).[20]

Then there is a vast array of alleged parallels and so-called allusions to the Gospel traditions. These range from the modest number of eight parallels allowed by Furnish (most of them in Romans 12–14, with three others in 1 Thessalonians 5),[21] to the extravagant assertions of Resch, who claimed to discover not far short of a thousand Pauline allusions to the Gospel traditions.[22] Despite Paul's obvious, if limited, use of material otherwise known to us from the Gospels, there is no generally accepted explanation of the phenomenon. Yet it must by any standards be an extraordinary state of affairs where we have just one or two explicit references to the Gospel traditions, combined with literally hundreds of real or imagined allusions and parallels.

One way of accounting for Paul's apparent reticence to mention the Gospel traditions is to suppose that an account of Jesus' life and teachings formed part of his initial missionary preaching, and therefore he had no need to repeat this when writing letters on matters of Christian belief and behavior.[23]

---

*Studies* (Manchester: Manchester University, 1968) 25 n. 3. Not all scholars see any significance in these links, of course (cf. G. Bornkamm, *Paul* [ET: New York: Harper & Row, 1971] 109-19, 183ff.), and according to P. Stuhlmacher, Paul never meant such formulations to be understood as referring to an actual saying of Jesus, but rather as a way of appealing to some ultimate authority ("Jesustradition im Romerbrief? Eine Skizze," in *TBei* 14 [1983] 243).

20. Cf. Walter, "Paul and the Early Christian Jesus-Tradition," 59; Schweizer, "The Testimony to Jesus."

21. *Theology and Ethics in Paul* (Nashville: Abingdon, 1968) 51-65.

22. A. Resch, *Der Paulinismus und die Logia Jesu,* TU 27 (Leipzig: J. C. Heinrichs, 1904), claimed to be able to identify even "unknown" sayings of Jesus alluded to by Paul. This is obviously a flight of imagination, though one does occasionally encounter imagery that one suspects may well have come from such a source: for example, the saying in 1 Cor 9:7 about a shepherd being entitled to some of the milk of the flock, coming as it does in the middle of other recognizable allusions to Gospel traditions.

23. "Some things are omitted from the Epistles . . . not because they were unimportant, but on the contrary just because they were fundamental; instruction about them had to be given at the very beginning and except for special reasons did not need to be repeated" (J. G. Machen, *The Origin of Paul's Religion* [New York: Macmillan, 1921] 151). Moule takes a similar line: "there is no reason why Paul should have shown an interest in the story of Jesus . . . in letters written, for highly specialised purposes, to persons who were already Christians" ("Jesus in New Testament Kerygma," 18). Common sense suggests that some kind of knowledge about Jesus must have been an essential part of evangelization in the early church: "It is quite unthinkable that Paul, or any other evangelist, could have preached the message of the cross without a lively concern for the facts about the crucified" (Moule, "Jesus in New Testament Kerygma," 25). Moule further argues from the evidence of Acts that an account of the life of Jesus formed part of early Christian preaching. He is fully aware of the difficulties with the Acts evidence, but "even if it amounts to

A variant on this is proposed by Walter, who observes that whereas Paul uses Jesus tradition to back up those parts of his own teaching that were most distinctive, he does not typically use it in relation to "the central content of his gospel."[24] Schweizer speculates that this may be related to the complex historical roots of early Christianity: in the Galilean context (of which we know next to nothing, of course), memories of the historical Jesus would naturally be more relevant than they would be in any mission context (whether related to Paul or other early missionaries), where the cross / resurrection and its meaning would arguably be more relevant topics.[25]

Theories of this sort obviously have many attractions, hence their popularity. But they will always fall short of proof, for in the final analysis they are based on a series of unsupportable assumptions and intuitions, which often fail to take adequate account of the complex nature of the methodological problem both from the Pauline side and from the perspective of the Gospel traditions themselves.[26]

---

nothing more objective than what seemed appropriate to a narrator of the ancient world," it "represents the apostolic message, outside Jerusalem, as containing the kind of material that is to be found in the Gospels" (23). Without going quite so far, Stanton holds a similar position (*Jesus of Nazareth,* 112).

24. Walter, "Paul and the Early Christian Jesus-Tradition," 63. The proposal advanced by Walter is certainly worth further exploration. He suggests that Paul used Jesus-tradition in two ways: (1) in giving specific instructions, he treats sayings of the Lord as teachers would handle wisdom traditions ("without reflecting upon those who formulated them before them") — and often treating them as a rabbi would regard sayings of a colleague ("he quotes them either in order to endorse them or to set another view over against them"); cf. 1 Corinthians 4, 7, etc. But (2) where it is a matter of firm convictions on basic issues as to how Christians should live, things are different; cf. Romans 14. At the same time, Walter insists that Paul does not quote Jesus-tradition in relation to his central soteriological or christological positions, implying that this (as distinct from his ethics) "is essentially independent of the early church's pre-Synoptic Jesus-tradition."

25. Schweizer, "Testimony to Jesus," 86ff. Schweizer still insists, however, that it was "very unlikely that there ever were Christian communities who lived only with the confession of [Jesus'] death and resurrection without knowledge of his earthly activity" (96). Wedderburn reaches a similar conclusion, when he asks whether the epistles were not written at a time when it was simply taken for granted that Christian spirituality as an experienced reality had to be related to the historical stories of Jesus, so that "there was then no question or possibility envisaged of cutting loose from that foundation story" ("Paul and the Story of Jesus," in *Paul and Jesus,* 179).

26. Other attempts to explain Paul's reticence to mention the Gospel traditions are even more problematic. Reisenfeld's argument that they formed part of an esoteric teaching handed down within a distinctive context in the church's life is unlikely, if only because of the great emphasis of the NT on the open declaration of the Christian message (cf. his essay "The Gospel Tradition and Its Beginnings"). Equally unlikely is Bruce's notion that "Paul was not an eyewitness of these events, and preferred to confine himself to those events of which he could speak at first hand" (*Paul and Jesus,* 55-56). If that had been the case, then he would never have made even limited allusions to the historical Jesus and his teachings.

## 4

Considering the amount of energy expended on it, the Paul-Jesus debate has produced remarkably insubstantial conclusions. Could it be that we are asking the wrong sort of questions, and instead of focusing on narrowly textual details we ought rather to be considering a much broader picture? I want to propose that instead of concentrating on narrow textual studies, a more broadly based model may help to give us clearer insight. In particular, I suggest that a more appropriate model for appreciating the relationship between Paul and Jesus may be found in Wittgenstein's concept of "family resemblances."[27] Wittgenstein proposed this notion in the context of his discussion of the characteristics of a game, observing that there are both similarities and differences between the various things we call "games," but that does not disqualify any of them from being recognized as games. The relationship between games is more complex than that, and despite many striking differences — for example, between the Olympic Games and ring-a-ring-a-roses — "similarities crop up and disappear . . . we see a complicated network of similarities, overlapping and criss-crossing." Wittgenstein called these similarities "family resemblances," on the analogy of the human family in which various constant features interrelate, while still producing quite unique individuals. Using this terminology, then, could Paul and Jesus be said to have a "family resemblance"? The answer seems to be yes.

Some recent studies have been groping toward this, though without using Wittgenstein's model as a frame of reference. Wedderburn has written of the importance of "continuity," and moves away from the search for detailed correspondences between this or that aspect of the teaching of Paul and Jesus, in favor of an approach which assumes that "Paul acts and preaches as he does because a tradition has come down to him either that Jesus acted and preached in a similar way or that such acting and preaching is the Christian way to act and preach."[28] In another study of Paul, C. Wolff identified four features of Paul's ministry that can be identified with attitudes typical of Jesus — namely, Deprivation, Renunciation of Marriage, Humble Service, and Suffering / Per-

27. L. Wittgenstein, *Philosophical Investigations* (Oxford: Blackwell, 1968) §§65-78.

28. Wedderburn, "Paul and the Story of Jesus," 180. Wedderburn first used the term "continuity" in his 1985 article, "Paul and Jesus: The Problem of Continuity" (*SJT* 38, 189-203; reprinted in *Paul and Jesus,* 99-116), and further elaborated it in "Paul and Jesus: Similarity and Continuity," *NTS* 34 (1988) 161-82. Though laying more stress on those things that were not common to Jesus and Paul (such as "the kingdom of God," understanding of the Spirit, or of the church), Marshall made a similar assumption in his inaugural lecture, identifying a unity of purpose between the two in their adoption of the love ethic, as well as claiming that "Jesus' openness to the poor and the outcasts . . . issues in an openness to the Gentiles" ("Jesus, Paul and John," 28). The view that Paul's message did not concern the kingdom has been challenged by Wedderburn, who claims that Paul was forced to drop it as a result of misunderstandings created in Corinth ("Paul and Jesus: The Problem of Continuity," 201).

secution.[29] These are not all of the same order: suffering / persecution, for instance, is clearly related to the choices of other people, not Paul, whereas the first three represent free choices made by the apostle himself. Notwithstanding this, however, these features do constitute the kind of thing Wittgenstein calls "family resemblances," and within this frame of reference, we might add a further family resemblance to the list supplied by Wolff — namely, that there is a style of evangelization common to Paul and Jesus that was quite different both from the traditions of Judaism and from other leaders in the life of the early church.

Krister Stendahl has demonstrated that Paul has often been misunderstood as a result of being viewed through the experience of Martin Luther.[30] But this is not the only distortion in modern perceptions of Paul. A false image of Paul has been created in the likeness of nineteenth-century Western imperialism, and he has been unjustly caricatured as the ultimate exponent of an oppressive and unappealing style of evangelization. It is undeniable that some of the worst excesses of Protestant missions in the last 200 years have claimed to find their inspiration in Paul, perceiving him as an abrasive retailer, purveying a pre-packaged religious product wherever he could find consumers gullible enough to buy it. This is, at best, a one-sided view of Paul, if not a complete misunderstanding of all that he stood for. The book of Acts and Paul's letters speak with a common voice at this point, and depict his missionary strategy as consisting of two major elements which we may describe as "going" and "waiting." Paul was undoubtedly committed to going out, and showed enormous enterprise in physically transporting himself over great distances at considerable personal cost. But he was not motivated by the mentality of the enterprise culture, driven by the desire for successful empire-building. On the contrary, his style of evangelization was so relaxed that he was constantly surprised at the extraordinary results it produced, something to which the thanksgiving sections of his letters frequently testify. Paul's method was not a form of megaphone diplomacy, nor was it based on authoritarian principles, and he always spoke *with* people rather than *at* them. Whether in the synagogue or, as at Ephesus, in a hired lecture hall, Paul was always open to challenge and debate (Acts 19:8-10), and when he describes his own procedures in 1 Thess 2:1-12 he goes to some lengths to emphasize that he was not interested in bullying people to make them accept his message. Paul can on occasion use military metaphors, but when he writes of evangelization he uses the language of the nursery, not of the battlefield. Paul recognized the importance of going out. But far from interpreting this in triumphalist terms, he saw it as a way of expressing solidarity

29. C. Wolff, "Humility and Self-denial in Jesus' Life and Message and in the Apostolic Existence of Paul," in *Paul and Jesus,* 145-60.

30. K. Stendahl, "The Apostle Paul and the Introspective Conscience of the West," *HTR* 56 (1963) 199-215; reprinted in *Paul among Jews and Gentiles* (Philadelphia: Fortress, 1976) 78-96.

through his own vulnerability, as he willingly chose to operate on territory where other people felt more at home than he did. As well as going, his was also a strategy of waiting: creating a space in which people could be themselves, and as themselves could decide without coercion how and when to respond to the challenge of the gospel.[31]

The same style generally characterizes all the Gospel portraits of Jesus, but Luke in particular emphasizes these traits in his presentation of Jesus' teaching.[32] It is often remarked that Luke's equivalent to the "great commission" which completes the Gospel of Matthew (28:16-20) is held over until his second volume, the Acts of the Apostles. But there is at least one passage in the Gospel of Luke which highlights precisely these features that are so characteristic of Paul's evangelizing style. No doubt Luke uses this as a means of alerting the reader to the fuller exposition which follows in his second volume. But it occurs in a passage so distinctive that there can be no doubt it also reflects authentically some key aspects of the style of the Jesus of history.

In Luke 15 we find three parables relating to lostness. The lost sheep is the only one of the three which appears anywhere else, and by comparison with Matthew's version (Matt 18:12-14) Luke undoubtedly intended to accentuate the job of the shepherd over and above the predicament of the sheep. The shepherd's calling is to go out. The same motif emerges, if anything even more strongly, in the parable of the lost coin where by definition the coin is unable to make any moves to enable itself to be found, and is therefore wholly dependent on the earnestness of the seeker. But the third parable is quite different. There is still an obvious emphasis on the one who has lost something — in this case, the father who has lost a son. But unlike either the shepherd or the woman, the father makes no moves at all to rescue the lost son. Instead, the father's role is one of expectant waiting, looking for the son to return — and then creating a space to receive him with no strings attached when the son feels the right moment has come. All the commentators are agreed that by including these three parables grouped together like this Luke or his special source (it makes little difference which) intended to make a significant point, and most suggest that the key idea relates to what was lost. Without detracting from that, it is also possible and necessary to see here an equal emphasis on the methodology of finding — or, to put it another way, on a model of evangelization which encapsulates the two dynamics of "going" and "waiting."[33]

There has been much debate on what distinguished Jesus from the Jewish

31. Cf. R. F. Hock, *The Social Context of Paul's Ministry: Tentmaking and Apostleship* (Philadelphia: Fortress, 1980); E. Best, *Paul and His Converts* (Edinburgh: T. & T. Clark, 1988).

32. On the close interconnections between Paul and Luke, see Dale C. Allison Jr., "The Pauline Epistles and the Synoptic Gospels: The Pattern of the Parallels," *NTS* 28 (1982) 1-32.

33. I owe this observation to my friend Raymond Fung, former Evangelism Secretary to the World Council of Churches, though the application of it here is different from the use he makes of it.

teachers of his day.[34] At least one element seems to have been his willingness to accept people as they were, challenging them only to follow him, but then leaving them with personal space to work out in their own time and way precisely what that might involve. As a result, repentance quite often became the second act rather than (as in conventional Jewish piety) the first.[35] Jesus did not impose a closely circumscribed model of discipleship, but allowed those who would follow him the space to determine for themselves the meaning of discipleship in relation to their own thinking and personality. In that sense, Bultmann's insistence that Paul had an essentially existential understanding of the gospel could also be applied to Jesus, for they are both characterized by a strong emphasis on personal freedom, which significantly distanced and distinguished them from typical Jewish models of evangelization.[36] "[Jesus] did not train his disciples to be 'well-plastered cisterns, never losing a drop' — the ideal set before the pupils of the rabbis — but rather to be His apprentices, sharing His ministry with His own creative freedom."[37] This is precisely the policy that Paul espoused in 1 Thessalonians 2, and all the evidence shows that he carried it through in practice, for it was his insistence on people having personal freedom to respond to Christ for themselves that led to most of the problems to which his letters bear such eloquent testimony. Had he not allowed this freedom to the converts in Corinth, for example, then the whole course of his ministry and theology might well have been different. It is obvious that many of the profound heartaches that emerge in other letters were also related to the tensions involved in allowing and encouraging converts to develop their own sense of spiritual maturity, rather than imposing a ready-made framework on them.

Given that Paul himself emerged from a religious background where tradition was all-important, he would need strong encouragement to become the kind of evangelist that he was. And given that Jesus is the only other clear example of this open-ended model in the NT, it would be perverse not to draw the obvious conclusion that what Paul knew of Jesus had a considerable influ-

34. Indeed, this has been a major concern of writers in the "Third Quest" for the historical Jesus (the term "Third Quest" was coined by T. Wright; see S. Neill and T. Wright, *The Interpretation of the New Testament 1861-1986*, 2d ed. [Oxford: Oxford University, 1988] 379ff.), and incorporates the lines of investigation begun by M. J. Borg, *Conflict, Holiness and Politics in the Teachings of Jesus* [New York: Harper & Row, 1984]; A. E. Harvey, *Jesus and the Constraints of History* [London: S.P.C.K., 1982]; B. F. Meyer, *The Aims of Jesus* [London: SCM, 1979]; E. Rivkin, *What Crucified Jesus?* [Nashville: Abingdon, 1984]; E. P. Sanders, *Jesus and Judaism* [London: SCM, 1985]).

35. A particularly striking example is the case of Peter, who was summoned to "follow Jesus" without any further demands placed upon him (Mark 1:17; Matt 4:19), and for whom in all the Gospel traditions repentance was a significant part of spiritual growth rather than the beginning of discipleship.

36. Cf. Sanders, *Jesus and Judaism*, 174-211.

37. F. F. Bruce, *Tradition Old and New* (Grand Rapids: Zondervan, 1970) 27. Cf. A. Fridrichsen, "Jesus, St John and St Paul," in *The Root of the Vine* (London: Dacre, 1953) 37-62.

ence on his own style, and this is why they share a family resemblance. The existence of these two possible styles of evangelization actually illuminates many of the controversies in the life of both Paul and Jesus. The conflicts of Paul with James and other Jerusalem leaders, for example, are readily explicable in terms of tension between these two models.[38] Jesus himself was not immune from the same criticism, not only from the Pharisees but also on occasion from his own disciples (Luke 9:49-50). The church has struggled with this tension throughout the centuries, but has generally found it easier to adopt a narrow understanding of the gospel than to handle the kind of freedom to which Jesus and Paul both bear witness. The same concerns have also to a large extent dominated the modern discussion of the relationship between Paul and Jesus, with the agenda set either by the understandable desire to establish a detailed correspondence between Paul and Jesus in terms of their message or theology (tradition), or by the opposite insistence, of which Bultmann is the best example. The search for continuity of tradition seems doomed to futility.[39] Yet we cannot dismiss it out of hand, for the points where Paul's praxis seems to reflect that of Jesus are precisely the places where that was most distinctive. Nor can we dismiss absolutely Bultmann's claim that Paul had no interest in tradition — while at the same time acknowledging that Paul displays just enough interest in it to undermine the existentialist interpretation which Bultmann wanted to impose on him. And we also need to recognize that both concerns ultimately stem from the rationalist-materialist outlook of the European Enlightenment that is now largely discredited and in process of being superseded.

Perhaps the present crisis in modernity, and all that that will entail for the future of Western culture, may yet point this debate in new directions. For there can be no doubt that both Jesus and Paul would be less convinced by rationalist ideologies than most of their twentieth-century admirers — both liberal and conservative — have usually been.

The story of this quest is a good example of the Western methodology that believes it is possible to understand things by taking them to pieces — a reductionist mind-set that is largely responsible for the present crisis of Western

38. It is striking that while Jesus regularly lifted up and affirmed even the most unlikely of people, the one exception was in his dealings with Pharisees — just as Paul was able to accept an extraordinary amount of squabbling from Gentile converts, but had no hesitation in squashing the Judaizers or even, on occasion, recognized Jewish Christian leaders such as James or Peter. Presumably there was more at stake here than mere personality clashes: they were different (and incompatible) understandings of the nature of belief. Indeed, Wedderburn suggests that Paul's apparent reluctance to quote the teaching of Jesus may have been related to the fact that it was " 'in enemy hands' in the sense that it was being used in a legalistic way by his Judaizing opponents," and therefore endorsing it could have given the impression of accepting either their teaching or their authority ("Paul and Jesus: The Problem of Continuity," 190-91).

39. Despite his overall optimism, Marshall really admitted as much when he observed that because of the Evangelists' own theology, "we cannot simply compare the Gospels with Paul if we are trying to compare Jesus and Paul" ("Jesus, Paul and John," 22).

culture. Today's rising culture and the more interconnected intellectual climate that it heralds may offer new possibilities for breaking out of this largely sterile approach and discovering a more authentic understanding of Jesus and of Paul by the use of a more holistic methodology, which will avoid setting them in opposition to each other and will instead hold both the diversity and unity in creative tension. Asking new questions may well open up hitherto unseen doors of perception, which will enable us to understand more clearly both the individuality and the shared heritage of each of them within a more dynamic framework than has so far been possible. And if the renewed concern for an ecumenical theology of mission provides the matrix within which this can be done, then for the Christian scholar there is the added advantage of redirecting us to a concern that was undoubtedly a priority for both Jesus and Paul. Perhaps our struggles to understand the relationship between Paul and Jesus owe more than we realize to our inbred inability to allow ourselves that open-ended flexibility and freedom which both of them deliberately placed at the center of the gospel.

# The Story of Jesus Known to Paul

David Wenham

No one disputes that Paul was familiar with the story of Jesus' passion and resurrection. The evidence lies primarily in 1 Corinthians, since he reminds the Corinthians in ch. 11 of the tradition of the Last Supper and in ch. 15 of the resurrection traditions. There are plenty of intriguing questions to discuss in connection with those traditions: How does Paul's version of the Last Supper relate to the Gospel narratives? Was Paul unfamiliar with the story of the women finding the empty tomb? How much did he know about the trial and crucifixion of Jesus? These important questions are not the subject of this article. One comment is, however, worth making in passing, and that is that silence on the part of Paul about something may not be taken to be a sign of ignorance. Had the Corinthian church not had acute problems over the observance of the Lord's Supper, we might have concluded that the Supper was unknown in the Pauline churches; had the Corinthians not had mixed-up ideas about the resurrection of the dead, we would not have discovered the extent of Paul's knowledge of the resurrection traditions.

No one disputes that Paul had some knowledge of Jesus' teaching. Again 1 Corinthians is vital evidence, with explicit references to Jesus' teaching on divorce in 1 Cor 7:10-12 and on mission in 1 Cor 9:14. How extensive Paul's knowledge was of the sayings of Jesus is hotly debated among scholars. It is not the purpose of this article to go into that debate, but there is a good case for saying (1) that Paul knew much of the teaching of Jesus and (2) that he saw it as of great importance, echoing it frequently.[1]

But what evidence is there for Paul knowing anything about the pre-passion life and ministry of Jesus, apart from the sayings? Common sense suggests that, if he knew about the passion and resurrection and if he was

1. See, e.g., my "Paul's Use of the Jesus Tradition: Three Samples," in *Gospel Perspectives*, vol. 5, ed. D. Wenham (Sheffield: JSOT, 1985) 7-37; and now especially M. Thompson, *Clothed with Christ* (Sheffield: JSOT, 1991). (I am grateful to Dr. Thompson for comments on this paper.) For a contrary opinion see F. Neirynck, "Paul and the Sayings of Jesus," in *L'Apôtre Paul*, ed. A. Vanhoye (Leuven: Leuven University, 1986) 265-321.

familiar with the sayings of Jesus, he must also have known about Jesus' life before "the night on which he was betrayed." But this does not inevitably follow. Scholars have presupposed (1) that the passion narrative was the earliest narrative of Jesus to circulate, probably being used liturgically, and (2) that the teaching of Jesus may well have been collected together very early, as sayings not in a narrative. Given these admittedly speculative hypotheses and the lack of any explicit reference to Jesus' pre-passion ministry in Paul's writings, it is at least an open question as to whether he knew much about Jesus' life and ministry. The purpose of this article is to gather and briefly review some of the evidence that may suggest that Paul knew more than he openly reveals.

## 1. The Birth of Jesus

To suggest that Paul probably knew the story of Jesus' virginal conception may seem audacious, given the massive scholarly uncertainty that there is about the historical value of the infancy narratives of Matthew and Luke. It is widely held that those narratives represent a relatively late development in the christological thinking of the early church, and Paul, like Mark, is cited as an early Christian writer who knows nothing of the Virgin Birth story.

However, C. E. B. Cranfield has recently challenged this view, referring to Rom 1:3 ("the gospel concerning his Son, who was descended from David according to the flesh"); Gal 4:4 ("God sent forth his Son, born of a woman, born under the law"); Phil 2:7 ("emptied himself, taking the form of a slave, being born in human likeness . . ."). Cranfield notes how in each context Paul uses the Greek verb γίνομαι in preference to the more usual "birth" verb γεννάομαι (with its frequent connotations of being begotten by a father), and comments that this does not prove that Paul knew of the Virgin Birth, but "it seems to me highly likely."[2]

The inference does not seem at all likely to other commentators. Thus J. D. G. Dunn does not even mention the interpretation in question when commenting on Rom 1:3; he explains the use of the verb γίνομαι as follows: "Since γίνεσθαι ('become, come to be') merges into εἶναι ('to be'), the participle phrase has in view more the state of man (= 'born of woman' — Job 14:1; 15:14; 1 QS 11.20-21; 1QH 13.14; 18.12-13, 16) than the event of giving birth itself, for which γεννάω would be the more appropriate word."[3] F. F. Bruce notes Cranfield's view when commenting on Gal 4:4, but concludes that "Paul's word-

2. "Some Reflections on the Subject of the Virgin Birth," *SJT* 41 (1988) 177-98. For others arguing similarly see W. C. Robinson, "A Re-Study of the Virgin Birth of Christ," *EvQ* 37 (1965) 198-212; and J. McHugh, *The Mother of Jesus in the New Testament* (London: Darton, Longman and Todd, 1975) 274-77. A few manuscripts do have the verb γεννάομαι for γίνομαι in Rom 1:3 and Gal 4:4, but the overwhelming majority of texts have γίνομαι.

3. *Romans 1–8*, WBC 38 (Dallas: Word, 1983) 12.

ing . . . throws no light on the question whether he knew of Jesus' virginal conception or not." Bruce speaks of "a well-attested use of γίνομαι as a quasi-passive of γεννάω," and refers to 1 Esdr 4:16; Tob 8:6; Wis 7:3; Sir 44:9; John 8:58.[4] Ronald Fung and R. N. Longenecker argue similarly in their recent Galatians commentaries.[5]

The argument against Cranfield's view is powerful. But it is not conclusive. (1) There is no question that γίνομαι is used in the way Bruce suggests, but the overwhelmingly common verb for "being born," both in the NT and the LXX, is γεννάομαι. Some of the examples of γίνομαι which Bruce cites are in a rather special category, including John 8:58, where Jesus' comment "Before Abraham was (γενέσθαι) I am" refers to Abraham's time of life generally rather than to his birth specifically. (2) Dunn's explanation that in Rom 1:3 the participle γενομένου has in view more the state of a human than the event of birth could be correct,[6] but it is perhaps more plausible in Phil 2:7 (where the contrast is between the divine form and the human form) than in Rom 1:3, where the participle is followed by ἐκ σπέρματος Δαυείδ; and Gal 4:4, where the following phrase is ἐκ γυναικός. It is interesting that in the two LXX verses cited by Dunn to make his point, Job 14:1; 15:14, the "born of woman" phrase is γεννητός γυναικός — the same phrase as is used in Matt 11:11 / Luke 7:28 of John the Baptist — not a participle of γίνομαι. Paul, when speaking of Jesus, specifically avoids this phraseology. It is also interesting that in Galatians 4, when he goes on to speak of Sarah and Hagar and their giving birth, he uses some of the same sort of language as he uses in Gal 4:4 and Rom 1:3 of Jesus (compare ἐκ γυναικός in Gal 4:4 with ἐκ τῆς παιδίσκης and ἐκ τῆς ἐλευθέρας in 4:22, 23; also κατὰ σάρκα in 4:23 with Rom 1:3), but the verb that he uses of Jesus is γίνομαι and of Sarah's and Hagar's sons is γεννάομαι. So compare:

- Gal 4:23 ὁ μὲν ἐκ τῆς παιδίσκης κατὰ σάρκα γεγέννηται
- Gal 4:29 ὁ κατὰ σάρκα γεννηθεὶς ἐδιῶκεν τὸν κατὰ πνεῦμα

with similarly phrased texts about Jesus:

- Gal 4:4 γενόμενον ἐκ γυναικός
- Rom 1:3 γενομένου ἐκ σπέρματος Δαυεὶδ κατὰ σάρκα . . . κατὰ πνεῦμα[7]

4. *The Epistle to the Galatians,* NIGTC (Grand Rapids, Michigan: Wm. B. Eerdmans, 1982) 195.

5. R. Y.-K. Fung, *The Epistle to the Galatians,* NICNT (Grand Rapids, Michigan: Wm. B. Eerdmans, 1988) 182; R. N. Longenecker, *Galatians,* WBC 41 (Dallas: Word, 1990) 171.

6. It might reflect an incarnational understanding of Jesus on Paul's part (hence the stress on his "becoming" human), as well as perhaps a consciousness that Jesus' birth was out of the ordinary.

7. The argument about the different verbs used is propounded by Robinson, "Virgin Birth,"

(3) In addition to Paul's consistent use of the verb γίνομαι, where we might expect γεννάομαι (or γεννητός), we note that in Gal 4:4 and Rom 1:3 the participle follows and describes "his Son" (τὸν υἱόν / τοῦ υἱοῦ αὐτοῦ). The one who is born of the seed of David and of a woman is in both contexts called "God's son." In itself it proves nothing that Paul refers to Jesus' divine Father (often) and to his human mother (once), but never to a human father. And yet his choice and combination of language (including the verb he uses) would certainly be in keeping with a belief in the Virgin Birth. It seems to be readily assumed that Paul could have believed in Jesus' natural conception and at the same time in his divine sonship; but it is by no means certain that his remarkable belief in Jesus as the preexistent Son who came forth from God (probably expressed in Philippians 2 and quite possibly implied in Rom 1:3 and Gal 4:4) would have been compatible in his thinking with a normal human birth.

Not wholly unrelated is the observation that Paul speaks occasionally of Jesus' humanity in an interestingly qualified way — "in the likeness of . . ." (Phil 2:7; Rom 8:3). It is widely agreed that Paul wants to assert the true humanity of Jesus, while affirming his distinctiveness, particularly as far as sin is concerned. Whether Paul's view of Jesus' sinless humanity had any corollary in his understanding of Jesus' birth cannot be proved, but it is not at all improbable.

(4) The language used by Paul in Rom 1:3-4, and also in Gal 4:4, is reminiscent of the infancy narratives of Matthew and Luke. In particular the combination of divine sonship and Davidic lineage is found both in Matthew and especially in Luke — e.g., Luke 1:32, "he will be great, and will be called the Son of the Most High; and the Lord God will give to him the throne of his father David." (Compare Matt 1:1; 2:15; note also "Christ the Lord" language in Rom 1:4; Phil 2:11; Luke 2:11. The emphasis in Gal 4:4 on Christ as born "under the law" is reminiscent of the Lukan infancy narrative, for example, 2:21-24, 27, 39.) This may prove nothing; it could be that the direction of any relationship between the Pauline theology and the Gospel infancy narratives is from Paul to the Synoptic tradition, with Paul's theological ideas being developed into the stories of the Virgin Birth; but it may be that Paul or the tradition that he is using — since he is often thought to be using tradition in Rom 1:3-4 and Philippians 2 — is drawing on an early form of the Virgin Birth story. The fact that Matthew and Luke have such different infancy narratives, but a common core of ideas (including ideas of divine conception and sonship), suggests that the story of the virginal conception was one known independently to both

---

and McHugh, *Mother of Jesus,* and rejected as inconclusive by R. E. Brown, *The Birth of the Messiah* (London: Chapman, 1977) 519. For a survey of differing opinions, showing that commentators have been divided on the interpretation of the evidence from earliest days onward, see E. de Roover, "La maternité virginale dans l'interpretation de Gal 4:4," in *Studiorum Paulinorum Congressus Internationalis Catholicus,* AnBib 17-18 (Rome: Pontifical Biblical Institute, 1963) 2:17-37.

Evangelists and that it goes back very early. This is confirmed by the primitive and highly Semitic character of the infancy narratives.[8]

Paul, we suggest, may well be a witness to this early tradition, contrary to what is commonly thought.[9] It is well known that Paul does have a number of traditions in common with Luke (e.g., the Last Supper and the resurrection appearance to Peter); his traditions may very well have included a narrative of Jesus' birth. This argument stands, irrespective of whether the traditional authorship of the Gospel is maintained. If the traditional authorship is accepted — with the Gospel of Luke being written by a companion of Paul by about 70 C.E., as I. H. Marshall suggests in his commentary on Luke — then the probability that Paul will have been familiar with the story of the Virgin Birth is obviously increased.[10]

## 2. The Baptism and Temptations

It is impossible that Paul, having resided in Palestine in the first half of the first century, will not have known of John the Baptist and his ministry, although, of course, he makes no mention of them. But did he know anything about Jesus' baptism by John?

There is a strong probability that the baptism was common knowledge, and indeed that it was an embarrassment to the early church, since some people, including followers of John, could claim that it proved Jesus to be an inferior to John. This quite probably lies behind Matt 3:14, where Matthew specifically records John's acknowledgment of Jesus' superiority, and the similar emphasis on Jesus' greatness in John 1:20. This may also be why the Synoptists fail to mention Jesus' baptizing ministry in Judea, which the Fourth Gospel mentions: it looked a little at that stage as though Jesus was just a follower of the Baptist.[11]

But although it may seem *a priori* likely that Paul was familiar with the story of Jesus' baptism by John, is there any way of showing that he was? Certainly nothing direct. However, a number of considerations about Paul, his

8. On the similar ideas in Luke 1 and Rom 1:3-4 see G. A. Danell, "Did St Paul Know the Tradition about the Virgin Birth?" *ST* 4 (1951) 94-101. Also Brown, *Messiah,* 312-13.

9. It is also possible that Mark and John attest the tradition indirectly; so Cranfield, "Virgin Birth," 178-79.

10. *The Gospel of Luke,* NIGTC (Exeter: Paternoster, 1978) 33-35. R. J. Cooke, *Did Paul Know of the Virgin Birth?* (London: Epworth, 1926), argues that the question of Jesus' birth must have been one of great interest in the early church and makes much of the link between Luke and Paul. A. Legault, "Saint Paul a-t-il parlé de la maternité virginale de Marie?," *ScEccl* 16 (1964) 481-93, denies that Paul betrays knowledge of the tradition of the Virgin Birth, and supposes that Luke came across the tradition during Paul's Caesarean imprisonment.

11. See among other discussions that of J. R. Michaels, *Servant and Son* (Atlanta: John Knox, 1981) 1-24.

ministry, and his churches add to the likelihood that he did. First, there is the simple observation that the Pauline church, as indeed the church as a whole, was a "baptist" movement, for whom baptism (as the expression of faith) was the normative initiation rite and so very important. This by itself proves little for the question of Paul's knowledge of Jesus' baptism, but the fact that the Christian movement was in many ways so similar to the older Jewish baptist movement of John (and indeed was known to have grown out of the old movement) means that the question of the relationship of the two movements and of their two leaders could hardly have been avoided, at least if the two movements coexisted and had any contact with each other.

The second observation follows from that last point, namely that there is evidence in the book of Acts that the Pauline church and indeed Paul himself had contact with the disciples of John the Baptist and will therefore have had to address the question of John and Jesus. Thus Acts 18:24-28 describes Apollos as one who knew only John's baptism until he was further instructed about Jesus by Paul's friends and colleagues, Priscilla and Aquila. Then Acts 19:1-10 refers to Paul meeting twelve disciples of the Baptist in Ephesus and instructing them about Jesus. There has been much scholarly discussion of the two Acts passages, but, whatever the precise historical background of the passages is, the tradition that Paul had contact with people who were associated with John the Baptist is thoroughly credible.[12] If the traditional location of John's Gospel in Ephesus is accepted, then the case is strengthened, since, as we observed, it probably alludes to controversy about the relative greatness of Jesus and John.

As far as Apollos is concerned, 1 Corinthians confirms that Paul had contact with the eloquent Alexandrian (see 1 Corinthians 1–3 and 16:12). It does not, of course, associate him with John the Baptist. But it is an interesting, if unprovable, hypothesis that Paul's slightly defensive comments on baptism in 1 Cor 1:13-17 may have been in response to some of his critics in Corinth, who preferred Apollos to Paul and who emphasized not only "wisdom / eloquence" and "spirituality," but also baptism.[13] It may be that these Corinthians compared Paul unfavorably with Apollos on all these points; certainly Acts 18:24-25 portrays Apollos as (1) a follower of the Baptist, (2) eloquent, and (3)

12. On the Acts texts and for bibliography, see F. F. Bruce, *The Acts of the Apostles,* 3d ed. (Grand Rapids, Michigan: Wm. B. Eerdmans; Leicester: Apollos, 1990) 401-6. C. K. Barrett, "Apollos and the Twelve Disciples of Ephesus," in *The New Testament Age,* ed. W. C. Weinrich (Macon: Mercer University, 1984) 29-39, suggests a background of controversy over whether it was enough to be baptized with John's baptism (as was Jesus himself) or whether it was necessary to be baptized in the name of Jesus in order to receive the Spirit.

13. It is possible that 1 John addresses a related church situation involving false teachers who emphasized baptism ("water"), spiritual anointing, and knowledge, but who failed to give proper emphasis to the cross ("the blood"). Whether their teaching had any connection with current ideas about the Baptist and Jesus is impossible to prove, though there is reason to believe that the Johannine community was aware of controversy about John and Jesus. (I am indebted to the Rev. Ray Porter for suggestions relating to 1 John.)

"boiling in spirit." It does not indicate that his "baptist" tendencies carried over into his Christianity, but it is possible that Paul's remarks playing down the importance of the baptizer and commenting on his own nonbaptist priorities — "Christ did not send me to baptize but to preach" — could have been in response to some followers of Apollos who emphasized baptism more than Paul. We may note also 1 Cor 10:1-5, where Paul warns against misplaced confidence in the sacraments.

The argument so far has still been mostly at the level of *a priori* probabilities. Is there any more concrete evidence that Paul knew the story of Jesus' baptism, as the Gospels describe it? Again the answer must be that there is no direct evidence. However, the third point to note is that the Gospels' description of Jesus' baptism and Paul's understanding of Christian baptism have several features in common. Jesus' baptism in the Gospels is (1) a baptism with water, (2) accompanied by the descent of the Spirit, and (3) associated with divine sonship — hence the words of royal adoption, "You are my Son." For Paul Christian baptism is (1) with water, (2) in the Spirit, and (3) associated with adoption as "sons" of God.[14]

To jump too quickly from this observed parallelism to the conclusion that Paul derived his view of Christian baptism from the story of Jesus' baptism would be to ignore all sorts of questions and issues. There are differences as well as parallels. Paul, for example, has a distinctive emphasis on Christian baptism as "into Christ" and in particular as into Christ's death. Furthermore, the parallelism that there is does not necessarily prove Paul's knowledge of the Jesus tradition; it could alternatively be argued that the Gospel tradition of Jesus' baptism has been influenced and shaped by church tradition and practice rather than vice versa.

Despite these complications, there is still a case for making the suggested connection. It is true that for Paul Christian baptism is "into Christ" in a way that Jesus' own baptism could not be, but that may simply be to recognize that for Paul Jesus' experience is primary and Christian experience is derivative from that of Jesus.[15] It is true that Paul associates baptism with the death of Jesus and that this introduces an idea that is not explicit in the Gospel narratives of Jesus' own baptism (though it may conceivably be implicit). But to recognize that is only to admit that Paul's understanding of baptism is not only based on

14. Some scholars have questioned whether certain Pauline texts, such as 1 Cor 6:11; 12:13, do refer to water baptism, or only to baptism in the Spirit. G. R. Beasley-Murray, *Baptism in the New Testament* (London: Macmillan, 1963) 167-71, argues persuasively for a double reference (but see also J. D. G. Dunn, *Baptism in the Holy Spirit* [London: SCM, 1970] 120-32). On the connection of baptism and sonship, see most directly Gal 3:23–4:6 (cf. Romans 8). For discussion of the relationship of Jesus' baptism and Christian baptism see, among others, Beasley-Murray, *Baptism*, 63-67; Dunn, *Baptism*, 32-37.

15. If Jesus' baptism was seen as the occasion and / or means of his experiencing and being anointed with the eschatological Spirit (as the anointed Messiah), so for the disciples baptism is the occasion and means of receiving kingdom, Messiah, and Spirit.

the story of Jesus' baptism: his post–death / resurrection perspective has enriched his understanding, and he may also have been influenced by the sayings of Jesus about "taking up the cross" and sharing his baptism of death (Mark 8:34; 10:39).[16] Baptism has to do not just with sharing the Spirit and the sonship, but also the cross that went with it for Jesus.

As for the argument that the dependence, if there is any, may be from Paul to the Gospel tradition rather than vice versa, it is not possible to rule out this possibility. But that the dependence and influence go the other way is suggested (1) by the way Paul clearly sees the Christian as being incorporated into Christ and his experience, including his death and resurrection, but also into his experience of the Spirit and of sonship; and (2) by Paul's use of "Abba," this being a clear-cut case of a Christian experience that is derivative from the experience of the earthly Jesus. Paul speaks of God sending the Spirit of his Son into our hearts (Gal 4:6). The genitive "of" here could suggest the Spirit given by the risen Jesus or acting for Jesus; but the context, speaking of Jesus' Sonship and our sonship and referring to the crying of "Abba," suggests that the reference is to the Spirit of sonship that was Jesus' experience and is now his followers' experience; we are Jesus' fellow-heirs, having the same Spirit.

The evidence does not add up to proof that Paul knew the story of Jesus' baptism; the dependence, if it does exist, could be via church tradition (unless we are to say that Paul was the first or the only one in the early church to associate water baptism, the Spirit, and sonship). But to argue that would be to admit that Paul is an indirect witness to the Gospel tradition, and, given our earlier *a priori* argument about Paul's probable knowledge of the story of Jesus and John, the possibility of direct dependence is real.

There are no definite verbal echoes of the Gospel tradition, though Paul's language in 1 Cor 12:13 (ἐν ἑνὶ πνεύματι . . . ἐβαπτίσθημεν) is similar to that of John the Baptist in the Q and Johannine traditions (αὐτὸς ὑμᾶς βαπτίσει ἐν πνεύματι ἁγίῳ . . . — Matt 3:11; Luke 3:15; John 1:33). Paul may well be familiar with the Baptist's contrast of his own baptism ἐν ὕδατι (cf. 1 Cor 10:2) and Jesus' baptism ἐν πνεύματι.

The evidence for Paul's familiarity with the story of Jesus' temptation is just as meager. Paul believes in Satanic temptation (e.g., 1 Cor 7:5; Gal 6:1; 1 Thess 3:5), and he believes that the Christian may overcome temptation (1 Cor 10:13). But he does not associate the ideas specifically with Jesus. He does, however, speak of Jesus as one "who knew no sin" (τὸν μὴ γνόντα ἁμαρτίαν, 2 Cor 5:21; compare also other Pauline passages, such as Romans 5, where Jesus is seen as the specifically righteous one). This is a most significant comment for the purposes of this essay, since, although it can be argued that Jesus' sinlessness in 2 Cor 5:21 has more to do with his sacrificial death (he being the perfect offering) than with any historical recollection of his life, it is hard to

16. See Thompson, *Clothed with Christ,* 85.

imagine Paul speaking thus if Jesus' moral uprightness was not part of the tradition of Jesus' earthly life that he knew.[17] Certainly it is part of the Gospel tradition (e.g., John 7:18; 8:46; Matt 3:13-15).

It could be that the phrase "who knew no sin" represents a general recollection of Jesus' moral goodness, but it could also be that the phrase has a more specific reference to the overcoming of particular temptation. There is a parallel phrase in Heb 4:15: "tempted in every way as we are, yet without sin"; presumably the author of Hebrews has in mind, among other things, the agony of Gethsemane (cf. 5:7), and it is probably true that Jesus' sinlessness was particularly associated in Christian thought with his passion (cf. 1 Pet 2:22-23; Matt 27:23-24 *et passim;* Luke 23:4, 47; etc.). But whether Paul had anything specific in mind and whether it included something like the Q or the Markan temptation narratives is impossible to prove.[18]

## 3. The Ministry and Miracles of Jesus and the Apostles

There is reason to believe that Paul was familiar with the kingdom teaching of Jesus (see, e.g., 1 Cor 6:9-10; 4:20; Rom 14:17),[19] but what did he know about the historical context of that teaching — that is, about Jesus' ministry? There is reason to believe that he was familiar with Jesus' teaching about mission (e.g., 1 Cor 9:14), but what did he know, if anything, about the apostolic missions described in the Gospels?

In view of his contacts with the apostles Peter and John and with James the Lord's brother (see Galatians 2), it is highly probable that he knew a great deal. The evidence within his letters of what he knew is fairly meager, but not nonexistent or without interest. Among the relevant data are the following points.

(1) In Rom 15:8 he describes Christ as having "become a servant of the circumcised." Although Paul himself was so keen to have his mission to the

17. M. Casey, *From Jewish Prophet to Gentile God* (Cambridge: Clarke, 1991) 125, argues for a purely sacrificial sense. C. Wolff, "True Apostolic Knowledge of Christ: Exegetical Reflections on 2 Corinthians 5:14ff.," in *Paul and Jesus,* ed. A. J. M. Wedderburn (Sheffield: JSOT, 1989) 96, speaks of Paul endorsing "the widespread Christian idea of Christ's sinlessness . . . ; that presupposes a knowledge of a corresponding conduct on the part of the earthly Jesus."

18. Paul's reference to Jews "seeking signs" is reminiscent of the Gospel accounts concerning Jesus' opponents testing him and asking for a sign (cf. 1 Cor 1:22; Matt 16:1-4 par.). The temptation to do marvelous signs is there also, arguably, in the Q temptation narrative (Matt 4:1-11 par.). Paul's use of "Abba" could derive from the Gethsemane narrative, the term being used in Mark 14:36, and this could be evidence of Paul's knowledge of that scene of temptation; but it is probable that "Abba" was more widely used in the Jesus tradition, including in the Lord's Prayer.

19. See G. Johnston, "'Kingdom of God' Sayings in Paul's Letters," in *From Jesus to Paul,* ed. P. Richardson and J. C. Hurd (Waterloo: Wilfrid Laurier, 1984) 143-56. Also A. J. M. Wedderburn, "Paul and Jesus: The Problem of Continuity," in *Paul and Jesus,* 99-115.

Gentiles recognized, he here indicates his awareness of the thoroughly Jewish context of Jesus' ministry. This fits with the Gospels' picture of Jesus' almost exclusive concentration on mission in Jewish areas, as expressed also in the hard saying of Matt 15:24: "I was sent only to the lost sheep of the house of Israel." Paul knew that it was historically a case of "the Jew first," and he could not and did not wish to deny it.

He does not, of course, regard the Gentile mission as in any way incompatible with the mission of Jesus. On the contrary, he sees it as the theologically logical continuation of the coming of Jesus' mission to Israel and as the completion of God's purpose of mercy for all (see, e.g., Rom 15:8-9: "to confirm the promises made to the ancestors so that the Gentiles may glorify God for his mercy"; also Romans 11, etc.). It is not unlikely that he found encouragement for this view within the teaching and practice of Jesus, perhaps in incidents like that of the Syrophoenician or Canaanite woman described in Matt 15:21-28, in parables like that of the Good Samaritan, or in eschatological sayings such as Matt 24:14 / Mark 13:10; Luke 21:24 (compare Rom 11:25); had Jesus been wholly negative to non-Jews, it could have been difficult for Paul to justify his mission.[20] But, although that may well be correct, the fact is that Paul endorses the Gospels' picture of the Jew coming very much first, and only then the Greek. Paul is aware that the Gentile mission is in some sense an innovation, in which he (Paul) has a particular God-given role.

(2) Paul is aware of the status of "the twelve" (1 Cor 15:5) and of the special position of Simon Peter (1 Cor 15:5; Gal 2:7). So far as Peter in particular is concerned, Paul speaks of him as "one entrusted with the gospel for the circumcised," comparing this with his own commission to the uncircumcised.

These references may at first sight seem to prove little about Paul's knowledge of the ministry of Jesus: he could simply be reflecting on the church situation as he knew it — on the special position of the Twelve in the church and on Peter's leadership in the Jewish-Christian church. However, (a) it is arguable that, when Paul was writing 1 Corinthians, the Twelve as a group were more a historical body than a currently functioning leadership team. In any case, Paul in 1 Cor 15:5 speaks of them in connection with the resurrection appearances — that is, historically.[21]

(b) Paul implies that apostleship — his own as well as others' — has its basis in seeing Jesus (this being understood historically rather than mystically) and in being "sent out" and "entrusted" with a mission by Jesus (1 Cor 9:1; 15:8-9; Gal 2:7-8). The Gospels describe precisely such a "sending out" of apostles by Jesus in his ministry, and, although it is not possible to prove that this sending is what is

20. On the basis in Jesus' teaching for Paul's Gentile mission see C. H. H. Scobie, "Jesus or Paul? The Origin of the Universal Mission of the Christian Church," in *From Jesus to Paul,* 47-60.

21. At the time of the writing of 1 Corinthians, the Twelve had been depleted by the death of James (cf. Acts 12:1-2). For an interesting, if oversubtle, argument about the concept of the Twelve, see E. P. Sanders, *Jesus and Judaism* (London: SCM, 1985) 103.

implied by Paul, it is surely the simplest explanation, especially since Paul shows himself familiar with parts of the mission discourse recorded in the Gospels. Paul refers to the itinerant mission of apostles in his own day (1 Cor 9:5), and this may well have had its roots in the ministry of Jesus.

(c) Paul describes Peter as "entrusted with the gospel *for the circumcised*" (Gal 2:7), though he also associates James and John with this specifically Jewish commission (2:9). He implies that this limited focus of their mission was something they recognized; otherwise Paul's claim to be apostle to the Gentile could have been seen as a challenge to Peter and the others and could itself have been open to challenge. Paul also implies that Peter's commissioning to go to the Jews was somehow comparable to his own dominical call to go to the Gentiles (even if his apostleship was out of due time). What are we to make of this? A plausible explanation is that Paul was familiar not only with Jesus' saying about his own mission to Israel (see above), not only with Q or Markan elements in the mission discourse (e.g., 1 Cor 8:9), but also with Jesus' specific instruction to the Twelve found in Matt 10:5, where he sends them only to the "lost sheep of the house of Israel." It seems also that Paul knew of the singling out of Peter as the leader of the Twelve, and quite possibly of the commissioning described in Matt 16:17-19. The evidence for this does not simply lie in Paul's acknowledgment of Peter's preeminence, but also in some of the language he uses in Galatians 2 to assert his own special call. Paul's explanation that he, Paul, had a "revelation," not from "flesh and blood" but from God, may well be phrased in that way deliberately, in order to make it clear that his commissioning was equivalent to that of "Cephas" (the rock), described in Matt 16:17-19.[22] It is notable that Paul regularly uses the name "Cephas" — rather than Simon — presumably being aware of the tradition of Jesus giving this name to Simon (Matt 16:18; John 1:42).

The conclusion that Paul may well have known three widely disputed pieces of M tradition (Matt 10:5; 15:24; 16:17-19) may go against the grain for those wedded to a rather wooden version of the two-source hypothesis, but the idea that Matthew has retained early tradition which Mark has not reproduced is quite plausible, especially in the case of Matt 10:5; 15:24, where Mark's Gentile interest would have made the sayings concerned problematic.

(3) There is no specific reference to Jesus' miracles in Paul's letters. It is just possible that Paul's reference to the σπλάγχνα Χριστοῦ in Phil 1:8 could be connected to the Gospel stories (including miracle stories) that speak of Jesus having "compassion" (σπλαγχνίζομαι) on those in need (e.g., Matt 9:36; 14:14; 15:32; 20:34; par.).[23] More significantly, Paul knows that apostleship and

22. See more fully in my "Paul's Use," 24-28. See below for Paul's possible knowledge of the inner three — Peter, James, and John.

23. For discussion of the term see P. T. O'Brien, *The Epistle to the Philippians*, NIGTC (Grand Rapids, Michigan: Wm. B. Eerdmans, 1991) 71-72.

miracle-working go together; thus in 2 Cor 12:11-12, where Paul is asserting his equality with the "super-apostles," he says, "The signs of a true apostle were performed among you with utmost patience, signs and wonders and mighty works." It seems to have been a regular tactic of Paul's opponents to contrast him unfavorably with those they regarded as the true and original apostles; they probably questioned his apostleship both on the grounds that he was not an eyewitness of the risen Christ (hence his rhetorical questions in 1 Cor 9:1, "Am I not an apostle? Have I not seen Jesus our Lord?") and because of his supposed lack of miracle-working prowess (hence the comment in 2 Cor 12:11).

The assumption, evidently accepted by Paul, is that the apostolic mission included healing. Where did this assumption come from? We have already seen evidence of Paul's familiarity with some of the contents of the mission discourse (including the "laborer is worthy of his hire" and "go . . . to the lost sheep of the house of Israel"), and it is probably not accidental that the discourse includes the command to "proclaim" and to "heal" (cf. Matt 10:7-8; Luke 9:2; 10:9). The discourse is plausibly seen as constitutive of the apostolic mission: "these twelve Jesus sent out" (ἀπέστειλεν) (Matt 10:5; cf. Luke 9:1-2), and Paul accordingly has to defend his mission in those terms.[24] In Rom 15:18 Paul speaks of his mission as "by word and deed," and he speaks of the power of signs and wonders accompanying his proclamation of the gospel.

Given (1) the cumulative evidence of Paul's familiarity with the traditions of the Synoptic mission discourse — in addition to the sayings mentioned, there are others, including the Matthean "You have received freely, give freely" (10:8) and the Lukan "Eat whatever is set before you" (10:6) — and (2) the evidence which points to the existence of a very early pre-Synoptic version of the discourse, it is reasonable to infer that Paul knew not just isolated sayings of Jesus about mission, but probably a whole discourse.[25] Since Paul associated miracles specifically with the apostles, it is also reasonable to infer that Paul knew of the apostolic mission itself as the context of the teaching.

If Paul knew that the apostolic mission was a miracle-working one, he must have thought of Jesus' mission in similar terms. His own mission (with its signs and wonders) was, as he says, "Christ working through me" (Rom 15:18). On the other hand, when speaking of the "lawless one" in 2 Thess 2:9 Paul refers to his deceptive "power, signs, lying wonders"; if the antichrist figure had such powers, we may confidently assume that Paul believed in the miracles of Jesus even though, with the exception of the overwhelmingly important miracle of the resurrection, he does not directly mention them. Paul's failure to mention Jesus' other miracles need cause no surprise; they were presumably

24. V. P. Furnish, *II Corinthians,* AB 32A (Garden City, New York: Doubleday, 1984) 553, connects 2 Cor 12:11-12 with both Matt 10:1, 8 and 16:17-18.

25. On the mission discourse see D. Dungan, *The Sayings of Jesus in the Churches of Paul* (Oxford: Blackwell, 1971) 41-75; and B. Fjärstedt, *Synoptic Tradition in 1 Corinthians* (Uppsala: Teologiska Institutionen, 1974) 66-99; also my "Paul's Use," 36.

common knowledge, and not a matter of controversy. Apostolic miracles were, however, controversial because of the questions concerning Paul's own ministry.

## 4. The Transfiguration

An interesting case has been made recently by A. D. A. Moses for Paul's knowledge of the Transfiguration story.[26] He looks at that richly complicated chapter 2 Corinthians 3, and notes (among other things) the theme of Moses' shining face on the mountain (compare Jesus on the Mount of Transfiguration), the use of the verb μεταμορφούμεθα in v 18, and the description in 4:6 of God "who has shone in our hearts to give the knowledge of the glory of God in the face of Jesus Christ." The last verse has been taken by scholars as a reference, in the first instance, to Paul's Damascus Road experience; A. D. A. Moses suggests that Paul is defending his ministry against his critics (see 2 Corinthians 3), and is doing so in terms of the Transfiguration, because his critics have been elevating Peter in particular and citing the Transfiguration as setting Peter and his colleagues above others. Paul insists that he (and others) have also seen the glory of the face of Jesus.

The idea is speculative, but not improbable. The importance of the Transfiguration as far as the status of Peter is concerned is suggested by 2 Pet 1:16-18 (irrespective of authorship), and it is possible that sharing in the Transfiguration experience (more than anything else) gave Peter, James, and John a special position within the Twelve. They seem to have such a position in the Synoptic Gospels. Did Paul know of their position? Interestingly Paul refers in Gal 2:9 to Peter, James, and John as the "pillars" of the Jerusalem church; the James concerned this time is the Lord's brother, not the apostle, and so this trio may have nothing to do with the trio of Jesus' ministry (except two common members). However, F. F. Bruce has suggested that James the brother may have succeeded James the apostle within the privileged group of "pillars" after the latter's execution.[27] This theory is not as farfetched as it may at first sound, and if there is anything in it, then the reputation of "the reputed pillars" of the Jerusalem church may in part at least have been based on the Transfiguration. Paul may then be responding to the claims of a "Peter party" in 2 Corinthians 3 and 4, who made much of the Transfiguration; this would fit in with what

26. See A. D. A. Moses, "The Significance of the Transfiguration in Matthew's Gospel Seen in Its Jewish and Early Christian Context" (Ph.D. thesis, Westminster College, Oxford [CNAA], 1992) 234-45. Note also Thompson, *Clothed with Christ,* 84, endorsing J. S. Banks's view that Rom 12:2 may also be seen as a Transfiguration echo.

27. Bruce, *Galatians,* 123. For further discussion of this view and of certain interesting related ideas (e.g., about a possible connection between the "pillars" language of Gal 2:9 and the saying about "those standing" in Mark 9:1 par. and between the "reputed ones" of Gal 2:2, 6, 9 and Mark 10:42, the last verse being addressed particularly to James and John), see a forthcoming article planned by myself and A. D. A. Moses.

was suggested about Galatians 2, where again Paul is affirming his parity with Peter by comparing his experience with that of Peter.

## 5. The Mary / Martha Story and Other Evidence

What other evidence may be adduced? It is possible to argue that Paul's attitudes toward celibacy, poverty, and Christian service may reflect his knowledge of Jesus' own lifestyle.[28] Paul's rather liberated (though often misunderstood) view of women may be a reflection of Jesus' outlook and practice.[29]

One particular example of a Gospel narrative about women which may be echoed in Paul's letters is the story of Mary and Martha (Luke 10:38-42). C. F. D. Moule and others have observed how the description of Mary sitting at the feet of Jesus and of Martha worrying and distracted has striking verbal and conceptual similarities to Paul's discussion of the merits of singleness in Christian service in 1 Cor 7:32-35.[30] Paul sees married persons as potentially more worried and divided in their concerns, and the unmarried person as having the opportunity for undistracted devotion to the Lord. It is some of the vocabulary used that makes the case for connecting the Lukan and Pauline versions attractive here. In particular, Paul speaks of the single person εὐπάρεδρον τῷ κυρίῳ ἀπερισπάστως. The word εὐπάρεδρος is not found in the Lukan story, but its etymological meaning is "sitting well beside" — compare Mary in the story. The word ἀπερισπάστως, "undistractedly," does have a parallel in Jesus' word in Luke 10:40, where it is said of Martha that "she was distracted," περιεσπᾶτο. The case is nowhere proven, but there is at least a good possibility that this Lukan tradition of Jesus was known to Paul.

## 6. Conclusion

The picture that emerges is of Paul knowing, or possibly knowing, a remarkable range of Jesus traditions. He may well have known of Jesus' family (Mary, James, and Jesus' Davidic lineage), of the virginal conception, the baptism, the Jewish

28. See C. Wolff, "Humility and Self-Denial in Jesus' Life and Message and in the Apostolic Existence of Paul," in *Paul and Jesus,* 145-60.

29. See W. Klassen, "Musonius Rufus, Jesus, and Paul: Three First-Century Feminists," in *From Jesus to Paul,* 185-206. He brings out well the similarity between Jesus and Paul, but unnecessarily concludes that 1 Tim 2:9-15 represents a non-Pauline and unliberated attitude.

30. C. F. D. Moule, *The Birth of the New Testament,* 3d ed. (London: Black, 1981) 118-19. Marshall notes the parallel in the *Gospel of Luke,* 452. B. Pixner notes that Mary, Martha, and Lazarus appear to be unmarried, and argues interestingly that they may have been an Essene family; see his *Wege des Messias und Stätten der Urkirche* (Giessen / Basel: Brunnen, 1991) 209. If this was their background, they might very well and appropriately have come to mind when Paul was discussing the advantages of singleness (even if Martha is a negative example).

limits of Jesus' ministry, the choosing and sending of the Twelve, the commissioning of Peter, the miracles, the Transfiguration before the inner three, the incident with Mary and Martha, and something of Jesus' lifestyle and attitude toward women. The evidence is not enormous in quantity or in strength. But what is not very weighty evidence when Pauline parallels to the pre-passion narrative of the Gospels are considered by themselves becomes much more significant when put alongside the far weightier evidence for Paul's knowledge of (1) Jesus' teaching and (2) the passion and resurrection narratives. In addition, we suggested that there is a strong *a priori* possibility that Paul will have been informed about Jesus' ministry, and all we needed to find were clues confirming the probability, not evidence on which to build an unlikely case.

The evidence adduced is interesting in that it points to Paul's familiarity with some of the Gospel traditions concerning which scholars have had most doubts, both traditions that form critics would categorize as "legendary" (i.e., the infancy, baptism, and Transfiguration narratives) and traditions that some source critics would regard as doubtfully authentic (i.e., M and L traditions). The evidence will probably be dismissed by some for exactly these reasons, but it should not be so dismissed. We argued that, quite apart from the Pauline evidence, there was reason to think that the tradition of the virginal conception goes back much earlier than is sometimes supposed; the story of Jesus' baptism (a Q and Markan tradition) has an obvious claim to being primitive, and the story of the Transfiguration has a similar claim. If there is a tacit assumption that such stories must have evolved after the time of Paul, that assumption deserves questioning, as does the tendency to discount the historical value of M and L traditions.

We noticed that Paul's explicit references to the Last Supper, the resurrection stories, and Jesus' teaching on divorce were all evoked by particular things going on in the Corinthian church. And this is true of at least some of the evidence examined in this essay. In particular we saw how it was controversy about Paul's apostolic status that called forth Paul's comments on apostolic ministry and his allusions to the commissioning of Peter and the Transfiguration. Paul presupposes knowledge of the stories concerned, and indeed it seems that the Jesus traditions had been used by others against Paul.[31] In view of this evidence, nothing significant can be made of Paul's silence about other incidents in the ministry of Jesus; it is in one sense fortuitous that he mentions anything at all. The probability is that in the Pauline allusions to Jesus and his teaching we see only the tip of an iceberg that was quite as big as the Gospel mediated to us by Matthew, Mark, Luke, and John.[32]

31. See my "Paul's Use"; also "2 Corinthians 1:17, 18: Echo of a Dominical Logion," *NovT* 28 (1986) 271-79.

32. It could be that Paul's knowledge was as extensive as we have suggested, but still that Paul was not very interested in the story of Jesus. However, his evident interest in Jesus' teaching on divorce and on the Lord's Supper and in Jesus' resurrection — issues that happen to have been raised directly in Corinth — is probably illustrative of the high importance that he attached to Jesus tradition in general.

# Christology and Pneumatology in Romans 8:9-11 — and Elsewhere: Some Reflections on Paul as a Trinitarian

Gordon D. Fee

Most discussions of christology in Paul, as elsewhere in the NT, are primarily concerned with the twin issues of how Paul perceived Christ's deity and how he perceived Christ's relationship with the Father. The concern of this essay is to come at the other side of the christological / trinitarian issue in Paul, namely how he perceived the relationship of Christ to the Spirit, an issue on which much in fact has been written,[1] but at times with what appears to be far more confidence than the data or methodology seems to allow. The contention of this essay is that the idea, common in some quarters, that Paul blurred the relationship of the Risen Lord with the Spirit with a kind of "Spirit christology" is in fact the invention of scholarship, and that Paul himself knew nothing about such.[2]

1. In addition to the studies cited below in section 1, see G. W. Bromiley, "The Spirit of Christ," in *Essays in Christology for Karl Barth,* ed. T. H. L. Parker (London: Lutterworth, 1956) 135-52; and F. F. Bruce, "Christ and Spirit in Paul," *BJRL* 59 (1976-77) 259-85 (= *A Mind for What Matters: Collected Essays of F. F. Bruce* [Grand Rapids, Michigan: Wm. B. Eerdmans, 1990] 114-32). There are many other works on this subject which deal primarily with the historical Jesus and the Spirit, as the avenue to a Spirit christology, which are not included here, since my concern in this essay is with Pauline theology. See, e.g., among many others, G. W. H. Lampe, "The Holy Spirit and the Person of Christ," in *Christ, Faith and History: Cambridge Studies in Christology,* ed. S. W. Sykes and J. P. Clayton (Cambridge: Cambridge University, 1972) 111-30. Among many other studies whose interests are primarily from the standpoint of systematic theology, see N. Hook, "Spirit Christology," *Theology* 75 (1972) 226-32; P. Rosato, "Spirit Christology: Ambiguity and Promise," *TS* 38 (1977) 423-40; and O. Hansen, "Spirit Christology: A Way out of Our Dilemma?" in *The Holy Spirit in the Life of the Church,* ed. P. Opsahl (Minneapolis: Augsburg, 1978) 171-98.

2. Any more than he would have understood one's speaking of God in terms of a "Christ theology" or a "Spirit theology," because he sometimes interchanges the functions of Christ or the Spirit with those of God the Father.

After a brief survey, therefore, I propose (1) to critique both the exegesis and methodology of much of this discussion,[3] (2) to offer an exposition of the one text that is always mentioned in this discussion — Rom 8:9-11 — but which is never carefully analyzed in light of it, and (3) to contend for a methodological alternative which is much more in keeping with the instincts of the early church that led finally to Chalcedon.[4]

## 1

That Paul perceived the closest kind of ties between the exalted Christ and the Holy Spirit can scarcely be gainsaid. Just as the coming of Christ forever marked Paul's understanding of God,[5] so also the coming of Christ forever marked his understanding of the Spirit. The Spirit of God is now also denoted as the Spirit of Christ (Gal 4:6; Rom 8:9; Phil 1:19),[6] who carries on the work of Christ following his resurrection and subsequent assumption of the place

3. I am grateful to the editors for graciously calling my attention to an article by M. Turner that deals with some of these same issues, and comes to many of the same conclusions ("out of the mouth of two witnesses"?) — although the basic concern of that paper is quite different from mine. See "The Significance of Spirit Endowment for Paul," *VE* 9 (1975) 56-69. My attention has also been called to K. Stalder, *Das Werk des Geistes in der Heiligung bei Paulus* (Zürich: Evz-Verlag, 1962) esp. 26-69, who also makes many of the points made in this essay. Cf. also H. D. Hunter, *Spirit-Baptism: A Pentecostal Perspective* (Lanham, Maryland: University Press of America, 1983) 212-30, in an excursus on "Spirit Christology," which, although it overviews the biblical data, comes at the question from the urgencies of systematic theology.

4. I am delighted to offer these musings in honor of my friend Howard Marshall, whose work has been both a model and inspiration to me ever since his "The Synoptic Son of Man Sayings in Recent Discussion," *NTS* 12 (1965-66) 327-51. A presuppositional word about references and the Pauline corpus: (1) Although no argument will hinge on such, I will regularly include references to the entire Pauline corpus, on the grounds that Colossians, Ephesians, 2 Thessalonians, and the Pastorals are first of all Pauline, whatever else. In every case, the inclusion of references from these letters will only serve to demonstrate that the same theology is at work in these matters (the one great exception being Tit 3:6, where, alone in the Pauline corpus, the Spirit is understood to be poured out through the agency of Christ). (2) All references will appear in their chronological order, as I perceive that to be (1-2 Thessalonians, 1-2 Corinthians, Galatians, Romans, Colossians, Philemon, Ephesians, Philippians, 1 Timothy, Titus, 2 Timothy).

5. So that the transcendent God of the universe is henceforth known as "the Father of our Lord Jesus Christ" (2 Cor 1:3; Eph 1:3) who "sent his Son" into the world to redeem (Gal 4:4-5).

6. Some would add 2 Cor 3:17, "the Spirit of the Lord." But despite arguments for this based on v 14 — "because in Christ [the veil] is abolished" — the contextual evidence would seem to support a reference to Yahweh: Paul is citing the LXX in v 16, where "the Lord" refers to Yahweh; the passage is not christological at all, but pneumatological, and Paul far more often refers to the "Spirit of God" than to "the Spirit of Christ"; the use of τὸ πνεῦμα κυρίου, with its articular πνεῦμα and anarthrous κυρίου, is unique to the Pauline corpus, and is best explained as Paul's picking up the reference to Yahweh in v 16; and finally — and decisively for me — the "glory" of the Lord in v 18 almost certainly refers to Christ, as 4:6 makes certain, so that the Lord of whom Christ is the "glory" is Yahweh of the Exodus passage.

of authority at God's right hand. To have received the Spirit of God (1 Cor 2:12) is to have the mind of Christ (v 16). For Paul, therefore, Christ also gives new definition to the Spirit: Spirit people are God's children, who by the Spirit address God in the language of the Son ("Abba") and are thus his fellow heirs (Rom 8:14-17), for whom the Spirit also serves as the ἀρραβών, σφραγίς, or ἀπαρχή ("down payment, seal, firstfruits") of their final inheritance. At the same time Christ is the absolute criterion for what is truly Spirit activity (e.g., 1 Cor 12:3). Thus it is fair to say that Paul's doctrine of the Spirit moves toward christocentricity,[7] in the sense that Christ and *his* work often give definition and focus to the Spirit and his work in the Christian life.

So much is this so that it became popular in NT scholarship — and still is in some quarters — to speak of this relationship in a way that tends to blur the distinctions between Christ and the Spirit. This tendency is due primarily to a (mis)understanding of a few Pauline texts (especially 2 Cor 3:17 and 1 Cor 14:45; sometimes 1 Cor 6:17; Rom 1:4; and Rom 8:9-11); but it is also partly due, one suspects, to a predilection not to take the *person* of the Spirit very seriously in Pauline thought and experience and therefore to resolve both of these matters — the texts and personhood — by suggesting that Paul thought of some kind of loose identification between the Risen Lord and the Holy Spirit — that the Holy Spirit received "personality" by his identification with the Risen Lord.[8]

One can trace this tendency at least as far back as H. Gunkel's brief but seminal work on the Spirit.[9] It was carried forward with special vigor in the influential work of A. Deissmann[10] and W. Bousset,[11] so much so that by 1923 E. F. Scott could say that "in many presentations of Paulinism it has become customary to assume, almost as self-evident, that in Paul the Spirit and Christ are one and the same."[12] The post–World War II impetus to this theological

7. But not absolutely so, as is often asserted; see section 2 below.

8. Cf. J. D. G. Dunn, *Jesus and the Spirit* (Philadelphia: Westminster, 1975) 324-25.

9. By which he "felled the giant" of nineteenth-century liberalism, wherein the Spirit had been identified with consciousness. See *Die Wirkungen des heiligen Geistes nach der populären Anschauung der apostolischen Zeit und der Lehre des Apostels Paulus* (Göttingen: Vandenhoeck & Ruprecht, 1888); ET: *The Influence of the Holy Spirit: The Popular View of the Apostolic Age and the Teaching of the Apostle Paul* (Philadelphia: Fortress, 1979). The giant-killing analogy is from the introduction to the ET by R. A. Harrisville (x). Gunkel's discussion can be found on 112-15; his supporting texts, in his order, are 1 Cor 15:45; 6:7; and 2 Cor 3:17.

10. See esp. *Die neutestamentliche Formel "in Christo Jesu"* (Marburg: N. G. Elwert, 1892). For English readers a succinct overview of his position can be found in *St. Paul: A Study in Social and Religious History* (London: Hodder and Stoughton, 1912 [Ger. original 1911]) 123-35.

11. In *Kyrios Christos* (Göttingen: Vandenhoeck & Ruprecht, 1913); ET: *Kyrios Christos* (Nashville: Abingdon, 1970) 154-55, 160-64.

12. *The Spirit in the New Testament* (London: Hodder and Stoughton, 1923) 178. In keeping with the nature of the book this is stated without documentation.

perspective came especially from N. Q. Hamilton,[13] I. Hermann,[14] and, more recently, J. D. G. Dunn.[15]

The common thread in all of these studies, from Gunkel to Dunn — and in many whom they have influenced[16] — is to start by noting the Pauline texts, usually beginning with 2 Cor 3:17, and then to use such language as "identification,"[17] "equation" (Gunkel, Dunn), or "merge" (Bousset) to speak about this relationship.[18] To be sure, in most cases all of this is said with the proper

13. In his published Basel dissertation (under O. Cullmann), *The Holy Spirit and Eschatology in Paul,* SJT Occasional Papers 6 (Edinburgh: Oliver and Boyd, 1957). In his first chapter (3-16), Hamilton offers a (much too brief to be convincing) analysis of the key texts (2 Cor 3:17; 1 Cor 12:3; Rom 8:9; Gal 4:6; Phil 1:19; Rom 1:3-4; 1 Cor 14:45) so as to demonstrate that "Christology [is] the key to pneumatology." One can trace the influence of this study in almost all the subsequent literature.

14. *Kyrios und Pneuma: Studien zur Christologie der paulinischen Hauptbriefe* (München: Kösel, 1961). This study has also had considerable influence, but only among those who really do think that 2 Cor 3:17 is saying something christological, since in effect Hermann's whole case is based on a demonstrable misunderstanding of this passage.

15. First in articles on two of the key texts ("Jesus — Flesh and Spirit: An Exposition of Romans i.3-4," *JTS* 24 [1973] 40-68; and "I Corinthians 15.45 — Last Adam, Life-giving Spirit," in *Christ and Spirit in the New Testament: Studies in Honour of C. F. D. Moule,* ed. B. Lindars and S. S. Smalley [Cambridge: Cambridge University, 1973] 127-41); later in summary form in *Jesus and the Spirit,* 318-26; and *Christology in the Making* (Philadelphia: Westminster, 1980) 141-49. On the other hand, Dunn also wrote specifically against finding support for this view in 2 Cor 3:17 ("II Corinthians 3.17 — 'The Lord is the Spirit,'" *JTS* 21 [1970] 309-20). For those who write on this issue, and have been influenced by these various scholars, one can trace a parting of the ways between those who follow Hermann and Dunn as the result of this latter article.

16. See, among others, H. Berkhof, *The Doctrine of the Holy Spirit* (London: Epworth, 1964) 21-28; D. Hill, *Greek Words and Hebrew Meanings,* SNTSMS 5 (Cambridge: Cambridge University, 1967) 275-83 — although Hill, to be sure, does so with considerable qualification.

17. This is the obviously operative word; see, e.g., Gunkel, Scott (hesitantly), Hamilton, Hermann, Berkhof, Hill ("virtual identification"); cf. Walter Kasper: "That is why Paul can actually identify the two (2 Cor 3.17)" (in *Jesus the Christ* [New York: Paulist, 1976] 256).

18. Another thread common to many of these studies is the assertion that Paul's "in Christ" and "in the Spirit" formulas amount to one and the same thing, a view which in particular may be traced back to Deissmann *(Formel),* whose thesis in part depends on this interchange; cf. Bousset (160): "The two formulas coincide so completely that they can be interchanged at will." Cf. Hill, *Greek Words,* 276. But this seems to be a considerable overstatement, since in fact there are some significant differences: Paul always uses the preposition (ἐν) with "Christ"; he alternates between πνεύματι / ἐν πνεύματι with "Spirit"; this reflects the fact that the predominant usage of πνεύματι / ἐν πνεύματι is instrumental, whereas the predominant usage of "in Christ" is locative. The differences are demonstrated in Rom 9:1, the one sentence where both formulas appear together. In his asseverations as to his own truthfulness, Paul "speaks the truth [as one who, with them] is in Christ Jesus"; moreover, his own conscience, "by the [inner witness of] the Holy Spirit," bears witness to the same. Thus the two formulas are scarcely interchangeable, except for those places where the soteriological activity of Christ and the Spirit overlap, such as "sanctified in / by Christ Jesus" in 1 Cor 1:2, where the emphasis lies on Christ's redemptive activity, and "sanctified by the Holy Spirit" in Rom 15:16, where the emphasis is on the appropriation by the Spirit of the prior work of Christ. Cf. the more detailed critique of Deissmann in F. Büchsel, "'In Christus' bei Paulus," *ZNW* 42 (1949) 141-58; F. Neugebauer, "Das paulinische 'in Christ,'" *NTS* 4 (1957-58) 124-38; and M. Bouttier, *En Christ: Etude d'exégèse et de théologie pauliniennes* (Paris: Presses Universitaires, 1962).

demurrers, that Paul does indeed also recognize the distinctions,[19] that the identity is "dynamic" rather than "ontological,"[20] or that the identity is not so complete that the one is wholly dissolved in the other.[21] But there can be little question that "identification" is the stronger motif, especially at the level of Christian experience of the Risen Christ and the Spirit, which is asserted for all practical purposes to be one and the same thing.[22]

That the emphasis clearly lies with "identification" rather than "distinction" is evidenced by another thread that runs through these studies as well, namely the rather strong denial that Paul's experience and understanding of God can be properly termed "trinitarian." This is pressed vigorously by Hermann, who goes so far as to argue that the identification of Christ with Spirit is so complete that one can no longer press for a personal identity to the Spirit, separate and distinct from Christ, hence distinct in traditional trinitarian terms.[23] The demurrers of Hamilton and (especially) Dunn are not far from this, so much so that in effect to speak of trinitarianism in Paul is probably to use inappropriate language altogether.[24]

But one may properly question whether all of this is a genuine reflection of Paul's own christology and pneumatology. Three matters give reason to pause: the data from the Pauline Spirit texts taken as a whole; an analysis of the key texts used to support a Spirit christology; and the methodological issue of finding a proper starting point in talking about Paul's understanding of God, including his understanding of Christ and the Spirit. To each of these we turn in brief.

19. Scott, *Spirit,* 183, in fact stands apart from the others mentioned above in that he thinks the "identification" was not deliberate on Paul's part, that it was "forced upon him in spite of himself."

20. Hamilton, *Holy Spirit,* 6, 10.

21. This is the demurral language of H. Ridderbos, *Paul: An Outline of His Theology* (Grand Rapids, Michigan: Wm. B. Eerdmans, 1975) 88, who takes a position similar to the one argued for in this essay, except that he is willing to allow that some of these texts point toward "a certain relationship of identity with each other" (87).

22. Cf. Dunn, "*If Christ is now experienced as Spirit, Spirit is now experienced as Christ* [emphasis his]" (*Jesus and the Spirit,* 323).

23. *Kyrios und Pneuma,* 132-36.

24. Thus Hamilton (*Holy Spirit,* 3): "An attempt to deal with the Spirit in the traditional way as an aspect of the doctrine of the Trinity would be inappropriate to Paul. This is not to deny that the Spirit is for Paul a distinct entity over against the Father and the Son. The problem of the Trinity, which is the occasion of the doctrine of the Trinity, was for Paul no problem." Thus "to deal with the Spirit in the tradition of the New Testament is to avoid all speculation about the nature of the being of the Spirit." (One of course could say the same about Paul's assertions about Christ, which means therefore that one in effect should cease christological discussion altogether!) Dunn ("1 Corinthians 15.45," 139): "*Immanent christology is for Paul pneumatology* [emphasis mine]; in the believer's experience there is *no* [Dunn's emphasis] distinction between Christ and the Spirit. This does not mean of course that Paul makes no distinction between Christ and Spirit. But it does mean that later Trinitarian dogma cannot readily look to Paul for support at this point." If by "immanent christology" Dunn denotes the traditional sense of "Christ as he is in himself," then this statement seems far removed from Pauline realities.

## 2

We noted above that the coming of Christ forever marked Paul's understanding of the Spirit.[25] But what does *not* seem to cohere with the data is the oft-repeated suggestion that "we have to think of the Spirit in *strictly* christocentric terms."[26] The data themselves indicate that this is something of an overstatement.

The use of πνεῦμα and πνευματικός language, referring specifically to the Holy Spirit, occurs over 140 times in the Pauline corpus,[27] the vast majority of which occur in the so-called *Hauptbriefe*. The full name, Holy Spirit, occurs in 17 instances. Depending on how one understands "the Spirit of the Lord" in 2 Cor 3:17, Paul refers to "the Spirit of God" / "His Spirit" 16 (or 15) times, and to "the Spirit of Christ," or its equivalent, but 3 (or 4) times. Some observations about these statistics:

(1) Paul refers to the Holy Spirit as a full name in the same way as, and at about the same ratio that, he refers to Christ by the full name, our Lord Jesus Christ. This use of the full name in itself suggests "distinction from," not "identity with," as the *Pauline presupposition.*

(2) Despite suggestions to the contrary, Paul thinks of the Spirit *primarily* in terms of the Spirit's relationship to God (the Father, although he never uses this imagery of this relationship). Not only does he more often speak of the "Spirit of God" than of the "Spirit of Christ," but God is invariably the subject of the verb when Paul speaks of human reception of the Spirit. Thus God "sent forth the Spirit of his Son into our hearts" (Gal 4:6), or "gives" us his Spirit (1 Thess 4:8; 2 Cor 1:22; 5:5; Gal 3:5; Rom 5:5; Eph 1:17), an understanding that in Paul's case is almost certainly determined by his OT roots, where God "fills with" (Exod 31:3) or "pours out" his Spirit (Joel 2:28), and the "Spirit of God" comes on people for all sorts of extraordinary ("charismatic") activities (e.g., Num 24:2; Judg 3:10).

Two passages in particular give insight into Paul's understanding of this primary, presuppositional relationship. In 1 Cor 2:10-12 he uses the analogy of human interior consciousness (only one's "spirit" knows one's mind) to insist that the Spirit alone knows the mind of God. Paul's own concern in this analogy

25. One must put it that way, of course, because even though the *experience* of the Spirit for the earliest believers followed their experience with Christ, Incarnate and Risen, their *understanding* of the Spirit begins with the OT, and it is that understanding which is being transformed by Christ, just as was their understanding of what it meant for Jesus to be Messiah, not to mention their understanding of God himself.

26. This is the language of Berkhof, *Doctrine,* 24 (emphasis mine). Cf. M. E. Isaacs, *The Concept of Spirit: A Study of Pneuma in Hellenistic Judaism and Its Bearing on the New Testament,* HeyM 1 (London: Heythrop College, 1976) 124: "For all N.T. writers the power and presence of God, signified by πνεῦμα, is grounded exclusively in Jesus, the Christ."

27. For a full discussion of these data on usage in Paul, see ch. 2 in my forthcoming monograph, *God's Empowering Presence: The Holy Spirit in the Letters of Paul* (Peabody, Massachusetts: Hendrickson).

is with the Spirit as the source of *our* understanding the cross as God's wisdom; nonetheless the analogy itself draws the closest kind of relationship between God and his Spirit. The Spirit alone "searches all things," even "the depths of God";[28] and because of this singular relationship with God, the Spirit alone knows and reveals God's otherwise hidden wisdom (1 Cor 2:7).

In Rom 8:26-27 this same idea is expressed obversely. Among other matters, Paul is here concerned to show how the Spirit, in the presence of our own weaknesses and inability to speak for ourselves, is able to intercede adequately on our behalf. The effectiveness of the Spirit's intercession lies precisely in the fact that God, who searches our hearts, likewise "knows the mind of the Spirit," who is making intercession for us.

(3) Given these data, the cause for wonder is that Paul should *also* refer to the Spirit as "the Spirit of Christ." That he does so at all says something far more significant about his christology than about his pneumatology — although the latter is significant as well. Here is evidence for Paul's "high christology," that a person steeped in the OT understanding of the Spirit of God as Paul was, should so easily, on the basis of his Christian experience, speak of him as the Spirit of Christ as well.[29]

(4) A careful analysis of all the texts in which Paul identifies the Spirit either as "the Spirit of God" or "the Spirit of Christ" suggests that he chose to use the genitive qualifier when he wanted to emphasize the activity of either God or Christ that is being conveyed to the believer by the Spirit. Thus the church is God's temple because God's Spirit dwells in their midst (1 Cor 3:16),[30] or God gives his Holy Spirit to those he calls to be holy (1 Thess 4:8), and so on. So also in the three texts in which the Spirit is called the Spirit of Christ, the emphasis lies on the work of Christ in some way. We will note below how this is so in Rom 8:9. In Gal 4:6 the emphasis is on the believers' "sonship," evidenced by their having received "the Spirit of God's Son," through whom they use the Son's language to address God; and in Phil 1:19 Paul desires a fresh supply of the Spirit of Christ Jesus so that when on trial Christ will be magnified, whether by life or by death.

(5) Finally, in Rom 8:9-11 Paul clearly and absolutely identifies "the Spirit of God" with "the Spirit of Christ"; on the other hand, as will be noted momentarily, nowhere does he make such an identification of the Risen Christ with

28. An idea that reflects Paul's background in the OT and Jewish apocalyptic (cf. Dan 2:22-23).

29. It is of some interest that this point is so seldom made in the literature.

30. This is an especially important *theological,* vis-à-vis christological, understanding of the experience of the Spirit, where the OT motif of God's presence (from Sinai, to the tabernacle, to the temple, and finally in the promised new covenant) is seen to have been fulfilled by the Spirit's presence in the gathered community (and also in the life of the individual believer in 1 Cor 6:19). One wonders in light of such passages about the language of the Spirit as "exclusively christocentric" in Paul.

the Spirit, including the handful of texts that might appear to suggest otherwise. To these we now turn.

### 3

We cannot here examine the several texts at full length. My aim is simply to offer some exegetical conclusions, supported elsewhere in more detail.[31]

(1) *2 Corinthians 3:17.* This is the text which lies at the root of all Spirit christology talk. Indeed, Hermann rests his whole case on this passage. But in fact Paul's words, "Now the Lord is the Spirit," do not even remotely suggest that the Spirit is to be identified with the Risen Lord — as Dunn himself, the most vigorous advocate of Spirit christology in the English-speaking world, acknowledges.[32]

Similar to what he does in 1 Cor 10:4 and Gal 4:25, Paul here uses a form of midrash pesher to offer biblical support for what is said in v 16 — by the anaphoric use of ὁ δὲ κύριος, which picks up and interprets this word from the preceding pesher citation of Exod 34:34 (LXX). Thus he has "cited" Exodus to the effect that "whenever anyone [not Moses] turns to the Lord [so as to be converted], the veil is removed." "Now," he goes on to interpret, for the sake of his point in context, "ὁ κύριος in that passage stands for the Spirit."

Once this literary device has been observed, much of the debate over Paul's language in this text becomes irrelevant. By "the Lord," Paul does not intend either God or Christ; he intends the Spirit. That is, he is interpreting the text of Exodus in light of the present argument, which is, after all, a pneumatological passage, not a christological one. By this interpretative device he keeps alive his argument that his ministry is that of "the new covenant of the Spirit" (v 6). "The Lord" in the Exodus narrative, he is saying, is now to be understood (not literally, but in an analogical way) as referring to the Spirit — not because this is the proper identification of the Lord in Exod 34:34, but because in this argument that is the proper way to understand what happens at conversion. The Spirit, who applies the work of Christ to the life of the believer, is understood to be the one who removes the veil, so that God's people can enter into freedom.

This is further made clear by the clause that follows, where the Spirit is called "the Spirit of the Lord." By this further designation Paul himself seems intent on removing any misunderstandings brought about by his previous clause. That is, "in interpreting 'the Lord' in the Exodus passage as referring to the Spirit, I do not mean that the Spirit *is* the Lord; rather, the Spirit is, as always, the Spirit *of the Lord.*"

31. See the full exegetical discussion of all the Spirit texts in the Pauline corpus in Fee, *God's Empowering Presence.*

32. See Hermann, *Kyrios und Pneuma.*

Thus, in this crucial text, there is not a hint of "identity" between the Risen Lord and the Holy Spirit.

(2) *1 Corinthians 15:45.*[33] Here is the more difficult passage, and the one on which Dunn ultimately rests his case.[34] In a passage whose whole point is soteriological-eschatological, Paul is intent on one thing — to demonstrate from Christ's own resurrection that there must be a future, bodily resurrection of believers as well. Thus he begins by citing the LXX of Gen 2:7, in another expression of midrash pesher:[35]

| | | | |
|---|---|---|---|
| ἐγένετο ὁ | πρῶτος ἄνθρωπος | Ἀδὰμ εἰς ψυχὴν | ζῶσαν |
| ὁ | ἔσχατος | Ἀδὰμ εἰς πνεῦμα | ζῳοποιοῦν |

Several observations about this citation-turned-interpretation are needed: (1) Paul's *modifications* of the LXX in the first line — the additions of the adjective "first" and of the name "Adam" — seem specifically designed to lead to the second line, where his real concern lies. (2) The two words that describe

33. Cf. esp. the similar critique of Dunn on this passage by Turner, "Significance," 61-63, an article of which I was unfortunately unaware when I wrote my commentary, where the details of the following exegesis are worked out in more detail.

34. Even though Dunn recognizes that the crucial clause about Christ has been shaped by the former one about Adam, he insists that Paul intends something quite christological here. His points are: (1) v 45 is not an explanation of v 44, but advances the argument in its own right [I would say no and yes to this]; (2) that the ἐγένετο from the first clause must be read in the second as well [yes, but not with Dunn's intent]; (3) that therefore Paul understands a fundamental change to have taken place at Christ's resurrection, in which he is now to be identified with the Spirit whom the Corinthians have experienced, but in some aberrational ways [an especially questionable point, in that it has Paul inserting a red herring into an otherwise consistent and self-contained argument]; (4) that this identification is made certain by the qualifier "life-giving" with πνεῦμα, which is elsewhere attributed to the Holy Spirit (2 Cor 3:6); and that Paul's intent here is similar to 12:3, where by identifying the Spirit whom they have received with the Risen Christ, he gives christocentric content to their experience of the Spirit. Rather than refute this point by point, I will let the interpretation offered here (and given in more detail in my *The First Epistle to the Corinthians,* NICNT [Grand Rapids, Michigan: Wm. B. Eerdmans, 1987] 787-90; and *God's Empowering Presence*) stand as that refutation. But it does need to be noted that Dunn's primary assertion on the basis of Paul's use of "life-giving πνεῦμα" — namely, that the "believer's *experience of the life-giving Spirit* is for Paul proof that the risen Jesus is σῶμα πνευματικόν" (131; emphasis mine; Dunn emphasizes the whole sentence) — is just that, an assertion pure and simple; it is difficult to imagine anything further removed from Paul's intent than this, which in fact turns Paul's point quite on its head, namely that Christ's now assuming a "supernatural body" is the certain evidence that the Corinthian believers, too, will eventually "bear such a body."

35. Cf. E. E. Ellis, *Paul's Use of the Old Testament* (Edinburgh: Oliver and Boyd, 1957) 141-43; it is doubtful, however, whether Paul is here citing a midrash that had already taken hold in Christian circles (95-97). Paul himself is perfectly capable of such pesher. Dunn ("1 Corinthians 15.45," 130) argues that the whole sentence "stands under the οὕτως γέγραπται — including verse 45b, as the absence of δέ indicates." Yes and no. This is true of the pesher as such, but Paul hardly intends the second clause to be understood as Scripture — even in a targumic way — in the same sense that the first line is.

Adam and Christ respectively are the cognate nouns for the adjectives ψυχικόν and πνευματικόν in v 44. This in fact is *the only reason both for the citation and for the language used to describe Christ.* This clear linguistic connection implies that the *original bearers* of the two kinds of bodies mentioned in v 44 are Adam and Christ.[36] That is, the two "Adams" serve as evidence that even as there is a ψυχικός body (as the first Adam demonstrates; Gen 2:7), so also Christ, the second Adam, by his resurrection is evidence that there must be a πνευματικός body.[37] (3) Not only so, but Paul's *reason* for saying that Christ became "a life-giving πνεῦμα" is that the LXX had said of Adam that he became "a living ψυχή." That is, the *language of the citation* called for the *parallel language about Christ.* (4) Even though the content of the second line is neither present nor inferred in the Genesis text, it nonetheless reflects the language of the prior clause in the LXX, "and he *breathed* into his face the *breath of life* (πνοὴν ζωῆς)"; now in speaking about Christ, Paul makes a play on this language. The one who will "breathe" new life into these mortal bodies — with life-giving πνεῦμα (as in Ezek 37:14) and thus make them immortal — is none other than the Risen Christ himself. (5) The language "life-giving" thus repeats the verb used of Christ in the previous Adam-Christ analogy in v 22, indicating decisively, it would seem, that the interest here, as before, is in Christ's resurrection as the ground of ours ("in Christ all will be made alive"). Thus the argument as a whole, as well as the immediate context, suggests that even though Christ has now assumed his exalted position in a σῶμα πνευματικόν and is thus a "life-giving πνεῦμα," *his function in this particular role will take place at the resurrection of believers,* when he "makes alive" their mortal bodies so that they too assume a σῶμα πνευματικόν like his.

The concern of line 2, therefore, is not christological, as though Christ and the Spirit were somehow now interchangeable terms for Paul. Indeed, despite the combination of "life-giving" and πνεῦμα, he almost certainly does not intend to say that Christ became *the* life-giving Spirit, but a life-giving spirit.[38] Christ is not *the* Spirit; rather, in a play on the Genesis text, Paul says that Christ through his resurrection assumed his new existence in the spiritual realm, the realm of course that for believers is the ultimate sphere of the Spirit, in which they will have "spiritual" bodies, adapted to the final life of the Spirit.

(3) It seems evident, therefore, that in the two basic texts where Paul is alleged to identify the Risen Christ with the Spirit, he does not in fact do so at all. His language in both cases is dictated by his "interpretation" of OT passages, in light of the urgencies of the present contexts. And without these texts, the whole

36. As Dunn also notes ("I Corinthians 15.45," 130).

37. This is the point that Turner, "Significance," 62, makes especially strongly.

38. Grammar must still have its day in court. Paul tends to be very precise, and generally unambiguous with his use or non-use of the definite article with "Spirit." In the nominative, both as subject or as predicate noun (as here), when Paul intends the Holy Spirit he always uses the article. For a full analysis of Pauline usage see ch. 2 in *God's Empowering Presence.*

idea lies in shambles, because the rest of the texts are seen merely to support one or both of the other two. Thus, for example, *1 Cor 6:17* is often drawn in as support, "The one who joins himself to the Lord is one S / spirit[39] [with him]." Here again the language has been dictated by the argument and the immediately preceding sentence, "The one who joins himself to a prostitute is one body [with her]." Whereas the latter sentence makes perfectly good sense, and is based on the clear intent of Gen 2:24, the former sentence standing on its own is near nonsense and becomes meaningful precisely because of Paul's penchant to do this very thing — let a prior sentence or clause dictate how he expresses a contrasting clause. Paul's point seems perfectly clear, even if the language with which that point is made is less so, namely that the Spirit has forged a "uniting" relationship between the believer and the Lord of such a kind that absolutely prohibits an illicit "uniting" of the believer's body with that of a prostitute.

So also with *Rom 1:4,* and the phrase κατὰ πνεῦμα ἁγιωσύνης, every word of which, as Cranfield points out,[40] is full of difficulty. This is Dunn's second text by which he supports a Spirit christology; but he does so by circuitous and convoluted exegesis, which proceeds as if v 2 did not exist and as though a concern to establish "to the Jew first" were not a part of the letter. On this matter, the argument by E. Schweizer, that vv 3 and 4 reflect the two expressions of Christ's (the Messiah's) existence as earthly and heavenly and in that succession, is to be preferred at almost every point to that of Dunn.[41] And in any case, it is difficult to imagine how this phrase can be turned into: "The personality and the role of Jesus expand and swallow up the less well-defined personality and more restricted role of the Spirit. *Jesus becomes the Spirit* (1 Cor. xv.45); . . . the Spirit becomes the

39. For this translation see Fee, *First Corinthians,* 259-60.

40. See *The Epistle to the Romans,* ICC (Edinburgh: T. & T. Clark, 1975) 1:62-63.

41. See "Röm. 1:3f. und der Gegensatz von Fleisch und Geist vor und bei Paulus," *EvT* 15 (1955) 563-71. The position Dunn took in his 1973 article is only slightly moderated in his commentary (*Romans 1–8,* WBC 38A [Dallas: Word, 1988] 13). If reader criticism counts for anything, and it must in this case since the Romans for the most part had not heard Paul in person, then it is hard to imagine the circumstances in which they could have understood Paul as Dunn presents him to be arguing. In an otherwise useful overview of the use of σάρξ in Paul, Dunn concludes that the σάρξ / πνεῦμα contrast in vv 3-4 is primarily to be understood in Paul's more characteristically theological way, rather than as indicating two successive spheres of existence — so much so that to speak of Christ as "descended from the seed of David κατὰ σάρκα" is ultimately pejorative. He was thus "bound and determined by the weakness and inadequacy of the human condition, *allowed worldly considerations to determine his conduct* [emphasis mine], he was merely Son of David and no more — Messiah indeed, but a disappointing, ineffective, irrelevant Messiah" (57). And this in a Pauline sentence that begins: "The gospel of God which he promised beforehand through his prophets in Sacred Scripture"! How could the Romans have so understood κατὰ σάρκα? Or that κατὰ πνεῦμα ἁγιωσύνης has also (especially) to do with Jesus' earthly life ("In Paul's view the sonship of the earthly life was constituted by the Holy Spirit" [57])? Although this latter is clearly the view of Luke, and therefore may be assumed to be Paul's point of view, nowhere does Paul make such a point, and it can scarcely be asserted to be true by the circuitous means by which Dunn arrives at it in this article.

executive power of the exalted Christ."[42] That would indeed seem to be a bit more weight than κατὰ πνεῦμα ἁγιωσύνης can be made to handle.

(4) The final text is *Rom 8:9-11,* which we need to look at in slightly more detail, since in fact it not only does *not* support an identification of Christ with the Spirit, but also offers some keys to getting at this relationship in Paul.

## 4

On the surface, and especially in English translation, the set of clauses in Rom 8:9-11 can seem very confused — and confusing. But a couple of observations about Pauline style and present urgencies may help us to unpack both the argument and its Spirit talk. First, a Pauline stylistic observation. As in the passages just noted, where an OT text about which he is going to make a Christian application sets up both the language and pattern of his second sentence or clause, so too Paul tends at times to let his own rhetoric dictate *the way some things are said,* which *on their own* would almost certainly have been said with much less ambiguity.[43] The present set of sentences is particularly noteworthy in this regard.

Second, as to the argument itself, several observations are pertinent: (1) Both the argument as a whole (from 7:6, picked up at 8:1-2) and the paragraph itself make it clear that Paul's primary interest is in the role the Spirit plays in "the righteousness of God" that comes "apart from Torah through faith in Christ Jesus" (3:21-22); and in this instance the clear emphasis is on the role / function of the *indwelling* Spirit.[44] In v 2 Paul had said (in a kind of thesis statement for 8:1-11) that "the 'law' of the Spirit of life has . . . freed you from the 'law' of . . . death." This paragraph elaborates that point.[45]

(2) At the same time the linguistic ties to 6:4-14 are so unmistakable[46]

42. "Jesus — Flesh and Spirit," 59 (emphasis mine).

43. Note, e.g., the notoriously un-Pauline sentiment expressed in the final clause in 1 Cor 6:13, that "the Lord is for the body." This has been set up by the double rhetoric of vv 12 and 13, the latter expressing the Corinthian position (with which Paul probably agrees): "Food for the stomach and the stomach for food." But this is not true of the body itself, he goes on: "The body is [not for sexual immorality but] for the Lord, and the Lord for the body." Seen as rhetoric, and as his own construct to balance the former clause, the sentence makes perfectly good sense. It is not that the Risen Lord exists for the sake of our bodies, in the same way that the stomach exists for food, but that the resurrection of Christ has singularly marked our human bodies as not irrelevant but as belonging to him and destined for resurrection (as v 14 goes on to explain).

44. Evidenced by the thrice repeated, "the Spirit dwells in you," plus the language "have the Spirit of Christ" and thus "Christ in you."

45. Just as vv 3-8 elaborate the first point, "freedom from the 'law' of sin."

46. This takes place esp. in the apodoses of vv 10-11. (1) "The body is dead because of sin" echoes "the body of sin" and "sin reigning in our mortal bodies" in 6:6, 12; (2) "the Spirit is life because of righteousness" echoes 6:13, where we are to present ourselves as "alive" from the dead (because of Christ's death and resurrection in which by faith we participate) and our members as instruments "of righteousness" for God; (3) "He who raised Christ from the dead shall also give

that it is hard to escape the conclusion that Paul is here intentionally tying together what was said there about Christ with what is said here about the Spirit. The singular difference between this passage and that one is that the "death / resurrection" motif in the former has primarily to do with sin and righteousness in terms of behavior, while this one has to do with present and future eschatology in terms of future bodily resurrection. Thus, just as he does in vv 1-4, Paul seems intent to tie together what has been said earlier in the argument about the work of Christ with what he now says about the life of the Spirit.

(3) The present passage is thus another excellent example of the eschatological tension in Paul between the "already" (the indwelling Spirit of God / Christ means life *now*, predicated on the righteousness Christ has provided) and the "not yet" (even though sin means death for the present mortal bodies [cf. 5:12, 21], the indwelling Spirit means life both now and forever, through resurrection). Thus it is *because* of the Spirit's presence now, not through the Spirit's power later, that our future resurrection is guaranteed.[47]

With this passage, therefore, Paul seems intent to tie together both the

---

life to our mortal bodies" echoes "Christ was raised from the dead through the glory of the Father" in 6:4 and "if we died with Christ . . . we shall live with him" in 6:8.

47. Thus the logic of the argument itself, as well as the weight of both external and internal evidence favors the reading τὸ ἐνοικοῦν αὐτοῦ πνεῦμα ("will live *because of* his Spirit who dwells in you"; read by B D F G K Ψ 33 181 1241 1739 1881 lat MajT Origen); the alternative, τοῦ ἐνοικοῦντος αὐτοῦ πνεύματος ("*through* the Spirit who dwells in you"), is read by ℵ A C 81 88 104 326 436 2495 pc and NA[26] / UBS[3]. The UBS committee made its choice first of all by negating the witness of B ("in the Pauline corpus the weight of B when associated with D G . . . is quite considerably lessened") and then favoring the genitive "on the basis of the combination of text-types, including the Alexandrian (ℵ A D 81), Palestinian (syr[pal] Cyril-Jerusalem), and Western (it[61?] Hippolytus)" (B. M. Metzger, *A Textual Commentary on the Greek New Testament* [London: United Bible Societies, 1971] 517). But that will scarcely do in this case. The same combination of text-types exists even more strongly for the alternative reading (B 1739, which in combination more often represent the "Alexandrian" text than otherwise; the preponderance of Western witnesses, early and widespread; and several "Palestinian" Fathers [Methodius, Origen, Theodoret]). The issue therefore must be decided on the grounds of transcriptional probability, since the variation can only have been deliberate, not accidental. Here the evidence weighs altogether in favor of the accusative, since that is not what one expects when διά modifies a verb for resurrection (cf. 6:4; 1 Cor 6:14) — all the more so when agency would make such perfectly good sense. Despite Cranfield, *Romans*, 1:392, to the contrary (who suggests that it might have been changed to the accusative on the basis of the accusatives in v 10), one cannot in fact imagine the circumstances in which the very natural genitive would have been changed so early and often to the much less common accusative — especially so in light of 6:4, where the διὰ τῆς δόξης τοῦ πάτρος not only reflects Paul's ordinary habits but also, by its very difficulty, begs to be changed to the accusative (which would seem to make so much more sense) — yet no one ever did so. Intrinsic probability — the argument as here presented — only adds to the weight of this conclusion.

It should perhaps be pointed out in passing that this textual decision also does away with the one place in the Pauline corpus which suggested that the Spirit was involved in the resurrection of Christ. All other passages (e.g., 1 Cor 1:14; Eph 1:1-21), which are sometimes brought into this purview, are dependent on reading the genitive in this passage. Paul's point in v 11 is not on the Spirit's agency, but on the indwelling Spirit as eschatological guarantor.

work of the Spirit with that of Christ, as well as the ethical life of righteousness effected by Christ and the Spirit with the final eschatological inheritance gained through the resurrection of the "mortal" body. The Spirit obviously plays the leading role, both in appropriating the work of Christ previously argued for and as evidence and guarantee of the future — despite present weaknesses and suffering (a matter to be taken up in detail in vv 18-27).

Thus one can trace the flow — and concerns — of the argument through an (abbreviated) display of its basic structure:

| | | | | |
|---|---|---|---|---|
| | 9 But (as for you) you are not in the flesh | | | |
| | | but in the Spirit, | | |
| [A] | since indeed | the Spirit of God | dwells in you. | |
| [B] | Now if anyone does not have | | the Spirit of Christ, | |
| | this person is not of him | | [Christ]. | |
| [B′] | 10 But if Christ is in you, | | | |
| | [C] that means: μέν | | the *body* is *dead* | because of sin, |
| | [D] | δέ | the *Spirit* is *life* | because of righteousness. |
| [A′] | 11 Now if | the Spirit of him [God] | who raised Jesus . . . dwells in you, | |
| | then | he | (who raised Christ Jesus from the dead) | |
| | [(C) / D′] | will also give *life* to your *mortal bodies,* | | |
| | | | because of his *Spirit* who dwells in you. | |

The *point* of the paragraph seems obviously aimed at the two "D" clauses in vv 10 and 11, which express the net result of the reality of the indwelling Spirit. First (v 10), since the Spirit is none other than the Spirit of Christ, that means "life" for us as the direct result of the "righteousness" effected by the Christ whose Spirit now indwells the believer — despite the fact that the "body is dead" because of sin. Second (v 11), since the indwelling Spirit is none other than the Spirit of the God who raised Christ from the dead, the Spirit therefore is also God's own surety in our lives that, just as Christ was raised, so too our "mortal" bodies are going to live again through resurrection.

The middle portion [B / B′], on the other hand, seems aimed at tying what is about to be said in A′ with what he has already said about Christ in 6:1-14. The awkwardness of the μέν / δέ contrasts, especially following the protasis, "but if Christ is in you," is the result of *these* contrasts. That is, Paul intends, "If Christ is in you, the Spirit means life for you, because of the righteousness effected by Christ." But since the concern here is with "life" also (especially) in terms of the future resurrection, he inserts — awkwardly for us — that "the body is dead because of sin." This obviously cannot mean that Christ's indwelling by his Spirit brings about the mortality of the body; sin alone has done that. Rather, he intends something like this (paraphrased to keep Paul's arrangement, but to get at his meaning): "But if Christ by his Spirit is in you, that means that *even though* the body is destined for death because of sin, the presence of Christ by his Spirit also means that the body is destined for life (because of Christ's own resurrection and the presence of the Spirit)."

Thus the A clause, a kind of "afterthought" protasis to v 9a, simply states the reality of the indwelling Spirit — designated the Spirit of God both because this is Paul's primary understanding of the Spirit and because of the emphasis he intends to make in v 11. In Pauline theology, God is the initiating subject of the saving action of Christ, mediated to believers through the Spirit. The second clause [B] functions in three ways: (1) It serves to reinforce the point of the preceding clause; (2) in typical fashion it sets up a "not / but" contrast so as to make the point of the "but" clause all the stronger; and (3) by changing the designation "Spirit of God" to "Spirit of Christ" Paul not only makes a considerably important point about his new understanding of the Spirit, but also makes the closest possible ties between the clearly distinct, but inseparably joined, activities of the three divine persons in bringing about our salvation — thought of in this case in terms of its eschatological culmination, the resurrection of believers from the dead.

That leads, then, to a final word about the apparently confusing switch from "having the Spirit of Christ" to "Christ in you." Both the structure of the argument as displayed above and the flow of thought between vv 9 and 10 make it certain that Paul did *not* in fact perceive the Risen Christ to be one and the same as the Spirit, or that he thought of both as indwelling "side by side," as it were. The expression "Christ in you" is to be understood as shorthand for "having the Spirit of Christ" from the preceding clause. The reason for the shorthand is that the emphasis in the argument has momentarily shifted to the work of Christ; since "Christ dwells in you by his Spirit, that means life is at work in you based on his gift of righteousness." That he comes back to the language "Spirit of God" in the final clause is the clear evidence that Paul saw the Spirit and his role as distinct from that of Christ and his role, even though in terms of "indwelling," Paul seems also clearly to understand that since the Spirit is both "of God" and "of Christ," this is how God and Christ both indwell the believer in the present aeon — by the Spirit.

Thus, just as in Eph 2:21-22, where the church is a "habitation for God, by his Spirit," so here — and elsewhere where Paul speaks about "Christ in me / us / you"[48] — he means "Christ by his Spirit dwells in me / us / you." All told, therefore, not only does this passage not support a Spirit christology, but it serves as one more link in a long chain that suggests quite the opposite. To this longer chain we now turn by way of conclusion.

48. Which he does not in fact do very often: only here, 2 Cor 13:5 (probably); Gal 2:20; and Eph 3:16. The passage in Col 1:29 ("Christ in you the hope of glory") probably means, "Christ in you Gentiles."

## 5

In light of these data, a final word is needed, a methodological word. Another common denominator of those who claim for Paul a "Spirit christology" is that they all begin with this handful of texts, mostly obscure texts full of notorious exegetical difficulties, which can be demonstrated not to carry any of the weight they wish to give them. What is important here is that *these* texts, which serve as the starting point, also serve not simply as the *primary* basis but as the *only* basis for Paul's alleged "Spirit christology," as though it were clear to all who would read Paul. In turn, the clear and certain trinitarian texts are then either negated by disclaimers or in some cases not even considered at all. Thus they begin with what they *assume* Paul to be saying in a few obscure texts and either avoid or treat with diffidence what he unambiguously says elsewhere, and in all kinds of unmistakable ways.[49]

Paul, on the other hand, began at a different point. Here is a thoroughgoing monotheist, whose encounter with Christ on the Damascus Road, and subsequent encounter with the Holy Spirit, forever radically altered his understanding of God and of his (now Christian) existence. At the heart of Pauline theology is his gospel, and his gospel is primarily *soteriology* — God's saving a people for his name through the redemptive work of Christ and the appropriating work of the Spirit. It is his encounter with God soteriologically — as Father, Son, and Holy Spirit — that accounts for the transformation of Paul's theological language and finally of his understanding of God — although this is simply never worked out at the level of immanent, or doxological, trinitarianism. In light of this reality and the preponderance of texts that support it — and do so with trinitarian language — one would think that these texts should serve as the methodological starting point, and that the more obscure ones should be interpreted in light of these, not the other way about.

That Paul's understanding of God had become functionally trinitarian and that the distinctions between Father, Son, and Spirit were presuppositional for him[50] may be demonstrated in three ways: the trinitarian texts themselves (2 Cor 13:13; 1 Cor 12:4-6; Eph 4:4-6); the many soteriological texts that are expressed in trinitarian terms; and the passages in which in close proximity the *functions* of Christ and the Spirit are expressed in ways that presuppose clear distinctions.

(1) The grace-benediction with which Paul singularly concludes

49. Dunn, therefore, seems to work at cross purposes with a methodology he has himself spoken against (*Baptism in the Holy Spirit,* SBT 15 [London: SCM, 1970] 103-4). Cf. his similar critique of Hermann in "II Corinthians iii.17," 309; yet he seems to turn about and do this very thing on the basis of his own exegesis of 1 Cor 15:45 and Rom 1:3-4.

50. On this whole question, and especially on Paul as a trinitarian, see the section entitled "What about the Trinity?" by D. Ford, in F. Young and D. Ford, *Meaning and Truth in 2 Corinthians* (Grand Rapids, Michigan: Wm. B. Eerdmans, 1987) 255-60.

2 Corinthians is so well known that it is easy to miss its several remarkable features: first, that Paul elaborates his concluding grace at all — which he does not do anywhere else, either in his earlier or later letters; second, that he does so with this trinitarian formulation, which appears here in such a presuppositional way — not as something Paul argues for, but as the assumed experienced reality of Christian life. That it is an *ad hoc* elaboration, and not part of the church's existing liturgical tradition, seems certain from its third remarkable feature: the order — Christ, God, and Spirit — which can only be explained because Paul began his standard benediction, and then felt compelled in this letter[51] to add words about the Father and the Spirit. That the three expressions are precisely the Pauline understanding of the soteriological functions of the Trinity seems to clinch the matter.

The second feature in particular, its presuppositional nature — not to mention that this is said as a form of prayer — suggests that this is *the proper place to begin all discussions about Paul's understanding of God.* For here is a text that by its very off-handed, presuppositional expression reveals Paul's theology — both his theology proper and his soteriology, which is foundational for the former.

First, it serves to encapsulate what lies at the very heart of Paul's singular passion — the gospel, with its focus on salvation in Christ, equally available by faith to Gentile and Jew alike. That the *love of God* is the foundation of Paul's soteriology is expressly stated, with passion and clarity, in such passages as Rom 5:1-11; 8:31-39; and Eph 1:3-14. The *grace of our Lord Jesus Christ* is what gave concrete expression to that love; through Christ's suffering and death in behalf of his loved ones, God effected salvation for them at one point in our human history. The *participation in the Holy Spirit* expresses the ongoing appropriation of that love and grace in the life of the believer and the believing community. The κοινωνία τοῦ ἁγίου πνεύματος (note the full name!) is how the living God not only brings people into an intimate and abiding relationship with himself, as the God of all grace, but also causes them to participate in all the benefits of that grace and salvation, indwelling them in the present by his own presence, guaranteeing their final eschatological glory.

Second, this text also serves as our entrée into Paul's theology proper, that is, into his understanding of God himself, which had been so radically affected for him by the twin realities of the death and resurrection of Christ and the gift of the eschatological Spirit. Granted that Paul did not wrestle with the ontological questions which such statements beg to have addressed. Nor does he here *assert* the deity of Christ and the Spirit. But what he does is to *equate the activity of the three divine persons* (to use the language of a later time) *in concert*

51. This may very well be related to 11:4, that those were currently troubling the church, in effect by their insistence on Jewishness offered them another Jesus, thus meaning the reception of another Spirit, both of which in effect denied Paul's preaching of the gospel.

*and in one prayer,* with the clause about God the Father standing in second place. This would seem to suggest that Paul was truly trinitarian in any meaningful sense of that term — that the one God is Father, Son and Spirit, and that in dealing with Christ and the Spirit one is dealing with God every bit as much as one is with God the Father.

Thus this benediction, with its affirmation of the distinctions of God, Christ, and Spirit, also expresses in shorthand form what is found everywhere elsewhere in Paul, that "salvation in Christ" is in fact the cooperative work of God, Christ, and the Spirit. Such affirmations would seem to shut down all possibilities that Paul could ever identify the Risen Christ with the Spirit so that in Paul "immanent christology is pneumatology."[52]

(2) That this "soteriological trinitarianism" is foundational to Paul's understanding of the gospel is further evidenced by the large number of soteriological texts in which salvation is expressed in similar trinitarian formulation. This is especially true of the larger, explicit passages such as Rom 5:1-8; 2 Cor 3:1–4:6; Gal 4:4-6; or Eph 1:3-14 (cf. Tit 3:5-7). But it is also true of many other texts, primarily soteriological, in which salvation is either explicitly or implicitly predicated on the threefold work of the triune God, as encapsulated in 2 Cor 13:13. Thus:

*1 Thess 1:4-5,* where the love of God has brought about the realization of election through the gospel (the message about Christ) empowered by the Holy Spirit.

*2 Thess 2:13,* where God's people are "beloved by the Lord [through his death]," because God elected them for salvation through the sanctifying work of the Spirit.

*1 Cor 1:4-7,* where God's grace has been given in Christ Jesus, who in turn has enriched the church with every kind of Spirit gifting.

*1 Cor 2:4-5,* where Paul's preaching of Christ crucified (v 2) is accompanied by the Spirit's power so that their faith might rest in God.

*1 Cor 2:12,* where "we have received the Spirit that comes from God," so that we might know the things given to us (in the cross is implied in context) by God.

52. Cf. the two other most clearly trinitarian passages in the corpus: 1 Cor 12:4-6 and Eph 4:4-6. In the former, at the beginning of a long argument (12:4-30) urging the need for diversity (over against their apparently singular interest in glossolalia), Paul insists that such diversity reflects the character of God himself and is therefore the true evidence of the work of the one God in their midst. The trinitarian implications of these three sentences seem undeniable. In Eph 4:4-6, another creedal formulation is expressed in terms of the distinguishable activities of the triune God. The basis for Christian unity is God himself. The one body is the work of the one Spirit (cf. 1 Cor 12:13); we live our present eschatological existence in one hope, effected for us by the one Lord, in whom all believe (= "one faith") and to which faith all have given witness through their "one baptism." The source of all these realities is the one God himself, "who is over all and through all and in all."

*1 Cor 6:11,* where God is the conceptual subject of the "divine passives" (you were washed, justified, sanctified), effected in the name of Christ and by the Spirit.

*1 Cor 6:19-20,* where the believer has been purchased (by Christ; cf. 7:22-23) so as to become a temple for God's presence by the Spirit.

*2 Cor 1:21-22,* where God is the one who has "confirmed" believers in a salvation effected by Christ, God's "Yes" (vv 19-20), evidenced by his giving the Spirit as "down payment."

*Gal 3:1-5,* where Christ crucified (v 1, picking up on 2:16-21) is conveyed to believers by the Spirit, whom God "supplies" even yet among them (v 5).

*Rom 8:3-4,* where God sent his Son to do what the law could not in terms of securing salvation, and the Spirit does what the law could not in terms of effecting righteousness in behavior ("walking" = living in the ways of God).

*Rom 8:15-17,* where the God-given Spirit serves as evidence of "adoption" as children, and thus "joint-heirs" with Christ, who made it all possible.

*Col 3:16,* where in worship it is all played in reverse — as the message of Christ "dwells richly among them," they worship the God from whom salvation has come, by means of a Spirit-inspired hymnody.

*Eph 1:17,* where the God of our Lord Jesus Christ gives the Spirit of wisdom and revelation so that they may understand the full measure of the work of Christ in their behalf.

*Eph 2:18,* where "through [the death of] Christ" (vv 14-16) Jew and Gentile together have access to God by the one Spirit, whom both alike have received.

*Eph 2:20-22,* where Christ is the "cornerstone" for the new temple, the place of God's dwelling by his Spirit.

*Phil 3:3,* where believers serve (God is implied) by the Spirit of God and thus boast in the effective work of Christ Jesus.

(3) As final evidence that Paul is presuppositionally trinitarian and that he could never therefore have confused or "identified" the Risen Christ with the Spirit are several other kinds of (nonsoteriological) texts, where the activities of the Risen Christ and the Spirit are clearly kept separate in the apostle's understanding. We have already noted this kind of distinction in Rom 9:1, where the formula "in Christ" and "by the Spirit" function quite differently — but characteristically — in one sentence. Similarly, in Rom 15:30 ("through our Lord Jesus Christ and through the love of the Spirit") the repeated διά indicates that Paul's appeal has a twofold basis. First, it is "through our Lord Jesus Christ," meaning "on the basis of what Christ has done for us all as outlined in the argument of this letter"; second, it is "through the love of the Spirit," meaning "on the basis of the love for all the saints, including myself, that the Spirit engenders."

Perhaps the most significant text in this regard, thinking only of passages where Christ and the Spirit appear in close approximation, is the combination of Rom 8:26-27 (the Spirit intercedes for us) and 8:34 (Christ intercedes for us). On the surface one could argue for "identification" in function; but what one gets rather is the clearest expression not only of "distinction" but of the fact that the Risen Christ is *not* now understood by Paul to be identified with the Spirit. The role of the Spirit is on earth, indwelling believers so as to help them in the weakness of their present "already / not yet" existence and thereby to intercede in their behalf. The Risen Christ is "located" in heaven, "at the right hand of God, making intercession for us."[53] The latter text in particular, where Paul is not arguing for something but asserting it on the basis of presuppositional reality, would seem to negate altogether the idea that the Spirit in Paul's mind could possibly be identified with the Risen Christ, either ontologically or functionally, which means, of course, that there seems to be no warrant of any kind that Paul had a "Spirit christology."

## 6

The net result of this study, therefore, is that Paul would not so much as recognize the language nor the theological assertions made by those who consider him to have had a Spirit christology. His presuppositions lay elsewhere, with the one God, now bringing salvation through the cooperative work of the three divine persons: God, Christ, and Spirit. At points where the work of any or all overlaps, so could Paul's language tend to be flexible — precisely because salvation for him was the activity of the one God. If his trinitarian presuppositions and formulations, which form the basis of the later formulations, never move toward calling the Spirit God and never wrestle with the ontological implications of his own presuppositions and formulations, there is no real evidence of any kind that he lacked clarity as to the distinctions between, and the specific roles of, the three divine persons who effected so great salvation for us all.

53. Cf. A. W. Wainwright, *The Trinity in the New Testament* (London: S.P.C.K., 1962) 260.

# Christ as Bearer of Divine Judgment in Paul's Thought about the Atonement

Stephen H. Travis

"Paul's vocabulary expresses the results of Christ's death rather than its character, and this fits in with New Testament thought in general, which is more concerned with the nature of salvation than the precise way in which it has been achieved."[1] Though most would agree with these words of I. H. Marshall, the history of exegesis and of dogmatic theology is laden with attempts to explain in detail the rationale of Paul's understanding of the death of Christ. My aim here is to explore to what extent statements in Paul's letters can bear the weight of those interpretations of Christ's death which speak in terms of "Christ bearing our punishment."

In *Christ and the Judgment of God*[2] I argued that in Paul's understanding of divine judgment ideas of "punishment" or "retribution" lie on the periphery of his thought. He thinks not so much of God imposing a retributive penalty for human sins, but of people experiencing the God-given consequences of their choices and actions. He understands both salvation and condemnation primarily in relational terms: people's destinies will be a confirmation and intensification of the relationship with God or alienation from him which has been their experience in this life. In that study, for fear of overcomplicating the argument, I chose not to discuss passages in Paul which seem to bring retributive ideas into relation with the death of Christ. In attempting now to make good the omission I hope to clarify some aspects of Paul's view of the atonement, as well as to complement my earlier discussion of Paul's statements about divine judgment.

1. I. H. Marshall, "The Development of the Concept of Redemption in the New Testament," in *Jesus the Saviour: Studies in New Testament Theology* (London: SPCK, 1990) 250.

2. Basingstoke: Marshall, Morgan and Scott, 1986.

## 1. History and Definitions

In Anselm's understanding of the atonement it is axiomatic that if injustice remains unpunished the integrity and credibility of God are in question. Sinners cannot put themselves right with God, yet justice requires the "satisfaction" of God's demands. The death of Jesus, offered freely as a gift to the Father, outweighs in value and therefore compensates for all the sins of humanity.[3] The Reformers shifted the focus from satisfaction to more strictly penal categories by speaking of Christ undergoing vicarious punishment to meet the claims of God's punitive justice, as when Calvin writes: "This is our acquittal: the guilt which held us liable for punishment was transferred to the head of the Son of God."[4]

Among twentieth-century writers who speak of Christ bearing the penalty or punishment for sin are E. Brunner and K. Barth. Peter Stuhlmacher sees in Rom 4:25 the idea that "the death of Jesus is the punishment 'for our trespasses.'" And L. Morris insists on a retributive understanding of the penalty which Christ has borne on behalf of humanity.[5]

Before proceeding to a study of certain texts in Paul's letters, we need to clarify what we are looking for. The word "retribution" is often used loosely to refer to any kind of unpleasant consequences which arise from human actions. But in what follows I shall use the word in its strict sense, to refer to a penalty which is inflicted on the offender *from outside,* not intrinsically "built into" the acts to which it is attached; and to imply some *correspondence* or *equivalence* between punishment and the deed which has evoked it.[6] To what extent, then, do such ideas underlie Paul's references to the saving significance of Christ's death? The following discussion takes these passages in their probable order of writing, though nothing crucial hangs on their being taken in this order.

## 2. Key Passages in Paul's Letters

> Christ redeemed us from the curse of the law, having become a curse for us — for it is written, "cursed be every one who hangs on a tree." (Gal 3:13)

This text forms part of Paul's argument against those who would insist that Gentiles submit to circumcision and the food laws — those marks of Jewish

3. See C. E. Gunton, *The Actuality of Atonement: A Study of Metaphor, Rationality and the Christian Tradition* (Edinburgh: T. & T. Clark, 1988) 87-93.

4. *Institutes* 2.16.5.

5. Brunner, *The Mediator* (London: Lutterworth, 1934) 473; Barth, *Church Dogmatics,* 4.1: *The Doctrine of Reconciliation* (Edinburgh: T. & T. Clark, 1956) 253 (but on 230ff. he rejects the theory of penal substitution); Stuhlmacher, *Reconciliation, Law and Righteousness* (Philadelphia: Fortress, 1986) 79; Morris, *The Cross in the New Testament* (Exeter: Paternoster, 1966) 382-88.

6. See further Travis, *Christ and the Judgment of God,* 2-5.

identity referred to as "works of the law" (v 10). The intention is to show that it is "in union with Christ Jesus" and "through faith" that Gentiles may share in the blessings promised to Abraham (v 14). N. T. Wright has illuminated in the following way the route whereby Paul moves from v 10 to v 14. Paul is working with the theme of the covenant: Genesis 15 and Deuteronomy 27, both quoted here, are great covenant passages. In line with Jewish writers of the period (e.g., CD 1:5-8) he believed that the Jewish people were still experiencing the curse of exile predicted in Deuteronomy 27, and this left in doubt how the blessings to Gentiles, promised to Abraham, could ever be fulfilled. But now the problem has been dealt with. "The covenant has reached its climax in the death of the Messiah." When Paul says, "Christ has redeemed *us*," he means Jews, who were under the judgment decreed by the law. And the purpose of their redemption was that their exile — their being distanced from God and his blessing — should be ended and the blessing be conveyed to Gentiles.

It is important to recognize here that Paul is concerned not so much with the sins of individuals incurring God's judgment, but with Israel as a whole which has failed to observe the Torah. And he can say that Christ has endured the curse on Israel's behalf because he sees him as representative of Israel. "Christ, as the representative Messiah, has achieved a specific task, that of taking on himself the curse which hung over Israel and which on the one hand prevented her from enjoying full membership in Abraham's family and thereby on the other hand prevented the blessing of Abraham from flowing out to the Gentiles."[7] Paul's argument is not a statement about atonement in general or about the salvation of individuals. His concern is not so much to explain how the death of Christ makes atonement for individual sinners as to show how it makes possible the coming of God's blessing to Gentiles (v 14).

So we must not read v 13 as a general statement about atonement. If it is to shed light on our understanding of the atonement this must be by extrapolation from Paul's argument, which is here specific to the situation of Israel-in-exile. We may say, perhaps, that just as Jesus, Israel's representative Messiah, through his death finally exhausted the curse of exile for the Jewish people and thus brought about the renewal of God's covenant with Israel (cf. 1 Cor 11:25) and opened the way for Gentiles to enter into union with Christ (Gal 3:14), so he took upon himself for all of us the consequences of our sinfulness and identified with our alienation from God in order to bring us into union with him.

Moreover, we may wonder whether Paul — despite the very specific reference of Gal 3:10-14 to the situation of Israel-in-exile — had not already been doing some such theologizing himself. The fact that other NT writers allude to Deut 21:23 (as is evidenced by the description of the cross as a "tree" in Acts 5:30; 10:39; 13:29; 1 Pet 2:24), though without making use of the covenant

7. Wright, *The Climax of the Covenant* (Edinburgh: T. & T. Clark, 1991) 137-56 (143, 151).

theology found in Galatians 3, suggests that there had already been some debate among Christians about the significance of that text in relation to the death of Jesus. There is evidence also in the Qumran Scrolls of the application of Deut 21:23 to instances of crucifixion. So it is likely that the question whether someone who had been "hanged on a tree" in crucifixion and had thereby apparently come under God's curse could possibly be the Messiah had already been a point of controversy between non-Christian Jews and followers of Jesus.[8] In view of the likelihood of such debate among Christians and between Christians and Jews, it seems plausible that Paul was aware of broader interpretations of Deut 21:23 than that which suited his specific purpose in Galatians 3. But we cannot be sure whether he would have found it appropriate to apply this theme of the covenant curse to Gentiles, or whether he felt that the "curse of the law" was something peculiar to Jews. Certainly we do not find him re-using this particular imagery in any other letter.

Did Paul regard the curse of the law as a retributive punishment? It is true, of course, that the curses of Deuteronomy 27 are followed in Deuteronomy 28–31 with threats of retribution — predictions of exile and numerous warnings that "the Lord will smite you . . . ," "the Lord will cause you to be defeated . . . ," etc. On the other hand, divine judgment is also expressed there in nonretributive terms of God's "hiding his face" (Deut 31:17-18; 32:20) so that his people, deprived of his protection, become oppressed by enemies of all kinds.[9] We can hardly know whether such details were in Paul's mind. But we can observe that in his citation of Deut 21:23 Paul alters "accursed by God" to "cursed" (ἐπικατάρατος). Is this because he wants to put a certain distance between Christ's experience of forsakenness and the thought that this is specifically inflicted by God?

There is of course a certain equivalence or correspondence (part of my definition of retribution) expressed in Gal 3:13 between the curse which threatened Israel and the curse which Christ endured on their behalf. But this does not imply a quantitative equivalence between the sins of men and women and the sufferings of Christ. It is part of the rhetoric by which Paul makes his point, an expression not of equivalence but of "interchange," as M. D. Hooker has expressed it. And she notes that "the experience of Gal 3:13 is not a simple exchange. It is not that Christ is cursed and we are blessed. Rather he enters into our experience, and we then enter into his, by sharing in his resurrection."[10]

In saying that Christ "became a curse for us" Paul is showing knowledge of the Hebrew text of Deut 21:23, which says that a hanged person is "a curse

8. See B. Lindars, *New Testament Apologetic* (London: SCM, 1961) 232-34; M. Wilcox, "'Upon the Tree' — Deut 21:22-23 in the New Testament," *JBL* 96 (1977) 85-99.

9. See Travis, *Christ and the Judgment of God,* 12.

10. "Interchange in Christ," in *From Adam to Christ: Essays on Paul* (Cambridge: Cambridge University, 1990) 16.

of God" or "an affront to God" (קללת אלהים; cf. Jer 24:9; 42:18; Zech 8:13). Such daring use of language is found also in the next passage to be considered.

Having spoken of Christ's death "for us" (ὑπὲρ ἡμῶν), Paul moves on to speak of blessing "in Christ Jesus." This combination of "representation" or "substitution" language with "participation" language is something else to which we shall return.

* * *

> For our sake he made him to be sin who knew no sin, so that in him we might become the righteousness of God. (2 Cor 5:21)

Here again Paul uses extremely paradoxical language to speak of Christ's saving work. He is probably reworking traditional material.[11] But the formulation is consistent with Paul's own love of paradoxical expressions: in 2 Corinthians we find, for example, power through weakness (12:9), life through death (4:12), wealth through poverty (8:9).

God made (n.b. the divine initiative, cf. v 19) to "be sin for our sake" (ὑπὲρ ἡμῶν again) the one who "knew no sin." Several commentators understand this clause as an allusion to the sin-offering — either to the unblemished animal sacrifice of Leviticus 4 or to the metaphorical use of sacrificial language (אשׁם) in Isa 53:10. Others insist that it would be impossible for Paul to use ἁμαρτία in two different senses in the space of three words and that the shocking mystery of Paul's language should be left to make its own impact.[12] But in either case the essential point is that Christ has experienced the sinner's estrangement from God; he has absorbed and thereby taken away sin, so that we might be brought into a right relationship with God.

Once again language about Christ being offered "for us" is linked with the statement that "in him" we find righteousness. In identifying with sin for us as our representative Christ breaks its power and thereby frees those who are in him to share his righteousness (cf. the similar ideas in Rom 5:19; 6:10-11).

In his discussion of this passage Marshall comments: "It is hard to understand this [Christ's becoming sin for us] in any other way than that in dying

11. See discussion in P. Stuhlmacher, *Gerechtigkeit Gottes bei Paulus* (Göttingen: Vandenhoeck & Ruprecht, 1965) 74-77; R. P. Martin, *2 Corinthians,* WBC 40 (Waco, Texas: Word, 1986) 138ff., 156.

12. In favor of "sin-offering" are, e.g., Martin, *2 Corinthians,* 157; V. P. Furnish, *2 Corinthians,* AB 32a (Garden City, New York: Doubleday, 1984) 351; J. D. G. Dunn, "Paul's Understanding of the Death of Christ as Sacrifice," in *Sacrifice and Redemption: Durham Essays in Theology,* ed. S. W. Sykes (Cambridge: Cambridge University, 1991) 42-43. The word was so interpreted by patristic commentators such as Cyril of Alexandria (*PGM* 77.209) and Augustine (*PLM* 40.253). Against it are P. E. Hughes, *2 Corinthians,* NICNT (London: Marshall, Morgan & Scott, 1962) 214-15; C. K. Barrett, *2 Corinthians* (London: Black, 1973) 180; M. D. Hooker, *From Adam to Christ,* 13.

Christ exhausted the effects of divine wrath against sin."[13] But God's wrath is not mentioned in the context, and the focus is in fact on Christ's death absorbing or neutralizing the effects of sin. And that does not involve notions of retribution.

The formal correspondence of language between "knew no sin" and "righteousness" and between "sin" and "sin" evokes the same comment as was made above on Gal 3:13. It is a stylistic device, not an expression of equivalence between sin and suffering. It could provoke eloquent expressions of worship, as in the *Letter to Diognetus:* "O sweet exchange! O unsearchable operation! O benefits surpassing all expectation! that the wickedness of many should be hid in a single Righteous One, and that the righteousness of One should justify many transgressors" (ch. 9). But that is, appropriately, the language of wonder and worship rather than of theological precision.

* * *

> . . . Christ Jesus, whom God put forward as an expiation by his blood, to be received by faith. This was to show God's righteousness, because in his divine forbearance he had passed over former sins; it was to prove at the present time that he himself is righteous and that he justifies him who has faith in Jesus. (Rom 3:24-26)

Here is yet another passage in which Paul makes use of traditional formulations in an exposition of the meaning of Christ's death.[14] The particular questions which concern us are the meaning of ἱλαστήριον (v 25), and the implications of the double reference to God's righteousness in v 26.

The debate as to whether ἱλαστήριον should be translated as "expiation," "propitiation," or "mercy-seat" has become something of a war of attrition.[15] Clearly Paul is using sacrificial imagery to express the significance of Christ's death. But is he saying that this death serves to expiate or take away sin, or that it turns away God's wrath? The main arguments of those who opt for "propitiation" are that the word-group has this meaning at least sometimes in the OT (e.g., Num 16:46; Dan 9:16), and that the whole context of Paul's exposition, beginning with the revelation of God's wrath in Rom 1:18-32, *requires* reference

13. "The Meaning of Reconciliation," in *Jesus the Saviour,* 264. He is influenced partly by the use of "reconciliation" language in 2 Maccabees, on which we shall comment in connection with our next passage.

14. Discussion is summarized in J. D. G. Dunn, *Romans 1–8,* WBC 38a (Dallas, Texas: Word, 1988) 163-64. There is dispute about precisely where the traditional material begins and ends, and how Paul has adapted it. But it seems misguided to suggest, as some do, that in v 26 Paul is deliberately correcting earlier tradition. One may safely assume that Paul uses the tradition because he is happy to make it his own — or at least that if he were correcting it he would have made this a little more obvious to his Roman readers!

15. Dunn, *Romans 1–8,* 161-62, 171-72, gives references to most of the relevant literature.

to the turning away of that wrath in the explanation of Christ's saving work in 3:21-26. Arguments in favor of "expiation" are that in many OT instances of the related verb ἱλάσκομαι the object is not God but human beings or their sins (e.g., 2 Kgs 5:18; Ps 24:11); and that Paul here has God as the subject of the action. "If God is the subject, then the obvious object is sin or the sinner. To argue that God provided Jesus as a means of propitiating *God* is certainly possible, but less likely."[16] Dunn has made out a strong case for the view that according to Paul's "theology" of sacrifice Christ's death cancels out human sin by destroying it. However, the *effect* of sin being destroyed in this way is of course that the wrath of Rom 1:18-32 no longer hangs over those who identify with Christ as their representative. So it is possible to say that expiation leads to propitiation, and to avoid polarizing the two ideas.[17]

However, to admit that a reference to God's wrath underlies Paul's use of ἱλαστήριον is not to introduce the idea of retribution. For if we ask what is the nature of the wrath described in Rom 1:18-32, we find that it is not the retributive inflicting of punishment from outside, but God's allowing of people to experience the intrinsic consequences of their refusal to live in relationship with him. "God gave them up . . ." (Rom 1:24, 26, 28). God's wrath is his judgment experienced as alienation from God.[18] As ἱλαστήριον Christ does not suffer punishment from God and thereby avert his wrath; he enters into humanity's experience of sin's consequences to destroy sin and thus restore people to relationship with God.

Several scholars have sought to shed light on Paul's use of ἱλαστήριον here by appealing to the martyr theology of 2 and 4 Maccabees, where the deaths of the Maccabean martyrs are understood as having atoning, or propitiatory significance. In 2 Macc 7:37-38 the youngest of the seven brothers says to his enemies:

> I, like my brothers, give up body and life for the laws of our fathers, appealing to God to show mercy (ἵλεως γένεσθαι) soon to our nation and by afflictions and plagues to make you confess that he alone is God, and through me and my brothers to bring to an end the wrath (ὀργή) of the Almighty which has justly (δικαίως) fallen on our whole nation.

In 4 Macc 6:28-29 Eleazar prays:

> Be merciful (ἵλεως γενοῦ) to your people and let our punishment be a satisfaction on their behalf (ἀρκεσθεὶς τῇ ἡμετέρᾳ ὑπὲρ αὐτῶν δίκῃ). Make my blood their purification and take my life as a ransom (ἀντίψυχον) for theirs.

16. Dunn, "Paul's Understanding," 49.

17. Cf. C. K. Barrett, *Romans* (London: Black, 1957) 78.

18. See Travis, *Christ and the Judgment of God,* 31-33, 36-38; and *idem,* "Wrath of God (NT)," in *ABD* 6:996-97.

And 4 Macc 17:20-22 says that the seven martyrs

> became, as it were, a ransom (ὥσπερ ἀντίψυχον) for the sin of our nation. Through the blood of these righteous ones and through the propitiation of their death (διὰ . . . τοῦ ἱλαστηρίου [τοῦ] θανάτου αὐτῶν) the divine providence rescued Israel.

I do not wish to dispute the suggestion that Jewish martyr theology of this kind influenced early Christian thinking about the death of Jesus. But it seems to me a mistake of method to look to such texts for an explanation of what Paul's use of ἱλαστήριον means. The fact that the retributive ideas of 2 and 4 Maccabees are not explicit in Romans 3 strongly suggests that he does not accept the assumptions of those writers.[19] In contrast to 2 and 4 Maccabees, but in line with the sacrificial cult of the OT, he stresses God's initiative in providing the sacrifice. Hence it is likely that his primary reference is to the Jewish sacrificial cult itself as an image of Christ's death.

To elucidate the issues in vv 25b-26 I will summarize two contrasting interpretations represented by the commentaries of C. E. B. Cranfield and J. A. Ziesler. According to Cranfield,

> Paul is saying in these two verses that God purposed (from eternity) that Christ should be ἱλαστήριον, in order that the reality of God's righteousness, that is, of His goodness and mercy, which would be called in question by his passing over sins committed up to the time of that decisive act, might be established.

He is taking εἰς ἔνδειξιν to mean "to prove," and πάρεσις to mean "passing over, leaving unpunished." God's patient holding back of his wrath might have been interpreted to mean that he was indifferent to human sins — which would be a denial of his own nature. But now he demonstrates through the cross his decisive dealing with sin. God has done this so that he might be righteous even in justifying the one who believes in Jesus (v 26b). He has maintained his own righteousness without compromise because in Christ's work as ἱλαστήριον he has himself borne the intolerable burden of evil and disclosed both his full hatred and his complete forgiveness of human evil.[20] Cranfield does not say that Christ was bearing the punishment for sin, though he does insist on "propitiatory sacrifice" as the meaning of ἱλαστήριον. But others who follow

19. Whereas these and other Jewish writers often suggest that the persecutions experienced by God's people are divine punishment for their sins, Paul nowhere expresses this assumption about the persecution of Christians. Is that because he believes that Christ has taken on himself the sufferings which would otherwise be due to Christians, or simply because he is working with a different set of assumptions? See Travis, *Christ and the Judgment of God,* 83-85.

20. See his whole discussion in *The Epistle to the Romans,* vol. 1, ICC (Edinburgh: T. & T. Clark, 1975) 211-18 (212).

this general line of exegesis do make explicit use of retributive language. N. T. Wright says: "Justification in the present depends on the achievement of an objective atonement in which sins are not ignored but dealt with in the proper way, by punishment. That punishment had not been meted out before (3:24ff). Now, on the cross, it has." And Morris concludes that the NT writers "see Christ as suffering in such a way as to remove from God the stigma of being unjust in remitting our penalty."[21]

Ziesler, on the other hand, views each instance of "righteousness" and "righteous" in vv 25 and 26 as expressing the same meaning as the initial declaration of God's righteousness in Rom 1:17. It is, as we have learned from the OT scholars, his loyalty to his covenant by which he commits himself to restore and sustain Israel; but now in the gospel this covenant loyalty is seen to embrace a saving purpose for *all* who have faith — Gentiles as well as Jews (1:16-17). Taking πάρεσις to mean "forgiveness," Ziesler sees God's saving righteousness as being demonstrated by his forgiving the sins formerly committed by people who are now receiving the gospel. To say that God "is righteous (δίκαιον) and that he justifies (δικαιοῦντα) the one who has faith in Jesus" means that he demonstrates his faithfulness and promise of salvation by accepting those who trust in Jesus.[22]

How is one to choose between these two basic approaches, both of which could be elaborated with lists of supporting scholars and with details of argument about the numerous exegetical dilemmas lurking in this dense passage? For our present purposes, we may suggest that the first approach has an inner consistency and a long pedigree of interpretation. But its consistency does seem to depend on understanding ἱλαστήριον as the turning away of retributive wrath. And we have seen reason to question whether that is what Paul intends. The second approach does not underplay the seriousness of the human condition apart from divine grace, and sees the death of Christ as the supreme demonstration of God's commitment to bring human beings into relationship with himself. But it does not imply a retributive understanding of the sufferings which Christ endured on the cross.

* * *

> Since, therefore, we are now justified by his blood, much more shall we be saved by him from wrath. For if while we were enemies we were reconciled to God by the death of his Son, much more, now that we are reconciled, shall we be saved by his life. (Rom 5:9-10)

21. Wright, *The Great Acquittal* (London: Collins, 1980) 24; Morris, *Cross,* 388. Cf. J. Piper, *The Justification of God* (Grand Rapids: Baker, 1983) 115-30; D. Hill, *Greek Words and Hebrew Meanings* (Cambridge: Cambridge University, 1967) 158.

22. *Paul's Letter to the Romans* (London: SCM, 1989) 115-16. See further his *The Meaning of Righteousness in Paul* (Cambridge: Cambridge University, 1972) 193-94.

Here again Paul moves from sacrificial language ("blood") to the idea of sharing Christ's life. The juxtaposition of a reference to wrath ("of God" is not in the Greek text, despite the RSV) and to the reconciliation of enemies raises the question whether the enmity lies entirely on the human side, or whether Paul thinks of a hostility of God toward human beings.[23] Most scholars deny that there is any hostility on God's part, pointing out that he never uses the verb "to reconcile" with God as the object. This is in contrast to passages such as 2 Macc 1:5; 7:33; 8:29, which certainly speak of God being reconciled to his people after expressing his wrath toward them.

As in the case of ἱλαστήριον, it would be dangerous to allow meanings in 2 Maccabees to determine exegesis of Paul. But since the logic of Paul's argument is that the sacrificial death of Christ was necessary to bring about our justification and reconciliation, there is more than a hint here of a hostility on God's part toward human sinfulness. Certainly in Rom 11:28 God is said to be the subject of hostility toward people. But that hostility is not to be conceived of as desire to inflict punishment. Rather is it an absence of relationship between God and human beings, which he has taken the initiative to overcome.

## 3. Some Further Considerations on Paul's Understanding of the Death of Christ

We have now, I believe, considered all of the passages in Paul's letters where a retributive understanding of the sufferings of Christ on the cross may be considered a serious possibility. And we have seen reason to believe that in each case a retributive interpretation is not the most likely one. This is not to deny that, according to Paul, God takes human sin with absolute seriousness, or that Christ on the cross experienced divine judgment on our behalf. But it is to suggest that to speak of Christ on the cross suffering our "punishment," or enduring a retributive penalty for our sins, is to go further than Paul himself goes.

It is true, of course, that Paul has many allusions to Christ's death which *might* be interpreted in line with a retributive understanding of what he suffered. For example, if a retributive understanding were established on other grounds, all the statements that Christ died "for our sins" (ὑπὲρ τῶν ἁμαρτιῶν ἡμῶν, e.g., Rom 4:25; 1 Cor 15:3; Gal 1:4) or "for us" (ὑπὲρ ἡμῶν) or similar expressions (e.g., Rom 5:6; 8:32; 1 Cor 8:11; 11:24; Eph 5:2; 1 Thess 5:10) could be regarded as expressions of the same theological perspective. But such brief statements do not on their own establish such a doctrine, and they are capable of other interpretations. I want now therefore to make some observations about

23. E. Käsemann lists scholars on either side of this debate, *Commentary on Romans* (London: SCM, 1980) 139.

Paul's understanding of the death of Christ in order to try to set the passages discussed above in a broader framework.

(1) Paul has more than one framework for understanding the significance of Christ's death. For instance, he can speak of Christ's sufferings as the beginning of the "messianic woes" which herald the new age of salvation.[24] Or he can use the image of sacrifice. Although attempts are made occasionally to minimize the significance of sacrificial imagery for Paul, it is difficult to deny that he sometimes compares the death of Christ to the sin-offering (Rom 8:3), the Passover sacrifice (1 Cor 5:7), and the covenant sacrifice (1 Cor 11:25).[25] As we have seen, sacrificial imagery crops up particularly when Paul is making use of traditional formulas, but it is by no means confined to these. He makes some use of the suffering servant theme — already itself a metaphorical application of sacrificial ideas — as when he uses phrases such as "he was given up for our trespasses" (Rom 4:25) and "God gave him up for us all" (Rom 8:32; cf. κύριος παρέδωκεν αὐτὸν ταῖς ἁμαρτίαις ἡμῶν, Isa 53:6 LXX; διὰ τὰς ἁμαρτίας αὐτῶν παρεδόθη, Isa 53:12 LXX). Or he can refer often to our participation in Christ's death and resurrection (e.g., Rom 6:3-4) — a theme to which we shall return. In the context of the range of language and imagery used by Paul, it is important to notice how comparatively few are the passages where we have been able to find even the possibility of a retributive framework of understanding.

(2) Insofar as it is possible to discern a rationale of sacrifice in Paul's use of this imagery, the rationale seems not to be one that fits comfortably with a retributive framework. There is, notoriously, no clear rationale of how the Jewish sacrificial system worked within the OT itself. But Dunn believes he can reconstruct Paul's understanding of what sacrifice signified from his references to Christ's death as sacrifice. He finds that the sin-offering, like Jesus' death in Rom 8:3, was meant to deal with sin; that, as Jesus in his death represented humanity in its fallenness ("in the likeness of sinful flesh," Rom 8:3), so the sin-offering represented the sinner in his or her sin; and that the death of the sacrificial animal was seen as the death of the sinner *qua* sinner, that is, the destruction of that person's sin (in Rom 8:3 it is *sin* which is "condemned," i.e., destroyed, done away with).[26]

If this explanation holds good, there is no place for the popular idea that in the sacrificial ritual God is somehow *punishing* the animal so that the punish-

24. D. C. Allison Jr., finds allusions to this idea in, e.g., Col 1:24; 2 Cor 1:5; *The End of the Ages Has Come* (Edinburgh: T. & T. Clark, 1987) 65-66.

25. See E. Käsemann, *Perspectives on Paul* (London: SCM, 1969) 43-44, for a denial that Paul ever clearly calls Christ's death a sacrifice. For the view that the sin-offering is referred to in Rom 8:3 see Wright, *The Climax of the Covenant*, 220-25.

26. Dunn, "Paul's Understanding," 43-47. He acknowledges that aspects of his argument are vigorously contested, but his understanding of the matter does seem to fit with the hints given by Paul himself.

ment should not fall on the sinner who presents the sacrifice, or for the inference that something parallel to that is happening in the sacrificial death of Christ. The point is rather that as the sinner identified with the sacrificial victim his or her sin was transferred to the animal and destroyed through its death.[27]

(3) Already within the OT and Jewish literature sacrifice had begun to be spiritualized in terms of obedience. The prophetic demand for obedience *rather than* sacrifice is well known (Isa 1:10-17; Jer 7:21-23; Hos 6:6; Amos 5:21-25; Mic 6:6-8; Pss 40:6-8; 50:7-14; 51:16-17). But a passage such as Ecclus 35:1-5 expresses the idea that obedience to the moral demands of God "fulfills" or "serves as" or "substitutes for" sacrifice: "He who keeps the law makes many offerings; he who heeds the commandments sacrifices a peace offering. He who returns a kindness offers fine flour, and he who gives alms sacrifices a thank offering. . . ." Within the NT the Letter to the Hebrews, for all its detailed allusion to priesthood and sacrifice, explains that the sacrificial system has been superseded by Christ's obedience, citing Psalm 40: "Sacrifices and offerings thou hast not desired. . . . Then I said, 'Lo, I have come to do thy will, O God'" (Heb 10:5-10).[28]

In the Pauline literature the obedience of Christ is perhaps not explicitly described in terms of the fulfillment of sacrifice (though 2 Cor 5:21 and Eph 5:2 come close). But certainly Christ's obedience is a key motif in his presentation of the significance of Christ's death in Rom 5:18-19. (Is there here an allusion to Isa 53:11, which also speaks of "the many" being made "righteous" — through the "sacrificial" self-giving of the servant?) In obedience to the Father, Christ identified with Adam's race, shared in Adam's death, and attained to vindication and resurrection as the head of a new humanity. "The many" share in his vindication and new life by identification with him as their representative Head.

(4) This brings us to the connection between Christ's death and our "union with him" or "participation in him." Although D. E. H. Whiteley overemphasized this theme in Paul in his anxiety to minimize the notion of substitutionary atonement, Paul is particularly fond of it as a way of talking about how Christ's death affects men and women.[29] It is notable how often Paul refers to Christ's death with a brief sacrificial allusion and then goes on to elaborate its purpose in terms of participation in Christ. Several times he uses sentences in the form: "Christ gave himself for our sins [or similar] *in order that* we might live in him [or some such "participationist" expression]." For example:

27. Cf. Gunton, *The Actuality of Atonement*, 120.

28. Cf. G. B. Caird, *The Language and Imagery of the Bible* (London: Duckworth, 1980) 71-72.

29. See Whiteley, *The Theology of St. Paul* (Oxford: Blackwell, 1964) 130-51. E. P. Sanders has been somewhat unfairly criticized for implying that Paul's "participationist" language has not been properly integrated with his "juristic" language. See *Paul and Palestinian Judaism* (London: SCM, 1977) 466, 507-8, 519-20.

". . . Christ, who died for us so that . . . we might live with him" (1 Thess 5:9-10; cf. Rom 8:3-4; 14:9; 2 Cor 5:15, 21). An alternative formulation is found in 2 Cor 5:14, "One has died for all; therefore all have died." And if Paul can say, "We are justified by his blood" (Rom 5:9), he can equally well speak of our being "justified in Christ" (Gal 2:17).

Two things should be noted here. First, "participation in Christ's death and resurrection" is a central theme in Paul's presentation of Christ's death and its effect on humanity. When he talks about our being "crucified with Christ" (Gal 2:19) or "buried with him by baptism into death" (Rom 6:4), he means that we enter into his obedience so that we may also share in his resurrection life. "Participationist" language such as this is far more frequent in Paul than language which might be understood as retributive in the sense discussed earlier.

But, second, the formulation of those sentences in the form "Christ gave himself for our sins *so that* . . ." (1 Thess 5:9-10, etc.) implies that in his death Christ achieved something objectively *before* the fruits of it were available to the subjective experience of those who have faith in him. Our "participation" in Christ crucified and risen *depends* on his first "dying for us." It was while we were "helpless," "ungodly," "sinners," "dead" that Christ died for us (Rom 5:6, 8; Col 2:13-14). The varieties of Paul's language about Christ's death cannot simply be collapsed into the theme of participation.[30] Rather, it should be recognized that the varieties of expression find their unity in the idea of Christ as representative Man, who identifies with sinful humanity and with whom we may identify ourselves — in whose death and resurrection we may participate — through faith.

## 4. Conclusions

I have argued that Paul's understanding of the death of Christ does not include the idea that he bore the retributive punishment for our sins which otherwise would have to be inflicted on us. To understand the atonement in those terms is to misunderstand what Paul means by "the wrath of God." It is to press too far the implications of his legal metaphor. It is to risk driving a wedge between the action of God and that of Jesus.[31]

Rather than saying that in his death Christ experienced retributive punish-

30. Cf. J. I. Packer, "What Did the Cross Achieve? The Logic of Penal Substitution," *TynB* 25 (1974) 31-34. For a helpful exploration of the need for balance between "objective" and "subjective" in theories of the atonement, see P. S. Fiddes, *Past Event and Present Salvation: The Christian Idea of Atonement* (London: Darton, Longman & Todd, 1989).

31. Cf. Gunton, *The Actuality of Atonement,* 165. For forceful statements on the difficulties involved in retributive language see G. W. H. Lampe, "The Atonement: Law and Love," in *Soundings,* ed. A. R. Vidler (Cambridge: Cambridge University, 1962) 173-91; *idem,* "The Saving Work of Christ," in *Christ for Us Today,* ed. N. Pittenger (London: SCM, 1968) 141-53.

ment on behalf of humanity, Paul says that he entered into and bore on our behalf the destructive consequences of sin. Standing where we stand, he bore the consequences of our alienation from God. In so doing he absorbed and exhausted them, so that they should not fall on us. It is both true and important to say that he "was judged in our place" — that he experienced divine judgment on sin in the sense that he endured the God-ordained consequences of human sinfulness. But this is not the same as to say that he bore our punishment. It is a perspective on the atonement which, I believe, confirms the understanding of divine judgement for which I argued in *Christ and the Judgment of God:* that judgment is not inflicted by God "from outside," but is the intrinsic outworking, under God's control, of the consequences of human choices and actions, and that Paul's primary category for understanding salvation and condemnation is that of relationship or nonrelationship to God.

Such an approach does not regard the human condition as any less serious than approaches which rely on retributive categories. But it is more in line with Paul's understanding of sin as a relational concept. It is very striking that Paul almost always uses his normal word for "sin" (ἁμαρτία) in the singular. Of sixty-two instances, only nine are in the plural and at least four of these are in OT quotations or are dependent on early Christian tradition (Rom 4:7; 11:27; 1 Thess 2:16; 1 Cor 15:3). This is because he understands sin not as a collection of individual acts but as a relationship of hostility toward God.[32] It is that hostility, that whole mass of opposition to God, which Christ absorbed in his death. The danger with a retributive framework of thought is that it tends to regard sins as individual deeds, each requiring a corresponding penalty.

The retributive doctrine is right in its insistence that forgiveness cannot take place without a cost being borne. It is no light or easy thing to forgive and to restore broken relationships. Those who forgive others take into themselves the hurt and the pain which has been caused, rather than throw it back at the offenders in retaliation. The meaning of the cross is that in Christ God himself took responsibility for the world's evil and absorbed its consequences into himself. He was not punishing his Son in order to avoid punishing his creatures. Admittedly, we may sometimes speak of athletes or academics "punishing themselves" in order to achieve some great goal, but we know we are using such language in a highly figurative way. And it would not clarify our understanding of the atonement to use such extreme imagery with reference to God. Rather may we speak of him "absorbing the cost" of remaking our relationship with him.[33]

32. Cf. W. Grundmann, "ἁμαρτάνω," in *TDNT* 1:309-10.

33. Cf. C. F. D. Moule, "The Theology of Forgiveness," in *From Fear to Faith: Studies of Suffering and Wholeness,* ed. N. Autton (London: SPCK, 1971) 61-72. Also significant here is Marshall's helpful distinction between "price" and "cost" in language about redemption (*Jesus the Saviour,* 251 n. 4).

# Jesus Christ: "Head" of the Church (Colossians and Ephesians)

Clinton E. Arnold

In this essay I will address the long-standing debate over the source of the concept of Christ as the head of the church: Was Jesus initially regarded as "head" of a cosmic body? Or is there an alternative background to the head-body imagery that better explains its usage in Colossians and Ephesians?[1]

My thesis is that a noncosmological interpretation of the head-body imagery best explains the texts in Colossians and Ephesians. Specifically, I will contend that a simple metaphorical interpretation of the imagery based on Greek physiological explanations of the function of the literal head of the physical body gives the best explanation of the biblical passages. One of the contributions of this essay will be to demonstrate that a noncosmological interpretation of head-body imagery had a precedent in the Judaism contemporary with Paul.[2]

In his popular book *The Work of Christ*, I. H. Marshall says that Jesus' title "head" "indicates His position of authority as Lord, but at the same time it means that He is the source of the spiritual life which flows through the body and nourishes the members."[3] This is a very apt description of the meaning of the metaphor as it is used through Colossians and Ephesians. In the course of this essay, I intend to provide further support for Marshall's conclusion. I will

1. In an indirect way, this essay will have implications for current discussion on the meaning of Paul's use of κεφαλή in passages where he discusses husband-wife relationships. However, my primary concern is to interpret the meaning of Christ as "head" of the church.

2. I will use "Paul" to refer to the author(s) of Colossians and Ephesians. Although it seems to me that the apostle is the most likely author of the letters, there is nothing in my presentation that imposes this conviction on the details of the theme under consideration.

3. I. H. Marshall, *The Work of Christ* (Palm Springs: Ronald N. Haynes, 1981; originally, Exeter: Paternoster, 1969) 86. It is a pleasure for me to write this essay in honor of my *Doktorvater*. I look back with fond memories to the years I spent in Aberdeen working under Professor Marshall's tutelage.

use the expressions "leadership" and "source of provision" to summarize the meaning of the metaphor.

## 1. Head of a Cosmic Body?

Colossians 1:18 is normally seen as the most productive starting point for interpreting the head-body imagery in Colossians and Ephesians. The verse occurs within the context of a passage commonly regarded as poetic or hymnlike: "He [Christ] is the head of the body, the church." The vast majority of interpreters have regarded the final words of the line, "the church," as the letter writer's addition to a preexisting hymn reflecting Hellenistic or Hellenistic-Jewish influence. Specifically, the original form of the hymn is thought to be an ascription of praise to Christ as the head of his body — *which is the universe.* Whereas the alleged gnostic roots of the hymn have largely been discounted,[4] many interpreters now explain that the original hymn reflects the Hellenistic notion of the universe as a cosmic body (or "macroanthropos") guided and controlled by a wise and ruling head.[5] In support of this, interpreters refer to texts such as an Orphic Fragment (Fragment 168), where Zeus is depicted as head of the cosmos which he permeates with his divine power, or Plato's *Timaeus,* which portrays the cosmos as a living body which is directed by a divine soul (*Timaeus* 31b; 32a, c; 39e; 47c–48b).[6]

4. Not all have jettisoned the gnostic view. H. Conzelmann, "Der Briefe an die Kolosser," in *Die Briefe an die Galater, Epheser, Philipper, Kolosser, Thessalonicher und Philemon,* NTD 8, 16th ed. (Göttingen: Vandenhoeck & Ruprecht, 1985) 184, for example, continues to speak of an Iranian source for the head-body imagery. With regard to Col 1:18, he notes, "Indeed in the original sense, Jesus is the 'head' of the 'cosmos' which constitutes his body — a body of a special sort! It has nothing to do with the form of the human body. At the root of this lies a mythical teaching about the origin and essence of the world which can be traced to Iran and India: the world is the body of the primitive person *(Urmensch)*" (translation mine)."

5. Most recently, see A. T. Lincoln, *Ephesians,* WBC 42 (Dallas: Word, 1990) 69: "So, it is likely that the relation between 'head' and 'body' entered Pauline thought in this way via Hellenistic ideas about the cosmos." P. Pokorný, *Colossians: A Commentary* (Peabody, Massachusetts: Hendrickson, 1991) 82, notes: "The conception of the Macroanthropos and its members, or of a supra-individual head, has also found entrance in Gnosticism and in Christianity. . . . In Col. 2:19 this conception is applied to the church . . . [where it is] construed to a large extent, as a discussion on the correct application of this conception." See also C. Colpe, "Zur Leib-Christi-Vorstellung im Epheserbrief," in *Judentum, Urchristentum, Kirche,* ed. W. Eltester, BZNW 26 (Berlin: de Gruyter, 1964) 172-87, esp. 179-82; E. Lohse, *Colossians and Philemon,* Hermeneia (Philadelphia: Fortress, 1971) 54-55; E. Schweizer, *The Letter to the Colossians* (London: S.P.C.K., 1982) 58-59, 82-83; *idem,* "σῶμα," *TDNT* 7:1054-55; *idem,* "Body," in *ABD* 1:771; *idem,* "Die Kirche als Leib Christi in den paulinischen Antilegomena," in *Neotestamentica. Deutsche und Englische Aufsätze, 1951-1963* (Zürich and Stuttgart: Zwingli, 1963) 293-316; H.-M. Schenke, *Der Gott "Mensch" in der Gnosis: Ein religionsgeschichtlicher Beitrag zur Diskussion über die paulinische Anschauung von der Kirche als Leib Christi* (Göttingen: Vandenhoeck & Ruprecht, 1962) 153-56; H. Hegermann, *Die Vorstellung vom Schöpfungsmittler im hellenistischen Judentum und Urchristentum,* TU 82 (Berlin: Akademie, 1961) 138-57; *et al.*

6. See Lohse, *Colossians,* 53; Schweizer, "σῶμα," 7:1029-30, 1032, 1074-77.

Many interpreters contend that this concept was mediated to the composer of the original hymn through Hellenistic Judaism and not directly through pagan thought. Philo is then seen as holding the key for unlocking the appropriate understanding of the head-body imagery of the hymn. In particular, Philo's cosmic interpretation of the vestment of the high priest (cf. Exodus 28) is regarded as the most relevant background.[7]

In his most detailed allegorization of the vestment (*Vit. Mos.* 2.117-35), Philo explains that the air is represented by the priest's robe, the earth by the flowers on the robe, heaven by the ephod, the twelve houses of the zodiac by the twelve stones on the breastplate (with the four seasons represented by the four rows into which the stones were organized). On the priest's head is a turban which indicates his superiority to all others (even kings) as he fulfills his consecrated duties. Philo here regards reason (λόγος) as a function of "the reason seat" (τὸ λογεῖον) located in the breastplate (cf. Exod 28:30).

In another passage (*Fug.* 108–11) Philo refers to the high priest as a "divine word" (λόγος θεῖος) who puts on the world (κόσμος) as a garment — that is, he "arrays himself in earth and air and water and fire." His "head" (κεφαλή) functions as the ruling faculty (τὸ ἡγεμονικόν), and upon it is placed a symbol of his ruling authority (ἡγεμονία).

Finally, in *Quaest. in Exod.* 2.117, Philo responds to the question, "Where is the head of the world?" by saying: "The head of all things is the eternal Logos of the eternal God, under which, as if it were his feet or other limbs, is placed the whole world." The passage then goes on to identify Christ the Lord as this eternal Logos, thereby betraying this section as a Christian interpolation.[8] After discounting this passage, we are then left with only two passages in Philo which give symbolic meaning to the cosmic vestiture of the high priest.

In response to this conception, it is necessary to acknowledge that Philo does indeed speak of the universe as a giant cosmic body (e.g., *Plant.* 7; *Spec. Leg.* 1.210) which was controlled by the Logos (e.g., *Spec. Leg.* 1.96; *Vit. Mos.* 2.127, 133, 134). It must be observed, however, that nowhere does Philo explic-

7. See Hegermann's discussion of the vestiture in Section A.3 ("Der Hohepriester im Kosmosgewand") of *Schöpfungsmittler,* 47-67.

8. R. Marcus, *Philo,* LCL, supp. vol. 2, 168, places in brackets the entire section beginning with the introductory rhetorical question, "'But where, O theologian,' someone may say, 'is the head of the world?'" Colpe, "Leib-Christi," 180 n. 22, thus rightly comments, "Es sei bemerkt, daß die ganze Stelle höchstwahrscheinlich christlich interpoliert oder mindestens überarbeitet." Hegermann, *Schöpfungsmittler,* 58-59, argues that the inserted material is not as extensive as Marcus indicates. Some interpreters use this passage to illustrate Col 2:19 without ever acknowledging the possibility that it is a Christian interpolation; see Lohse, *Colossians,* 54; Lohmeyer, *Kolosser,* 179; Dibelius-Greeven, *Kolosser,* 36. For a case against the relevance of this passage for interpreting Col 1:18 and 2:19, see N. Kehl, *Der Christushymnus im Kolosserbrief,* SBM 1 (Stuttgart: Katholisches Bibelwerk, 1967) 96-98. Kehl, in fact, concludes: "daß sie [the Colossian hymn] keine Schöpfungsmittlerbezeichnungen enthalten." He contends that "head" needs to be understood in the passage in a juridical sense (cf. Col 2:10).

itly refer to the Logos as κεφαλή (except *Quaest. in Exod.* 2.117, likely a Christian interpolation). There are additional difficulties that need to be registered regarding the appropriateness of appealing to Philo's cosmic interpretation of the head-body imagery, especially as represented by the cosmic vestiture of the high priest, as background to the concept of Christ as "head of his body, the church." First, the garments of the priest, not the priest's physical body, are interpreted as having cosmological significance. The head-body imagery in Colossians and Ephesians never occurs in conjunction with garments, only with members (τὰ μέρη / τὰ μέλη) of a body. Second, in *Vit. Mos.* 2.117-35, reason (λόγος) is not ascribed to the head, but to the breastplate of the priest. The only time "head" (κεφαλή) is mentioned in this passage is for the sake of describing where the turban is placed. The term κεφαλή is given no metaphorical interpretation in this passage. Most importantly, "head" and "body" are not coordinated and imbued with some metaphorical significance. Third, in *Fug.* 108–11, it is the high priest himself, not his "head," which is described as the "divine word" (λόγος θεῖος).

The single greatest objection to a cosmic interpretation of "head" and "body" in Col 1:18a is the fact that Paul does not present Christ as the head of a cosmic body. Otherwise, he would not have added "which is the church" (τῆς ἐκκλησίας) as an explanation of the body. Even if he is citing a preexisting hymn in which "head" and "body" are given cosmic significance, he clearly limits the referent of body to the church and later develops the ecclesiological significance in the letter (Col 2:19). The "body" is explicitly defined as the church, certainly viewed in its more comprehensive sense as the conglomerate of all those who have exercised faith in Christ — perhaps quite a large company of believers, but by no means cosmic or universal in scope. The difficulty, however, is that some interpreters think that the Hellenistic conception of the cosmic body has influenced the development of the imagery throughout Colossians and then in Ephesians.[9]

What then inspired Paul to develop this concept of Christ as "the head" in relation to a "body" which represents his people? We must look beyond the OT since the specific idea does not occur there, namely God as the κεφαλή in relation to his people who represent his σῶμα.[10] Neither is it likely that Paul developed the concept based on precedents in Stoic thought.[11] Furthermore,

9. E.g., see Lohse, *Colossians,* 55, who contends, "The author of the letter gives this cosmological train of thought a new direction by designating the church as the place where in the present Christ exercises his rule over the cosmos."

10. The more general concept of God as the leader of his people is certainly present and assuredly influenced Paul. Ernest Best has argued that Paul is here influenced by the OT concept of corporate personality where there is an oscillation between the one and the many, the individual and the corporate; see E. Best, *One Body in Christ* (London: SPCK, 1955). See also P. T. O'Brien, *Colossians, Philemon,* WBC 44 (Waco: Word, 1982) 50.

11. This view has recently received a fresh exposition by J. D. G. Dunn, "'The Body of Christ' in Paul," in *Worship, Theology and Ministry in the Early Church: Essays in Honor of Ralph P. Martin,* ed. M. J. Wilkins and T. Paige, JSNTSS 87 (Sheffield: JSOT, 1992) 146-62. He contends that the

rather than beginning with the Colossian hymn for interpreting the head-body imagery in Colossians and Ephesians, perhaps the best starting point is the two passages where the metaphor is elaborated: Col 2:19 and Eph 4:15-16. Both of these passages extend the imagery beyond the head and body to joints (ἁφαί) and ligaments / sinews (σύνδεσμοι) which nourish (ἐπιχορηγέω, ἐπιχορηγία), hold together (συμβιβάζω), and fit together (συναρμολογέω) the entire body. The metaphor in these two passages has been elaborated to a far greater degree than the simple cosmic body image that appears in some of the Hellenistic and Jewish-Hellenistic sources. Starting with these two passages points us in the direction of the medical writers.

## 2. Head-Body in the Medical Writers and Plato

Prior to the turn of the century, J. B. Lightfoot suggested that Paul himself developed the metaphor based on the common physiological conceptions of his time. He describes the physiology of the ancient doctors Hippocrates of Cos (*c.* 460-370 B.C.E.) and Galen of Pergamum (129-99 C.E.) with regard to the role of the head in relation to the body.[12] Lightfoot contended that this background not only explained the additional physiological metaphors, but also helped interpret the meaning of Christ's "headship." For Lightfoot, Christ as "head of the church" means that he is "the inspiring, ruling, guiding, combining, sustaining power, the mainspring of its activity, the centre of its unity, and the seat of its life."[13]

This view has more recently been taken up and argued by M. Barth in his massive two-volume commentary on Ephesians. Barth also contends that the head-body imagery needs to be seen in the light of the common physiology of antiquity as found in the writings of Hippocrates, but especially Galen whose works interact with the accumulated progress of medical knowledge attained between 300 B.C.E. and 100 C.E. Barth concludes:

---

emphasis on Christ as head emerged from the fact that in Stoic thought "both state and cosmos as a body could include also the thought of the ruler of the state or the divine principle of rationality in the cosmos (Zeus or the logos) as the head of the body." This interpretation, however, ignores the elaboration of the head-body imagery in Col 2:19 and Eph 4:16 with more extensive physiological imagery. Furthermore, the concept of the state as a body with a controlling head present in its leadership was not exclusively the domain of Stoic thought. This was likely a more common conception than Dunn acknowledges. For example, according to Pliny, an enormous human skull was found during the laying of the foundations for the temple of Jupiter Capitolinus in Rome. This was regarded as an omen that Rome would be the head of the world and the capitol would be the seat of its power (Pliny *Natural History* 23.4). Cf. M. Merslin, "Head: Symbolism and Ritual Use," in *The Encyclopedia of Religion*, vol. 6 (New York: Macmillan, 1987) 222.

12. J. B. Lightfoot, *Saint Paul's Epistles to the Colossians and to Philemon* (Grand Rapids: Zondervan, 1959; originally published in 1879) 198-201. See also J. A. Robinson, *St. Paul's Epistle to the Ephesians*, 2d ed. (London: Macmillan, 1904) 43, 103.

13. Lightfoot, *Colossians*, 157.

> By his acquaintance with physiological insights Paul could ascribe to the head more than a representative and dominating function. He could attribute to it the power to perceive, to interpret, to coordinate, and to unify all that went on in the body and its several members. Because the head is the "greatest power" of the body, causation and coordination can be ascribed to nothing else. There is but one source, throne, and acropolis of all members, including their movements and perceptions — the head. In other words, by its power the head is omnipresent in the whole body; its relation to the body is as a "dynamic presence."[14]

One could say that for both Lightfoot and Barth, Christ's headship implies both *leadership* and *source of provision*. Their description accurately represents the medical writers.

The study of medicine, in the scientific sense, began with Hippocrates. His rational approach to the investigation of disease led him to make giant strides in understanding human physiology. His influence was felt for centuries through his legacy in the Hippocratic schools of medicine.[15] Hippocrates regarded the head as the most important part of the body. The head contains the brain (ἐγκέφαλος), which coordinates and controls all the parts of the body. It is appropriate to attach the functions of the "brain" (ἐγκέφαλος) to the "head" (κεφαλή) not only because the head contains the brain but also because Hippocrates speaks of them as an integral union (see *Morb. Sacr.* 13.27-28). The importance of the head / brain is well illustrated in a passage from *The Sacred Disease* (= *Morb. Sacr.*):

> Κατὰ ταῦτα νομίζω τὸν ἐγκέφαλον δύναμιν ἔχειν πλείστην ἐν τῷ ἀνθρώπῳ· οὗτος γὰρ ἡμῖν ἐστι τῶν ἀπὸ τοῦ ἠέρος γινομένων ἑρμηνεύς, ἢν ὑγιαίνων τυγχάνῃ· τὴν δὲ φρόνησιν ὁ ἀὴρ παρέχεται. οἱ δὲ ὀφθαλμοὶ καὶ τὰ ὦτα καὶ ἡ γλῶσσα καὶ αἱ χεῖρες καὶ οἱ πόδες οἷα ἂν ὁ ἐγκέφαλος γινώσκῃ, τοιαῦτα πρήσσουσι· γίνεται γὰρ ἐν ἅπαντι τῷ σώματι τῆς φρονήσιος, ὡς ἂν μετέχῃ τοῦ ἠέρος. ἐς δὲ τὴν σύνεσιν ὁ ἐγκέφαλος ἐστιν ὁ διαγγέλλων. (*Morb. Sacr.* 19.1-10)

> In these ways I hold the brain is the most powerful organ of the human body, for when it is healthy it is an interpreter to us of the phenomena caused by the air, as it is the air that gives it intelligence. Eyes, ears, tongue, hands and feet act in accordance with the discernment of the brain; in fact the whole body participates in intelligence in proportion to its participation in air. To consciousness the brain is the messenger.[16]

14. M. Barth, *Ephesians*, AB 32 (New York: Doubleday, 1974) 1:190.

15. See J. Kollesch, "Medizin (Nachträge)," in *Der Kleine Pauly* (München: Deutscher Taschenbuch, 1979) 5:1625.

16. Text and translation from W. H. S. Jones, *Hippocrates*, LCL, vol. 2 (Cambridge: Harvard University, 1953) 178. This passage is also quoted (without translation) in Lightfoot, *Colossians*, 200-201.

In the Hippocratic conception, the brain functions like a control center for all the various parts of the body. Because it is the interpreter of sense perception, the brain is able to coordinate the responses of the members of the body.

For Hippocrates, the head also is the source of supply for the members of the body. He describes the head as the starting point of the four thickest pairs of veins in the body (σῶμα). From the head, the veins reach to every part of the body and give nourishment (ἡ τροφή) and provide (διαδίδωμι) what the body needs (*Nat. Hom.* 19.11).[17] By this description, Hippocrates is not supplanting the role of the heart as the organ that pumps blood; rather, he is stressing that the head controls the supply of blood to all the parts of the body. He says that "neither [the heart or the diaphragm] has any share of intelligence (φρονήσιος), but it is the brain (ἐγκέφαλος) which is the cause of all the things I have mentioned" (*Morb. Sacr.* 20.27-29).

Plato (429-347 B.C.E.) demonstrates a significant dependence on the Hippocratic tradition for his understanding of physiology. In line with this school, he ascribes to the head a ruling function in relationship to the body. His position can be seen most clearly in the *Timaeus:*

> Τὰς μὲν δὴ θείας περιόδους δύο οὔσας, τὸ τοῦ παντὸς σχῆμα ἀπομιμησάμενοι περιφερὲς ὄν, εἰς σφαιδοειδὲς σῶμα ἐνέδησαν, τοῦτο ὃ νῦν κεφαλὴν ἐπονομάζομεν, ὃ θειότατόν τ' ἐστὶ καὶ τῶν ἐν ἡμῖν πάντων δεσποτοῦν. ᾧ καὶ πᾶν τὸ σῶμα παρέδοσαν ὑπηρεσίαν αὐτῷ ξυναθροίσαντες θεοί (*Tim.* 44d).
>
> The divine revolutions, which are two, they bound within a sphere-shaped body, in imitation of the spherical form of the All, which body we now call the "head," it being the most divine part and reigning over all the parts within us. To it the gods delivered over the whole body they had assembled to be its servant.[18]

This passage is one of the clearest references to Plato's concept of a cosmic body (σῶμα) governed by a head (κεφαλή) which serves as the pattern, or idea, for the constitution of each individual.[19] For Plato, the principle of the head's leadership is expressed with the word δεσποτέω. The leadership (ἡ ἡγεμονία) is carried out according to the forethought of the soul (ἡ προνοία τῆς ψυχῆς; *Tim.* 45b).

17. See W. H. S. Jones, *Hippocrates,* LCL, vol. 4 (Cambridge: Harvard University, 1953) 30-33.

18. Translation by R. G. Bury, in *Plato,* LCL, vol. 7 (Cambridge: Harvard University, 1952). See also *Timaeus* 45a.1-2, 69d6-e3.

19. In contrast to the presentation of Christ in Col 1:15-20, Plato's "World-Soul" in the *Timaeus* is not the creator, which is properly the function of the demiurge. Plato views the "World-Soul" strictly as a maintainer of order against the natural tendency for the material creation to move toward chaos. See R. D. Mohr, "The World-Soul in the Platonic Cosmology," in *The Platonic Cosmology,* Philosophia Antiqua 42 (Leiden: E. J. Brill, 1985) 170-77.

The head, as the leading member, coordinates all the other members of the body. The sinews (νεῦρα) provide the connection between the head and the body: "God set the sinews at the bottom of the head round about the neck and glued them there symmetrically . . . and the rest of the sinews He distributed amongst all the limbs (τὰ μέλη), attaching joint to joint (ἄρθρον ἄρθρῳ)" (*Tim.* 75c-d). The veins provide the additional means of connection between the head and the body and furnish all the essential nourishment to the body (τροφὴν διδὸν τῷ σώματι) from what the head, namely, the mouth, takes in (*Tim.* 77c-e). Through these connections to the body, the head is also able to communicate sense impressions from one part of the body to all the other parts. For these reasons, Plato can describe the "head" in terms of the acropolis of a country (*Leg.* 969b-c).

Galen's works are especially important for perspective on this issue. Galen gives us testimony of an ongoing debate between certain philosophers and medical writers on the governing part of the body. Aristotle (384-322 B.C.E.) and some Stoic writers (esp. Zeno and Chrysippus) argued that the heart was the governing part of the body.[20] Against them, Galen defended the position of Hippocrates and Plato that the head was the ruling part of the body. Plato's notion of the head's leadership is reaffirmed by Galen in his work *On the Doctrines of Hippocrates and Plato* (Latin: *De Placitis Hippocratis et Platonis*), as he describes the relationship of the head to the body:

> Nor is it necessary that because the brain, like the Great King, dwells in the head as in an acropolis, for that reason the ruling part of the soul is in the brain (οὐδὲ γὰρ ὅτι καθάπερ ἐν ἀκροπόλει τῇ κεφαλῇ δίκην μαγάλου βασιλέως ὁ ἐγκέφαλος ἵδρυται, διὰ τοῦτ' ἐξ ἀνάγκης ἡ τῆς ψυχῆς ἀρχὴ κατ' αὐτόν ἐστιν), or because the brain has the senses stationed around it like bodyguards (δορυφόρους), or even if one should go so far as to say that as heaven is to the whole universe, so the head is to man, and that therefore as the former is the home of the gods, so the brain is the home of the rational faculty.[21]

In another work, *On the Usefulness of the Parts of the Body,* Galen asserts that the notion of the head's sovereignty over the body was an opinion that was commonly held:

20. C. J. Singer and A. Wasserstein, "Anatomy and Physiology," in *OCD*², 59, note: "Among the noteworthy errors of Aristotle is his refusal to attach importance to the brain. Intelligence he placed in the heart. This was contrary to the views of some of his medical contemporaries, contrary to the popular view, and contrary to the doctrine of the *Timaeus*." See also F. W. Bayer, "Anatomie," *RAC* 1 (Stuttgart: Hiersemann, 1950) cols. 430-37.

21. P. de Lacy, *Galen: On the Doctrines of Hippocrates and Plato,* CMG V4, 1, 2, Pt. 1 (Berlin: Akademie, 1978) 120.1-10. H. Schlier, "κεφαλή," *TDNT* 3:674, cites still another passage from Galen *(De Remediis)* which compares the head to an acropolis: αὕτη γὰρ καθάπερ τις ἀνθρώποις αἰσθήσεων οἰκητήριον.

Ἡ δὲ δὴ κεφαλὴ τοῖς μὲν πλείστος ἔδοξε διὰ τὸν ἐγκέγαλον γεγονέναι, καὶ διὰ τοῦτο καὶ τὰς αἰσθήσεις ἁπάσας ἔχειν ἐν αὐτῇ, καθάπερ τινὰς ὑπηρέτας τε καὶ δορυφόρους μαγάλου βασιλέως. (Galen *De Usu Partium* 1.445.14-17)[22]

To most people the head seems to have been formed on account of the encephalon and for that reason to contain all the senses, like the servants and guards of a great king.

For Galen, the ἐγκέφαλος (the brain) is the control center for all of the senses. Furthermore, the ἐγκέφαλος is the source of the senses (αἰσθήσεις), of the nerves (νεῦρα), and of all voluntary motion (κινήσεις) (*De Usu Partium* 1.453.13-15). Galen clearly did not have the advanced understanding of the neurological system that we possess today. What is important for us to note, however, is that he was firmly convinced that the ἐγκέφαλος, located in the κεφαλή,[23] was the command and supply center for the body. Notice how Galen regards the head, or, more specifically, the ἐγκέφαλος, as the body's source of provision by his use of ἀρχή:

(1) ἀρχὴν νεύρων (*De Usu Partium* 1.453.13)
(2) ἀρχὴν αἰσθήσεώς τε καὶ κινήσεως (*De Usu Partium* 1.453.22)
(3) ἀρχὴ προαιρέσεως καὶ κινήσεως (*De Usu Partium,* 1.456.8-9)

(1) [The brain is] the source of the nerves
(2) [The brain is] the source of sensation and voluntary motion
(3) [The brain is] the source of the will and motion

The functions of the body most people would refer to as belonging simply to the "head," Galen attributes to the ἐγκέφαλος, thus providing more precision. For Galen, the κεφαλή is important because it contains the ἐγκέφαλος.[24] Galen is most concerned, however, to prevent functions properly belonging to the head / brain from being attributed to the heart (*contra* Aristotle). He emphatically argues that all the instruments of the senses communicate with the ἐγκέφαλος (*De Usu Partium* 1.451.26-27).

A similar opinion regarding the function of the head was shared by Rufus of Ephesus (*c.* 100 C.E.). In his work "On the Names of the Parts of the Human

22. G. Helmreich, *Galenus: De Usu Partium (*ΓΑΛΗΝΟΥ ΠΕΡΙ ΧΡΕΙΑΣ ΜΟΡΙΩΝ ΙΖ*),* vol. 1 (Amsterdam: Hakkert, 1968 [= Leipzig: Teubner, 1907]) 445. ET by M. T. May, *Galen: On the Usefulness of the Parts of the Body,* vol. 1 (Ithaca, New York: Cornell University, 1968) 387.

23. Galen points out that the brain is called the ἐγκέφαλος because it lies ἐν τῇ κεφαλῇ ("in the head"). He is careful to distinguish the ἐγκέφαλον from the κεφαλή, however, by clarifying that the former is the command and supply center, while the latter is merely the location of the brain in most living beings (except the crustaceans) (*De Usu Partium* 1.454.1-14).

24. He points out that crabs and other crustacea do not have a head. The part controlling the senses and voluntary motion is contained in the thorax (*De Usu Partium* 1.445.19-20).

Body" (Περι Ονομασιας Των Του Ανθρωπου Μοριων [= *Onom.*]), Rufus puts the head at the beginning of the list of the most important parts of the body (Ἔστι δὲ τὰ μέγιστα μέρη τοῦ σώματος, κεφαλὴ, καὶ αὐχὴν, καὶ θώραξ, καὶ χεῖρες, καὶ σκέλη; 135.1-2).[25] Rufus regards the heart as the source of heat, life, and the pulse (*Onom.* 155.11-12), but he considers the brain, located in the head, to be the source of the nerves and senses: "the processes springing from the brain (ἐγκέφαλος) are the sensory and voluntary nerves (νεῦρα),[26] through which feeling and voluntary movement — in fact, all the activities of the body — are carried out" (*Onom.* 163.12-14).[27] Rufus's opinion is important because he taught anatomy and physiology at the end of the first century C.E.[28] Such opinion was surely well known in Asia Minor, which was famous in antiquity for its advanced medical science and excellent medical schools (Pergamum, Smyrna, Ephesus, Miletus, Tralles, Laodicea, and elsewhere).[29]

Without further multiplying the number of examples, one may safely conclude that for the medical writers (and for philosophers like Plato), the head not only exercised sovereignty over the physical body, but was also the source of its sensations and movement. The leadership role of the head stemmed precisely from the fact that it was the source of sensation, movement, and decision making. It is also likely that the opinion of Hippocrates, Galen, and Rufus regarding the function of the head in relationship to the body reflects the common physiological understanding of the time (with due respect to the variant opinion of Aristotle and the Stoics).

## 3. Head-Body in Hellenistic Judaism

Philo clearly reflects this common physiological understanding of the relationship of the head to the body. Without doubt, his conceptions are also dependent on Plato (whom Galen defends).[30] He is certainly aware of the debate over whether

25. C. Daremberg and E. Ruelle, *Oeuvres de Rufus d'Éphèse* (Amsterdam: Adolf M. Hakkert, 1963 [= Paris, 1879]).

26. According to A. J. Brock, *Greek Medicine* (New York: E. P. Dutton, 1929 [reprint ed., New York: AMS, 1972]) 125, Rufus uses the terms "nerves" (νεῦρα) to refer to tendons as well as nerves proper (which Rufus distinguished into sensory and motor).

27. Translation from Brock, *Greek Medicine,* 127.

28. J. Ilberg, *Rufus von Ephesos: Ein griechischer Arzt in Trajanischer Zeit,* Der Abhandlungen der philologisch-historischen Klasse der sächischen Akademie der Wissenschaften 1 (Leipzig: S. Hirzel, 1930) 7.

29. Ilberg, *Rufus von Ephesos,* 1, notes: "Die Anfänge griechischer Heilwissenschaft liegen im Osten, auf der kleinasiatischen Küste und in ihrer Nähe, wie die Anfänge wahrer Wissenschaft überhaupt." See also W. Elliger, *Ephesos: Geschichte einer antiken Weltstadt* (Stuttgart: Kohlhammer, 1985) 85.

30. See D. T. Runia, *Philo of Alexandria and the Timaeus of Plato* (Amsterdam: VU Boekhandel, 1983) esp. 229-30.

the seat of control lies in the head or the heart (*Somn.* 1.32; cf. *Quaest. in Exod.* 2.100), but he clearly aligns himself with the position that sees the head as sovereign. In fact, Philo frequently uses the word ἡγεμονικός and its cognates (the "dominant" or "leading" part) to characterize the head (e.g., *Op. Mund.* 119; *Fug.* 110, 182; *Somn.* 2.207; *Vit. Mos.* 2.30, 82; *Spec. Leg.* 3.184; *Quaest. in Gen.* 1.3, 10; 2.5; *Quaest. in Exod.* 2.124).[31] He can also refer to it as "the master limb of the members" (ὁ κυριώτατος τῶν μελῶν; *Spec. Leg.* 1.147). The head is "the first, highest and principal part"; it is the "chief" (*Quaest. in Exod.* 1.17). For Philo, "the head, like the citadel of a king, has as its occupant the sovereign mind" (τὸν ἡγεμονικὸν νοῦν; *Quaest. in Gen.* 2.5). The head is so important to Philo because it is the residence of the "mind" (νοῦς).[32] Elsewhere, Philo speaks of the head as the dwelling place of "reason" (λόγος):

> λόγῳ μὲν ὡς ἡγεμόνι τὴν ἄκραν ἀπένειμαν οἰκειότατον ἐνδιαίτημα κεφαλήν, ἔνθα καὶ τῶν αἰσθήσεων αἱ τοῦ νοῦ καθάπερ βασιλέως δορυφόροι τάξεις παρίδρυνται. (*Spec. Leg.* 4.92)

> To reason as sovereign they [the philosophers, namely, Plato] assigned for its citadel the head as its most suitable residence, where also are set the stations of the senses like bodyguards to their king, the mind.

In his discussion of the function of the head, Philo prefers to speak of it as the location of the "mind" (νοῦς) or "reason" (λόγος) instead of the "brain" (ἐγκέφαλος). Whereas Galen was using more precise language physiologically, Philo was more concerned to draw out the philosophical / theological implications.

The head not only exercises "reason" as a function of the "mind," it also controls the sense perceptions of the body.

> The soul innervates and strengthens sense perception by directing its energies (ἐνεργείας) to what is suitable for it, with the participation of the parts of the body. And the centre, in one meaning, is the chief and head, as is the leader of a chorus. (*Quaest. in Gen.* 1.10)

In this passage both the leadership of the head and its ability to provide for the body are stressed. Elsewhere, Philo makes it clear that he regards the head as the ruling part of the soul (*Somn.* 2.207; cf. also 1.128, 146). The head, therefore,

31. J. A. Fitzmyer, "Another Look at ΚΕΦΑΛΗ in 1 Corinthians 11.3," *NTS* 35 (1989) 509-10, cites four of these passages to illustrate his contention that κεφαλή can mean "authority" or "supremacy" in Hellenistic Judaism. He is certainly correct in what he affirms, and as we have demonstrated, there are many additional passages in Philo that verify this assumption. The simple idea of "authority," however, does not exhaust the meaning of κεφαλή in Philo, especially when it occurs in connection with "body."

32. Runia, *Philo,* 229, therefore observes that for Philo, as well as for Plato, "the head, and in particular the face, is the most principal part of the body because it is the location of the rational soul and of the senses which serve the mind."

is the ultimate source of supply for all of the body's needs. This passage highlights that the head directs "energies" (ἐνεργείαι) to the various members of the body. This conception sounds quite similar to Eph 4:16 (and Col 2:19), which speaks of the body (the church) drawing its nourishment and provisions from Christ for the building up and increase of the body. Although Philo does not explicitly say that the body grows (αὐξάνω) as a result of the head's provision, he does affirm the body's total dependence on the head because it is "innervated" and "strengthened" by the head. Growth could certainly be implied as a natural by-product of dependence on the head.

This thought is similarly expressed in a passage where Philo is commenting on Deut 28:13 ("The Lord will make you the head, not the tail"):

> καθάπερ γὰρ ἐν ζῴῳ κεφαλὴ μὲν πρῶτον καὶ ἄριστον, οὐρὰ δ' ὕστατον καὶ φαυλότατον . . . τὸν αὐτὸν τρόπον κεφαλὴν μὲν τοῦ ἀνθρωπείου γένους ἔσεσθαί φησι τὸν σπουδαῖον εἴτε ἄνδρα εἴτε λαόν, τοὺς δὲ ἄλλους ἅπαντας οἷον μέρη σώματος ψυχούμενα ταῖς ἐν κεφαλῇ καὶ ὑπεράνω δυνάμεσιν. (*Praem. et Poen.* 125)

> For as in an animal the head is the first and best part and the tail the last and meanest . . . so too he [Moses] means that the virtuous one, whether single man or people, will be the head of the human race and all the others like the limbs of a body which draw their life from the forces in the head and at the top.

On one level, the head of the physical body is regarded as the source of life (ψυχούμενα) to all of the individual members (μέρη σώματος). At the same time, Philo stresses the prominence of the head by describing it as "the first" and "best" part (πρῶτον καὶ ἄριστον). Philo, however, uses this physiology to develop a metaphorical meaning. Specifically, "the virtuous one" (σπουδαῖος) is a source of spiritual life to all true members of his group or association. For Philo, this is a blessing for all good people who fulfill the laws by their deeds (*Praem. et Poen.* 126). This passage is very significant for our investigation because the physiology is metaphorically applied to one person (κεφαλή) in relationship to a group of other people (μέρη σώματος). This compares to how Paul uses the imagery in Colossians and Ephesians. Furthermore, the dual notion of leadership and source of provisions is present.

The metaphorical use of "head" in relationship to a "body" is nonexistent in the LXX and is exceedingly rare in the pseudepigraphal literature. An examination of all the passages listed under κεφαλή in A.-M. Denis's concordance turns up only one relevant reference.[33] The passage, which appears in the *Testament of Zebulun,* never explicitly mentions σῶμα, but it is certainly implied:

33. A.-M. Denis, ed., *Concordance Grecque des Pseudépigraphes d'Ancien Testament* (Louvain: Université Catholique de Louvain, 1987) 472-73. Admittedly, the concordance only covers Greek documents and Greek fragments of documents that may be extant in other languages. I am aware of no other relevant passages, however.

> Do not be divided into two heads (κεφαλάς), because everything the Lord has made has a single head (κεφαλήν). He provides two shoulders, two hands, two feet, but all members (τὰ μέλη) are subject to (ὑπακούει) one head (κεφαλῇ). (*T. Zeb.* 9:4)

The writer of the Testament then illustrates the principle of division into two heads by calling attention to Israel's demise under the divided kingdom when they followed after two *kings.* The author says this action resulted in Israel committing every abomination and worshiping every idol (*T. Zeb.* 9:5). This use of κεφαλή reflects the function of head as the "guiding center in the body,"[34] as we saw in the use of κεφαλή as ἡγεμονικός in Philo. Surprisingly, this passage has seldom figured in the discussion of the head-body imagery in Paul in spite of the fact that it describes the function of a "head" in relation to the members of a body. Here the notion of leadership is stressed without any thought of provision by the head to the members. The passage also employs the common Pauline expression τὰ μέλη with reference to the members of the body.

Outside of Philo, head-body imagery was not especially common in Hellenistic Judaism. We have noticed two related characteristics of the usage of the imagery in Philo: (1) Philo may emphasize *the leadership* and *position of authority* that the head exercises and holds in relationship to the body, or (2) he may stress the function of the head as the *source of provision* for the body, enabling it to function properly. On most occasions both of these aspects are present in the same passage.

Philo, no doubt, was directly dependent on Plato for this concept. However, his use of the imagery was reinforced and enriched by the common physiological explanation of the relationship of the head to the body. Also, as we observed earlier, Philo never ascribes a cosmic function to κεφαλή when he elaborates on the world soul. In fact, D. Runia notes that Philo deliberately avoids even referring to the cosmos as a body in many instances where it would be quite natural to do so.[35]

## 4. Christ as Head of the Church in Colossians and Ephesians

We are now in a position to draw out the implications of this material for the interpretation of the head-body imagery in Colossians and Ephesians. In place of the cosmic interpretation of the head-body imagery, I have reasserted Light-

34. So H. W. Hollander and M. de Jonge, *The Testaments of the Twelve Patriarchs,* SVTP 8 (Leiden: E. J. Brill, 1985) 270, note on v 4.

35. Runia, *Philo,* 165, observes, "where Plato speaks of the body of the cosmos, Philo prefers to refer simply to the cosmos. . . . The avoidance of the notion of the body of the cosmos would seem quite deliberate."

foot's view that the source of the imagery is rooted in a common physiological understanding of the function of the head in relationship to the body.

Up to this point, this view has attracted few followers.[36] Perhaps one of the difficulties that has hindered acceptance of this view is the difficulty of determining how Paul would have been familiar with such physiological discussions. This is really not an insuperable difficulty if we imagine that the basic anatomical terminology and concepts observed in Hippocrates, Galen, and Rufus were part of common belief (Galen notes that this was the case).[37] We have seen, however, that the views of the doctors penetrated Hellenistic Judaism, particularly in the writings of Philo.

Paul may therefore have developed the concept of Christ as "head" of his "body," the church, in direct dependence on the common physiological understandings of his day (so Lightfoot and Barth) or based on the use of the imagery in Hellenistic Judaism, or in dependence on both. It is doubtful that Paul would have been unaware of either stream of thought.

In my discussion of the following passages, I will limit my remarks to demonstrating the implications of the proposed background to the interpretation of the texts. For a full exegesis of each passage, I would refer the reader to the commentaries.

*4.1. Col 2:19.* I begin with Col 2:19 because it is appropriate that the more fully elaborated concept of "head" and "body" as evidenced here should inform our interpretation of Col 1:18a rather than vice versa. This is not to deny the possibility of a preexisting piece of tradition in Col 1:15-20, but rather to stress that the physiological connotations of the present passage are more important to the interpretation of Col 1:18a than the assumption of a cosmic head and body.

Paul employs the imagery as part of his polemic against a new teaching which was influencing the church at Colossae. "The philosophy," as the competing teaching was called (2:8), appears to have been highly syncretistic, drawing aspects of its practice and belief from Judaism, local Phrygian religion, magic, and astrology.[38] Paul regards the teaching as dangerous to the health of the church, labeling it "vain

36. Although see K. Usami, *Somatic Comprehension of Unity: The Church in Ephesus,* AnBib 101 (Rome: Biblical Institute, 1983) 140-42; and F. F. Bruce, "The 'Christ Hymn' of Colossians 1:15-20," *BibSac* 141 (1984) 105.

37. Lightfoot, *Colossians,* 201, appealed to Paul's acquaintance with Luke, "the physician," as the source of the imagery. Although this suggestion is assuredly speculative, it is often too quickly (and unfairly) dismissed as absurd.

38. I am currently engaged in writing a monograph on the nature of the competing teaching at Colossae. The general direction of my thinking on this issue may be seen in *Powers of Darkness: Principalities and Powers in Paul's Letters* (Downers Grove, Illinois: InterVarsity, 1992) ch. 10: "Christ and No Other." The bibliography for this topic is immense and the views are diverse. For the most recent treatment of the problem, see T. J. Sappington, *Revelation and Redemption at Colossae,* JSNTSS 53 (Sheffield: JSOT, 1991), who argues that the background to the teaching of the opponents is best illustrated by the ascetic-mystical piety of Jewish apocalypticism.

deceit" and warning the congregation not to be taken captive (συλαγωγέω) by it (2:8). In the paragraph consisting of 2:16-19, Paul issues two warnings: "do not let anyone judge you" (μὴ οὖν τις ὑμᾶς κρινέτω) and "do not let anyone . . . disqualify you for the prize" (μηδεὶς ὑμᾶς καταβραβευέτω). Each of these warnings is followed by a brief description of some of the practices of the variant teaching followed by Paul's response. After the second warning and description, Paul delivers two judgments about those who advocate the teaching: (1) such a person is extremely arrogant, and (2) "this person is not holding tight to the head (κεφαλήν)."

The head is then described as the source of the body's growth: ἐξ οὗ πᾶν τὸ σῶμα . . . αὔξει τὴν αὔξησιν τοῦ θεοῦ (2:19). Earlier in his polemic, Paul indicated two alternatives for the Colossians: follow the teaching of Christ (κατὰ Χριστόν) or follow the teaching of the elemental spirits (κατὰ τὰ στοιχεῖα τοῦ κόσμου) (2:8).[39] Here he builds on this thought by accusing the opponents of not receiving their teaching and practices from Christ. By employing head-body imagery here, Paul is able to elaborate on the role of the risen Christ in relationship to his church.[40] He appears to draw on the contemporary physiological understanding of the head in relationship to the body to communicate his message to the congregation. In the first place, Christ alone is *the leader* of the church. He alone possesses authority over his people. The teachers of the "philosophy" therefore have no right to judge the Colossians (κρίνω; 2:16), disqualify them (καταβραβεύω; 2:18), and impose their teaching and practices on them. Their teaching does not have its source in Christ, but in "elemental spirits" who are attempting to assert their deceptive influence on the church (2:8). Christ has disarmed these spirits, however, exposing their weakness, and has led them in his triumphal procession by his work on the cross (2:15).

Secondly, Christ is *the source of provision* for the church. It is from him (ἐξ οὗ) that the entire church (πᾶν τὸ σῶμα) draws its nourishment for growth. "Body" is here modified by three expressions (one prepositional phrase and two participles). The body is able to grow "through the mutual contact of the limbs and through the ligaments" (διὰ τῶν ἁφῶν καὶ συνδέσμων). The term σύνδεσμος was the common one in the medical writers to refer to the ligaments.[41] The correspond-

39. With this interpretation, κατὰ τὴν παράδοσιν τῶν ἀνθρώπων becomes the means through which these spirits influence the church. The concept of false teaching as ultimately stemming from "evil spirits" was common in Judaism and in the early church.

40. Some interpreters have attempted to explain the use of σῶμα here in cosmic terms; see, e.g., M. Dibelius and H. Greeven, *An die Kolosser, Epheser, an Philemon*, 3d ed., HNT (Tübingen: J. C. B. Mohr [Paul Siebeck], 1953) 84. Such an interpretation drastically misses the point of the admonition to the Colossian believers and does not fit the context. Furthermore, the author of Colossians has already limited the σῶμα to ἡ ἐκκλησία in 1:18.

41. See, e.g., Galen *De Usu Partium* 1.442.22; 2.202; Rufus of Ephesus Περι Ονομασιας 142.11-12; 157.6. Note esp. Galen *On the Doctrines of Hippocrates and Plato* 94.11-19:

> There are three structures similar to each other in bodily form but quite different in action and use. One is called "nerve" (νεῦρον), another "ligament" (σύνδεσμος), and the third, "tendon" (τένων).

ing term in this passage, ἁφή, is often translated "joint," and is virtually a synonym for τὰ ἄρθρα.[42] It is not clear if Paul expects the reader to interpret the ἁφαί and σύνδεσμοι as part of an extended metaphor and, especially, as some have thought, as a reference to church leaders.[43] Many recent commentators think no referent is intended; he only seeks to emphasize the unity of the body.[44] It is possible, however, that Paul is thinking of the entire body (πᾶν τὸ σῶμα) in these terms. If so, he would be stressing the role of the individual members as channels of provision to the rest of the body based on their relationship to Christ and close contact with one another (thus ἁφή). Each of the members is also an important source of unity to the rest of the body (thus σύνδεσμος). The terms ἁφαί and σύνδεσμοι then become an alternative way of referring to the parts (τὰ μέρη) of the body (cf. 1 Cor 12:27).

The source of the imagery changes when Paul speaks of the body being "constantly supplied" (ἐπιχορηγούμενον) and "held together" (συμβιβαζόμενον). Neither of these terms is common in the medical writings. The former stresses provision, as a husband would provide for his wife,[45] while the latter stresses unity ("to be put together," "to be knit together," "framed"[46]). Christ is ultimately the source of both provision and unity for the church, but he accomplishes this through his people living in dependence on him.

The apostle wants the Colossian believers to know that those who advocate this new "philosophy" are not depending on Christ, but spirits of deception (στοιχεῖα τοῦ κόσμου; 2:8). The teachers whom they are enticed to follow are detached from a relationship to Christ as their head — a head who provides direction, nourishment, and unity. The church can only mature as it submits to Christ's leadership and receives his nourishing strength and support.

***4.2. Eph 4:16.*** Very similar imagery appears in Eph 4:16, but there is not the same pressing danger of a specific false teaching threatening the church at the moment of his writing. Although the overall context is much more positive, focusing on the principle of Christian growth, there is a clear stress on the general threat of false teaching (Eph 4:14).

The imagery is introduced by the exhortation, "let us grow up into him [Christ] in every way" (4:15). This aim of growing into maturity is facilitated

42. Lightfoot, *Colossians,* 198-99. See his commentary for the relevant references.

43. Theodoret asserted that the terms refer to apostles, prophets, and teachers (Theodoret [cited in Lohmeyer, *Kolosser,* 179 n. 6]). J. Gnilka, *Der Epheserbrief,* HTKNT 10.2 (Freiburg: Herder, 1971) 220; and R. Schnackenburg, *The Epistle to the Ephesians* (Edinburgh: T. & T. Clark, 1991) 189, both regard the term ἁφαί as a reference to church officers (cf. v 11). The emphasis of the verse, however, is on every individual in the body receiving grace from God and then contributing to the growth of the body.

44. Lohmeyer, *Kolosser,* 179, stresses that the main point of comparison is the relationship between the head and body.

45. The word appears often in marriage and divorce contracts with the meaning "to provide for," "to support" (for examples, see Lohse, *Colossians,* 122 n. 62).

46. *LSJ,* s.v.

by the risen Christ endowing the church with gifted people (4:11-13).[47] The people of Christ speak the truth and manifest love to one another; they do not propagate erroneous teaching for evil, self-centered motives. Furthermore, as the body of Christ matures, it will not be taken in by those who disseminate such destructive and deceptive teachings (4:14-15).

The context of the head-body imagery here is therefore comparable to Col 2:19. Whereas a concrete problem faced the Colossian church, the apostle is here preparing the readers for incursions of a similar kind. If Ephesians was written shortly after Colossians, and given the close proximity of Colossae to the readership of Ephesians, it is understandable why Paul would have taken up this theme once again and applied it to a different setting.

Paul develops Christ's headship of the body in a very similar way with a few variations that in the end make little difference to the meaning. The similarities and differences can be easily noted by displaying the two passages side-by-side (verbal parallels are noted with a double-underline; cognate terms with a single underline):

| **(Col 2:19)** | **(Eph 4:15-16)** |
|---|---|
| καὶ οὐ κρατῶν τὴν κεφαλήν, | ὅς ἐστιν ἡ κεφαλή, Χριστός, |
| ἐξ οὗ πᾶν τὸ σῶμα | ἐξ οὗ πᾶν τὸ σῶμα |
| διὰ τῶν ἁφῶν καὶ συνδέσμων | συναρμολογούμενον καὶ συμβιβαζόμενον |
| ἐπιχορηγούμενον καὶ συμβιβαζόμενον | διὰ πάσης ἁφῆς τῆς ἐπικορηγίας |
| αὔξει τὴν αὔξησιν τοῦ θεοῦ. | κατ' ἐνέργειαν ἐν μέτρῳ |
| | ἑνὸς ἑκάστου μέρους |
| | τὴν αὔξησιν τοῦ σώματος ποιεῖται |
| | εἰς οἰκοδομὴν ἑαυτοῦ ἐν ἀγάπῃ. |

I will comment on a few of the differences. (1) The Ephesian passage drops σύνδεσμος and joins ἐπιχορηγία (the noun cognate of ἐπιχορηγέω) to ἁφή in a descriptive genitive relationship. The resultant meaning is not significantly different. The ἁφαί, the parts of the body viewed in their contact with the other parts, are still seen as channels of provision that extend nourishment to the other parts from the head. The change to the singular and the addition of πᾶς stress the contribution of each individual part. The phrase κατ' ἐνέργειαν ἐν μέτρῳ ἑνὸς ἑκάστου μέρους, unique to Ephesians, also highlights the importance of the active contribution of each individual member. (2) The stress on unity is not lost, in spite of the absence of σύνδεσμοι and the switch of ἁφή to the singular. The members are viewed as a corporate unity both at the beginning of the passage (πᾶν τὸ σῶμα) and at the end (τὸ σῶμα, ἑαυτός). (3) The introduction of συναρμολογέω, used earlier in the author's temple imagery (2:21), further heightens the theme of unity and the notion of the believers

47. See the excellent discussion of this passage by Lincoln, *Ephesians*, 248-57.

growing together as a collective whole. (4) The final phrase, εἰς οἰκοδομὴν ἑαυτοῦ ἐν ἀγάπῃ, merely reiterates in different terms (again a change to architectural imagery) the notion of growth as stated in the previous line, "the increase of the body is made" (τὴν αὔξησιν τοῦ σώματος ποιεῖται). The addition of ἐν ἀγάπῃ furthers the writer's emphasis on the theme of love throughout the letter (cf. esp. 4:2, 15). (5) Finally, God's provision of divine enabling power to each individual member of the church is implicit in the expression κατ' ἐνέργειαν (cf. Col 1:29; cf. also Eph 1:19; 3:7).[48]

Here again the dual notion of *leadership* and *provision* is present in the head-body imagery. This corresponds to the common notion of the function of the head in relationship to the body in the contemporary physiological understandings, and especially as represented by Philo.

These passages demonstrate the elasticity of the apostle's "body" concept as it is seen in comparison to 1 Corinthians 12 and Romans 12. He introduces the notion of Christ as "head" of the body because of the situational exigency. The church at Colossae as well as the readership of his letter to the Ephesians need to draw on Christ alone for leadership and strength in order to resist the influence of cunning and deceitful false teachers.

***4.3. Col 1:18a.*** As I indicated earlier, Col 1:18a is usually taken as the starting point for interpreting all the other references to the head-body imagery throughout Colossians and Ephesians. It is better, however, to start with the passages which give the full elaboration of the theme, as we have done, than to begin with a passage where it is only briefly mentioned and not developed. Furthermore, this approach avoids the pitfall of misconstruing the author's intent by explaining this part of the hymn as an exposition of Christ as head of a cosmic body. Whether or not we are dealing with a piece of pre-Pauline traditional material which may or may not have included τῆς ἐκκλησίας, it is clear that Colossians and Ephesians restrict the interpretation of σῶμα to the church. Some have questioned whether the cosmic function was ever really present in the hymn. N. T. Wright has shown that τῆς ἐκκλησίας may very well have been part of the original hymn.[49]

My interpretation of the meaning of the head-body imagery in Col 1:18a is not dependent on any particular strophic arrangement of the hymn. In the final form of the hymn, as it appears in the letter, σῶμα must refer to the church

48. See my *Ephesians: Power and Magic,* SNTSMS 63 (Cambridge: Cambridge University, 1989) 160. See also Lincoln, *Ephesians,* 263; and Gnilka, *Epheserbrief,* 220.

49. N. T. Wright, "Poetry and Theology in Colossians 1.15-20," *NTS* 36 (1990) 447-48. The strength of his argument is twofold: (1) the close similarity of line lengths based on syllable counts when τῆς ἐκκλησίας is retained, and (2) by taking the two καὶ αὐτός ἐστιν statements as introducing the central members of a chiasmus (A = 15-16; B = 17; B′ = 18ab; A′ = 18c-20), he provides a compelling explanation for the overall structure of the hymn (or, as he prefers with good reason, "some kind of poem").

because of the presence of the genitive of apposition. Christ is therefore seen as "head" of the church, not as "head of the world." This use of the imagery early on in the letter therefore has an epistolary function of introducing a theme that will be developed in the course of the letter.

***4.4. Col 2:10 and Eph 1:22.*** Paul uses the term κεφαλή again in a metaphorical sense in Col 2:10 when he says, "Christ is the head of every principality and authority" (ὅς ἐστιν ἡ κεφαλὴ πάσης ἀρχῆς καὶ ἐξουσίας). In this instance, σῶμα does not appear because Paul is not referring to Christ's relationship to the church, but to evil angelic powers. Neither is he implying that the angelic powers are a part of his cosmic body.

As it is used here, the term κεφαλή does not reflect the medical parallels which describe the function of the head in relation to the body. This is a special metaphorical use of κεφαλή which is in line with OT and Hellenistic Jewish usage expressing the idea of "authority over," "superior," or "ruler."[50] No doubt this usage is ultimately related to the concept of the "head's" function in relation to the physical "body." In usage, the term "head" could be detached from the full metaphor of head-body and the ruling, authoritative concept (ἡγεμονία) associated with the term emphasized.

The context here strongly militates against interpreting the meaning of κεφαλή as "source" — either in the sense of "origin" or "source of provision." One of the theological emphases of Paul's polemic against the opponents is Christ's defeat of the powers and his resultant supremacy over them (see esp. Col 2:15, 20). To interpret Col 2:10 as affirming that Christ is the "source" of the hostile powers is not at all appropriate to the context. In Col 2:10, Paul is trying to communicate to the Colossians that they share in his fullness by virtue of their union with Christ. This means that they, too, share in his authority over the powers of darkness and can resist their evil influence by depending on the resources in Christ.

The head-body imagery also appears at the beginning of the Ephesian letter, namely, in the introductory prayer-thanksgiving (Eph 1:15-23). It appears as fourth in a list of affirmations about Christ: God raised him from the dead, he seated him at his right hand, he subjected everything under his feet, and "he gave him [as] head over everything to the church, which is his body" (αὐτὸν ἔδωκεν κεφαλὴν ὑπὲρ πάντα τῇ ἐκκλησίᾳ, ἥτις ἐστὶν τὸ σῶμα αὐτοῦ).

There are two senses in which "head" is used in this passage: its meaning in connection with the expression ὑπὲρ πάντα, and its meaning in relationship to "the church / his body." With regard to ὑπὲρ πάντα we can be certain that Paul is painting Christ's "headship" in cosmic terms. "Everything" needs to be understood in the broadest sense. However, there is one aspect of the cosmos

50. See my *Ephesians*, 79. See also, more recently, Fitzmyer, "ΚΕΦΑΛΗ," 503-11.

over (ὑπέρ) which Paul is especially concerned to assert Christ's supremacy, namely, the principalities and powers. In the second affirmation about Christ in this context (1:21), Paul elaborates on Christ's exaltation by declaring that he has been exalted "high above (ὑπεράνω) every principality and authority and power and dominion and every name that is named." Colossians 2:10 therefore becomes the best commentary on this part of the passage. Paul is once again asserting Christ's supremacy over the powers, using the term κεφαλή to express his ruling authority. Here again the meaning of "source" for κεφαλή is inappropriate to this context. In fact, the following ὑπὲρ πάντα would be inexplicable if one tried to interpret κεφαλή as source.

The passage also affirms that Christ is head of the church. For the full significance of the meaning of this concept, one needs to interpret this passage in the light of Eph 4:1-16, especially v 16. As with Col 1:18a, Paul's brief employment of head-body imagery at this point in the letter serves an epistolary function.

One must observe the precise wording of the passage. Paul does not simply say, as in Colossians, that Christ is "head of his body which is the church." Rather, he says that God gave Christ as head "over all things" to the church. Christ is given in his exalted status to the church. He has defeated the powers on the cross and now possesses full authority over them. The head of the church is a victorious Lord. For this reason Christ can impart all of the empowering resources the church needs to resist the attacks of Satan and his evil minions (Eph 6:10-20).

Therefore, in relationship to the cosmos, and particularly the evil powers, Christ as "head" means he is the ruling authority. For the church, he is the ruling authority, but in the sense of providing positive leadership for the fulfillment of his purposes. But he is also the source of provision for the church, especially empowerment for resisting the principalities and powers and for growth.

***4.5. Eph 5:23, 29-30, 32.*** The final appearance of head-body imagery is in the portion of the Ephesian household code treating the relationship between husbands and wives (Eph 5:21-33).[51] Paul uses the relationship of Christ to the church, the head to the body, as one means of defining the respective roles of husbands and wives.

The concept of "head" as providing both leadership and sustenance is prominent in this passage, both with respect to Christ's role in relationship to the church and the husband's toward his wife. The notion of leadership is implied in the fact that the church subjects itself to Christ (ἡ ἐκκλησία ὑποτάσσεται τῷ Χριστῷ; 5:24). This, in turn, serves as an example of how the wife should respond to her husband. The nature of Christ's leadership is, of

51. See the excellent discussion of this passage in Lincoln, *Ephesians,* 350-94.

course, governed by selfless love (5:2, 25) with the welfare of the church always in view.

Christ is also presented in this passage fulfilling his role as "head" by providing for the church. The husband is called "to nourish" (ἐκτρέφω) and "cherish" (θάλπω) his wife because this is what Christ does for the church (5:29-30). The verb ἐκτρέφω is cognate to the noun τροφή ("nourishment") which the medical writers say the head supplies to the body. Paul also uses the verb later in the passage to express the responsibility of parents, especially the father, to nourish and provide for their children as they raise them up (6:4). Similarly, Paul uses θάλπω in 1 Thess 2:7 to refer to the nurse's care of children. A. T. Lincoln points to a papyrus marriage contract which states the husband's duties to his wife using this terminology: θάλπειν καὶ τρέφειν καὶ ἱματίζειν αὐτήν, "to cherish and nourish and clothe her."[52] Christ is therefore thought of as the source of provision for the church. This idea is therefore comparable to ἐπιχορηγία / ἐπιχορηγέω in Col 2:19 and Eph 4:16. It is also in line with common notions of how the physical head functions in relationship to the body as expressed in the medical writers and Philo.

## 5. Conclusion

The head-body imagery used by Paul in Colossians and Ephesians does not have its root in the tradition of the macroanthropos governed by a cosmic head as illustrated by certain Hellenistic texts and Philo. In fact, it is questionable whether Philo ever uses "head" in a cosmic sense. Paul draws on the current physiological understandings of the head in relationship to the body as exhibited in the medical writers to enrich his notion of the church as a corporate body (Romans 12; 1 Corinthians 12). The medical writers describe the head not only as the ruling part of the body, but also as the supply center of the body, since it is the source of sensation, movement, and will. Philo reflects the same concept of the function of the head, but develops the metaphorical usage of the imagery. For Philo, the head gives leadership (ἡγεμονία), but also provides the animating energy and life force.

In Colossians and Ephesians, both aspects of the function of the head are present in the head-body passages. As head of the church, Christ provides the necessary leadership and direction for his people. Christ is also the supplier, the source of the church's life energy, for its growth to maturity.

52. Lincoln, *Ephesians,* 379-80.

# The Christological Basis of the Johannine Footwashing

Ruth B. Edwards

The Fourth Evangelist is well known for his habit of describing incidents which can be interpreted at more than one level.[1] One such happening is the miracle at Cana (John 2:1-11), often seen as an act of kindness to a family in trouble at a village wedding, but which has a deeper meaning as a sign of Jesus' glory and messiahship, and as a foretaste of the joy of the kingdom. Another is the miraculous feeding of the 5,000 (John 6), which was both an act of compassion to a hungry multitude who were physically fed and satisfied, and a deeply symbolic act of spiritual feeding (with overtones of Jesus' role as divine Wisdom, as Messiah, and as the one who is to feed the church sacramentally). Throughout his Gospel John makes use of ambiguity and double meaning to convey his picture of Jesus as the revealer and savior.

The problem with this allusive way of writing is that sometimes people either miss the underlying symbolic meaning, or read more into a text than the author intended. Once the door is opened to understanding a text symbolically, there seem to be no limits to the "spiritual" or allegorical interpretations which human ingenuity can devise. Thus some of the deeper meanings mentioned in our opening paragraph could be disputed, while further symbolic interpretations for them could readily be proposed. In reading John it is essential to keep a firm grip on what the text actually says, observing any indications, either explicit or implicit, that the author may give as to his own interpretation, while noting any symbolic connotations which his language might reasonably be expected to convey in the society in which he lived. At the same time we need to root our exegesis in John's broader theology and purpose.

1. This essay draws on a paper given to St. Andrews University Theological Society in April 1991, and to the Aberdeen University New Testament Postgraduate Seminar in February 1992. I am grateful to all who contributed to the discussion on those occasions, and to the editors of this *Festschrift* for their helpful suggestions and comments.

An important episode in the Gospel of John which can be understood at more than one level is Jesus' washing of the disciples' feet (13:1-20). At least three different interpretations have been put forward, which may be succinctly categorized as (1) exemplary or moral, (2) sacramental, and (3) christological and soteriological. It is the purpose of this essay to consider, first, how far the author intended these interpretations; second, how they relate to one another; and third, what insights they might bring to our understanding of John's distinctive christology.[2]

## 1. The Validity of the Different Interpretations

***1.1. The Exemplary or Moral Interpretation.*** Beyond any shadow of a doubt Jesus' washing of the disciples' feet was intended by the author of ch. 13 in its final form as a moral example of humble service. This is proved by Jesus' explicit command to those with him at the meal: "If I your Lord and Teacher have washed your feet, you ought also to wash one another's feet. I have set you an example: you are to do as I have done for you" (vv 14-15). This understanding is reinforced by Jesus' subsequent reference to slaves (δοῦλοι) and masters (v 16).

The significance of this humble action should not be underestimated. In the ancient world the washing of guests' feet was normally the work of slaves. B. Kötting has collected an array of evidence to this effect from both the Jewish and Greco-Roman worlds.[3] What is not always appreciated is that footwashing was regarded as particularly suitable work for women and female slaves. According to rabbinic sources Jewish *male* slaves were exempt from doing it, though it might be required of a Gentile male slave. On the other hand, both Jewish and Gentile *female* slaves could be required to wash their masters' feet. Jewish wives were also expected to do this humble service for their husbands; apparently footwashing was regarded as a wifely act of personal service, like preparing a husband's meals or making his bed.[4] Sometimes a husband protested at his wife performing such a humble task: in *Joseph and Asenath* (20:1-4) Asenath, the model proselyte and wife, insists on washing her new husband's

2. The essay is offered as a tribute to Howard Marshall, both as a scholar who has contributed so much to the study of NT christology, and as a friend and colleague, whom I have known for nearly thirty years.

3. See B. Kötting, "Fusswaschung," in *RAC,* 8, esp. 744-61; cf. also J. C. Thomas, *Footwashing in John 13 and the Johannine Community* (Sheffield: JSOT, 1991) esp. 26-56.

4. The Bible makes several references to a host's duty to provide water for the washing of guests' feet, but the texts do not always make it clear whether this was done by the guests themselves or someone else; see Gen 18:3-5; 19:1; 24:32; 43:24; Luke 7:44. For the rabbinic evidence see Str-B 1:527, 706-7; 2:557; 3:663; citing sources from *Mek.* Exod 21:2, the *'Abot R. Nat.* 16, the Babylonian and Palestinian Talmuds (see esp. *b. Ketub.* 61a), the *Sipra* Deut 33, 24, and the Tosepta (*Qidd.* 1:11); further details are given in Kötting, "Fusswaschung," 753-59. Some of these sources go back to the Tannaitic period, but others are considerably later.

feet on their marriage, "because you are my Lord from now on, and I am your maidservant." "Your feet are my feet . . . and another woman will never wash them." Similarly in 1 Sam 25:41 the virtuous Abigail shows her extraordinary humility by offering to wash the feet of David's slaves.

Footwashing was not always women's work. Jewish children might do it for their parents, and sometimes, we are told, devoted rabbinic students performed this service for their teachers (just as they often carried out other personal tasks for them); but they were not *required* to do so. When footwashing was done for another, it was always performed by one regarded as an inferior for a superior; hence John the Baptist's modesty when he said he was not worthy even to bend down and undo Jesus' sandal straps (Mark 1:7 par.). So when Jesus washes his own disciples' feet he is reversing the world's values and doing the work of the lowest of the low — Gentile slaves, women, children, and students! On this interpretation John is offering us a vivid acted parable, illustrating the teaching familiar from the Synoptics that "the Son of Man did not come to be served, but to serve . . ." (Mark 10:45 par.). We may compare also Jesus' words in Luke 22:27, in the context of the Last Supper: "I am among you as one who serves" (ὁ διακονῶν).

But some scholars have found problems in seeing humble service as the primary meaning of the footwashing. Nowhere else in this Gospel does John lay stress on Jesus' role in performing practical service for others. When he creates wine, or feeds the crowd miraculously, the stress is rather on his role as God's authoritative agent or Messiah. The Johannine Jesus is constantly obedient to his Father, but in relation to his disciples he is the authoritative Teacher and Master, who expects obedience from them. Some have even suggested that Jesus' role as a servant here is somehow in tension with the rest of the Gospel, and many have sought more subtle ways of understanding the text.

***1.2. Sacramental Interpretations.*** Another significant approach to John 13 has been to suggest that it is designed to convey some kind of sacramental teaching. But those who take this view differ as to which sacrament they believe lies behind the narrative. Many scholars, noting the prominent place of the footwashing in John's account of the Last Supper, together with the absence of any words of "institution" of the Eucharist in John, have suggested that the footwashing must refer to the Lord's Supper. In support of this has been adduced the fact that it seems to be some kind of symbol of unity, when Jesus says to Peter, "If I do not wash you, you have no part with me" (v 8). Particular attention has been drawn to Jesus' enigmatic words in v 10: "Anyone who has bathed does not need to wash [except the feet], but is clean all over." A. J. B. Higgins suggested that the word "bathed" (λελουμένος) refers to the unrepeatable "bath" of baptism, and the partial washing (νίψασθαι) to the periodic "purification from post-baptismal sins in the Eucharist."[5] Others too, on various grounds,

5. A. J. B. Higgins, *The Lord's Supper in the New Testament* (London: SCM, 1952) esp. 84-85;

have found here an allusion to the Eucharist. But if this is the meaning, the symbolism is very obscure. The Eucharist, or Lord's Supper, plainly represents the giving and receiving of Christ himself, as our savior, and feeding on him as spiritual food in the context of a shared fellowship meal. Footwashing is simply not a natural symbol for this. The eucharistic interpretation has therefore been dismissed as "farfetched" or even "grotesque";[6] it also has to assume the longer reading in v 10, which is rejected by many leading Johannine scholars.

Others, especially Roman Catholic commentators, have sought to link the footwashing with the forgiveness of postbaptismal sin in "penance," but this seems to be reading back into John the sacramental practice of the later church.[7] One may also ask why the washing of the *feet* should stand for this forgiveness (the Church Fathers devised some allegorical explanations, more ingenious than convincing). This understanding, too, requires the longer text.

Other exegetes have argued that the sacrament in question is baptism. Noting the omission of the phrase "except the feet" in some manuscripts of v 10, they argue for the shorter reading, and see this verse as polemic against second baptisms — "whoever has been washed does not need to wash [*sc.* again]." This was a view of many Latin Church Fathers, who sometimes cited this passage, including the words *rursus* and *iterum* ("again").[8] But one suspects that they had an axe to grind. It is improbable that the Fourth Evangelist was concerned with the issue of second baptism, and in any case no word for "again" is to be found in the Greek. Others see the verse as polemic against Jewish purification rites, but there is no basis for this in the text.

Yet other scholars draw attention to the fact that footwashing was more than a social custom at meals. It was also practiced in ancient cultures as an act of symbolic cleansing before sacred service, as it still is in modern Islam. There is some evidence for its ritual use in the Greco-Roman world,[9] but more important is its regular practice — along with handwashing — by priests before cultic service (e.g., Exod 30:17-21; 40:30-32), and by laity before entering the sacred temple area (cf. *m. Ber.* 9.5; P.Oxy. 840). Drawing on this evidence E. Lohmeyer suggested that Jesus' washing of the disciples' feet served as their

---

cf. O. Cullmann, *Early Christian Worship* (London: SCM, 1953) 105-10. For other scholars who hold a eucharistic interpretation see G. Richter, *Die Fusswaschung im Johannesevangelium* (Regensburg: Pustet, 1967) 254-56; also Thomas, *Footwashing,* 13 n. 1. Very recently a link with the Lord's Supper has been argued by F. J. Moloney, "A Sacramental Reading of John 13:1-38," *CBQ* 53 (1991) 237-56.

6. So C. K. Barrett, *The Gospel according to St. John,* 2d ed. (London: SPCK, 1978) 442; R. Bultmann, *The Gospel of John* (Oxford: Blackwell, 1971) 469 n. 2. On the eucharistic interpretation see further R. E. Brown, "The Johannine Sacramentary," in *New Testament Essays* (London/ Dublin: Chapman, 1965) 62-63.

7. See further Richter, *Fusswaschung,* 257.

8. See N. M. Haring, "Historical Notes on the Interpretation of John 13:10," *CBQ* 13 (1951) 355-80. Another factor in the baptismal theory was the Fathers' idea that the apostles must, at some stage, have been baptized by Jesus.

9. See Thomas, *Footwashing,* 42-44.

symbolic ordination to a "priestly apostolate."[10] This cultic background to footwashing as a rite of purification and consecration for divine service has been rather neglected in studies of John 13; but while it may have some bearing on our understanding of the theological significance of the footwashing, it needs to be stressed that there is no evidence that John thought of the disciples as priests in the sense in which this term is normally understood in "Catholic" Christianity. Cultic footwashing as a ritual purification was practiced by lay-people as well as priests, and normally individuals washed their own feet for this purpose. Nor did it have any place in rabbinic ordinations.

This leaves the possibility that if John 13 refers to any sacrament, it might be a new one, *sui generis,* not to be identified with any other sacrament of the church (either Roman Catholic or Protestant). This was proposed in the last century by certain liberal Protestant exegetes, and more recently has been upheld by B. W. Bacon and H. Weiss.[11] Bacon, somewhat implausibly, suggested that the rite symbolized the washing of the feet of Christ's bride, the church, in preparation for her sacral marriage, but there is no trace of such thought in John's Gospel. Weiss proposed that it represented the consecration of the disciples for martyrdom. While he makes some sound points about footwashing as an act of dedication and preparation, one feels that he presses too much the specific connection with martyrdom. J. C. Thomas argues that footwashing was practiced in the Johannine community to signify "the cleansing of believers from post-conversion sin," not in the Catholic sense of sacramental penance, whereby a priest absolves a penitent in "confession," but with the idea that it was carried out for one another by ordinary members of the Johannine community in the context of mutual confession and intercession, taking place perhaps in house churches (cf. 1 John 5:16-18). Some of Thomas's arguments are sound, but like others before him who have postulated "new" sacraments, he fails to provide precise evidence for their actual practice.[12] Nor does he bring out with sufficient clarity the relationship between the footwashing and the Johannine view of Jesus' death. This leads us to consider yet another way of understanding John 13, which may prove more fruitful.

10. See E. Lohmeyer, "Die Fusswaschung," *ZNW* 38 (1939) 74-94. The same idea has recently been put forward (though without reference to Lohmeyer) by D. Tripp in "Meanings of the Footwashing," *ExpTim* 103 (1991-92) 237-39, speaking of "a sort of sacerdotal ordination."

11. B. W. Bacon, "The Sacrament of Footwashing," *ExpTim* 43 (1931-32) 218-21; H. Weiss, "Foot Washing in the Johannine Community," *NovT* 21 (1979) 298-325. For further criticisms of these views see Richter, *Fusswaschung,* 258; Thomas, *Footwashing,* 150-53.

12. See Thomas, *Footwashing,* esp. 184-85. There are problems with Thomas's interpretation: he nowhere defines what he means by a "sacrament," and in citing the Church Fathers he fails to make a sufficiently clear distinction between footwashing as an act of, or metaphor for, practical service (cf. 1 Tim. 5:10), as a figurative expression for spiritual cleansing, and as a cultic rite. In his "historical reconstruction" (126-85) there is sometimes confusion between the cultic use of footwashing as a subsidiary part of ancient baptismal ceremonies, as a demonstration of monastic hospitality, as a symbol of priestly humility (e.g., in Maundy Thursday ceremonies), and as a possible sign of, or aid to, the forgiveness of inherited, prebaptismal, or postbaptismal sins.

***1.3. Christological and Soteriological Interpretations.*** In its Johannine context the footwashing is part of an elaborately constructed episode. It comes at a turning point in the Gospel. In the first twelve chapters Jesus has shown himself as the heavenly Revealer, demonstrating his divine sonship by miraculous signs and by teaching. He has also come into conflict with the Jewish leaders. Allusions have been made to his coming "hour," when he is to be "glorified"; but this hour was "not yet." In ch. 12, Jesus announces: "The hour has come for the Son of Man to be glorified," and speaks of his anguish in spirit (12:27). It becomes clear that Jesus' hour of "glory" is also a time of suffering, as an astute reader might have already guessed from earlier allusions (e.g., 2:19-22; 3:14-15; 6:51). At the start of ch. 13 the author reemphasizes that the hour has come for Jesus to depart to the Father (i.e., to die), and he speaks of his unfailing love, which endures "to the end" (εἰς τέλος).[13] Then he describes how Jesus lays aside his garments, girds himself with a towel, pours water, and washes his disciples' feet. When he has finished, he resumes his garment (i.e., puts it back on). The vocabulary here is quite distinctive. The word for laying aside is τίθημι — not the usual term for taking off a garment:[14] it is the same verb as was used repeatedly, a few chapters earlier, for the Good Shepherd laying down his life for the sheep (10:11, 15, 17, 18 *bis*); it will also be used later in ch. 13 for Peter's willingness to lay down his life (13:37, 38). The verb for "resuming" the clothing, λαμβάνω, is also unusual in the sense which John gives it here,[15] but is again paralleled in the Good Shepherd discourse, where Jesus speaks of taking up his life again in the resurrection (10:17, 18). Some commentators think it "fanciful" to see in the "laying aside" and "taking up" of Jesus' outer garments a symbol of Jesus' death, but others, including Hoskyns, Brown, and Culpepper, argue

13. The Greek is ambiguous, and can mean either "completely" or "to the end." Most commentators believe that John intended both nuances; cf. Jesus' cry, "τετέλεσται" (19:30).

14. The simple, active τίθημι for a person taking off or laying aside a garment is very rare; there are no similar uses elsewhere in the NT or LXX, though there is a parallel in Plutarch *Alcibiades* 8.2. One would have expected the compound ἀποτίθημι, in the middle (cf. Acts 7:58), or ἀποβάλλω (cf. Mark 10:50), or ἐκδύομαι (cf. 1 Sam 19:24 LXX), or another compound of δύομαι; see J. P. Louw and E. A. Nida, *Greek-English Lexicon of the New Testament Based on Semantic Domains* (New York: United Bible Societies, 1988), 1:49.21, with their note commenting on "this seemingly unusual use of τίθημι." This must strengthen the case for a deliberate echo of the Good Shepherd laying down his life in John 10; cf. also John 15:13.

15. This use of the active λαμβάνω in the sense of "taking up" or "putting on" one's own garment is also unexpected; normal LXX and NT usage would be ἐνδύομαι (e.g., Acts 12:21), ἀμφιέννυμαι (e.g., Luke 7:25), or περιβάλλομαι (e.g., Acts 12:8), or even διαζώννυμαι (e.g., John 21:7). Louw and Nida (*Lexicon,* 1:49.10) again comment on the "unusual sense," this time postulating an "ellipsis." The two classical examples (from Herodotus 2.37 and 4.78) cited by BAGD 464 are not directly parallel, since they concern the adoption of particular styles of dress, rather than the physical putting on of a garment. John's distinctive use of τίθημι and λαμβάνω with ψυχήν (10:17, etc.) may perhaps be explained as a Latinism (like τίθημι τὰ γόνατα in Mark, Luke, and Acts); cf. *vitam ponere* and *animam ponere,* "to lay down one's life," paralleling *vestem ponere,* to take off one's clothes, and *vestem capere,* to put on clothes.

that the choice of vocabulary may well be deliberate.[16] Garments are indeed often used with symbolic significance in the ancient world, and reclothing is a frequent symbol of new status, both socially and spiritually.[17] It would therefore seem quite reasonable to understand in John's use of these verbs an indirect allusion to Jesus voluntarily laying aside his life on the cross, and resuming it in the resurrection.

It is possible that Jesus' girding of himself with a towel (διαζώννυμι, v 4) was also intended to be understood symbolically. Girding oneself, or being girt with an apron or towel, was a regular sign of preparation for menial service (cf. Luke 12:37; 17:8; 1 Pet 5:5).[18] In his *Life of Caligula* (ch. 26) Suetonius tells us that when the emperor wanted to insult some highborn senators he made them gird themselves with a linen cloth and wait on him at table (the Latin word he uses for "linen cloth," *linteum,* is the same as the Greek λέντιον — a loanword from Latin — used here by John). A midrash on Gen 21:14 makes a similar point in connection with Abraham's dismissal of Hagar, when he ceased to treat her as his wife: "Abraham dismissed her with a bill of divorcement and took a cloth and girded it about her loins, that people might know her to be a slave."[19] And in John 21:18-19 Peter's being girded by another symbolizes his death by martyrdom. It is then at least possible that Jesus' self-girding with a towel is a double symbol, both of his willingness to perform menial service for others and of his humiliation in death by crucifixion (a penalty commonly afflicted on slaves as well as traitors and bandits).

If we are on the right track here, the thought would be very close to that of the famous Philippian "hymn," where Paul speaks of Christ emptying himself, taking the form of a slave (μορφὴν δούλου λαβών), and humbling himself to become "obedient to the point of death, even death on a cross" (Phil 2:6-8). It could also relate to Jesus' words to his disciples in Mark 10:44-45, where service

16. See E. C. Hoskyns and F. N. Davey, *The Fourth Gospel,* rev. ed. (London: Faber and Faber, 1947) 436-39; R. E. Brown, *The Gospel according to John,* vol. 2 (Garden City, New York: Doubleday, 1966) 551; R. A. Culpepper, "The Johannine *Hypodeigma:* A Reading of John 13," *Semeia* 53 (1991) 133-52, esp. 137. (I am grateful to the Rev. R. Maccini for drawing my attention to this work.) For the opposite view see B. Lindars, *The Gospel of John,* NCBC (London: Oliphants, 1972) 450.

17. See Luke 15:22 (restoration of Prodigal Son); Exod 29:5-9 (priestly ordination of Aaron and his sons); and the metaphorical uses in Sir 6:29, 31, and in the NT of "putting on" new life in baptism (Gal 3:27), or a heavenly body in resurrection (1 Cor 15:53-54; 2 Cor 5:2, 4; cf. Rev 3:4-5; 6:11; 7:9). There are numerous parallels to the idea of the (heavenly) body as a garment in Jewish apocalyptic writings and gnosticism; see R. H. Charles, *The Revelation of St. John,* ICC, vol. 1 (Edinburgh: T. & T. Clark, 1920) 184-88.

18. One might draw the analogy of a Victorian maid wearing a white apron and cap as a sign that she is a domestic servant.

19. See Str-B 2:557, citing *Yal.* 1:25 (on Gen 21:14); cf. Hoskyns and Davey, *Fourth Gospel,* 437; and G. R. Beasley-Murray, *John,* WBC 36 (Waco, Texas: Word, 1987) 233. The date of the relevant midrash cannot be determined. It occurs in a medieval Jewish compilation, which drew on earlier sources; the detail of the cloth is not found in the *Midrash Rabba.*

and death are closely linked: "Whoever wishes to become great among you shall be your servant (διάκονος), and whoever wishes to be first among you shall be the slave (δοῦλος) of all. For the Son of Man did not come to be served, but to serve and to give his life a ransom for many." A symbolic understanding of the footwashing itself in relation to Jesus' death might have been further encouraged by the parallel of Mary's anointing of Jesus' *feet*, described in the preceding chapter (12:1-8), where Jesus explicitly interprets her action with reference to his impending death. It would also make excellent sense of Jesus' words to Peter (v 7): "You do not now know what I am doing, but you will understand later," if by "later" Jesus meant after his death and resurrection (cf. 2:22) or even at the time of Peter's own martyrdom (21:19), rather than merely when he had completed the footwashing and explained it as an example of humble service (vv 14-17).[20]

The interpretation of the footwashing as a christological or soteriological sign does not rest solely on the symbolism postulated in the last few paragraphs. It is also implied by the place of the episode in John's passion narrative, by the reference to Jesus' "hour" and his love for his own in the opening verse of the chapter, and by the allusion to cleansing (v 10), which almost certainly refers to the cleansing power of Jesus' death (or of his word) rather than to mere physical cleaning of the feet.[21] Thus Dunn, Lindars, Beasley-Murray, Schnackenburg, and many others affirm a soteriological significance for the footwashing without necessarily accepting a special symbolic significance in the use of the words τίθημι, λαμβάνω, and διαζώννυμι.[22]

Jesus' dialogue with Peter now takes on a new significance. It will be remembered that when Jesus first approached Peter to wash his feet, Peter protested in horror, saying, "Lord, are *you* going to wash *my* feet?" Jesus solemnly replied, "If I do not wash you, you have no part (μέρος) with me," and then Peter exclaimed, "Lord, not my feet only, but also my hands and my head" (vv 7-9). Taken at its face value, this is just another instance of Peter's well-known impetuosity and tendency to misunderstanding. Interpreted at a deeper level, it illustrates John's fondness for ambiguity or double meaning. The word μέρος,

20. On John 13 and the Philippian "hymn" see G. F. Hawthorne, *Philippians,* WBC 43 (Waco, Texas: Word, 1983) 78-79. On the relation to Mark 10:44-45, see Barrett, *John,* 436; and J. A. T. Robinson, "The Significance of the Footwashing," in *Twelve More New Testament Studies* (London: SCM, 1984) 77-80 (originally in *Neotestamentica et Patristica* [Leiden: E. J. Brill, 1962]). On Mary's anointing of Jesus see Hoskyns, *The Fourth Gospel,* 414-17; M. Sabbe, "The Footwashing in Jn 13 and Its Relation to the Synoptic Gospels," *ETL* 58 (1982) 279-308, esp. 298-305.

21. In support of the cleansing power of the cross we might mention the blood and water which flowed from Jesus' side in 19:34; for cleansing through the word, cf. 15:3.

22. See J. D. G. Dunn, "The Washing of the Disciples' Feet in John 13:1-20," *ZNW* 61 (1970) 247-52, esp. 252, and the commentators *ad loc.* H. Weiss goes so far as to say that, since Hoskyns, "most commentators have adopted a view of the foot-washing as an interpretation of the significance of Jesus' death on the cross" (see "Foot Washing," 299; references in his n. 9). This trend continues in the most recent work, e.g., D. A. Carson, *The Gospel according to John* (Grand Rapids, Michigan: Wm. B. Eerdmans; Leicester: Inter-Varsity, 1991) 459-68.

usually translated "part," means "lot" or "portion." Along with its cognate μερίς, it is used in the Greek Bible for "inheritance," sometimes a physical inheritance, like that of the Prodigal Son (Luke 15:12), but more often a spiritual inheritance — the equivalent of Hebrew חֵלֶק.[23] What John is saying is that those who wish to share a spiritual inheritance with Jesus must accept his "footwashing," that is, both his practical service and his sacrificial death on the cross. They must also wash the feet of others as a sign of their willingness to participate in his service and death.

All this throws light on the problems of v 10: "He who has bathed (ὁ λελουμένος) does not need to wash (νίψασθαι) except the feet." Many editors, translators, and commentators have been puzzled as to what to do about the phrase "except the feet." It is omitted in the Codex Sinaiticus and various old Latin witnesses and Fathers, but is found in an early papyrus (𝔭[66]) and, with slight variations of word order, in many other good and early witnesses, including major uncials and most of the versions. The majority of modern commentators are inclined to adopt the shorter reading. Thus C. K. Barrett suggests that λούω and νίπτομαι are used by John as synonyms:

> The intention of the saying was to point out the foolish misunderstanding of Peter, who supposed that, because Jesus' act in washing his feet represented the humble ministry of his death, he would get more good by having his hands and head washed also, as if washing with water were in itself a religious benefit. Against this Jesus points out that once one has received the benefit of his love and death ("has been baptized into his death") he is "entirely clean" (καθαρὸς ὅλος); further washings are pointless.

Barrett suggests that the longer reading arose because it was not appreciated that λούω and νίπτομαι were synonyms, and it was assumed that reference was being made to the custom of having a full bath before going out to dinner and then just a footwash on arrival to remove the dust of the journey from one's feet.[24] Bultmann, Brown, Schnackenburg, Lindars, and Beasley-Murray likewise favor the shorter reading.

On the other hand, the longer reading has been accepted by many older commentators, by most modern editors of the Greek text (as well as many older ones), and by a substantial proportion of both older and more recent translators. In recent years it is also been defended by Sanders and Mastin, Morris, Haenchen, Bruce, and Carson among Johannine commentators, by Owanga-Welo in a 1980 dissertation, and by Robinson, Thomas, and Segovia in articles.[25]

23. E.g., Pss 16:5; 73:26 (μερίς); Matt 24:51; Rev 20:6; 21:8; 22:19 (μέρος); 1 Pet 1:3-4 uses κληρονομία in the same sense; cf. Tit 3:7.

24. C. K. Barrett, *John*, 442.

25. References in J. C. Thomas, "A Note on the Text of John 13:10," *NovT* 29 (1987) 46-52; and *idem, Footwashing*, 19-25; cf. F. F. Segovia, "John 13:1-20: The Footwashing in the Johannine Tradition," *ZNW* 73 (1982) 31-51, esp. 44.

The strongest argument in its support is its excellent manuscript attestation, plus the fact that it is in some ways the "harder reading." Thomas argues that (1) λούω and νίπτομαι are not synonymns, but were carefully distinguished even in the Hellenistic period, so that the latter must refer to a washing of some part of the body; (b) if the "bathing" implied by λούω refers either to baptism, or to cleansing through the cross, or even to cleansing through the "word," then the partial washing implied by νίπτομαι could refer to cleansing from postbaptismal sin. The shorter reading could be explained as an accidental omission, or as an attempt to smooth away apparent difficulties in the longer reading. It might even have arisen for dogmatic reasons (cf. above on possible polemic on second baptisms).

The arguments for the two readings are so nicely balanced that it may seem impossible to judge between them with any degree of confidence. If we retain the longer reading, λούω may be understood as referring to cleansing through Jesus' word (cf. 15:3), or (proleptically) through the cross, and νίπτομαι as referring to a further cleansing through acceptance of Jesus' service and death, and through serving others in identification with him. If the shorter reading is preferred — and it has received strong scholarly support in recent years — then "being bathed" would most naturally be taken as referring to the "once-for-all" nature of the cleansing through the cross, while the footwashing itself could still be understood as a prophetic sign of the believing disciples' unity with Jesus (Judas is explicitly excluded from this). It is to be noted that either the shorter or the longer reading of v 10 is consistent with the idea that John intended this identification of believers with Jesus in the way suggested here.

We conclude that both an exemplary and a christological / soteriological meaning was intended by the author of our final text of John. It is also possible, though not certain, that some kind of sacramental significance was implied, though probably not with reference to either baptism or the Eucharist or the forgiveness of postbaptismal sin.

## 2. The Interrelationship of These Interpretations

How do the different interpretations so far discussed relate to one another? The scholars' theories here are quite complicated, and depend very much on their view of John's method of composition. One group supposes that the account of the footwashing in ch. 13 is built up from a basic source to which new material has been added, including a fresh interpretation of the original narrative. (Much ingenuity has been expended on reconstructing the hypothetical *Grundschrift*, as can be seen, e.g., in Schnackenburg's commentary.) A second group (going back to Wellhausen) supposes that there were once two separate sources, which differed in their understanding of the footwashing and which were in tension with one another. Whatever view is taken of the composition, there is no agreement as to which interpretation was the earlier and which was the later. For example, Richter and Brown both consider the christological interpretation to be more original (and the work of the Evangelist himself), while they see the "moralizing" or exemplary interpretation as being added later, possibly by someone of the Johannine "school." On the other hand, Boismard presupposes the reverse, namely that the exemplary understanding represents the oldest strand, to which further materials have been added (by more than one author). In contrast to all the preceding, Barrett and Lindars conclude that both interpretations go back to the main author, though they accept the possibility of some secondary additions (e.g., vv 2b, 10b, 11, 16, 20).[26]

I would like to suggest that the narrative makes sense as a theological whole, and has been shaped by the Evangelist with a definite purpose in mind. This is not to deny the possibility of separate sources, or of later redaction to the main text. But the nature of the evidence makes it impossible to identify the stages of composition with certainty. It seems probable (with Boismard) that the moral interpretation is historically the earliest. It is the one most plainly in the text, and the simplest to grasp; and it coheres admirably with what we know about Jesus' teaching on service from the Synoptics. We may leave open the question of whether it represents a vivid dramatization of Synoptic teaching on service (so Barrett), or an authentic tradition concerning Jesus' actions which has not been preserved in the other Gospels (so Robinson). We should, however, note that there are other places where John appears to preserve historically reliable material,[27] and that where John wishes to convey his own interpretations, he normally does it by the addition of dialogue or discourse to a narrated action, rather than by transforming teaching into action.[28] It has also been pointed out that in what many consider to be the closest Synoptic parallel (Jesus' teaching on service in Luke 22:26-27) the term used for "serving" is διακονέω, whereas in the Johannine footwashing the stress is on the work of the slave (δοῦλος). This would strengthen the argument that the Johannine footwashing is not literarily dependent on Luke, but it still leaves open the question of the

26. A further complication is that some of the verses which look "secondary" in a literary sense (e.g., vv 16, 20) have close parallels in the Synoptic tradition and may have a good claim to stem from authentic words of Jesus. On the various theories of composition see the discussions in Schnackenburg and Brown (with references); for a particularly complex hypothesis see M.-É. Boismard and A. Lamouille, *Synopse des quatre évangiles en Français 3: Évangile de Jean* (Paris: du Cerf, 1977) 329-46.

27. E.g., the ideas that Jesus' first disciples were originally followers of John the Baptist, that Jesus' and John's ministries overlapped, that Jesus baptized, that he visited Jerusalem several times before his last visit, and that Nicodemus anointed his body.

28. Compare, e.g., the dialogue following the temple cleansing and the "bread of life" discourse / dialogue after the feeding miracle (ch. 6). It should be noted, however, that more radical critics have suggested a number of instances where teaching may have been transformed into action; see, e.g., B. Lindars on the miracle at Cana (John 2:1-11) and the raising of Lazarus (11:1-44).

relationship with Mark.[29] Whatever the origins of the "moral" or exemplary interpretation, the verses in which it is expressed cannot be removed from the text without doing violence to the narrative, which is all the more reason for regarding them as an integral part of the Evangelist's composition.

We would further suggest that the christological or soteriological interpretation is also the work of the Evangelist himself. We have already noted his liking for double meanings. The narrative as a whole contains many hallmarks of his style — for example, the references to Jesus' "hour" (v 1), to his "departing" from "this world" to the Father (vv 1, 3), and to the disciples' knowing "later" the meaning of his actions (v 6). It also fits in with John's very special emphasis on the person of Jesus, and on the significance of his death for believers.

As for sacramental interpretations, if those scholars were right who relate the narrative to either baptism or the Eucharist, this might suggest that it belongs to a late strand of composition (especially if Bultmann's view were accepted that [ἐξ] ὕδατος καί in 3:5 and the eucharistic allusions in 6:51c-58 are later additions by an "ecclesiastical redactor"). But we have seen reasons for doubting whether the passage refers directly to either of these sacraments, or indeed to the postbaptismal forgiveness of sins, whether through "penance" (as argued by many Roman Catholic commentators) or through mutual confession by believers, as argued by Thomas. There is, however, another option for a sacramental interpretation. Once one accepts the presence of two understandings — one of the footwashing as an example of practical, humble service, and one of it as a prefiguration of Jesus' death on the cross — then the footwashing could readily be interpreted as *a sacrament of identification with Jesus in his humble service and death.*

Before we develop this point, it may be worth thinking more fully about what the term "sacrament" means. Definitions vary in the different Christian churches, but most are agreed that a sacrament is a rite instituted by God, or Christ himself, as an outward sign of something which God does for us — what the Anglican *Book of Common Prayer* calls "an inward and spiritual grace."[30]

29. Compare carefully Robinson, "Footwashing"; J. Roloff, "Anfänge der soteriologischen Deutung des Todes Jesu (Mk. X.45 und Lk. XXII.27)," *NTS* 19 (1972-73) 38-64; F. Schnackenburg, *The Gospel according to John,* vol. 3 (New York: Crossroad, 1982) 40-42; M. Sabbe, "Footwashing"; J. B. Green, *The Death of Jesus: Tradition and Interpretation in the Passion Narrative,* WUNT 2:33 (Tübingen: J. C. B. Mohr [Paul Siebeck], 1988) 111-20. It is doubtful whether one can press the point about the absence of the term διακονέω from the footwashing; see John 12:26, and note the alternation between διάκονος and δοῦλος in Mark 10:44-45. It is beyond the scope of this essay to enter further into the complex question of the relationship of John to the Synoptics. If Jesus really did tell his followers to wash one another's feet, it is remarkable that the NT nowhere else refers to this custom (apart from 1 Tim 5:10, where it is confined to widows).

30. The *Book of Common Prayer* defines a sacrament as "an outward and visible sign of an inward and spiritual grace given unto us, ordained by Christ himself, as a means whereby we receive the same, and a pledge to assure us thereof." The Westminster Confession similarly describes

The dominical command is plain enough in John 13:14-15, and so is the outward sign. But questions might be raised as to the nature of the "inward grace." Here the dialogue with Peter provides the clue, when Jesus says: "If I do not wash you, you have no *part* with me" (v 8). Mutual footwashing is, then, a sign of belonging to Christ and sharing in his work of loving service and willingness to die.[31]

We may, then, go along with Weiss, Thomas, and others, who have argued that footwashing was practiced as a sacramental rite in the Johannine community, even though this left comparatively few traces in later Christian tradition.[32] Where we would differ from them is in our understanding of the significance of this rite for those who practiced it. We propose that participation in Christ's service and death is the true meaning of the "sacrament" of footwashing, and that it serves as a dramatic and vivid illustration to the church of the two primary meanings which we have already accepted, namely Jesus' role as Servant and as Savior who dies for the sins of all.

## 3. Implications for Johannine Christology

The Gospel of John is generally seen as having a very "high" christology, with Jesus presented as the preexistent Word, in union with God, having foreknowledge and autonomy over his own destiny. He is the Son, who acts with his Father's full authority, and as God's agent in both life-giving and judgment. He is also in some sense identified with God: "The Word was with God, and the Word was God" (1:1).

For some Christians this "high" christology is problematic. The Johannine Christ seems so exalted that he almost ceases to be a human being. Thus E. Käsemann speaks of the unsolved problem of the "divine glory of the Johan-

sacraments as "holy signs and seals of the covenant of grace, immediately instituted by God, to represent Christ, and His benefits; to confirm our interest in Him: as also, to put a visible difference between those that belong to Christ, and the rest of the world; and *solemnly to engage them to the service of God in Christ, according to His Word*" (italics added). Footwashing admirably fulfills these definitions, as it does also the traditional Roman Catholic teaching, found in Aquinas and elsewhere, of sacraments as sacred realities which sanctify men and women.

31. The potential objection that mutual footwashing requires a double action at the human level — both passive (having one's own feet washed) and active (washing the feet of another) — can be met with the thought that it also takes at least two (besides God) to perform a baptism, to celebrate the Eucharist, or to effect a marriage.

32. For the evidence compare Kötting, "Fusswaschung," 761-63; and Thomas, *Footwashing*, 129-49, 158-79. Footwashing appears to have been understood as a sacramental rite by both Augustine and Ambrose, the latter attesting to its practice as part of the baptismal liturgy at Milan, where it seems to have represented purification from inherited ("original") sin. We can only speculate on how it might have been practiced in the Johannine community; one possibility might be as a preparation for the Lord's Supper (cf. the Seventh Day Adventists today), but there is no external evidence to confirm this.

nine Christ going about on earth," and asks: "In what sense is he flesh, who walks on the water and through closed doors. . . ?" Käsemann claims that Jesus' passion must be described as a triumphal procession rather than a *via dolorosa;* even on the cross Jesus maintains his majesty. Such a figure, as Käsemann himself realizes, could easily become someone with whom it is impossible to identify: "The [Johannine] Son of Man is neither a man among others, nor the representation of the people of God or of the ideal humanity, but God, descending into the human realm and there manifesting his glory."[33]

But this is not the whole picture. As other scholars have pointed out, Jesus in John is also a man who knows weariness and hunger, who weeps at the death of a friend, and experiences anguish of spirit as he prepares to face his own death (12:27). He prays to God, and is dependent on God. He speaks of the Father as greater than himself. In a rather neglected study of Johannine christology J. E. Davey acutely observed that the author of John "was capable of holding together in his mind, as true, views which seem to us to clash"; he speaks of "a union of opposites" (the phrase is E. F. Scott's) — divine and human, universal and particular, infinite and limited.[34] We might add to these the images of king and servant.

The washing of the disciples' feet represents Jesus' role as servant *par excellence* and contrasts with his role as king (1:49; 18:33-37; 19:19-22). But it should not be seen as something which stands in isolation from the rest of the Gospel. All through the work Jesus is depicted as someone under authority, as well as someone with authority. He is in constant obedience to his Father (see esp. 14:28; cf. 4:34; 5:19; 7:28; etc.). As Davey has stressed, he is dependent on God for his power, knowledge, mission, message; for his being, nature, destiny, authority, and office; for his love, glory, honor, witness; for guidance and the gift of the Spirit; even for the disciples whom God has entrusted to him. His "subordinate" or serving role is also indicated by many of the images applied to him, for example, the "door," the "path" or "way" (i.e., the means by which people have access to God), and the "vine," dependent on God as the gardener; even the pictures of Jesus as light, truth, and life rest ultimately on the idea of God as Light, Truth, and Life. Subordination and service (as well as authority) are implied by Jesus' title of Son. One notes especially 20:17, where the risen Jesus still associates himself with the disciples as his "brothers" (and sisters).[35] Even Jesus' role as Teacher, so often seen as a sign of his authority, is also an aspect of his service, for he taught on the authority of God (7:16, etc.). There is, then, no real tension between Jesus' serving role in John 13 and his autonomy and lordship elsewhere in the Gospel.

33. E. Käsemann, *The Testament of Jesus* (London: SCM; Philadelphia: Fortress, 1968) 9-18.

34. J. E. Davey, *The Jesus of St. John* (London: Lutterworth, 1958) esp. 14-15 and 90-157. On Jesus' humanity see further M. M. Thompson, *The Humanity of Jesus in the Fourth Gospel* (Philadelphia: Fortress, 1988), with further criticisms of Käsemann.

35. Cf. C. K. Barrett, *Essays on John* (London: SPCK, 1982) 22, citing and developing Davey's work.

And what of his death? How does this fit into the picture? If we are right in our soteriological interpretation of the footwashing in ch. 13, then Jesus' death can in no way be separated from his service. Like the prophets before him, "the servants of Yahweh," Jesus suffered for his testimony. In recent years there has been much discussion about the role of the cross in the Fourth Gospel. Rudolf Bultmann understood John as depicting Jesus primarily as a Revealer, and minimized the significance of the cross, which he saw as almost an appendix to the story: "In John, Jesus' death has no pre-eminent importance for salvation, but is the accomplishment of the 'work' which began with the incarnation: the last demonstration of the obedience which governs the whole life of Jesus."[36] J. F. Forestell tried to redress the balance by pointing out the logical necessity of the cross as a manifestation of Jesus' and God's love.[37] Others have sought to find in John traces of a more traditional theology of atonement, suggesting that the author might have held this side by side with his "complementary insight" of salvation through revelation; we may mention here especially the work of Max Turner.[38]

Did the Fourth Evangelist see Jesus' death as an atoning sacrifice? It is true that a sacrificial interpretation of it is much more obvious in 1 John than in John (see esp. 1 John 1:7; 2:2; 4:10), but there are signs that it was known also to the Fourth Evangelist (see John 1:29; 6:51; 10:11, 15; 11:50-52; 15:13; 17:19; 18:14). Even Lindars, who sees the sacrificial interpretation as a "secondary issue," nevertheless recognizes that it is "not wholly unintegrated to his [*sc.* John's] thought."[39] Whatever the precise significance attached to Jesus' death, it is clear that the theme of the cross is integrated into the warp and woof of the narrative, and cannot be removed except by destroying the whole. Since the evidence for this has been disputed, it is worth summing up the relevant passages.

The cross is signaled already in the opening chapter by the Baptist's recognition of Jesus as "the lamb of God that takes away the sin of the world" (1:29), a phrase which almost certainly implies an allusion to both the paschal lamb and the Isaianic "suffering servant," led like a lamb to the slaughter.[40] It is picked up

36. R. Bultmann, *Theology of the New Testament,* vol. 2 (London: SCM, 1955) 52; cf. Käsemann, *The Testament of Jesus,* 7.

37. J. F. Forestell, *The Word of the Cross: Salvation as Revelation in the Fourth Gospel* (Rome: Pontifical Biblical Institute, 1974).

38. M. Turner, "Atonement and the Death of Jesus in John: Some Questions to Bultmann and Forestell," *EvQ* 62 (1990) 99-122.

39. B. Lindars, "The Passion in the Fourth Gospel," in *God's Christ and His People: Studies in Honour of Nils Alstrup Dahl,* ed. J. Jervell and W. A. Meeks (Oslo: Universitetsforlaget, 1977) 71-86, esp. 72-74. See also D. Senior, *The Passion of Jesus in the Gospel of John* (Collegeville, Minnesota: Liturgical, 1991), arguing that "the death of Jesus drives the story from start to finish," and that the flow of blood and water from Jesus' side signifies the "salvific effects" of his death (see esp. 30-39, 120-29).

40. See C. K. Barrett, "The Lamb of God," *NTS* 1 (1954-55) 210-18. There has been a tendency in recent years to minimize the influence of the Isaianic Servant on NT christology (e.g., M. D. Hooker, *Jesus and the Servant* [London: SPCK, 1959] esp. 147-63). But one does wonder whether the reaction against older piety which naively equated Jesus with "the Servant" has not

in the references to Jesus' "hour" (2:4; 7:30; 8:20; 12:23; 13:1), to his being "lifted up" (3:14; 8:28; 12:32, 34) or "glorified" (7:39; 12:23; 13:31; etc.).[41] It is part of the deeper meaning of the Johannine cleansing of the temple, where John quotes Scripture to show that Jesus will be "consumed" (i.e., destroyed) by zeal for God's house, but will rise within three days (2:17-22). It is implied in the famous affirmation that God so loved the world that he gave his only Son that those who believe might have eternal life (3:16), as well as in Jesus' identification of the bread of heaven as his flesh given for the life of the world (6:51). It lies behind the Samaritans' confession of Jesus as the "savior of the world" (4:42), Caiaphas's prophetic reference to one man dying "for the people" (11:50-52; cf. 18:14), and Jesus' (proleptic) proclamation that he has "overcome the world" (16:33). It is made explicit in the Good Shepherd discourse when Jesus affirms that the shepherd lays down his life "for the sheep" (10:11). It dominates the passion narrative, from the introduction to the account of the footwashing, with its allusion to Jesus' loving his own "to the end," through the references to his "departure" to the Father, so that the Paraclete might come, and his prayer of self-consecration (where the verb ἁγιάζω has sacrificial overtones), to the actual description of his crucifixion "on the day of preparation for the Passover" (19:14), with its remarkable insistence on the fact that both blood and water flowed from Jesus' side (19:34). Some scholars believe that the Evangelist made so much of this last incident because he wanted to assure his readers that Jesus really had died, and they may well be correct. But it is most unlikely that this exhausts its meaning: Lindars (and others) are surely right to see also in the blood and water a symbolic reference to the atoning efficacy of Jesus' death, and the fountain of grace which it opened up, bringing new life to believers. We may further point out that in John 17:17-19 Jesus consecrates not only himself but also his disciples in preparation for their being sent out in mission into a hostile world. If footwashing is taken to be a rite of preparation for holy service (cf. Lohmeyer and Weiss), this would fit in well with such a theme. For mission to the world includes the holy worship of God as well as the practical service of others.

## 4. Conclusion

We may then conclude that the interpretation of the footwashing as symbolizing both Jesus' humble service and his atoning death is in no way inconsistent with

---

gone too far. While the precise degree of dependence on individual texts may be disputed, a general influence of the Isaianic passages (esp. 52:13–53:12) seems inescapable. Even Hooker acknowledges that "in St. John's Gospel it is possible that the theme of Isaiah 52–53 underlies his emphasis upon the exaltation and glory of Christ, achieved in and through his sufferings," though she regards this as involving a radical reinterpretation of the original passage (151).

41. On the "lifting up" sayings and Jesus' glorification, see esp. G. C. Nicholson, *Death as Departure* (Chico, California: Scholars, 1983).

the general thrust of John's Gospel. Indeed, it harmonizes excellently with it. Like so many incidents in this Gospel it may be interpreted at more than one level, and the different interpretations — moral, sacramental, and soteriological — complement one another. The whole picture of Jesus as Servant complements traditional christologies in which Jesus is seen as prophet, priest, and king.[42] In a vivid narrative the Evangelist brings home his lesson that all who seek to imitate Christ must take on the task of humble service to others and identify themselves with Christ in his death. This may involve martyrdom, as it did for Peter and has done for those who more recently have died in witness to the faith. But for most Christians this will mean the wholehearted dedication of their lives in service to God and humanity. It is probable that the Evangelist intended this identification to be symbolized sacramentally by the rite of footwashing, which may well have been practiced by the Johannine community. Whether or not this is the case, this whole chapter provides a profound theological and practical teaching, which Christians of all traditions should take to heart. We leave the last word to John (and to Jesus):

> Unless a grain of wheat fall to the earth and die, it remains alone; but if it dies, it bears a rich harvest. Those who love their lives will lose them, but those who "hate" their lives in this world will preserve them into eternal life. Whoever serves me, let them follow me, and where I am, there shall my servant be also. Whoever serves me, the Father will honor them. (12:24-26)

42. Cf. D. T. Williams, "The Four-fold Office of Christ," *ExpTim* 100 (1988-89) 134-37.

# Territorial Religion, Johannine Christology, and the Vineyard of John 15

Gary M. Burge

It is perhaps the Palestinian Christians, theologians like Riah Abu El Assal of Nazareth,[1] Naim Ateek of Jerusalem,[2] and Mitri Raheeb of Bethlehem,[3] who will help us to look at one theme in biblical theology in a new way. Just as Latin American writers have challenged us to rethink the biblical meaning of righteousness and justice, so Palestinian Christians are asking us to rethink what the NT says about "The Land" (i.e., the land of Israel / Palestine). Fueled by the political crises of the twentieth century and the eschatological zeal of many Western evangelical churches, land confiscation in Israel and the Occupied Territories[4] has grown at an unprecedented rate and has been chronicled by researchers and writers for years.[5] And the Christian communities in this part

1. El Assal is Archdeacon of the Jerusalem Diocese of the Episcopal Church and pastor of Christ Evangelical Church in Nazareth. He is currently at work on a volume which traces the history of the Arab people within the earliest days of the Jewish-Christian communities of the first century.

2. Ateek is Canon of St. George's Cathedral in Jerusalem and pastor of its Arabic-speaking congregation. In 1989 he authored *Justice and Only Justice: A Palestinian Liberation Theology* (Maryknoll, New York: Orbis, 1989). More recently he coedited with M. Ellis and R. Ruether, *Faith and the Intifada: Palestinian Christian Voices* (Maryknoll, New York: Orbis, 1992).

3. Raheeb has taught church history at Bethlehem Bible College since completing his Ph.D. at Marburg University (published as *Das reformatorische Erbe unter den Palaestinensern: Zur Entstehung der Evangelische Lutherischen Kirche in Jordan* [Gütersloh, 1990]). He also pastors the Evangelical Lutheran Christmas Church in Bethlehem. His book on the history of the Christian church in Israel / Palestine will be published this year by Fortress.

4. "Occupied Territories" is used today to refer to those regions conquered by Israel in 1967, particularly the West Bank and Gaza. For 25 years the Arab residents in these areas have not been integrated into Israeli society, have not possessed freedom of movement in the country, have not been allowed to vote in national elections, and have been kept under strict military rule.

5. Land confiscation in Israel / Palestine is a remarkable story. Since 1967 approximately 55 percent of the West Bank and 30 percent of Gaza have been nationalized by the Israeli government. See S. Jiryis, *The Arabs in Israel* (New York: Monthly Review, 1976); E. T. Zureik, *The Palestinians*

of the world are facing a troubling dilemma. Arab pastors have witnessed the Bible becoming the vehicle of devastation for them and their congregations. Both the campaigns of Joshua and the predictions of the OT prophets have been used to justify the wholesale taking of land.

The Palestinian church is in the grip of a hermeneutical crisis as it wonders how to reclaim its scriptures. As Canon Naim Ateek puts it, if the Bible becomes the instrument of death for his people, it cannot also offer them life and light and hope.[6]

The subject of The Land in biblical theology is complex. Those with a keen interest in eschatological fulfillment or Jewish or Christian Zionism will find in the Bible an unbreakable triad: God, Israel, and The Land. For them, The Land is at the heart of the Israelite faith. As A. Hertzberg has said, "The observant Jew in the Diaspora is, from the very beginning, a less obedient one, a truncated version of the fulness of Judaism."[7] But W. D. Davies has shown persuasively that such a monolithic view of Judaism is incorrect.[8] The *Tanak* (the Christian OT), Qumran literature, the apocrypha and pseudepigrapha, the literature of rabbinic Judaism, and even modern Zionism all bear witness to a considerable diversity of thought. For many Jews, as a well-known rabbinic saying puts it, the appropriate triad for Jewish faith is different: God, Israel, *and Torah.* The Land is not *necessarily* mentioned.[9] The practical realities of nomadic beginnings, frequent conquest, exile, and foreign occupation forced Israel to rethink God's intentions for his people. Thus after the war of 70 C.E. Johanan ben Zakkai asked Vespasian if he could found a school devoted to the law and spiritual development — a school void of any political pretensions.

---

*in Israel: A Study in Internal Colonialism* (London: Routledge and Kegan Paul, 1979); I. Lustick, *Arabs in the Jewish State: Israel's Control of a National Minority* (Austin, Texas: University of Texas, 1980); R. Shehadeh, *Occupier's Law: Israel and the West Bank* (Washington, D.C.: Institute for Palestinian Studies, 1985); U. Davis, *Israel: An Apartheid State* (London: Zed, 1987); R. and H. Ruether, *The Wrath of Jonah: The Crisis of Religious Nationalism in the Israeli-Palestinian Conflict* (New York: Harper & Row, 1989). On a more popular level, see E. Chacour, *We Belong to the Land: The Story of a Palestinian Israeli Who Lives for Peace and Reconciliation* (San Francisco: Harper & Row, 1990); and G. M. Burge, *Who Are God's People in the Middle East? What Christians Are Not Being Told about Israel and the Palestinians* (Grand Rapids, Michigan: Zondervan, 1993).

6. *Justice and Only Justice,* 3.

7. "Symposium Comments," in W. D. Davies, *The Territorial Dimension of Judaism* (Minneapolis: Fortress, 1992) 106. This is the second edition of Davies's well-known book (*The Gospel and the Land: Early Jewish Territorial Doctrine* [Berkeley: University of California, 1974]), which includes critical comments by seven other scholars.

8. *Territorial Dimension,* 97: ". . . any endorsement of a simple literal understanding of the promise [of land] is critically unacceptable."

9. It is for this reason that many orthodox Jews even in Israel have objected to the construction of the nation of Israel itself as a *political entity.*

## The New Testament and The Land

No doubt the seminal study of The Land in the NT belongs to W. D. Davies.[10] Davies makes clear that the subject of The Land witnessed an intense debate in the NT era. Some looked to an aggressive messianism in which land would be conquered and secured forever; others saw it as a transcendent order in the age to come. Either way, The Land played a central role in the Jewish consciousness as a metaphor, eschatological promise, or political goal. Even after Jamnia, the rabbis insisted that the *Eighteen Benedictions* be said three times each day as a perpetual reminder of Jerusalem and The Land (see esp. *Benedictions* 14, 16, and 18).

In the culture of first-century Palestinian Judaism, land ownership was one of the critical measurements of wealth and economic security. To be landless — to be hired by another as a laborer, or to be a merchant or craftsman — signaled some deficiency, some failing in life. This is symbolized, for instance, in the two great promises extended to Abraham: he will gain children (to end his childlessness) and he will gain land (to end his landlessness). Hence, even the holiness code protected land ownership (for families and tribes) so that one generation's mismanagement would not unduly handicap the next generation. Land would always return to its original owner (Leviticus 25). "Possession of the land" reads like a refrain throughout the book of Deuteronomy, suggesting that this is one of the central aims of Jewish faith. These communities affirmed the OT notion of The Land of Israel as the center of the earth (Ezek 38:12). Ezekiel 5:5 confirms: "Thus says the Lord God: This is Jerusalem; I have set her in the center of the nations, with countries round about her." This commitment to The Land was underscored in later periods, as attested in *Ethiopic Enoch* 26:1 (where travel to Jerusalem is understood as coming to the earth's center) and *Jub.* 8:12 (where Shem's portion of land is at the earth's center). *Jubilees* goes further, even describing Mt. Zion as the "center of the earth's navel" (8:19)! Israel was the center of the world, Jerusalem stood at the centerpoint of The Land, and the temple was the center of Jerusalem.[11] Even Jews living in the Diaspora sought to be buried in The Land: it was like being buried on an altar of atonement.[12]

In light of this background we should expect the NT to address the question of what could be called "territorial religion." To neglect Judaism's "land consciousness" is to neglect a critical aspect of the culture that shaped the NT. Should Christians still look to The Land of Israel as a place of redemption? Is

10. *The Gospel and the Land.* See also F. W. Marquardt, *Die Juden und ihr Land* (Gütersloh: Gerd Mohn, 1975); and R. Rendtorff, *Israel und sein Land* (München: Kaiser, 1975).

11. The evidence of land commitment in the apocrypha, pseudepigrapha, Qumran literature, and the rabbis is conveniently surveyed in Davies, *Gospel and the Land,* 49-74.

12. M. Wilson, *Our Father Abraham, Jewish Roots of the Christian Faith* (Grand Rapids, Michigan: Wm. B. Eerdmans, 1989) 260. Today this same passion for "historic land ownership" pervades the cultures of the Middle East and lies at the heart of the Israel / Palestinian struggle. Western culture has few parallels to this experience.

Israel more than real estate, more than a mere place to live? Is it *the place* of revelation and redemption?

Even though the NT does not address the subject of The Land directly, still, Davies's book gives us an index of the rich and varied metaphors which spoke to Israel's land consciousness and how the NT uses them. In fact, if we could comprehend Judaism's passion for The Land in the first century, we would discover new hermeneutical windows into the text of the NT itself. Krister Stendahl and W. D. Davies have remarked how Christian interpreters have too often intellectualized Jewish and Jewish-Christian theology, neglecting the practical things expected through faith.[13] For instance, while Paul does not refer to The Land *per se* and shows little interest in geography, nevertheless his concentration on "the promises of Abraham" and the extent to which Christians are heirs, shows that he is close to the heart of Jewish land expectations. These "promises" include the Jewish heritage of nation and land.[14]

Walter Brueggemann has also written a penetrating analysis of The Land as a theological symbol in biblical theology.[15] Brueggemann understands that The Land is included among those things that will experience "radical reversal" in the Gospels. Those who are hungry will be filled, mourners will rejoice, the powerless will be empowered, the blind will see, *the meek will be given land.* Those who grasp after life, demanding the benefits of their religious privileges, will walk away empty (Luke 9:24; 13:30; 14:11). Characters in conflict, according to Brueggemann, should be seen as those who are powerful and landed opposing those who are landless and without hope. Thus, in Luke 7:36-50, Jesus demolishes the security of the Pharisee in favor of a landless woman — a radical reversal of what we might expect. In Luke 19:9 Zacchaeus's repentance leads him to aid the poor — and then as a result Jesus affirms that Zacchaeus is still heir to Abraham's promises, alluding to "land" once more.

Therefore Jesus challenges the assumption of the religiously powerful that they can continue to be heirs to God's promises. His kingdom means that a radical reversal is afoot. The gospel is a scandal for those who are empowered and landed. Brueggemann concludes, "The land being newly given is land presented in an acutely dialectical way. The way to land is by loss. The way to lose land is to grasp it."[16] We can be sure that the poor who followed Jesus and

13. W. D. Davies, *The Gospel and the Land,* p. 161; K. Stendahl, as cited by M. Wilson, *Our Father Abraham,* 260.

14. Paul refers to Jerusalem in Gal 4:26 along with his discussion of Abraham. In this case Paul understands that Christian believers belong to "a Jerusalem above, for she is our mother." This spiritualizing of The Land follows a well-established trend in diaspora Judaism (see below).

15. W. Brueggemann, *The Land: Place as Gift, Promise, and Challenge in Biblical Faith* (Philadelphia: Fortress, 1977) 167-75.

16. *Land,* 175. Brueggemann continues, ". . . the New Testament has discerned how problematic land is; when the people are landless, the promise comes; but when the land is secured, it seduces and the people are turned toward loss. Thus the proclamation of Jesus is about graspers losing and those open to gifts as receiving" (175).

later populated the early church noted as well that Jesus himself was *landless,* and yet God had bestowed on him tremendous blessing as Messiah. Even in his temptation, one offer from Satan extends the promise of land to Jesus — the kingdoms of the world — but Jesus resists.

For the most part the NT does not view The Land as the object of messianic promise. Typically, Stephen's speech in Acts 7 seems to reject "land messianism" outright. Revelation and salvation can be found anywhere from Egypt to Mesopotamia, according to Stephen. Frequently The Land is spiritualized so that, as in Hebrews 4, Canaan becomes the place of heavenly reward. But this entails another difficulty. The NT is also concerned to preserve the historical, geographical, reality of revelation. To spiritualize the objective record of Christ would play directly into gnostic hands. Therefore The Land is often treated as a place of historical record and its objective reality is never denied. Both concerns — land as spiritual metaphor and land as place of revelation — live in tension in the NT.

## The Fourth Gospel and The Land

The Fourth Gospel likely provides the most creative response to Judaism's concern for land and promise. John neither spiritualizes the reality of land (his incarnational theology would not permit it) nor makes it a literal object of promise. The Fourth Gospel reinterprets the promise of land in the historic presence of Christ. In the words of Davies, John "Christifies" The Land.[17]

Today few scholars would deny that the Fourth Gospel is deeply anchored in Judaism and conversant with the geographical particulars of The Land. And yet John's penchant for double meaning suggests that he is willing to create an ironic drama in order to disclose something new about Jesus. In particular, John uses the concrete gifts of The Land (Jerusalem's temple with its festivals, Israelite cities, and holy places) in order to show that what these places promise can be found in abundance in Christ. Thus Jesus cleanses the temple and announces that his body is a temple (2:21). He is the place where God's glory is viewed, where God "pitches his tent" (1:14). He appears at Tabernacles and says that he is water (7:37) and light (8:58), two ritual symbols in this festival. He is arrested at Passover and becomes that celebration's sacrifice (19:31-37). Thus Jesus supplies and surpasses what the temple offers. Jesus replaces the temple and its festivities as the place where God is revealed. Simply put, Jesus is the new "holy space" where God can be discovered.[18]

Therefore the Fourth Gospel, rather than dismissing the importance of Holy

17. Davies remarks, ". . . for the holiness of place, Christianity has fundamentally, though not consistently, substituted the holiness of the Person: it has Christified holy space" (*The Gospel and the Land,* 368).

18. Davies, *The Gospel and the Land,* 367.

Places, shifts their content to Jesus Christ who is The Holy Place. John finds in his christology an answer to the Jewish yearning for *place.* Christ is *the place* of God's promise.

This shift is particularly clear in all of those passages where Jesus appears at "holy sites" in The Land and contrasts himself with what these places offer. Thus *Bethel* is on Jesus' mind in 1:51 when he says to Nathanael, "Very truly, I tell you, you will see heaven opened and the angels of God ascending and descending upon the Son of Man." The experience of Jacob here (Gen 28:10-17) will be surpassed. In *Samaria* Jesus tells the woman that his water exceeds in value that which Jacob's ever gave (4:1-15). The sacred pool of *Bethesda* (5:1-9) cannot heal like Jesus; nor can the blind man be healed by the waters of *Siloam* (9:1-7): he is only healed because Jesus the "Sent One" (LXX, *Siloam;* Hebrew, *Shiloah*) has touched him. The pattern is clear. John's christology replaces Holy Spaces with Jesus Christ.

These observations are hardly new, as any commentary will indicate. However, one thing is less clear. What is the central concern that these passages address? For some, this christological emphasis veils a religious rivalry between the Johannine church and first-century synagogues. It is a literary motif, a replacement motif, showing that the festivals and institutions of Judaism are being supplanted by Christ. Indeed, the relevance of Judaism's rituals — like the value of Bethesda's waters — disappears at the coming of Christ.

But what if a second, more basic nuance is present? It is our view that Johannine christology is directly addressing the question of territorialism in first-century Judaism. Jesus replaces festivals, institutions, and The Land with all that it promises as Holy Space.

## The Fourth Gospel and Diaspora Judaism

The Hellenistic Jewish communities of the Diaspora which contributed to the Johannine outlook also had serious concerns about Jewish territorialism. The Land of Israel / Palestine, they argued, was not the only appropriate place of residence for a Jew. They experienced a marked ambivalence when they considered their homeland, Israel. On the one hand, Jerusalem was the center of faith, the genesis of the Jewish story. And yet the Diaspora had provided an endless number of other centers since the Babylonian exile. Jews loved Jerusalem and idealized its religious value, but many did not return there. Jerusalem became a place of pilgrimage, but not always a place of permanent residence. The Land was given high place in literature, but not occupied.

Philo's comments on the land promises of Genesis show the extent to which diaspora Jews could spiritualize The Land of Israel. In Gen 15:7-8 The Land is called a symbol of wisdom and virtue.[19] In fact, even the messianic age

19. Philo *Questions on Genesis;* cited in Davies, *The Gospel and the Land,* 122.

would not witness the centrality of The Land. The world's inheritance would be the law enjoyed in every land on earth. Thus the stage was set for the full spiritualization of The Land and the promises to Abraham.[20] From Philo we can point to the little-known *Testament of Job* as evidence that those who reinterpreted scriptural allusions to The Land were open to substantial criticism (v 33).[21]

Even Jerusalem was spiritualized so that as Jewish eschatology looked forward, a "heavenly Jerusalem" could be anticipated. The conception first appears in *1 Enoch* 90 and recurs with marked frequency particularly following the Jewish War of 66-70 C.E. (see *2 Apoc. Bar.* 4:1-7; 4 Ezra 7:26; 8:52-53; 9:38–10:57). In many of these texts, Jerusalem becomes a city that existed before creation, that transcends the earthly city that suffers destruction. This was strong consolation no doubt for a Judaism that had just witnessed its conquest by Roman legions.

And so Judaism lived with two minds. There was this reality of the historic land — the Land of Israel / Palestine — and there was the wider diversity of the Diaspora that invited eager spiritualization of the historic promises. This ambivalence likely explains why during the War of 66-70 C.E. diaspora Judaism did not support the campaign against Rome in earnest. Something of The Land could be had without living within the historic perimeters of Judea, Samaria, and Galilee.

The Fourth Gospel, reflecting these territorial concerns of diaspora Judaism, may be making a direct and simple comment about Christians and "holy geography," about sacred territory. John's debate is not simply with Judaism and the synagogue, nor is John just contrasting Judea and Galilee in a theological drama. *John is saying that the heritage of the people of God is no longer territorial.* In this sense John is echoing the concerns of diaspora Jews, many of whom have joined the Johannine church. Just as the definition of "children of Abraham" is open to redefinition in light of the messianic presence (8:33-44; cf. Matt 3:9; Luke 3:8), so too, the *heritage of Abraham* has changed for all time. The people of God are no longer to be concerned either "with this mountain or with Jerusalem" (4:21).

Already R. Gundry has made a somewhat similar case where "place" is spiritualized using John 14.[22] Tracing the lexical history of μονή in 14:2, he

20. The Diaspora's spiritualization of the promises to Abraham has been discussed by N. Calvert, "Abraham Traditions in Middle Jewish Literature: Implications for the Interpretation of Galatians and Romans" (Ph.D. diss., Sheffield University, 1992).

21. Davies (*The Gospel and the Land,* 125) cites the edition of S. P. Brock, *Testamentum Iobi* (Leiden: E. J. Brill, 1967) 43-44.

22. R. Gundry, "In My Father's House Are Many Μοναί (John 14:2)," *ZNW* 58 (1967) 68-72; cf. M. McNamara, " 'To Prepare a Resting Place for You,' Targumic Expression in Jn 14:2f," *Milltown Studies* [Dublin] 3 (1979) 100-108; for a history of interpretation, see G. Fischer, *Die himmlische Wohnung: Untersuchungen zu Joh 14,2f* (Bern / Frankfurt: Lang, 1975).

has shown this shift at work. Note the text: "In my father's house are many *rooms;* if it were not so, I would have told you. I am going there to prepare a *place* for you." On one level, the "place" of promise is certainly eschatological: what was sought as a future place in heaven becomes a realized place in the present. Eschatological places of dwelling become places of indwelling (14:27). Thus, as Gundry shows, μονή is used cleverly in 14:2 and 14:23 to make an eschatological adjustment. But μονή means more than this. The desire for place, a holy place, is anchored initially in the Holy Land. John exploits territorial images of place, acknowledges their use in eschatology, and then absorbs them in christology. Indeed, God promises *a place* where he dwells with his people — and this place is coming with the messianic era. Jesus' surprise is that this "Holy Place" is that disciple's life wherein the Father and the Son make their dwelling.

## John 15 and The Land

Most interpretations of the vine homily in John 15 echo the sentiments of Barrett, who discovers here a primary connection with the Christian Eucharist.[23] Even Brown, who is generally cautious with a sacramental interpretation of the Fourth Gospel, finds a eucharistic interpretation most satisfying.[24] To be sure, the search to unravel the meaning of the vine metaphor has been exhaustive, combing gnostic, Mandean, OT, and Jewish sources.[25] Even when commentators acknowledge the substantial OT vineyard parallels (Isa 27:2-6; 5:1-7; Ps 80:9; Ezekiel 17; etc.), still, because the parallels are not exact, they deduce that the eucharistic setting has been formative.[26]

But perhaps the more important question is *not* about the precision of parallels, but the *cultural weight* of the metaphor itself and how it served the communities who used it. The vine — regardless of its metaphorical application — was widely used in a variety of ways throughout Hebrew literature. Thus it seems appropriate for us to question the certainty of the eucharistic interpretation. Most commentators give only two reasons for this eucharistic view: John 15 finds its setting in the upper room and the "vine" appears in the Synoptic eucharistic sayings ("Truly I tell you, I will never again drink of the fruit of the

23. C. K. Barrett, *The Gospel according to St. John,* 2d ed. (London: SPCK, 1978) 393.

24. R. E. Brown, *The Gospel according to John,* 2 vols., AB 29- 29A (Garden City, New York: Doubleday, 1970) 2:673-74.

25. J. Behm, "ἄμπελος," *TDNT* 1:342-43; Brown, *John,* 2:669; G. Johnston, "The Allegory of the Vine," *CJT* 3 (1957) 150-58; R. Borig, *Der wahre Weinstock* (München: Kösel, 1967); J. Rosscup, *Abiding in Christ: Studies in John 15* (Grand Rapids, Michigan: Zondervan, 1973). See the bibliography in G. R. Beasley-Murray, *John,* WBC 36 (Waco, Texas: Word, 1987) 265; and E. Haenchen, *John,* 2 vols., Hermeneia (Philadelphia: Fortress, 1984) 2:129-30.

26. Thus Brown complains that nowhere in the OT is the vine a *source of life* for the branches (*John,* 2:261).

vine until that day when I drink it new in the kingdom of God" [Mark 14:25]). This second point is true, but nowhere is "the vine" used to describe *disciples* drinking "the fruit of the vine" in a eucharistic setting.[27]

But the vine had a far more diverse and popular usage, particularly in agrarian societies like Israel. In addition to representing The Land (see below), Judaism used it metaphorically both for wisdom (Sir 24:27) and the Messiah (*2 Apoc. Bar.* 39:7). A golden vine even served as a prominent decoration on the gates of Herod's temple to represent the flourishing of Israel in The Land (Josephus *J.W.* 5.210). Even the early Christians, who were no strangers to the eucharistic setting, could use the vine as a symbol for other things *in their eucharist liturgies* (*Did.* 9:2).

Interpreters of John 15 may be strongly influenced by what they bring to the text by way of presupposition about the early church's worship and how its experience formed the content of the Gospels. But it may be that an earlier, more basic concern now foreign to us was at the center of Jesus' thinking. It was a concern about The Land and place and sacred space so central to the Jewish consciousness.

*John 15:1-6 is the Fourth Gospel's most profound theological relocation of Israel's "Holy Space."* This suggestion, offered once by A. Jaubert, has generally been overlooked by interpreters.[28] The central interpretative reference point is Israel's belief that *the land itself is a source of life and hope and future.* And a principal metaphor describing this rootedness in the land is the vineyard. The vineyard and the grapevine both in antiquity and today have supplied Middle Eastern culture with abundant pictures of life.[29] Thus Ps 80:8-13 describes Israel as a vine transplanted from Egypt to Canaan — Canaan, which is God's vineyard.

> Restore us, O God of hosts; let your face shine, that we may be
> saved.
> You brought a vine out of Egypt;
> You drove out the nations and planted it.
> You cleared the ground for it; it took deep root and filled the land.
> The mountains were covered with its shade, the mighty cedars
> with its branches;
> It sent out its branches to the sea, and its shoots
> to the River.
> Why then have you broken down its walls,
> So that all who pass along the way pluck its fruit?

27. D. Carson, *The Gospel according to John* (Grand Rapids, Michigan: Wm. B. Eerdmans, 1991) 512-13.

28. A. Jaubert, "L'image de la Vigne (Jean 15)," in *Oikonomia: Heilsgeschichte als Thema der Theologie. O. Cullmann zum 65,* ed. F. Christ (Hamburg: Reich, 1957) 93-99.

29. R. Bultmann, *The Gospel of John* (Philadelphia: Westminster, 1971) 529-32, gives ample evidence for the use of this metaphor. Cf. Behm, "ἄμπελος."

> The boar from the forest ravages it, and all that move in the field
> feed on it.
> Turn again, O God of hosts; look down from heaven, and see;
> Have regard for this vine, the stock that your right hand planted. (Ps. 80:7-15)

Hosea 10:1 makes the analogy explicit: "Israel is a luxuriant vine that yields its fruit." The OT prophets Jeremiah (2:21; 5:10; 12:11-12), Ezekiel (15:1-8; 17:1-10; 19:10-14), and Isaiah (27:2-6) all make ample use of this imagery, as do Sirach (24:27) and *2 Apocalypse of Baruch* (39:7). Occasionally the metaphor becomes elastic, making Israel not simply a vine, but the vineyard itself in The Land. This is seen in Isaiah's well-known song of the vineyard: "For the vineyard of the Lord of Hosts is the House of Israel" (5:7). Thus the primary OT metaphor depicts The Land as a vineyard cultivated by Yahweh. The people of Israel are the vines planted within this vineyard, upon The Land. Taken together the cultivated vineyard (filled with vines) is "the House of Israel" tended by Yahweh, Israel's vinedresser.

Similarly in the Synoptic Gospels Jesus tells a parable making the Land of Israel a vineyard which is visited by the vineyard owner (Mark 12:1-11). Jesus' use of the vineyard as metaphor for The Land shows that he has adopted this common usage well-known in Judaism. And yet here Jesus typically changes the terms of the metaphor in important ways. The people of Israel are not vines in the vineyard but tenants. The vines, therefore, are part of the vineyard itself. The vines carry the symbolic value of Israel-as-Land, vines and vineyard working closely together to make a composite image.

The crux for John 15 is that *Jesus is changing the place of rootedness for Israel.* The commonplace prophetic metaphor (The Land as vineyard, the people of Israel as vines) now undergoes a dramatic shift. God's vineyard, the Land of Israel, now has only one vine (ἄμπελος),[30] Jesus. The people of Israel cannot claim to be planted as vines in The Land; they cannot be *rooted* in the vineyard unless first they are *grafted* into Jesus. Other vines are not true (15:1). Branches that attempt living in The Land, the vineyard, which refuse to be attached to Jesus will be cast out and burned (15:6). In John 15 we are given a completely new metaphor: God the vinedresser now has one vine growing in his vineyard. And the only means of attachment to The Land is through this one vine, Jesus Christ.

30. Brown notes that the Old Latin, Old Syriac, Eth. Tatian, and some Church Fathers understood ἄμπελος to be "vineyard" in 15:1 (*John,* 2:660). In first-century Koine ἄμπελος (vine) can take on the meaning of ἀμπελών (vineyard). This would compare favorably with 15:6, which describes withered branches being "cast out" (i.e., cast out of an assumed vineyard). In this case, Jesus himself is God's new vineyard in which believers are called to take root. Jesus replaces The Land of Israel itself as God's place of life and growth. However, the bulk of evidence supports ἄμπελος as *vine* in the present context.

This christological emphasis is simply the Johannine replacement motif at work once more. Jesus replaces festivals like the Passover (John 6) and institutions like the temple (John 2). As Messiah he sweeps up principal themes in traditional Judaism and reinterprets them, replacing their conventional meaning. He is living bread (6:35), living water (4:10; 7:38), and the light of life (8:12). Jewish ritual sources for these in ceremony and tradition are now obsolete. Now in John 15 we learn that Jesus is the vine, a potent metaphor for Israel itself. He offers what attachment to The Land once promised: rootedness and hope and life.[31] As the final "I AM" saying, John 15:1 therefore is the culmination of the images paraded throughout the Gospel showing that Jesus replaces what is at the heart of Jewish faith. The Fourth Gospel is transferring spatial, earthbound gifts from God and connecting them to a living person, Jesus Christ.

God the Father is now cultivating a vineyard in which only one life-giving vine grows. Attachment to this vine and this vine alone gives the benefits of life once promised through The Land. And as Isaiah and the other prophets pressed the vine metaphor to show Israel's lack of good fruit, Jesus promises that fruitbearing will be natural to all those growing in him (15:2-5).

The family of concepts that draws together John 15 and The Land centers on Israel's quest for life and fruitfulness under the watchful eye of Yahweh. The Johannine christology urges that this quest will not be satisfied with religious territory, with the real estate of Judea, Samaria, or Galilee, any more than it will be satisfied with religious ritual. In the messianic age, God's vineyard has one vine, Christ, and all must be grafted into him. Those who pursue territory, religious turf, motivated by the expectation that it is theirs by privilege, hoping that God will bless their endeavor, are sorely mistaken. Johannine christology could not be clearer. Only one person, Jesus, is the way to such nearness to God. He alone is attached to God's vineyard. He alone is the way to God's Holy Space, to God's Holy Land. "The way" is not territorial. It is spiritual. It is to be in the Father's presence (John 14:1-11). Just as the Samaritan woman of John 4 learned that Jerusalem was no longer *a place* of true worship (and that worship in Spirit is what the Father seeks), so now The Land as *holy place* cannot be an avenue to the blessings of God.

Edwin Hoskyns caught this nuance in John 15 and wisely avoided purely eucharistic applications. For him, the Eucharist may have been the setting for Jesus to disclose something powerful about himself *and Israel.*

> Jesus, the Son of God, is the incorruptible vine, His faithful disciples are the living and fruit-bearing branches, Judas and all other apostates are branches, broken off, withered, and fit only as fuel for the fire. *I am the true vine* is therefore not an illustration of the assimilation of Christian language to the

31. Bultmann, *John,* 530.

> formulae of Oriental mysticism; it is, rather, a formal denial of Jewish claims and the fulfillment of prophecy. Jesus, not Israel, is the vine of God; the disciples, not the Jews, are the branches of the vine. The synagogue is superseded by the Christian Ecclesia, and the true and genuine vine is contrasted with all that is counterfeit, false and inadequate for salvation.[32]

Therefore John 15 is in fact a careful critique of the territorial religion of Judaism. The prophets of the OT employed the vine metaphor to urge Israel to greater righteousness — to cultivate the vineyard. In some cases they used the metaphor to encourage Israel, saying that The Land itself was God's vineyard and his gift to the people. In a way reminiscent of diaspora Judaism, Jesus points away from the vineyard as place, as a territory of hills and valleys, cisterns and streams. *In a word, Jesus spiritualizes The Land.*

But if we are to be grafted into Jesus, we might ask the next logical question: What has happened to the vineyard? Is Jesus then rooted in the vineyard, The Land of Israel? Is Jesus the means of getting The Land? On the contrary, Jesus is *rooted* in the Father; he is one with the Father (John 17:11). The Johannine replacement motif characteristically exploits those elements which the Jewish ritual offers and then ignores any further application of the symbols found there. Thus Jesus empties Tabernacles of its ritual significance and then leaves the ceremony behind offering the light and water once offered there. In John 15, Jesus exploits the vineyard metaphor in order to take from it what Judaism had sought from The Land. Now Jesus is the sole source of life and hope and future. The Land, as holy territory, therefore should now recede from the concerns of God's people. The vineyard is no longer an object of religious desire as it once had been.

## Implications

Exegesis frequently has implications with a direct bearing on our world. This is a case in point. The discussion of "holy space" and "territorial religion" is not merely academic in today's Holy Land. On the basis of divine right, "holy land" is being taken in an effort to restore a religious vision of an earlier biblical era.[33] But we are mistaken if, as Christians, we promote the land of Israel / Palestine into a place of divine presence. We are mistaken if, as Christians, we say that rootedness in God will now be discovered by people who wish to build another "vineyard" on the OT order of things.

Christians — especially Western evangelicals — have been quick to endorse modern Israel's territorial agenda for theological reasons. Generally a zeal

32. E. C. Hoskyns, *The Fourth Gospel,* ed. F. N. Davey (London: Faber and Faber, 1947) 475.

33. Specifically, the modern state of Israel is taking land illegally from its neighbors to recreate a vision of a biblical nation, and this is justified on theological, biblical grounds.

for eschatological fulfillment has inspired Christian commitments to Israeli nationalism. But to do so is to read the land promises of the OT without incorporating the radical changes brought about through Jesus Christ. Jesus said, "I AM the *true* vine." To neglect this aspect of NT christology is also to neglect the Palestinian Christian church which is suffering through these theologically fueled injustices.

New Testament christology — indeed, Johannine christology — has forever changed the *place* of God among men and women.[34] As Jesus predicted, Israel's vineyard was devastated (Mark 12:9a). But instead of being rebuilt again, it was "given to others" (Mark 12:9b). John's homily of the vineyard tells us that God's new vineyard contains one vine, Jesus Christ, and in him and him alone will be found all the benefits of the heritage of The Land.

34. I think, e.g., of the many Christian pilgrims whom I have seen in Jerusalem proclaiming that God is nearer to them in this city. They walk in Capernaum and "feel the presence of Jesus" in a new way. I do not wish to deny to them an emotional or historical experience of being in "the Holy Land." This goes beyond enjoying historical (biblical) reminiscences and becomes a theological conviction for many. But theologically — spiritually — Jesus has proclaimed that this sort of spatial residence for God is no longer appropriate. The "tongues of fire" in Acts 2 makes this explicit: the dwelling place of God (seen in fire) is found no longer in the structures of the temple. It resides in the hearts of men and women. The NT, on the other hand, speaks against any such "territorial" spirituality.

# The Christology of Revelation

†Donald Guthrie

The aim of this essay will be to attempt to put the christological emphases in the book of Revelation in the context of NT christology generally. Such a quest at once faces a difficulty since the genre of the book is so evidently different from any other literature within the NT. We are faced with a symbolic approach which must involve some theory of interpretation. Indeed, the wide variety of such interpretations for this book is testimony enough to the major obstacles facing our quest.

A further problem is the many negative opinions about this book, not only generally but more particularly of its christology.[1] Too many have sympathized with Martin Luther's opinion that this book is a "dumb prophecy" which speaks too little of both Christ and the gospel. If this were a correct assessment, we should be fully justified in ignoring it and our quest would immediately become a waste of time. A more positive assessment of this book, however, is not only possible but much more convincing. Once the strangeness of the genre is accepted, the presentation of Christ may be claimed to be of the highest order. This does not mean to say that it presents a complete account of the nature and work of Christ, but its contribution to NT christology is nevertheless considerable.

Many scholars have not taken seriously its christology on the grounds that it is a mixture of Jewish and Christian ideas.[2] Theories of different literary

1. Cf. C. H. Dodd, *The Apostolic Preaching and Its Development,* 3d ed. (London, 1963) 49; R. Bultmann, *Theology of the New Testament,* vol. 2 (New York: Charles Scribner's Sons, 1955) 175.

2. Cf. S. A. Edwards, "Christological Perspectives in the Book of Revelation," in *Christological Perspectives,* ed. R. F. Berkey and S. A. Edwards (New York: Crossroad, 1982) 139-54. J. M. Ford (*Revelation,* AB 38 [Garden City, New York: Doubleday, 1975]) believes that the christology supports a two-document theory. She argues for two Jewish apocalypses from John the Baptist and from his school. The redactor is seen as a Christian disciple of John. This theory has been criticized by E. S. Fiorenza on the grounds of the strong linguistic unity of the book ("Composition and Structure of the Revelation of John," *CBQ* 39 [1977] 347). Cf. the brief discussion by G. R.

sources, popular in some quarters, have seemed to support such a reduction of the christological presentation, but these theories play down the strong linguistic unity of the book. It is not possible here to discuss in detail these literary theories, but in any case we are concerned with the christology of the finished product, not of its parts. We shall look first of all at the evidences within the book and then discuss any comparisons with other NT literature.

## 1. The Christological Material within the Book

It is best to present this material under two sections — (1) Revelation 1–3 and (2) Revelation 4–22.[3]

*1.1. The Christology of Revelation 1–3.* The central position of Christ is seen in the opening words. The book purports to be "the revelation of Jesus Christ." It is therefore christocentric. This is the key to understanding the book. Indeed, the opening chapter contributes some valuable insights into the christology of the whole book. The threefold description of 1:5, which presents Christ as faithful witness, firstborn from the dead, and ruler of the kings of the earth, points to three important elements of Revelation's christology. Christ is essentially portrayed as the witness to the truth of God throughout Revelation.[4] He is also seen as the risen Christ and as the King of kings. This statement prepares us for a consistent presentation linking the first section with the following visions.

It is not accidental that the title "Jesus Christ" occurs three times in the first chapter but nowhere else in the book. The first Christian readers would need to be led from Jesus Christ to the Lamb, the name which dominates the second part of the book. It is significant that the messianic title for Christ, in the sense of the Anointed One, is introduced at the beginning but occurs again only three times in the rest of the Apocalypse.[5] It is as if the writer is leading

---

Beasley-Murray, "How Christian Is the Book of Revelation?," in *Reconciliation and Hope: Essays Presented to L. L. Morris,* ed. R. J. Banks (Grand Rapids, Michigan: Wm. B. Eerdmans, 1974) 275-84.

3. There has been much recent discussion regarding the structure of this book, but a decision on this question does not affect our discussion of christology. For various opinions on the matter, cf. J. Lambrecht, "A Structuration of Rev. 4:1–22:5," in *L'Apocalypse johannique et l'Apocalyptique dans le Nouveau Testament,* ed. J. Lambrecht, BETL 53 (Leuven: Leuven University, 1980) 77-104. Cf. also Fiorenza, "Composition and Structure," 344-66. For a different approach to the book's christological teaching see D. Guthrie, *The Relevance of John's Apocalypse* (Exeter: Paternoster, 1987) ch. 2.

4. Cf. M. de Jonge, "The Use of the Expression ὁ Χριστός in the Apocalypse of John," in *L'Apocalypse johannique,* 267-81. This expression cannot be understood only in a purely Jewish sense (cf. Ford, *Revelation,* 13-14), although it undoubtedly has Jewish undertones.

5. For the significance of this expression, cf. de Jonge, "Expression"; he draws attention to the fact that this form of title is used only in contexts with future reference.

his readers to concentrate on an even more significant title, that of the Lamb, who is not, however, introduced until ch. 5.

Another interesting point about the presentation in the first chapter is that God introduces himself as "Alpha and Omega" (1:8),[6] while this all-inclusive title is not used of Christ until 22:13. It is as if the writer delays such an identification until consideration of the triumph of Christ at the consummation of human history has convinced his readers that what is true of God is equally true of Christ.

The most significant contribution of the opening chapter to the christology of the whole book is the vision of the one "like a son of man" among the candlesticks (1:12-16). It sets out a glorious picture of Christ which seems at first sight far removed from the portrait of Christ in the Gospels. There he was approachable, but here overawing. Of course it was the resurrection which made the difference, but no one can proceed further into this book without an impressive view of the glorified Christ. The symbolic details are all aimed to enhance this view. The dignified robe, the golden sash, the pure white hair, the blazing eyes, the burning feet, the majestic voice, the powerful hands, the sharp, two-edged sword, and the shining face at once set this figure apart from ordinary mortals. The reader with a knowledge of the OT will not fail to see the allusions to the "Son of Man" of Daniel 7; nor is it accidental that the figure there, as here, is remarkably "like" the Ancient of Days himself, or the theophanic figure of Ezekiel 1. But in portraying Christ this way, does Revelation present a docetic picture? Taken on its own this is a possibility, but the sequence corrects all fear of this. True, John's initial reaction of being overawed points to an intimidating effect, but the right-handed touch and the assurance that he was dead but is now alive firmly link the vision to the historical Jesus. The human life of Jesus may find few echoes in the book, but the reality of the death and resurrection cannot be denied. Furthermore, no consideration of this vision would be complete without recognizing that this exalted figure of Christ is nonetheless standing in the midst of the candlesticks. He is as central to the life and activities of the churches on earth as he is in dealing with the enemies of God.

We cannot appreciate the force of the vision in ch. 1 without considering the kind of presentation of Christ seen in chs. 2 and 3. In spite of the fact that the introductions to the letters draw heavily from details in the vision in ch. 1, the christology is not of the overawing type. In all the letters the messages show a deep concern for the churches in spite of the fact that all but two contain criticisms. There is an invitation to repentance. There are strong assurances for the overcomers. There is no suggestion that Christ is in any way remote. Moreover, he is portrayed as having knowledge of what was happening in the

6. Cf. the note in G. R. Beasley-Murray, *The Book of Revelation,* NCBC (Grand Rapids, Michigan: Wm. B. Eerdmans, 1974) 60-63, on the early Christian word-square which incorporated the Alpha and Omega symbol.

churches (note the repeated "I know"). In addition, there are elements in the introductions which fill in the vision with further details (e.g., the key of David, the Amen, the Ἀρχή,[7] and the Son of God).[8]

Another factor to observe is the exhortation at the end of all the messages for the hearers to listen to what the Spirit says.[9] As in the teaching of Jesus (John 14, 16), the Spirit is the witness to the teachings of Jesus. This feature is of importance when considering the relationship between the christology here and that of other parts of the NT.

It must be noted that this section of the book places great emphasis on the exalted Christ but little on the human Jesus.[10] This is a pattern followed in the remainder of the book. Its implications will need further discussion later.

***1.2. The Christology of Revelation 4–22.*** Without doubt the central feature of the christology of this latter part of the book is the presentation of Christ as "the Lamb,"[11] a title which occurs nearly 30 times. Since it does not occur in chs. 1–3, some explanation needs to be found for this fact. Is the Lamb imagery inappropriate for addressing the churches? What is the significance of the Lamb imagery in the visions of worship and of judgment? Why is the Lamb title generally lacking from other NT books?

Our first task must be to note the various aspects of the Lamb imagery which occur in this book. Its first appearance is linked with lion imagery (ch. 5). In spite of the fact that lion imagery would be more appropriate in scenes of conflict and triumph, this title does not occur elsewhere in the book. Clearly the writer is not intending to portray Christ in an overmastering fashion. The Lamb is essentially a sacrificial symbol, as is seen from the description of its "looking as if it had been slain" (5:6). Since this description occurs in a section in which the Lamb is said to have purchased men and women for God through his blood it can hardly be denied that the Lamb is here sacrificial (cf. 7:14). It has been pointed out, however, that, although the symbol may have been taken

7. G. Delling, "ἀρχή," *TDNT* 1:484, is not certain whether ἀρχή is used here in the same sense as in Col 1:18, but agrees that Rev 21:6 and 22:13 point to that likelihood. I. T. Beckwith, *The Apocalypse of John* (New York: Macmillan, 1919) 488, understands ἀρχή as pointing to the one from whom creation took its beginning.

8. E. Schweizer, "υἱός κτλ," *TDNT* 8:389, argues that for the writer of Revelation "Son of God" is to be understood only within the limits of Jewish understanding. But this seems an inadequate explanation of the reference in 2:18, the context of which cannot be regarded as Jewish.

9. Cf. E. Schweizer, "Die sieben Geister in der Apokalypse," *EvT* 11 (1951-52) 502-12; F. F. Bruce, "The Spirit in the Apocalypse," in *Christ and Spirit in the New Testament*, ed. B. Lindars and S. S. Smalley (Cambridge: Cambridge University, 1973) 333-44.

10. In order to maintain her theory that "Jesus" does not occur in the apocalyptic section, Edwards ("Perspectives," 149) is obliged to regard all these references as glosses. But there are no textual evidences for such a view, as she admits.

11. If, of course, the apocalyptic section is divorced from the Christian section (as it is by Edwards, "Perspectives"), the Lamb ceases to be the key to the christology of the whole book.

from the Jewish Passover lamb, there is no evidence in this book of familiar Passover imagery. It has alternatively been suggested that the imagery is indebted to Jewish apocalyptic literature since in the *Testament of Joseph* (19:8-9) the twofold Messiah is represented in terms of both lion and lamb. Nevertheless in that book the Messiah is a powerful conqueror: either the lamb imagery has been dominated by the lion imagery, or the "lamb" in question is the bellwether of the flock of Israel. In the *Testament of Joseph* it is not a sacrificial lamb at all. Of course, it is possible that John has himself fused the two different lamb imageries — the powerful bellwether who overcomes Israel's enemies, and the sacrificial lamb — perhaps to make the point that it is precisely *as* the *slain* lamb that Christ conquers and rules. But such a point is left implicit, and the author prefers rather to direct our attention to other features of the Lamb.

Particularly noteworthy is that the Lamb is seen as worthy[12] of worship (ch. 5) in a sense parallel to that of God (ch. 4).[13] This is significant for a correct view of the christology of this book. Although the lamb imagery may suggest qualities of gentleness, the Lamb in this book is in no sense weak but fully capable of overthrowing the enemies of God (like the lamb of the *Testament of Joseph*). Moreover, he is presented at the end as a Bridegroom receiving his bride (ch. 19). It is only the Lamb who is capable of opening the book of visions (5:9), which shows a christology containing a revelatory element, and only he can open the seals of the scroll of destiny, which points to a christology of full sovereignty.[14] Apart from the presentation of the Lamb as a victorious conqueror,[15] we must note a more severe and solemn side as represented by the phrase "the wrath of the Lamb" (6:16), which is parallel to the more frequent reference to the wrath of God.[16]

12. Cf. K.-P. Jörns, *Das hymnische Evangelium,* SNT 5 (Gutersloh: Gerd Mohn, 1971) 56-73, for a full discussion of this point. The view that ἄξιος was related to the imperial cult was advanced as long ago as 1926 by E. Peterson, *Eis Theos: Epigraphische, formgeschichtliche und religionsgeschichtliche Untersuchungen,* FRLANT 41 (Göttingen: Vandenhoeck & Ruprecht, 1926) 176-79. R. H. Mounce, "Worthy Is the Lamb," in *Scripture, Tradition and Interpretation: Essays Presented to Everett F. Harrison,* ed. W. W. Gasque and W. S. LaSor (Grand Rapids, Michigan: Wm. B. Eerdmans, 1978), in commenting on this ascription, maintains that no christology could be superior.

13. Cf. W. C. van Unnik, " 'Worthy is the Lamb,' the Background of Rev. 5," in *Mélanges Bibliques en hommage au R. P. Béda Rigaux,* ed. A. Descamps and A. de Halleux (Gembloux: Duculot, 1970) 445-61.

14. Cf. D. Guthrie, "The Lamb in the Structure of the Book of Revelation," *VE* 12 (1981) 64-71. Cf. also D. R. Carnegie, "Worthy Is the Lamb: The Hymns in Revelation," in *Christ the Lord,* ed. H. H. Rowden (Leicester: Inter-Varsity, 1982) 243-56.

15. Beasley-Murray, *Revelation,* 125, comments, "The warrior-Lamb then has conquered through accepting the role of the passover-Lamb." If, of course, the Lamb is identified with Israel, as suggested by Edwards, "Perspectives," 144, it would have no significance for christology. Cf. also R. E. Brown, *The Gospel according to John,* vol. 1, AB (Garden City, New York: Doubleday, 1966) 59.

16. R. H. Mounce, *The Book of Revelation,* NICNT (Grand Rapids, Michigan: Wm. B. Eerdmans, 1977) 163, has drawn attention to the fact that only once in the Gospels is the word

The Lamb is not only involved with judgment in this book but also with salvation, which belongs both to God and to the Lamb (7:10). In the New Jerusalem the Lamb is closely linked with God (22:3), which points to similar characteristics. Indeed, the climax of the book is not the final overthrow of the enemies, but the marriage supper of the Lamb and the establishment of the New Jerusalem (chs. 19–20). Although there is no mention of the cross in this book, its shadow is everywhere present. The theme of redemption is prominent in the worship passages. The christology is linked with a clear picture of the work of Christ on behalf of his people.

Two other characteristics of the Lamb are worth mentioning. There is an association with shepherd imagery in 7:17, where the shepherd leads his people to springs of living water. This portrays the gentler aspect of the person of Christ and gains special significance because it parallels the claims of Jesus himself to be the Good Shepherd (John 10). Another feature of great significance is the Lamb as the keeper of the records (13:8); he knows his people and he knows their deeds.

In addition to the Lamb imagery other titles used of Christ in the latter section of the book throw considerable light on the christology of Revelation. The title "King of kings and Lord of lords" (19:16) is set in the context of the victory over the kings of the earth. The absolute superiority of Christ over all other powers, including Satanic forces, is one of the overwhelming emphases of this book.

Among the other significant christological titles used in the latter part of this book are "Word of God" and "Alpha and Omega." The first of these occurs in the vision of the conquering warrior in 19:11ff.[17] It is not immediately clear why this title is used in this context. Some have suggested that it may be indebted to the passage in the book of Wisdom (18:15-16) in which the Word leaps from heaven with a sharp sword.[18] But it is more likely to have come from the same background as the Word in John 1:1, a parallel which is further discussed below. The phrase "Alpha and Omega" has already appeared in the opening section, but the significant difference is that by the end of the book the title is applied to Christ himself in the same way in which it is earlier used of God. Both "Word" and "Alpha and Omega" portray Christ as the channel of communication from God to humanity.[19]

---

"wrath" used of Jesus (Mark 3:5). The term is not characteristic of the main portrait of the Gospels. There would be less difficulty here, as Mounce points out, if the Lamb figure is messianic rather than sacrificial. A. T. Hanson, *The Wrath of the Lamb* (London, 1957) 159-80, regards wrath as a process of retribution. For a full discussion of the wrath of God, cf. R. V. G. Tasker, *The Biblical Doctrine of the Wrath of God* (London, 1951).

17. Edwards, "Perspectives," 282 n. 13, disagrees with G. Kittel, "λέγω," *TDNT* 4:127, who identifies the Word of God here with Jesus. She thinks this warrior of the white anger of God is far removed from the Christ who prays, "Father, forgive!" (142). On the significance of "Word of God" in Rev 19:13 in comparison with "Logos" in the Fourth Gospel, cf. W. F. Howard, *Christianity according to St. John* (London, 1943) 41, 54.

18. Cf. Edwards, "Perspectives," 142.

19. For the connection between Christ as "Word" and as "the Beginning," cf. J. D. G. Dunn, *Christology in the Making* (London: SCM, 1980) 247.

***1.3. Summary of Christological Material in This Book.*** It will be seen that the christological presentation in this book is of a high order. Christ is portrayed in his full resurrection glory. His functions are parallel to those of God himself. His power is all-pervading. His ultimate victory is assured whatever the opposition. Most strikingly, according to 5:6-13, he takes his position on *God's* throne, and receives a universal *worship* that would be regarded as entirely blasphemous to offer any creature.[20] He is nonetheless the Savior and Protector of his people, for whom the New Jerusalem is prepared. He is fully aware of the developments within the Christian communities, is portrayed as in their midst, and holds them in his hands. The two parts of the book are complementary in their view of Christ. Theories which maintain that this book presents only the severe aspect of Christ as Judge do not account for the integral connection between the messages to the churches and the visions. Nevertheless it must be admitted that there is little evidence in this book for an incarnational christology. If anything the emphasis falls on the revelatory character of the work of Christ.

## 2. Comparison with Johannine Christology

It is of considerable importance to determine where the presentation of Christ in Revelation stands in comparison with the rest of the NT. Our prior question is: What is its relation to the other Johannine literature?[21] We shall consider this irrespective of any decisions regarding the authorship of either the Fourth Gospel or the book of Revelation. Of course, if strong parallels are found, this evidence would be valuable in considering the author question for both books. But is the

20. As R. J. Bauckham ("The Worship of Jesus in Apocalyptic Christianity," *NTS* 27 [1981] 322-41) has pointed out, the worship offered to Jesus in so thoroughly Jewish a writing implies a *divine christology.* Larry Hurtado (*One God, One Lord* [London: SCM, 1988]) has shown the degree to which the exalted Jesus of Revelation 1–5 is paralleled and prepared for by the way exalted angels, or ascended and glorified patriarchs, are depicted in Jewish apocalypses and other related pseudepigraphal writings. Hurtado, however, considers the fundamental *difference* between Revelation and these other writings to rest precisely on the matter of the worship of Jesus. This was the one thing not permitted of even the most exalted beings in the Jewish parallels: worship could be offered to God alone. Significantly, in seeking to explain how Christians came to believe that it was appropriate to offer Jesus the kind of worship that should only be offered to God, Hurtado points especially to visions such as those in Revelation 1–3 and 5 (117-23). It is this sort of vision of Christ in the midst of God's throne, he believes, which was largely responsible for the early Christian recognition of Jesus' divinity, and the transformation from Jewish exclusive monotheism to Christian inclusive (trinitarian) monotheism. While this alone is probably too narrow a basis to explain the development entirely (see, e.g., the essays by Ellis [192-203] and Turner [413-36] in this volume for other partial explanations) it highlights the very high christology of the Apocalypse.

21. For a brief summary of the relationship between Revelation and the other Johannine literature, cf. D. Guthrie, *New Testament Introduction,* 4th ed. (Leicester: Inter-Varsity, 1990) 937-38. Cf. also O. Böcher, "Das Verhältnis der Apokalypse des Johannes zum Evangelium des Johannes," in *L'Apocalypse johannique,* 289-301.

Christ of John's Gospel identifiable with the Christ of Revelation? In order to answer this we may note the following points of comparison — the parallel use of Logos (the Word), the shepherd imagery,[22] the Lamb imagery, and the salvation theme.

We have noted above the use of the "Word" in Revelation 19 and connected it with John 1. The major difference in Revelation 19 is the addition of the genitive "of God."[23] But since in John 1 the Word is said to be God, the difference is not significant. In both it is God communicating with humanity, but in Revelation that communication is portrayed visually. When we link with this the "Word of life" mentioned in 1 John 1:1, we have a strong pointer to a revelatory christology. But we cannot isolate these references from John 1:14, where the incarnation of the Word is linked with the same theme.

The occurrence of Shepherd imagery in the Fourth Gospel forms an important part of the presentation of Christ in that Gospel, not only because of the "I am" saying about the Good Shepherd in John 10, but also because the risen Christ uses shepherd imagery in his communication with the recalcitrant Peter (John 21). In Rev 7:17 the Lamb is predicted as the shepherd who will lead his people to springs of living water. There seems to be a parallel with the living water mentioned in John 7:38, although here the main point is the shepherd's concern for the flock, a thought more closely paralleled in John 10. It is important to set this gentler image of Christ alongside the wrath of the Lamb (Rev 6:16). This aspect is also in agreement with the picture of God wiping away the tears of his people in the New Jerusalem (Rev 21:4). Another striking similarity between the christology of the Fourth Gospel and that of Revelation is in their distinctive use of Lamb imagery. It is only in these two books of the whole NT that "the Lamb" or "the Lamb of God" actually serves as a *title* for Jesus. While "the Lamb" is the regular christological title for Jesus in Revelation 4–21, it appears only twice in the Fourth Gospel (1:29, 32) and there with a different Greek word (ἀμνός, not ἀρνίον). But these differences should not be emphasized too strongly. John 1:29, 32, as part of the proem of John, provide the spectacles through which the person and work of Christ in that Gospel will be understood. And the switch from ἀρνίον to ἀμνός may well be occasioned by John's wish to portray Jesus' death (so central to the theology of this Gospel) as a fulfillment of Isaiah 53 (where the same Greek word is used in the LXX) too, as well as his hope for a powerful "lamb" who will overcome Israel's predatory enemies.[24]

22. Howard, *St. John*, 137-40, brings out the significance of the shepherd imagery in the Johannine presentation of the ministry.

23. Cf. Howard, *St. John*, 41-54, for comment on this genitival use.

24. For "the Lamb (of God)" in the Gospels, see I. H. Marshall, "Lamb of God," in *Dictionary of Jesus and the Gospels*, ed. J. B. Green and S. McKnight (Downers Grove, Illinois: InterVarsity; Leicester: Inter-Varsity, 1992) 432-34. On the relations of this to "the Lamb" of Revelation, see, e.g., G. R. Beasley-Murray, *John*, WBC 36 (Waco, Texas: Word, 1987) 24-25; and M. M. B. Turner, "Atonement and the Death of Jesus in John — Some Questions to Bultmann and Forestell," *EvQ* 62 (1990) 99-122 (esp. 119-22).

Whereas the book of Revelation may give the superficial impression of being concerned mainly with judgment rather than salvation, a closer examination shows this to be a wrong opinion. Not only are the visions of judgment sandwiched between visions of heavenly worship, but the whole book moves on inexorably toward the final uniting of the Lamb with the Bride in the New Jerusalem. The salvation theme is introduced most clearly in ch. 5, but the deep interest of the risen Christ in his people in chs. 2 and 3 and the calls for repentance show that the main emphasis is not to be judgment. Salvation is linked to the power of God in 12:10, as also in 19:10. It is impossible to construe the christology of this book without taking into account his saving work.[25] The combination of judgment and salvation is also a feature of John's Gospel, as a comparison of John 5:30 with John 3:16ff. demonstrates.

In addition to these main points of comparison many other incidental parallels build up a strong indication of a similar christology. In both books Christ is linked with life. The purpose of the Fourth Gospel is that those who believe may have life. In Revelation, in addition to the references to the tree of life and the crown of life in the opening chapters (2:7, 10), and the book of life (3:5), there are also references at the end of the book to the tree of life and book of life (22:2, 14, 19). Moreover, the allusion to the water of life in 21:6; 22:1, 17 finds a close parallel in the water imagery of John 4:14 and 7:37-38. Similarly, another theme found in the Johannine prologue and running through the Gospel is the connection between Jesus and light (1:5; 8:12), and this finds parallels in Revelation (cf. 22:4; 21:23). This comparison is reinforced by the emphasis in both books on the clash between light and darkness.[26] In John 10:7 Jesus claims to be the gate, while in Rev 3:20 he stands outside the gate. There are parallels in the close connection between Jesus and the Spirit in both books (cf. John 3:5-8; 7:39; 14–16; Rev 1–3; 21:10; 22:17). In both books there are anticipations of a second coming (John 14:3; Rev 19:11ff.; 22:20).

When these considerations are properly weighed it is difficult to avoid the conclusion that the christology is similar. But is there no justification for the view that the Jesus of the Gospel, who can be weary (ch. 4) and can weep (ch. 11), is very different from the all-conquering warrior of Revelation 19 who comes as the agent of God's wrath? The difference is more apparent than real when it is borne in mind that early Christians recognized the immense importance of the resurrection. Is it reasonable to expect that the same picture of Jesus would be presented before and after that event? The alleged differences between John's christology and the christology of Revelation are no greater than the difference between the approach of the disciples before and after Pentecost.

25. Cf. G. B. Caird, *The Revelation of St. John the Divine* (London: Black, 1966) 296, for a succinct summary of the theme of salvation in this book.

26. The antithesis between light and darkness, which occurs in both Revelation and the Fourth Gospel, and is strongly paralleled in the Qumran writings, shows how prevalent this kind of imagery was in contemporary society. It sets this book in particular against a background of conflict.

## 3. Comparison with Pauline Christology

It is perhaps of greater importance to discuss in what sense the christology of Revelation ties in with Paul's views. Our concern will not be to compare these two christologies to establish which has exerted the greater influence, for none would dispute that the decision would go to Paul. But it is important to discover whether the christology of Revelation in any sense conflicts with Paul's views. There are undoubtedly some significant parallels. The concentration on the exalted Christ finds clear support from the great christological hymns of Col 1:15ff. and Phil 2:6ff.[27] The reference to Christ's creative activity in the former passage is significant because it focuses on the powers, rulers, and authorities of this age and is reminiscent of the triumphant position of the Lamb in Revelation. Paul's christological statement is more specific in declaring Christ to be the image of the invisible God, but the close connection in Revelation between the functions of God and of Christ are in line with this exalted christology. Although Paul links to this a statement about the reconciling activity of Christ, it must be admitted that Revelation does not highlight this aspect. Nevertheless Paul himself sees the work of Christ in terms of redemption as well as reconciliation and in this respect his views are more closely aligned to Revelation. It may justly be claimed that whereas Paul's christology is stated in profound affirmations, that of Revelation portrays the glorious reality in more visual terms.

The idea of Christ as Son of God is strong in Paul's writings, although not so prominent in Revelation. Nevertheless the presence of father-son terminology testifies to a similar conviction.[28] Paul looks ahead to the time when Christ will deliver the kingdom to the Father (1 Cor 15:24), whereas in Revelation there is an angelic announcement of the kingdom of the world becoming the kingdom of our Lord and his Christ (11:15; cf. also 12:10).[29] Although it may be said that the eschatological aspect of the kingdom is more prominent in Revelation than in Paul, it cannot be said that this eschatological view would have been alien to the apostle's teaching. Certainly Paul looked ahead to the consummation of the age (e.g., Rom 8:19-23), and Revelation fills in some of the details.

The concept of conflict which so dominates Revelation is also stressed in Paul's letters. The battle between the forces of the devil and the people of God is particularly seen in Eph 6:10ff. Whereas Paul speaks of "the spiritual forces

27. On the Colossians passage, cf. H. Ridderbos, *Paul* (Grand Rapids, Michigan: Wm. B. Eerdmans, 1975) 78-86. On the Philippians passage, cf. R. P. Martin, *Carmen Christi,* 2d ed. (Grand Rapids, Michigan: Wm. B. Eerdmans, 1983).

28. Note especially the occurrence of "my Father" three times in the letters in Revelation (2:27; 3:5, 21).

29. It is important to recognize that the idea of kingdom here, as in the teaching of Jesus, is not of a sphere over which a king rules, but of the act of ruling. Cf. M. E. Boring, *Revelation* (Louisville: John Knox, 1989) 148; also P. Prigent, "Le temps et le Royaume dans l'Apocalypse," in *L'Apocalypse johannique,* 231-45.

of evil in the heavenly realms," Revelation sets the conflict out in visual representation. The great antagonist of the exalted Christ and his people is Satan, the personification of all evil. As in Revelation there is no uncertainty in Paul that Christ will be ultimately victorious (cf. 1 Cor 15:25). Another feature Revelation shares with Paul is the conviction that there will be a day of judgment. Paul speaks of the judgment seat of Christ (2 Cor 5:10), whereas Revelation focuses on the great white throne (Rev 20:11ff.).[30] Some have insisted that the two are not to be identified, but in view of the close association between the functions of God and Christ in Revelation it is difficult to maintain this distinction. Moreover, there is no suggestion in Revelation of a double judgment, one for believers and one for unbelievers.

## 4. Comparison with the Christology of the Rest of the New Testament

Since much has been made of the difference between the presentation of the historical Jesus and the Christ of Revelation,[31] some comment is necessary on the relationship between the Synoptics and Revelation. Although there is little literary connection, can it be said that the picture of the earthly Jesus giving his vivid teaching and doing works of compassion is so far removed from the presentation of Christ in Revelation that it is impossible to find any relationship between the two? The comparative absence of allusions to the historical Jesus in Revelation provides the main difficulty. The human figure of flesh and blood has largely been replaced by the Lamb. The main historical interest is in the fact of the death and resurrection of Christ. It is not easy to find a satisfactory solution to the absence of other historical details. But there is no doubt that the writer assumes that the Lamb figure will be recognizable to his readers. There would be no explanation of the Lamb "looking as if it had been slain" (5:6) if such an allusion were totally alien to the readers. Since the concentration of ideas is so clearly eschatological it is by no means clear where more allusions to the historical Jesus could have been introduced. We must conclude that the purpose of Revelation is so entirely different from that of the Synoptics that this sufficiently explains the difference of presentation. Nevertheless there are a few significant points of comparison. The eschatological discourse with its focus on future events and its reference to the end of the age shows that projections into the future are not alien in the teaching of

30. Caird, *Revelation*, 258, links the great white throne to Paul's reference in 1 Cor 15:24-28. Some scholars distinguish between the judgment seat of Christ in 2 Cor 5:10 and the great white throne in Rev 20:11ff., but the notion of two judgment seats is difficult to maintain. That there is a close connection between the two can hardly be denied.

31. For studies of parallels between the Synoptic Gospels and Revelation, cf. R. J. Bauckham, "Synoptic Parousia Parables and the Apocalypse," *NTS* 23 (1977) 162-76; and L. A. Vos, *The Synoptic Tradition in the Apocalypse* (Kampen: J. H. Kok, 1965).

Jesus.[32] It reminds us that no christology would be complete without taking into account the teaching of Jesus concerning his return and its implications. It is not too much to claim that Revelation expands on a theme which is found in embryo in the apocalyptic discourse of Jesus.

There are a few interesting parallels between the christology of Revelation and the Epistle to the Hebrews. The most striking is the view of God as a consuming fire (Heb 12:29) in a letter which sets out so clearly the mediatorial work of Christ.[33] Both aspects are seen in Revelation, although the severer side may appear to be the most dominant. We may also observe that Hebrews mentions the New Jerusalem which forms the climax of the book of Revelation (cf. Hebrews 12). It is noteworthy that in Hebrews much is made of the effectiveness of the "blood of Christ," a theme that runs through Revelation. Moreover, the picture of the victorious Christ in Rev 19:11ff. links the title "Word of God" with the idea of a sharp sword coming from the conqueror's mouth, a parallel to the description of the Word of God in Heb 4:12. There is also the suggestion of the antagonistic work of Satan as the adversary in Heb 2:14, 15 and of his overthrow by Christ, which may be seen as a commentary on the book of Revelation. It may also be claimed that the christological presentation in Hebrews 1 is fully in line with the exalted christology of Revelation.

One or two interesting parallels may be noted between the Petrine epistles and the book of Revelation. In 1 Peter the theme of redemption is linked with the Shepherd figure (cf. 1 Pet 1:18; 2:28; 5:2) in a way similar to the christology of Revelation. The light versus darkness theme so prominent in Revelation finds an echo in 1 Peter (2:9). The destruction of the heavens and the earth which forms the climax of Revelation is predicted in 2 Pet 3:10.

## 5. Conclusion

It may reasonably be claimed that the christology of Revelation belongs to the mainstream of early christological thought, although it is expressed in highly individualistic terms. It does not appear to be the end product of a long series of development.[34] It is the presentation of a visionary, but he has not created

32. Cf. the several cross-references to the book of Revelation in G. R. Beasley-Murray, *A Commentary on Mark Thirteen* (London: Macmillan, 1957).

33. As F. F. Bruce, *The Epistle to the Hebrews,* NICNT (Grand Rapids, Michigan: Wm. B. Eerdmans, 1964) 385, points out, "Reverence and awe before His holiness are not incompatible with grateful trust and love in response to His mercy." Both awe and mercy are featured in the book of Revelation. The author of Hebrews does not hesitate to draw attention to the awesomeness of divine wrath (cf. H. W. Montefiore, *A Commentary on the Epistle to the Hebrews,* HNTC 14 [New York: Harper & Row, 1964] 237).

34. V. Taylor, *The Atonement in New Testament Teaching,* 2d ed. (London: Epworth, 1945) 34ff., took the view that the teaching of the Apocalypse should be included in the primitive period. He shows the close connection between christology and atonement in this book.

a Christ of his own making. The early Christians may have had some difficulties with this book, but there is no evidence that there were any hesitations about its christology. It was viewed therefore as belonging to the diverse body of literature which set out what early Christians believed.

Some of the modern difficulties occasioned by this book have been the result of the adoption of a realized eschatology which has called into question any futuristic views.[35] Nevertheless a christology which finds no place for a future consummation is defective in an important area, for it is essential that some notion of Christ's part in the winding up of history should be included in an adequate christology. Far from being "a dumb prophecy," then, Revelation may be claimed to be the capstone of NT christology, leaving us with a glorious vision of a New Jerusalem in which the person of Christ will be supreme.

35. Caird, *Revelation*, 298, rightly points out that John distinguishes two types of eschatology — the promise for the individual and the promise for the vindication of God's people. The concluding promise in this book, "I am coming soon," makes no sense apart from a future coming of Christ. This is wholly in harmony with the similar promise in John 14:3, 18, 28.

# III. New Testament Christology: Wider Issues

# The Spirit of Christ and "Divine" Christology

Max Turner

## 1. Introduction

The origins of "divine" christology — where and in what terms it is to be found in the NT, and how it is to be explained — remain a center of NT studies, as the lively and provocative studies by *(inter alios)* Dunn,[1] Hurtado,[2] Casey,[3] and Barker[4] clearly attest. This article seeks to explore further a potentially relevant area of the debate that has been curiously overlooked: the contribution to christology made by the NT church's understanding of Jesus' relationship to the gift of the Spirit poured out on believers. In an earlier study of Peter's Pentecost speech I suggested that in Acts 2:33, as elsewhere in the NT, we find evidence that the exalted Jesus is regarded as standing in that sort of relationship to the Spirit of God that in Judaism and early Christianity normally characterizes *God's own* relationship to the Spirit; that is, the Spirit mediates the person and actions of the exalted Lord, thereby making the risen Christ a saving, empowering, and directing "presence" for the disciples on earth, and the Spirit of God has thus become "the Spirit of Christ" too.[5] Where such a view was held, I suggested, it was bound almost inevitably to entail a strong type of "divine" christology. The study thus raised the possibility of explaining the development of a major and virile form of divine christology fundamentally in terms of the early church's *experience* of God's Spirit. The term " 'divine' Chris-

1. J. D. G. Dunn, *Christology in the Making* (London: SCM, 1980); *idem, The Partings of the Ways* (London: SCM, 1991) esp. chs. 9–12. I am grateful to Professor Dunn for critical comments on an earlier draft of this essay.

2. L. Hurtado, *One God, One Lord* (London: SCM, 1988).

3. M. Casey, *From Jewish Prophet to Gentile God: The Origins and Development of New Testament Christology* (Cambridge: Clarke, 1991).

4. M. Barker, *The Great Angel: A Study of Israel's Second God* (London: SPCK, 1992).

5. M. M. B. Turner, "The Spirit of Christ and Christology," in *Christ the Lord: Studies in Christology Presented to Donald Guthrie*, ed. H. H. Rowdon (Leicester: Inter-Varsity, 1982) 168-90.

tology" is of course itself ambiguous, and could connote anything from the divine agency of *any* messianic figure to a full trinitarian christology. Here I shall use it in a restricted sense to mean a christology which appears to push the unity between Jesus and the Father beyond anything Judaism could envisage of any (mere) creature, *however exalted*, and thus potentially even to breach exclusive monotheism as Judaism understood it.

We may briefly summarize the main arguments of the former article relevant to our present task (page numbers refer to the above article):

(1) According to the pre-Lukan tradition of Acts 2:33, the exalted Jesus "received" the promise of Joel 2:28-32 (= Acts 2:17-21) in the sense that "he now has the power to administer the operation of the Spirit as the Spirit of prophecy" (180).
(2) From Luke's perspective this means Jesus has somehow achieved that "lordship" in respect of the gift of the Spirit (in the church) which Joel predicates of *God* (cf. 2:36, 38-39); the Spirit of God (as "the Spirit of prophecy")[6] has become "the Spirit of Jesus" (Acts 16:7), and *Jesus* (with God) is now seen as directing, gifting, and empowering the church through visions, prophecy, and charismatic wisdom afforded by the Spirit (180-81).
(3) The perceived activities of Jesus through the Spirit and the inferred relationship of Jesus to the Spirit are unparalleled by anything said in Judaism with respect to the Spirit and the Messiah (or the Spirit and any exalted being other than God himself). The Messiah of the Spirit may be inspired and empowered by the Spirit, but (despite claims made) is in no analogous sense "lord" of the gift of the Spirit (181-83).
(4) As the claim made in Acts 2:33 is made in the context of a Judaism for which the Spirit is not a second heavenly being, but a way of speaking of *God's own* "vitality," "life," or "self-expression," of God *himself* in action or of the extension of his personality, to speak of Jesus as (somehow) "lord" of the Spirit, or of the Spirit as (e.g.) "the Spirit of Jesus / Christ" (or as Jesus' "executive power"), is tantamount to making a divine claim for Jesus (183).
(5) Jesus' sharing with the Father in the work of the Spirit in the disciples "finds its most luminous expression in the Paraclete discourses of the Fourth Gospel which announce the coming of the Son and the Father to live in the disciple (14:23), and to direct him in the truth (16:13) through the gift of the Spirit given jointly by the Father and the Son (14:26; 15:26; 16:7)" (187). But it is also found in the Johannine circle in the Apocalypse:

6. For the scope of charismata of this gift, see R. P. Menzies, *The Development of Early Christian Pneumatology with Special Reference to Luke-Acts*, JSNTSS 54 (Sheffield: JSOT, 1991) chs. 1–11; M. M. B. Turner, "The Spirit of Prophecy and the Power of Authoritative Preaching in Luke-Acts: A Question of Origins," *NTS* 38 (1992) 66-88; *idem*, "The Spirit and the Power of Jesus' Miracles in the Lucan Conception," *NovT* 33 (1991) 124-52.

"Jesus has 'the seven spirits of God sent out into all the earth' (5:6) and he gives his word (e.g., 2:1) to the churches through the Spirit of prophecy (e.g., 2:7a; cf. 19:10)."

(6) Paul's pneumatology is similar. He regards the Spirit as "an ambassador acting on behalf of both God and Christ, and thus as the power of Christ exercising his lordship in the church" (188). In the light of this, such expressions as "the Spirit of Christ" (Rom 8:9), "the Spirit of his Son" (Gal 4:6), and "the Spirit of Jesus Christ" (Phil 1:19) should be understood after the analogy of the expressions "the Spirit of God" or "the Spirit of the Lord," "and were used to express the belief that the Spirit acted on behalf of God and of Christ, and under the sovereignty of both" (188).

(7) This claim on behalf of Jesus is grounded in (a) the general "Jesus" character of the experience of the Spirit; (b) Jesus' own teaching (John 14–16; Luke 21:15), (c) the conviction that Jesus was continuing his "ministry" through the Spirit, and (d) the experience of charismata in which the risen Lord appeared or seemed to speak to the church (from Acts 7:55; 9:3-6, 9-16 and *passim,* through to Rev 1:1 and *passim*).

It is surprising that this potentially fruitful avenue of approach to the development of divine christology remains substantially unresearched, when others receive such detailed attention.[7] For example, while nearly all works on the development of christology recognize that the Fourth Gospel has departed from Jewish exclusive monotheism in the direction of a Christian inclusive (trinitarian) monotheism, this is explained almost entirely in terms of John's incarnational Logos / Wisdom doctrine, while the christological consequences of the motif of Jesus' exalted role with respect to the Spirit are largely overlooked. Logos / Wisdom christology may dominate the first half of John, but the motif of Jesus as giver of life through the Spirit gradually builds up from 1:33; 4:10, 14; 6:63; and 7:37-39 to a major contribution in John 14–16, and a climax in 20:22 where Jesus insufflates with the Holy Spirit of new creation (cf. Gen 2:7: LXX ἐνεφύσησεν), preparing for Thomas's confession, "My Lord and my God" (20:28). This surely raises the question as to whether John's high christology is fundamentally to be explained in terms of his Logos christology, or whether it is not the Johannine church's experience of Christ as the wisdom revealed by the Spirit, and of the Spirit as the ongoing presence of Christ (and of the Father), that gave the fundamental impetus to John's particular development of incarnational Logos christology.

We find a similar bypassing of the question in various works seeking to explain the development of christology more broadly. On the one hand, L. Hur-

7. G. Fee (in this volume, 318, n. 29) observes that the christological import of speaking of the Spirit of God as the Spirit of Christ is seldom spelled out. Cf. A. J. Hultgren, *Christ and His Benefits* (Philadelphia: Fortress, 1987): "The experience of the disciples' being encountered by the Spirit and the Spirit's working in and among them is a neglected factor in the search for origins" (32).

tado's excellent monograph shows that while intertestamental Judaism's exalted "chief agent" figures prepared in some ways for the Christian descriptions of Jesus at God's right hand, Christians attributed to the risen Jesus an unparalleled degree of participation in the divine glory, including *worship*[8] — thus breaking with Jewish exclusive monotheism. When he seeks to *explain* what motivated this binitarian christology, he attributes it ultimately to visionary experiences such as Stephen's (Acts 7:55), or, more precisely, such as that in Revelation 5, where Jesus shares the divine throne and receives heavenly worship, with the Father's approbation.[9] But these visionary experiences, while significant, can barely have been so commonplace as (alone) to trigger the christological development Hurtado (correctly) describes, and it is unlikely that such "justification" would have been unopposed unless it had a much broader base. Hurtado might have provided a more convincing account had he explored the significance of the visions along with the more widespread and varied claims to experience Christ as God's saving presence in the Spirit. But he failed to examine the latter.

On the other hand, Hultgren's monograph on christology asserts that of the four hard historical facts we know about Jesus, one is that the disciples experienced him after the crucifixion "in majestic power and glory" and another is that "they believed themselves to be endowed by the Spirit sent from God and *mediated to them by the risen Christ* (Acts 2:33; John 20:22 . . .)."[10] These two are enough (Hultgren insists) to explain a redemptive understanding of the cross and resurrection. However, and despite his own lament that the Christo-soteriological significance of this experience of the Spirit has not yet adequately been researched,[11] in the final analysis Hultgren himself fails to press the question of christological consequences beyond the assurance that (for the NT writers) the risen Christ continues to be active in salvation.

More remarkable perhaps is Casey's sidestepping of the issue:

> With Jesus at the right hand of God, Acts 2.33 holds him in some sense responsible for the events of Pentecost. This is a very elevated function, though we should not regard it as evidence of deity. We have seen abundant evidence that messianic and intermediary figures took on functions which were previously those of God, and this did not make them divine. This verse occurs in a context where God himself is the overall author of the event. The main importance of this development is that it attributes a perceptible event on earth to the work of Jesus in heaven, thereby validating the community's belief in his exaltation.[12]

8. Dunn, *Partings*, 203-6, argues Hurtado has overemphasized this; his own corrective goes too far in the reverse direction.

9. Hurtado, *God*, 118-21.

10. Hultgren, *Benefits*, 32 (our italics).

11. See above, n. 7.

12. *Prophet*, 107.

Casey assumes, without examination, that if some divine prerogatives may be delegated or shared with other beings, *all* must (at least potentially) be — though as he himself draws some kind of line on the right to receive worship, one might have expected him to consider more carefully whether there were not other exclusively divine prerogatives, and whether the kind of relationship between Jesus and the Spirit implicit in holding Jesus "in some sense responsible for the events of Pentecost" was not among them.

While many have touched on our subject, especially from the different perspective of systematic theology, or the narrower one of Pauline theology,[13] the only writer who has so far given extensive, detailed, and cautious consideration to the relevant issues of Christian origins is J. D. G. Dunn. Since Dunn offers an alternative (sometimes qualifying, sometimes opposed) view to our own, the rest of this essay will develop the argument largely by critical interaction with his work.

## 2. Professor Dunn's Understanding of the Relation of the Spirit to the Exalted Christ in the New Testament Church

Dunn's elucidation of this issue is made in periodic contributions spanning some twenty years, and provided in the context of quite different debates.[14] It should not be surprising that his emphases shift with time and context,[15] even

13. For brief accounts and bibliography see G. Fee's essay in this volume, and cf. M. M. B. Turner, "The Significance of Spirit Endowment for Paul," *VE* 9 (1975) 56-59 (though I would express myself rather differently at a number of points now, and should certainly have clarified that important aspects of the position traced back to Deissmann [on p. 61] were anticipated by Gunkel).

14. J. D. G. Dunn's main contributions on the subject (in chronological order of publication) are:

(1) *Baptism in the Holy Spirit* (London: SCM, 1970);
(2) "Rediscovering the Spirit," in *ExpTim* 84 (1972-73) 7-12, 40-44;
(3) "Jesus — Flesh and Spirit: An Exposition of Romans I:3-4," *JTS* 24 (1973) 40-68;
(4) "1 Corinthians 15.45 — Last Adam, Life-giving Spirit," in *Christ and Spirit in the New Testament*, ed. B. Lindars and S. S. Smalley (Cambridge: Cambridge University, 1973) 127-42;
(5) *Jesus and the Spirit* (London: SCM, 1975);
(6) *Christology* (1980);
(7) "Rediscovering the Spirit (2)," in *ExpTim* 94 (1982-83) 9-18; and
(8) *Partings* (1992) chs. 9–11.

15. Occasionally the shifts are conscious revisions of earlier positions, e.g., the move away from the Spirit-christology of his earlier writing (for which see, e.g., "Rediscovering," 12; "Jesus," where he concludes, "The 'deity' of the earthly Jesus is a function of the Spirit, is, in fact, no more and no less than the Holy Spirit" [58]; and *Jesus,* 325, where he sums up, "the dynamic of the relationship between Spirit and Jesus can be expressed epigrammatically thus: *as the Spirit was the 'divinity' of Jesus . . . , so Jesus became the personality of the Spirit*" [Dunn's italics]) to a specific repudiation of this in, e.g., "Rediscovering (2)," 14-16 (summarizing positions argued mainly in his *Christology*). Other shifts emerge more gradually and apparently less consciously. Thus while

if this unfortunately makes "Dunn's 'position'" a little more difficult to describe. But we may begin by summarizing where he agrees, and where he disagrees, with the conclusions of our 1982 article summarized above.

There are significant points of (at least partial) agreement: Dunn essentially accepts that Luke and John portray Jesus as in some way "lord" of the Spirit (arguments 1, 2, and 5), though he tends to limit this to authority to *bestow* the Spirit.[16] Concerning such authority he concedes (in a section on "exaltation to divine functions"), "the most striking function of the exalted Christ might seem to be his power to bestow the Holy Spirit upon others."[17] *But,* Dunn remains unsure whether this moves in the direction of a "divine" christology (in the sense mooted above, and our argument 4), suggesting (a) that Jesus' prerogative may find analogy in the transfer of other divine functions to exalted figures in intertestamental Judaism, (b) that Judaism and John the Baptist anticipated a Messiah bestowing the Spirit (but would not have thought of him *ipso facto* as "divine" in any sense that transcended the categories of creaturely agency), and (c) that *Christians* too can be thought of as "bestowing" the Spirit (cf., e.g., Acts 8:17-20).

More significantly, Dunn argues that even the qualified "lordship" of the Spirit envisaged by, for example, Acts 2:33 cannot confidently be traced earlier than the late witness of Luke-Acts and John. It is not found in the earlier (and more central?) Paul, or held by believers before him; thus, "where Luke and John seem happy to attribute the gift of the Spirit equally to God and to the exalted Christ, Paul thinks only to attribute it to God."[18] Similarly, "For Paul it would not be true to say that the exalted Christ was Lord of the Spirit; by his

---

*Baptism,* 23-27, argues (against Pentecostals) that Jesus' Jordan experience of the Spirit was *primarily* that of (prototypical) Sonship and entry to new covenant / new age relationship to the Father (and only *secondarily* empowering), and while Jesus' experience of eschatological sonship by the Spirit is still a notable emphasis in *Jesus,* 15-39, 62-67, there is latterly a much fuller recognition of the Spirit as the inspiration and empowering of Jesus as eschatological *prophet* (cf. "Rediscovering [2]," 15). Indeed, the section in his *Christology* on "Jesus the man of the Spirit" (136-41) rather surprisingly has virtually no mention of "sonship" by the Spirit (*contrast* his comments on Rom 8:15-16 and Gal 4:6 [esp. 26-27, 145]), and concludes rather that (as with Jesus himself, and the Jerusalem kerygma) *"the Evangelists also understood the relation between Jesus and the Spirit in terms primarily of one inspired and empowered, a prophet like Moses"* (140; Dunn's italics). This is the position we earlier argued *against* Dunn (cf. M. M. B. Turner, "Jesus and the Spirit in Lukan Perspective," *TynB* 32 [1981] 3-42).

16. Cf. *Christology,* 142, where he claims of Luke and John "their testimony is clear: *by virtue of his resurrection and exaltation Jesus the man of the Spirit became Lord of the Spirit*; . . . or more precisely, by his resurrection he began to share in God's prerogative as the giver of the Spirit" (142, Dunn's italics).

17. *Partings,* 187.

18. *Christology,* 143 (all in italics; compare also "Rediscovering [2]," 16). Dunn qualifies the contrast between Luke and John on the one side, and Paul on the other, by noting that it would be more accurate of the former pair to say the Spirit is given by the Father *through* the Son (Acts 1:5 [divine passive]; 2:33; John 15:26) (*Christology,* 147-48 [cf. 142]).

resurrection he did not gain the authority of the one God to dispense the Spirit to men."[19] Rather,

> Paul seems to think of the Spirit as in some sense determined by Christ — not in the sense that Christ himself has taken control of the Spirit . . . , but in the sense rather that the Spirit has been shaped and characterized by its relationship to Jesus, both the earthly Jesus . . . and the exalted Christ (particularly Rom. 8.29; I Cor. 15.49).[20]

We shall need, later, to inquire more precisely what this means, and how Dunn justifies it; here it suffices to say that he offers as a principal analogy for such expressions as "the Spirit of Christ" (in Paul, Acts [16:7] and 1 Pet 1:11) Jewish usage "where the Spirit of God could be linked with a particular example of one inspired" (e.g., "the spirit . . . of Elijah").[21] In sum, in earliest Christianity and Paul the Spirit is not so much under Jesus' lordship, as stamped with his personality; and since this does not break the mold of Jewish analogies it does not entail a full divine christology.

In the two main sections which follow we shall examine Dunn's case, that the kind of "lordship" of the Spirit envisaged in Luke-Acts and John does not necessarily imply a transcendent "divine" christology, and that Paul makes a "lesser" claim than "lordship" of the Spirit.

## 3. Does "Lordship" of the Spirit Not Imply a Divine Christology?

Casey and Dunn ask the perfectly legitimate question whether the claim made, for example, in Acts 2:33; John 14–16 is not comprehensible within the kind of exclusive Jewish monotheism which portrays exalted figures sharing in divine functions. In reply we must make four points.

(1) Despite Dunn's claim, no convincing parallel has yet emerged to justify the claim that Judaism expected a Messiah who *bestows* the Spirit (whether individually or corporately).[22] Both Dunn[23] and Webb[24] have recently contended that at the very least John the Baptist's promise of one who will "baptize with Holy Spirit-and-fire" points in such a direction. But the Baptist's promise is better understood within the framework of the strong *traditional* expectation

19. *Christology,* 146. Note again the effective restriction of "lordship" of the Spirit to power to bestow the Spirit.

20. *Christology,* 145.

21. *Partings,* 201.

22. Against Dunn's appeal (based on 1QIsa 52:15 conflated with 1QS 4:21; CD 2:12 and *T. Judah* 23.4) in "Spirit-and-fire Baptism," *NovT* 14 (1972) 89-91, see Turner, "Spirit of Christ," 181-83.

23. *Partings,* 187.

24. R. L. Webb, *John the Baptizer and Prophet,* JSNTSS 62 (Sheffield: JSOT, 1991) 289-95.

of a messianic figure powerfully fulfilling Isa 11:1-4 (and 9:2-7 — as in *1 Enoch* 49:2-3; 62:1-2; *Pss. Sol.* 17:37; 18:7; 1QSb 5:24-25; 4QpIsa 3:15-29; etc.). The expectation of the arrival of such a figure to rule, with his decisively authoritative Spirit-imbued command, burning righteousness, and dramatic acts of power, effecting both judgment and salvation, *would itself* be sufficient to explain the metaphor of his unleashing a deluge of Spirit-and-fire on Israel (compare, e.g., *Tg. Neb.* Isa 4:4, where the "Spirit of judgment" and "Spirit of fire" become the Messiah's powerful command of judgment and of extirpation respectively,[25] and compare also the anticipation of a stream of flame and fiery *breath* from the Messiah in 4 Ezra 13:8-11). In short, the tenor of the metaphor is the historical impact of a Spirit-anointed Messiah, not the bestowal of a gift of the Spirit *by* a Messiah.[26]

(2) Dunn suggests that bestowal of the Spirit by *Christians* (in, e.g., Acts 8:17-20; cf. 19:6) undermines the claim that Jesus' lordship of the Spirit (understood as power to bestow the gift) is necessarily an exclusively divine prerogative.[27] This seems an unhelpful comparison. In the case of Peter and John in Samaria it is simply a matter of prayerful human incorporative invocation of the Spirit (cf. 8:15, at least partially misunderstood by Simon as "power to bestow"), with no ongoing relationship between the apostles and the Spirit imparted to the Samaritans. Even if Simon's perception were correct, and the act was essentially like a tactile transfer of *mana,* the nature of the bestowal of the Spirit by Jesus in Acts 2:33 remains qualitatively entirely different. Jesus' gift of the "Spirit of prophecy" is what enables his *ongoing* relationship and communication with his disciples.[28] This leads to our next point.

(3) The limitation of the discussion of "lordship" of the Spirit *to power to bestow* the Spirit is an unjustified (and possibly unintentional) restriction that focuses on a significant, but by no means the most important, aspect of the presentation in Luke and John. Strictly speaking, *God alone* is described as "giving" the Spirit in Luke-Acts (cf. Luke 11:13; Acts 5:32; 15:8), and Jesus only sends / commissions / pours out the Spirit *as* the gift of the Father (Luke 24:48; Acts 2:33). It is not so much his power to *bestow* the gift that constitutes Jesus' "lordship" over the Spirit (if that is appropriate language), as the relationship he *sustains* to the gift bestowed. Jesus acts and reveals *through* the Spirit — that is, *he becomes the author of charismata afforded by the Spirit;* not least in Acts 2:33, where what is said to be poured out by Jesus is not simply the gift of the Spirit, but more precisely the prophetic charismatic *activities* that the audience

25. I am indebted for this observation to Menzies, *Development,* 138-81.

26. Cf. M. M. B. Turner, "Holy Spirit," in *Dictionary of Jesus and the Gospels,* ed. J. B. Green and S. McKnight (Leicester: Inter-Varsity, 1992) 341-51, esp. 342, 344.

27. *Partings,* 187.

28. For "the Spirit of prophecy" as the organ of communication in Judaism and early and Lukan Christianity see G. J. Haya-Prats, *L'Esprit Force de l'Église* (Paris: Cerf, 1975), and esp. the works cited in n. 6 above.

has seen and heard. But the picture is certainly not confined to Acts 2:33; thus, for example, Luke carefully conflates the wording of the assurance of the Holy Spirit's help in time of trial (Luke 12:12) with that of the promise that the risen Lord will give wisdom that none can withstand (Luke 21:15) in his redactional portrayal of Stephen in Acts 6:10.

Similarly, dreams and visions (programmatically traced to the Spirit in Acts 2:17) now regularly have the character of christophanies in which Jesus is seen acting on behalf of the disciple (7:55 [reemphasizing the Spirit as the "means" of such phenomena]), instructing the disciple (9:10-17; cf. 16:6-7), or bringing encouragement and protection (18:10). This last, with its promise ἐγώ εἰμι μετὰ σοῦ, was formerly seen as something of a breach of Luke's (alleged) more typical "absentee christology," but more recently R. O'Toole, and others, have made a convincing case that it is precisely texts such as Acts 18:10 (with, e.g., Luke 21:15; Acts 9:5, 34; etc.) that most truly represents Luke's christology, which is one of soteriological omnipresence.[29] For Luke, the ascension-exaltation gives Jesus the promised eternal throne of David from which he actively rules in the affairs of "the house of Jacob" (Luke 1:32-34; 22:42-43; Acts 2:25-36), and one of the chief (if not the exclusive) means of his presence and activity is through the Spirit he pours out (Acts 2:33; 16:7). Similarly, but in more developed fashion, for John, the Paraclete sent / commissioned by Jesus (15:26; 16:7; cf. 4:10, 13-14; 7:38-39; 20:22) from the Father (15:26; cf. 14:26) brings not only charismatic wisdom which interprets the Christ-event to the believer (14:26 [cf. 2:22]; 16:12-14), and leads the disciple deeper into its truth (16:13), but he also (a) brings the words of the risen Lord (16:13-14), and (b) becomes the means of Jesus' ongoing self-manifestation to the disciples (and through them to the world), and of the promised indwelling of the Father and the Son in the disciple (the *inclusio* of 14:15-17 and 25-26 providing the explanation of the otherwise riddling promises in 14:19b, 21b, 23).[30] If for Luke-Acts and John the Spirit acts on behalf of Jesus, and brings his activity and presence into and through the disciples' lives, then the picture of the Spirit's relation to the exalted Jesus corresponds very closely indeed to the way in which the Spirit relates to God in the OT and Judaism. We clarify this in the next point.

29. R. F. O'Toole, *The Unity of Luke's Theology,* GNS (Wilmington: Glazier, 1984) esp. chs. 2–3. Douglas Buckwalter, one of Professor Marshall's research students, has argued that the evidence on which it is normally claimed that Jesus is "absent" in heaven (e.g., he is only glimpsed from earth in visions, and occasionally "present" to his disciples by *substitutes* such as his "name" or δύναμις) well matches biblical descriptions of *God,* and is actually part of Luke's tendency to portray Jesus as multifariously *omnipresent* (so "The Character and Purpose of Luke's Christology" [Ph.D. diss., University of Aberdeen, 1991] 211-31).

30. For fuller justification see briefly Turner, "Holy Spirit," 349-50; *idem,* "The Significance of Receiving the Spirit in John's Gospel," *VE* 10 (1977) 24-42 (esp. 26-28); but esp. R. E. Brown, "The Paraclete in the Fourth Gospel," *NTS* 13 (1966-67) 113-32; G. M. Burge, *The Anointed Community: The Holy Spirit in the Johannine Community* (Grand Rapids, Michigan: Wm. B. Eerdmans, 1987) 137-47.

(4) In Judaism the Spirit is related to Yahweh in a way that makes such "lordship" of the Spirit by a (mere) creature virtually inconceivable. That is, in the Judaism out of which Christianity sprang, the Spirit is so integrally an aspect of God's being, "life," surging rational power or activity — like the "breath" of his mouth (Job 33:4; 34:14; Ps 33:6; Wis 11:20) — that any attempt to speak of "lordship" over God's Spirit would almost inevitably sound like a (preposterous) claim to "lordship" over God himself. Whereas there is some evidence that intertestamental Judaism hypostatized Wisdom and Logos, this never convincingly happens with the Spirit. God's "Spirit" is virtually always synecdoche for God himself, and is usually a way of speaking of God's *presence* while preserving his transcendence (from Isa 63:10 and Ps 143:10 through to Josephus [*Ant.* 8.114] and the rabbis [*Exod. Rab.* 1:22; *Num. Rab.* 20:19; *Deut. Rab.* 6:14; *Ruth Rab.* Proem 7]). While targumic language can seem at first glance to distance the Spirit from God (in, e.g., the common expression "the Spirit of prophecy from before [קדם] the Lord" [*Tg. Onq.* Gen 41:38; *Tg. Neb.* Judg 3:10 and frequently thereafter]) or "a / the Spirit of power from before the Lord" (*Tg. Neb.* Judg 6:34; 11:29; 13:25; 14:6; 1 Sam 11:6; 16:13-14])[31] and the rabbis occasionally indulge in dramatic literary personification of the Spirit (most strikingly in *Pes. Rab.* 3:4, where God rebukes the tarrying Spirit, "Must Joseph long remain in grief? Foot it speedily, and enter into Jacob that he might bless them," and then sums up the affair, "I [the Lord] forced the holy spirit to foot it back [to Jacob], so that he could bless Ephraim"; cf. *Gen. Rab.* 97; *Lev. Rab.* 6:1; *Deut. Rab.* 3:11), these (as is widely acknowledged) are merely linguistic and literary devices. One might also suspect distancing when, for example, *Jubilees* and Qumran turn God's Spirit (of Ezek 36:26-27) into "a holy spirit" (*Jub.* 1:20-25; 1QS 4:20-23),[32] and when Wis 1:7 almost appears to confuse πνεῦμα as Stoic immanent substance with more traditional Jewish concepts of Spirit (1:5; 7:7; 9:17; 12:1; 15:11),[33] but in no such cases is either hypostatization of the Spirit (on the one hand) or systematic reduction of God's Spirit to a mediating fluid substance or power (on the other hand) a plausible explanation. This last assertion would require at least another paper to justify adequately, but we need not press the issue here, for Dunn's own provisional survey is in *substantial agreement.*[34] So we may press the *significance:* we suggest that the

31. But "'from before' the Lord" here still means "of the Lord"; cf. M. L. Klein, "The Preposition קדם (Before): A Pseudo-Anthropomorphism in the Targums," *JTS* 30 (1979) 502-7.

32. See A. E. Sekki, *The Meaning of RUAḤ* at Qumran (Atlanta: Scholars, 1989) ch. 8.

33. Dunn, *Christology,* 130 (cf. 135), speaks of Spirit being identified with Wisdom at 1:4-5, 7; 9:17. Against Dunn (and Menzies, *Development,* 49-50), the last merely expresses in a parallelism the general Jewish view that the Spirit, as the Spirit of prophecy, affords charismatic wisdom. There is no formal identification at all. See Turner, "The Spirit of Prophecy," 84 n. 36. Wisdom 1:4-5 is as readily explained by analogy with Philo's view of the prophetic Spirit as divine rational power, or, as in 1:5, ἅγιον . . . πνεῦμα παιδείας merely qualifies Wisdom as *a* (holy) spirit.

34. *Christology,* 129-36.

irony of Isa 40:13-14 would be equally transparent to Jews of the first century and later (cf. *2 Apoc. Bar.* 75:3-4), "Who has understood the Spirit of the LORD, or instructed him as his counsellor? Whom did the LORD consult to enlighten him? . . . " The LORD and his "Spirit" are one, and no (mere) person (nor any other exalted creature attested) can instruct or commission God's Spirit.

Against assertions by Dunn and Casey that Jesus' "lordship" of the Spirit is not unique, but analogous to the transfer of other divine prerogatives to chief agents, we are inclined to respond that the prerogatives in question are not strictly comparable. There is little problem with conceiving how God's theophanic "glory" may be *shared* by beings he creates (especially those in closest relationship to him in the heavens); similarly there is no conceptual problem with the *delegation* (in part or whole) of divine tasks such as judgment (as with Abel in *Testament of Abraham* 13, etc.) — and the same applies to participation in God's *rule* by a chief agent in communion or conference with God (for which Israel's kingship and some of its messianic expectations offered analogies enough).[35] There is not even a fundamental problem with the conception of Wisdom and Logos participating in creation (given that they receive their authority and power from or in God). But, we submit, there most probably *would* have been a problem in speaking of any created being (however awesome) coming into the sort of controlling position we have described above with respect to God's very "inner life," his Spirit (even if only in operations *ad externam*). It is thus not surprising that while Judaism may envisage an exalted figure mounting the very throne of God (Moses, in Ezekiel the Tragedian, *Exagōgē* 68–80, albeit there only in a dream the interpretation of which [85] applies to his earthly "rule" among Israel on behalf of God), *there is simply NO analogy for an exalted human* (or any other creature) *becoming so integrated with God that such a person may be said to "commission" God's Spirit, and through that to extend that exalted person's own "presence" and activity to people on earth.* For the Jew, such relationship to, and activity in or through, the Spirit appears to be necessarily, inalienably, and so distinctively, *God's.*

We conclude that arguments (1)-(5) of our original argument largely stand, despite the attempted qualifications offered by Dunn. When Luke and John present the Spirit as mediating not merely the Father, but *the risen Lord too,* they have broken the mold of Jewish analogies. In maintaining that (in some sense) Jesus has become "lord" of the Spirit (which Dunn accepts) their assertions appear necessarily to move beyond Jewish exclusive monotheism, and to take the first steps towards an *inclusive* monotheism. Indeed, if Jesus' "lordship" of the Spirit in the sphere of salvation promotes the conclusion that Jesus must somehow be fully one with God, that same experience of lordship would also press in the direction of a trinitarian understanding of the Spirit (for it

35. For the relation between divine eschatological rule and messianic rule, see G. R. Beasley-Murray, *Jesus and the Kingdom of God* (Exeter: Paternoster, 1986) chs. 1–8 (esp. ch. 8), and his essay in this volume (22-36).

otherwise led either to the blasphemous assertion of the Son's "lordship" over the Father, or to demotion of the Spirit to a nondivine mediating power — neither of which pertains).

## 4. Does Paul Not Consider That Jesus Became "Lord" of the Spirit?

Dunn's most detailed discussion of Paul's understanding of the relation of the exalted Christ to the Spirit came in his articles on Rom 1:3-4 and 1 Cor 15:45 (1973). In both he says (implicitly and explicitly) that for Paul Jesus became Lord of the Spirit. His more recent works have merely abbreviated, clarified, and revised the emphases and specific conclusions of these pioneering articles, but from his (1980) *Christology* onward he denies this "lordship" of the Spirit to Paul. This shift, the significance of which we must explore, is not the result of offering new exegetical evidence, but of increasing emphasis on *aspects* of his former description, refocused by his growing conviction that earliest Christianity only very slowly came to breach exclusive monotheism.

Dunn's argument on Rom 1:3-4 is complex and far-reaching. In the first two parts[36] Dunn attempts to establish that:

> It is entirely probable . . . that the κατὰ σάρκα / κατὰ πνεῦμα antithesis of Rom. i.3f. not only describes two distinct and successive phases in the life of Jesus separated by the resurrection, but refers also to the pre-resurrection life of Jesus as a life lived both according to the flesh and according to the Spirit. In so far as Jesus lived on the level of the flesh, was bound and determined by the weakness and inadequacy of the human condition, allowed worldly considerations to determine his conduct, he was merely Son of David and no more — Messiah indeed, but a disappointing, ineffective, irrelevant Messiah. . . . But in so far as Jesus lived on the level of the Spirit, refused to allow merely human considerations, fleshly suffering, or Jewish expectations to determine his course . . . he manifested that he was indeed Son of God, and thereby proved his right to be installed as Son of God with power as from the resurrection of the dead. (57)

To derive this from Rom 1:3-4 (given that Paul says *nothing* explicit in any of his epistles about the Spirit in the earthly life of Jesus) Dunn has read the (distinctively) Pauline exposition of Christian life κατὰ σάρκα / κατὰ πνεῦμα into an otherwise simple confession of Jesus' messianic sonship as the legitimate Davidid, vindicated through resurrection exaltation (largely on the basis of a lexical study of σάρξ and κατὰ σάρκα which appears to raise fundamental questions of linguistics).[37] Dunn subsequently builds from this (in

36. "Jesus — Flesh and Spirit," 40-57.
37. Dunn attacks the interpretation offered by E. Schweizer, "Röm. 1,3f, und der Gegensatz

the third part of his article), protecting himself against the possible misunderstanding that Jesus thereby merely becomes the first to possess the Spirit in a distinctively Christian way by insisting that (for Paul) Jesus was uniquely "full of the Spirit" in his earthly ministry, and that, as a consequence, through resurrection exaltation, he "impressed his character and personality on the Spirit" (59). The Spirit thereafter inspires the believers' confession of Jesus' lordship (1 Cor 12:3) and reproduces Jesus' character in them (2 Cor 3:18). This leads Dunn to acknowledge that Rom 1:4 asserts something like Jesus' "lordship" of the Spirit:

> Jesus from being a man under the direction of the Spirit, Son of God κατὰ πνεῦμα, becomes by virtue of his resurrection Son of God in full power of his sonship, that is, in full power of the Spirit. . . . in Paul's view whereas the earthly Jesus was ruled by the power of the Spirit, *now the Spirit becomes the executive power of the exalted Christ.* (58-59; our italics)

---

von Fleisch und Geist vor und bei Paulus," *EvT* 15 (1955) 563-71. Schweizer argued that in Rom 1:3-4 the flesh / Spirit antithesis cannot signify its normal Pauline pejorative ethical contrast, but (neutrally) designates the realm of humanity, over against the heavenly world of Spirit. Dunn replies that κατὰ σάρκα must always have a pejorative sense or "bad connotation" (44) because (over against W. D. Davies who argued that we must distinguish, e.g., σάρξ[1] = "physical flesh" from σάρξ[6] = "human nature (moral)" [superscripted numbers refer to senses defined in the *Greek-English Lexicon of the New Testament,* 2 vols., ed. J. P. Louw and E. A. Nida (New York: UBS, 1988)]), σάρξ does not have a set of discrete senses, but "a spectrum of meaning, and individual uses are often less like a point in the spectrum and more like a range of meanings within the spectrum" (44). This enables Dunn to interpret the sense of σάρξ at 1:3 in the light of other contexts where undoubtedly it frequently carries negative connotations, and leads to his wildly improbable attempt to see the reference to Jesus' Davidic claim κατὰ σάρκα as deprecatory (44-49). He then further insists that the κατὰ σάρκα / κατὰ πνεῦμα antithesis must always signal the superiority of the latter, not neutrality (which Schweizer would barely deny) and concludes Rom 1:3-4 should be read in accordance with the usual Pauline soteriologically antithetical sense. But since he cannot allow a Jesus experiencing "flesh" (in *malam partem*) alone (1:3) he rereads 1:3-4 to speak of *overlapping* period of flesh and Spirit (50-59). The whole eisegesis appears substantially to be built on unacceptable linguistics. By all the canons of modern lexical semantics Davies was absolutely *right,* and Dunn's coalescing of senses fundamentally wrong: lexemes usually have several distinct (point) senses, some of which may be related (polysemy), others of which may not (homonymy). Each distinguishable sense is more closely related in meaning to other quite *different* words in the same semantic domain than to the other meanings of the "same" word: i.e., σάρξ[1] = "physical flesh" is more closely related to words like σπλάγχνα (intestines), αἷμα (blood), and ἁφή (ligament) than it is to σάρξ[3] = "human beings" (belonging to the same domain as words like ἄνθρωπος[1], ἀνήρ[2], etc.) or to σάρξ[5] = "nation" (in a domain with words like γένος[2], φυλή[1], συγγενής[1], etc.) or to σάρξ[6] = "human nature" (in which the trait "sinful" may or may not be present, and belonging to the domain of psychological faculties with ψυχή[1], νοῦς[1], πνεῦμα[5], etc.). The different senses do *not* "leak" across the domains into each other, though there is commonly a shared *component*(s) of meaning (but this is not "weakness," "independence," or "sinfulness" in the case of σάρξ); see F. P. Cotterell and M. M. B. Turner, *Linguistics and Biblical Interpretation* (London: SPCK, 1990) chs. 4–5. The sense of κατὰ σάρκα in 1:3 is probably the neutral "by human descent" or "in the human sphere," and, since it does not qualify the same event or state as the κατὰ πνεῦμα of 1:4 (contrast all other Pauline uses), *the two phrases are not strictly antithetical* at all.

Later in the same article he specifically affirms that (for the NT writers, including Paul) through his resurrection "Jesus took over the Spirit . . . and *became Lord of the Spirit*" (69; our italics).

But we need to recognize that these italicized statements, so significant for our inquiry, do not represent the heart of Dunn's understanding of the relationship between Jesus and the Spirit in Paul. The real center is Dunn's fusion of what he understands as the *prototypical aspect* of Jesus' relation to the Spirit (i.e., the earthly Jesus' experience of eschatological sonship by the Spirit; this enhanced through destruction of the [competing] "flesh" and consequent resurrection) with the *unique aspect,* namely, that in and through his obedience, death, and, most specifically, resurrection, the Spirit receives the stamp of Jesus' character. It is this line of thought which leads to his epigram, "if the Spirit [in the ministry] gave Jesus his power, Jesus gave the Spirit his personality" (59). Here the emphasis is not on Jesus exercising some kind of lordship over the Spirit but on a transformation *of the Spirit* wrought by all that led up to (and included) the resurrection-exaltation. Implied is that such expressions as "the Spirit of Christ," "the Spirit of his Son," etc. should be taken to mean, not (as it would be understood in Luke and John) the Spirit who proceeds from the risen Christ, and thereby brings Christ's transforming word, presence, and activity (as he does God's), but the Spirit whose own character has been stamped by the whole Christ-event in the transforming experience of the resurrection,[38] and now impresses that same character on the believer.

It should be clear this latter emphasis is capable of being spelled out in a virtually unitarian sense, which makes the post-resurrection Christ all but irrelevant for the continuing work of the Spirit. Jesus can be the "definition of the Spirit," and the Spirit can have the character of Christ and be recognized as the power transforming into Christ's eschatological image — all ways Dunn typically defines the Spirit of Christ[39] — because *God* (not Christ himself), *as Spirit,* is active in the lives of believers *in the same way* that he was "concretely exhibited in Christ."[40] And such an understanding of "the Spirit of Christ" would indeed make the analogy of "the Spirit of Elijah" especially appropriate. It will also be evident, however, that it is precisely the statements about Jesus' lordship of the Spirit which most clearly prevent such an understanding, along with the various kinds of identification of Christ and Spirit which threaten to

38. Cf. *Jesus,* 447 (n. 117), where Dunn explains Paul's alleged unwillingness to say that Jesus was (prototypically) resurrected *by* the Spirit on the grounds that "it was precisely *in and by the resurrection* that the relationship between Jesus and the Spirit was reversed — instead of 'Jesus and the Spirit' we have 'the Spirit of Jesus'."

39. *Jesus,* 319-21; *Christology,* 144-46.

40. This mirrors G. W. H. Lampe's definition of the Christ-Spirit (*God as Spirit* [Oxford: Clarendon, 1977] 114), though the italics are ours. Dunn directly compares it with his own position (*Christology,* 320 n. 78). The most important attempt at a Spirit Christology since Lampe's is that of P. W. Newman, *A Spirit Christology* (London: University Press of America, 1987).

collapse christology into pneumatology.[41] It is only if Jesus' active "lordship" of the Spirit is disclaimed, and if the risen Christ is formally identified with the Spirit, that "the Spirit of Christ" is in danger of being understood merely as the Christified Spirit or as Lampe's Christ-Spirit.

What, then, are we to make of Dunn's own repeated claim (on the basis of 1 Cor 15:45) that Paul did indeed identify the Spirit and the risen Lord? In his 1973 article, Dunn gives the detailed exegesis of the verse and immediate context which provides the basis for his claim, and elucidates its significance. Essentially he argues that Paul provides his answer to gnostic skepticism about the resurrection body (1) by distinguishing σῶμα as "neutral" from σάρξ and ψυχή (which gnostics would be inclined to regard as inimical to spiritual life), (2) from his argument (15:35-44) that different types of existence have different and appropriate σώματα, (3) by his application of this to the case of Adam and Christ who stand at the head of different creation orders (hence the parallel formulation based on Gen 2:7 in 1 Cor 15:45), and (4) by his careful identification of Christ with the Holy Spirit in 15:45b (ὁ ἔσχατος Ἀδὰμ εἰς πνεῦμα ζῳοποιοῦν) designed to underscore the prototypical / representative character of Jesus' resurrection — that is, with respect to this formulation the Corinthians are expected to recognize:

(a) (from 15:45b taken with v 44) that Jesus is a σῶμα πνευματικόν;
(b) (from the wording πνεῦμα ζῳοποιοῦν) that the Last Adam / Jesus is experienced as the Holy Spirit who gives them new creation "life";
(c) (from their experience of (b)) that the Spirit is stamped by the pattern of the Christ-event, and recapitulates Jesus' life in them; that is, the Spirit makes Jesus' sonship prototypical for them; so
(d) (as conclusion) that Jesus' existence as σῶμα πνευματικόν is prototypical too, and yet to be accomplished in them by the same πνεῦμα ζῳοποιοῦν.

When Dunn explains the crucial "identification" of Christ as life-giving Spirit he insists it is not ontological (he had earlier argued against such a conclusion drawn by I. Hermann's work on 2 Cor 3:17),[42] but "functional" —

41. H. Berkhof, *The Doctrine of the Holy Spirit* (London: Epworth, 1964) 13-26, comes close to such a collapse (though a mirror image of Lampe's) before eventually insisting that he nevertheless believes that "the risen Lord transcends his own functioning as life-giving Spirit" (28), and finally defining the Spirit (in Barth's words) as "the presence and action of Jesus Christ Himself" and (in his own) as "the risen Christ, reaching out to the *totum,* to conform us to his image" (29). These latter statements effectively make Christ "Lord of the Spirit" (in the sense we understand that term).

42. Against I. Hermann, *Kyrios und Pneuma: Studien zur Christologie der paulinischen Hauptbriefe* (Munich: Kösel, 1961) esp. 132-36, see J. D. G. Dunn, "II Corinthians 3.17 — 'The Lord Is the Spirit'," *JTS* 21 (1970) 309-20, arguing that "the Lord" here denotes Yahweh of Exodus 34, not Christ (similarly C. F. D. Moule, "2 Corinthians 3:18b, καθάπερ ἀπὸ κυρίου πνεύματος," in *Neues Testament und Geschichte,* ed. H. von Baltensweiler and B. Reicke [Tübingen: J. C. B.

that is, while Paul believes Christ himself sustains a relationship to God that is not expressed in terms of Spirit (e.g., 1 Cor 15:24-28), and so has a theology Dunn describes as incipiently trinitarian,[43] 1 Cor 15:45b implies that at least "in the *believer's experience* there is no distinction between Christ and the Spirit."[44] It is the Jesus content, and character of the experience of the Spirit, that once again provides the basis for the identification.[45] As in his study on Rom 1:3-4, this actually leads him to make statements which amount to Jesus' "lordship" of and through the Spirit, thus:

> Such experiences they could only attribute to *the risen Jesus acting upon them through the Spirit;* there was a spiritual power moving in them which they could describe equally well as 'Christ in me' or 'the Spirit in me', or, most striking of all, as 'the Spirit of Christ' (Rom. 8:9), 'the Spirit of his Son' (Gal. 4:6), 'the Spirit of Jesus Christ' (Phil. 1:19). . . . It was this Jesus-relatedness, this Jesus content in their spiritual experience which constituted proof for the early believers that it was *the exalted Jesus who was acting upon them* — Jesus had become πνεῦμα ζῳοποιοῦν. (134; our italics)

In other words, while in both early articles Dunn explains the relationship of Spirit to the exalted Christ largely in terms of the Jesus-character and Jesus-content of the believer's experience, he still at this stage plainly understands the consequent Christ-mysticism as an *ongoing* action of the risen Christ effected *through* the Spirit, and within such a framework Christ's relationship to the Spirit mirrors that of God's (as in Luke and John).

How should we evaluate this contribution? As a general comment on Paul's pneumatology we might broadly agree with the statement quoted above. But we must doubt whether it can be securely based in 1 Cor 15:45. Dunn's exegesis of that verse seems to us as implausible as it is ingenious; far too subtle and compact for the Corinthians to follow, and demanding too many presuppositional concessions of them.[46] Least probable is the central affirmation that πνεῦμα ζῳοποιοῦν "can only refer to the early believers' experience of new life [by the Spirit]" (132), which Dunn justifies by affirming that had Paul meant a reference to Christ's own mode of being as "a spirit" (in contrast to Adam, "a (living) soul"; 15:45a) he would have written πνεῦμα ζῶν (not ζῳοποιοῦν, which one would more naturally refer to the Spirit, as in John 6:63; 2 Cor 3:6

---

Mohr (Paul Siebeck), 1972] 231-37); also W. Thüsing in K. Rahner and W. Thüsing, *A New Christology* (New York: Seabury, 1980) 183-89.

43. See esp. *Christology,* 146-49; "Rediscovering (2)," 16-17; *Partings,* 202-3. Dunn thus rejects Lampe's unitarianism, which dispenses with the "post-existent" Christ.

44. "1 Corinthians 15.45," 139 (our italics). He immediately adds, "this does not mean . . . that Paul makes no distinction between Christ and Spirit."

45. "1 Corinthians 15.45," 138-41; cf. "Rediscovering (2)," 16.

46. See our earlier critique ("Significance of Spirit Endowment," 61-63), and the similar one by G. Fee in this volume (312-31).

[132]).[47] In fact, ζῳοποιέω has no special collocational relationship to "the Spirit"; *God* and *Jesus* are equally ζῳοποιοῦν in John 5:21; God is at Rom 4:17; 8:11 (as is the Christ of, e.g., Phil 3:21, though ζῳοποιέω is not the term used), and, most important, both the contrast with Adam here, and the use of the adjective ζῳοποιοῦν, take up the contrast in 1 Cor 15:22: ἐν τῷ Ἀδὰμ πάντες ἀποθνῄσκουσιν . . . ἐν τῷ Χριστῷ πάντες ζῳοποιηθήσονται. Given this cotext, and the immediate parallel of v 45b with v 45a ('Εγένετο ὁ πρῶτος ἄνθρωπος Ἀδὰμ εἰς ψυχὴν ζῶσαν), the Corinthians would be bound to interpret the πνεῦμα of v 45b as a statement about Christ's own mode of being, not about the Christ-character *the Spirit* has taken on (to signal which the definite article at very least would be required, if not the epexegetic addition of τὸ πνεῦμα τὸ ἅγιον). In addition, Dunn's case that the identification of Christ and Spirit is only "functional" (not ontological) requires that the verse be read from the believer's perspective, whereas it is in fact written from the perspective of an omniscient narrator contrasting the beginnings of two creation orders in their respective representatives.

We are forced to conclude that the appeal (made regularly from Gunkel to Dunn) for some form of identification of Christ and Holy Spirit based in 1 Cor 15:45 is at best insecure. And if it cannot be found here, it cannot really be found anywhere else. While Paul most certainly believes that "Christ" is experienced through the Spirit, no text reduces this to an identification of Christ and Spirit (not 2 Cor 3:17 [as Moule and Dunn have shown],[48] nor 1 Cor 6:17, nor Rom 8:9-11).[49]

In our discussion of his 1973 articles we have seen that Dunn was at that stage willing to explain the "Christ" character of the Spirit ultimately in terms of the exalted Jesus' "lordship" with respect to the Spirit. But, as we have noted, from 1980 onward he rejects that (for Paul) Christ "has taken control of the Spirit" or that (with God) Christ exercises some kind of "lordship" over the Spirit. While Luke and John may have believed such, "in Paul, Christ is Lord, but never explicitly in relation to the Spirit";[50] for him rather the Spirit of Christ is the Spirit shaped and characterized by Jesus. We must now assess the significance of this shift.

Given the explicit contrast just mentioned, the most natural way to read this denial of Jesus' lordship in respect of the Spirit would at first appear to be that Dunn no longer thinks Paul considered the exalted Christ personally to

47. Cf. Dunn's assertion, "Paul identifies the exalted Jesus with the Spirit — not with a spiritual being (πνεῦμα ζῶν) or a spiritual dimension or sphere (πνευματικόν), but with the Spirit, the Holy Spirit (πνεῦμα ζῳοποιοῦν)" (139).

48. See n. 42 above.

49. Cf. Turner, "Significance of Spirit Endowment," 64; and Fee, in this volume (323-26), who rightly points out that Rom 8:9-11 equates "the Spirit of God" and "the Spirit of Christ"; not "Christ" and "the Spirit."

50. *Christology,* 143. Perhaps, but he is never explicitly this in Luke or John either.

undertake activities through God's Spirit, and that he has largely retreated to the view that Jesus merely provided a pattern of eschatological sonship which God incorporates into and repeats through the Spirit. One could then explain the functional equation between Christ and Spirit to mean that (for Paul) the believer encounters "Christ" *only* in the sense that he encounters the Spirit shaped by the Christ event, the Spirit who "has himself taken on the character of Christ."[51] On such an understanding the "Christ" character of the Spirit is the product not of union with the postexistent Christ himself (encountered *through* the Spirit), but the new character imparted *to* the Spirit (by God?) through the Christ event, and specifically at the resurrection. A number of features of Dunn's later works point in the direction of this interpretation. Thus, from 1975 onward there are no clear references to the Spirit as the exalted Christ's executive power (or the like); by contrast, if, in his *Christology,* he still maintains that the "Spirit of Christ" denotes "the Spirit of the exalted, living Christ," nothing suggests that he necessarily means more by this than that "the Spirit as the life-giver is . . . determined by the character of Christ's *resurrection.*"[52] And Dunn regularly speaks of, for example, the character of the Spirit taking "its shape from the impress of Jesus' own [earthly] relationship to God,"[53] or of the Spirit taking on the character or personality of Christ. The strong assertion that 1 Cor 15:45 offers an identification between Christ and Spirit that should be read in *both* directions,[54] and the increasing emphasis on the analogy between "the Spirit of Christ" and such expressions as "the Spirit of Elijah" would also support such a reading. Ultimately this would give us a pneumatology similar in important respects to Lampe's (even if with a very different christology).

However, not only has Dunn assured me that this is not what he intended,[55] but there are strong reasons for disbelieving this simple (and so potentially attractive) reading of Paul — considerations which *at the same time* suggest that we should resist any attempt to deny Jesus' "lordship" of the Spirit to Paul.

(1) Any suggestion that Christ gives the impress of his character to the Spirit through the Christ event, but is otherwise inactive with respect to the Spirit, would

51. *Jesus,* 322.

52. *Christology,* 146 (our italics). Similarly, in the passage from *Christology,* 145, quoted above (419, above), the only shape the *exalted* Jesus gives to the Spirit (to judge by the references to Rom 8:29 and 1 Cor 15:49) is precisely as the prototype of our resurrection.

53. *Jesus,* 320.

54. *Jesus,* 322-23.

55. In commenting on the first draft of this essay Dunn indicated that he had not intentionally retracted his view that the Spirit was the executive power of the exalted Christ, and that he still understood 1 Cor 15:45 to imply roughly that. This means that his position is closer to that of Berkhof (while rejecting Berkhof's dependence on I. Hermann's exegesis). In this case we must press the urgent question: What then does it *mean* to deny Jesus' lordship of the Spirit to Paul?

not conform to the evidence. By Dunn's own admission, the risen Lord is indicated as the source of the διαιρέσεις διακονιῶν of 1 Cor 12:4 (alongside God, and the Spirit, as in different senses sources of the same spiritual gifts under the complementary descriptions ἐνεργήματα and χαρίσματα),[56] a view reemphasized by Eph 4:7-16. Moreover, the Christ who rules at God's right hand (Psalm 110; 1 Cor 15:20-28) continues (with the Father) to be a source of spiritual χάρις and "peace" in the church according to most Pauline letter introductions (Rom 1:7; 1 Cor 1:3; 2 Cor 1:2; Gal 1:3; Eph 1:2; Phil 1:2; 2 Thess 1:2) and occasional benedictions (2 Cor 13:14; 1 Thess 5:28), and it is difficult to believe that his "grace" (cf. 2 Cor 12:8-10) is mediated in any other way than through the Spirit who imparts the Father's. By the same token, when Paul says "may the Lord make you increase and abound in love for one another" immediately after his prayer that "our God . . . and our Lord Jesus direct our way to you" (1 Thess 3:11-12), he thereby identifies Jesus as the "lord" active in the guidance and spiritual growth of Christians, and this in turn implies that he sees Jesus as participating fully in the Father's lordship of the Spirit. Again, we observe that while Paul is adamant that our future resurrection is accomplished by the Spirit of God (Rom 8:9-11; 1 Corinthians 15; etc.), Phil 3:21 can speak of it as an act of *Jesus,* who will transform us "by the power which enables him to subject all things to himself." It would be perilous here to argue that because Paul does not *explicitly* state that this is the Spirit (why should he?), he was *theologically reticent* to do so, or that he had in mind some means of present and resurrection power *other* than the Spirit. But if the Spirit is this power, then Jesus is surely in a very real sense "lord" of the Spirit.

(2) We may allow that the genitives in such phrases as "the Spirit of (Jesus) Christ" deliberately imply a certain "Christ" character and content to the operation of the Spirit envisaged (certainly at Gal 4:6; Rom 8:9-11), but the readiest explanation of this is not the reductionist one, that the Spirit has become identified with Christ, or that the Spirit has undergone some fundamental transformation through the resurrection, becoming stamped by the Christ event, receiving his personality from Jesus, and so emerging as "the Spirit of Christ." Indeed, all such formulations would prove inherently problematic. For Paul the Spirit was and remains the Spirit *of God,* and, as such, was and shall ever be the extension of *his* personality (cf. his love in Rom 5:5; his fatherhood in Rom 8:14 [where our "sonship" is evidenced precisely in willing submission to πνεῦμα θεοῦ]; his self-revelation in 1 Cor 2:10-12; his presence in 1 Cor 3:18; etc.). However much Christ has been displayed at the center of God's redemptive purpose, Paul does not narrow the Spirit down to "the Spirit of Christ" so that every experience of Spirit is exclusively of Jesus[57] (as though a vision like

56. *Jesus,* 324; reaffirmed in *Christology,* 145; and cf. the affirmation, "the experience of new life and of charismatic endowment can be referred equally to God, the Spirit, and the exalted Christ" (146).

57. *Contra* Dunn, *Jesus,* 322.

Ezekiel's or that of Revelation 4 is now theologically precluded). The Spirit has not suffered some metamorphosis, some fundamental change of character *from* Spirit of God *to* Spirit of Christ. Rather, the way Paul subtly changes the theological focus within the Spirit material suggests that he thinks of the Spirit's mediation as at times focusing the Father and his activity, usually accentuating the-Father-with / through-the-Son, but at other times expressing the Son's prototypical significance, lordship, or activity. This dynamic interchange of focus more readily suggests that Paul thinks of the Father and the exalted Christ as dynamically sharing in lordship through the Spirit, than that, for example, the Spirit has been "stamped with" the character of Christ, or completely "functionally identified" with Christ at resurrection. Indeed, the "Spirit of Christ" sayings in Rom 8:9-11 and Phil 1:19 are as well, if not better, explained on such an understanding. The latter surely means not merely that Paul hopes for support (in his suffering) from a Holy Spirit who is now understood to impress on him the character of Christ and of the Christ-event; important as such an idea is in the context, Paul's thought goes beyond that. It is fellowship (*through* the Spirit) with Christ himself who suffered (not merely union with the Christified Spirit), and the support of him who now has the power to sustain all things, and transform him into his own likeness at resurrection (3:21), that assures Paul of his σωτηρία.[58] We might extend the comment to cover the whole "Christ mysticism" in Paul, with its lively sense of unity with the risen Lord, and of the same Lord himself addressing the believer (e.g., 2 Cor 12:8-9), and promoting the quality of life in his people that he himself had lived out (e.g., 1 Thess 3:12). An explanation in terms of a substitution for Christ by a Christ-stamped Spirit would hardly be convincing; the more natural explanation is that *the Spirit is now also thought to act as the dynamic extension of the risen Christ's personality, and activity, as formerly he had been thought to act as God's.* In other words, we can entirely agree with Dunn's affirmations that for Paul the Spirit "is the medium for Christ in his relation to men" and that Christ can be experienced now only in and through the Spirit,[59] and even with his qualification "indeed only *as* Spirit,"[60] providing the latter is not restricted to mean "in the Spirit once-for-all stamped with Christ through the Christ-event" and intended to exclude "by the Spirit proceeding from, and mediating the ruling activities of, the exalted Christ." *But this latter surely means that Jesus shares in the Father's "lordship" through the Spirit.* The same applies in Rom 1:4, where Dunn in 1973 was undoubtedly right to see that it was precisely the Spirit acting as Christ's *executive power* that could attest he had been appointed "Son-of-God-with-

58. This interpretation would be necessary, not merely more probable, if the σωτηρία in question were deliverance from prison (as advocated by G. Hawthorne, *Philippians,* WBC 43 [Waco, Texas: Word, 1983] 40).

59. Unless by the sort of heavenly ascent hinted at in 2 Cor 12:2-4.

60. *Christology,* 146; cf. *Partings,* 202.

power" since the resurrection. A mere christification of the Spirit (as in Lampe's analysis) would clearly not necessarily attest such an appointment. But, once again, what can it mean to deny Jesus' "lordship" of the Spirit if one still maintains that the Spirit is Jesus' "executive power" — that is, that Jesus is the *subject* of the wide range of saving actions and blessings performed in the Spirit?

(3) Dunn himself clearly avoids Lampe's own understanding of "the Spirit of Christ" (which dispenses with the exalted Lord, and explains the phrase in unitarian terms, namely that God, who through the Spirit wrought the special obedience and sonship of the paradigm Jesus, now continues to work the same way in believers) by speaking of a unique transformation at the resurrection, by which *Jesus gave the Spirit his personality.* Paul, of course, neither explicitly says, nor really suggests, quite such a thing; it is Dunn's creative way of "explaining" how we pass from Jesus inspired by the Spirit to "the Spirit of (Jesus) Christ." But we need to ask how a Jew could possibly entertain such an explanation, and what it would mean. In fact, phrases of the form "Spirit of X" (where X stands for a name other than God's, and the reference is nevertheless to the divine Spirit) are rare in Judaism. As far as I know, the only uses are "the Spirit of Elijah" (*Tg. Ps.-J.* 2 Kgs 2:9-10, simply following MT), meaning the gift of the Spirit of prophecy in the same strength and power as was on Elijah, the "Spirit of Moses" (Philo *Gig.* 24, 26 and *Num. Rab.* 13:20), meaning the gift of the Spirit of prophecy God had given Moses and was sharing with the seventy elders, and "the Spirit of the Messiah" (*Gen. Rab.* 2:4), apparently meaning the Spirit with which the Messiah of Isa 11:2 will eventually be anointed. In none of these cases does "the Spirit of X" mean "Spirit with the personality of X," far less that the named person impresses his character on the Spirit transferred to others. At most such examples would support a purely unitarian explanation of "the Spirit of Christ"; namely, as a gift of prophetic-messianic inspiration like that experienced *by* Jesus. *Were* a Jew to come up with the new concept that an exalted being, B, "gave his or her personality" to the Spirit (or "became the definition of the Spirit"), and if that Jew meant that *B* so acted (not simply that God, as Spirit, began to act in others as he had acted in B's case, and so to conform others to B), then I do not see that this person could mean much less than that B became in some way "lord" of the Spirit — and (as a corollary) that B must somehow be "God" (in a way that breached exclusive monotheism). For how could such a claim to "define" the Spirit *differ* from one to the exercise of some kind of lordship of the Spirit? And what kind of being, other than God, could be expected to effect such transformation in God's Spirit?

But we do not need Dunn's difficult explanation of "the Spirit of Christ" when a simpler lies close to hand. The *only* parallels we have for "Spirit of N," meaning Spirit extending the personality N, are precisely references to the Spirit *"of God"* or *"of the Lord,"* and this makes it more likely that "the Spirit of Jesus Christ" means the Spirit who mediates the presence, character, redemptive activities, and rule of Jesus Christ, in a way analogous to that in which he mediates God's.

We conclude that while there are certainly distinctives to Paul's elucidation of the relation of the Spirit to the exalted Jesus — including a much clearer focus on the Spirit as impressing Jesus' eschatological sonship on the believer — he is essentially in agreement with Luke-Acts and John in presenting Jesus as in some fundamental sense "lord" of the Spirit. That is, like those writers, Paul believes that the Spirit relates the presence and actions of the exalted Christ to the believer in ways that immediately evoke the analogy of the Spirit's extension of *God's* person and activity to humankind. It is difficult to see how such a claim would stop short of some form of "divine" christology. Finally, we may suggest that our reading of Paul's pneumatology fits better the *development* of pneumatology from the earliest period through to the later writings; this is the subject of the next section.

## 5. How Early May We Trace Claims to Jesus' "Lordship" of the Spirit?

Space permits but the sketchiest remarks. We have noted that by 1980 Dunn had come to the opinion that the earliest we find such claims is in post-Pauline formulations of Luke-Acts and John.[61] With respect to Acts 2:33 he states that we cannot be certain it is derived from early tradition,[62] and that while early Christians probably cherished Pentecost (and other outpourings of the Spirit) as the fulfillment of the Baptist's promise, nevertheless, "whether they thought of Jesus as the baptizer in the Spirit is put in doubt by the 'divine passive' form of Acts 1:5 and 11:16."[63] Dunn is right that the oral tradition of the Baptist's promise was probably remembered from the earliest stages at least partly because believers considered it to have been fulfilled among them. But if these Christians thought of Pentecost as the fulfillment of the Baptist's prediction (the earliest form of which we find in the Q tradition; Luke 3:16 par.), then they would *inevitably* have thought Jesus was the "baptizer in Spirit," except in the unlikely event they referred the "Coming One" to someone *other* than Jesus. That the promise referred to a messianic figure rather than to God himself is convincing,[64] and early *Christians* were not liable to find an alternative to Jesus. As for the references to the promise in Acts 1:5 and 11:16, they are evidently

61. In *Partings* he plays down even these (see 187), and explains phrases of the type "the Spirit of Christ" uniformly in terms of Jesus having become the definition of the Spirit, the Spirit of God manifesting the character of Jesus (201) — apparently including even Acts 16:7 and 1 Pet 1:11, for both of which such explanation is unwarranted.

62. *Christology*, 143.

63. *Christology*, 143.

64. See Webb, *John*, 282-89.

*ad hoc* (quite possibly Lukan) adaptations, and the passives follow naturally the required change of topicalization signaled by the fronting of ὑμεῖς δέ; they are not necessarily semantically "*divine* passives" at all. What christological significance would follow from the claim that Jesus fulfilled the Baptist's prediction is unclear, however, since we do not know how they conceived Jesus to relate to the gift of the Spirit with which he "baptized" them (it need not require that he was considered to be at the source of its charismata).

Acts 2:33 is more pertinent. Of course, "certainty" as to its origins (as on so many issues) is elusive, but traits of the Pentecost speech suggest that it is pre-Lukan.[65] More important, however, is the real plausibility of the Acts 2 account, with the Spirit in the church presented very much in terms of Jewish expectation of the Spirit of prophecy, not the distinctively Christian "Spirit of Sonship" which Dunn reads back through his interpretation of Rom 1:3-4. The latter notion, a characteristically *Pauline* emphasis, *must have been built on something like the former.* That is, it can only have been as the Spirit of prophecy was experienced mediating and elucidating Jesus and his benefits, and bringing his direction to the church, and as the impact of all this on individuals and the shaping of the church was gradually perceived, that a meta-explanation like "the Spirit has become the Spirit of sonship" could emerge. But the very charismata that eventually provided the basis for such an understanding would much more rapidly, indeed (in instances of, e.g., words from the risen Lord) *intuitively,* evoke the conclusion that Jesus was (with the Father) *their source.* So even if one (unwarrantably) discounts Luke 12:11-12 par.; 21:15; 24:49; John 14–16; and Acts 2:14-38 as entirely baseless tradition, it nevertheless seems virtually inevitable that the experience of Jesus through the church's charismata would quickly have led to the *kind* of theology embodied there (indeed John 14–16 is transparently a christologically focused version of the Jewish Spirit of prophecy).[66] And in such development, the claim that Jesus shares with God in the execution of Joel's promise (the claim of Acts 2:33) would have been a very obvious preliminary deduction. We have argued that Paul, too, regards Jesus as sharing in God's lordship of and through the Spirit (and that his more distinctive pneumatology can be explained as a theologizing of the Jewish concept of Spirit of prophecy in the light of its ecclesiological impact is especially inviting in, e.g., 1 Corinthians 12).

How soon this led to well-formulated *christological* conclusions is also uncertain. Acts 2:33-36, 38-39 suggest that Jesus' share in God's "Lordship" through the Spirit was an immediately perceived corollary. Those who consider the Pentecost speech more Lukan (or traditional) than genuinely Petrine will be inclined to put the step later. But whatever one's critical stance with respect

65. Dunn mentions only Zehnle's conclusions, but contrast Turner, "Spirit of Christ," 184-86.

66. See Turner, "Holy Spirit," 347-51.

to Acts 2, it must be said that the step from recognition of Jesus (with the Father) as the source of charismata to some sort of recognition of his share in God's divine lordship would have been a short one — precisely because Judaism made the Spirit so exclusively God's *own* "influence," not merely an Agent who might act on behalf of other exalted beings too (or a substance God merely used). In favor of the view that Acts 2:33-36, 38-39 represents a very traditional position is the fact that the ancient confession of Jesus as "Lord of all" (Acts 10:36; Rom 10:12), and the equally ancient tradition of calling on the name of the Lord Jesus (Acts 2:38; etc.), are precisely grounded together in Joel 2:28-32 (LXX 3:1-5), as is clear not only in Acts 2 but also in the (pre-Pauline) formulation in Rom 10:12.[67]

The argument of this essay is that the understanding of Jesus as sharing in God's lordship of the Spirit — that is, of the Spirit extending the presence and activities of the risen Lord to disciples in and through diverse charismata — can be traced to the earliest forms of Christianity we may claim to know anything about, and that this understanding was liable to provide a decisive impulse toward "'divine' Christology" and to open up the way to the worship of Jesus with the Father as the One God. To what extent this was left as an implicit christology, and how it interacted with more explicit formulations, deserves further study.

67. See J. Dupont, "'Le Seigneur de tous" (Ac 10.36; Rm 10.12)," in *Tradition and Interpretation in the New Testament,* ed. G. F. Hawthorne and O. Betz (Tübingen: J. C. B. Mohr [Paul Siebeck], 1987) 229-36.

# The Making of Christology — Evolution or Unfolding?

James D. G. Dunn

There is no question that we have to speak of the development of christology in the earliest decades of Christianity. At the beginning of that period and within the area where Christianity began there was no thought of a messiah figure being crucified, raised from dead, and designated θεός. Less than one hundred years later such claims were being made regarding Jesus (particularly in John 20:28), and indeed already being taken for granted (at least in Ign., *Eph.* inscr; 1:1; 7:2; 15:3; 18:2; 19:3; etc.).1 Clearly something was being said at the end of the period which had never been said before. In that sense at least we must speak of development of ideas and usage.

But that conclusion simply opens up the more important question: What do we mean by "development?" Do we mean the outworking of what was always there in principle or *in nuce* — the organic development of the seed into the plant, of the acorn into the oak? The fuller christology of the late first century and early second century (and beyond) could then be said to be simply the recognition of what had always been true of Jesus and only awaited the eye of faith to see with increasing clarity. Just as the rabbinic (oral) tradition could be defined by the rabbis as the "Torah received by Moses at Sinai" and handed down through Joshua, elders, and prophets to the great assembly (*m. 'Abot* 1.1), so the developed christological formulations of later centuries could be traced back to Jesus and the apostles. This in effect has been the classic view of christological development, defended in more extensive principle by Newman,[2] and in recent NT scholarship by Moule.[3] The claim by Hengel that "more happened" in christology in the first two decades of Christianity "than in the

1. Further details in W. R. Schoedel, *Ignatius of Antioch,* Hermeneia (Philadelphia: Fortress, 1985) 39.

2. J. H. Newman, *An Essay on the Development of Christian Doctrine* (first published 1845).

3. C. F. D. Moule, *The Origin of Christology* (Cambridge: Cambridge University, 1977).

whole of the next seven centuries,"[4] amounts to the same thing.[5] And the present volume's dedicatee follows a similar line in *The Origins of New Testament Christology:* "Behind the development there stands the figure of Jesus and the claim, indirect or direct, which he made for himself"; "the divinity of Jesus . . . emerged as the inescapable corollary of Jesus' position."[6] For want of a better label I put this perspective under one of Newman's terms, "unfolding."

The alternative view is that earliest christology developed by accretion, that is, in crude terms, by adding on new ideas and claims which were not implicit in or native to the earliest response to Jesus. This can be characterized more carefully as the model of "evolution" — that is, development by inner change, from one species to another, where there is, of course, continuity between what went before and what develops out of it, but where changing environment makes it necessary for the organism to adapt and thus to evolve into something different. This in effect was the classic rationalist response to traditional christology. It naturally found a definitive precedent in the emergence of a clear model for "evolution" in the work of Darwin and was variously espoused in the Liberal Protestantism of Harnack and the *religionsgeschichtlich* approach of Bousset and Bultmann.[7] However, reaction to the particular theses of the latter in the intervening decades of NT scholarship has tended to cloud the hypothesis of evolutionary development and to detract from its credibility. And it is only in the last few years that it has gained a new champion and a fresh, sophisticated version.

I refer to the revised version of M. Casey's Cadbury Lectures delivered at the University of Birmingham in 1985 and now published under the title *From Jewish Prophet to Gentile God: The Origins and Development of New Testament Christology.*[8] The issues it raises are so important that I propose to devote the rest of this essay to discussion of Casey's thesis.

4. M. Hengel, *The Son of God* (London: SCM, 1976).

5. See, e.g., Hengel, *Son of God,* 71: "There was an inner necessity about the introduction of the idea of pre-existence into christology."

6. I. H. Marshall, *The Origins of New Testament Christology* (Leicester: Inter-Varsity, 1976) 128-29. Other recent monographs which focus largely on the initial impact of Jesus and his resurrection include P. Pokorny, *The Genesis of Christology* (Edinburgh: T. & T. Clark, 1987); and M. de Jonge, *Christology in Context: The Earliest Christian Response to Jesus* (Philadelphia: Westminster, 1988).

7. A. Harnack, *What is Christianity?* (first published 1900); W. Bousset, *Kyrios Christos: A History of the Belief in Christ from the Beginnings of Christianity to Irenaeus* (1913; [2]1921; ET, Nashville: Abingdon, 1970); R. Bultmann, *Theology of the New Testament,* vol. 1 (London: SCM, 1952) §15.

8. P. M. Casey, *From Jewish Prophet to Gentile God: The Origins and Development of New Testament Christology* (Cambridge: James Clarke; Louisville: Westminster, 1991). I am grateful to Dr Casey, my former colleague at Nottingham, for his readiness to comment on the first draft of this essay and to help remove possible misrepresentations or misunderstandings of his argument.

## 1

Casey begins by proposing a new way of analyzing the evidence, which he then uses to elaborate a new theory to explain why NT christology developed as it did. The major concept is that of *identity.* The identity of a group is "everything which is perceived[9] to make it that group and not another group" (11). What that means in practice is the recognition of a sequence of *identity factors,* whose distinctiveness either characterizes or focuses or encapsulates or together builds up to embody the group's identity. For the purposes of his study he specifies eight identity factors of Second Temple Judaism — ethnicity, Scripture, monotheism, circumcision, Sabbath observance, dietary laws, purity laws, and major festivals. He notes that it is not a simple matter of all or nothing. Ethnicity is obviously a key factor, and indeed may be an overriding factor: "People may be perceived as Jewish if it is the only one of the eight identity factors that they have, and they may be perceived as Gentile if they have all the other seven identity factors, but not ethnicity" (14). The fact that five of the eight identity factors "may reasonably be perceived as social factors which have received religious legitimation" (16) leads to the further observation that "when a religion is coterminous with an ethnic group, its identity factors are both social and religious" (17). He also maintains that "a concept of orthodoxy is necessary," with "orthodox Jews" defined as those who, in opposition to threats of assimilation, sought to ensure the observation and application of the law to the whole of life — the law thus elaborated and enacted being seen in this way to embody Jewish identity (17-19).[10]

On this base Casey's thesis can be stated in straightforward terms. As long as the earliest Christian community was Jewish in self-identity, the crucial developments in christology of affirming the deity and incarnation of Jesus could not happen. The crucial identity factor of Jewish monotheism inhibited and limited the development of christology. That limiting factor was only finally removed in the Johannine community. There the sharpness of the confrontation with "the Jews" indicates that the author had Gentile self-identification. This implies in turn that the identity factor of monotheism either was no longer such a constraining factor or was no longer operative at all. "The removal of the Jewish restraint after A.D. 70, leaving the Johannine community with Gentile self-identification, was the decisive step which ensured that Jesus was hailed as God. . ."; "this Gentile self-identification was a necessary cause of belief in the deity of Jesus, a belief which could not be held as long as the Christian community was primarily Jewish" (37-38). Here, clearly, the evolutionary hypothesis receives very strong statement. It is not simply the case

9. The use of the passive voice at this foundational point in Casey's procedure is significant. It naturally raises the question: "perceived" by whom? As we shall see, this simple question has important ramifications.

10. Note also Casey, *Jewish Prophet,* 61-64: Jesus was in conflict with "the orthodox wing of Judaism."

of a changing environment permitting a development which would have been inhibited elsewhere, but of the changed environment actually *causing* the development — a development, that is, which would not have taken place without that change from Jewish to Gentile self-identity.

## 2

We can be grateful to Casey for bringing the category of identity into play so fully. As others have recognized, the question of how individuals and groups saw themselves, and defined themselves over against others, is bound to be critical in any attempt to sketch out the history of a movement, particularly in its beginnings.[11] Moreover, within the list of identity factors selected (somewhat arbitrarily) by Casey, ethnicity was undoubtedly a crucial factor. It could indeed be said that that alone was sufficient to ensure that Christianity became something different from Judaism. That is, as more and more Gentiles joined what started as a Jewish sect, without becoming Jews (proselytes), it was inevitable that a Judaism for which ethnic Jewishness remained the fundamental identity factor would have to disown that sect. We should note nevertheless that a vital and continuing *Jewish* Christianity meant that the process was much more drawn out than is normally recognized.[12]

A more important point of critique, however, is Casey's failure to recognize the extent to which there was (and still is) a tension between ethnic and religious identity in Judaism. Ethnicity may be fundamental, but is it decisive? Orthodox and the various branches of hasidic Judaism today in Israel would certainly want to raise questions here. "Who is a Jew?" is as lively an issue as it has ever been. Are nonreligious Jews (apostates), or Gentiles who have converted to liberal Judaism, or Jews who have become Christians, really "Jews"? And, more to the immediate point, the issue was just as lively in the first century also. It is relevant here to recall that Josephus uses the name "Jews" for the exiles returning from Babylon, rather than for those who had remained in Judea throughout (*Ant.* 11.173), that he shows clear disapproval of the Samaritans calling themselves "Jews" (*Ant.* 11.340-41), and that he refrains from calling the apostate Tiberius Alexander a "Jew" (cf. *Ant.* 20.100). It is still more relevant to recall that Paul is able to dispute the definition of "Jew" (Rom 2:28-29) while both speaking of his life "within Judaism" as something belonging to the past (Gal 1:13-14) and claiming still to be an "Israelite" (Rom 11:1). In all these cases religious and ethnic identity are being held in uncomfortable tension.

11. See, e.g., E. P. Sanders et al., ed., *Jewish and Christian Self-Definition,* 3 vols. (London: SCM, 1980-82); J. Neusner and E. S. Frerichs, *"To See Ourselves as Others See Us": Christians, Jews, "Others" in Late Antiquity* (Chico: Scholars, 1985).

12. See my *The Partings of the Ways between Christianity and Judaism* (London: SCM, 1991) ch. 12.

The problem is exacerbated by introduction of the concept of "orthodoxy." For the reality of the matter is that different groups within late Second Temple Judaism regarded themselves as in effect the only truly "orthodox," the only truly loyal to the covenant and to the law. Their faithfulness to a Zadokite priesthood, their observation of (what they regarded as) the (only) correctly calculated feasts, their commitment to their own sectarian halakah (interpretation of the law), all carried the corollary in different degrees that the other sects, and probably the larger mass of Jewish people, were "unorthodox," or, in their own terms, "sinners," "impious," "ungodly." Such factionalism within Second Temple Judaism can be clearly seen not only in the writings of the Qumran Essenes, but also in such writings as *1 Enoch, Jubilees,* the *Psalms of Solomon,* and the *Testament of Moses.*[13] By using the term "orthodox" of the Pharisees (61-64) Casey is viewing the time of Jesus from a post-70 rabbinic perspective, with inevitably distorting effect.

The point is this: with such disagreement and dispute so obvious within the Jewish writings of the period, can we speak so straightforwardly of "Jewish identity"? In fact many historians of the period, not least Jewish scholars, find it necessary to speak of Second Temple Judaisms (plural) rather than simply of Judaism (singular), or indeed, if the word is appropriate for the time of Jesus, of competing orthodoxies. In other words, Casey is running the danger of postulating a too simplified and uniform concept of Jewish identity. Of course he recognizes the dangers, and tries to meet them by speaking of "an identity scale" (12). But nonetheless he does not really grapple with the problem of an identity which was itself developing (or evolving), or of identity factors disputed in what they amounted to and in their degree of relevance. Hence the earlier question: "perceived" by whom?[14] For an outsider might perceive "Judaism" to be more coherent and internally consistent than an insider.[15] On the other hand, an insider could well be more concerned with internal boundaries, and regard them as in effect more important than the external boundaries which marked out all Jews.[16] Identity markers as perceived from outside might well have different values from the way they were perceived from inside.

Here it may be significant that Casey ignores what surely must be regarded as one of the chief identity factors of Second Temple Judaism — that is, the Second Temple itself.[17] Judea was a temple state — a political entity whose

13. I may refer again simply to my *Partings,* 102-7.

14. See above, n. 9.

15. This is the implication of Mark 7:3-4, where the note added assumes that Pharisaic halakhah was followed by all Jews.

16. The most striking example of this within Second Temple Judaism are the Qumran Essenes, who regarded themselves as "the sons of light" and (apparently) all others, including all other Jews, as "the sons of darkness."

17. Contrast my *Partings,* ch. 2, where I designate the temple as one of the four pillars of Second Temple Judaism.

identity (political, social, economic, and religious) was wholly bound up with the temple. But, of course, the direct relevance of the temple as then constituted to the practice of Judaism was one of the more disputed features of Second Temple Judaism, as, once again, the Dead Sea Scrolls and such writings as the *Psalms of Solomon* attest, given also, not least, that the majority of Jews lived outside Israel and would probably have been unable to attend the temple more than once or twice in their lives. Yet the loss of the temple in 70 C.E. was not a fatal blow to Judaism; instead, it led into the greatest inner transformation of Judaism (should we say unfolding or evolution?) that Judaism recognizes — from a religious system dominated by priest and cult, to one dominated by rabbi and rabbinic interpretation of the Torah. Fully to appreciate the transformation of a Jewish sect into Christianity, one has to be able to compare these two transformations (from Second Temple Judaism to Christianity, and from Second Temple Judaism to rabbinic Judaism) with each other. Otherwise the concept of "Jewish identity" is being given artificial value and unhistorical coherence and consistency.

And if Jewish identity in the Second Temple period was that much less clear-cut, it should further warn us against a too simple juxtaposition and antithesis of "Jewish identity" with "Gentile identity." This is particularly pertinent in the case of the Fourth Gospel. Casey's whole thesis, in fact, swings on his assertion that the Fourth Evangelist "wrote as a member of a group who had Gentile self-identification" (27), and whose christology therefore breached the constraints of *Jewish* monotheism. But given the complexities and tensions already noted, the issue needs much more careful handling. It is not settled, for example, by noting that John speaks of "the Passover of the Jews" (John 2:13); the presence of even a minority of Gentiles among the recipients of the Gospel would be sufficient to explain such notes of explanation. And talk of "your / their law" when Jesus is speaking to or about "the Jews" (8:17; 10:34; 15:25) need only imply a group of Jews whose identity as Jews was closely bound up with the law (as interpreted by them).

Even the frequent references to "the Jews" do not settle the matter. The many hostile references surely indicate a breach with those so designated; but most scholars identify "the Jews" in these passages with the Jewish authorities in the area where the Johannine congregations were meeting. And it still leaves a similar range of references where "the Jews" in question are the common people, the crowd. What is interesting about them is that they stand in the middle between Jesus on the one hand and "the (hostile) Jews" (= the authorities) on the other. They are presented as a shifting, ambivalent mass, for whose loyalty Jesus and the authorities are in competition, and where the clear hope is that many of them, like Nicodemus and the blind man of John 9 (even the many "authorities" of 12:42), will take their courage in both hands and declare for Jesus. In other words, the drama being played out in the Fourth Gospel, above all in existential terms for the Johannine communities themselves, is still an intra-Jewish drama, where Jews (and Gentiles) were contesting with other Jews the common Jewish heritage and the allegiance of still uncommitted Jews.[18]

It should be said that Casey is not oblivious to this problem — the problem of identifying identity in too clear-cut terms, the problem of defining self-identity. Unfortunately, however, his allusions to the problem only help to compound it. For he speaks of "assimilating Jews" (32-34) and even of "former Jews" (33). At what point an "assimilating Jew" becomes a "former Jew" (= a Gentile?) is not clear. How can an ethnic Jew become a "former Jew"? Nor does he say anything of the blurring of boundaries from the other side, that is, in the cases of proselytes and God-fearers; or indeed of the other Jews (*minim* = heretics) rejected by the post-Yavnean sages. In other words, the concepts of "Jewish identity" and "Gentile identity" can simply not be drawn as sharply as he strives to do. And, in particular, the arguments that there was in effect a shift in identity between the earlier and other Christian (diaspora) communities and the Johannine community, and that the Johannine community had a "Gentile," that is, non-Jewish identity,[19] are altogether too casually drawn, not least when they are the hinge on which his overall argument turns. This alone would be sufficient to put a very large question mark against Casey's thesis of christological development.

## 3

Casey is also to be commended for his analysis of other messianic and intermediary figures in Second Temple Judaism (ch. 6), which provide parallels or analogies with earliest Christian evaluation of Jesus. The presence and significance of such parallels has been one of the major subjects of debate in regard to NT christology over the past twenty years. But Casey has added a potentially helpful distinction between "static parallels" and "dynamic parallels." The former indicate a category which may simply have been transferred to Jesus from another figure; the latter denote "an intermediary figure (which) was involved in a process which increased its status, or function, or both" (78). Instances of the former are "Lord," "Messiah," and "Son of God," and, more suprisingly, preexistence; more surprisingly, since it is at least arguable that preexistence was a more dynamic category as it itself developed from a concept of "ideal" preexistence to one of "real" preexistence.[20] Under the heading of

18. For fuller detail see my "The Question of Anti-semitism in the New Testament Writings of the Period," in *Jews and Christians: The Parting of the Ways* AD *70-135,* ed. J. D. G. Dunn (Tübingen: J. C. B. Mohr [Paul Siebeck], 1992) 177-211; here 195-203; more briefly in *Partings,* 156-60. For the two levels on which John's Gospel must be read, see particularly J. L. Martyn, *History and Theology in the Fourth Gospel,* rev. ed. (Nashville: Abingdon, 1979).

19. "Gentile," of course, is itself a *Jewish* term of identification.

20. As the recent study of J. Habermann, *Präexistenzaussagen im Neuen Testament* (Frankfurt: Peter Lang, 1990) 26, notes, this distinction goes back at least to W. Beyschlag's *Christologie des Neuen Testaments* (1866).

"dynamic parallels" he lists no less than sixteen figures who were held by some Jews "to be of unusually elevated status," including the future Davidic king, Abel, Elijah, Enoch, Jacob, Melchizedek, Michael, Moses, Wisdom, and Word. A common feature is that "most of them were closely associated with the identity of the Jewish people, and they underwent striking developments of their status and functions during the Second Temple and early rabbinical periods" (85), especially Enoch and Wisdom.

There are two features of this inner-Jewish development on which Casey focuses as of particular significance for his thesis. The first is that "we can detect a social subgroup attached to each of them (Enoch and Wisdom), and each of them in some way indicates or embodies the identity of that group. This illuminates the nature of the cause of these developments. They were caused by the needs of the community." Such parallels lead us naturally to expect that the figure of Jesus would develop in status similarly in accordance with the needs of the early Christian community (92). This is all posited in a logical and winning way. But it involves a number of significant jumps, where the claim is simply stated and neither worked through nor defended. From observing that a subgroup can be hypothesized behind each of the figures of Enoch and Wisdom, the deduction is made that the figures indicate or embody (two significantly different claims) the identity of these subgroups, and then the further jump is taken to the claim that the developments in these figures were *caused* by the *needs* of these subgroups. The argument is certainly plausible. But when it is so fundamental and vital to Casey's thesis one would have hoped that it might be argued with more documentation and detail, rather than being simply asserted. Of course Casey would readily admit that very little is known about these subgroups (86-89). But that simply reinforces the imprudence of drawing such firm and clear conclusions on the basis of so little hard evidence.

The second important feature about this inner-Jewish development of intermediary figures for Casey is that it was "inner-Jewish"; that is, it was held within the constraints of Jewish monothism. "No other serious limitation may be observed. In particular, there was no general bar to prevent the transfer of status and functions from one intermediary figure to another" (93). At this point I am in substantial agreement with Casey. I too am persuaded that monotheism was one of the "four pillars" of Second Temple Judaism, and that it was the Christian redefinition of this fundamental axiom of Judaism which resulted in the most decisive partings of the ways between Christianity and Judaism.[21]

At the same time, however, we should note that there are not a few scholars who would question whether Jewish monotheism was quite so firm and unyielding as both Casey and I claim. The most thoroughgoing examples are the recent contributions by Hayman and Barker, who argue that in fact Israel was

21. *Partings,* chs. 2, 11.

never as monotheistic as is usually assumed.[22] Rather, they claim, the more ancient belief was of a High God *('El 'Elyon)* who had several Sons of God, of whom Yahweh was one, to whom Israel was given as his heritage (as in Deut 32:8-9 LXX), and this ancient belief lies behind subsequent talk in particular of a supreme angel. The significance of such a thesis for developments in christology is clear. "The fact that functionally Jews believed in the existence of two gods explains the speed with which Christianity developed so fast in the first century towards the divinization of Jesus."[23] "Yahweh, the Lord, could be manifested on earth in human form, as an angel or in the Davidic king. It was as a manifestation of Yahweh, the Son of God, that Jesus was acknowledged as Son of God, Messiah and Lord."[24]

This is not the place to engage in a thorough study of the arguments mounted by Hayman and Barker. It must suffice to note that the perception of a strong monotheism at the heart of Judaism from the exile onward remains hard to discount to the extent that Hayman and Barker argue for. It is not a matter simply of the evidence of the Shema (Deut 6:4) and Second Isaiah (especially Isa 45:20-25). The same common self-perception is evident also in such worldly wise Jews as Philo and Josephus,[25] and witnessed in the Jesus tradition (cf. Mark 12:29-30 par.). Judaism was similarly perceived from without by those who found its monotheistic denial of other gods a mark of atheism — as in the case of Celsus: "The goatherds and shepherds who followed Moses as their leader were deluded by clumsy deceit into thinking that there was only one God . . . (and) abandoned the worship of many gods. . . . The goatherds and shepherds thought that there was one God called the Most High, or Adonai, or the Heavenly One, or Sabbaoth, or however they like to call this world; and they acknowledged nothing more" (*Contra Celsum* 1:23-24). Philo, we should note, was a prominent exponent of the sort of language and conceptuality which Barker cites as evidence for a strong strand of apocalyptic (non-Palestinian) Judaism.[26] And Celsus, too, was obviously well aware of the range of titles used for God within Judaism. But neither saw any contradiction between that wider conceptuality and usage and the assertion / recognition of Judaism's strong and consistent monotheism. Since those named were capable of highly sophisticated thought and nuanced expression, we should give such assertions / recognitions full weight.

Others have used much of the same evidence to draw less radical conclusions:

22. P. Hayman, "Monotheism — A Misused Word in Jewish Studies?," *JJS* 42 (1991) 1-15; M. Barker, *The Great Angel: A Study of Israel's Second God* (London: SPCK, 1992).

23. Hayman, "Monotheism," 14.

24. Barker, *Great Angel*, 3.

25. Philo *Decal.* 65: "Let us, then, engrave deep in our hearts this as the first and most sacred of commandments, to acknowledge and honour one God who is above all, and let the idea that gods are many never even reach the ears of the man whose rule of life is to seek for truth in purity and goodness"; Josephus, *Ant.* 5.112 — "to recognize God as one is common to all the Hebrews."

26. Barker, *Great Angel*, ch. 7.

that the LXX of Dan 7:13 ("came *like* the Ancient of Days," instead of "came *to* the Ancient of Days") indicates a readiness within apocalyptic Judaism to recognize a heavenly being like God;[27] that the glorious angel of such passages as Ezek 8:2 and Dan 10:5-6 indicates a "bifurcation" within the Jewish conception of God;[28] or, more commonly, that the figure(s) of divine Wisdom (and Logos — Philo) mark already the hypostatization of a divine attribute.[29] Again, I beg to disagree: in such characterizations not enough allowance is being made for the vigor and flexibility of Jewish apocalyptic writing or Wisdom speculation.[30] Certainly the language indicates a willingness to explore different ways of speaking of the reality of God and of God's interaction with his world. But evidently a Philo could engage in such speculation and still say, and fully mean, the Shema.

The real point to emerge from all this is not that Judaism contained a large and prominent segment which had abandoned monotheism, but that (prior to the second century C.E. at least) Judaism's monotheism was able to contain within itself a vigor of metaphorical language and apocalyptic vision which indicates how rich and diversely textured that monotheistic axiom actually was. I do not exclude the probability that many Second Temple Jews were functionally polytheistic; that is, that the more speculative language or visionary experience in unsophisticated hands effectively resulted in a breach of Jewish monotheism. In the same way I suspect that many Christians today who think they are Trinitarians are actually tritheists (or Christotheists), because the highly technical distinctions within the doctrine of the Trinity pass them by. Nor do I ignore the fact that sometime early in the second century rabbinic Judaism took fright at the possible deduction to be drawn from visions of glorious heavenly figures and denounced the declaration that there are two powers in heaven as heresy.[31] But it seems to me still to be a proper and accurate summary of Second Temple Judaism, as expressed in the writings which have come down to us from that period or which bear witness to that period, that Second Temple Judaism was through and through monotheistic in character.

It should be clear enough where all this bears upon Casey's thesis. At the very least, it means that Jewish monotheism is a much less clearly defined or, indeed, much less firm identity marker than Casey assumes. If the arguments of Hayman and Barker, or the other less radical views, have any substance in them, then we must acknowledge a legitimate dispute as to whether Judaism was wholly mono-

27. Cf. S. Kim, *"The 'Son of Man'" as the Son of God,* WUNT 30 (Tübingen: J. C. B. Mohr [Paul Siebeck], 1983) 22-24.

28. C. Rowland, *The Open Heaven: A Study of Apocalyptic in Judaism and Early Christianity* (London: SPCK; New York: Crossroad, 1982) 96-97, 100.

29. E.g., M. Hengel, *Judaism and Hellenism,* 2 vols. (London: SCM, 1974) 1:154-57, 312.

30. See further my *Christology in the Making,* 2d ed. (London: SCM; Philadelphia: Trinity, 1989); also *Partings,* chs. 10–11.

31. See particularly A. F. Segal, *Two Powers in Heaven: Early Rabbinic Reports about Christianity and Gnosticism* (Leiden: E. J. Brill, 1977).

theistic at all. And if monotheism had never wholly carried the day within Judaism, or if Jewish monotheism had been decisively eroded or diluted well before Jesus appeared on the scene, then it is quite possible to accommodate the developing christology of the first two Christian generations wholly within Judaism. If, alternatively, as Casey and I believe, Jewish monotheism remained as a strong identity factor throughout Second Temple Judaism, the consequences differ only slightly for Casey's thesis. For then we are confronted with a monotheism which contained within it richly diverse ways of speaking of divine immanence. In particular, it becomes quite possible to accommodate the developments marked by the Christian apocalypse of John (Revelation) wholly within the stream of *Jewish* apocalyptic visionary speculation. And even the rich developments of the Gospel of John's christology can be seen primarily as an extension of the Jewish fascination with divine revelation which was the driving force of apocalyptic and mystical trends *within Judaism* at that time. To be sure there were Jews ("the Jews" = the Jewish authorities of the region) who believed that John's Christ had threatened the unity of God (John 5:18; 10:33); but it was probably the same Jews (the early rabbis) who believed that the apocalyptic and mystical concerns of other Jews with glorious heavenly beings other than Yahweh was equally threatening to the unity of God. The point is that such developments could, and did, take place wholly within a Jewish context. It is simply not true that "the deity of Jesus is a belief which could have developed only in a predominantly Gentile church," and at least highly questionable whether "the deity of Jesus is . . . *inherently* unJewish."[32] Once again the transition from Jewish identity to Gentile identity has been too casually drawn. The development within the NT is not so much from Jewish prophet to *Gentile* God, as from Jewish prophet to *Jewish* God; it is precisely that development and the problems it caused within Judaism which is reflected in the Fourth Gospel.

## 4

A third element of his thesis on which Casey is vulnerable is in his postulation of what can only be characterized as a rather one-sided and reductivist development schema. It revolves around what Casey sees as the interaction of identity, social cohesion, and christology, in what boils down to an explanation of the development of christology as the result of essentially social factors. The schema depends on two principal assertions.

The first is that "the whole of Jesus' ministry could be perceived" "to embody Judaism as a religion," "as the embodiment of Judaism as it should be" (72) — and not only "could be," but was so perceived. "Jesus offered people the spiritual centre of Judaism"; "from the disciples' perspective he was the embodiment of Judaism itself." Consequently the group around him could also be perceived to have

32. Casey, *Jewish Prophet,* 169, 176.

embodied Judaism as it should be; as a result Jesus "was himself the visible embodiment of Jewish identity, and the source of the recreation of the Jewish identity of his disciples" (73-74). This claim is central to Casey's thesis, for in his view it is Jesus' embodiment of the identity of Judaism which was the original driving force behind early Christian belief in the resurrection of Jesus (100, 105) and which thus set the whole development in train. Likewise it was his first disciples' perception that he embodied "all that was right, all that was religious and salvific, in Judaism, without ethnic customs such as circumcision and dietary laws (which) drove christology upwards, and drove it more vigorously than comparable figures because of the uniqueness of the community" (136). This aspect of the thesis is summarized in the final chapter: "the relationship between identity and christological development is to some extent one of cause and effect" (162).

The penultimate quotation, however, brings in the other key feature in the schema. The Gentile mission was the additional driving force behind christological growth. It was this mixed community of Jews and Gentiles which needed the figure of Christ to be powerful enough to hold it together (137). Again the development is one of cause and effect: the "decline in the observance of the Jewish Law in the Christian community drastically increased the requirement for a higher christology"; "the conflicts intensified by war between Israel and Rome drove christological development up to the deity of Jesus" (138); the secondary material expressing higher christology "has been produced most extensively at those points where the community needed it most" (153). In short, "the development of christology . . . was, and has remained, a means of holding together a large social group" (176).

This reconstruction is open to a number of criticisms. One is the degree of arbitrariness with which the first assertion is introduced and the lack of fit between the reconstruction and the data. With what justification can it be claimed that Jesus was perceived as "the embodiment of Judaism itself"? The claim is fundamental and far-reaching, but it is simply asserted, and the material reviewed by Casey (72-73) does hardly anything to justify the claim itself. It is certainly fair to argue that Jesus and the disciples' commitment to him is what marked them off from the rest of Judaism (74); but that is not the same as saying that they perceived Jesus to embody Judaism itself. We have already noted that the category of Judaism and Jewish identity was much more contested and much less clearly drawn at that time than most (including Casey) assume. And while it is highly probable that Jesus was seen by the Evangelists as replaying the role of Israel (as in Matt 4:1-11), it is less clear that Jesus was so seen during his ministry.[33] Rather the implication of Jesus' having chosen twelve disciples is that *he* saw *them* as embodying Israel, and himself as somehow over against them. At the very least Casey has to argue his case, not simply assert it.

33. Casey himself attributes the reference to Jesus of the manlike figure ("one like a son of man" = the saints of the Most High) of Dan 7:13-14 to post-Easter reflection.

There is also a degree of tension between the two postulated causes of christological development which requires more clarification than Casey provides. For the more it is claimed that Jesus was seen as the embodiment of Judaism the less easy is it to explain how and why the movement focused on this Jesus first opened the door to Gentiles. The second cause (mixed community, growing Gentile self-identity) is itself not explained, and cannot be explained from the first cause (Jesus as embodying Jewish identity). Jesus was not remembered as advocating outreach to the Gentiles; nor is he ever remembered as saying anything whatsoever on the most crucial issue of all (whether Gentile converts should be circumcised) — a surprising fact if indeed other passages in the Synoptic Gospels have been produced to meet the community's need. And while passages like Matt 5:17-20 and 10:5-6 could be explained as occasioned by a (self?)-perception of Jesus embodying Jewish identity, their presence in the Jesus tradition simply serves to underline the difficulty of explaining the Gentile mission on Casey's thesis. In other words, Casey's postulated causes are insufficient to explain developments which he sees as fundamental to the growth of christology, and indeed, if anything, make these developments harder to explain.

This reflection leads into the second main point of criticism: that Casey's reductivist sociological explanation needs at least to be supplemented and corrected by the hypothesis of other causes. Has Casey actually uncovered the dynamic of the development of earliest christology? He has indicated social factors which must have played some role in contributing to and shaping that development. It may be that he has indicated a necessary cause of the development. But has he uncovered the necessary and sufficient cause, sufficient to explain all the relevant data which make up NT christology? Was there not also a more important inner dynamic within the christological development, which no doubt interacted with the social forces but which is not to be wholly explained by them?

For instance, Casey's discussion of the category of "messiah" operates with a too static category (42-43) and allows too little for the impact of Jesus himself on the designation giving it his own evolutionary twist to a fluid Jewish messianology.[34] We could also note that Casey's assertion that Jesus was perceived to embody Judaism itself introduces an element of internal dynamic which he ignores. The more that claim can be pushed, the more we have to ask whether Jesus' first disciples could reach such a conclusion without any stimulus or encouragement from Jesus himself ("Jesus offered people the spiritual centre of Judaism"), and the more we have to reckon with the possibility that Jesus saw himself as in some sense a focus for Israel and its people's hopes, with all

34. Casey's assertion that "the messiah was not a title in Second Temple Judaism" (42) is strictly correct, but the usage of *Pss. Sol.* 17:32 and 1QS 9:11 and 1QSa 2:20 is surely sufficient indication of belief in a royal Davidic messiah; see further my "Messianic Ideas and Their Influence upon the Jesus of History," *The Messiah: Developments in Earliest Judaism and Christianity,* ed. J. H. Charlesworth (Minneapolis: Fortress, 1992) 365-81.

that that implies in terms of Jesus' own self-understanding as a representative figure. An *individual* who thus expresses the corporate identity of Israel / Judaism ("embody" is Casey's term) immediately suggests a royal or priestly figure, or indeed an image like the suffering servant of Isaiah 53 or the human-like figure of Dan 7:13-14. In other words, Casey himself may open the door to the recognition that Jesus made or implied high claims for his own significance, claims which would themselves be sufficient cause to explain much of the subsequent development in christology. At the very least, Casey needs to explicate his own hypothesis with greater care.

The analysis of the crucial belief in Jesus' resurrection is similarly incomplete. Casey is surprisingly confident that only "resurrection was the culturally relevant form of vindication" which Jesus could have looked for (52, 102-3). What of the exaltation or translation long ago attributed to Enoch and Elijah, or to the martyred righteous in Wisdom 5, or implied in the triumph of the saints of the Most High in Daniel 7, or attributed to such great saints as Moses, Baruch, and Ezra at around this time?[35] It is by no means clear that Jesus was bound to use the category of resurrection (Aramaic קום) in expressing a hope of vindication, or that the first disciples seeing visions of Jesus after he was dead should conclude therefrom that he had been resurrected rather than taken to heaven. On the contrary, given that Jesus' resurrection was self-evidently *not* part of the general resurrection at the end of time, the conclusion of the first Christians that that is what had happened to Jesus is all the more surprising — precisely because a less problematic category lay close to hand (postmortem exaltation to heaven). Again we are forced toward the conclusion that external factors and availability of suitable categories were not the sufficient cause to explain the earliest belief in Jesus' resurrection. Rather we must assume an inner dynamic which shaped the categories as well as being shaped by them. Without more allowance for that inner dynamic than Casey allows the development of christology cannot be adequately grasped.[36]

Other elements within the inner dynamic of developing christology could be mentioned. For example, Casey refers at one point to "the gift of the Holy Spirit" and to the "religious and emotional experience of new revelation" (108), without apparently considering what this might have meant for christological development. And he is so confident that the changing character of earliest mission (to Gentiles as well as Jews) was the cause of developments in christology that he fails to consider whether the influence was not as much or more

35. See further, e.g., my *Partings*, 186-87.

36. Casey's discussion of the resurrection narratives leaves a good deal more to be desired. For example, he notes that the discrepancies between the different Gospel accounts "are too great to have resulted from accurate reporting of a perceptible event" (99); he does not seem to allow the possibility of *confused* reporting of a perceptible event! And he ignores such questions as why the report of an empty tomb should be attributed to women, and why there was no early tomb veneration at an undisturbed tomb.

the other way: that it was the christology which resulted in the opening to the Gentiles, as the NT writers certainly believed (e.g., Matt 28:18-20; Gal 1:15-16). Putting the same point in other terms, Casey seems to assume that Paul's own experience was simply a confirmatory factor, that is, presumably, of developments determined entirely by social pressures, without asking whether Paul's experience (as Paul himself understood it, of Christ) was not itself one of the major factors which achieved the revolution of the Gentile mission (e.g., again Gal 1:15-16).[37]

Above all, Casey has ignored the whole dynamic of early Christian worship. This is most serious since it is precisely the thesis of the other recently published monograph, which also seeks to explain the transition from Jewish monotheism to Christian belief in the deity of Christ, that this transition can only be explained in terms of the cultic veneration of Christ and the generative power of religious experience.[38] And it is all the more serious since worship and religious experience are such common factors in the other apocalyptic and mystical explorations of divine transcendence and immanence, of which Casey is well aware, as it is, for example, of Revelation and the christological hymns in the NT. Casey may mean, of course, to include all this within his social description of such communities. But the factors are surely of too obvious importance to be so absorbed within or reduced to social forces. And without taking them into account it is highly dubious whether any explanation of christological development could be counted adequate.

## 5

In short, Casey's monograph is a stimulating and provocative attempt to trace the development of christology in evolutionary terms, as the effect of social causes — namely, the way in which Jesus embodied the identity of the new movement, and the way in which the expansion of that movement to include Gentiles caused the movement's primary identity factor (Christ) to gain increasing significance, until the predominance of Gentiles within the movement made it possible / inevitable that the constraint of Jewish monotheism be slackened and abandoned. The thesis is to be welcomed precisely because it highlights the social factors so clearly, and can therefore serve as a standing reminder not to ignore or unwisely discount such factors.

Unfortunately, however, Casey works with a too simplified concept of Judaism and of Jewish identity, and thus with a too simplified appreciation of

37. But I am not sure that I have understood Casey's logic here: "Paul's christological developments can be traced without much reference to experience because they were so closely related to experience that they were confirmed by experience" (131).

38. L. W. Hurtado, *One God, One Lord: Early Christian Devotion and Ancient Jewish Monotheism* (Philadelphia: Fortress, 1988).

the richness and diversity of reflection on divine immanence which was possible and is attested within Jewish monotheism. Moreover, his social analysis does not sufficiently explain all the relevant data and discounts to a serious degree what arguably were the principal factors in the development of christology — namely (using theological shorthand), the impact of Jesus, the impact of Jesus' ministry and teaching, the impact of the resurrection of Jesus, the impact of the Spirit of God, and the generative power of religious experience and of worship of God through Christ particularly in and through the preaching and teaching of religious geniuses like Paul and John.

That such a process is not simply to be described as "evolution" should be clear enough. Whether it can be described simply as an "unfolding" is less clear, since the process of conceptuality in transition within historical contexts themselves undergoing change is not easily categorized, as I have tried to explain elsewhere.[39] But that it involved an inner dynamic (the inner dynamic of religious experience and worship) and that it was understood by the participants as an unfolding of the truth of Christ is sufficiently clear, and with that we probably have to be content.[40]

39. See the Foreword to the second edition of my *Christology,* xiv-xvi. But Newman's idea of development / unfolding (*Essay*) was also nuanced and reflected changing circumstances.

40. It is a pleasure to contribute this small offering in honor of Howard Marshall, whose thoroughness and integrity of scholarship has long set a standard by which all evangelical contributors to larger debates can measure themselves.

# Christology in Luke, Speech-Act Theory, and the Problem of Dualism in Christology after Kant

Anthony C. Thiselton

## 1

The above title, with its three diverse points of reference, may appear to be so far-ranging as to necessitate an explanatory defense at the beginning of the argument. First, I have chosen to focus a good part of this essay on Luke partly because I. Howard Marshall, whom this volume duly honors and congratulates, has made Luke, as well as christology, one of his own special areas of interest and expertise. Within his work on Luke, he has also refused to accept an artificial dualism between theology and history; to attack the supposed inevitability of such a dualism thus constitutes part of the agenda of this essay as well.

But at a still more important level in terms of the present argument, I propose that what has traditionally been termed "Luke's interest in history" should more constructively be termed, from the standpoint of hermeneutics and contemporary philosophical theology, Luke's concern about the importance of *the public domain.* The public domain constitutes a necessary context for Luke's christology. In this respect it is arguable that Luke stands in contrast, at least in terms of emphasis, to Mark's concern to call attention to more enigmatic features which signal transcendence, and to Matthew's concerns about particular communities, particular traditions, and eschatology.

Second, speech-act theory sharpens the importance of the extra-linguistic features which lie in the stream of life out of which language operates, but may not always be "said." Speech-act theory in the tradition of J. L. Austin and J. R. Searle draws a careful distinction between what is "said" as a propositional *content* and the illocutionary *force* of an utterance in which an *act* is performed *in* the saying of the utterance or *in* the writing of a text. An appraisal of the force may "show" (if not "say") that certain presuppositions or implications must hold if this illocutionary force is to be successfully operative. This gives us the clue to what Marshall in *The Origins of New Testament Christology* (1976) has termed "the indirect approach to Christology."[1] As Marshall suggests, here we may distinguish between the question: "Did Jesus *say that* he was the Messiah?" (a question of propositional content) and the different question: "Did Jesus *act* and speak *as* Messiah?" This latter question concerns performative force and implies a presupposition about an institutional status and role. This might, in turn, be translated into a theological proposition, but now one of a different order, about christology.

In a very recent essay "The Son of Man and the Incarnation" (1991), Marshall distinguishes, by way of analogy, between the proposition "George was King," and the *implicature* which may be derived from a proposition which asserts a different matter of content: "King George died in 1952." He comments, "The use of the term 'King' carries a whole set of implications regarding the status and functions of the person thus described, and this aspect of the statement is distinguishable from the statement made about the subject, namely that he died."[2] On this basis, for example, Marshall disentangles issues about the messianic self-consciousness of Jesus from the question of whether he explicitly made assertions about his own messianic status and role. To confuse these two distinct issues, he points out, is quite simply "illogical."[3]

I propose to pursue this approach further, developing particular aspects of my work on speech-act theory in *New Horizons in Hermeneutics*.[4] In these pages I have argued, for example, that in the triple tradition of the Synoptic Gospels, the utterance of Jesus, "My son, your sins are [hereby] forgiven you" (Mark 2:5; par. Matt 9:2; Luke 5:20), depends for its operative effectiveness on the presupposition that outside language Jesus possesses a particular institutional role and status.[5] Matthew and Mark use the present tense which normally (but not always) characterizes performative utterance (e.g., "I give and bequeath . . ."), but on Luke's use of the perfect Marshall rightly observes that ἀφέωνται expresses "the abiding force" *(sic)* of the forgiveness.[6]

Marshall notes in his commentary on this passage in Luke that the question posed in the minds of the witnesses, "Who can forgive sins except God?" (Luke 9:21) consciously raises the issue of "whether Jesus has any authorization

1. I. H. Marshall, *The Origins of New Testament Christology* (London: Inter-Varsity, 1976) 55.

2. Marshall, "The Son of Man and the Incarnation," *Ex Auditu* 7 (1991) 30; cf. 29-43.

3. Marshall, *Origins*, 55.

4. A. C. Thiselton, *New Horizons in Hermeneutics: The Theory and Practice of Transforming Biblical Reading* (London: HarperCollins, 1992) 16-19, 274-75, 282-312, 361-67, 389-90, 559-60, 597-604.

5. Thiselton, *New Horizons*, 286.

6. Marshall, *The Gospel of Luke: A Commentary on the Greek Text* (Exeter: Paternoster, 1978) 212.

to speak in this fashion."[7] In *New Horizons in Hermeneutics* I have urged that there is a crucial difference, developed in speech-act theory by Austin, Evans, Searle, and Recanati, between *institutional* authority of an extralinguistic nature and mere *causal* authority which may rest on little more than the force of self-assertion. Christology in the NT represents an affirmation of the former and a denial of the latter, and it is this which gives rise to reticence if or when Jesus *asserts* propositions *about* himself, rather than *acts* and speaks *as* himself.

Two years after the publication of *The Two Horizons* (1980), in which I attempted (among other tasks) to explore the significance of Wittgenstein for hermeneutics, R. G. Gruenler published his book *New Approaches to Jesus and the Gospels: A Phenomenological and Exegetical Study of Synoptic Christology.*[8] Gruenler affirms both Marshall's exploration of "the indirect approach to Christology" and my own exploration of Wittgenstein's philosophy of language, although he also notes a certain difference of emphasis and area between his work and mine.[9] He does not explore in depth the philosophical issues which lie behind Wittgenstein's broadly Kantian concerns about the limits of language, nor does he appeal to a theory of speech-acts of the kind developed by Austin, Searle, or other post-Wittgensteinian writers. Nevertheless we share a common starting point concerning the interweaving of language and life, especially in first-person utterances. We both allude to D. M. High's interpretation of Wittgenstein.[10]

The third point of reference in the title is to the problem of dualism in christology after Kant. It is, to my mind, important to understand the dilemma posed by Kantian philosophy in order to see why from Kant and Strauss to Bultmann and Robinson a certain kind of dualism has bedeviled so many attempts to interpret the NT in such a way as to articulate a coherent christology in the modern world. We may readily allow that the two-natures christology of the patristic era and the Chalcedonian creeds had to steer a careful path to avoid its own kind of dualism. But the problem has taken on a new urgency since Kant. The point is made with acute perceptiveness by H. Frei in his carefully argued essay on D. F. Strauss. Frei writes:

> The dilemma is at least as old as the fourth- and fifth-century endeavour to describe the indivisible unity of the person of Christ and the presence of two unabridged natures, divine and human, in him. The modern shift in categories from those of substantialist personhood to self-conscious, inward, and

7. Marshall, *Gospel of Luke,* 214.

8. R. G. Gruenler, *New Approaches to Jesus and the Gospels: A Phenomenological and Exegetical Study of Synoptic Christology* (Grand Rapids, Michigan: Baker, 1982).

9. Gruenler, *New Approaches,* 11, 109.

10. Gruenler, *New Approaches,* 20; A. C. Thiselton, *The Two Horizons: New Testament Hermeneutics and Philosophical Description* (Exeter: Paternoster; Grand Rapids, Michigan: Wm. B. Eerdmans, 1980) 425; *idem, New Horizons,* 617.

at the same time historical personality, gave the problem new urgency and changed its expression.[11]

If rational inquiry, as Kant claimed, cannot move beyond that which the activity of the mind shapes and conditions in terms of the categories and structures of space, time, and causality through which it apprehends the phenomenological world of objects, persons, and events within the historical continuum, how can Jesus Christ simultaneously constitute a full *manifestation of the divine and eternal,* while also remaining a full participant *in the nexus of historical life within the world?*

This form of epistemological dualism poses sharper and more complex problems than the simpler pre-Kantian dualism imposed between contingent history and universal reason by Lessing's "ugly ditch." It constitutes a far more fundamental challenge to the attempt, sustained by Marshall and others, to hold together theology and history in the interpretation of christological data than more empirical fine-tuning concerning, for example, the accuracy of Luke's work as a historian. It is noteworthy that Marshall writes in his book aptly entitled *Luke: Historian and Theologian* (1970) that Luke's "view of theology led him to write history."[12] In the tradition of rationalism, from I. Newton's *Mathematical Principles* (1687) through Locke's *Reasonableness of Christianity* (1695) to Lessing's *Wolfenbüttel Fragments* (1777-78) and *The Education of the Human Race* (1780), *"history"* might seem to add nothing which might not also be apprehended by universal reason, even if the paradigm of mathematics seemed to some to assign to *"reason"* a purity and universality to which the accidental might-or-might-nots of history could never aspire. But in principle natural theology and special revelation might in the event cohere together. With the publication a year later of Kant's *Critique of Pure Reason* (1781, 2d ed., 1787), a watershed was reached, and the nature of the problem of a dualism between history and reason passed a nodal point of transition.

In a clear essay on Kant, E. Fackenheim draws attention to some sentences from Kant which most sharply focus the problem:

> Even if God really spoke to man, the latter could never know it was God who had been speaking. It is radically impossible for man to grasp the Infinite through his senses. . . . If such an immediate intuition happened to me . . . I should still have to use a concept of God as a standard by which to decide whether the phenomenon in question agreed with the necessary characteristics of a Deity.[13]

11. H. Frei, "David Friedrich Strauss," in *Nineteenth-Century Religious Thought in the West,* ed. N. Smart, et al., 3 vols. (Cambridge: Cambridge University, 1988 [1985]) 1:254.

12. Marshall, *Luke: Historian and Theologian* (Exeter: Paternoster, 1970) 52; see 21-52 *et passim.*

13. E. L. Fackenheim, "Immanuel Kant," in *Nineteenth-Century Religious Thought,* 31-32,

It is no answer to appeal to religious mysticism, for there is no way to know whether what is experienced or found "are the products of its own imagination mistaken for the divine."[14]

It would be a mistake, however, to relegate this problem to the peculiarities of a Kantian critical philosophy which could readily be discarded, or at least disregarded. It is quite clear that in the work of Strauss and many Hegelians, a dualism persisted between the raw data of the causal nexus of *Historie,* or "objective history" as it lay open to the scrutiny of reconstructive historical research, and "myth" or "idea" or "spirit" (depending on the writer) which might express a "value" dimension for the kind of christology which might serve theology. The story is too well known to need to be retold. F. C. Baur resolved the dualism by giving priority to the social forces of the causal nexus of history. Strauss, when pressed, despaired of what history could offer, and saw the choice as lying between a mythological idea and the recognition of fiction for what it was. Kähler opted for the side of the dualism which exalted the preached Christ at the expense of the so-called historical Jesus. Bultmann insisted that *Historie* possessed a certain importance, but so closely identified the appeal to history with an anti-Lutheran appeal to justification by the "works" of historical inquiry that the "history" side of the dualism was effectively minimized.

If it is thought that recent British scholarship fails to be touched by this legacy of philosophical theology, we may recall some sentences from J. A. T. Robinson in the well-known volume *Christ, Faith, and History* (1972). He seizes at once on the alleged dualism of the Chalcedonian formulas as giving the impression that "Jesus was a hybrid . . . a sort of bat-man or centaur, an unnatural conjunction of two strange species."[15] But the transposition into a different kind of linguistic dualism which he suggests simply reflects the tradition of D. F. Strauss. Following M. Wiles, Robinson declares: "What we are talking about are not two storeys *(sic)* but two stories. The one is natural, scientific, descriptive. The other is supernatural, mythological, and interpretative."[16]

There remains, no doubt, an element of truth in what Robinson is seeking to convey. In the context of his firmly stated title *I Believe in the Historical Jesus* (1977) Marshall himself readily concedes: "The historical facts of the earthly ministry of Jesus were not by themselves sufficient to lead to Christian faith."[17] But his solution does not rest on the retelling of a supposedly mythological

---

cited from *Conflict of Faculties* in the Prussian Academy edition of Kant, *Werke: Akademie-Textausgabe* (Berlin: de Gruyter, 1968) 7:63 and 8:142.

14. Fackenheim, "Kant," 32; *Werke,* 6:83.

15. J. A. T. Robinson, "Need Jesus Have been Perfect?" in *Christ, Faith, and History: Cambridge Studies in Christology,* ed. S. W. Sykes and J. P. Clayton (Cambridge: Cambridge University, 1972) 39.

16. Robinson, "Need Jesus Have Been Perfect?" 40. Cf. M. F. Wiles, "Does Christology Rest on a Mistake?" in *Christ, Faith, and History,* 3-12.

17. Marshall, *I Believe in the Historical Jesus* (London: Hodder & Stoughton, 1977) 239.

layer of events, as if to suggest that a story of empirical cause and effect and of social agency takes care of historical research and the philosophical criterion of falsification, while a story of mythological theology transcends the empirical world, but leaves points of contact with it problematic. Such a conceptual scheme hardly leaves room for a theology of "incarnation" and renders the notion more conceptually embarrassing than it was even in earlier times.

## 2

We may begin perhaps to clarify the issue and to make some tentative advance if we transpose Kant's critique of the limits of *thought* into parallel terms representing a critique of the limits of *language*. Although Mauthner had earlier formulated a critique of language, the classic formulation in terms reminiscent of Kant can be found in the early Wittgenstein. In his early *Tractatus* he writes: "The sense of the world must lie outside the world. . . . *In* it no value exists [his italics]. . . . If there is any value that does have value, it must lie outside the whole sphere of what happens and is the case. For all that happens and is the case is accidental."[18] He continues: "God does not reveal himself *in* the world . . . . There are indeed things that cannot be put into words. They *make themselves manifest* . . . . What we cannot speak about we must pass over in silence [Wittgenstein's italics]."[19]

A clue is given, however, about whether or how the Kantian fact-value disjunction can be bridged: what transcends the phenomenal world of spatio-temporal states of affairs (e.g., that Jesus lived at Nazareth and was crucified) may make itself "manifest" (e.g., that Jesus speaks as the word and presence of God). Wittgenstein earlier observed, "A proposition is a description of a state of affairs"; and "What *can* be shown, *cannot* be said."[20]

The contrast between "saying" and "showing" takes us a little way forward in our understanding of how christology finds expression in the Synoptic Gospels. Almost everyone, including Marshall, notes that even for Bultmann "Jesus' call to decision implies a christology."[21] The *authority* of Jesus to call is implicitly analytic, or grammatically internal, to the speech-act of calling in this context. Many of the parables of Jesus similarly "show" what cannot, with precisely the same effect, be "said." In the case of certain parables (though certainly not all parables) an "explanation" by its very nature undermines the suggestive and transcendent function of what is being "made manifest" with

18. L. Wittgenstein, *Tractatus Logico-Philosophicus* (London: Routledge & Kegan Paul, 1961) 6.41 (p. 145).

19. Wittgenstein, *Tractus,* 6.432, 6.4321, 6.522 and 7 (pp. 150-51).

20. Wittgenstein, *Tractus,* 4.023 and 4.1212 (pp. 41, 51).

21. R. Bultmann, *Theology of the New Testament* (London: SCM, 1952) 1:42; and Marshall, *Origins,* 29.

the same kind of clumsy inappropriateness as the uncomfortable experience of being asked to "explain" a joke. If the hearer does not "see" it, it is better left aside.

Literary theorists have drawn attention repeatedly to this feature in Mark, although some utterly misconstrue Mark's theological and christological purpose. The most notorious example is F. Kermode's tragically unfortunate reading in *The Genesis of Secrecy,* which fully appreciates Mark's reluctance to "say" certain propositions, but misconstrues this as a device for turning readers into "insiders" who can supposedly "see" what the manipulative Evangelist wishes them to "see," and "outsiders" who cannot or will not play the ecclesial game. Thus Kermode believes that Mark is "polyvalent" as a matter of strategy and principle; that he offers only "riddling parables"; that he "banishes interpreters from the secret places"; and that just as the reader begins to glimpse a vision Mark closes "the door of disappointment."[22] "Interpretation . . . is bound to fail."[23] Graham Shaw attributes to Mark the same manipulatory ecclesial motives, driving a wedge, once again, between Jesus and the work of the Evangelists or redactors.[24]

A far more sensitive and perceptive account of the contrast between saying and showing in Mark is offered by P. Grant in his excellent study *Reading the New Testament* (1989). In Mark, he observes, "on the one hand we are summoned by the signs and promises to affirm a transcendent, beneficent reality, even as, on the other hand, we are warned against naïve interpretations of signs. . . . The cross is the sign which stands for the failure of signs to provide solace or certainty."[25] The reason for reticence about how much can be "said" depends on the nature of christology in Mark, and on a dialectic between revelation and hiddenness of the transcendence of Jesus prior to the resurrection.

Although Luke does not hesitate to retain elements of Mark's tradition which witness to this emphasis, Luke's "showing" of a christology which Jesus seldom seems to "say" takes the form of a more explicit portrayal of action and speech-acts based on institutional roles visible in the public domain. Before we examine Luke's material, however, more needs to be said about the development and conceptual tools of speech-act theory. We may trace the following stages or aspects of development.

(1) Wittgenstein himself became dissatisfied with the unresolved dualism which had marked his earlier work in the *Tractatus,* although it is important to note that his vast accumulation of material and in particular the *Philosophical Investigations* "could be seen in the right light only by contrast with and against

22. F. Kermode, *The Genesis of Secrecy: On the Interpretation of Narrative* (Cambridge, Massachusetts: Harvard University, 1979) 34, 141, 145.

23. Kermode, *Genesis of Secrecy,* 27.

24. G. Shaw, *The Cost of Authority: Manipulation and Freedom in the New Testament* (London: SCM, 1983) 190-268, esp. 255-57.

25. P. Grant, *Reading the New Testament* (London: Macmillan, 1989) 19, 21.

the background of my old way of thinking."[26] Wittgenstein in his later work saw propositions not as part of a logical calculus, but as embedded in a variety of concrete situations in the stream of life from which they derived particular currency. The notion of a "language-game" calls attention to a "whole, consisting of language and the actions into which it is woven."[27] Language about "love," "belief," "promise," or "expectation" draws its currency from actions and attitudes which precede and follow such language. To say "I love you" is to perform a speech-act of implied attitude or even commitment which would be undermined if my conduct before and after the utterance betrayed hostility or indifference. Similarly, Wittgenstein observes, "If there were a verb meaning 'to believe falsely,' it would not have any significant first person present indicative. . . . My own relation to my words is wholly different from other people's."[28] My attitude and actions "show" whether my words function as an operative and authentic speech-act.

(2) We have already earlier introduced the distinction between propositional *content* and illocutionary *force.* Such a distinction is fundamental to the work of J. L. Austin, J. Searle, and F. Recanati. Propositions describe states of affairs, and may be true or false. But, Austin argues, it is logically odd to use "true" or "false" of performative speech-acts: "We do not speak of a false bet or a false christening."[29] An illocutionary act, in contrast to a bare locutionary act, is in Austin's terms the performing of an act *in* the saying of an utterance. Typically it entails a lack of logical symmetry between first-person and third-person utterances. If I say, "I hereby promise to . . . ," and my subsequent actions stand behind my speech act, it becomes operative. But, as Austin observes, the anxious mother's assurance to an aggrieved neighbor, "He promises, don't you, Willie?" does not have the same *performative* force at all (at least not as *Willie's promise,* as against a veiled threat to Willie by the speaker).

Searle allows readily that "in performing an illocutionary act one characteristically performs propositional acts and utterance acts,"but this does not invalidate the key distinction between "force indicators" and "proposition indicators."[30] Force indicators may need to be explicated logically — for example, "I promise (Force, "F") that I shall be there (Proposition, "p")" — when, as Austin and Recanati observe, everyday language may use an abbreviated form which may conceal the force indicator: "I'll be there" still assumes the same *logical* form, "*F (p).*"

(3) Normally speech-acts presuppose roles and carry consequences in the *extralinguistic world.* That is to say, if I declare to my class, "I promise to assess your essays by next week," for this speech-act to function operatively, the act of

26. L. Wittgenstein, *Philosophical Investigations,* 2d ed. (Oxford: Blackwell, 1967) xe.

27. Wittgenstein, *Philosophical Investigations,* sect. 7.

28. Wittgenstein, *Philosophical Investigations,* II.x.190e, 192e.

29. J. L. Austin, *How to Do Things with Words* (Oxford: Clarendon, 1962) 11.

30. J. R. Searle, *Speech Acts: An Essay in the Philosophy of Language* (Cambridge: Cambridge University, 1969) 24, 31.

promising presupposes that I have the right, status, and capacity to make the assessment, and it further constrains me from using my time entirely for other purposes during the period of time in question. My status as assessor is presupposed but need not be stated; how I spend the next week conditions the level of trust which will be placed in future promises as operative speech-acts. I have given this matter some considerable attention with reference to biblical material in *New Horizons in Hermeneutics,* drawing in particular on Searle's illuminating essay "The Logical Status of Fictional Discourse," on N. Wolterstorff's consideration of "the fictive stance" in his *Works and Worlds of Art,* and on some comments from F. Recanati.[31]

In christological terms, the *operative effectiveness* of "My son, your sins are forgiven" (Mark 2:5; Luke 5:20; cf. Matt 9:2) depends on *a state of affairs about the identity, role, and authority of Jesus.* The same principle applies to a speech-act of exorcism: "Be silent; come out of him" (Mark 1:25). In the triple tradition the "point" lies less in the miraculous or supernatural nature of the act than in the issue of *who* could be in a position to "plunder the goods" of the "strong man" (Mark 3:23-27; par. Matt 12:22-30; Luke 11:14, 15, 17-23). Similarly the command of Jesus in the triple tradition "Peace! Be still!" to the wind and waves (Mark 4:35-41; par. Matt 8:23; Luke 8:22-25) constitutes what Austin termed an "exercitive" speech-act, giving rise to the question (which is "the point"): "Who, then, is this that even the wind and sea obey him?" (cf. Matt 8:27, "What sort of person is this. . . ?").

(4) We come now to a crucial issue in speech-act theory. Austin's disciple D. D. Evans rightly draws a very careful distinction between *institutional authority* and *causal force.* In *New Horizons in Hermeneutics* I have followed the respective subclassifications of Austin and Searle with reference to biblical material in parallel with what Searle grandly calls "a taxonomy of speech-acts."[32] J. L. Austin and D. D. Evans used the term "exercitive" to denote a subcategory of performative utterances in which the uttering of a speech-act by an appropriately authorized person in an appropriate language situation served to constitute an act of (for example) appointing, commanding, commissioning, authorizing, and so forth. In Austin's terminology, exercitives identify "the exercising of powers . . . warning, ordering, choosing, enacting, claiming, directing."[33] For technical linguistic and

31. Thiselton, *New Horizons,* 26-27, 128-30, 289-90, 352-54, 355-72, 388, 485, 527, 566, 570-75, 598-99, 615-16. More broadly in relation to textuality in Barthes and in Derrida, 92-141. The work of Searle and Wolterstorff is fundamental for parts of this argument as a whole. Cf. N. Wolterstorff, *Works and Worlds of Art* (Oxford: Clarendon, 1980) 198-239, esp. 231-34; J. R. Searle, "The Logical Status of Fictional Discourse," in *Expression and Meaning: Studies in the Theory of Speech Acts* (Cambridge: Cambridge University, 1979) 58-75. Cf. further F. Recanati, *Meaning and Force: The Pragmatics of Performative Utterances* (Cambridge: Cambridge University, 1987) esp. 260-66. It would constitute a digression from the present argument to consider the status of speech-acts in plays and fiction.

32. Thiselton, *New Horizons,* esp. 298-300.

33. Austin, *Things with Words,* 150, 154-55.

philosophical reasons which need not detain us here, Searle prefers to use the term "directive" in place of Austin's "exercitive." The term functions with greater precision and symmetry within the system which Searle proposes and has generally superseded Austin's terminology in such writers as Recanati, Levinson, and Leech.[34] Searle's "directives," include such characteristic speech-acts as "appointing," "choosing," "commanding," "commissioning," "forgiving," "guaranteeing," "inviting," "naming," "ordaining," and "sending." (This is not an exhaustive list.) But to *"appoint"* with operative effectiveness I need to be *the holder of some appropriate institutional office,* such as dean, principal, captain, manager, committee chairperson, or even professional client. The notion of "guaranteeing" provides a powerful example in the commercial world: who stands behind the guarantee, and what is its official or legal status? Has someone the right to "send" me where I may not wish to go?

The same claim that an authoritative or *authorized status or role* must be *presupposed* if the speech-act is to operate effectively *as* a speech-act (i.e., not merely by the *causal* force of persuasion) applies equally to the subcategory defined as that of "verdictives" by Austin, and as "declaratives" by Searle. The *verdict* of a judge, jury, referee, or umpire *determines* whether the player is *counted as* "out" or "offside," or whether an accused person *is* guilty. Thus Austin includes "reckoning, requiting, ruling, assessing" as "verdictives," while Searle includes the same examples under his subcategory of "declaratives."[35]

The *force* of *these* utterances as *acts* depends entirely on there being an *institutional* state of affairs in which the judge, jury, referee, or umpire is recognized as having a duly *authorized status and role.* In this case the performative force is identified by Austin and Searle as *illocutionary* force. This is distinct from that of the barrister, advocate, counsellor, or spectator who tries to persuade someone *causally* by *rhetoric* concerning the verdict. This rhetoric, if it was sufficiently persuasive, would constitute an example of *perlocutionary* force. In this case, the referee or judge would pronounce *legally* or *constitutionally* what is the case, even if the relatively recent and regrettable phenomenon of "disagreeing with the referee" represents an attempt to override *illocutionary* force by *perlocutionary* force.

The distinction is crucial for our interpretation of the christology of the Synoptic Gospels on the basis of the words and deeds of Jesus and how these were perceived by Luke and other Evangelists. Explicit rhetoric urging christological claims risks subordinating illocutionary to perlocutionary force. On the other hand, operative illocutions raise the christological question (which may result in the inquirer's reaching a christological confession): "Who has the right,

34. Searle, *Expression and Meaning,* 13-23; Recanati, *Meaning and Force,* 154-63; S. C. Levinson, *Pragmatics,* CTL (Cambridge: Cambridge University, 1983) 240-42; G. Leech, *The Principles of Pragmatics* (London: Longmans, 1983) 205-12.

35. Austin, *Things with Words,* 152; Searle, *Expression and Meaning,* 16-20; Recanati, *Meaning and Force,* 138-54.

status, and institutionally validated role to "acquit," to "judge," to "justify," or to "reckon as"? Is there not a veiled or "implicit" christology in the verdict of the parable in Luke concerning the tax collector and the Pharisee that "this man . . . was justified rather than the other" (Luke 18:14)?

Clearly such language can be found in the utterances of Jesus. The climax of Matthew portrays an act of authorization and commission: "All authority in heaven and on earth has been given me. Go, therefore, and make disciples . . ." (Matt 28:18-20). The classic instance of the conversation between Jesus and the centurion whose servant was in need of healing (Luke 7:1-10) turns on notions of institutional authority. The centurion tells Jesus that he himself understands what is entailed in standing in a derivative chain of command: "I also am *under* authority," that is, "*derive* authority from my institutional status and role"; hence, "only *say the word* and my servant will be *healed*" (Luke 7:7-8).

On the basis of examples such as these it can readily be seen that the relation between perlocutionary language, on the one hand, and illocutionary speech-acts on the other, is radically different for christology. The language not only of verdict ("your sins are hereby forgiven") but also of *promise* and *gift* depends for its operative effectiveness on the self-commitments, authority, and status of the speaker (Is the gift his to give? Will he stand behind, and execute, the promise?) Indeed we must go further. *Their respective significance for christology is one of almost complete opposition and contrast.* For the performing of acts on the basis of *causal force* constitutes in essence an *act of power through self-assertion.* On the other hand, illocutionary acts which rest on institutional roles serve their purpose as *acts which point by implication away from the self to some source of authority which lies beyond the self alone.* In Kantian terms, they presuppose a transcendent dimension of christology which seems all-too-readily to elude neat rational or conceptual packaging.

One of the few nineteenth-century thinkers to appreciate the logically contradictory character of Jesus' "saying" his own role and status, and thus risk the possibility of a self-assertive stance which would stand *in contradiction to the cross,* was Kierkegaard. Kierkegaard's christology rested on the "paradoxical" notion of Christ as "the God-Man," in which we may behold "the divine and the human together in Christ." But this "togetherness" could be revealed only through indirect communication.[36] Kierkegaard amplifies this by commenting that, if a witness of Jesus is not *present,* the communication for a later generation must be indirect. Presumably disclosure occurs *either* through such forms as parable, irony, and paradox, *or* in some sense in which that which lies "hidden" in terms of *description* may be "*shown*" in *action.*[37] In this sense, Christ remains

36. S. Kierkegaard, *Philosophical Fragments* (Princeton: Princeton University, 1936) 44; *idem, Training in Christianity* (Princeton: Princeton University, 1941) 28.

37. Kierkegaard, *Training in Christianity,* 96; on this passage see also John Macquarrie, *Jesus Christ in Modern Thought* (London: SCM, 1990) 243.

for later generations of believers "just as contemporary with His presence on earth as were those [first] contemporaries. This contemporaneousness is a condition of faith." For Christ is "the inviter," who says "come"; but "from the seat of His glory he has not spoken one word. Therefore it is Jesus Christ in his humiliation, in the state of humiliation, who spoke these words."[38] The hiddenness of what cannot be "said" directly arises from the transvaluation of authority and power as determined by the nature of the cross. Hence, Kierkegaard writes, "Christ never desired to conquer in the world; He came to the world to suffer, *that* is what He called conquering."[39]

It is not surprising, therefore, if the primary data for christology which may genuinely reflect the period before the resurrection arises not in the main from what Jesus "says" about his own power or identity, but from what has to be *presupposed* about his identity and authority on the basis of those speech-acts which rest on a more-than-earthly transcendent role and status, and point both to God and to the relation between God and Jesus. Admittedly the relation of presupposition entails more than strictly formal logical inference, since the institutional status and role in question is a more than "natural" one. In terms of speech-act theory this may be described analogically as an institutional role and status, in as far as Christ is duly appointed and authorized by God. Indeed, it also reflects a certain *sharing* of a divine role and function, even if, in direct terms, this remains hidden. The role of theological propositions in such a christology is not, in such a case, simply to describe the faith and experience of the earliest communities (Bultmann), or even the unconditioned religious experience of the ecclesial community (Schleiermacher). It is to describe those institutional features which the nonpropositional force of the speech-acts of Jesus presupposes. In language which Marshall sometimes uses, such propositions serve to explicate an "implicit" christology.

A theological counterpart to this kind of endeavor can be seen in certain areas of Barth's *Church Dogmatics.* Especially in volume II, part 2, Barth begins with the "institutional" concepts of divine *election* and *covenant* as the basis of the authorization under which Christ enacts the work of redemption and reconciliation. Barth asserts: "Election . . . is the first . . . and decisive thing. . . . It is God's choice that under the name of Jesus Christ He wills to give life to the substance of his people's history . . . constituting Himself its Lord and Shepherd."[40] For Bultmann, as for Kant, what is beyond time and space is effectively unspeakable, except through the distorted and misleading language of anthropomorphic myth. But for Barth, it is a presupposition and implicate of the active work of Jesus that "before time and space as we know them," Christ

38. Kierkegaard, *Training in Christianity* ( = *A Kierkegaard Anthology,* ed. R. Bretall [London: Oxford University, 1947] 375, 377, 387).

39. Kierkegaard, *Training in Christianity,* 218.

40. Barth, *Church Dogmatics,* vol. II, pt. 2 (Edinburgh: T. & T. Clark, 1957) 54.

is the "Elected of His Father . . . elected in his oneness with man," elected "in His pre-temporal eternity . . . election which is absolutely unique, but which in this very uniqueness is universally meaningful and efficacious."[41]

Like Kierkegaard, Barth rightly urges the importance of the principle that "the *crucified* Jesus is the image of the invisible God" (Barth's italics).[42] Both the humiliation and humble self-emptying of Jesus and his authority to forgive, to invite, and to reconcile are caught up, through divine election and appointment, into "the eternal will of God," in such a way that the two sides of the dualism of the eternal and the finite, the transcendent and the this-worldly, "together acquire one name and the name of one person . . . the christological centre."[43] In his brief *Dogmatics in Outline* Barth adds: "The work of the Son of God includes the work of the Father as its presupposition."[44]

If we penetrate so deeply into the realm of Christian theology, however, is it still appropriate to distinguish between "institutional" authority (borrowed from social history or from sociology) and "causal" force? The work of Austin, Evans, and Searle amply demonstrates the validity of the contrast. Someone whose work is unsatisfactory may respond to the warning of a friend by dint of causal force (persuasion); but this is different in official terms from a formal warning by the manager, which carries with it certain potential consequences in British employment law. An institutional status carries with it rights, obligations, and a delegated authority, as well as a representational character; institutional roles generate patterns of action which may operate with legal and social effect in accordance with the status in question. Whether the performative utterances "You are fired" or "I acquit you of blame" have extralinguistic consequences is bound up with the institutional status and role of the speaker. In this light, we may be hesitant to drive too sharp or large a wedge between so-called "functional" and "titular" christologies. Perhaps, after all, Cullmann's comments about the titular status of the "rightful lord" acquire fresh point in this context.

(5) The aspect of Searle's speech-act theory which I have explored with most profit in *New Horizons in Hermeneutics* is his careful distinction between *two "directions of fit" between words and the world.*[45] In the case of what Searle and Recanati term *"the logic of assertion"* the "direction of fit" which is entailed is that of *words reflecting the world.* The "control" is the world, and the words which depict or report states of affairs perform their required function insofar as they "fit" the world which they describe. The reverse is the case in *"the logic of promise." Here the world, or states of affairs, must be changed in order to "fit" the word of promise.* The language of biblical texts and of Christian theology

41. Barth, *Church Dogmatics,* vol. II, pt. 2, 101, 103, 104, 117.
42. Barth, *Church Dogmatics,* vol. II, pt. 2, 123.
43. Barth, *Church Dogmatics,* vol. II, pt. 2, 146, 147, 149.
44. Barth, *Dogmatics in Outline* (London: SCM, 1949) 71.
45. Thiselton, *New Horizons,* 294-307.

operates in both directions. The important direction of fit in terms of *cash value for the process of salvation* is that *the promissory language of Jesus can transform states of affairs to fit the messianic word of promise.*Here the promissory *word* is primary and life-changing. But this can be so, as we noted in our discussion of illocutions, only because certain *truths about the status, authority, and role* of Jesus can in principle be asserted — that is, that the word fits the state of affairs which it portrays.

Existential approaches to christology may well be helpful in pinpointing the self-involving dimension of confession: human persons who make christological confessions from the heart are not left unchanged. Nevertheless the capacity for change is not self-generated; it rests on the possibility of accounting, even if retrospectively, for the basis beyond human persons which makes promissory language effective. On the other hand, it is equally only half of the story to reduce christology to mere description alone. Christology has to do with an interplay between assertions which "fit" states of affairs and changes in states of affairs to make them "fit" a promissory word. The Fourth Gospel, partly because of its more explicit retrospective and cosmic perspective, allows equal prominence to be given to both directions of fit. The Synoptic Gospels make promissory language explicit, leaving the possibility of christological assertion to lie hidden *implicitly* behind the overt speech-acts of Jesus as that which gives them currency.

In one case, the world shapes the words. Here descriptive report constitutes the primary model. In the other case, *directives,* or *directive speech-acts,* may function like a shopping list which I may carry with me around the stores: the words on the list ("peaches," "milk," "bread") determine how I shape the world in terms of what I remove from the shelves; whereas a store detective rehearsing a report when I forgot to pay uses words which describe a state of affairs in the world as he or she observed it to be.[46] Here a key paradigm suggested and developed by Searle and in *New Horizons* is that of *promise.*

What could be more central to an account of christology than the notion of a *status and role appropriate to a mission to "change the world to match the word of promise"*? The many utterances, therefore, of what Jesus came to do carry presuppositions about his authorization and authority to put verbal promises, especially the promises of God, into *operative effect,* where prophets, wise people, and others had failed to do so. It is at this point that Luke's concern for the world as a public domain of action and transformation comes into play as a contribution to christological understanding which characterizes his Gospel.

46. Searle, *Expression and Meaning,* 3-4.

## 3

In his detailed and thorough commentary on the Greek text of Luke, Marshall comments concerning Luke's choice of style for his preface (Luke 1:1-4): ". . . Luke was claiming a place for Christianity on the stage of world history. How far his predecessors had made such claims we do not know."[47] The often-discussed triple dating of Luke 3:1, 2, with its six historical allusions, likewise, Marshall notes, serves "to give the Christian gospel its setting in imperial and local history."[48] In contrast to supposed or actual elements of secrecy in Mark, S. Brown urges in his essay on Luke's prologues (1978) that "Luke is telling his readers *all* there is to tell" (his italics).[49] While in certain parts of his argument he may well overstate a case, U. Wilckens rightly sees a contrast between Luke's concern for the public domain of history and tradition, and an existentialist emphasis among Bultmann and other interpreters on the individual, on personal decision, and on the transitory present moment.[50]

Many features which have traditionally been regarded as evidences of Luke's "universalism" may perhaps more strictly reflect his concern to present the gospel and his christology as truth in the public domain. The tracing of the genealogy of Jesus back to Adam rather than forward from Abraham may reflect not so much some particular attitude about Jews and Gentiles, but Luke's concern to disengage the gospel from any supposedly sectarian ghettolike tradition (Luke 3:38). The same comment might be offered concerning Luke's extension of the quotation from Isaiah: "and all flesh shall see the salvation of God" (Luke 3:6), and perhaps the small touch in Luke which adds "from north and south" to Matthew's "from east and west" (Luke 13:29; par. Matt 8:11).

Conzelmann's uneven work, with its idiosyncratic blend of the perceptive and the speculative, well underlines Luke's interest in public or "secular" history. As Conzelmann observes, "the State is here to stay," and Luke, far from seeing the world as a realm out of which the believer is to be taken, understands it as a public stage on which witness can be viewed, and as a sociopolitical reality which invites structure and order both inside and outside the Christian community.[51] It is perhaps less central an issue whether it is Jewish or Roman authorities who find Jesus innocent of any crime than a distinctive concern of Luke to place on public record that the duly appointed sociopolitical authorities who oversee law and order "find no crime in this person" (distinctive to Luke 23:4, of Pilate) or are simply frustrated in their misguided attempts to do so

47. Marshall, *Gospel of Luke,* 40.

48. Marshall, *Gospel of Luke,* 132.

49. S. Brown, "The Role of the Prologues in Determining the Purpose of Luke-Acts," in *Perspectives on Luke-Acts,* ed. C. H. Talbert (Edinburgh: T. & T. Clark, 1978) 105; cf. 99-111.

50. U. Wilckens, "Interpreting Luke-Acts in a Period of Existentialist Theology," in *Studies in Luke-Acts,* ed. L. E. Keck and J. L. Martyn (London: S.P.C.K., 1968) 60-83.

51. H. Conzelmann, *The Theology of Luke* (London: Faber, 1960) 138.

(distinctive to Luke 23:9-11, of Herod and "Herod's jurisdiction," v 7). Three times the representative of Imperial government, as Conzelmann and others note, confirms the legal and political innocence of Jesus.[52]

What has often traditionally been regarded as Luke's "social concern" should also be seen in the light of its significance for the public domain. First, the universally recognized concerns about women, the poor, and the outcasts, serve to deprivilege any suggestion that the gospel is addressed primarily to some "inner" religious elite. The non-religious and the outsider are involved. Second, Luke's interest in the stewardship of riches, land, and property calls attention to the public face of otherwise "inner" response. Hence Luke alone includes what one writer over-grandly called the "sociological" teaching of John the Baptist (Luke 3:10-14): repentance is to make an observable difference in the public world for tax collectors and for soldiers as well as for "the multitudes" (Luke 3:10, 12, 14). Kodell's comment that "Luke is not soft and easy-going" reflects not a character judgment, for Luke is an outstandingly warm and generous writer; but Luke's theological recognition that unless the Christian community can "show" where the transcendent dimension makes a difference in the public world, the credibility of the gospel becomes undercut.[53]

This does not lead Luke to underplay eschatological concerns, as H. W. Bartsch, S. G. Wilson, and others have pointed out.[54] Wilson is surely right to see a double pastoral concern on Luke's part in this respect (cf. Luke 12:38-48). But it may help to account for a perplexing ambivalence of emphasis on what many describe as Luke's preoccupation with "evidential" activities of the Holy Spirit in relation to Jesus as well as to the church.

Peculiar to Luke is Jesus' application of his synagogue reading of Isaiah 61:1-2: "The Spirit of the Lord is upon me, because he has anointed me to preach good news to the poor. He has sent me to proclaim release to the captives and recovering of sight to the blind, to set at liberty those who are oppressed, to proclaim the acceptable year of the Lord" (Luke 4:18-19). James Dunn describes this as "almost certainly a Lukan construction on the basis of Mark" in which Luke brings forward in anticipation an earlier reference to messiahship than is historically probable, on the basis of Isaiah 61.[55] Dunn sees the reference to "the poor" in the Beatitudes as a further allusion to Isaiah 61 (Matt 5:3; Luke 6:20), and more especially a third allusion in Jesus' reply to John the Baptist in Luke 7:18-23, par. Matt 11:2-6). On the basis of the second and third examples Dunn concludes that "Isa. 61:1 played an important role in Jesus' own thinking,"

52. Conzelmann, *Theology of Luke,* 140.

53. J. Kodell, "The Theology of Luke in Recent Study," *BTB* 1 (1971) 119.

54. H. W. Bartsch, *Wachet aber zu jeder Zeit! Entwurf einer Auslegung des Lukasevangeliums* (Hamburg-Bergstedt, 1963); S. G. Wilson, *The Gentiles and the Gentile Mission in Luke-Acts* (Cambridge: Cambridge University, 1973) 59-87.

55. J. D. G. Dunn, *Jesus and the Spirit* (London: SCM, 1975) 54.

after a rigorous examination of theories about the original authenticity of 7:18-23.[56]

At first sight it may seem difficult to reconcile Dunn's comment that Jesus' "own experience of God, of divine power and inspiration" make him aware of the applicability of Isaiah 61:1-2 to himself, with C. K. Barrett's earlier penetrating conclusion that "Jesus acted under the necessity of divine constraint. Lack of glory and a cup of suffering were his Messianic vocations, and part of his poverty was the absence of all the signs of the Spirit of God. They would have been inconsistent with the office of a humiliated Messiah."[57] Indeed, can these two comments be reconciled, or does Dunn capture Luke's emphasis while Barrett communicates Mark's?

As both Barrett and Dunn confirm, the "anointing" of Jesus for his messianic office took place at his baptism. The Spirit "descends" onto Jesus in all three traditions; although while the allusion to the dove in Matt 3:16 and Mark 1:10 may suggest a parallel with divine creativity in Genesis, Luke's addition of "in bodily form" (σωματικῇ εἴδει, Luke 3:22) may perhaps hint at the notion of "visible appearance," which Marshall sees as potentially a possible interpretation of Mark 1:10, here "heightened by Luke."[58] At all events, three points are clear. First, as Dunn urges, in this experience Jesus recognized an awareness of the Spirit, which he understood as also a consciousness of sonship. Second, Marshall stresses, this constituted an act in which "Jesus is commissioned and equipped for his task."[59] Third, as Barrett emphasizes, part of the total act is the initiation of Jesus into the temptation experience from which "Jesus returns from victory with the conviction that the way of God's Chosen is the way of humility and weakness, and from that time references to the Spirit are very few indeed."[60] It may be a different matter, Barrett adds, after the vindication and exaltation of Jesus.

Although it may be strictly justified, Dunn's language concerning Jesus as a "charismatic figure" may perhaps risk the possibility of confusions between *institutional authorization* to act as Spirit-anointed divine presence in the name of God and *causal power* to perform supernatural feats. This would once again open the door to the problems of a dualistic approach to christology which we have been trying to avoid. It is considerably more helpful when in his *Christology in the Making* Dunn focuses on "Jesus' sense of sonship" with reference to issues about his messianic consciousness and of his sense "of eschatological significance, unique in the degree and finality of the revelation and authority accorded to him."[61]

56. Dunn, *Jesus,* 55-60.

57. C. K. Barrett, *The Holy Spirit and the Gospel Tradition* (London: S.P.C.K., 1958) 158; Dunn, *Jesus,* 61.

58. Marshall, *Gospel of Luke,* 153.

59. Marshall, *Gospel of Luke,* 154.

60. Barrett, *Holy Spirit,* 159.

61. J. D. G. Dunn, *Christology in the Making: An Inquiry into the Origins of the Doctrine of the Incarnation* (London: SCM, 1980) 29; cf. 22-28.

So we return to specific examples of speech-acts in Luke which may "show" but not necessarily "say" christological dimensions of authorization, status, and institutional role in the purposes of God for the world, even if as presupposition or implicates they may, in turn, give rise to christological propositions or even indirectly seem to presuppose the propriety of certain "titles." As we earlier conceded, such presupposition may entail more than a formal logical relation of implication, because a judgment about the transcendent nature of the authorization has still to be made. Further, whether Jesus explicitly "claimed" such titles transforms the agenda into something different from whether his speech-acts might presuppose their candidature for consideration. Some central examples in the triple tradition have already been mentioned: "My son, your sins are forgiven" (Mark 2:5; Matt 9:2; Luke 5:20); "Peace! Be still!" (Mark 4:35-41; Matt 8:23-27; Luke 8:22-25); "Be silent, come out of him" (Mark 1:25; cf. Mark 3:23-27; Matt 12:22-30; Luke 11:14-23).

Some substantial further examples, however, remain peculiar to Luke. One of the most important is the raising of the widow's son at Nain: "Jesus came and touched the bier, and the bearers stood still. And he said, 'Young man, I say to you, arise.' And the dead man sat up, and began to speak" (Luke 7:14-15). Howard Marshall rightly calls attention to the sequel in which the witnesses reflect on what this might imply about the identity and role of Jesus. Jesus himself does not "say" what this is; but the bystanders speculate on the themes of "a great prophet" and "a divine visitation," and at very least conclude from what they see that "God has acted in the mighty work done by Jesus."[62]

The act of healing a crippled woman in the speaking of an utterance (Luke 13:10-17) also remains peculiar to Luke: "She was bent over and could not fully straighten herself. And when Jesus saw her, he called her and said to her, 'Woman, you are [hereby] freed from your infirmity', and immediately she was made straight, and she praised God" (13:12-13). Marshall rightly comments that both the immediate response of the woman (v 13) and the second climax of the episode (v 17, "rejoiced at the glorious things . . .") stress "that the deeds of Jesus are the work of God."[63] They therefore reflect the institutional authority, status, and role, defined by what Barth (we saw) called the divine election of Jesus, rather than Jesus' reliance on unmediated causal power as such. Thereby his status as humiliated Messiah who points to God is not transposed into premature exaltation before the resurrection, but remains a cruciform mediation of divine presence and power. Jesus' christological status is sufficiently hidden to shift the focus to God; but sufficiently presupposed to give rise to themes of glory through his speech-acts.

It would be possible to multiply further instances from the triple tradition or from Luke. It is worth noting, for example, that in the triple tradition Jesus

62. Marshall, *Gospel of Luke*, 287.
63. Marshall, *Gospel of Luke*, 559.

performs the act of giving sight to Bartimaeus, but only in Luke does this take the explicit form of a speech-act — "Receive [hereby] your sight" (Luke 18:42) — rather than a report of a healing (Matt 20:34) or a reference to the man's faith with a different utterance (Mark 10:52, although "go your way" might equally be said to constitute a speech-act). Without doubt, the most explicit example of a speech-act which becomes operative *on the basis of institutional authority rather than causal power* occurs in the material peculiar to Luke in the healing of the centurion's servant (Luke 7:1-10). The whole basis of the centurion's grasp of the situation is, as Marshall suggests, that Jesus "can use his delegated authority to give orders that others must obey."[64] This expresses the heart of the matter.

Some might be tempted to associate this approach with an "adoptionist" christology. But such a categorization would be crude and inaccurate, since what is at issue is a feature of language which allows the unity of the divine and human to be "shown," in terms of implicature, without risking a separation of the Jesus of history from the eternal Word or the Christ of faith. However, such a separation might be said to have characterized so-called "adoptionist" christologies in the early church.

By contrast, I hope that the above arguments have sign-posted a possible approach that allows NT texts to engage with those horizons of our own day which are inevitably colored by the problems bequeathed by Kant, without inviting the difficulties of a Kantian dualism. John Macquarrie's magisterial book *Jesus Christ in Modern Thought* (1990) confirms, if any confirmation is needed, the pervasive difficulty posed by this Kantian legacy throughout most major strands in modern christology. Kant himself, Macquarrie demonstrates, gave priority to the notion of Christ as "archetype" rather than as a historical figure in terms which were "fundamentally docetic."[65] Schleiermacher's hope to expound the incarnation "as a natural fact" was so heavily qualified as to frustrate his own intentions.[66] Hegel's privileging of speculative thought in the dialectical process led him to give priority to the "speculative Good Friday" over "the historical Good Friday."[67] Strauss, as we have noted, presided over a "collapse of the historical record," but whether entirely seriously or not also argued that "faith can survive unscathed."[68]

In our own century some, like Tillich, have entertained the hypothesis that a Christ without reference to history could still sustain faith. For the most part, however, writers have stressed the other side of the dualism, and J. A. T. Robinson's book *The Human Face of God* (1973) represents one of the most

64. Marshall, *Gospel of Luke,* 282.

65. J. Macquarrie, *Jesus Christ in Modern Thought* (London: SCM, 1990) 185.

66. Macquarrie, *Jesus Christ,* 208.

67. Macquarrie, *Jesus Christ,* 220.

68. Macquarrie, *Jesus Christ,* 229. On Hegel and on the period from Ritschl to Troeltsch, cf. also A. McGrath, *The Making of Modern German Christology* (Oxford: Blackwell, 1986) 32-93.

powerful and moving statements of the reality of the humanness of Jesus of Nazareth. But the sense of unease and discomfort about a dualistic chasm that can scarcely be bridged generates various symptoms, including the contemporary difficulty that too often biblical specialists and systematic or philosophical theologians tend simply to "talk past" each other on the basis of a different agenda.

The approach outlined in this essay does not claim to resolve this problem. Indeed, it would be foolish to attempt to view this approach as a comprehensive or fully rounded model for christology. The Fourth Gospel approaches matters from a different angle, even though we should not underplay the significance of *delegated* (and in this sense "institutional") authority focused in a Christ whose glory is seen in terms of humiliation, suffering, and self-giving service: "As the Father has sent me, even so I send you" (John 20:21).

In Luke, however, Searle's notion of a certain category of speech-act which operates with a "world-to-word" direction of fit touches a central nerve of christology, and perhaps allows some progress toward softening the problem of dualism in modern christology. By virtue of an institutional status and role which is seldom "said" but often presupposed, the humiliated Messiah on his way to the cross begins decisively to transform the world in accordance with divine promise. His acts, and especially his speech-acts, "show" themselves in the public domain on the stage of historical life. What could be nearer to the heart of christology than that Jesus begins to change the world in accordance with the divine word of promise, and that his speech and his acts "make themselves manifest" as the speech and acts of God?

# The Foundational Conviction of New Testament Christology: The Obedience / Faithfulness / Sonship of Christ

Richard N. Longenecker

Numerous attempts have been made throughout the course of the church's history to capture the essence of the gospel by means of highlighting some supposedly central NT concept or expression. Much that has been proposed has been enlightening and helpful — though when isolated and treated in an exclusivistic fashion, all too often that supposedly central feature has been used to truncate the fulness of the gospel or to deflect Christian thought and action into subsidiary paths, so skewing the Christian message.

One early attempt at capturing the essence of the gospel was that encapsulated by what has been called the "Victory Motif," which G. Aulén (*Christus Victor,* 1931) and R. Leivestad (*Christ the Conqueror,* 1954) have labeled the "classic idea" of the atonement: that God through the work of Christ on the cross won victory over the evil cosmic powers, thereby freeing believers from sin, death, the law, and condemnation. Later in the third and fourth centuries, in response to such seemingly logical questions as Victory over whom, where and how?, this emphasis on victory became the basis for the "Devil Ransom" theory and the "*Descensus ad Inferos*" doctrine (so the Nicene Creed: "He descended into hell"). Another attempt has been to focus on the "Body of Christ" — which as a metaphor carries important corporate nuances regarding the relationship of believers to Christ and to one another, but has been seen in certain circles to have ontological significance as well. So in Roman Catholic theology the fact that the church is spoken of in the Pauline letters as the "Body of Christ" has been spelled out to mean that just as Christ walked the hills of Palestine in his physical body so he exists corporally today in his church with its center at Rome, with the result that there now exist (1) two forms of revelation (Scripture and Tradition), the latter being more explicit and the prescribed means for understanding the former, and (2) two forms of redemptive activity (Christ's work and the church's work), the latter being a redoing and application of the former. Most rigidly expressed, the church is God's sole agent of revelation and redemption today, with no salvation available to men and women apart from the ministrations of the church.

The watchword of the Protestant Reformation was "Justification by Faith." What Luther and his reforming colleagues desired was that people be brought back to a lively consciousness of what Christ had already done on their behalf, thereby putting an end to all thoughts about attaining righteousness by one's own efforts or acceptance before God by one's own actions. So they focused on the fact of God's justification of the unrighteous by means of the work of Christ, with concomitant emphases on "Scripture alone" (apart from ecclesiastical dogma) and "faith alone" (apart from works). Later as these Reformation principles took root, the idea of "imputation" was viewed, particularly in Reformed circles, as being also a central motif of the gospel — both that of God's imputation of Adam's sin to each individual and God's imputation of Christ's righteousness to the elect. In other circles, however, such concepts as "salvation," "reconciliation," or even "transfer of merit" became important auxiliary ideas to be joined to the central theme of justification.

The twentieth century, too, has witnessed a number of attempts to capture the essence of the gospel in a central motif or expression. One prevalent way has been to focus on the eschatological factor of early Christian proclamation, with various schemes proposed. Chief among these often quite diverse eschatological proposals are those that go under such names as "Consistent" or "Thoroughgoing Eschatology," "Realized Eschatology," "Proleptic Eschatology," "Inaugurated Eschatology," "Participationistic Eschatology," and "Fulfilled Messianism." Another quite prevalent approach has been to focus on the christological titles of the NT, with particular attention to one or the other of these titles as incorporating the substance of the early Christians' conviction regarding Jesus of Nazareth and so the essence of their first preaching and teaching. Chief among these titular proposals have been those that focus on the title "Messiah" or "Christ," or the title "Son of God," or that of "Lord," or "Son of Man," or some combination of the above — with often quite diverse understandings set forth as to what each of these titles meant among early believers, and so quite diverse implications drawn as to what any one central title or complex of titles might have signified as to the essence of the earliest Christian proclamation.

The above listing sets out in rough outline only some of the most prominent proposals that have been put forward over the course of the past two millennia in an endeavor to capture the essence of the Christian gospel. But even such a rough-hewn sketch raises questions as to the possibility, feasibility, and / or capability of scholars to carry out such an endeavor. Amid all of the various features within the proclamation of the NT, can we, in fact, identify a central affirmation or some foundational conviction that resides at the heart of things? Or to pick up on an expression coined by J. Moffatt, Is there an identifiable "sense of center" in all that is variously affirmed in the NT? Even more important for our consideration here — and particularly since we believe that conviction regarding Jesus of Nazareth lies at the heart of all Christian proclamation: Is there some basic understanding of the work and person of Jesus of Nazareth that underlies the christology of the NT?

The thesis of this article is that the various terms and expressions used in the NT with respect to Christ are to be understood as pictorial representations, graphic metaphors, and / or similes that stem ultimately from a basic conviction that has to do with the obedience, faithfulness, and sonship of Christ — with its corollary being the trustful obedience of the believer in response. In the case of Christ, I suggest that all the titles ascribed to him in the NT and all the metaphors used in description of the nature and effects of his work are founded ultimately on the early Christians' conviction regarding the full obedience and entire faithfulness of Jesus of Nazareth, God's Son *par excellence,* with this complete filial obedience seen as having been exercised throughout his life and coming to ultimate expression in his death on the cross. In the case of believers, response is in terms of relationship with that Obedient One — or, in Pauline terms, being "in Christ."

Long ago in his quasi-popular English lectures *The Religion of Jesus and the Faith of Paul* (1923), A. Deissmann attempted to mark out the path that scholars should take in dealing with the various theological terms in Paul's letters. So, for example, when speaking of Paul's teaching on justification, Deissmann wrote:

> According to my conception, the doctrine of justification is not the quintessence of Paulinism, but one witness among others to his experience of salvation. Justification is one ancient picture-word, alongside many others. Justification is one note, which, along with many others — redemption, adoption, etc. — is harmonised in the one chord that testifies to salvation. (271)

Similarly, on the variety of terms used by Paul, Deissmann wrote:

> The impression of complexity has only arisen because we have not understood the similes as similes which were synonymous with one another, though to the mind of antiquity they would easily have been so understood. The single so-called Pauline ideas have been isolated by us, and then the attempt has been made to reconstruct a chronological order of salvation, an 'ordo salutis', as our ancestors called it. As a matter of fact, the religion of Paul is something quite simple. It is communion with Christ. (222-23)

Deissmann's statements, of course, must be seen in the context of his own agenda: that of the primacy of being "in Christ" or "Christ mysticism" in Pauline thought — which is an understanding of Paul that cannot be easily set aside, though it is not the focus of our discussion here. Nonetheless, whatever is thought of Deissmann's overall thesis, his comments regarding the nature of Paul's theological language (as well as of NT language generally) are suggestive and helpful.

More recently M. Barth, in his 1971 work on *Justification*, focused his analysis of Paul's understanding of Christ's work on the theme "Jesus Christ comes, demonstrating faithfulness to God and man" (38-39). Barth's emphasis in that central part of his work is stated in the following words:

> The Son is not only sent out by the Father and Judge to be a passive tool, as it were, of God. He also renders *obedience* to his commission by *coming* to fulfil his office. With his advent, 'faith came'. . . . Thus faith in God (or better, faithfulness to God) and love for men are realized in Jesus Christ at the same time in the same deed. (39, italics his)

In what follows, I want to spell out the above thesis by way of a rather elemental survey of the major NT materials, dealing with them in rather rough chronological fashion: first with some of the early Christian confessions that are incorporated within the NT writings, then with Paul's letters, then with the canonical Gospels, and finally with the Letter to the Hebrews. The reader needs to be alerted to the fact that, due to the scope of the subject here treated, I have opted to omit the citing of support for the various statements made, since any attempt at proper footnoting would have to be extensive — consuming, in fact, the article's greater amount of space. I can only beg the indulgence of the reader, particularly so since my intent is more suggestive than definitive. Furthermore, the reader needs to be aware that throughout what follows I am using the terms "obedience," "faithfulness," and "son / sonship" with reference to Christ in a roughly equivalent fashion. My hope is that such an equivalency of concepts will be seen to be demonstrable from the data cited below.

## 1. The Early Christian Confessions

That there existed within the early church certain rather fixed confessional formulas is suggested by references in the Pauline corpus (1) to "the traditions" that Paul passed on to his converts (2 Thess 2:15), (2) to kerygmatic material that was commonly used within the early church, which Paul received and passed on (1 Cor 15:3; see also v 11), (3) to "the form of teaching" to which believers were committed (Rom 6:17), and (4) to "the good confession" made by Timothy (1 Tim 6:12). The presence of such confessional formulas is also pointed to by statements in Hebrews that speak of "confessing" Jesus (3:1), "confessing the faith" (4:14), and "confessing" one's Christian hope (10:23), as well as those in Jude that refer to "the faith" and "the most holy faith" (3, 20). Exactly what criteria are to be used for establishing the presence of such early Christian confessional material in any particular NT portion has been a matter of continued debate ever since the first proposals made by E. Norden in his *Agnostos Theos* of 1912. Likewise, how to distinguish between liturgical formulations, creedal statements, traditional sayings, and hymns — as well, of course, as identifying the provenance of each of these confessional fragments — are matters on which scholars have often been divided. Nonetheless, almost all are agreed that the needs of proclamation, worship, and instruction among the early believers in Jesus must have brought into existence various Christian confessional materials, and most believe it possible to identify at least some of these within the pages of the NT.

The first early Christian confession to be identified within a NT passage, and the one that has been accepted by almost everyone to be the most obvious, is the hymnodic portion found in Phil 2:6-11. One need not here rehearse the reasons why this passage is usually seen to be a pre-Pauline Christian hymn, nor attempt to analyze its stropic structure or identify its exact provenance. Nor need we enter here into any of the many theological debates that have been based on this passage or that use it as the fulcrum for their arguments — for example, whether the nature of the Son is the same as *(homoousios)* or similar to *(homoiousios)* that of the Father; whether preexistence is an attribute of Christ; whether a Kenosis theory of the Incarnation legitimately derives from this passage, and, if so, how it should be understood; whether a docetic view of the Incarnation is expressed in this passage; and issues regarding Christ's exaltation, ultimate universal lordship, and even the meaning of the title "Lord" itself.

All of the above critical and theological matters are important for any proper analysis of this passage. For if in these verses we have the remnants of an early pre-Pauline Christian confession that is set within the strophic structure of a hymn, then it is of the greatest import to deal with these matters seriously when trying to understand the attitudes and commitments of at least one congregation of early Christian believers, whatever may be said about their exact conceptual orientation or geographical location.

All this being so, however, it yet remains necessary to highlight one datum of importance that is central in this passage — not just because it is suitable for our purposes, but also because it is so often overlooked: that in his actions on behalf of humanity, the one of whom the hymn speaks "became obedient unto death" (γενόμενος ὑπήκοος μέχρι θανάτου). At the very heart of this early Christian hymn is an affirmation regarding the complete obedience of Christ. It is an obedience expressed not just "in death," as is so often mistakenly assumed, but an obedience that characterized his entire life and so extended even to the inclusion of death, as the preposition μέχρι suggests in its emphasis on degree, measure, and / or extent.

That such an obedience is the focal point of the hymn is signaled by what appears to be Paul's inserted exclamation at this point: "Even death on a cross!" The words should probably be seen as Paul's own emotive interjection, for they break the stropic structure of the hymn, however that structure is set out. Certainly they reflect (1) a general Jewish horror of the exposure of a dead corpse on a tree, which came during the Second Temple period to include the impalement or crucifixion of a living person on a pole or cross (cf. Deut 21:22-23), (2) the central problem of early Christians as to how to understand Jesus of Nazareth as both Messiah and accursed by God because of having died on a cross, which they resolved by the proclamation of an "exchange curse" (cf. 2 Cor 5:21), and (3) Paul's own early revulsion against any thought of a crucified Messiah, which he knew to be scandalous to Jews (cf. 1 Cor 1:23; Gal 5:11). More importantly, however, Paul's interjected words should be seen as signaling the point of emphasis in this early Christian confessional hymn — at least the emphasis in the κατάβασις or "lowering" section, which makes up the first half of the hymn: that the work of Christ is to be understood preeminently in terms of his complete obedience, with that obedience being present throughout his life and extending even to the inclusion of death. And it is this kind of obedience that is appealed to throughout the rest of Philippians, first in showing how it was present in the ministries of Paul himself, his colleague Timothy, and the church's emissary Epaphroditus, and then in urging that such a paradigm of obedience be worked out in the lives of believers at Philippi as well.

In Gal 4:4-5 there appears another early Christian confessional portion that Paul seems to have drawn, either in whole or in part, from the church's proclamation:

> When the time had fully come, God sent his Son, born of a woman, born under the law, to redeem those under the law, that we might receive the full rights of sons.

It is a confession that seems based, as narrative analysis suggests, on the gospel story as told by the earliest Jewish Christians. And it is a confession used by Paul to support his emphases in Galatians on (1) a believer's true sonship when related to God by means of the work of Christ, apart from "the works of the law," and (2) Gentile believers' freedom from the supervision of the Mosaic law.

These verses seem to stem from a Jewish Christian confessional affirmation, for Paul quotes them to Gentile converts by way of countering judaizing agitators who claimed to be supported by the Jewish Christian congregation at Jerusalem. But what needs to be noted here is that central to this confessional portion is a stress on the sonship of Christ, which in a Jewish Christian context probably carried not so much an ontological nuance as signaled primarily the factor of loving obedience rendered by the Son to the Father.

The statement "God sent his Son" may very well have been a formula drawn from Jewish Wisdom writings and used by the early Christians to associate Wisdom with Christ (cf. 1 Cor 1:24, 30), as E. Schweizer and many others have argued — whether with ontological or functional nuances, or both. But when this formulaic statement was used among Jewish Christians in the context of a confession, Gal 4:4-5 tells us that they spoke of Christ as not only being truly human ("born of a woman") and possessing a representative quality ("the Man") but also as offering a perfect obedience to God the Father ("born under the law," "the Son") on behalf of all those "under the law," that is, all Jews.

Also of importance when dealing with the sonship of Christ in the early Christian confessions is the title "Son of God" in the salutation of Paul's letter to the Romans. Romans 1:3-4 is often seen as an early confession that Paul used to explicate what he means by "his Son": (1) "the one who was a descendant of David, as to his human nature"; but also (2) "the one who was declared to be the Son of God with power, according to the spirit of holiness, by the resurrection of the dead." A two-stage understanding of Christ seems to be here set out. The first identifies him as David's descendant. The second speaks of what God declared him to be on the basis of the character of his life and as evidenced by his resurrection. And for that latter stage the title "Son of God" is used, which in an early Jewish Christian confession probably referred more to Christ's attitude and actions of obedience than to anything necessarily ontological — though, of course, such an ascription would fit well into later christological developments.

One other early confessional portion could perhaps be cited here in defense of the thesis that the obedience or faithfulness of the Son is the underlying conviction of the earliest christology — though, of course, as one moves on to analyze the various proposed early Christian confessions it becomes more and more difficult both to legitimize their presence and to set out their limits. That particular confessional portion in mind comes at the end of the thesis paragraph of Rom 3:21-26, which has been argued by R. Bultmann, E. Käsemann, *et al.* to be made up of vv 24-26 (starting with the participle δικαιούμενοι, "being justified") and by E. Lohse and others to comprise vv 25-26 (starting with the relative personal pronoun ὅν, "who"). Based on an analysis of structure, style, *hapax legomena,* and distinctive theological content, a compelling case has been made for the presence of an early Christian confessional portion that is here used by Paul in support of his thesis of Rom 3:21-23 (perhaps also v 24) regarding the manifestation of God's righteousness, the witness of Scripture, the work of Christ, and the necessity of faith — though scholars have been almost equally divided as to exactly where that confession begins (and to some extent ends).

For my part, I believe Bultmann and company to be right in taking the confession to begin with the present participle δικαιούμενοι, "being justified." Accepting such a view, the confessional portion may be seen as setting out three graphic metaphors in description of the work of Christ: (1) the legal metaphor of justification, "being justified freely by his grace" (v 24a); (2) the civil and social metaphor of redemption, "through the redemption that came about by Christ Jesus" (v 24b); and (3) the cultic metaphor of sacrificial atonement or propitiation / expiation, "God set him forth as a sacrifice of atonement [or propitiation, expiation] through faith in his blood" (v 25a). But what needs to be noted as well is that all three of these metaphors — as well as everything else said about God's salvific actions in the rest of vv 25b-26 — are based on the final statement of the confession, which serves as the climax of the whole: "In order that God might be just and the justifier of τὸν ἐκ πίστεως Ἰησοῦ."

That final expression τὸν ἐκ πίστεως Ἰησοῦ is, of course, notoriously difficult to translate. Taking Ἰησοῦ as an objective genitive, it may mean "the one who has faith in Jesus." More likely, however, as we will attempt to validate when discussing later the expression πίστις Ἰησοῦ Χριστοῦ in Paul's own thought, Ἰησοῦ should probably here be seen as a subjective genitive and the expression in question understood as "the one who is based on the faithfulness of Jesus." And if this be so, then it needs to be observed that in an early Christian confession that Paul uses in support of his thesis statements of Rom 3:21-23 regarding the present manifestation of God's righteousness, the metaphors "justification," "redemption," and "propitiation / expiation" are based on and stem from an underlying conviction regarding the faithfulness of Jesus.

## 2. Paul's Letters

The above four confessions have been drawn from three letters of Paul. In any full treatment of the early Christian confessional materials it is necessary to deal not only with what the early believers meant by such statements but also how the author who incorporates them into his writings understood them. It is possible, of course, for authors to quote material for their own purposes without giving full credence to all that is said in the quotation. But this was not the case in Paul's use of these four confessions — particularly with respect to their focus on Christ's obedient and faithful sonship. To a degree we have hinted at how Paul used the portrayals of Christ's obedience in his exhortations directed to believers at Philippi, Galatia, and Rome, thereby suggesting how intrinsic such a theme was to his own theology. And we believe that any more complete contextual study of these confessions and their use by Paul will bear such an understanding out. More directly relevant here, however, are the statements of Paul's own composition (via, of course, one or more of his colleagues or companions who served as his amanuensis or secretary) that focus on the obedience, sonship, and / or faithfulness of Christ.

The most obvious reference to the obedience of Christ in Paul's own writings is to be found in Rom 5:19:

> For just as through the disobedience of the one man were the many made sinners, so through the obedience of the one man will the many be made righteous.

In context, this statement must be seen as the second part of a doublet, the first part of which is set out in v 18. For in v 18 Paul speaks of the "one trespass" of

Adam that resulted in "condemnation for all humanity," countering it by Christ's "one act of righteousness" that brings about "righteousness of life for all humanity"; while in v 19 he speaks of "the disobedience of the one man [Adam]" that brought about the sinful condition of "the many," countering it by "the obedience of the one man [the Second Man = Christ]" that will make "the many" righteous. Also speaking contextually, vv 18-19 must be seen as the conclusion of Paul's rather convoluted argument that began back at v 12, as the joining of the particles ἄρα and οὖν at the beginning of v 18 suggests.

There are, of course, a number of issues that need to be dealt with in any full consideration of what Paul is saying in v 19 and its import for the argument of Romans. Immediately obvious is the question as to whether the parallel statements of vv 18 and 19 are to be taken as setting out two distinguishable, though clearly related phenomena (i.e., Christ's "passive righteousness" in his death and his "active righteousness" throughout his life) or should be seen in terms of the former being explicated by the latter (i.e., Christ's "one act of righteousness" in his death is to be understood in the context of his complete obedience). Furthermore, exactly how 5:12-21 functions in the course of Paul's argument throughout Romans 1–8 is an important issue for any real contextual and exegetical study of Romans. Most commentators believe that there is a break in Paul's argument in these chapters that occurs either between chs. 4 and 5 or between chs. 5 and 6, and so (1) view chs. 1–4 and 5–8 as two phases of the argument (the first on justification; the second on sanctification) or (2) take chs. 1–5 as the argument for justification by faith and chs. 6–8 as depicting the results of justification — with Luther, who favored this latter understanding, even suggesting 5:12-21 to be an excursus appended by Paul to his portrayal of justification in 3:21–5:11. On the other hand, some have proposed that the argument of the first eight chapters of Romans should be seen as being set out in two somewhat overlapping or parallel sections, with the break coming between 5:11 and 5:12: the first, that of 1:18–5:11; the second, that of 5:12–8:39 (so, e.g., Melanchthon, Zahn, Leenhardt, Black).

I personally favor taking 5:12-21 as the beginning of the central section of Paul's argument in Romans, with this new section of 5:12–8:39 building on what has gone before in 1:18–5:11 but going on beyond that to present a series of relationships that culminate in the state of being "in Christ." On such a view, Paul's reference to the obedience of Christ, who is the Second Man, has an important place in the overall argumentation of Romans, for it appears in material that starts off the new, central section of the letter in 5:12–8:39. But even if the place of 5:12-21 in the overall argument of Romans should be viewed differently, at least it needs to be noted that reference to the obedience of Christ in v 19 has a vital place in the argument of 5:12-21 itself, for it is the basic feature that Paul highlights when he speaks about the work of Christ — whether the parallel statements of vv 18-19 are to be seen as depicting two related phenomena that come to climax in the latter (cf. the phenomena of "death" and "life" in Rom 5:10) or as the former being explicated by the latter.

Admittedly, apart from its appearance in the confession of Phil 2:6-11, only here in Rom 5:19 does Paul use the noun "obedience" when speaking about the work of Christ. But theology is more than mathematics, and one does not just appeal to frequency counts in support of significance. Furthermore, one needs to couple with this term the cognate expressions and statements that appear in Paul's letter for the idea of obedience. Chief among such cognate ways of expressing Christ's obedience in Paul's writings are the expression "the faith / faithfulness of Jesus Christ [or Christ Jesus, or simply Christ]" and the titles "Son" and "Son of God."

Of late, many have come to see that Paul's use of πίστις Ἰησοῦ Χριστοῦ has much to do with the subject of Christ's obedience, and that, further, it should be seen as signaling something of vital importance for Paul's own christological thought. Usually, of course, the genitive occurrence of the name "Jesus Christ," "Christ Jesus," or simply "Christ" in the expression is taken as an objective genitive, and so translated "faith in Jesus Christ." Some still insist on that as the only possible translation. Others, however, find in the expression a great deal of christological significance, though without minimizing the importance of human faith as called for in many of Paul's other uses of πίστις.

In addition to its appearance in the confessional material of Rom 3:26b, the expression πίστις Χριστοῦ Ἰησοῦ appears in Paul's own writings six times (with 𝔭[46] having a seventh at Gal 3:26):

- Rom 3:22 — "The righteousness of God [is manifested] διὰ πίστεως Ἰησοῦ Χριστοῦ to all who believe."
- Gal 2:16 (twice) — "Knowing that a person is not justified by the works of the law but διὰ πίστεως Χριστοῦ Ἰησοῦ, even we have believed in Jesus Christ in order to be justified ἐκ πίστεως Χριστοῦ.
- Gal 3:22 — "The scripture has consigned all things under sin in order that the promise, which is ἐκ πίστεως Ἰησοῦ Χριστοῦ, might be given to those who believe."
- Eph 3:12 — ". . . in whom we have boldness and confidence of access διὰ τῆς πίστεως αὐτοῦ."
- Phil 3:9 — ". . . not having a righteousness of my own that is based on the law, but that which is διὰ πίστεως Χριστοῦ, the righteousness of God that depends on faith."

It is admittedly a difficult expression. But when πίστις is understood in terms of the Hebrew term אֱמוּנָה, which means both "faith" and "faithfulness," then it is not too difficult to view Paul as using πίστις Ἰησοῦ Χριστοῦ in much the same way as he uses πίστις τοῦ θεοῦ ("the faithfulness of God") in Rom 3:3 and πίστις Ἀβραάμ ("the faith of Abraham") in Rom 4:16. And this may be the case as well in that very enigmatic expression ἐκ πίστεως εἰς πίστιν of Rom 1:17, so reading "a righteousness that is *based on* [a divine] *faithfulness resulting in* [a human response of] *faith.*"

In effect, Paul seems to use πίστις Ἰησοῦ Χριστοῦ as something of a set phrase — perhaps drawn from the confessional expression ἐκ πίστεως Ἰησοῦ that he incorporated in Rom 3:26 — to signal the basis for the Christian gospel: that its objective basis is the perfect response of obedience that Jesus rendered to God the Father, both actively in his life and passively in his death. Taking such a view, it needs to be noted that in three of the passages cited above Paul nicely balances the objective basis for Christian faith ("the faith / faithfulness of Jesus Christ") and humanity's necessary subjective response ("by faith"): Rom 3:22, "this righteousness of God is 'through the faith / faithfulness of Jesus Christ' and 'extends to all who believe' "; Gal 3:22, "so that the promise, 'which is based on the faith / faithfulness of Jesus Christ,' 'might be given to those who believe' "; and Phil 3:9, "a righteousness 'that is based on the faith / faithfulness of Christ' " and "that depends on faith." Though it is often claimed that here we have simply cases of redundancy in Paul's vocabulary, it is probably better to see in these three verses Paul attempting to set out both the objective and the subject bases for the Christian life — that is, both the objective "faith / faithfulness of Christ" in obedience to God the Father and the subjective "faith" of those whom God reconciles to himself through the work of Christ.

Also of pertinence when attempting to grasp that which underlies Paul's christological thought are the titles "Son" and "Son of God," which among the earliest Jewish believers seem to have been used in a more functional manner to denote Jesus' unique relationship with God and his obedience to the Father's will. Admittedly, Paul does not use these titles for Christ as much as do the canonical Evangelists or the writer to the Hebrews (whose usages will be treated below). Nonetheless, in addition to references to "his Son" and "Son of God" in the confessional materials that he includes in Gal 4:4-5 and Rom 1:3-4, Paul does use these titles some thirteen times in his letters:

- "His Son": Rom 1:3, 9; 5:10; 8:3, 29, 32; 1 Cor 1:9; Gal 1:16; 4:6; 1 Thess 1:10;
- "The Son": 1 Cor 15:28; and
- "Son of God": 2 Cor 1:19; Gal 2:20.

And often these thirteen occurrences, in context, reverberate with the more functional nuance of obedience — particularly when combined with the motif of Christ's faith or faithfulness or when juxtaposed with statements regarding his death, which function to highlight the extent of Christ's obedience and faithful sonship.

### 3. The Canonical Gospels

That sonship is a dominant motif in the portrayals of Jesus in the canonical Gospels is beyond dispute. He is presented as speaking about God and to God in such a manner as to indicate that God was uniquely his Father, and as referring to himself in both direct and allusive fashion as the "Son" and "Son of God" — not just during or at the end of his ministry but also as a twelve-year-old in the Jerusalem temple, which he called "my Father's house" (Luke 2:49). Even Satan is represented as recognizing this fundamental factor in Jesus' self-consciousness, for two of his three temptations recorded in Matt 4:1-11 and Luke 4:1-13 use such a consciousness as their point of departure ("If you are the Son of God"). In fact, as portrayed in the Gospels, it was this filial consciousness that undergirded all of Jesus' ministry and from which he worked in the carrying out his messiahship.

As well, the Evangelists themselves evidence a lively consciousness of the unique sonship of Jesus, particularly Mark, Matthew, and John. Such a consciousness is to be seen not only in their explicit editorial comments, but also in how they arranged their materials and what they emphasized in their portrayals. Indeed, it is not going beyond the evidence to argue that it was this consciousness of Jesus' unique filial relation with God that served as the foundational conviction for all they wrote.

Mark, for example, begins his Gospel with the caption: "The beginning of the gospel about Jesus Christ, the Son of God" (1:1). The first half of his Gospel is concerned with the question of the identity of Jesus, and concludes with the affirmation of Peter: "You are the Christ!" (8:29). The second half spells out the nature of Jesus' ministry as being that of a suffering Messiah, and concludes with the acclamation of the Roman centurion: "Surely this man was the Son of God!" (15:39). Exactly what it was that impressed the centurion and what he meant by "Son of God" may be debated, for he was a Gentile and so probably used the title in something of a polytheistic manner. It is doubtful that he was thinking along the lines of Jesus' full obedience to the Father's will. Nonetheless, even though the centurion may have nuanced his acclamation differently than the early Jewish believers in Jesus would have, Mark evidently considered that he spoke better than he knew. So Mark makes the point — whatever the centurion himself might have meant by such an honorific outburst — that in calling Jesus "Son of God" the centurion used the proper title. In fact, Mark highlights this acclamation by putting it as the climax of the second half of his Gospel that deals with the unfolding secret as to the nature of Jesus' messiahship. For in his teaching about the nature of his messiahship (8:31–10:52), during his Jerusalem ministry (11:1–13:37), and throughout his Passion (14:1–15:39), Jesus evidenced that he was indeed God's obedient Son *par excellence.*

Furthermore, it needs to be noted that all three Synoptic Evangelists make a point of focusing on the unique sonship of Jesus in their depictions of Jesus' baptism and Transfiguration. In the baptism narrative the "voice from heaven," which is a locution for God himself, identifies Jesus as "my beloved Son" (ὁ υἱός μου ὁ ἀγαπητός) and commends his sonship — Mark 1:11 and Luke 3:22 reading "You are my beloved Son; with you I am well pleased"; Matt 3:17, "This is my beloved Son, with whom I am well pleased." In the Transfiguration narrative, the "voice out of the cloud," which again stands for God, speaks of Jesus as "my beloved Son" (ὁ υἱός μου ὁ ἀγαπητός) or "my chosen Son" *(ὁ υἱος μου ὁ ἐκλελεγμένος)* and exhorts the disciples to "listen to him" (with the Matthean version also including a divine commendation) — Mark 9:7, "This is my beloved Son; listen to him"; Matt 17:5, "This is my beloved Son, with whom I am well pleased; listen to him"; Luke 9:35, "This is my chosen Son, listen to him!" Undoubtedly, all three Evangelists felt that they were reproducing the acclamation of the heavenly voice just as they found it in the Gospel tradition, if not verbatim *(ipsissima verba)* at least in essence *(ipsissima vox).* But the redactional changes that each of them makes in their respective presentations show that they were not just trying to reproduce a tradition about what happened but also that they were attempting, each in his own way, to highlight for their readers the fundamental importance of the sonship of Jesus. They were saying, in effect, "To understand Jesus, one must see his divine Sonship as basic to all that he did!"

And John's Gospel, while devoid of any baptism or Transfiguration narrative, says much the same thing in speaking of Jesus as God's "one and only Son" in 3:16 (ὁ υἱὸς ὁ μονογενής; cf. 1 John 4:9) and 3:18 (ὁ μονογενὸς υἱός), as well as in ascribing the same title to the Logos in 1:14 and 18 of the Gospel's prologue (though, admittedly, textual support varies as to whether the adjective "one and only" in these latter verses modifies "Son" or "God," or with the article alone is used substantively). For this is the One who as both God's Son and the divine Logos not only reveals the Father's purposes, but is in complete compatibility with the Father's will and so expresses true filial obedience.

Among the Evangelists, it is Matthew who seems to have been most dominated by a consciousness of Christ's obedience. For throughout his Gospel, particularly in the first half, Matthew appears to be often paralleling the life of Jesus and the life of the nation Israel — with that paralleling evidently meant to portray Jesus as *the Jew* who recapitulated the experiences of the nation, obediently responding to God in a manner that Israel had not. Matthew's Gospel, of course, has a number of themes (some major and some minor), with many of these themes being used to organize the presentation (sometimes extensively and at other times in more limited fashion). It cannot be claimed, therefore, that an emphasis on Jesus' sonship entirely molded or fashioned all of the material presented by the Evangelist. On the other hand, however, many commentators believe that they can detect echoes and reminiscences of Israel's earlier experiences, particularly in the first half of Matthew's Gospel. Some of the parallels between Jesus and the nation are as follows: (1) a child of promise

(1:18ff.); (2) delivered from Herod's slaughter (2:1ff.); (3) coming out of Egypt (2:15, 19ff.); (4) passing through the waters (3:13ff.); (5) entering the wilderness for testing (4:18ff.); (6) calling out the "twelve sons of Israel" (4:18ff.); (7) giving the law from the mountain (chs. 5–7); (8) performing ten miracles (chs. 8–9); (9) sending out the Twelve to "conquer" the land (10:1ff.); (10) feeding the multitudes with "manna" from heaven (14:15ff. and 15:32ff.), and (11) being transfigured before his disciples (17:1ff.). Not all of these features, of course, are equally evident or compelling. But the general parallelism between Jesus and the nation that is set out in Matthew's Gospel cannot easily be set aside.

Much more could be cited from the Gospels in support of the thesis that the Evangelists themselves possessed a lively consciousness of the unique sonship of Jesus and that they wrote from the perspective of such a foundational conviction. What we have done above is simply to highlight some of the most obvious data in support of such a thesis. We must leave it to others to deal with the more allusive and inferential evidence.

One cannot, however, leave the witness of the Gospels in this regard without referring to what in the Synoptic Gospels is presented as Jesus' last great spiritual struggle before enduring the agony of the cross — with, in particular, the Evangelists' focus on his response of obedience. For in the Gethsemane narrative Jesus is presented as crying out in anguish: "Father, if you are willing, take this cup from me!" But immediately coupled with this cry is his response of obedience: "Yet not my will, but yours be done!" (Luke 22:42; cf. Mark 14:36; Matt 26:39). An echo of this event appears in John's Gospel in the words of Jesus: "Now my heart is troubled, and what shall I say? 'Father, save me from this hour'? No, it was for this very reason I came to this hour. Father, glorify your name!" (John 12:27-28). Though the details of the Gethsemane experience differ somewhat in the three Synoptic Gospels (e.g., Matthew: "he fell on his face"; Mark: "he fell on the ground"; Luke: "he knelt down"; also note Luke's addition of an angel being present to strengthen him and his sweat being "like great drops of blood"), and though John's Gospel puts this response in a different context, all of the Evangelists agree in focusing on Jesus' attitude of complete obedience — which is the only fitting way to express his divine sonship.

## 4. The Letter to the Hebrews

The argument of the first ten chapters of Hebrews is built on the framework of (1) a thesis statement in 1:1-2, (2) what appears to be an early Christian confessional portion quoted in support in 1:3-4, and thereafter (3) five biblical portions drawn from the LXX: a catena of passages (Ps 2:7; 2 Sam 7:14; Deut 32:43; Pss 97:7; 45:6-7; 102:25-27) on which the exposition of 1:5–2:4 is based; Ps 8:4-6 on which 2:5-18 is based; Ps 95:7-11 on which 3:1–4:13 is based; Ps 110:4 on which 4:14–7:28 is based, and Jer 31:31-34 on which 8:1–10:39 is based. Chapters 11–13 then exhort the readers to move forward in their Christian commitments, focusing attention on Jesus "the Pioneer and Perfecter" of their faith (2:9-10; 12:2-3) and being prepared to follow Jesus even to the point of leaving their former Jewish allegiances, if need be (13:11-14).

The substance of the argument, however, has to do with Christ as "the Son," by whom God "in these last days" has revealed himself and acted redemptively on behalf of his people. And the point of the argument that comes to the fore repeatedly throughout the first ten chapters of the letter is that the Son — while in continuity with all of God's past words and actions — is to be seen as being superior to all of God's previous revelations and redemptive activities. In particular, as the argument of the letter unfolds, the Son is superior to angels in his exaltedness (1:5–2:4), to angels in his lowliness and humiliation (2:5-18), to Moses and the law (3:1-6), to Joshua and the possession of the land (3:7–4:13), to the Levitical priesthood (4:14–5:10), to the Melchizedekian priesthood (7:1-28), and to the old covenant and its cultus (8:1–10:39).

One of the interesting features of the Letter to the Hebrews is its placement of the theme of the Son's obedience in the context of both (1) ontological affirmations regarding Jesus' divine status and sinlessness, and (2) functional portrayals of his redemptive activities on behalf of men and women. The statement of the writer in 5:8-9 appears, at first glance, somewhat startling in its joining of ontology and function: "Although he was a son, he learned obedience from what he suffered; and once made perfect, he became the source of eternal salvation for all who obey him." That this reference to the Son's obedience being perfected during his earthly life is no inadvertence on the part of the author is evidenced by the fact that the same point appears in briefer fashion in 2:10, where it is said that "in bringing many sons to glory it was fitting that God . . . should make the Pioneer of their salvation perfect through suffering," and 7:28, which speaks of "the Son, who has been made perfect forever." However difficult it may be for scholars today to understand the conjunction of the categories of ontology and function, or to reconcile a "Christology from Above" with a "Christology from Below," the writer to the Hebrews seems to have had no problem with bringing together both status and process when speaking about Christ, the Son — that is, with putting forward a christology that has to do with both being and becoming.

But however the ontological and functional categories are to be related in the portrayals of sonship in Hebrews, the important point to note here is that at the heart of the writer's argument about the work of Christ stands the concept of the Son's obedience. This can be seen throughout the first ten chapters of the letter. But it appears in a particularly explicit and forceful manner in the final chapter of that sustained argument, in 10:5-7 quoting Ps 40:6-8:

> Therefore, when Christ came into the world, he said: "Sacrifice and offering you did not desire, but a body you prepared for me; with burnt offerings and sin offerings you were not pleased. Then I said, 'Here I am — it is written about me in the scroll — I have come to do your will, O God.'"

For the writer of Hebrews, therefore, the fundamental factor that underlies both the incarnation of the Son and his earthly ministry is that of obedience: "To do your will, O God."

## 5. Conclusion

The thesis of this article is that all of the christological titles and all of the metaphors used in description of Christ's work are founded ultimately on the early Christians' conviction regarding the full obedience and entire faithfulness of Jesus of Nazareth, God's Son *par excellence*, with this complete filial obedience seen as having been exercised throughout his life (his so-called "Active Obedience") and coming to ultimate expression in his death on the cross (his so-called "Passive Obedience"). That does not mean that we should disregard the titles or neglect the metaphors. Much can be learned that is of profit for Christian theology by a contextual and historical study of each of the titles and metaphors, for they are given to flesh out the gospel message and highlight areas of significance in different contexts. Furthermore, the impact of the gospel is often greatly enhanced by the proclamation of its message in terms of one or the other of these titles or metaphors, especially when suited to the needs of a particular audience or situation. But what needs to be appreciated is that behind all of these pictorial representations, graphic metaphors, and / or similes stands the foundational conviction of the early Christians about the obedience, faithfulness, and sonship of Christ — with its corollary being the trustful obedience of the believer in response.

Validation for the above thesis is not just to be found in the frequency with which the terms "obedience," "faithfulness," and "Son / Son of God" appear in the NT. Rather, it is to be found in their strategic use by the NT letter writers and Evangelists, appearing, as we have noted above, in such significant places as an early Christian confessional portion that has been incorporated into a letter (e.g., Phil 2:8; Gal 4:4-5; Rom 1:3-4; 3:26), the thesis of a letter (e.g., Rom 3:21-23; Heb 1:1-2), the propositional statement of a letter (e.g., Gal 2:15-21), a major argument of a letter (e.g., Rom 5:19; Gal 3:22), the caption and conclusion of a Gospel (e.g., Mark 1:1; 15:39), or woven into the warp and woof of the presentation of a Gospel or letter (e.g., Matthew and Hebrews). Likewise, validation is to be found in the multifaceted way in which this concept of Christ's obedient, faithful sonship undergirds a great many of the crucial discussions of the NT writers, for it informs matters that are not only christological in nature but also soteriological, ecclesiological, eschatological, ethical, and sacramental — though to demonstrate how this foundational conviction undergirds the presentations in each of these areas would take a monograph, which is a task that must be left to others.

# Christology: Synchronic or Diachronic?[1]

Paul Ellingworth

## 1

With typical modesty, Howard Marshall described his admirable survey of the Son of Man literature as "especially sketchy."[2] Its sketchiness is as nothing compared with the sketchiness of the remarks which follow. These will attempt, not a substantive contribution to christology, but a few reflections on the christological task. If theology is the science or theory of faith in God, and christology the theory of faith in Jesus Christ, what follow are some thoughts about the process of christological construction itself. One might call it metachristology, if that were not far too pretentious a polysyllable.

To be fair, the sketchiness will not derive only from the limitations of the present writer. Scientists tell us that we can never know at the same time both the exact position of a particle and its precise velocity. Similarly, linguists generally feel obliged to choose between a diachronic and a synchronic approach to language; between tracing the historical development of (for example) a word, and studying how that word interacts with other words in the vocabulary of a particular speech community. Sometimes they opt for one, sometimes for the other; there are fashions in this as in most things. But it is methodologically impossible to do both at the same time.

In the same way, *mutatis mutandis*, it is extremely difficult to hold together the synchronic and the diachronic dimensions of christology. On the one hand, one may focus on the christology of a particular writer, such as Luke or Origen, or a particular text, such as the Definition of Chalcedon. On the other hand, one may follow through time the growth of a particular christological motif,

1. I am most grateful to Professor D. A. S. Fergusson and to Dr. M. Turner for their comments on a draft of this paper; I remain solely responsible for its remaining inadequacies.

2. I. H. Marshall, *The Origins of New Testament Christology*, 2d ed. (Leicester: Apollos, 1990) 63.

such as devotion to the humanity of Christ.[3] The two tasks are, it would seem, theoretically almost impossible to combine.

## 2

It is interesting to speculate for a moment on possible reasons why this should be the case. First, a particular scholarly tradition may favor one method rather than the other; for example, the typically English history-of-doctrine approach rather than a typically German systematic construction; or a typically Western analytic approach rather than a typically Eastern Orthodox synthesis. Second, within a particular tradition, an individual scholar may have a predominantly synchronic or diachronic cast of mind. Karl Barth is a towering example of one who at different times attempted both approaches, but there is no doubt that in his work as a whole, the diachronic was generally used in the service of the synchronic.

Third, there are the increasing demands of academic specialization. No one knows better than Howard Marshall how to delimit an area of research; no one is more aware of the need to do so at an early stage if one is to get anywhere. These are qualities for which generations of research students stand up and call him blessed. In *The Origins of New Testament Christology,* for example, he states programmatically:

> On the one hand . . . our concern is with the task of laying bare what the New Testament says about Jesus, not with what the modern theologian does with the material provided by the New Testament scholar. . . . On the other hand, our task must be differentiated from that of the historical study of the life of Jesus.[4]

Conversely, J. P. Meier's work on the historical Jesus "prescinds from what Christian faith or later Church teaching says about Jesus, without either affirming or denying such claims."[5] Such an approach may provide only raw material for christology, yet christology will ignore such data at its peril.

A fourth aspect of the problem may be more fundamental, in the sense of preceding and underlying the others which we have mentioned so far. It is the theoretical and practical impossibility of moving in two directions at the same time. Words follow one another two-dimensionally, as lines on a page. If they are spoken rather than written, they may radiate out in all directions

3. "Eros: or, Devotion to the Sacred Humanity: An Epilogue," in G. L. Prestige, *Fathers and Heretics* (London: SPCK, 1940) 180-207.

4. *Origins,* 11-12.

5. J. P. Meier, *A Marginal Jew: Rethinking the Historical Jesus,* vol. 1 (Garden City, New York: Doubleday, 1991) 1.

through the air; but what matters for the individual hearer is the line between the speaker's mouth and his or her own ears. If this is true of words in general, how much truer must it be of christology, the science of the Word incarnate?

Indeed, the christological task is more arduous than anything we have yet mentioned. It is not three-, but at least[6] four-dimensional. Its scope embraces, first, the time line from the Bible to the present day; second, the dimension of space, the "Christ of the Indian road"[7] and all the other culturally conditioned responses to the one Christ (including our own); third, the dimension in which the faith of the individual believer interrelates with that of his or her believing community; and fourth, the transcendent dimension from which, as Christians hold, Christ entered history, and in which he now "lives for ever to plead with God" for those who "come to God through him."[8] Surely it is beyond the powers of any individual, even any team of scholars, to encompass it all at the same time. Yet the problem will not go away; for all this, and more, is part of christology, the theoretical expression of faith in Christ.

## 3

One response to this situation would be simply to admit defeat; to acknowledge that a fully adequate, multidimensional christology is an unachievable aim. In the same way, on a humbler level, one might conclude that translation is impossible,[9] that all *traduttori* are to some extent *traditori*. Yet people continue to practice both translation and christology, however inadequately, and the demand for both remains unabated.

An apparently somewhat less defeatist (and more realistic) response is to choose one dimension of the christological data, and explore it as thoroughly as one can. This is what most people appear at first sight to be doing. Yet this is an oversimplification, and in this fact there may be a ray of hope.

More precisely, what students of christology commonly do is to *focus* as far as possible on a particular point in this multidimensional complex; but this focusing by no means excludes what one might call peripheral vision of adjacent areas of the christological continuum.

To take a concrete example, one may set out to study the christology of John's Gospel: just one theme in a mere booklet of thirty pages or so. Yet even

6. The list is certainly not exhaustive: for any kind of completeness, one would need at least to add dimensions relating to the significance of Christ for unbelieving humanity and for the cosmos.

7. The title of a well-known book, published in 1925, by E. S. Jones (1884-1973).

8. Heb 7:25. Biblical quotations, unless otherwise indicated, are from the Good News Bible (Today's English Version).

9. This appears to be the conclusion of G. Steiner's sensitive and intricate *After Babel: Aspects of Language and Translation* (London: Oxford University, 1975).

this limited task inevitably involves study of the various factors which may have influenced the way in which John writes of Christ; the diachronic development from (perhaps) the life and teaching of Jesus himself, through the various stages of composition of John's Gospel, and outward from the Gospel itself to the situation, presuppositions, needs, and expectations of the Johannine community. The task may also usefully involve delimitation of John's christology, by reference to aspects which John presents more weakly than other NT writers, or not at all.

Moreover, whether one likes it or not, the task cannot exclude the scholar's own situation, presuppositions, etc. Librarians have to decide whether a book on Origen's christology is likely to be mainly about Origen or mainly about christology, and a similar question might arise in less acute form about (say) R. Bultmann's commentary on John, or indeed anyone else's. Yet the distinction between the dimensions remains valid in theory, and the need to focus, albeit nonexclusively, on one of them remains compelling in practice.

Despite all this, this most common christological strategy remains ultimately unsatisfying; semidefeatist, one might call it; a strategy of truce. The reason for this is that it fails to take account of two essential facts; facts which relate respectively to the beginning and the end of christology.

## 4

First, the beginning. No student can fail to be impressed by the extraordinary theological creativity of the NT period: as M. Hengel has put it, "this development in christology progressed *in a very short time*."[10] One is reminded irresistibly of the cosmological "big bang."[11] First Thessalonians is widely held to be the earliest of the NT writings. It is often dated to the early 50s, though a date as early as 41 has been proposed;[12] say broadly between ten and twenty-five years after the crucifixion. Yet already, Paul is describing Jesus as the one who died and rose again (4:14; cf. 1:10; 2:15), and who as God's Son (1:10) will play a crucial role in the coming judgment (1:10; 3:13; 4:14-16), so that the "Day of the Lord" (5:2) becomes the Day of the Lord Jesus.[13] Further, in this same early letter Paul is describing Jesus as at least the instrument of God's salvation (5:9); as at least the immediate source of grace (5:28); and of Paul's authority to give moral instruction (4:2; cf. 1:6); as the one who will punish those who offend

10. M. Hengel, *The Son of God: The Origin of Christology and the History of Jewish-Hellenistic Religion* (Philadelphia: Fortress, 1976) 77; Hengel's italics.

11. The same parallel is drawn independently by Meier, *Marginal Jew,* 6.

12. I. H. Marshall, *1 and 2 Thessalonians,* NCBC (Grand Rapids, Michigan: Wm. B. Eerdmans; London: Marshall, Morgan, & Scott, 1983) 20-23; cf. L. Morris, *The First and Second Epistles to the Thessalonians,* rev. ed., NICNT (Grand Rapids, Michigan: Wm. B. Eerdmans, 1991) 12-15.

13. Marshall, *Thessalonians,* 133; cf. Morris, *Thessalonians,* 150-51.

against such teaching (4:6); and most of all as one closely associated with God the Father and with the Holy Spirit (1:3-5). Moreover, Paul can assume that his readers in Thessalonica already hold at least the tradition that "Jesus died and rose again" (4:14);[14] like their fellow-Christians in Judea, they belong to Christ and live in union with him (2:14; 3:8, 13; cf. 4:16).

It is perhaps not quite impossible to find parallels for such rapid developments among followers of other religious leaders;[15] but it is difficult to imagine such a range and depth of expressions of faith being attached, at the date of publication of this *Festschrift,* to someone who had died around 1970 at the earliest.

The point may be illustrated even more clearly from pre-Pauline tradition. Intensive research has left standing the probability that "Jesus is Lord" was indeed the earliest Christian confession.[16] This suggests that already in primitive Christianity the historical Jesus was inseparable from the Christ of faith. The language of that last sentence is of course modern: it betrays among other things the Western tendency to distinguish and divide what most other generations and peoples would hold inseparably together. But it makes explicit something which was already implicit in that primitive confession. And it strongly suggests that, very soon after the christological "big bang," Christians did not share the difficulty, which most students of christology find virtually insuperable, of speaking in the same breath of all the dimensions of faith in Christ. Their faith, so to speak, was tightly compacted, like matter (according to current theory) in the first few nanoseconds of our universe.

If this is so, it may incidentally point toward understanding a difference of approach between Howard Marshall and, for example, J. P. Meier. Professor Marshall, in the spirit of primitive Christianity, dares to entitle one of his most challenging books *I Believe in the Historical Jesus.*[17] He is of course fully aware that the compacted credal synthesis which sprang so naturally to the lips of the first Christian generation poses problems for twentieth-century scholars. He addresses the problem directly in ch. 4: "Historical Jesus or Christ of Faith?", concluding with a statement which appears to express, not conceptual identity, but a strong *communicatio idiomatum* between the two: "The person who has Christian faith is a believer in the historical Jesus as the one who is now alive as the risen Lord."[18]

Professor Meier, by contrast, draws a firm distinction between, first, the

14. Even if the "we" of v 14a is semantically exclusive, like the we's of vv 13, 15, it is clear that in vv 14-15 Paul is moving from traditional to less familiar teaching, though even the latter is identified as "the Lord's teaching."

15. For example, followers of Simon Kimbangu and other founders of independent African churches and syncretistic sects; but most of these are subject to strong Christian influence.

16. Marshall, *Origins,* 104-8.

17. London: Hodder and Stoughton; Grand Rapids, Michigan: Wm. B. Eerdmans, 1977.

18. *Historical Jesus,* 84.

collection of historical data about Jesus; second, "highlight[ing] and appropriat[ing] those aspects of this historical knowledge that would be significant for us today," and third, "faith-knowledge of Jesus as Lord and Christ, the faith-stance that prompts me to call Jesus my Lord and my Savior."[19] Meier, however, emphasizes that this is a distinction methodologically important in defining the scope of his research; it is not a theological opposition: "We abstract from Christian faith," he writes, "because we are involved in the hypothetical reconstruction of a past figure by purely scientific means."[20] In other words, Meier, unlike Marshall, is not, at least directly, engaged in the christological task.

To return to the main point: the first Christians put their trust in someone whom, not long before, some of them had known (better than we shall ever know him) as a real though extraordinary human being. Normally, no questions arose about his real humanity; when, quite exceptionally, questions did arise, it was when he is recorded as doing quite exceptional things, such as walking on water,[21] or appearing in physical form after his crucifixion.[22] Even such exceptions are only apparent, for what was in doubt was not Jesus' true humanity, but whether the figure seen in such exceptional circumstances was indeed Jesus, whom his followers knew to be a person of flesh and blood. Nowhere in the Gospels do we find anyone, even an opponent, remotely suggesting that, because of certain extraordinary things which Jesus did, his humanity had been only a simulacrum all the time.

Yet this was the one to whom, if not in his lifetime at least not very long after the resurrection, his followers were applying, naturally and apparently uncontroversially, language previously used of God: titles such as "Lord," OT texts such as Ps 45:6-7 (MT: 45:7-8), activities and functions such as salvation and judgment. True, we find in the NT, perhaps most clearly in Rom 1:3-4, indications of what (avoiding the technicalities of later christological definition) one might call the duality of Christ, together with the strongest indications (explicitly in Rom 1:4) that the resurrection was the hinge on which that duality turned; but *nowhere do we find that either the duality or the resurrection was a problem for believers.*

In NT Christianity, the various dimensions of the Christ event are seen as what dimensions are: aspects of a single whole. One almost wrote ". . . a single object"; but an external object was precisely what Christ for NT Christianity was not: believers were "in Christ," and he in them. The four dimensions referred to above are all implicit in the confession "Jesus is Lord." An amplified paraphrase of it might read: "We Christians are united in the belief that in Jesus, God fulfilled his eternal purpose for humanity, and by raising him from the

19. *Marginal Jew,* 29-30.
20. *Marginal Jew,* 30-31.
21. Mark 6:45-52 par.
22. John 20:24-29.

dead demonstrated his Lordship over the whole of creation and the whole of human life."

The language in which this belief was expressed varied with astonishing adaptability. As Christianity moved in widening circles into the Hellenistic world, the title "Son of Man," for example, became not only mysterious but incomprehensible, so it was jettisoned with the same ruthlessness with which Christians discarded almost all of Jesus' teaching in its presumably[23] original Aramaic form; other titles, such as "Lord," became central; and new titles, such as "high priest" in Hebrews, were applied to him to meet particular needs. But the common faith in Christ remained; and within that faith, the resurrection was not a problem but its organizing center.

## 5

How does all this relate to the end of christology: to its temporal end and also to its purpose, both of which consist in providing *an intellectually coherent account of faith in Jesus Christ at the present time?*

From one point of view, the problems appear insuperable.

On one level, they are practical. A postgraduate student who proposed to her supervisor as her area of research the italicized words above would probably be told, first, that she must choose between the Departments of New Testament, Systematic Theology, and possibly Practical Theology; and, second, that her subject would have to be considerably narrowed. Similar choices would have to be made by a staff member proposing to lecture on the same subject; and, in addition, he would be exposed to attack from various sides by colleagues who felt that their own specialties had been neglected or misrepresented in this interdisciplinary task.

Yet in the proposed object of such a study, that is, in the living faith of Christians and Christian communities today, one finds the same multidimensionality as in the NT: it is not limited to a few seconds, or a few years, after the "big bang."

True, one cannot expect to find the same primal creativity as in the first Christian century; the situation is different, and present-day Christianity depends on the Bible in a different and more absolute sense than first-century Christianity may be said to depend on the OT.

True, one may expect to find among present-day Christians deviation from NT norms which cannot be fully or legitimately explained by reference to contemporary needs: images of Christ which are not only different from but inconsistent with the NT data; indifference to the cultural differences between

23. On the question "What language did Jesus speak?", see Meier, *Marginal Jew,* 255-68, with further references 289-300.

NT times and our own; individualistic faith insufficiently rooted in a believing community (often allied to an introspective, "that will be glory for me" faith indifferent to mission and evangelism); transcendentalism insufficiently rooted in the here and now.

Yet when all these and other allowances have been made, one finds, in expressions of living Christian faith from every period including our own, something of the same multidimensional richness of NT christology. Indeed, it may be argued that this is, despite all imbalances or deviations, the norm, and that any christological analysis which ignores one or more of these dimensions does less than full service to the Christian community, whose faith it purports to describe.

The contrast between faith in Christ on the one hand, and christology, its theoretical counterpart, on the other, appears at first sight irreducible: to express the contrast in its simplest form, faith synthesizes while christology analyzes. If this were the end of the matter, one would have to conclude that christology is fundamentally incapable of performing the task for which it is specifically designed. Which is absurd.

## 6

One possible way out of the dilemma is to recognize that it has at least partial analogies in other fields of human endeavor.

Take, for example, a large engineering construction, such as an oil rig or the Forth Road Bridge. I suppose, on the basis of absolutely no specialized knowledge, that such a construction requires cooperation between a large number of people, each with specialized knowledge and skill: for example, experts in various branches of applied physics, chemistry, and mathematics; soil science, meteorology, quantity surveying, budgeting, financial control, etc., plus people whose task is to ensure that each part of the construction, each bolt and weld, is in conformity with specified standards, and others responsible for effective coordination and management from first design to final acceptance and operation. Specialization and coordination are equally essential to the finished product: each person engaged in the project must *both* have his or her own clear job description *and* use clearly defined lines of communication with others.

It is this kind of cooperation between specialists, this sense of working together to produce something useful, which often appears lacking in reflection on faith in Christ. Yet the need for such a product is clear, as Christians in one area may find it difficult to say in what respect Jesus was more than a good person, and in another area may express their devotion to him by passionately kissing even a photograph of an icon on the cover of a book in a closed shop window.

Or take a somewhat less remote example, about which I do admit to some specialized knowledge. In order to produce a good translation of the Bible, contributions are required from a number of specialists (translators, reviewers, maybe a stylist, publishers, typographers, printers), possessing various technical skills and personal qualities (ranging from adequate knowledge of the source and receptor languages to the ability to work together), and working to agreed principles and procedures, within an agreed budget, under some form of coordination. Within this complex structure, the translators, who are ultimately responsible for the form of the translated text, must combine two qualities which might appear theoretically incompatible: on the one hand, perfect understanding of the meaning of the original texts, and on the other hand, the ability to think and feel themselves into the situation of readers who are totally dependent on the translation, and to whom the translators' understanding of the original must therefore be transmitted in an appropriate (usually quite different) form. How these two qualities are combined in a good translator would be a complex interdisciplinary study in itself: the model of a two-phase movement back into the original text, and then forward into the receptor language, is almost certainly oversimplified. But the immediate point is that the human mind is in principle able to transcend, and thus relate to one another, processes which, as it were on a level, two-dimensional plane, appear mutually exclusive. Perhaps, after all, our minds, though not our bodies, do have the gift of moving in two or more directions at once.

## 7

It is at this point, as we return to the central theme of this symposium, that we turn for guidance to A. C. Thiselton's contribution on christology in Luke,[24] which, though rigorously theoretical in scope, addresses and helps to resolve a problem similar to that which we have outlined. A central strand in Thiselton's thesis may, at the risk of oversimplification, be summarized as follows. Many statements attributed to Jesus, especially in Luke, presuppose not only "causal power" but "institutional authorization," for example, to forgive, to heal, even to bring a dead person back to life; more generally, "to act as Spirit-anointed divine presence in the name of God."[25]

Thiselton's use of the word "institutional," illuminatingly transferred from social history or sociology to christology, prompts further questions concerning the nature and basis of the "institution" in question, and the "authority" which it confers. On the highest level, as Thiselton points out, this authority is *"delegated"*[26]: in Johannine language, "As the Father has sent me, even so I send you"

24. In this volume, 453-72. I am grateful to M. Turner for kindly making available to me an advance draft of this contribution.

25. Thiselton, above, 469.

26. Thiselton, above, 472.

(John 20:21). Yet such a statement, almost by definition, lies beyond the reach of direct human validation. It is therefore probably more realistic to move to a slightly lower level, one to which the language of the social sciences may apply more directly, and to speak of institutional authorization, implicit in the words and acts of Jesus, and confirmed in his resurrection, which a community of believers (a church, and thus in the best sense an institution) recognizes, freely though under divine impulsion, as deriving ultimately from beyond themselves, and to which they freely respond in faith.

It is of course true that such a recognition and response lie beyond autonomous human proof, and that this situation is not fundamentally changed by appeal to the faith of a community; for the voice of a people is not necessarily the voice of God. But this is not the point. Nor is faith in Christ to be placed in a unique, privileged category in which normal rules of evidence are relaxed. In the last analysis, very little, perhaps nothing, is amenable to autonomous human proof; for the further one goes in questioning presuppositions, the closer one comes to the possibility that the sum of human perceptions may be an illusion.

The point is rather that faith in Christ has this in common with human knowledge in general: that it proceeds by the recognition of organic coherence[27] within a growing body of data. The exegete hesitating between different interpretations of a biblical text will normally choose that option which best coheres with the immediate and the wider context. Only in extreme cases, where all attempts to discover that coherence have failed, will one as a last resort regretfully conclude that the text itself is corrupt or otherwise incoherent.

Similarly, the first followers of Jesus perceived a coherence between the status implicit in some of his statements, and the related effectiveness of his actions; between the statement, "Young man, I say to you, arise," and the dead man sitting up;[28] between promise and fulfilment. In the same way also, the NT writers perceived a wider organic coherence between the Christ event as a whole and the earlier biblical tradition: despite the qualitative newness of the Christ event, it was "according to the scriptures," within the coherent purpose of the one God.

*These are the data which it is the task of christology to interpret, and this interpretation must ultimately stand the test of organic coherence with the faith of Christians today, seeking to make sense of the world in which they live.*

27. The following discussion owes much to the idea of *Horizontverschmelzung* or "fusion of horizons" developed in H.-G. Gadamer, *Truth and Method* (London: Sheed & Ward, 1975) esp. 269-74, 337-41; and A. C. Thiselton, *The Two Horizons* (Exeter: Paternoster, 1980) esp. 307-10, though different language is used.

28. Luke 7:14-15; cf. Thiselton, above, 470.

## 8

Two qualifications to this thesis are, however, necessary as we conclude.

The first, more obvious, and less important, is that such coherence, though it may provide a fully adequate basis for practical Christian living, will never be complete. In traditional terms, the finite cannot contain the infinite; the creature is not intended to become independent of its creator, or fallen human nature independent of its savior. Some aspects of reality appear to us to be incoherent (dysteleological) in themselves. Our beginning and our end, like the beginning and the end of the universe in which we find ourselves, are largely hidden from us; it is enough that we hold to the center, which is Christ.

The second and more important qualification is that the organic coherence of which we speak is always open, in principle like any hypothesis or *Weltanschauung,* to critical challenge by new data, or by a fresh assessment of old data. The more broadly based the coherence, the less radical one may generally expect the reassessment to be; but it is always possible that, for example, a new evaluation of the christology of Luke may somewhat change the character of the present-day believer's perception of, and faith in, Jesus Christ. It is in such a setting that critical, analytic studies of NT christology find their rightful place. But if academic specialists view their work as an end in itself, it will be ultimately unfruitful; and if they succumb to the temptation to view their research as of a higher order than the (first-, sixteenth-, or twentieth-century) data with which they work (as a finished product may be thought superior to its raw materials), their *hubris* will in due course incur its corresponding *nemesis.*

It is appropriate that such questions should be raised in a tribute to the work of Howard Marshall, distinguished *inter alia* among NT scholars for his equal concern for the most rigorous scholarly standards, and for the life and mission of the church today.

# Index of Ancient Sources

## OLD TESTAMENT

## APOCRYPHA

## NEW TESTAMENT

**Luke**

## PSEUDEPIGRAPHA AND EARLY CHRISTIAN WRITINGS

## DEAD SEA SCROLLS AND RELATED TEXTS

## TARGUMIM



## RABBINIC LITERATURE AND TRACTATES

## OTHER ANCIENT AUTHORS AND WRITINGS

# Index of Modern Authors